# the Joy of CREATIVE CUISINE

ORACLE BOOKS

Publisher: Rick Bailey; Editorial Director: Elaine R. Woodard
Editor: Jeanette P. Egan; Art Director: Don Burton
Typography: Cindy Coatsworth, Michelle Carter
Director of Manufacturing: Anthony B. Narducci

**Published by Oracle Books, a division of HPBooks, Inc.**
P.O. Box 5367, Tucson, AZ 85703   602/888-2150
ISBN 0-89586-392-8
Library of Congress Catalog Card Number 85-80862
© 1985 HPBooks, Inc.
Printed in Italy by A. Mondadori Editore - Verona
1st Printing

Portions of this book originally published as Four Seasons Salads, The Fun Food Book, The Busy Cook's Book, Suppers and Snacks, Delicious Desserts, Special Occasion Casseroles, Chinese Cookery, Cooking for Your Freezer, Good Home Baking, Chocolate Cooking, Cooking for Christmas

© 1983, 1984 Hennerwood Publications Limited

Microwave chapter from Microwave Cookbook
© 1983 HPBooks, Inc.

Cover Photo: Chicken & Crab Rolls with Wild Rice, page 151

# the *Joy of* CREATIVE CUISINE

## Table of Contents

# Introduction

This is not just a basic cookbook. It is *more* than a basic cookbook. There are recipes for every occasion from quick meals to elegant impressive desserts. There are 14 chapters ranging from *Appetizers* to *Microwave*. Explore the cooking opportunities that await you!

## APPETIZERS

This chapter has a variety of appetizers from soufflés to an easy cheese ball. Appetizers are a great way to entertain friends or to get a meal off to an impressive start. First impressions can be lasting ones.

## SOUPS

Recipes in the soup chapter range from broth-based soups to chilled fruit soup. There are soups for every occasion from starters to main dishes. All recipes are easy and delicious.

## SALADS

This chapter is based on the four seasons of the year. Even in mid-winter, there are ingredients available to make interesting and unusual salads. Many salads can be served as main dishes and starters, as well as dinner salads.

## MAIN DISHES

Whether you want a main dish that is easy and elegant or a slow-simmered pot roast, you're sure to find a recipe that fits your needs. There are several recipes for poultry, beef, pork, veal, game and fish. There are many one-dish meals.

## LIGHT MEALS & SNACKS

Here's the answer to what can I serve for lunch or supper, or what can I serve as an easy snack. There are numerous recipes for easy main dishes and tasty sandwiches. This chapter is sure to be a favorite.

## BREADS

Nothing is more rewarding than making bread. Treat your family and friends to the delicious aroma and taste of just-baked breads. There are muffins, biscuits, scones, coffeecakes, rolls and yeasts breads. Start baking today!

## DESSERTS

Desserts are the perfect way to end a meal. This chapter has everything from cookies to elegant tortes and gâteaux. If you need a dessert in a hurry, check the *Quick & Easy* section. Or, make one of the impressive pastries using frozen puff pastry.

## CHOCOLATE

Smooth, luscious chocolate, one of the world's great delights! This is a chapter that you won't want to miss. There are 26 pages of helpful information and recipes using chocolate.

## CHINESE

Chinese seems to be everyone's favorite ethnic food. There's an introduction brimming with information to help you become an expert Chinese cook. The recipes are easy-to-do and delicious!

## PARTY TIME

Everyone enjoys entertaining family and friends. Food is an important part of any social occasion. This chapter will help you celebrate social occasions from the Christmas holidays to family birthdays.

## QUICK & EASY

Whether you have only 15 minutes or 60 minutes to cook dinner, this is the chapter for you! In each section, recipes are selected that can be prepared within the time given. You'll even find menus to help you plan ahead.

## MAKE-AHEAD MEALS

Meal time is more relaxed if some dishes are made ahead. This chapter helps you cook ahead and refrigerate or freeze the dishes until needed. Instructions are given for storage times, thawing and serving.

## MICROWAVE COOKING

This is a basic guide to using that greatest timesaver of all—the microwave oven. There are recipes for appetizers, main dishes, vegetables and desserts.

# Appetizers

Appetizers include spicy dips, smooth pâtés, crunchy salads, warm quiches and much more. They can be served as a starter for a meal or as a snack with drinks. This chapter contains recipes for several types of appetizers from pâtés to filled crepes. There's even a frozen gazpacho, the perfect appetizer for a hot summer day! In addition, check the index for recipes in other chapters that can be served as appetizers.

## CHOOSING APPETIZERS

Anytime people get together, food plays an important role whether it's an informal dinner, a cocktail party or an open house. The type of appetizers selected will depend on the occasion. For a stand-up cocktail party, choose foods that are easily eaten with one hand. Small pastries, cheese cubes, small pieces of fruit or vegetables are good choices for these occasions. Or, choose a pâté that can be spread on an interesting selection of crackers and breads. *Easy Cheese Ball* would be an excellent item that could be made ahead.

A selection of several appetizers will be more interesting than only one or two. Use the same guidelines in choosing appetizers that you would in planning a menu. Balance color, flavor, texture and temperature of the food. Choose some items that can be made ahead to avoid a last-minute panic. Don't forget your budget. If you're serving an expensive item, such as smoked salmon or shrimp, choose other less-expensive foods to keep within your budget. If you know the preferences of your guests, take them into consideration when planning a party. Don't serve all new and exotic items if your guests would really prefer cheese and crackers. However, if your guests like to experience new foods, let your imagination go.

The time of the party and whether a meal is to be served will also determine the type and number of appetizers. If you are serving a large meal, limit the number of appetizers and the length of the cocktail hour. Don't fill your guests with appetizers and then sit down to dinner!

If a meal is not being served, appetizers should be more substantial. Plan on everyone eating more of each item. Let your guests know in advance what type of party to expect.

For a dinner at the table, the appetizers can be more elaborate. Perhaps a small serving of a meat or fish salad, such as Ham-Stuffed Papaya or Smoked-Trout & Orange Salad would be ideal. If you want to make the appetizer ahead, choose a mousse, such as Smoked-Salmon Mousse, or a pâté that waits in the refrigerator. The appetizer should complement the rest of the menu. Don't repeat flavors of the appetizer in other courses. If the main dish is light, choose a heavier appetizer. However if the main dish is hearty, choose a light, delicate appetizer or perhaps even a light soup.

## SERVING APPETIZERS

Decide on the type of appetizers to be served. If several appetizers are being served, special utensils and equipment may be needed. If food is to be served hot, warming trays, chafing dishes or fondue pots will be needed. Small electric skillets or slow cookers are also useful for keeping food hot. Food that must be kept chilled can be placed in a bowl nestled in a bed of ice cubes. Make sure that the ice container doesn't leak as the ice melts. If heavy serving pieces are chilled before arranging the food, they will keep food cool for some time. Plan some items that can be served at room temperature.

Do a trial run the day before the party. Arrange serving equipment on the table to make sure everything fits and looks attractive. Arrange food attractively on serving plates and trays. Don't crowd food on plates. Choose larger plates or refill plates as needed. It's helpful to arrange plates in advance; bring out a fresh one when needed.

Garnish food attractively. Food that looks attractive is more appealing. Garnishes need not be elaborate; simple parsley sprigs, tomato wedges and lemon slices may be enough. If possible, make garnishes ahead of time.

**Bon appétit!**

Top to bottom: Ham-Stuffed Papaya and Italian Platter, page 8

# Italian Platter

*Dressing:*
3 tablespoons red-wine vinegar
1 tablespoon lemon juice
1 small garlic clove, crushed
1-1/2 teaspoons prepared coarse mustard
1/2 cup olive oil or other vegetable oil
Salt
Freshly ground pepper
*Platter:*
4 medium new potatoes, boiled in skins
1/4 cup mayonnaise
1 tablespoon chopped fresh parsley
1 (14-oz.) can artichoke hearts, drained
1 (14-oz.) can cannellini beans or
   white kidney beans, drained
1 (4-1/2-oz.) can sardines in oil, drained
10 salami slices, rolled into cornets
2 hard-cooked eggs, quartered
2 medium tomatoes
1 (2-oz.) can anchovy fillets in oil, drained

---

1. To make dressing, in a small bowl, combine vinegar, lemon juice, garlic and mustard. Gradually whisk in oil until thickened. Season with salt and pepper.
2. To make potato salad, cut potatoes into thick slices; place in a medium bowl. Stir in mayonnaise, parsley, salt and pepper.
3. Arrange artichoke hearts, beans, sardines, salami, hard-cooked eggs and potato salad around edge of a large platter like spokes of a wheel.
4. Slice tomatoes; place tomatoes in center of platter. Cover with an anchovy lattice.
5. Drizzle dressing over whole platter; serve with crusty bread. Makes 4 servings.

# Ham-Stuffed Papaya

4 large papayas, about 8 oz. each
2 teaspoons fresh lime juice
12 oz. cooked ham, cut into 1/2-inch cubes
1 red bell pepper, chopped
1/2 cup mayonnaise
2 teaspoons prepared horseradish
Finely grated peel of 1 lime
Buttered bread triangles

*To garnish:*
Lime twists

---

*Sometimes called pawpaws, papayas, with pink-orange flesh, are somewhat similar to melons. Serve half a papaya per person for an unusual starter.*

1. Slice papayas in half lengthwise; scoop out and discard seeds. Carefully scoop out flesh with a melon baller, or cut into small cubes, leaving shells intact.
2. In a medium bowl, combine papaya balls or cubes, lime juice, ham, bell pepper, mayonnaise, horseradish and lime peel.
3. Spoon papaya-and-shrimp mixture into reserved shells. Place 2 filled shells on each of 4 individual serving plates.
4. Refrigerate 30 minutes or until slightly chilled before serving. Serve with buttered bread. Garnish with lime twists. Makes 4 servings.

---

A papaya resembles an elongated melon. A papaya is ripe when the skin turns yellow and feels tender when lightly pressed at the stalk end.

To prepare a papaya, halve lengthwise; scoop out seeds with a metal spoon. The seeds have a very peppery taste and are usually discarded. After removing the seeds, scoop the flesh from the shell. Or, the papaya can be peeled and sliced.

Cheese & Watercress Flan

# Cheese & Watercress Flan

Pastry for a 9-inch pie crust
1 (8-oz.) pkg. cream cheese, room temperature
1/2 cup dairy sour cream
2 eggs, separated
Salt
Freshly ground pepper
1 (1/4-oz.) envelope unflavored gelatin (1 tablespoon)
1/4 cup chicken stock or water
1 bunch watercress (about 2 oz.), washed, shaken dry
1/4 cup finely chopped green onions

1. Preheat oven to 400F (205C). On a lightly floured surface, roll out pastry to an 11-inch circle. Use pastry to line a 9-inch quiche pan or flan pan with removable bottom. Line dough with foil; fill with pie weights or dried beans.

2. Bake in preheated oven 10 minutes. Remove foil and pie weights; bake 5 minutes more. Cool on a wire rack.

3. In a medium bowl, beat cream cheese, sour cream, egg yolks, salt and pepper until blended. Set aside.

4. In a small saucepan, combine gelatin and chicken stock or water. Stir well; let stand 3 minutes. Stir over low heat until gelatin dissolves; set aside to cool. Stir into cheese mixture; set aside.

5. Remove coarse stems and any discolored leaves from watercress; finely chop. In a medium bowl, beat egg whites until stiff but not dry. Set aside 2 tablespoons chopped watercress for garnish. Fold beaten egg whites, remaining chopped watercress and onions into cheese mixture. Spoon mixture into cooled pastry shell; smooth top.

6. Refrigerate 2 to 3 hours or until set. Sprinkle top of flan with reserved chopped watercress.

7. To take on a picnic, leave flan in pan. Wrap with plastic wrap or foil; keep chilled. Makes 4 to 6 servings.

# Cucumber, Melon & Ham Salad

1 small honeydew or other melon
8 oz. cooked ham
4 tomatoes, quartered
1 cup black grapes, halved, seeded
1/4 cucumber, thinly sliced

*Dressing:*
1/4 cup dairy sour cream
2 tablespoons chopped green onion
1 teaspoon chopped fresh mint
Salt
White pepper

*To garnish:*
Fresh mint sprigs

**1.** Slice melon in half; scoop out and discard seeds. Remove flesh with a melon baller, or cut into 1-inch cubes. Reserve melon shells for serving, if desired.
**2.** Cut ham into thin julienne strips. In a medium bowl, combine ham strips, melon ball or cubes, tomatoes, grapes and cucumber.
**3.** To make dressing, in a small bowl, combine sour cream, green onion, mint, salt and white pepper. Dressing can be made 24 hours ahead, if desired. Cover and refrigerate if not using immediately.
**4.** To serve, pour dressing over salad; toss until coated with dressing. Spoon into a serving bowl or melon shells.
**5.** Garnish with mint sprigs. Makes 4 servings.

Left to right: Cucumber, Melon & Ham Salad; Midsummer Chicken; Smoked-Trout & Orange Salad

# Smoked-Trout & Orange Salad

12 oz. smoked-trout fillets, skinned
1/2 cucumber, thinly sliced
3 oranges, sectioned
3 celery stalks, thinly sliced

*Dressing:*
1/2 medium apple, grated
1 tablespoon lemon juice
3 tablespoons mayonnaise
1-1/2 teaspoons prepared horseradish

*To serve:*
Few lettuce leaves
Red (cayenne) pepper

**1.** Flake trout into small pieces. In a medium bowl, combine flaked trout, cucumber, orange sections and celery.
**2.** To make dressing, in a small bowl, combine apple, lemon juice, mayonnaise and horseradish.
**3.** To serve, line individual serving dishes with lettuce leaves. Top with salad. Spoon dressing over salad.
**4.** Cover and refrigerate until chilled. Garnish with red pepper. Makes 4 servings.

# Midsummer Chicken

1 lb. cooked chicken, skinned, boned
1/2 cup dry white wine
1 teaspoon lemon juice
2 teaspoons grated onion
1 teaspoon chopped fresh tarragon
Pinch of onion salt
4 oranges, sectioned
1/4 head endive or leaf lettuce, torn into bite-sized
   pieces
1 bunch watercress, large stems removed
1/2 cup toasted pine nuts or walnuts

*Dressing:*
1 (3-oz.) pkg. cream cheese, room temperature
1/2 pint dairy sour cream (1 cup)
3 drops hot-pepper sauce
Salt
Freshly ground pepper

*To garnish:*
Blanched orange peel, cut into julienne strips

**1.** Slice chicken into thin strips. In a medium bowl, combine chicken strips, wine, lemon juice, onion, tarragon, onion salt and orange sections. Cover and let stand 20 minutes to blend flavors.
**2.** Meanwhile, toss lettuce or endive with watercress; line a serving plate with watercress mixture.
**3.** Drain marinade from chicken mixture, reserving marinade. Stir pine nuts or walnuts into chicken mixture. Spoon chicken mixture over watercress mixture on plates.
**4.** To make dressing, in a small bowl, combine cheese, sour cream, hot-pepper sauce, salt and pepper. Add about 2 tablespoons marinade or enough to give dressing a thick pouring consistency. Pour dressing over chicken mixture.
**5.** Garnish with orange peel. Makes 4 servings.

# Tropical Curried-Chicken Salad

12 oz. cooked chicken, skinned, boned
2 ripe bananas, sliced
1 tablespoon lemon juice
1/2 cup cashew nuts
1/4 cup raisins
1/4 cup chopped dried apricots

*Dressing:*
3 tablespoons mayonnaise
1 tablespoon finely chopped onion
1/2 teaspoon hot Madras curry powder
1/2 teaspoon lemon juice
2 tablespoons grated apple
1 teaspoon mango chutney
Pinch of salt

*To garnish:*
2 tablespoons shredded coconut, toasted

---

*For special occasions, serve this salad on plain or spiced poppadums. Poppadums, a thin bread from India, are available in specialty stores. If poppadums are not available, use corn tortillas that have been shaped into bowls and fried.*

1. Cut chicken into small pieces. In a serving bowl, combine chicken pieces, bananas and lemon juice. Stir in cashews, raisins and dried apricots.
2. To make dressing, in a small bowl, combine mayonnaise, onion, curry powder, lemon juice, apple, chutney and salt.
3. Spoon dressing over salad; toss to coat with dressing.
4. Cover and refrigerate until chilled. Garnish with toasted coconut. Makes 4 servings.

# Spicy Mexican Salad

1 (12-oz.) can whole-kernel corn, drained
1 (15-oz.) can red kidney beans, drained
1 small onion, thinly sliced into rings
1 small green bell pepper, thinly sliced
6 oz. cooked chorizo sausage, skinned, sliced,
    or salami, chopped

*Dressing:*
1/4 cup mayonnaise
2 tablespoons chili salsa
1/2 teaspoon mild chili powder
1 tablespoon finely chopped red bell pepper
Pinch of salt

*Use this spicy dressing in salads and sandwiches, or as a delicious topping for baked potatoes.*

1. In a large salad bowl, combine corn, kidney beans, onion, green bell pepper and chorizo or salami.
2. To make dressing, in a small bowl, combine mayonnaise, chili salsa, chili powder, red bell pepper and salt.
3. Spoon dressing over salad; toss to coat with dressing.
4. Cover and refrigerate until chilled. Serve with tortillas, corn chips or crisp crackers. Makes 4 servings.

# Seafood Pasta

6 oz. pasta twists (about 1-1/2 cups)
1 ripe avocado, sliced
2 teaspoons lemon juice
6 oz. shrimp, cooked, peeled, deveined
1 (8-3/4-oz.) jar mussels, drained
3 tomatoes, cut into wedges
4 or 5 mushrooms, sliced

*Dressing:*
2 tablespoons mayonnaise
2 tablespoons dairy sour cream
1 garlic clove, crushed
2 teaspoons chopped chives
Salt
Freshly ground pepper

*To garnish:*
3 or 4 whole unpeeled cooked shrimp

---

1. Cook pasta twists in a large saucepan of boiling salted water according to package directions until tender. Do not overcook. Drain and cool.
2. In a medium bowl, toss avocado slices in lemon juice. Stir in cooled pasta, shrimp, mussels, tomatoes and mushrooms until combined.
3. To make dressing, in a small bowl, combine mayonnaise, sour cream, garlic, chives, salt and pepper.
4. Fold dressing into salad; spoon into a serving dish. Cover and refrigerate until chilled. Garnish with whole shrimp. Makes 4 servings.

Top to bottom: Seafood Pasta, Tropical Curried-Chicken Salad served in a poppadum

# Chicken & Ham Loaf

1 unsliced sandwich-bread loaf
6 tablespoons butter or margarine
2 small onions, finely chopped
8 oz. mushrooms, thinly sliced (about 3-1/4 cups)
1 tablespoon chopped fresh parsley
Salt
Freshly ground pepper
6 bacon slices, crisp-cooked, crumbled
2 cups chopped cooked ham (about 8 oz.)
1/4 teaspoon rubbed sage
1/4 teaspoon dried leaf thyme
2 tablespoons dry sherry, if desired
2 cups chopped cooked chicken

*To garnish:*
Cilantro

---

1. Preheat oven to 375F (190C). Cut a 1/2-inch slice lengthwise off top of loaf. Carefully pull out soft bread inside, leaving a 1/2-inch-thick wall. Make bread crumbs from soft bread.
2. Melt 1/4 cup butter or margarine; brush loaf, inside and out, with melted butter or margarine. Replace lid; brush lid with remaining butter or margarine. Place on a baking sheet.
3. Bake in preheated oven 10 minutes or until crisp and golden.
4. Melt remaining 2 tablespoons butter or margarine in a medium skillet. Add onions; sauté 5 minutes or until soft. Add mushrooms; cook 2 minutes. Stir in parsley, salt and pepper. Remove from heat.
5. In a medium bowl, combine bacon, ham and 3 tablespoons bread crumbs. Stir in sage, thyme and sherry, if desired.
6. Press 1/2 of ham mixture into bread case. Cover with 1/2 of mushroom mixture. Cover with chicken; cover chicken with remaining mushroom mixture. Press remaining ham mixture over mushroom mixture. Replace lid; wrap loaf in foil.
7. Bake in preheated oven 50 minutes or until center is hot. Serve loaf hot or cold. Cut into thick slices to serve. Garnish with parsley. Makes 6 to 8 servings.

# Pear Waldorf Salad

8 oz. cooked chicken, skinned, boned
1 head lettuce, shredded
2 celery stalks, chopped
1 red bell pepper, sliced
1/4 cup walnut halves
1 cup seedless green grapes, halved
1 pear, peeled, cored, sliced

*Dressing:*
2 tablespoons plain yogurt
2 tablespoons mayonnaise
2 tablespoons grated cucumber
1 teaspoon grated onion
1/2 teaspoon chopped fresh tarragon
Salt
Freshly ground pepper

*To garnish:*
1 pear, cored, sliced
Fresh tarragon sprigs

---

*This is a variation of classic Waldorf Salad, so called because it was invented by the chef of the Waldorf Hotel in New York. Pear Waldorf Salad combines pears with classic ingredients and a tasty cucumber-and-tarragon dressing.*

1. Cut chicken into small pieces. In a large salad bowl, combine lettuce, celery, bell pepper, walnuts, grapes, pear and chicken pieces.
2. To make dressing, in a small bowl, combine yogurt, mayonnaise, cucumber, onion and tarragon. Season with salt and pepper.
3. Spoon dressing over salad ingredients; toss to coat with dressing.
4. Garnish with pear slices and a few tarragon sprigs. Makes 4 servings.

### Variation
**Pear Waldorf Salad with Sour-Cream Dressing:** To make dressing, in a small bowl, combine 2 tablespoons dairy sour cream, 2 tablespoons mayonnaise, 1 tablespoon grated zucchini or cucumber, 2 teaspoons grated onion, 1 tablespoon chopped peanuts, salt and freshly ground pepper.

Left to right: Chicken & Ham Loaf, Pear Waldorf Salad

# Smoked-Salmon Mousse

1 lb. smoked-salmon trimmings
2 tablespoons lemon juice
1/2 cup mayonnaise
1 medium onion, grated
2 tablespoons chopped chives
1 (1/4-oz.) envelope unflavored gelatin (1 tablespoon)
1/4 cup chicken broth or water
3/4 cup whipping cream
Salt
White pepper
Hot-pepper sauce
2 egg whites

*To garnish:*
Cucumber slices
Pimento-stuffed olives

1. In a blender or food processor fitted with a steel blade, process salmon pieces until almost smooth. Spoon into a medium bowl; stir in lemon juice, mayonnaise, onion and chives until thoroughly blended.
2. In a small saucepan, combine gelatin and broth or water. Stir well; let stand 3 minutes. Stir over low heat until gelatin dissolves; set aside to cool. Stir gelatin into salmon mixture.
3. In a medium bowl, whip cream until stiff peaks form. Fold into salmon mixture. Season with salt, white pepper and hot-pepper sauce. Refrigerate until mixture mounds when dropped from a spoon.
4. Beat egg whites in a medium bowl until stiff peaks form. Fold beaten egg whites into salmon mixture. Rinse a 4- to 5-cup decorative mold with cold water. Spoon mixture into mold; smooth top. Refrigerate 3 hours or until set.
5. To serve, run a knife tip around top of mold to loosen. Invert mold on a serving plate. Wet a clean dish towel with hot water; wring dry. Wrap hot towel around outside of mold a few seconds. Remove towel and mold. Garnish mousse with cucumber slices and pimento-stuffed olives. Serve with assorted crackers or cocktail breads. Makes 6 to 8 servings.

# Creamy Chicken Loaf en Croûte

*Pastry:*
1-1/2 cups all-purpose flour
1 teaspoon grated lemon peel
1/2 teaspoon salt
1/2 cup butter or margarine
3 to 4 tablespoons iced water
1 egg yolk beaten with 1 tablespoon water for glaze

*Filling:*
2 (5-oz.) cans white chunk chicken, well-drained
2 tablespoons butter or margarine, melted
2 tablespoons lemon juice
2 (3-oz.) pkgs. cream cheese, room temperature
1 egg, beaten
Salt
Freshly ground pepper
1 (4-oz.) jar sliced pimentos, drained
1 (2-oz.) jar capers, drained, coarsely chopped
1/3 cup chopped fresh parsley

*To garnish:*
Green-onion curls

1. To make pastry, in a medium bowl, combine flour, lemon peel and salt. With a pastry blender or 2 knives, cut in butter or margarine until mixture resembles coarse crumbs. Sprinkle with 3 tablespoons water; toss with a fork until mixture holds together, adding additional water if necessary. Gather dough into a flattened ball. Wrap in plastic wrap or waxed paper; refrigerate 30 minutes.
2. Preheat oven to 400F (205C). Lightly grease a 7" x 3" or 8" x 4" loaf pan. On a lightly floured surface, roll out 3/4 of chilled dough to a rectangle large enough to line loaf pan. Use rolled dough to line greased loaf pan.
3. To make filling, place chicken in a medium bowl; flake with a fork. Stir in butter or margarine. In a medium bowl, beat lemon juice, cream cheese, egg, salt and pepper until combined. Stir cheese mixture into chicken mixture.
4. Scatter pimentos in bottom of pastry-lined pan. Top with capers. Spoon 1/2 of chicken mixture over capers; spread with back of spoon. Sprinkle parsley over chicken. Top with remaining chicken mixture. Fold pastry edges over chicken mixture.
5. On a lightly floured board, roll out remaining 1/4 of pastry to make top crust. Cover loaf with rolled dough. Crimp and flute edges. Decorate top with pastry trimmings, if desired. Brush with egg glaze.
6. Bake in preheated oven 50 to 55 minutes or until pastry is golden brown. Cool completely in pan on a wire rack. Invert pan on a serving plate; refrigerate until served. To serve, cut into slices; garnish with green-onion curls. Makes 6 to 8 servings.

# Cheesy Onion Ring

*Pastry:*
2 cups all-purpose flour
1 teaspoon salt
3/4 cup butter or margarine
1 egg yolk
1/4 cup iced water
1 egg yolk beaten with 1 tablespoon water for glaze
Poppy seeds or sesame seeds

*Filling:*
2 cups shredded sharp Cheddar cheese (8 oz.)
1 cup finely chopped onions
1/2 teaspoon Italian seasoning
3 tablespoons mustard-pickle relish

*To garnish:*
Curly endive leaves

Left to right: Creamy Chicken Loaf en Croûte, Cheesy Onion Ring

1. To make pastry, in a medium bowl, combine flour and salt. With a pastry blender or 2 knives, cut in butter or margarine until mixture resembles coarse crumbs. In a small bowl, beat egg yolk and water until blended. Sprinkle over flour; toss with a fork until mixture holds together. Gather dough into a flattened ball. Wrap in plastic wrap or waxed paper; refrigerate 30 minutes.

2. Preheat oven to 400F (205C). Grease a baking sheet.

3. To make filling, in a medium bowl, combine cheese, onions, Italian seasoning and pickle relish.

4. On a lightly floured surface, roll out pastry to a 16" x 12" rectangle. Spread cheese filling over pastry to within 1/2 inch of edges. Brush 1 long edge of pastry with egg glaze. Roll up, jelly-roll style, starting from long unglazed edge. Press seam to seal. Lift filled roll carefully; place roll, seam-side down, on greased baking sheet.

5. Cut roll at 1-1/2-inch intervals with scissors, cutting almost through to opposite side of roll. Shape roll into a ring. Brush ends with glaze; press firmly to seal. Raise each cut section carefully; tilt back slightly to expose filling. Brush ring all over with egg glaze; sprinkle with poppy seeds or sesame seeds.

6. Bake in preheated oven 30 to 35 minutes or until golden brown. Cool on baking sheet on a wire rack 10 minutes. Slide ring off baking sheet carefully; cool on rack. Fill center with endive; serve warm. Makes 6 to 8 servings.

1/Brush 1 long edge of pastry with egg glaze.

2/Roll up, jelly-roll style, starting from long unglazed edge.

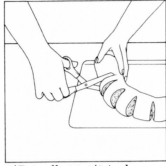

3/Cut roll at 1-1/2-inch intervals with scissors, cutting almost through to opposite side of roll.

4/Raise each cut section carefully; tilt back slightly to expose filling.

# Farmhouse Pâté

6 bacon slices
6 tablespoons butter or margarine
8 oz. pork liver, chopped
8 oz. salt pork, blanched, chopped
1 large onion, chopped
1 garlic clove, crushed
3 tablespoons all-purpose flour
1/2 cup milk
1/2 cup dry wine or apple cider
Salt
Freshly ground pepper
4 bay leaves
6 allspice berries

**1.** Preheat oven to 350F (175C). Grease a 1-quart terrine. Line bottom and sides of greased terrine with bacon.
**2.** Melt 1/4 cup butter or margarine in a large skillet. Add liver, salt pork, onion and garlic; cook 10 minutes. In a blender or food processor fitted with a steel blade, process liver mixture until smooth.
**3.** Melt remaining 2 tablespoons butter or margarine in a medium saucepan. Stir in flour; cook 1 minute, stirring. Gradually stir in milk and wine or cider. Bring to a boil; stirring constantly, cook 3 minutes. Season with salt and pepper. Stir into liver mixture. Spoon into terrine, leveling surface.
**4.** Top with bay leaves and allspice berries. Cover with buttered foil or a lid; place in a roasting pan. Add enough boiling water to roasting pan to come halfway up sides of terrine.
**5.** Bake in preheated oven 1 hour or until firm to the touch. Cool at room temperature 30 minutes. Cover and refrigerate until chilled. Pâté can be refrigerated up to 2 days or frozen up to 1 month. Thaw overnight in refrigerator before serving. Makes 8 servings.

Left to right: Stuffed French Bread, page 212; Farmhouse Pâté

# Crab-Filled Crepes

*Crabmeat Filling:*
**1 (6-1/2-oz.) can crabmeat, drained**
**2 tablespoons butter or margarine**
**2 tablespoons all-purpose flour**
**1 cup milk**
**1/2 cup shredded Swiss cheese (2 oz.)**
**1/4 cup dry vermouth or dry white wine**
**2 hard-cooked eggs, chopped**
**Salt**
**Freshly ground pepper**
**8 crepes**
**2 to 3 tablespoons half and half**
**1/2 cup dairy sour cream**

*If desired, refrigerate crabmeat filling overnight. Do not freeze.*

**1.** Pick over crabmeat; set aside.
**2.** Melt butter or margarine in a medium saucepan over medium heat. Stir in flour; cook 1 minute, stirring constantly. Slowly stir in milk; cook until slightly thickened, stirring constantly. Add cheese; stir over low heat until cheese is melted. Remove from heat; stir in vermouth or wine, crabmeat, eggs, salt and pepper.
**3.** Preheat oven to 350F (175C). Butter an 11" x 7" baking dish; set aside.
**4.** Spoon 1-1/2 tablespoons crabmeat mixture onto each crepe. Fold crepe over filling; place, seam side down, in buttered baking dish. Cover; bake 15 to 20 minutes or until heated through.
**5.** Stir 1 to 2 tablespoons half and half into sour cream. Place crepes on a serving dish; spoon sour-cream mixture across center. Makes 8 filled crepes.

# Crepes

**2 cups all-purpose flour**
**1/4 teaspoon salt**
**4 eggs**
**2 cups milk**
**1/4 cup butter or margarine, melted**
**Butter or margarine**

**1.** In a large bowl, combine flour and salt. In a medium bowl, with a whisk, beat eggs; beat in milk until combined. Slowly pour egg mixture into flour, beating constantly. Beat until mixture is blended and batter is smooth. Slowly add melted butter or margarine, beating until combined.
**2.** Or, place ingredients in a blender or food processor. Process 1 to 2 minutes or until batter is smooth.
**3.** Pour batter into a pitcher. Cover and refrigerate at least 1 hour.
**4.** Stir refrigerated batter. If batter has thickened slightly, stir in a few teaspoons of milk.
**5.** Melt 1 teaspoon butter or margarine in a 6- or 7-inch skillet or crepe pan over medium heat. Pour in 3 tablespoons batter or enough to make a thin layer in bottom of pan. Cook over medium heat 1-1/2 minutes or until small bubbles begin to form on crepe's surface. With a spatula, turn crepe over; cook 1-1/2 minutes. Remove cooked crepe to a flat plate; repeat with remaining batter. Add more butter or margarine to skillet or pan as necessary. Makes about 34 crepes.

# Melon & Grape Cup

**1-1/2 lb. melon**
**4 oz. black grapes, halved, seeded**
**1/4 cup red-grape juice**
**1/2 cup tonic water**

**1.** Remove and discard seeds from melon; peel. Cut peeled melon into small cubes.
**2.** In a medium bowl, combine melon cubes, grapes and grape juice. Refrigerate until chilled. To serve, spoon into glass dishes; pour tonic water over fruit immediately before serving. Makes 4 servings.

Left to right: Ham & Smoked-Cheese Flan, Spanish Vegetable & Ham Quiche

# Ham & Smoked-Cheese Flan

**Pastry:**
1-1/2 cups all-purpose flour
1/2 teaspoon salt
1/2 cup vegetable shortening
3 to 4 tablespoons iced water

**Filling:**
1 cup chopped cooked ham (about 4 oz.)
1 cup shredded smoked cheese (4 oz.)
3 eggs, beaten
1/2 cup half and half
Pinch of salt
1/4 teaspoon freshly grated nutmeg

**To garnish:**
3 tomatoes, cut into wedges

**1.** To make pastry, in a medium bowl, combine flour and salt. With a pastry blender or 2 knives, cut in shortening until mixture resembles coarse crumbs. Sprinkle with 3 tablespoons iced water; toss with a fork until mixture holds together, adding additional water if necessary. Gather dough into a flattened ball. Wrap in plastic wrap or waxed paper; refrigerate 30 minutes.
**2.** Preheat oven to 400F (205C). On a lightly floured board, roll out pastry to an 11-inch circle. Use to line a 9- or 10-inch pie pan or quiche pan. Crimp and flute pastry edge; prick bottom lightly with a fork. Line pastry with foil; fill with pie weights or dried beans.
**3.** Bake in preheated oven 15 minutes. Remove foil and pie weights or beans; bake 5 to 8 minutes or until golden. Set aside to cool. Reduce oven temperature to 375F (190C).
**4.** Sprinkle ham and cheese over bottom of cooled pastry shell. In a medium bowl, combine eggs, half and half, salt and nutmeg; carefully pour over ham and cheese.
**5.** Bake in preheated oven 35 minutes or until set. Serve flan warm or cold. Garnish with tomato wedges. Makes 6 servings.

# Quiche Lorraine

*Pastry:*
1-1/2 cups all-purpose flour
1/2 teaspoon salt
1/2 cup vegetable shortening
3 to 4 tablespoons iced water

*Filling:*
1/2 lb. bacon, crisp-cooked, crumbled
1-1/2 cups grated Swiss or Gruyère cheese (6 oz.)
3 eggs
1-1/2 cups half and half
1/4 teaspoon freshly grated nutmeg
Salt
Freshly ground pepper

1. To make pastry, in a medium bowl, combine flour and salt. With a pastry blender or 2 knives, cut in shortening until mixture resembles coarse crumbs. Sprinkle with 3 tablespoons iced water; toss with a fork until mixture holds together, adding additional water if necessary. Gather dough into a flattened ball. Wrap in plastic wrap or waxed paper; refrigerate 30 minutes.
2. Preheat oven to 400F (205C). On a lightly floured board, roll out pastry to an 11-inch circle. Use to line a 9- or 10-inch pie pan or quiche pan. Crimp and flute pastry edge; prick bottom lightly with a fork. Line pastry with foil; fill with pie weights or dried beans.
3. Bake in preheated oven 15 minutes. Remove foil and pie weights or beans; bake 5 to 8 minutes or until golden. Set aside to cool. Reduce oven temperature to 375F (190C).
4. Scatter bacon in bottom of cooled pastry shell. Sprinkle 1/2 of cheese over bacon.
5. In a medium bowl, beat eggs, half and half, nutmeg, salt and pepper until blended. Carefully pour into pastry shell. Sprinkle remaining 3/4 cup cheese on top.
6. Bake in preheated oven 35 to 45 minutes or until puffed and top is golden brown.
7. Cool in pan on a wire rack 15 minutes. Serve warm. Makes 6 servings.

### Variation
**Spinach Quiche:** Omit bacon. Thaw and drain 1 (10-ounce) package frozen chopped spinach. Heat 2 tablespoons butter or margarine in a medium skillet. Slice 1 bunch green onions; add to skillet. Cook 2 to 3 minutes. Stir in spinach; cook 1 minute. Scatter 3/4 cup cheese in bottom of cooled pastry shell. Spoon spinach mixture over cheese. Continue with step 5.

# Spanish Vegetable & Ham Quiche

*Pastry:*
1-1/2 cups all-purpose flour
1/2 teaspoon salt
1/2 cup vegetable shortening
3 to 4 tablespoons iced water

*Filling:*
2 tablespoons butter or margarine
1 small red bell pepper, sliced
1 small green bell pepper, sliced
5 oz. mushrooms, sliced (about 2 cups)
1 small zucchini, sliced
1 cup chopped cooked ham (about 4 oz.)
3 eggs
1-1/4 cups half and half
1/4 cup grated Parmesan cheese (3/4 oz.)
1/2 teaspoon ground cumin
Salt
Freshly ground black pepper

1. To make pastry, in a medium bowl, combine flour and salt. With a pastry blender or 2 knives, cut in shortening until mixture resembles coarse crumbs. Sprinkle with 3 tablespoons iced water; toss with a fork until mixture holds together, adding additional water if necessary. Gather dough into a flattened ball. Wrap in plastic wrap or waxed paper; refrigerate 30 minutes.
2. Preheat oven to 400F (205C). On a lightly floured board, roll out pastry to an 11-inch circle. Use to line a 9- or 10-inch pie pan or quiche pan. Crimp and flute pastry edge; prick bottom lightly with a fork. Line pastry with foil; fill with pie weights or dried beans.
3. Bake in preheated oven 15 minutes. Remove foil and pie weights or beans; bake 5 to 8 minutes or until golden. Set aside to cool. Reduce oven temperature to 375F (190C).
4. To make filling, melt butter or margarine in a medium skillet. Add bell peppers, mushrooms and zucchini; sauté 5 to 6 minutes or until tender.
5. Scatter ham in bottom of cooled pastry shell. Arrange cooked vegetables over ham. In a medium bowl, beat eggs, half and half, cheese, cumin, salt and black pepper until blended. Carefully pour egg mixture over vegetable mixture.
6. Bake in preheated oven 40 to 45 minutes or until center is set and top is golden brown. Remove from oven; cool slightly. Serve warm or cold. Makes 6 servings.

# Bacon & Liver Pâté

4 bacon slices, chopped
8 oz. turkey or chicken livers, chopped
1 hard-cooked egg
1 garlic clove, crushed
2 tablespoons brandy
1 tablespoon whipping cream
1/4 teaspoon dried leaf thyme
Pinch of ground mace
Salt
Freshly ground pepper

*To garnish:*
2 hard-cooked eggs, separated
Parsley sprigs

**1.** Place bacon in a large skillet over medium heat. Sauté until almost done. Add livers; cook 10 minutes, stirring occasionally.
**2.** In a blender or food processor fitted with a steel blade, combine cooked bacon-and-liver mixture and remaining ingredients except for garnish. Process until smooth. Spoon into 4 ramekin dishes. Refrigerate until chilled.
**3.** To garnish, with a knife, finely chop egg whites; press egg yolks through a sieve. Arrange chopped egg whites and sieved yolks in rings on top of pâté with a parsley sprig in center. Serve with hot toast. Makes 4 servings.

Clockwise from left: Blue-Cheese Soufflés, Country Chicken Pâté, Bacon & Liver Pâté

# Country Chicken Pâté

1 cup minced cooked chicken
1/4 cup minced cooked ham
1 teaspoon grated lemon peel
2 teaspoons chopped fresh parsley
1/4 teaspoon dried leaf tarragon
Salt
Freshly ground pepper
1/2 cup butter, melted

*To garnish:*
Lettuce leaves
Tomato slices
Parsley or tarragon sprigs

1. In a medium bowl, combine all ingredients except garnish.
2. Press chicken mixture into 4 individual ramekin dishes or foil-lined custard cups.
3. Chill until mixture is firm. Refrigerate overnight.
4. To serve, turn out onto plates lined with lettuce leaves and tomato slices. Garnish with a parsley or tarragon sprig. Serve with Melba toast. Makes 4 servings.

**Variation**
**Potted Shrimp:** Substitute 8 ounces minced cooked shrimp for chicken and ham. Substitute a pinch of red (cayenne) pepper for tarragon. Substitute lemon wedges for tomato slices.

# Blue-Cheese Soufflés

1/4 cup butter or margarine
1/2 cup all-purpose flour
1-1/2 cups milk
3 eggs, separated
2/3 cup fresh bread crumbs
1/2 teaspoon dry mustard
White pepper
1 cup crumbled blue cheese

1. Heavily grease 6 (2/3-cup, 3-1/2-inch-diameter) freezer-to-oven ramekins.
2. Melt butter or margarine in a medium saucepan over medium heat. Stir in flour; cook 1 minute, stirring constantly. Gradually stir in milk; boil until sauce is thickened, stirring constantly. Cool slightly.
3. Beat in egg yolks, bread crumbs, mustard and white pepper until blended. Add blue cheese; stir until cheese is melted. Pour cheese mixture into a large bowl.
4. In another large bowl, beat egg whites until stiff peaks form. Fold beaten egg whites into cheese mixture. Divide mixture evenly among greased ramekins.
5. Place filled ramekins on a baking sheet. Open freeze. Wrap each frozen soufflé with foil; label. Freeze up to 1 month.
6. Preheat oven to 425F (220C). Unwrap; place frozen soufflés in preheated oven. Bake 35 to 40 minutes or until raised and golden brown on top. Serve immediately; this soufflé will not wait. Makes 6 servings.

# Smoked-Salmon Boats

1-1/4 cups all-purpose flour
1/2 teaspoon salt
7 tablespoons shortening
3 tablespoons iced water

*Filling:*
1/3 lb. smoked-salmon trimmings, finely chopped
1 tablespoon lemon juice
1/4 teaspoon dried dill weed
1 tablespoon mayonnaise
1/4 cup whipping cream, lightly whipped
Salt
Freshly ground pepper

*To garnish:*
Paprika
Fresh dill sprigs

1. Preheat oven to 400F (205C).
2. To make pastry, in a medium bowl, combine flour and salt. Using a pastry blender or 2 knives, cut in shortening until mixture resembles fine bread crumbs. Add water; toss with a fork until dough begins to hold together. Press dough into a ball.
3. Roll out dough on a lightly floured surface. Use to line 8 boat-shaped tart pans. With a fork, prick well; place on a baking sheet. Bake in preheated oven 15 minutes or until golden brown. Cool in pans 10 minutes. Remove from pans; cool completely on a wire rack.
4. To make filling, in a medium bowl, combine all filling ingredients. Refrigerate until chilled.
5. Stir filling; spoon into baked pastry boats. Sprinkle with paprika; garnish with fresh dill. Makes 8 pastries.

# Easy Cheese Ball

2 cups shredded Cheddar cheese (8 oz.)
1 (3-oz.) pkg. cream cheese, room temperature
2 oz. crumbled blue cheese, room temperature (1/2 cup)
1 garlic clove, crushed
1/2 teaspoon Worcestershire sauce

1. In a blender or food processor fitted with a steel blade, blend Cheddar cheese, cream cheese, blue cheese, garlic and Worcestershire sauce until smooth.
2. Shape cheese mixture into a ball. Wrap in plastic wrap or waxed paper. Refrigerate 2 to 3 days.
3. To serve, unwrap cheese ball. Place on a serving plate. Serve with crackers. Makes 6 to 8 servings.

**Variations**
Roll cheese ball in chopped nuts before wrapping. Or, roll in chopped parsley immediately before serving.

# Chicken-Liver Pâté

1 lb. chicken livers
1/4 cup rendered chicken fat, butter or margarine
1 onion, finely chopped
1 garlic clove, minced
2 tablespoons Marsala or sweet sherry
Salt
Freshly ground pepper
2 hard-cooked eggs, chopped

*To garnish:*
Chopped fresh parsley
Assorted crackers or cocktail bread

1. Lightly grease a 2-1/2-cup mold with butter or margarine; set aside.
2. Trim chicken livers; cut in half. Rinse liver halves under cold running water; pat dry with paper towels.
3. Melt chicken fat, butter or margarine in a medium skillet over medium heat. Add onion; sauté until transparent. Add garlic and chicken livers; sauté 5 minutes or until livers are no longer pink.
4. In a blender or food processor fitted with a steel blade, process liver mixture until almost smooth. Add Marsala or sherry, salt and pepper; process 1 minute. Add eggs; process 1 minute.
5. Spoon into prepared mold; smooth top. Cover and refrigerate until thoroughly chilled. Refrigerate up to 2 days.
6. To serve, unmold onto a serving plate; garnish with chopped parsley. Serve with crackers or cocktail bread. Makes 8 servings.

Left to right: Gazpacho Ice, Smoked-Salmon Boats

# Gazpacho Ice

1 medium tomato, diced
1 medium cucumber, peeled, diced
1 small green bell pepper, diced
1 small onion, diced
1 garlic clove, crushed
1 to 2 tablespoons red-wine vinegar
1 teaspoon paprika
1/2 (8-oz.) pkg. cream cheese, room temperature
1/2 cup whipping cream
1 (1/4-oz.) envelope unflavored gelatin (1 tablespoon)
1/4 cup water
Salt
Freshly ground black pepper
Hot-pepper sauce

*To garnish:*
Lettuce leaves
Chopped green olives

1. In a blender or food processor fitted with a steel blade, process tomato, cucumber, green pepper, onion and garlic until pureed. Stir in vinegar and paprika. Press pureed mixture through a sieve into a large bowl; set aside.
2. Without rinsing blender or food processor, process cream cheese and cream until smooth. Add pureed vegetable mixture, 1/2 cup at a time; process until blended.
3. In a small saucepan, combine gelatin and water. Stir well; let stand 3 minutes. Stir over low heat until gelatin dissolves; set aside to cool. Stir cooled gelatin into puree. Season with salt, pepper and hot-pepper sauce.
4. Pour into a 4-cup rigid freezer container; cover and label. Freeze 5 to 6 hours or until thoroughly frozen. Store up to 1 month.
5. To serve, place in refrigerator several hours, or let stand at room temperature to soften slightly before serving. Spoon into individual serving bowls. Place bowls on lettuce-lined plates; garnish with chopped olives. Makes 6 to 8 servings.

# Smorgasbord Pinwheel

1 bread loaf, 9 or 10 inches in diameter
Butter or margarine, room temperature
2 (8-oz.) pkgs. cream cheese, room temperature
4 oz. blue cheese, crumbled, room temperature
Freshly ground pepper
3 tablespoons mayonnaise
1 (3-oz.) jar red lumpfish caviar
1 (3-oz.) jar black lumpfish caviar
About 1 cup sliced pimento-stuffed olives

---

**1.** Cut 1 (3/4-inch-thick) slice from widest part of loaf. Spread bread slice with a thin layer of butter or margarine. Place buttered bread on a flat board or platter.
**2.** In a medium bowl, beat 1/2 of cream cheese until creamy. Beat in blue cheese and pepper.
**3.** Spread blue-cheese mixture evenly over buttered bread.
**4.** In a medium bowl, beat remaining cream cheese and mayonnaise.
**5.** Mark cheese-topped bread into 8 equal sections with a knife blade.
**6.** Fill a pastry bag fitted with a star tip with mayonnaise-and-cheese mixture. Pipe mixture into rosettes along marked lines and around outer edge of circle.
**7.** Fill 4 alternate sections with sliced olives. Fill 2 opposite sections with red caviar; fill remaining 2 sections with black caviar. See photo opposite. Makes 8 servings.

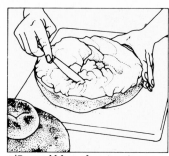

1/Spread blue-cheese mixture evenly over buttered bread.

2/Mark cheese-topped bread into 8 equal sections with a knife blade.

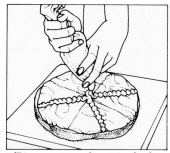

3/Pipe rosettes along marked lines and around outer edge of circle.

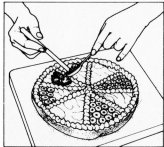

4/Fill sections with sliced olives, red caviar and black caviar. See photo opposite.

Smorgasbord Pinwheel

# Soups

We often think of a bowl of steaming soup as the perfect dish for a cold winter day. However soup can be served the year around. A creamy chilled soup can be the perfect first course on a sizzling summer day. This chapter includes recipes for cream soups, clear soups, hot soups and chilled soups. You're sure to find one that fits your needs. Check the index for soups that are included in other chapters.

## SOUP INGREDIENTS

Most soups are based on a broth. Broth can be made from poultry, meat, fish or vegetables. Make your own broth or buy canned broth or bouillon cubes. Most bouillon cubes and canned broths are salted. If using commercial products, taste the finished soup before adding additional salt.

Homemade broth can be quickly cooled and refrigerated up to 2 days. Remove fat before using. For longer storage, freeze cooled broth in ice-cube trays or freezer containers up to 3 months. Cubes of frozen broth are convenient because they can be used without thawing. Thaw frozen broth overnight in the refrigerator.

The other ingredients in soup will depend on what is available and when the soup is to be served. For a first course, a light broth may only need a few thin slices of meat or vegetable, for example, *Lime-Chicken Soup*. Use dried beans or peas, potatoes or pasta and fish or meat for a hearty soup or chowder that will be the main course. *Hearty Minestrone* and *Sunday-Night Pea Soup* are examples of soups that can be served as suppers or other light meals. Don't forget that great combination, soup and a sandwich!

Soups are a great way to use leftovers. Check your refrigerator; you may have the makings of a delicious soup. Because leftovers are already cooked, this is a quick way to make soup. Use your creativity in making soups; if a recipe calls for broccoli, substitute cauliflower or another vegetable that is available. Vary soups according to the season to take advantage of seasonal produce.

## SERVINGS SOUPS

Use your imagination in selecting serving containers for soups. Match the container with the soup. For example, Oriental soups seem to taste better when served in Oriental soup bowls with a ceramic spoon. Thick stews and heavy pottery go together. Mugs make excellent servers for soup. They are especially good for buffets or picnics.

Soup can be brought to the table in individual bowls or served from a tureen by the host or hostess. For a buffet, keep soup hot in a slow cooker or on a warming tray. A selection of soups and breads makes a great idea for a casual party. Remember to serve hot soups steaming hot and cold soups well-chilled.

Garnish soup attractively. Use a celery stalk in a mug of vegetable soup. Or, garnish cold soups with a lemon slice or a parsley sprig. For fruit soups, garnish with a small slice of fruit and a dollop of sour cream. Add hot tortilla chips to a chicken soup for a southwestern touch. Matching the garnish to the soup adds to its enjoyment.

# Chicken Minestrone

4 cups chicken stock
1 ham bone, with some meat
1 medium onion, chopped
2 carrots, thinly sliced
2 celery stalks, thinly sliced
1 cup chopped cooked chicken
4 oz. ziti or other thick macaroni
1/2 cup fresh or frozen green peas
1/2 teaspoon dried leaf oregano or marjoram
Salt
Freshly ground pepper
Grated Parmesan cheese

1. In a large saucepan, combine stock, ham bone, onion, carrots and celery. Bring to a boil. Reduce heat; simmer 20 minutes.
2. Remove ham bone; cut off and chop any meat. Add chopped ham and chicken to soup. Bring to a boil.
3. Add remaining ingredients except Parmesan cheese. Simmer 10 minutes or until macaroni is tender. Serve with Parmesan cheese. Makes 4 servings.

# Strawberry-Yogurt Soup

3 cups fresh or thawed frozen strawberries
3 cups water
1/3 cup sugar
1 tablespoon lemon juice
1/8 teaspoon salt
1 pint plain or strawberry-flavored yogurt (2 cups)

1. In a large saucepan, combine strawberries, water, sugar and lemon juice. Cook over medium heat, stirring, until sugar dissolves. Cool slightly.
2. In a blender or food processor fitted with a steel blade, process strawberry mixture until pureed. Pour into a large bowl. Cover and refrigerate until chilled.
3. To serve, stir yogurt into chilled strawberry mixture until blended. Ladle into individual bowls or a large serving dish. Makes 4 to 6 servings.

# Beef Stock

2 lb. soup bones
1 onion, chopped
1 celery stalk, chopped
1 carrot, chopped
2 bouquets garni
Salt
Freshly ground pepper
Water

*Freeze stock in 2-cup containers. Or, freeze in ice-cube trays; when frozen, pack in plastic freezer bags.*

1. Preheat oven to 425F (220C).
2. Put bones into a roasting pan; place in preheated oven. Roast 40 minutes, turning bones over once. Remove from oven.
3. Place browned bones, vegetables and seasonings in a large saucepan. Cover with water. Bring to a boil. Reduce heat; cover. Simmer 2 hours.
4. Strain stock into a large bowl, discarding bones, vegetables and bouquets garni. Refrigerate strained stock until cold. Lift fat from surface. Cover and refrigerate up to 3 days or freeze up to 3 months. To freeze, pour stock into a rigid freezer container or ice-cube trays. Cover and label.
5. Use for soups, stews, casseroles or gravy. Cubes may be added, still frozen, to hot soups. Bring to a boil before serving. Makes about 2 quarts.

**Variation**
**Chicken Stock:** Use 2 pounds chicken parts; do not brown. Proceed from Step 3.

Top to bottom: Chicken Minestrone; Melon & Grape Cup, page 19

# Chicken Chowder

4 bacon slices, chopped
1 onion, finely chopped
2 celery stalks, sliced
1-1/2 cups diced potatoes
1/2 cup whole-kernel corn
1-1/2 cups chicken stock
1 cup diced cooked chicken or turkey
Salt
Freshly ground pepper
Pinch ground mace
1/2 cup half and half

*Chowder is an American word thought to come from the name of the cooking pot that fishermen used to throw their catch into when they returned safely from the sea. The community shared in celebrating their homecoming. The thick soup/stew was a particular feature of New England cooking. Today, many ingredients other than fish are used to make chowder. Double recipe, if desired.*

**1.** Place bacon in a large saucepan over medium heat. Sauté until partially cooked. Add onion; sauté 5 minutes or until softened.
**2.** Add celery, potatoes, corn and stock. Bring to a boil; reduce heat. Cover; simmer 15 minutes.
**3.** Add chicken or turkey; cook 5 minutes longer. Season with salt, pepper and mace. Stir in half and half; heat but do not boil. Adjust seasoning, if necessary.
**4.** Serve with crackers or warm French bread and butter. Makes 4 servings.

Clockwise from upper left: Sunday-Night Pea Soup; Crab-Filled Crepes, page 19; Chicken Chowder

# Vichyssoise

3 large leeks, white part only
1/4 cup butter or margarine
4 medium potatoes (about 1-1/4 lb.)
5 cups chicken stock
1-1/2 cups half and half
Salt
White pepper

1. Cut leeks lengthwise; wash under running water to remove sand. Finely chop leeks.
2. In a large saucepan over medium heat, melt butter or margarine. Add leeks; sauté until softened, stirring occasionally.
3. While leeks are cooking, peel and chop potatoes. Add chopped potatoes and stock to leeks. Bring to a boil. Reduce heat; simmer until potatoes are tender. Cool slightly.
4. Process soup in a blender or food processor fitted with a steel blade until pureed. Pour into a large bowl; stir in half and half. Season with salt and pepper. Refrigerate until chilled.
5. Ladle into individual bowls or a large serving bowl. Makes 6 to 8 servings.

## Variation

To serve warm, place pureed leek mixture in a clean large saucepan; add half and half. Heat through; do not boil.

# Cream of Mushroom Soup

2 tablespoons butter or margarine
3 tablespoons chopped onion
2-1/2 cups finely chopped fresh mushrooms
2 tablespoons all-purpose flour
3 cups chicken stock
3/4 cup half and half
Salt
White pepper

1. In a medium saucepan over medium heat, melt butter or margarine. Add onion; sauté until softened. Add mushrooms; sauté 5 minutes.
2. Stir in flour; cook 1 minute stirring. Gradually stir in stock. Bring to a boil; reduce heat. Simmer about 15 minutes or until mushrooms are tender.
3. Stir in half and half. Season with salt and white pepper. Heat through; do not boil. Ladle into individual bowls or a large serving bowl. Makes about 6 servings.

# Sunday-Night Pea Soup

6 oz. dried peas
2 oz. dried lentils
About 6 cups water
1-1/2 lb. smoked ham hock
1 large onion, chopped
2 bay leaves
Freshly ground pepper

*This is a substantial soup. Serve as a main dish. Double recipe, if desired.*

1. Put peas and lentils in a large saucepan. Cover with cold water; let stand 12 hours.
2. Drain off and discard soaking water. Add ham, onion, bay leaves and pepper. Add enough water to cover.
3. Bring to a boil. Reduce heat; cover. Simmer 2 hours or until peas are tender.
4. Lift out ham. Remove skin and meat from bone; discard bone and skin. Cut meat into chunks; set aside.
5. In a blender or food processor fitted with a steel blade, process soup, in batches, until smooth. Process soup twice, if necessary. Add ham chunks to puree.
6. Heat soup in a large saucepan over medium heat. Bring to a boil, stirring occasionally. Taste; adjust seasoning, if necessary. Add a little milk if soup is too thick. Serve with whole-wheat rolls or toast. Makes 8 servings.

# Red-Pepper & Tomato Soup

3 tablespoons butter, melted
1 tablespoon vegetable oil
1 medium onion, chopped
3 small tomatoes, chopped (12 oz.)
2 red bell peppers, chopped
1 tablespoon all-purpose flour
1/4 teaspoon dried leaf basil
Salt
Freshly ground black pepper
2 cups water
1/2 cup half and half or milk

*To garnish:*
Chopped parsley

---

**1.** Heat butter and oil in a medium saucepan over medium heat. Add onion; sauté gently until soft. Stir in tomatoes and bell peppers; cook 5 minutes.
**2.** Stir in flour, basil, salt and pepper. Slowly stir in water. Bring to a boil, stirring constantly. Reduce heat; cover. Simmer 30 minutes, stirring frequently.
**3.** In a blender or food processor fitted with a steel blade, process soup until pureed. Rub puree through a sieve.
**4.** Place pureed soup in a medium saucepan over medium heat. Bring to a boil, stirring occasionally. Add cream or milk; heat, but do not boil. Season to taste. Garnish with chopped parsley. Makes 4 servings.

# Creamy Cabbage Soup

1/4 cup butter
3 cups finely shredded cabbage
3/4 cup chicken stock
1-1/4 cups milk
Salt
White pepper

*To garnish:*
Chopped chives or green-onion tops

---

*This basic soup is delicious. Any cooked vegetables, such as sliced button mushrooms, chopped asparagus tips, peas, carrots, and corn, or chopped cooked ham can be added. Make double or triple the amount to freeze.*

**1.** Melt butter in a medium saucepan over low heat. Add cabbage. Cover; cook about 30 minutes or until cabbage is soft, stirring occasionally.
**2.** Add stock to cooked cabbage. In a blender or food processor fitted with a steel blade, process cabbage and stock in batches until smooth.
**3.** Place cabbage mixture in a saucepan; bring to a boil, stirring occasionally. Add milk; season with salt and pepper. Garnish with chopped chives or onion tops. Makes 4 servings.

Left to right: Creamy Cabbage Soup; Red-Pepper & Tomato Soup; Whole-Wheat Soda Bread, page 275

# Lime-Chicken Soup

1 chicken-breast half, poached
1/2 small carrot
3 green-onion tops
6 cups chicken stock
2 tablespoons lime juice
Salt
White pepper

*To garnish:*
Fresh lime slices

1. Cut poached chicken into fine julienne strips; set aside. Cut carrot into fine julienne strips. Cut onion tops into strips the same size as carrot strips, keeping separate from carrot strips. Set onion and carrot strips aside.
2. In a medium saucepan, bring broth to a simmer. Add carrot strips; cook about 1 minute or until crisp-tender. Stir in chicken strips and onion strips; heat until hot.
3. Remove from heat; add lime juice. Season with salt and white pepper. Ladle soup into individual serving bowl. Top each bowl with a lime slice. Serve hot. Makes 6 servings.

# Chunky Gazpacho

2 bread slices, crusts removed
2 cups tomato juice
2 garlic cloves, crushed
1/2 cucumber, peeled, finely chopped
1 green bell pepper, chopped
1 red bell pepper, chopped
1 large onion, finely chopped
4 to 6 medium tomatoes, peeled, seeded,
    chopped (1-1/2 lb.)
1/4 cup olive oil
2 tablespoons red-wine vinegar
Salt
Freshly ground black pepper
1/4 teaspoon dried leaf marjoram
1/4 teaspoon dried leaf basil
Fresh cilantro sprig

*To serve:*
Croutons
Sliced pimento-stuffed olives
Coarsely chopped cucumber
Chopped green and red bell peppers
Chopped green onions

*A classic Spanish soup, Gazpacho makes a refreshing light supper or lunch dish. Guests sprinkle their bowls of soup with a little of each garnish before eating.*

**1.** Chop bread coarsely. Place chopped bread, tomato juice and garlic in a blender. Let stand 5 minutes; blend until smooth. Or, place bread, tomato juice and garlic in a medium bowl. Mash with a wooden spoon until blended.
**2.** In a medium bowl, combine bread mixture, cucumber, bell peppers, onion, tomatoes, olive oil, vinegar, salt, black pepper, marjoram and basil. Transfer to a chilled soup tureen or serving dish.
**3.** Refrigerate 1 hour or until chilled. Garnish with cilantro sprig. Serve with small bowls of croutons, olives, cucumber, bell peppers and green onions. Accompany with crusty French bread. Makes 4 servings.

---

To make *flavored croutons*, deep-fry bread cubes in hot oil until crisp and golden. Drain fried croutons on paper towels. Toss in coarse sea salt, freshly grated lemon peel, finely chopped fresh herbs, garlic salt, onion salt, finely grated Parmesan cheese or lemon pepper for delicious results.

---

# Hearty Minestrone

8 bacon slices, diced
2 garlic cloves, crushed
4 celery stalks, chopped
4 carrots, sliced
2 onions, chopped
2 potatoes, peeled, diced (about 12 oz.)
1 (1-lb.) can tomatoes
1 cup chicken stock
1 parsley sprig
1 bay leaf
1 tablespoon chopped fresh basil
Salt
Freshly ground pepper
1 (15-oz.) can white beans or garbanzo beans, drained
2 oz. spaghetti
8 oz. ham, cut into thin strips
1/2 small head cabbage, shredded
2 zucchini, sliced
1/2 (10-oz.) pkg. frozen green beans

*To garnish:*
4 to 6 tablespoons grated Parmesan cheese
4 to 6 fresh basil sprigs, if desired

**1.** Place bacon in a large flameproof casserole; cook until crisp. Drain off all but 2 tablespoons fat. Add garlic, celery, carrots, onions and potatoes; cook 5 minutes, stirring frequently.
**2.** Add tomatoes with their juice, stock, parsley, bay leaf, basil, salt and pepper. Cover and simmer 20 minutes.
**3.** Add canned beans; spaghetti, broken into small pieces; ham; cabbage; zucchini and green beans. Cover and cook 10 minutes or until spaghetti is tender.
**4.** Remove and discard parsley and bay leaf. Ladle soup into a warmed soup tureen or soup bowls.
**5.** Sprinkle with Parmesan cheese; garnish with a few basil sprigs, if desired. Makes 4 to 6 servings.

# Provence-Style Fish Chowder

3 tablespoons vegetable oil
3 large onions, finely chopped
1 garlic clove, crushed
1 (28-oz.) can tomatoes
1 parsley sprig
1 bay leaf
3 cups chopped peeled potatoes (about 1 lb.)
About 20 small black olives, pitted
2 tablespoons capers
1 cup tomato juice
2 cups chicken, vegetable or fish stock
Salt
Freshly ground pepper
1-1/2 lb. white fish, skinned, boned, cut into
   3/4-inch cubes

*To garnish:*
3 tablespoons finely chopped fresh parsley

**1.** Heat oil in a large saucepan. Add onions and garlic; sauté over low heat about 5 minutes or until lightly browned.
**2.** Add tomatoes with their juice, parsley and bay leaf. Bring to a boil. Reduce heat; simmer 5 minutes, stirring frequently to break up tomatoes.
**3.** Add potatoes, olives, capers, tomato juice, stock, salt and pepper. Cook, uncovered, 10 to 15 minutes or until potatoes are almost tender.
**4.** Stir in fish; simmer over low heat, uncovered, about 5 minutes or until fish tests done.
**5.** Remove and discard parsley sprig and bay leaf. Transfer to a warmed serving dish or tureen. Garnish with parsley. Serve hot with thick wedges of crusty bread. Makes 4 to 6 servings.

Clockwise from left: Chunky Gazpacho with accompaniments, Hearty Minestrone, Provence-Style Fish Chowder

# Salads

Gone are the days when salads were only served on hot summer days and always consisted of lettuce, tomato and cucumber. Now salads are served all year around and include numerous exciting ingredients. Salads are served for all occasions and range from substantial main courses to colorful side dishes and sophisticated starters. They may be simple to prepare, requiring only a few minutes to assemble before serving, or they may involve more elaborate preparations that can be done ahead.

Whichever type of salad you choose, it will always be fun to put together. Interesting salads consist of contrasting flavors, colors and textures. Preparing a salad is a wonderful excuse to indulge your imagination in arranging ingredients and in trying new garnishes. The presentation of a salad is all-important. Look for interesting plates and dishes for serving. Wooden salad bowls are perfect for green salads, but do not show off more elaborate salads to advantage. Use attractive glass, china or pottery serving plates, bowls and platters for these. It's fun to serve ethnic dishes in their native pottery. Many salads look their prettiest when arranged in individual dishes.

Recipes in this chapter are arranged according to the four seasons of the year. In each season you will find a selection of recipes for starters, main dishes and dinner salads. Starters are designed to stimulate the appetite; therefore, serving size should be smaller than those for most dinner salads and main dishes. Several light main-dishes are included; these are perfect for suppers and lunches. Dinner salads can vary from a simple tossed salad to a hearty bean or potato salad. The inspiration for these recipes comes from all over the world. This wide range of cuisines adds variety in flavor and texture, and introduces lots of new ideas for combining and presenting familiar and exotic ingredients.

Since most ingredients are fresh and seasonal, all the salads are healthy and nutritious. Some salads are ideal for those watching calories. But beware of calorie-laden ingredients, such as cheese, nuts, avocados and some dressings. Because salads are served chilled or at room temperature, they are excellent choices for make-ahead entertaining, as well as for family meals.

## SALAD DRESSINGS

The dressing is a vitally important element of any salad. It can literally make or break a salad's success. There are numerous types of dressing; choose one according to the ingredients you have available and the salad it is destined to dress. The classic vinaigrette or oil-and-vinegar dressing must be made with the best quality oil and vinegar. The exact proportions will depend on the types of oil and vinegar used and personal preference. This dressing should always be made to taste. A good oil-and-vinegar dressing is indispensable if you make salads regularly. Make and store it in a screw-top jar. Remember to shake the jar vigorously to combine the dressing before using. Oil-and-vinegar dressings can be refrigerated up to one week. Mayonnaise is another classic dressing that can be served with most salads. Homemade mayonnaise is not difficult to make and is more flavorful than commercially prepared ones.

Many other ingredients may be used in salad dressings. Yogurt, sour cream, cheeses, honey, sugar, garlic, herbs, citrus juices and other fruit juices are just a few. It's fun to experiment with different combinations.

Delicate fresh salad greens should be dressed immediately before serving; dressings cause them to wilt. The more robust greens and root vegetables can be dressed ahead. This will allow the vegetables to soften and flavors to blend. Starchy salad ingredients, such as potatoes, rice, pasta and dry beans, improve in flavor if dressed while still hot. This allows them to absorb more flavor from the dressing.

## SPRING

Spring is the season when the days grow warmer and light meals have more appeal. This is also a good time to lose any extra pounds that might have crept on during the winter months. Spring, however, is often the most difficult time of year to find salad ingredients, either in the markets or in the vegetable garden. The home-grown, common salad vegetables, such as lettuce, cucumbers and tomatoes, are not yet ready for eating. Only the more expensive greenhouse and imported varieties can be found.

Fortunately, there are other vegetables available

at this time with which to make delicious salads—for example, artichokes and asparagus. These are at their best in the spring. These two vegetables make luxurious salads. Cook simply and serve chilled with mayonnaise or oil-and-vinegar dressing. Or, combine these with other ingredients to make a more economical salad. In early spring, when there are few salad greens around, make use of root vegetables and green-leafy vegetables, such as carrots, potatoes and cabbage. Served in interesting dressings, these make excellent salads, either raw or cooked.

Dried legumes are another useful standby when fresh vegetables are scarce and expensive. Black-eyed peas, lima beans, kidney beans and lentils all make delicious economical starters and dinner salads. Cook and combine with contrasting ingredients and a good salad dressing. Bean sprouts and al-falfa sprouts are other valuable additions to salads when other vegetables are scarce. Small young spinach leaves can be used raw or lightly cooked to make nutritious salads. Other versatile ingredients include avocados, citrus fruits and pineapples. Later in the spring, delicious new potatoes and sweet young carrots increase the repertoire of salad vegetables.

## SUMMER

Summer is the time for eating outdoors, picnics and barbecues. As summer approaches, all fresh salad ingredients become more economical and more plentiful. Early summer is a good time to make salads from leaf lettuce and some of the spring vegetables that are still available.

Tomatoes, cucumbers, sweet peppers, zucchini, eggplant and other vegetables are featured in the markets and in vegetable gardens. These are all delicious additions to salads. Except for eggplant, most of these vegetables can be served either raw or cooked. Cook eggplant before using. Tomatoes are invaluable for evoking a wonderful Mediterranean-feel in salads. Summer is also the time for fresh green beans and peas. Fresh young lima beans, sugar peas and Chinese pea pods are excellent raw in salads. Cook green beans and more mature pea pods until crisp-tender before using. Beets and corn are ready for picking; when cooked, they make colorful additions to salads.

Fresh herbs are available throughout the summer. They add color and flavor to salads. Some, such as parsley, fennel and chives, can be chopped finely and included as an ingredient or as a garnish. Others, such as basil, sage, dill and marjoram, can be added to dressings in small quantities to add flavor.

## AUTUMN

Orchard fruits, such as apples and pears, herald the beginning of autumn. Grapes are also plentiful in early autumn. Combine these fruits with savory foods for salads. Or, use a combination of fruits to make a tasty fruit salad. Some summer vegetables, such as tomatoes, zucchini, eggplant, bell peppers and green beans, are also still in good supply in early autumn. When summer vegetables start to disappear, take advantage of those ingredients that are available in the markets all year long. One example of these is cultivated mushrooms. Look for new varieties, such as enoki mushrooms, that are becoming more widely available.

Celery, Chinese cabbage and fennel are plentiful now. Use these as interesting raw additions to autumn salads. Leeks are also beginning to reappear in the markets. A relatively new vegetable to look for is jicama. Its crisp texture adds a nice crunchiness to salads.

## WINTER

Winter sees the return of favorite vegetables which have been absent during the summer months. These include leeks; red, green and white cabbage; broccoli; cauliflower; and Brussels sprouts. Many of these vegetables are best after a frost. They can be finely shredded and eaten raw or lightly cooked. Root vegetables, such as carrots, celeriac, turnips and kohlrabies, are also good salad ingredients. Grate or finely chop these for eating raw, or cook these until crisp-tender. Chicory and cabbage are great winter-salad standbys and can be used instead of lettuce. They both keep well in the refrigerator. Radicchio, a very attractive, small red chicory, is an unusual and delicious addition to winter salads. It is not widely available and may be expensive, but a little adds color and flavor.

Sunchokes, also called Jerusalem artichokes, tend to be an underrated vegetable. They are also a delicious addition to salads. Around Christmas, there is an excellent supply of fresh nuts. These include chestnuts, pecans, almonds, Brazil nuts and walnuts. They are excellent in salads, especially when combined with dried fruits. Citrus fruits are in season. The tartness and flavor of oranges, tangerines and grapefruit make good contrasts to less assertive salad ingredients. Or, try other fruits, such as pomegranates and cranberries, to add color and flavor. For main-dish salads and starters, use the shellfish and fish that are available.

Ingredients for autumn and winter salads

# VEGETABLE CALENDAR

PEAK SEASON IS SHOWN IN GRAY.

**Legend (both tables):** SPRING, SUMMER, AUTUMN, WINTER

Months columns (left to right): MARCH, APRIL, MAY, JUNE, JULY, AUGUST, SEPTEMBER, OCTOBER, NOVEMBER, DECEMBER, JANUARY, FEBRUARY

## Left Table

| Vegetable | MAR | APR | MAY | JUN | JUL | AUG | SEP | OCT | NOV | DEC | JAN | FEB |
|---|---|---|---|---|---|---|---|---|---|---|---|---|
| ARTICHOKES | | | | | | | ● | ● | ● | ● | ● | ● |
| ASPARAGUS | ● | | | | | | ● | ● | ● | ● | ● | ● |
| AVOCADOS | | | | | | | | | | | | |
| BEAN SPROUTS | | | | | | | | | | | | |
| BEANS, GREEN | ● | ● | | | | | ● | ● | ● | ● | ● | ● |
| BEANS, LIMA | ● | ● | ● | | | | | | ● | ● | ● | ● |
| BEETS | ● | | | | | | | | ● | ● | ● | ● |
| BROCCOLI | | | | | | | ● | | | | | |
| BRUSSELS SPROUTS | ● | ● | ● | | | | ● | | | | | |
| CABBAGE | | | | | | | | | | | | |
| CABBAGE, CHINESE | | | | | | | | | | | | |
| CARROTS | | | | | | | | | | | | |
| CAULIFLOWER | | ● | ● | | | | | | | | | |
| CELERIAC | | | ● | | | | ● | | | | | |
| CELERY | | | | | | | | | | | | |
| CHICORY AND ENDIVE | | ● | | | | | ● | | | | | |
| CORN | ● | ● | | | | | ● | ● | ● | ● | ● | ● |
| CUCUMBER | ● | | | | | | | ● | | | | |
| EGGPLANT | | | | | | | | | | | | |
| FENNEL | | ● | ● | | | | ● | ● | | | | |
| GREENS, BEET, COLLARD, MUSTARD, TURNIP | | | | | | | | | | | | |
| JÍCAMA | | | | | | | | ● | ● | ● | | |
| KALE | | ● | | | | | | | | | | |
| KOHLRABI | | ● | ● | | | | | | | | | |

## Right Table

| Vegetable | MAR | APR | MAY | JUN | JUL | AUG | SEP | OCT | NOV | DEC | JAN | FEB |
|---|---|---|---|---|---|---|---|---|---|---|---|---|
| LEEKS | | ● | ● | | | | | | | ● | ● | ● |
| LETTUCE, HEAD | | | | | | | | | | ● | ● | ● |
| LETTUCE, LEAF | | | | | | | | | | | | |
| MUSHROOMS | | | | | | | | | | | | |
| OKRA | ● | ● | | | | | ● | ● | ● | ● | ● | ● |
| ONIONS | | | | | | | | | | | | |
| PARSNIPS | | | ● | ● | | | | | | | | |
| PEA PODS, CHINESE | | | | | | | | | | | | |
| PEAS, GREEN | | | | | | | | | | | | |
| PEPPERS, BELL | ● | ● | | | | | | | | ● | ● | ● |
| PEPPERS, CHILI | | | | | | | | | | | | |
| POTATOES, SWEET | ● | ● | ● | | | | | | | | | |
| POTATOES, WHITE | | | | | | | | | | | | |
| PUMPKINS | | ● | ● | | | | | | | | | |
| RADISHES | | | | | | | | | | | | |
| RUTABAGAS | ● | ● | ● | | | | ● | ● | | | | |
| SHALLOTS | | | | | | | | | | | | |
| SPINACH | | | | | | | | ● | ● | ● | ● | ● |
| SQUASH, SUMMER | | | | | | | | | ● | ● | ● | ● |
| SQUASH, WINTER | ● | ● | ● | | | | | | | | | |
| SUNCHOKES, JERUSALEM ARTICHOKES | | | | | | | | | | | | |
| TOMATOES | ● | ● | ● | | | | | | | ● | ● | ● |
| TURNIPS | ● | ● | ● | | | | | | | ● | ● | ● |
| WATERCRESS | | | | | | | | | | | | |

# UNUSUAL VEGETABLES

The following vegetables are unusual in one or two ways. Either they are not as familiar and widely available as the usual tomato, radish or cucumber, or they are not normally thought of as ingredients for salads—for example, lima beans and cauliflower.

## ARTICHOKE
Member of the thistle family. The fat bases of the leaves are edible, and artichoke bottoms and hearts are considered delicacies.

**Preparation**—Cut off stalks to make a level base. Pull off any tough outer leaves; cut off tips of remaining leaves. Cook in boiling salted water 30 to 40 minutes or until a leaf pulls out easily. Drain upside-down until cold. Remove choke, page 60.

**Serving ideas**—Serve as a starter with oil-and-vinegar dressing, mayonnaise or hollandaise sauce for dipping. Or, remove and discard chokes from cooked artichokes; stuff with a salad mixture. Serve hearts on their own or with other ingredients for hors d'oeuvres. Artichoke hearts are available frozen and canned.

## ASPARAGUS
Stalks 6 to 8 inches long. Asparagus can be green or white, thin or thick. Tips and most of stalk are edible.

**Preparation**—Wash; break off woody ends. Tie in bundles. Cook upright, so the stalks cook in the boiling water while the tips cook in the steam above. Stalks take longer to cook than tips. Cook in boiling salted water about 15 minutes or until crisp-tender. When cooking white asparagus, add a little lemon juice to the water to keep the asparagus white.

**Serving ideas**—Cooked asparagus can be eaten hot or cold. Serve as a starter with oil-and-vinegar dressing, mayonnaise or hollandaise sauce. Asparagus is also available canned and frozen.

## AVOCADO
A pear-shaped tropical fruit with a dark-green skin.

**Preparation**—Use raw for salads. Cut in half with a stainless-steel knife; remove seed. If only 1/2 of avocado will be used, do not remove seed. Rub cut surfaces with lemon juice immediately to prevent browning.

**Serving ideas**—Serve unpeeled halves filled with oil-and-vinegar dressing. Or, stuff with a seafood salad. Cube or slice peeled avocados for salads. This adds an interesting flavor and texture. Puree to make guacamole.

## BEANS, BROAD
Large beans with a whitish skin and bright-green flesh. They are usually sold in their pods.

**Preparation**—Remove from pods; peel more mature beans. Cook in boiling salted water 25 to 30 minutes, depending on age, or until tender. Drain and cool.

**Serving ideas**—Serve in an oil-and-vinegar dressing or a yogurt dressing with herbs. Serve as a dinner salad or as part of an hors d'oeuvre.

## BEANS, GREEN
Best in summer.

**Preparation**—Young tender green beans can be trimmed and left whole. Remove strings from more mature beans; slice diagonally. Boil in salted water about 10 minutes or until crisp-tender. Drain and cool. Canned and frozen green beans can also be used for salads.

**Serving ideas**—Serve alone in a dressing, or as part of an arranged salad, such as a salad Niçoise.

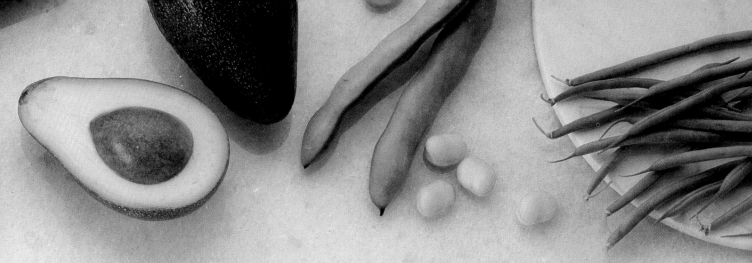

## BEAN SPROUTS
Sprouts from dried beans, usually mung or soy, page 57.
**Preparation**—Wash well; drain. Serve raw. Canned bean sprouts are not suitable for salads.
**Serving ideas**—Serve with oriental ingredients. Or, add to a tossed green salad to give extra crunchiness.

## BROCCOLI
Available year around; best during the cooler months. Buds should be tightly closed.
**Preparation**—Cut into small pieces; serve raw. Or, divide into flowerets; boil in salted water 5 to 8 minutes, depending on thickness of stalks, or until crisp-tender. Drain and cool.
**Serving ideas**—Serve as a starter with hollandaise sauce, or combine with other ingredients in a mixed salad.

## BRUSSELS SPROUTS
Member of the cabbage family. Best during cooler months.
**Preparation**—Finely shred raw Brussels sprouts. Or, boil in salted water about 5 minutes or until crisp-tender; cut in halves.
**Serving ideas**—Toss shredded Brussels sprouts in oil-and-vinegar dressing or mayonnaise as for coleslaw.

## CABBAGE, CHINESE
Crisp pale-green colored leaves in an elongated head. Sometimes called Napa cabbage in supermarkets.
**Preparation**—Wash and shred finely; serve raw. The leaves are rather bland.
**Serving ideas**—Serve with a well-flavored dressing and flavorful ingredients.

## CARROTS
Available year around.
**Preparation**—Coarsely grate raw carrots. Or, serve raw whole baby carrots as part of *Salade de Crudités*, page 54. Slice or dice more mature carrots. If desired, cook in boiling water 10 to 15 minutes, depending on age and size, or until crisp-tender.
**Serving ideas**—Combine grated carrots, mayonnaise and dried fruits, such as currants and raisins. Toss warm cooked carrots in an oil-and-vinegar dressing made with lemon juice instead of vinegar.

## CAULIFLOWER
A flowering cabbage. Available year around; best during cooler months. White is the usual color; but purple ones are occasionally available.
**Preparation**—Cut into small pieces or divide into flowerets. Serve raw, or boil in salted water 5 minutes or until crisp-tender. Drain; toss with dressing while still warm.
**Serving ideas**—Serve raw flowerets coated in a spicy dressing or plain as part of *Salade de Crudités*, page 54.

## CELERIAC (CELERY ROOT)
The edible root of a special celery variety. It has a mild celery flavor.
**Preparation**—Peel; toss in lemon juice immediately to prevent discoloration. Grate, shred or dice. Marinate in dressing to soften, or briefly boil shredded or diced celeriac in salted water. Boil shredded celeriac 1 minute; boil diced celeriac 5 minutes. Drain and toss in dressing while warm.
**Serving ideas**—It is traditionally cut into delicate julienne strips and served in a mustard-mayonnaise mixture. It blends well with carrots in salads.

## EGGPLANT
The large purple variety most common; white varieties also available.

**Preparation**—Trim off stem; cut into slices or dice. These are usually sprinkled with salt. Let drain in a colander 30 minutes to draw out any bitter juices. Rinse and pat dry with paper towels before cooking. Sauté sliced or diced eggplant about 5 minutes or until golden brown and tender. Drain on paper towels. Or, bake whole in a medium oven 30 to 60 minutes, depending on size, or until soft. Or, cook as part of ratatouille, a Provençal vegetable stew.

**Serving ideas**—Serve sautéed diced or sliced eggplant with a oil-and-vinegar dressing or yogurt dressing. Puree the pulp of baked eggplant to make a dip.

## FENNEL
White bulbs with green feathery leaves, a celery-like texture and a slight anise flavor.

**Preparation**—Slice thinly; serve raw.

**Serving ideas**—Include as part of *Salade de Crudités*, page 54. Combine with fruit or toss with salad greens.

## JÍCAMA
Large, round brown root with a crisp white interior.

**Preparation**—Peel and slice. Cut slices into strips.

**Serving ideas**—Add to tossed salads. Or, combine with citrus fruit for an unusual salad.

## KOHLRABI
White, pale-green or purple root vegetable. Looks and tastes similar to a turnip.

**Preparation**—Peel thickly; cut into slices or dice. Cook in boiling salted water 10 to 15 minutes or until tender. Kohlrabi can also be peeled, grated and served raw.

**Serving ideas**—Toss in oil-and-vinegar dressing.

## LEEKS
Large, mild member of the onion family. Can be used whole or sliced, raw or cooked.

**Preparation**—Wash well to remove all dirt. To eat raw, slice thinly; toss in oil-and-vinegar dressing. Cook whole leeks about 15 minutes in boiling salted water; cook sliced leeks 3 to 5 minutes. Or, poach in stock flavored with a bay leaf, peppercorns, coriander seeds and lemon slices.

**Serving ideas**—Serve poached leeks at room temperature as a starter. Serve dressed raw leeks as a dinner salad.

## LEGUMES
Includes kidney beans, navy beans, black-eyed peas and lentils.

**Preparation**—Soak overnight in enough water to cover. Or, boil water and beans 5 minutes. Drain soaked beans. Add fresh water; cover and simmer 1 to 2 hours or until tender. Lentils do not need soaking and cook in about 30 minutes. Drain cooked beans or lentils; toss in a parsley-flavored oil-and-vinegar dressing while still warm so that the dressing is absorbed.

**Serving ideas**—Combine with seafood and butter or margarine for delicious and economical starters. Legumes are a good protein source for vegetarians.

## LETTUCE, ENDIVE & OTHER SALAD GREENS
Common varieties of lettuce: leaf, Romaine, Boston or butter and iceberg. The chicory family, with a slightly bitter flavor, includes curly endive, Belgian endive and radicchio. Dandelion leaves, lamb's lettuce, mustard greens, sorrel and watercress can also be used.

**Preparation**—Wash and dry well. Keep covered in the refrigerator to retain crispness. Dress immediately before serving, or the dressing will wilt the leaves.
**Serving ideas**—Toss whole or shredded leaves in an herb-flavored dressing.

### MUSHROOMS
Available year around. Look for new varieties, such as enoki mushrooms, that are becoming available. Mushrooms are an excellent source of texture and flavor for salads.
**Preparation**—Wipe with a damp cloth, or rinse quickly in cold running water. Do not peel mushrooms. Use small succulent button mushrooms whole. Slice or chop larger mushrooms.
**Serving ideas**—Marinate in a lemon dressing; combine with seafood for a delicious starter. Or, try *Lemon & Thyme Mushrooms*, page 88.

### PEA PODS, CHINESE
Tender, green peas that are eaten pods and all.
**Preparation**—If young and tender, trim and serve raw. String more mature pea pods; boil in salted water 1 to 2 minutes or until crisp-tender. Chinese pea pods are also available frozen.
**Serving ideas**—For a starter, pea pods are especially delicious mixed with shrimp and an oil-and-vinegar dressing made with lemon juice instead of vinegar.

### PEPPERS, BELL
Available in green, yellow, red and purple. Red bell peppers are mature green bell peppers; they have a sweeter flavor.
**Preparation**—Remove stem and seeds. Cut into slices or rings. Or, grill whole peppers until skins blacken and blister. Cool slightly; remove skins. Cut into strips.
**Serving ideas**—Stuff whole bell peppers; bake until tender. Cool to room temperature. Bell-pepper slices and rings add flavor and texture to salads. Toss warm grilled bell-pepper strips in olive oil. Season with herbs, salt and black pepper. Use bell-pepper strips and rings as garnishes.

### SPINACH
Available year around.
**Preparation**—Prepare as for lettuce. Raw, young, small spinach leaves, tossed in dressing, make a delicious salad. Larger spinach stalks may be cooked and served like asparagus.
**Serving ideas**—Traditionally served with a hot bacon dressing as a starter. Add to any mixed green salad.

### SQUASH, SUMMER (YELLOW & ZUCCHINI)
**Preparation**—Wash and trim. Cut into thin circles or slice lengthwise. Serve raw, or steam 5 minutes or until crisp-tender.
**Serving ideas**—Toss in butter, margarine or yogurt dressing.

### SUNCHOKES (JERUSALEM ARTICHOKES)
A tuber, resembling a knobby potato, but with the flavor of artichokes.
**Preparation**—Must be cooked and peeled, either before or after cooking. Place in cold water and lemon juice or vinegar immediately after peeling to prevent browning. Boil in salted water with a little lemon juice or vinegar 10 to 15 minutes or until crisp-tender. Drain and cool.
**Serving ideas**—Slice and toss in an oil-and-vinegar dressing. Or, combine with mayonnaise, as for potato salad.

# Spring

## New-Potato Salad

1-1/2 lb. medium, new potatoes, scrubbed
2/3 cup Mayonnaise, page 112, or prepared mayonnaise
1 tablespoon white-wine vinegar
2 green onions, chopped
1 tablespoon chopped sweet pickle
1 tablespoon capers, drained
8 small pimento-stuffed olives, thinly sliced
Freshly ground pepper

*To garnish:*
Pimento-stuffed olives
Sweet pickles

1. In a large saucepan, cover potatoes with cold water. Bring to a boil; simmer 10 to 15 minutes or until tender but not soft. Drain; set aside to cool slightly.
2. Spoon mayonnaise into a large bowl. Stir in vinegar; stir in onions, chopped pickle, capers, sliced olives and pepper.
3. Do not peel potatoes. Leave small potatoes whole; cut larger potatoes into halves or quarters. Add warm potatoes to mayonnaise mixture; stir until coated with dressing. Refrigerate until chilled or up to 24 hours.
4. Spoon into a serving bowl. Garnish with olives and pickles. Serve with a cold-meat selection. Makes 4 dinner salads.

## Caribbean Shrimp Salad

1 small head lettuce
2 ripe avocados, peeled, sliced
1 ripe mango, thinly sliced
8 oz. medium shrimp, cooked, peeled, deveined
1/2 cup Thousand Island Dressing, page 112, or
    prepared Thousand Island dressing

*To garnish:*
2 tablespoons pumpkin seeds, if desired, toasted

1. Wash and dry lettuce; finely shred. Divide shredded lettuce among 4 to 6 salad plates.
2. Arrange avocado and mango slices, slightly overlapping, in a fan shape on lettuce.
3. Spoon dressing into a medium bowl. Stir in shrimp.
4. Spoon shrimp mixture over avocado slices and mango slices. Garnish with pumpkin seeds, if desired. Serve immediately. Makes 4 light main-dish servings or 6 starters.

### Variation
Substitute 1 cup seedless green grapes, halved, for mango. Arrange avocado slices over lettuce. Scatter grapes and pumpkin seeds, if desired, over top.

## Pineapple & Watercress Salad

1 bunch watercress, trimmed
1 small pineapple
1/3 cup coarsely chopped walnuts

*Dressing:*
2 tablespoons honey
2 tablespoons olive oil
2 tablespoons white-wine vinegar
Salt
Freshly ground pepper

1. Divide watercress among 4 salad plates.
2. Cut pineapple into 8 slices; peel slices. Cut each peeled slice in half; remove core.
3. Arrange 4 pineapple pieces on each plate; sprinkle with chopped nuts.
4. To make dressing, in a small bowl, combine honey, olive oil and vinegar. Season with salt and pepper; beat with a whisk until blended. Pour dressing over salads. Serve immediately. This is excellent with chicken dishes. Makes 4 dinner salads.

### Variation
Substitute 2 peeled, sliced large grapefruit for pineapple.

Top to bottom: Caribbean Shrimp Salad with mango, Caribbean Shrimp Salad with grapes

# Smoked-Fish & Bean Salad

1 cup uncooked dried black-eyed peas
Water
1 small onion, finely chopped
1 bay leaf
Freshly ground pepper
2/3 cup Oil & Vinegar Dressing, page 112, or
    prepared dressing
2 teaspoons prepared horseradish
Salt
1 tablespoon chopped fresh parsley
8 oz. smoked mackerel or other smoked fish, skinned,
    flaked
4 hard-cooked eggs, chopped

*To serve:*
2 or 3 lettuce leaves, if desired
2 lemon slices, twisted
1 or 2 parsley sprigs

1. Soak peas overnight in water to cover. Or, boil peas and water 2 minutes. Let stand 1 hour. Drain soaked peas; discard soaking water.
2. In a large saucepan, combine soaked peas, 2-1/2 cups water, onion, bay leaf and pepper. Cover; boil 10 minutes. Reduce heat; simmer 45 minutes to 1 hour or until beans are tender but not mushy. Drain; place in a medium bowl. Cool slightly.
3. In a small bowl, combine dressing, horseradish, salt and chopped parsley. Pour over drained cooled beans; toss gently.
4. Carefully stir fish and hard-cooked eggs into salad. Serve immediately, or cover and refrigerate up to 24 hours.
5. To serve, arrange lettuce in a serving dish or bowl, if desired. Spoon salad over lettuce. Garnish with lemon twists and parsley sprigs. Makes 4 main-dish servings or 6 starters.

**Variation**
Substitute 1 (15-ounce) can black-eyed peas, drained, for cooked black-eyed peas.

# Bouillabaisse Salad

*Rouille Mayonnaise:*
1-1/4 cups Mayonnaise, page 112, or
    prepared mayonnaise
6 oz. canned pimentos, drained
1 large garlic clove, crushed
1 tablespoon chopped fresh basil, thyme or parsley or
    1-1/2 teaspoons dried leaf basil, thyme or parsley

*Salad:*
1 onion, coarsely chopped
1 bay leaf
1 bunch fresh parsley or thyme
1 lemon slice or orange slice
Salt
Freshly ground pepper
1-1/4 lb. firm white fish (halibut, turbot or monkfish)
2 medium squid, cleaned
1-1/4 lb. assorted shellfish (mussels, scallops, unpeeled
    shrimp or crayfish tails)

1. To make Rouille Mayonnaise, in a small bowl, combine mayonnaise, pimentos, garlic and herbs. If desired, crush pimento, garlic and herbs to a paste in a mortar and pestle. Stir paste into mayonnaise. Cover and store in refrigerator; use within 2 days.
2. To make salad, in a large saucepan, combine 1 quart water, onion, bay leaf, parsley or thyme, lemon slice or orange slice, salt and pepper. Bring to a boil; boil 5 minutes.
3. Cut fish into 2-inch pieces. Add fish pieces to saucepan; simmer 5 to 6 minutes or until fish tests done. Do not overcook. Remove with a slotted spoon; set aside to cool.
4. Cut squid bodies crosswise into 1/4-inch rings. Cut tentacles crosswise in halves or quarters. Add squid pieces to boiling fish-cooking liquid; simmer 15 to 30 seconds or until squid turns opaque. Remove with a slotted spoon; set aside to cool.
5. Add scallops to boiling cooking liquid. Simmer about 5 minutes; remove with a slotted spoon.
6. Add shrimp or crayfish tails to boiling cooking liquid. Simmer 3 minutes or until firm. Remove with a slotted spoon; set aside to cool.
7. Add mussels to boiling cooking liquid; cover pan and simmer 4 to 8 minutes or until shells open. Remove mussels with a slotted spoon; discard any mussels that do not open. Set mussels aside to cool.
8. Place a small decorative bowl in center of a large platter; add mayonnaise. Arrange cooked fish and shellfish around bowl. Leave mussels in bottom shells, as shown.
9. Serve seafood with Rouille Mayonnaise and a green salad. Makes 4 main-dish servings.

**Variation**
Use any combination of fish and shellfish. Crab, lobster, clams and oysters are popular choices. Frozen shellfish can also be used.

# Spring Carrot Salad

**1-1/4 lb. small new carrots**
**Salt**
**Freshly ground pepper**

*Dressing:*
**2/3 cup plain yogurt**
**Grated peel and juice of 1/2 orange**
**2 tablespoons chopped fresh parsley or chives**
**Salt**
**Freshly ground pepper**

*This salad relies on the sweet flavor of young spring carrots. It is rich in vitamins and low in calories, making it an excellent choice for dieters.*

**1.** Scrub carrots; leave very small carrots whole. Cut larger carrots in half lengthwise.
**2.** Place carrots in a medium saucepan. Add 1 cup water; season with salt and pepper. Bring to a boil; simmer 5 to 8 minutes or until carrots are crisp-tender. Drain; set aside to cool.
**3.** To make dressing, in a small bowl, combine yogurt, orange peel, orange juice and parsley or chives. Season with salt and pepper.
**4.** Serve immediately, or cover and refrigerate carrots and dressing separately until served. To serve, place cooled carrots on a platter; top with dressing.
**5.** Serve with cold meats. Makes 4 dinner salads or 6 starters.

Left to right: Bouillabaisse Salad, Smoked-Fish & Bean Salad

# Salami, Bean & Tomato Salad

1 cup uncooked dried white beans
Water
1 lb. medium tomatoes (2 or 3)
1 tablespoon chopped fresh sage or 1 teaspoon rubbed
    sage
1 small onion, chopped
4 to 6 oz. thinly sliced salami

*Dressing:*
1 tablespoon white-wine vinegar
1 tablespoon olive oil
Salt
Freshly ground pepper

*To garnish:*
1 fresh sage sprig

---

**1.** Soak beans overnight in water to cover. Or, boil beans and water 2 minutes. Let stand 1 hour. Drain beans; discard soaking water.
**2.** In a large saucepan, combine 2-1/2 cups water and soaked beans.
**3.** Peel and chop 1/2 of tomatoes. Add chopped tomatoes to beans and water; add sage and onion.
**4.** Bring to a boil. Cover; simmer 1 to 1-1/2 hours or until tender but not mushy. Drain, reserving 1/3 cup cooking juice to use in dressing.
**5.** To make dressing, in a small bowl, combine reserved cooking liquid, vinegar and olive oil. Season with salt and pepper. Stir into cooked beans. Serve immediately, or refrigerate up to 24 hours.
**6.** To serve, arrange overlapping slices of salami around edge of a serving platter. Thinly slice remaining tomatoes; arrange tomato slices inside ring of salami slices. Spoon bean mixture in center of platter. Garnish with a sage sprig. Makes 4 main-dish servings or 6 to 8 starters.

**Variation**
Substitute 1 (15-ounce) can white beans for cooked beans. Drain; reserve 1/3 cup liquid for dressing.

# Lentil & Tomato Salad

1 cup uncooked lentils
1 small onion, finely chopped
1 qt. water (4 cups)
1 bay leaf
Salt
6 tablespoons Oil & Vinegar Dressing, page 112, or
    prepared dressing
1 large tomato, chopped
1 small green bell pepper, diced
4 green onions, chopped
8 black olives, if desired, chopped
1 tablespoon chopped fresh parsley

---

**1.** In a large saucepan, combine lentils, chopped onion, water, bay leaf and salt. Bring to a boil. Cover; simmer about 30 minutes or until tender but not mushy.
**2.** Drain; discard bay leaf. Pour lentil mixture into a salad bowl. Stir dressing into warm lentil mixture; set aside to cool. Serve immediately, or cover and refrigerate up to 24 hours.
**3.** To serve, stir in tomato, bell pepper, green onions and olives, if desired. Sprinkle with chopped parsley. Makes 4 to 6 dinner salads or 6 to 8 starters.

Left to right: Lentil & Tomato Salad; Salami, Bean & Tomato Salad; Cracked-Wheat Salad

# Cracked-Wheat Salad

1 cup uncooked cracked wheat
1 qt. water (4 cups)
6 tablespoons olive oil
1/4 cup lemon juice
6 tablespoons chopped fresh parsley
2 tablespoons chopped fresh mint or 2 teaspoons
  dried mint
6 green onions, thinly sliced
Salt
Freshly ground pepper

*To serve:*
1 head lettuce
4 tomatoes, cut into wedges
1 small cucumber, sliced
8 black olives
Parsley or mint sprigs
2 hard-cooked eggs, if desired, quartered

*In Lebanon, where this salad originated, preparation is highly individual and quantities of ingredients vary with each family.*

**1.** Soak cracked wheat in water 1 hour. Drain soaked wheat in a sieve; squeeze out any excess water.
**2.** Pour olive oil and lemon juice into a large bowl. Stir in parsley, mint, onions, salt and pepper. If using dried mint, let stand 15 minutes.
**3.** Stir drained wheat into dressing until combined. Cover and refrigerate until chilled or up to 24 hours.
**4.** To serve, arrange lettuce leaves on a serving plate or individual plates. Spoon salad into center of lettuce; garnish with tomatoes, cucumber, olives, parsley or mint sprigs and hard-cooked eggs, if desired. Or, spoon into a large serving bowl. Makes 6 dinner salads or 8 starters.

# Salade de Crudités

*Salad ingredients:*
1 head Bibb lettuce
1 head cauliflower
1/2 cucumber
4 firm tomatoes
1 bunch green onions
1 bunch radishes
8 carrots
12 mushrooms
1 fennel bulb
1 red bell pepper, cut into strips
1 green bell pepper, cut into strips

*Dips:*
1/2 cup Mayonnaise, page 112
1 cup Hummus, see below
1/2 cup Yogurt Dressing, page 113

---

**1.** Clean and trim vegetables. Arrange in a large shallow bowl. Spoon dips into small bowls.
**2.** Serve with small sharp knives for cutting vegetables as they are eaten with dips. Makes 6 to 8 appetizers.

# Hummus

---

1 cup uncooked garbanzo beans
Water
1/2 cup plain yogurt
2 tablespoons lemon juice
3 tablespoons tahini (sesame-seed paste) or
    peanut butter
1 garlic clove, crushed
Salt
Freshly ground pepper

*To serve:*
Paprika

---

**1.** Soak beans overnight in water to cover. Or, boil beans and water 2 minutes; let stand 1 hour. Drain beans; discard soaking water.
**2.** In a large saucepan, combine soaked beans and 2 cups water. Cover and boil 10 minutes. Reduce heat; simmer 1 to 1-1/2 hours or until beans are soft enough to mash, adding more water if necessary. Drain; reserve liquid.
**3.** Mash beans with 2 tablespoons cooking liquid. Beat in yogurt, lemon juice, tahini or peanut butter, garlic, salt and pepper. Or, place all ingredients in a blender or food processor fitted with a steel blade; process until smooth. Thin with an additional cooking liquid if necessary.
**4.** To serve, sprinkle with paprika; accompany with warm pita bread. Makes 4 main-dish servings or 6 to 8 starters.

### Variation
Substitute 1 (15-ounce) can garbanzo beans for cooked beans. Drain; reserve 2 to 4 tablespoons liquid.

Clockwise from left: Pita-bread rounds; Salade de Crudités with Hummus, Mayonnaise and Yogurt Dressing

# Spinach & Sardine Mold

1 (10-oz.) pkg. frozen chopped spinach, thawed
1 (1/4-oz.) envelope plus 1/2 teaspoon unflavored
   gelatin powder
1-1/4 cups water
1 chicken-flavored bouillon cube
1 (3-3/4-oz.) can sardines packed in olive oil
3/4 cup dairy sour cream
2 hard-cooked eggs, chopped
Salt
Freshly ground pepper

*This is an attractive and unusual way to prepare simple,
easily available ingredients. Use a fancy mold to provide a
touch of elegance.*

1. Squeeze as much liquid as possible from spinach; place in a medium bowl.
2. In a small saucepan, combine gelatin and water. Stir well; let stand 3 minutes. Stir over low heat until gelatin dissolves; stir in bouillon cube until dissolved. Set aside to cool. Pour cooled gelatin mixture over spinach; stir to combine.
3. Place undrained sardines in a small bowl; mash with a fork. Stir mashed sardines into spinach mixture until blended.
4. Fold in sour cream, hard-cooked eggs, salt and pepper. Rinse a 4-cup decorative mold with cold water; drain well. Spoon mixture into mold; smooth top. Refrigerate several hours or until completely set.
5. To serve, insert the tip of a knife around edge of mold. Invert mold on a serving plate. Wet a dish towel with hot water; wring dry. Place hot towel around mold a few seconds. Remove towel and mold. Serve with a tossed salad. Makes 6 to 8 main-dish servings.

Left to right: Spinach & Sardine Mold, Easter-Egg Salad, Curried
Vegetable Salad

# Curried Vegetable Salad

2 tablespoons vegetable oil
1 medium onion, thinly sliced
1 small apple, peeled, cored, chopped
1 garlic clove, crushed, if desired
1 tablespoon curry powder
1 cup chicken stock
Grated peel of 1/2 lemon
1-1/2 teaspoons lemon juice
6 to 8 new potatoes, scrubbed or peeled
4 carrots, scrubbed or peeled
1/2 head cauliflower, divided into flowerets
2 zucchini, cut into 1/4-inch slices
1/3 cup raisins

*To garnish:*
1/4 cup sliced almonds
1 tablespoon chopped fresh parsley
Lettuce, if desired
Cold cooked rice, if desired

1. Heat oil in a large saucepan over medium heat. Add onion, apple and garlic, if desired; sauté 5 minutes.
2. Stir in curry powder; cook 2 minutes. Stir in stock, lemon peel and lemon juice. Bring to a boil. Reduce heat; simmer 2 minutes.
3. Cut potatoes and carrots into 1/4-inch-wide strips. Add potato and carrot strips to curry sauce. Cover and simmer 10 minutes.
4. Add cauliflower, zucchini and raisins to pan; stir gently. Cover and simmer 6 to 8 minutes or until vegetables are crisp-tender. Cool to room temperature. Serve immediately, or refrigerate up to 24 hours.
5. To serve, toss vegetables gently to coat with curry sauce; spoon into a bowl. Sprinkle with almonds and parsley. Or, serve on lettuce or cold cooked rice. Makes 4 to 6 main-dish servings.

1/To chop parsley, hold knife horizontally; slice across parsley several times.

2/Holding knife by the handle and tip, finely chop parsley with an up-and-down cutting motion.

# Easter-Egg Salad

Skins from 2 to 3 large yellow onions
8 eggs
1 head lettuce, shredded
4 oz. bean sprouts (1 cup)
1 cup Green Mayonnaise, page 112, made
    with watercress

*To garnish:*
1 (4-oz.) jar lumpfish caviar, if desired

*For a color contrast, color only half of eggs; leave remaining eggs white.*

1. Pour water 3 inches deep into a medium saucepan. Add onion skins to water; bring to a boil. Water will turn a deep golden color.
2. Add eggs to pan; simmer 12 minutes. Remove eggs; reserve cooking liquid. Plunge cooked eggs into cold water.
3. Peel eggs; return to colored water. Simmer 3 minutes or until a rich golden color. Drain; refrigerate until served.
4. To serve, arrange lettuce and bean sprouts on a large plate to resemble a bird's nest. Place hard-cooked eggs on top.
5. Pour some mayonnaise over eggs; serve remaining mayonnaise separately. Garnish with caviar, if desired. Makes 4 main-dish salads or 8 starters.

To make your own bean sprouts, choose unsplit dried beans. Mung beans are the easiest to sprout. Soak 2 tablespoons dried beans in cold water to cover overnight. Drain well; place in a glass jar. Place jar in a cool, dark place. Rinse with room temperature water each morning and evening. Drain beans well after each rinsing to prevent molding. Repeat for 4 days or until sprouts are large enough to use. Mung-bean sprouts are ready to eat when 1 to 2 inches long. Refrigerate sprouts until used. Special perforated, plastic lids are available that fit standard canning jars to make draining easier. Or, cover the tops of the jars with cheesecloth or a piece of a clean nylon stocking; fasten with a elastic band. Alfalfa sprouts can be grown the same way.

# Duck, Red-Cabbage & Roquefort Salad

2 large duck breasts, about 1 lb. each
2 tablespoons honey
1/2 head red cabbage
1/2 head lettuce or endive
8 oz. Roquefort cheese
1/4 cup Oil & Vinegar Dressing, page 112, or
    prepared dressing

1. Preheat broiler. Place duck breasts in a baking pan; brush with honey. Cook under preheated broiler about 25 minutes, basting and turning until meat is done and skin is crisp and well-browned. Cool.
2. Slice red cabbage and lettuce or endive thinly; divide among 4 to 6 serving plates.
3. Thinly slice cooled duck; arrange on top of shredded cabbage and lettuce or endive.
4. Cut Roquefort cheese into small cubes; sprinkle over top of salad.
5. Pour 1 tablespoon dressing over each salad immediately before serving. Makes 4 light main-dish servings or 6 starters.

## Variation
Substitute 4 small or 2 large chicken breasts for duck.

This recipe is typical of *nouvelle cuisine* cooking where emphasis is on luxurious ingredients, carefully but simply arranged. It is very important that all components be of the best quality and in perfect condition and that extra care be taken in arranging the food.

To preserve the bright color of red cabbage, cut with a stainless-steel knife. If cabbage is cut ahead, toss in vinegar or an oil-and-vinegar dressing to prevent it turning blue.

Roquefort cheese has been produced since ancient time in southwestern France. Its unique and distinct flavor is derived from the humid limestone caves in which it is aged. If you prefer a milder-flavored blue cheese, use Stilton. Domestic blue cheeses are also available.

# Ham & Sprouts Salad

2 cartons radish sprouts
4 oz. alfalfa sprouts (1 cup)
8 oz. cooked ham, thinly sliced
4 hard-cooked eggs, chopped

*Yogurt-Tartar Dressing:*
1/2 cup plain yogurt
1 tablespoon capers
1 tablespoon chopped sweet pickles
1 tablespoon chopped pimento-stuffed olives
1 tablespoon chopped fresh parsley
Salt
Freshly ground pepper

*To garnish:*
1 carton radish sprouts
2 oz. alfalfa sprouts (1/2 cup), if desired

1. In a large bowl, combine radish sprouts and alfalfa sprouts.
2. Cut ham into 2-inch strips; add ham strips and hard-cooked eggs to sprouts. Toss to combine.
3. To make dressing, in a medium bowl, combine all ingredients. Pour dressing over salad; toss salad to coat with dressing.
4. Mound salad in center of a serving platter. Surround with a ring of radish sprouts and alfalfa sprouts, if desired. Serve immediately. Salad is excellent with warm, crusty whole-wheat bread. Makes 4 light main-dish servings.

# Chicory & Orange Salad

3 large or 4 small heads Belgian endive
3 medium oranges
1 shallot or small onion, cut in rings
1/4 cup Oil & Vinegar Dressing, page 112, or
    prepared dressing

*To garnish:*
6 large or 8 small pimento-stuffed olives

1. Cut endive crosswise into slices; place in a salad bowl.
2. With a small sharp knife, cut away peel and pith from oranges. Cut into sections, page 30; add to sliced endive. Squeeze any juice remaining in orange membranes into endive mixture.
3. Pour dressing over endive mixture; toss to coat with dressing.
4. Garnish with olives. This is excellent with cold cuts. Makes 4 servings.

# Cottage-Cheese Spring Salad

1 lb. cottage cheese (2 cups)
1 tablespoon chopped fresh parsley
1 tablespoon chopped fresh mint or 1-1/2 teaspoons
    dried mint
1 tablespoon chopped chives or green-onion tops, or
    1-1/2 teaspoons dried chives
4 large or 8 small pitted black olives, chopped
Salt
Freshly ground pepper
1 cup diced ham
1 cucumber, diced

*To serve:*
1 head lettuce or 1 head endive
Black olives
Mint or parsley sprigs

1. Place cottage cheese in a medium bowl. Stir in parsley, mint, chives or green-onion tops and chopped olives. Season with salt and pepper. If using dried herbs, let stand 15 minutes.
2. Stir ham and cucumber into cottage-cheese mixture.
3. Serve immediately, or cover and refrigerate up to 8 hours.
4. To serve, arrange lettuce or endive leaves in a bowl or on a serving platter. Spoon cottage-cheese salad in center; garnish with olives and mint or parsley sprigs. Makes 4 light main-dish servings or 6 starters.

### Variation
For special occasions, serve in hollowed-out cucumber boats or in avocado halves.

Left to right: Chicory & Orange Salad; Ham & Sprouts Salad;
Duck, Red-Cabbage & Roquefort Salad

# Artichokes Taramasalata

4 artichokes
Salt

*Taramasalata:*
1 (4-oz.) jar golden caviar
1/2 cup corn oil
1/2 cup plain yogurt
2 tablespoons lemon juice
Freshly ground white pepper
1 garlic clove, if desired, crushed

---

1. Wash artichokes; cut off stalks. As shown below, cut across tops and pull off any outer leaves that are dried or discolored. With kitchen scissors, cut tips from leaves.
2. Cook artichokes, uncovered, in a large pan of boiling salted water 30 to 40 minutes or until done. Artichokes are done when a leaf will pull off easily. Cooking time will depend on size and age of artichokes. Drain artichokes upside down on a plate.
3. To make Taramasalata, place caviar in a medium bowl. Gradually beat oil, yogurt, lemon juice and white pepper into caviar until smooth. Stir in garlic, if desired. Or, place all ingredients in a blender or food processor fitted with a steel blade; process until smooth. Refrigerate until served; mixture will thicken while chilling.
4. When artichokes are cool, remove chokes. To remove chokes, spread top leaves apart; pull out each central cone of small soft leaves. Scoop out and discard chokes, leaving hearts exposed.
5. Spoon Taramasalata into center of artichokes. To eat, pull off an outside leaf; dip fleshy base into Taramasalata. Makes 4 starters.

# Salad Sandwiches

4 large rye-bread slices
2 (3-oz.) pkgs. or 1 (8-oz.) pkg. cream cheese, room temperature
4 large crisp lettuce leaves
1/4 small cucumber, thinly sliced
4 oz. smoked salmon, sliced

*To garnish:*
1 carton radish sprouts
Lemon wedges

---

1. Spread bread slices with cheese.
2. Shred lettuce; arrange shredded lettuce on cheese.
3. Arrange cucumber and smoked salmon over lettuce in an attractive pattern.
4. Place open-faced sandwiches on a platter; garnish with radish sprouts and lemon wedges. Makes 4 servings.

# Artichoke-Heart Salad

4 cooked medium artichoke hearts
2 oz. mushrooms, thinly sliced
1/4 cup Oil & Vinegar Dressing, page 112, or prepared dressing
1 tablespoon chopped fresh parsley or chives
4 bacon slices

---

1. Place artichoke hearts and mushrooms in a serving dish.
2. In a small bowl, combine dressing and herbs; pour over artichoke hearts and mushrooms. Marinate 10 minutes.
3. In a medium skillet, sauté bacon until crisp. Drain on paper towels; cool. Crumble cooled bacon.
4. Immediately before serving, stir chopped bacon into salad. Serve artichokes on individual plates surrounded by mushroom mixture. Makes 4 starters.

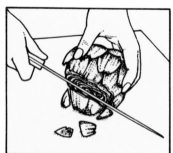

1/Cut across top of artichoke.

2/With kitchen scissors, cut tips from leaves.

3/Pull out central cone of small soft leaves.

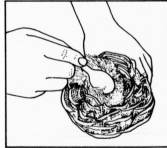

4/Scoop out and discard choke.

Top to bottom: Fresh artichokes, Fresh mushrooms, Artichokes Taramasalata, Artichoke-Heart Salad

# Spring Terrine

1/2 lb. lean bacon slices, blanched
1/4 cup butter or margarine
1 medium onion, chopped
1 garlic clove, crushed
1 (10-oz.) pkg. frozen chopped spinach, thawed,
    well drained
1/4 teaspoon freshly grated nutmeg
Salt
Freshly ground pepper
3 eggs
1/4 cup half and half
2 cups fresh bread crumbs
3 tablespoons grated Parmesan cheese
3 hard-cooked eggs

*To garnish:*
Chicory

1. Preheat oven to 350F (175C). Line bottom and long sides of an 8" x 4" or 7" x 3" loaf pan with bacon slices. Overlap slices slightly; drape ends over sides of pan.
2. Melt butter or margarine in a large skillet. Add onion and garlic; sauté until onion is transparent. Stir in spinach; cook 2 minutes. Season with nutmeg, salt and pepper. Set aside to cool slightly.
3. In another medium bowl, beat eggs and half and half until blended; stir in spinach mixture. Stir in bread crumbs and cheese until blended. Spoon 1/3 of spinach mixture into bottom of bacon-lined pan. Arrange hard-cooked eggs down center of spinach mixture. Spoon remaining spinach mixture into pan, covering eggs completely. Fold bacon slices over spinach filling; cover pan with foil.
4. Bake in preheated oven 1 hour 10 minutes. Remove foil; bake 10 minutes or until spinach filling is firm. Drain off fat; place pan on a wire rack to cool. Refrigerate if not served immediately. Bring to room temperature before serving.
5. To serve, invert terrine on a serving plate; remove mold. Garnish with chicory. Cut into 6 to 8 slices. Makes 6 to 8 servings.

# Asparagus Mousse

1 lb. fresh asparagus
1-1/2 cups water
Milk
2 tablespoons butter or margarine
2 tablespoons all-purpose flour
1 (1/4-oz.) envelope plus 1 teaspoon unflavored
    gelatin powder
1/4 cup cold water
Grated peel of 1/2 lemon
1 tablespoon lemon juice
1 hard-cooked egg, chopped
2/3 cup plain yogurt
Salt
Freshly ground white pepper

1. Wash asparagus; snap off and discard tough woody ends. Cut off stalks 1-1/2 inches below tips. Reserve stalks. Bring 1-1/2 cups water to a boil in a medium saucepan. Add asparagus tips; cook 6 to 8 minutes or until crisp-tender. Remove with a slotted spoon; set aside to cool. When cool, cover and refrigerate for garnish.
2. Chop reserved stalks; add to water in saucepan. Cover and cook 10 to 15 minutes or until soft. Drain stalks, reserving cooking liquid. Set stalks aside.
3. Pour cooking liquid into a 2-cup measuring cup; add enough milk to make 2 cups. Set aside. Melt butter or margarine in a medium saucepan. Stir in flour; cook over low heat 1 minute. Gradually stir in reserved cooking-liquid mixture; cook, stirring constantly, until mixture is thickened and comes to a boil. Add reserved stalks; cook 1 minute. Remove from heat; pour into a medium bowl.
4. In a small saucepan, combine gelatin and 1/4 cup water. Stir well; let stand 3 minutes. Stir over low heat until gelatin dissolves. Stir into cooled asparagus mixture. Set aside to cool.
5. Stir lemon peel, lemon juice, hard-cooked egg and yogurt into asparagus mixture until blended. Season with salt and white pepper. Rinse a 4- to 4-1/2-cup decorative mold in cold water. Pour in asparagus mixture; refrigerate several hours or until set.
6. To serve, insert the tip of a knife around edge of mold. Invert mold on a serving plate. Wet a dish towel with hot water; wring dry. Wrap hot towel around mold a few seconds. Remove towel and mold. Garnish with reserved asparagus tips. Makes 6 to 8 servings.

**Variation**
Substitute 2 (10-ounce) packages frozen asparagus spears for fresh asparagus. Cook according to package directions; cool. Cut off stalks to use in mousse. Reserve tips for garnish.

Left to right: Fresh asparagus, Asparagus Mousse, Spring Terrine

# Wilted Spinach Salad

8 oz. fresh, young spinach leaves (about 4 cups)
4 bacon slices, chopped
1 small garlic clove, if desired, crushed
1 tablespoon lemon juice

1. Wash spinach thoroughly; remove coarse stalks. Drain; pat leaves dry with paper towels. Leave smaller leaves whole; shred larger leaves. Place spinach in a large bowl.
2. To make dressing, combine bacon and garlic in a large skillet. Cook 5 minutes or until bacon is browned and crisp, stirring occasionally.
3. Remove from heat; carefully pour in lemon juice to avoid spatters. Stir quickly. Add spinach while dressing is still hot. Toss until all leaves are coated and have begun to wilt. Makes 4 dinner salads.

# Summer

## Chicken, Tarragon & Orange Salad

1 (2-1/2-lb.) broiler-fryer chicken
1 medium onion, thinly sliced
Grated peel and juice of 1 orange
1 tablespoon chopped fresh tarragon or 1-1/2 teaspoons
    dried leaf tarragon
1 bay leaf
Water
Salt
Freshly ground pepper
1 tablespoon vegetable oil
1/2 to 1 tablespoon white-wine vinegar

*To garnish:*
1 small orange, peeled, sliced
1 carton radish sprouts
Fresh tarragon sprigs, if desired

1. Place chicken, onion, orange peel, orange juice, tarragon and bay leaf in a large saucepan.
2. Add enough water to almost cover chicken; season with salt and pepper. Cover; bring to a boil. Reduce heat; simmer 45 minutes to 1 hour or until chicken is tender.
3. Lift out chicken; let cool. Discard bay leaf and onion.
4. Boil cooking liquid until reduced to 1 cup. Let cool; refrigerate until chilled.
5. When chicken is cool, remove meat from bones, discarding skin and bones. Cut meat into bite-size pieces; place in a medium bowl. Refrigerate while stock is chilling.
6. When stock is chilled, remove fat layer from top. Reheat stock; stir in oil and vinegar to taste. Pour over chicken pieces; toss well.
7. Serve at once, or cover and refrigerate up to 24 hours. To serve, spoon into a serving dish; garnish with orange slices, sprouts and tarragon sprigs, if desired. Makes 4 main-dish servings.

## Lettuce & Orange Salad with Almond Dressing

1 head iceberg lettuce
2 oranges
1/2 cup vegetable oil
1/2 cup slivered blanched almonds
1 tablespoon lemon juice
Salt
Freshly ground pepper

1. Tear lettuce into pieces; place in a salad bowl.
2. Remove peel and white pith from oranges; section peeled oranges. See box below. Add orange sections to lettuce pieces; squeeze orange juice from membranes over top.
3. Heat oil in a medium saucepan over medium heat. Add almonds; sauté, stirring constantly, about 3 minutes or until golden brown.
4. Cool almonds slightly; stir in lemon juice, salt and pepper.
5. Pour almond mixture over lettuce and orange segments; toss until well coated.
6. Serve immediately. Makes 4 to 6 dinner salads.

---

To make orange sections, cut a slice off top and bottom of an orange. Place orange on a cutting board. With a small serrated knife, make smooth downward cuts, following the curve of the orange. When all peel is removed, check that all white pith has also been removed. Cut away any remaining pith. To make sections, hold orange in the palm of one hand; with a sharp paring knife, cut down on either side of each membrane to the center of orange to free sections. Carefully lift out sections.

---

Top to bottom: Lettuce & Orange Salad with Almond Dressing; Chicken, Tarragon & Orange Salad

# Caesar Salad

5 tablespoons corn oil or olive oil
1 garlic clove, crushed
2 thick bread slices, cut into 1/2-inch cubes
1 head Romaine lettuce
1 (2-oz.) can anchovy fillets
1/4 cup grated Parmesan cheese
1 tablespoon lemon juice
Salt
Freshly ground pepper
1 egg

1. To make croutons, heat 2 tablespoons corn oil or olive oil in a medium skillet over medium heat. Add garlic and bread cubes; sauté until bread is crisp and golden brown. Drain on paper towels.
2. Tear or cut lettuce into bite-size pieces; place lettuce pieces into a salad bowl.
3. Chop anchovy fillets; add chopped anchovies and their oil to lettuce. Add Parmesan cheese; toss to combine.
4. Add remaining corn oil or olive oil, lemon juice, salt and pepper; toss well.
5. Cook egg in a small saucepan of boiling water 1 minute. Break egg over salad; toss gently. Add croutons; toss to combine. Makes 4 dinner salads or 4 to 6 starters.

# Italian Tomato Salad

6 small tomatoes, thinly sliced
6 oz. sliced Mozzarella cheese
10 to 12 small black olives
*Dressing:*
1/4 cup olive oil
1-1/2 tablespoons white-wine vinegar
2 tablespoons chopped fresh basil or 2 teaspoons
   dried leaf basil
Salt
Freshly ground pepper

1. Arrange sliced tomatoes in a shallow serving dish.
2. Place cheese slices in center of tomatoes, so that tomatoes are visible around edge of dish; see photo.
3. Arrange olives on tomatoes.
4. To make dressing, in a small bowl, combine olive oil, vinegar, basil, salt and pepper. If using dried basil, let dressing stand 15 minutes.
5. Pour dressing over tomatoes, cheese and olives. Serve immediately, or refrigerate 2 to 3 hours. Makes 4 dinner salads or 6 starters.

Left to right: Caesar Salad, Italian Tomato Salad,
Pipérade-Stuffed Tomatoes, Greek Salad with Tahini Dressing

# Pipérade-Stuffed Tomatoes

4 large tomatoes
1/4 cup butter or margarine
2 bacon slices, chopped
1 shallot, finely chopped
1 small red or green bell pepper, diced
4 eggs, slightly beaten
Salt
Freshly ground black pepper

*To serve:*
1 small head lettuce

---

1. Slice tops off tomatoes; reserve for lids.
2. Scoop out centers of tomatoes with a grapefruit knife or spoon. Chop centers; set aside. Place tomato cases, cut-side down, on a plate to drain.
3. Melt 2 tablespoons butter or margarine in a medium saucepan. Add bacon, shallot and bell pepper; sauté 5 minutes.
4. Add chopped tomatoes; simmer 10 minutes or until reduced to a thick puree, stirring occasionally.
5. In another saucepan, melt remaining butter or margarine over medium heat; pour in eggs. Cook gently, stirring with a wooden spoon, until eggs are scrambled.
6. Stir tomato mixture into scrambled eggs; season with salt and pepper. Cool to room temperature.
7. Fill tomato cases with cool mixture; replace lids. Separate lettuce into leaves; arrange lettuce leaves on a serving plate. Place stuffed tomatoes on lettuce. Makes 4 main-dish servings or 4 starters.

# Greek Salad with Tahini Dressing

1/2 large cucumber
3 small tomatoes, cut into thin wedges
1 small green bell pepper, sliced
1 small onion, thinly sliced
8 small pitted black olives, halved
4 oz. feta cheese

*Tahini Dressing:*
2 tablespoons tahini paste
1/4 cup plain yogurt
1 to 2 tablespoons water
2 tablespoons chopped fresh parsley
1 small garlic clove, if desired, crushed
Salt
Freshly ground pepper

---

1. Cut cucumber into 1/4-inch slices; cut slices into 1/4-inch-wide strips. Place cucumber strips into a salad bowl.
2. Add tomatoes, bell pepper, onion and olives. Cube feta cheese; set aside.
3. To make dressing, spoon tahini paste into a small bowl. Slowly beat in yogurt; thin with water if necessary. Stir in parsley and garlic, if desired. Season with salt and pepper.
4. Pour dressing over salad; toss well. Sprinkle cheese cubes over salad. Serve immediately.
5. This is excellent with cold roasted meats and pita bread. Makes 4 to 6 dinner salads.

# Mediterranean Bean Salad

1 lb. fresh green beans
Salt

*Dressing:*
6 tablespoons olive oil
Grated peel of 1 small lemon
2 tablespoons lemon juice
2 hard-cooked eggs, chopped
8 small black olives
1 small garlic clove, if desired, crushed
Salt
Freshly ground pepper

1. Trim and string beans. If beans are small, leave whole; cut beans in half crosswise, if large.
2. Place prepared beans and a little salt in a saucepan. Add enough boiling water to almost cover; simmer about 10 minutes or until crisp-tender.
3. Drain beans; rinse with cold water to cool quickly.
4. To make dressing, pour olive oil into a serving bowl large enough to hold beans. Stir in lemon peel, lemon juice, hard-cooked eggs, olives and garlic, if desired. Season with salt and pepper.
5. Add cooled beans to dressing; toss to coat beans with dressing. Serve immediately, or refrigerate several hours. Makes 4 dinner salads or 6 starters.

### Variation
For a richer Mediterranean flavor, add 1 (2-ounce) can anchovy fillets, chopped, with cooled beans.

# Bean & Bacon Salad

1 lb. shelled green lima beans or broad beans
    (about 2 cups)
1/2 cup plain yogurt
2 tablespoons chopped fresh parsley
1 teaspoon dried leaf oregano
1 tablespoon finely chopped onion
Salt
Freshly ground pepper

*To garnish:*
4 crisp-cooked bacon slices, crumbled

1. If using broad beans, remove skins. Place beans in a medium saucepan. Add enough boiling water to cover. Simmer lima beans about 15 minutes or until tender. Broad beans need 25 to 30 minutes. Drain cooked beans; rinse with cold water to cool quickly.
2. To make dressing, in a small bowl, combine yogurt, parsley, oregano and onion; season with salt and pepper.
3. Place cooled beans into a serving bowl; stir dressing into beans. Sprinkle with bacon. Serve immediately, or refrigerate several hours. Makes 4 to 6 dinner salads.

# Pasta & Pesto Salad

8 oz. uncooked pasta, any shape (about 2 cups)
Salt

*Pesto:*
1/2 cup fresh basil leaves, chopped
1/4 cup grated Parmesan cheese
1 garlic clove, crushed
About 6 tablespoons olive oil
1 tablespoon lemon juice
Salt
Freshly ground pepper
1/4 cup pine nuts or chopped blanched almonds

1. Cook pasta in a large saucepan of boiling salted water according to package directions until tender. Do not overcook.
2. Drain cooked pasta; rinse with cold water to cool quickly.
3. To make Pesto, place basil in a bowl large enough to hold pasta. Add cheese, garlic, 6 tablespoons olive oil, lemon juice, salt and pepper. Beat until blended. Or, place ingredients in a blender or food processor fitted with a steel blade; process until smooth.
4. Stir in pine nuts or almonds. Add cooled pasta; toss until pasta is coated with dressing. If pasta seems dry, add additional oil. Serve immediately, or cover and refrigerate up to 24 hours. Serve with ham or other cold meats. Makes 4 to 6 dinner salads.

### Variation
If fresh basil is not available, substitute 1/4 cup chopped fresh parsley and 2 tablespoons dried leaf basil for fresh basil.

Clockwise from left: Mediterranean Bean Salad, Pasta & Pesto Salad, Bean & Bacon Salad

# Salmon with Cucumber Sauce

4 salmon steaks, about 6 oz. each
Salt
Freshly ground pepper
1 lemon
4 parsley or dill sprigs
1/4 cup dry white wine or water

*Cucumber Sauce:*
1 cucumber, about 10 inches long
1/2 cup Mayonnaise, page 112, or prepared mayonnaise

*To serve:*
1 lettuce heart
Dill or parsley sprigs

1. Preheat oven to 350F (175C). Grease a baking dish large enough to hold salmon in a single layer. Place salmon steaks in greased baking dish; season with salt and pepper.
2. Grate peel from lemon; reserve for sauce. Cut lemon into thin slices; place 1 slice on each steak.
3. Place 1 parsley or dill sprig on each salmon steak; add wine or water. Cover with a lid or foil.
4. Bake in preheated oven 10 to 15 minutes or until salmon tests done. Set aside to cool; reserve cooking liquid.
5. To make sauce, dice cucumber. Place diced cucumber in a small bowl. Stir mayonnaise and reserved salmon cooking liquid into cucumber. Stir in reserved lemon peel, salt and pepper.
6. To serve, carefully remove skin and center bones from salmon, keeping steaks whole. Discard baked lemon slices and parsley or dill. Arrange steaks on a serving plate. Spoon sauce down center of each baked salmon where bone has been removed. Garnish with lettuce and a dill or parsley sprig. Serve immediately. Makes 4 main-dish servings.

### Variation
Substitute halibut, turbot or cod for salmon. If dill is not available, substitute the feathery leaves from fennel.

# Seafood-Stuffed Lettuce

1 large head lettuce
4 hard-cooked eggs, chopped
8 oz. shrimp, cooked, peeled, deveined
6 oz. cooked crabmeat
1/2 cup Anchovy Mayonnaise, page 112
1 tablespoon lemon juice
2 tablespoons chopped fresh chives
2 tablespoons chopped fresh parsley
Salt
Freshly ground pepper

1. Remove and discard outside leaves from lettuce; keep remaining leaves attached. Carefully wash lettuce; shake to remove excess water. Invert on paper towels or a clean dish towel.
2. To make stuffing, in a medium bowl, combine hard-cooked eggs, shrimp and crabmeat. Stir in Anchovy Mayonnaise, lemon juice, chives and parsley. Season with salt and pepper. Stuffing can be made several hours in advance; refrigerate until served. Stuff lettuce immediately before serving.
3. To serve, place lettuce on a large plate. Gently pull apart center leaves; remove lettuce heart.
4. Spoon stuffing into center of lettuce. Makes 4 main-dish servings or 6 to 8 starters.

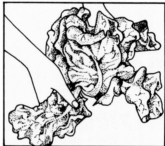
1/Remove and discard outside leaves from lettuce.

2/Remove lettuce heart.

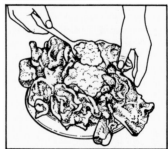
3/Spoon stuffing into center of lettuce.

# Eggplant Salad

1 (1-1/4-lb.) eggplant
1 tablespoon salt
5 tablespoons olive oil
1 medium onion, chopped
1 garlic clove, crushed
2 large tomatoes
1/2 cup chopped walnuts

*Dressing:*
1 tablespoon chopped fresh basil or 1-1/2 teaspoons
    dried leaf basil
1/2 cup Yogurt Dressing, page 113
Salt
Freshly ground pepper

*To garnish:*
1 tablespoon chopped fresh parsley

1. Cut eggplant into 1/2-inch cubes; place eggplant cubes in a colander. Sprinkle with salt; shake to distribute salt over all cubes. Place colander on a plate to drain; let stand 1 hour. Rinse; pat dry with paper towels.
2. Heat olive oil in a large skillet. Add rinsed eggplant, onion and garlic. Cook over medium heat 10 minutes or until eggplant is tender and browned, stirring frequently. Set aside to cool.
3. Spoon cooked eggplant mixture into a medium bowl. Dice tomatoes; stir diced tomatoes and walnuts into eggplant mixture.
4. To make dressing, in a small bowl, stir basil into Yogurt Dressing. Season with salt and pepper. Stir seasoned dressing into eggplant mixture until combined.
5. Spoon salad into a serving bowl; sprinkle with parsley. Serve immediately, or cover and refrigerate up to 24 hours. Bring to room temperature before serving. Makes 4 to 6 dinner salads.

Left to right: Salmon with Cucumber Sauce, Seafood-Stuffed Lettuce

# Midsummer Salad

1 small ripe melon, such as cantaloupe or honeydew
3/4 cup strawberries, hulled
1 (3-inch) cucumber piece
1 small head leaf lettuce, shredded

*Mint Dressing:*
1/4 cup Oil & Vinegar Dressing, page 112, or
    prepared dressing
2 tablespoons chopped fresh mint
Salt
Freshly ground pepper

*To garnish:*
2 tablespoons slivered almonds

---

1. Cut melon into quarters; remove and discard seeds and skin. Scoop into balls with a melon baller, or cut into 1/2-inch cubes.
2. Cut strawberries and cucumber into thin slices.
3. To serve, arrange lettuce on a large serving plate or 4 individual plates. Arrange melon balls or cubes, strawberry slices and cucumber slices over lettuce.
4. In a small bowl, combine oil-and-vinegar dressing, mint, salt and pepper. Pour over salad immediately before serving; sprinkle with almonds. Serve with a selection of hard and soft cheeses or ham. Makes 4 dinner salads or 4 to 6 starters.

**Variations**
Serve salad in small melon halves instead of plates. Substitute banana slices or kiwifruit slices for some or all of strawberries.

# Peperonata

2 tablespoons olive oil
1 large onion, sliced
4 to 6 red and green bell peppers, quartered
1 garlic clove, if desired, crushed
4 to 5 small tomatoes, peeled
Salt
Freshly ground black pepper

---

1. Heat olive oil in a large skillet. Add onion; sauté 5 minutes.
2. Cut bell peppers into 1/4-inch slices; add bell-pepper slices and garlic, if desired, to skillet. Cover skillet; simmer 10 minutes.
3. Cut each tomato into 8 wedges; add tomato wedges to bell-pepper mixture. Season with salt and black pepper.
4. Simmer, uncovered, 15 to 20 minutes or until vegetables are tender, stirring occasionally. Tomatoes should be tender but still hold their shape.
5. Spoon cooked vegetables and their juice into a serving bowl; cool to room temperature. Makes 4 dinner salads or 6 to 8 starters.

Clockwise from top: Midsummer Salad with Mint Dressing, Selection of cheeses, Zucchini-Timbale Salad

# Zucchini-Timbale Salad

1-1/2 lb. zucchini, trimmed, cut into
    1/2-inch thick slices
Salt
1 tablespoon freshly chopped basil or 1-1/2 teaspoons
    dried leaf basil
4 eggs
2/3 cup half and half
Freshly ground pepper
2 tablespoons grated Parmesan cheese

*To serve:*
3 to 4 tomatoes, sliced
1 carton radish sprouts
6 tablespoons Oil & Vinegar Dressing, page 112, or
    prepared dressing

---

1. Preheat oven to 350F (175C). Grease 6 (3/4-cup) ramekins.
2. Cook zucchini in a medium saucepan of lightly salted boiling water 5 minutes. Drain well; set aside to cool. In a blender or food processor fitted with a steel blade, process cooled zucchini and basil until smooth. Pour puree into a medium bowl.
3. In a small bowl, beat eggs and half and half until blended. Stir into zucchini puree until blended. Season with salt and pepper.
4. Spoon zucchini mixture into greased ramekins. Place filled ramekins on a baking sheet; sprinkle 1 teaspoon cheese over top of each ramekin.
5. Bake in preheated oven 45 to 50 minutes or until set. Remove from baking sheet; cool completely on a wire rack. Refrigerate timbales in ramekins until served.
6. To serve, run the tip of a knife around edge of each ramekin; invert ramekins on individual serving plates. Remove ramekins. Cut tomato slices in half; arrange around each timbale. Garnish with radish sprouts. Spoon 1 tablespoon dressing over each timbale. Makes 6 light main-dish servings.

# Marinated Mackerel

4 medium mackerel, ready to cook
1/2 cup white wine or apple juice
1/2 cup water
1 lemon slice
1 large parsley sprig
1 large thyme sprig or 1 teaspoon dried leaf thyme
1 bay leaf
Salt
Freshly ground pepper

*To garnish:*
1 tablespoon chopped fresh parsley
1 tablespoon chopped fresh chives
Shredded lettuce or cucumber slices

1. Preheat oven to 350F (175C). Place fish in a baking pan. Add wine or apple juice, water, lemon, herbs, salt and pepper. Cover with a lid or foil.
2. Bake in preheated oven 20 minutes or until fish tests done.
3. Set aside to cool. When fish is cool, remove and discard skin.
4. Pour cooking liquid into a small saucepan; boil until reduced to about 1/2 cup.
5. Place cooled fish in a shallow serving dish; add reduced cooking liquid. Cover and refrigerate until chilled.
6. To serve, sprinkle with chopped parsley and chives; garnish with lettuce or cucumber. Makes 4 main-dish salads.

# Beet & Orange Salad

1 (1-lb.) can cut beets, drained
1 medium orange
1/2 cup dairy sour cream
2 tablespoons chopped fresh chives
Salt
Freshly ground pepper

1. Arrange beets in a shallow serving dish.
2. Grate peel from 1/2 of orange; cut orange in half. Squeeze juice from grated orange half. Set orange peel and orange juice aside. Cut peel and white pith from remaining orange half; cut peeled orange half into sections. Scatter orange sections over beets.
3. In a small bowl, combine orange peel, orange juice and sour cream. Stir in chives, salt and pepper. Pour dressing over beets and orange; do not stir. Serve immediately. Makes 4 dinner salads.

# French Lamb Salad

1 lb. cold roast lamb, preferably medium rare
1/4 cup olive oil
2 tablespoons white-wine vinegar
2 tablespoons chopped fresh mint or 1 tablespoon dried leaf mint
Salt
Freshly ground pepper
4 green onions, chopped
1 cup cooked green peas

*To serve:*
1 head lettuce
Mint sprigs

1. Cut lamb into 3/4-inch cubes.
2. To make dressing, pour oil into a bowl large enough to hold lamb and vegetables. Whisk in vinegar, mint, salt and pepper.
3. Stir in lamb cubes and green onions until coated with dressing. Gently stir in peas. Serve immediately, or cover and refrigerate up to 24 hours.
4. Immediately before serving, shred lettuce; stir shredded lettuce into lamb salad. Spoon into a serving dish; garnish with mint sprigs. Makes 4 main-dish servings.

# Zucchini Ratatouille

2 tablespoons olive oil
1 medium onion, thinly sliced
1 garlic clove, crushed
1 lb. zucchini, sliced
2 or 3 small tomatoes, peeled, sliced
1 small eggplant, diced
1 green bell pepper, cut into thin strips
1 tablespoon chopped fresh oregano or 1-1/2 teaspoons
   dried leaf oregano
Salt
Freshly ground black pepper

*To garnish:*
1 tablespoon chopped fresh parsley

*This dish originates from Provence in southern France. Serve hot or at room temperature. The flavor is even better if prepared the day before serving.*

**1.** Heat olive oil in a large saucepan. Add onion and garlic; sauté 5 minutes.
**2.** Add zucchini, tomatoes, eggplant and bell pepper to pan. Sprinkle with oregano, salt and black pepper; stir gently.
**3.** Cover and simmer 10 to 15 minutes or until vegetables are tender but hold their shapes. Cool to room temperature. Serve immediately, or cover and refrigerate up to 24 hours. Bring to room temperature before serving.
**4.** To serve, turn into a serving dish; sprinkle with chopped parsley. Serve with grilled meats. Makes 4 dinner salads.

Left to right: Beet & Orange Salad, Marinated Mackerel

# Seafood Mousse

1 lb. white fish fillets
2/3 cup dry white wine
2/3 cup water
1 small onion, sliced
1 thick lemon slice
1 bay leaf
Parsley sprigs
Salt
6 peppercorns
Milk
2 tablespoons butter or margarine
2-1/2 tablespoons all-purpose flour
1/4 cup cold water
1 (1/4-oz.) envelope plus 1 teaspoon unflavored gelatin
   powder
1 tablespoon lemon juice
1 teaspoon anchovy paste
1 teaspoon paprika
1/2 pint dairy sour cream (1 cup)
1 egg, separated
Freshly ground white pepper

*To garnish:*
Thinly sliced cucumbers
1 carton radish sprouts
Green Mayonnaise, page 112

1. Preheat oven to 350F (175C). Place fish in a shallow baking dish. Add wine, 2/3 cup water, onion, lemon, bay leaf, parsley, salt and peppercorns. Cover with a lid or foil.
2. Bake in preheated oven 20 minutes or until fish tests done. Let cool slightly. Remove fish with a slotted spoon; set aside. Strain cooking liquid into a 2-cup measuring cup; add enough milk to make 2 cups. Set aside.
3. Melt butter or margarine in a medium saucepan. Stir in flour; cook over low heat 1 minute. Gradually stir in cooking liquid and milk; cook, stirring constantly, until sauce is thickened and comes to a boil. Lower heat; simmer 2 minutes, stirring occasionally. Set aside to cool.
4. Flake fish into a large bowl; mash with a fork. Stir in sauce until blended. In a small saucepan, combine 1/4 cup water and gelatin. Stir well; let stand 3 minutes. Stir over low heat until gelatin dissolves. Stir into fish mixture.
5. Stir in lemon juice, anchovy paste, paprika, sour cream and egg yolk until thoroughly blended. In a small bowl, beat egg white until stiff peaks form; fold into fish mixture. Season with salt and white pepper.
6. Rinse a 5- to 5-1/2-cup decorative fish mold with cold water. Pour in fish mixture; refrigerate several hours or until set.
7. To serve, run the tip of a knife around edge of mold. Invert mold on a large serving plate. Wet a dish towel with hot water; wring dry. Wrap hot towel around mold for a few seconds. Remove towel and mold. Garnish mousse with cucumber slices and radish sprouts. Serve with Green Mayonnaise. Makes 8 to 10 main-dish servings.

Seafood Mousse

# Oriental Pea-Pod Salad

1-1/4 lb. Chinese pea pods
Salt
4 oz. mushrooms, thinly sliced
1 small red bell pepper, finely chopped
8 oz. shrimp, cooked, peeled, deveined

*Dressing:*
3 tablespoons vegetable oil
1 tablespoon soy sauce
1 to 2 tablespoons lemon juice
1 teaspoon brown or white sugar, if desired

*To garnish:*
2 tablespoons sesame seeds

---

**1.** String pea pods, if necessary. Place in a medium sauce-pan of boiling salted water. Return to a boil; simmer 1 minute. Drain immediately; rinse with cold water to cool quickly. Drain again.
**2.** Combine drained pea pods, mushrooms, bell pepper and shrimp in a medium bowl.
**3.** To make dressing, in a small bowl, combine oil, soy sauce and lemon juice to taste. Stir in sugar until dissolved if a sweet dressing is desired.
**4.** Pour dressing over shrimp mixture; toss to coat with dressing. Cover and refrigerate up to 8 hours.
**5.** To serve, spoon into a large serving bowl or individual serving bowls; sprinkle with sesame seeds. Makes 4 light main-dish servings or 6 to 8 starters.

### Variation
Substitute sugar peas for Chinese pea pods. Sugar peas look like swollen pea pods. Do not cook; they are tender and deliciously sweet.

# Cucumber Salad with Dill

1 large cucumber
1 tablespoon salt

*Dressing:*
1/4 cup white-wine vinegar
1 tablespoon sugar
1 tablespoon chopped fresh dill or 1-1/2 teaspoons
  dried dill weed
Freshly ground pepper

*To garnish:*
1 tablespoon chopped fresh dill or parsley

---

*This refreshing Scandinavian salad is best made a day ahead. It is an excellent choice for a summer buffet party, especially one which has salmon on the menu.*

**1.** Score cucumber skin by running prongs of a fork down its length, all the way around.
**2.** Thinly slice cucumber with a sharp knife or a food processor fitted with a slicing attachment.
**3.** Place cucumber slices in a colander or sieve; sprinkle with salt. Shake to distribute salt over all slices. Place colander in a bowl to drain.
**4.** Let stand 1 to 2 hours, shaking occasionally, or until about 1/2 cup of liquid has drained off.
**5.** Rinse cucumber in cold water to remove excess salt; drain well on paper towels. Place drained cucumber in a shallow serving dish.
**6.** To make dressing, in a small bowl, combine all ingredients. Pour dressing over cucumber slices. Refrigerate until chilled or up to 24 hours.
**7.** To serve, sprinkle with chopped dill or parsley. Serve with cold salmon or other fish dishes. Makes 4 servings.

### Variation
**Tzatziki:** To make this refreshing Greek salad, substitute a mint-and-yogurt dressing for the dill dressing. To make mint-and-yogurt dressing, add 1-1/2 teaspoons dried leaf mint or 1 tablespoon fresh chopped mint to Yogurt Dressing, page 113.

Top to bottom: Oriental Pea-Pod Salad, Country Salad

## Zucchini & Mint Salad

1-1/2 lb. zucchini
2 teaspoons salt
1/2 cup pine nuts or slivered almonds
2/3 cup raisins
*Dressing:*
6 tablespoons olive oil
2 tablespoons lemon juice
2 tablespoons chopped fresh mint
Freshly ground pepper

**1.** Wash zucchini; coarsely grate into a colander. Sprinkle with salt; shake to distribute salt evenly. Place colander in a bowl to drain. Let stand about 1 hour to drain off excess juices. Rinse in cold water to remove excess salt. Drain and pat dry with paper towels.
**2.** Place drained zucchini in a medium bowl; stir in pine nuts or almonds and raisins.
**3.** To make dressing, in a small bowl, combine all ingredients; pour over zucchini mixture. Toss to combine. Serve immediately.
**4.** Serve with cold roasted lamb or chicken. Makes 4 dinner salads.

## Country Salad

1 small head lettuce
1 bunch dandelion leaves or 1/2 head curly endive
8 oz. lamb's lettuce
1 small bunch chives
1/2 cup Yogurt & Blue-Cheese Dressing, page 113, or
    prepared blue-cheese dressing

**1.** Wash lettuce; dry. Shred coarsely. Place shredded lettuce in a salad bowl.
**2.** Wash dandelion leaves, removing coarse stalks; dry. Add to lettuce.
**3.** Wash lamb's lettuce; dry. Separate into sprigs; add to lettuce mixture.
**4.** Chop chives; add to lettuce mixture.
**5.** Pour dressing over salad; toss to coat salad with dressing. Makes 4 dinner salads.

# Autumn

## Pears with Blue Cheese

2/3 cup plain yogurt
4 oz. Stilton cheese or other blue cheese,
   room temperature
Freshly ground pepper
1 small head lettuce
4 ripe pears

*To garnish:*
1 bunch watercress

---

1. In a small bowl, blend yogurt and 2 ounces cheese until smooth. Season with pepper.
2. Arrange lettuce leaves on 4 individual plates. Core and slice pears, arranging 1 pear on each plate.
3. Spoon dressing over pear slices. Crumble remaining cheese; sprinkle over dressing.
4. Garnish each plate with a few watercress sprigs. Serve immediately. Makes 4 dinner salads or 4 starters.

### Variation
For a more substantial salad, add 1 small ham slice to each serving.

## Peaches & Cream Salad

1 (8-oz.) pkg. cream cheese, room temperature
1 to 2 tablespoons half and half or milk
Salt
Freshly ground pepper
1 cup chopped mixed nuts, toasted
Lettuce leaves
4 ripe peaches or nectarines, halved, pitted

---

1. In a medium bowl, beat cheese until smooth; thin with half and half or milk, if necessary. Season with salt and pepper. Stir in 1/2 cup nuts.
2. Divide lettuce leaves among 4 individual plates; place 2 peach or nectarine halves on each plate.
3. Spoon some cream-cheese filling into center of each peach or nectarine half; sprinkle with remaining nuts. Makes 4 starters.

### Variation
**Pineapple & Cream Cheese:** Substitute 4 fresh or canned pineapple slices for peaches or nectarines. Mound cream-cheese mixture in center of slices.

## Melon & Prosciutto with Ginger Dressing

1 (2-lb.) honeydew melon
4 oz. thinly sliced prosciutto

*Ginger Dressing:*
2 pieces stem ginger preserved in syrup
2 tablespoons stem-ginger syrup
3 tablespoons vegetable oil
1 teaspoon lemon juice
Freshly ground pepper

---

1. Cut melon lengthwise into quarters. Discard seeds; remove peel. Cut each peeled melon quarter into 4 long slices, making a total of 16 slices.
2. Cut ham into long slices about 2 inches wide.
3. Arrange melon slices and ham slices alternatively on a serving platter.
4. To make dressing, finely chop stem ginger; place in a small bowl. Beat in ginger syrup, oil, lemon juice and pepper.
5. Pour dressing evenly over melon and ham. Cover and refrigerate 30 minutes before serving. Makes 4 starters.

Clockwise from top left: Pears with Blue Cheese, Peaches & Cream Salad, Melon & Prosciutto with Ginger Dressing

# Fennel & Apple Salad

2 fennel bulbs, about 1 lb. total weight
4 small or 3 large apples
1/2 cup coarsely chopped nuts
1/2 cup Mayonnaise, page 112, or prepared mayonnaise
5 tablespoons orange juice
Salt
Freshly ground pepper

---

1. Cut fennel bulbs in half lengthwise. Trim off feathery green leaves; reserve for garnish. Slice fennel very finely. Place fennel slices in a large bowl.
2. Quarter apples; remove cores. Cut apple quarters into thin slices. Add apple slices and nuts to fennel.
3. In a small bowl, combine mayonnaise and orange juice until smooth. Season with salt and pepper.
4. Pour dressing over salad; toss to coat with dressing.
5. Garnish with reserved fennel leaves. Serve immediately with cold roast meat or cold poached fish. Makes 4 to 6 dinner salads.

# Crunchy Green Salad with Blue-Cheese Dressing

1/4 head green cabbage
1/2 bunch broccoli
1 medium zucchini
1 small green bell pepper, thinly sliced
1 celery stalk, thinly sliced
1/2 cup Yogurt & Blue-Cheese Dressing, page 113, or
    prepared blue-cheese dressing

---

1. Slice cabbage very thinly, discarding any core. Place sliced cabbage in a large bowl.
2. Divide broccoli into flowerets; discard tough stalks. Add flowerets to cabbage.
3. Cut off and discard zucchini ends; slice trimmed zucchini as thinly as possible. Add to cabbage and broccoli.
4. Add pepper slices and celery to bowl. Pour dressing over vegetables; toss well.
5. Cover and refrigerate 1 hour before serving. Makes 4 to 6 dinner salads.

Left to right: Fennel & Apple Salad, Crunchy Green Salad with Blue-Cheese Dressing, Beef & Radish Salad

# Bread & Cheese Salad

2 cups plain croutons
1/2 cup Oil & Vinegar Dressing, page 112, or
    prepared dressing
1 teaspoon chopped fresh thyme or 1/2 teaspoon
    dried leaf thyme
8 celery stalks, sliced crosswise
4 tomatoes, cut into wedges
8 oz. Cheddar cheese or other hard cheese
Lettuce leaves or endive leaves, if desired

*To garnish:*
Celery leaves

1. Place croutons in a large bowl.
2. In a small bowl, combine dressing and thyme; pour over bread. Toss until croutons are coated with dressing.
3. Add celery and tomatoes; toss lightly.
4. Cut cheese into small cubes or strips; add to salad.
5. Serve immediately. Or, cover and refrigerate several hours.
6. Serve from bowl. Or, arrange lettuce or endive on a serving plate; top with salad. Garnish with celery leaves. Makes 4 main-dish servings.

# Beef & Radish Salad

1 lb. cold roast beef
1 bunch radishes with leaves
1/2 cup broken walnut halves
*Dressing:*
1/4 cup walnut oil or olive oil
2 tablespoons orange juice
1 tablespoon white-wine vinegar
Salt
Freshly ground pepper

1. Thinly slice beef; cut slices into 1-1/2" x 1/2" strips; place in a medium bowl.
2. Reserve 2 or 3 radishes and radish leaves for garnishing. For instructions on making radish roses, see illustrations below. Thinly slice remaining radishes; add sliced radishes to beef.
3. Add walnuts.
4. In a small bowl, combine dressing ingredients. Pour dressing over beef mixture. Toss to coat with dressing. Cover and refrigerate until served.
5. Spoon beef-and-radish salad into a serving bowl; garnish with radish roses and radish leaves. Makes 4 main-dish servings.

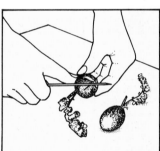

1/To make radish garnishes, cut vertically through center of radish almost to stem end. Give radish a 1/2 turn; make another cut. Repeat cuts at 1/8-inch intervals.

2/Place cut radishes in iced water until cuts open. Leave stem on, if desired.

# Seviche

1-1/2 lb. white fish fillets, skin removed
1/4 cup fresh lemon juice or lime juice
4 medium tomatoes
1 small green bell pepper
1 (4-inch) cucumber piece
2 tablespoons vegetable oil
1 tablespoon finely chopped onion
1 tablespoon ketchup
Salt
Freshly ground black pepper
Few drops hot-pepper sauce, if desired

*To serve:*
1 small head lettuce, shredded
Lime or lemon slices

1. Cut fish into thin strips; place in a medium bowl.
2. Pour lemon juice or lime juice over fish; stir until fish is coated. Cover and refrigerate at least 2 hours or until fish has turned white and opaque and looks cooked.
3. Meanwhile prepare vegetables. Peel tomatoes. Remove and discard seeds; dice tomatoes.
4. Cut bell pepper into quarters; remove and discard seeds. Dice bell pepper. Cut cucumber into slices; dice slices.
5. Combine marinated fish, diced tomatoes, diced bell pepper and diced cucumber
6. In a small bowl, combine oil, onion, ketchup, salt, black pepper and hot-pepper sauce, if desired. Stir dressing into salad. Serve immediately, or cover and refrigerate up to 8 hours.
7. To serve, divide lettuce among individual plates. Spoon Seviche over lettuce; garnish each serving with a lime or lemon twist. Makes 4 main-dish servings or 6 starters.

# Inca Salad

1/4 cup Oil & Vinegar Dressing, page 112, or
    other dressing
Few drops hot-pepper sauce
2 medium, ripe avocados
2 cups diced, cooked, peeled potatoes
1 (6-1/2-oz.) can tuna, water pack, drained, flaked
Lettuce leaves, if desired

*To garnish:*
4 small fresh chili peppers or cucumber slices

1. To make a hot-chili dressing, pour oil-and-vinegar dressing into a medium bowl; blend in hot-pepper sauce to taste.
2. Cut avocados in half. Remove seeds and peel. Cut peeled avocados into small cubes. Lightly toss avocado cubes in dressing.
3. Add potato cubes and tuna to avocado mixture. Toss gently; do not mash avocado cubes.
4. Line a serving dish or individual plates with lettuce leaves, if desired; mound avocado salad on top.
5. Garnish with chili flowers. To make chili flowers, see illustrations below. Or, garnish salad with cucumber twists. Makes 4 main-dish servings or 6 starters.

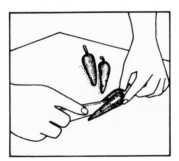

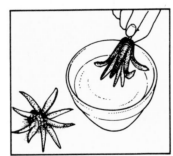

1/Make several longs cuts, starting 1/2 inch from stem end.

2/With scissors, make additional cuts for fine petals.

3/Place cut chilies in iced water until petals open.

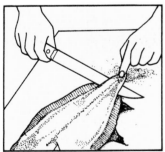
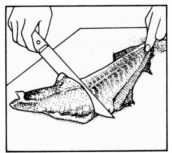

1/To skin a fish fillet, place fillet skin-side down. Starting at the tail, insert a knife between flesh and skin.

2/Carefully run knife towards the head, keeping blade slanting downwards. Sprinkle salt on the work surface to keep fish from slipping.

Left to right: Seviche, Inca Salad

# Russian Salad with Tongue

4 medium potatoes, peeled
2 large carrots
Salt
1 cup sliced celery, or 1 medium turnip, peeled, diced
1 (10-oz.) pkg. frozen green beans or green peas
8 to 10 thin slices cooked tongue

*Dressing:*
1/2 cup Mayonnaise, page 112, or prepared mayonnaise
2/3 cup dairy sour cream or plain yogurt
1 tablespoon chopped pickle
1 tablespoon capers

*To garnish:*
1 tablespoon capers
Pickle fans, see below

---

**1.** Place whole potatoes, carrots and salt in a large saucepan; cover with cold water. Bring to a boil; simmer 15 to 20 minutes or until tender but not soft. Drain; cool to room temperature.
**2.** In a medium saucepan, cook celery or turnip in boiling salted water about 15 minutes or until crisp-tender. Cook beans or peas 3 to 4 minutes in salted water. Drain vegetables; cool to room temperature.
**3.** Dice cooled potatoes and carrots; place diced vegetables in a large bowl. Stir in cooled celery or turnip and beans or peas.
**4.** To make dressing, in a small bowl, combine mayonnaise and sour cream or yogurt; stir in pickles and 1 tablespoon capers.
**5.** Pour dressing over vegetables; toss to coat with dressing.
**6.** Serve immediately. Or, cover and refrigerate up to 24 hours. To serve, arrange slices of tongue around edge of a platter. Pile Russian Salad in center; garnish with 1 tablespoon capers and pickle fans. Makes 4 main-dish servings.

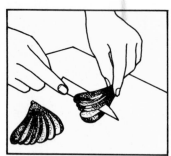

1/To make pickle fans, thinly slice pickle horizontally to within 1/2 inch of stem end. Spread slices apart to form a fan.

# Maryland Chicken Salad

1 tablespoon all-purpose flour
Salt
Freshly ground pepper
1 (2-1/2- to 3-lb.) broiler-fryer chicken, cut up
1 egg, beaten
1/2 cup dry bread crumbs
1/4 cup butter or margarine
1 tablespoon vegetable oil
4 small firm bananas
1 (12-oz.) can whole-kernel corn
1 bunch watercress
1 cup Yogurt Dressing, page 113

---

**1.** In a plastic bag, combine flour, salt and pepper. Add chicken pieces; shake to coat. Dip floured chicken in egg; coat with bread crumbs.
**2.** Heat butter or margarine and oil in a large skillet. Add coated chicken; sauté over medium heat 15 to 20 minutes, turning until chicken is golden brown and tender. With tongs, place cooked chicken on paper towels to drain. Reserve oil mixture for cooking bananas.
**3.** Peel bananas; cut in half lengthwise. Heat reserved oil mixture; add banana halves. Sauté, turning once, until lightly browned. Drain on paper towels.
**4.** Drain corn; set aside.
**5.** Arrange warm chicken on a large platter; top with warm bananas. Surround with drained corn. Garnish with watercress. Serve dressing separately. Makes 4 to 6 main-dish servings.

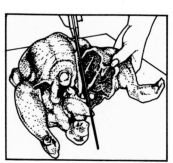

1/To cut up a chicken, cut through joints connecting thighs to body.

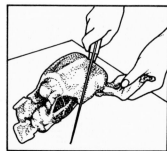

2/Cut through joints connecting wings to body.

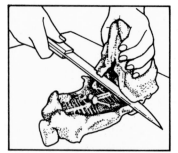

3/Remove breast by cutting along rib bones.

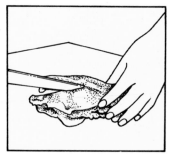

4/Cut through breast at breast bone.

# Corn Salad

2 (17-oz.) cans whole-kernel corn or 2 (10-oz.) pkgs.
  frozen whole-kernel corn
Salt
1/4 cup corn oil
1 tablespoon white-wine vinegar
1 tablespoon Worcestershire sauce
1 tablespoon ketchup
1 tablespoon brown sugar
1 tablespoon grated onion
1/3 cup raisins
1 red or green bell pepper, finely chopped

1. In a medium saucepan, cook frozen corn in salted boiling water according to package directions. Drain; cool to room temperature. If using canned corn; drain. Set aside.
2. Pour corn oil into a medium bowl. Beat in vinegar, Worcestershire sauce, ketchup, sugar and onion.
3. Stir in raisins and bell pepper. Stir in drained corn until combined.
4. Serve immediately, or cover and refrigerate up to 2 days. Serve with hamburgers or barbecued meat. Makes 4 dinner salads.

Top to bottom: Corn Salad, Maryland Chicken Salad with Yogurt Dressing

# Marinated Mushrooms

2 tablespoons olive oil or corn oil
2 onions, thinly sliced
1 celery stalk, thinly sliced
1 large garlic clove, crushed
2 bacon slices, chopped
1/2 cup red wine
2 medium tomatoes, peeled, quartered, seeded
1 tablespoon fresh thyme leaves or 1-1/2 teaspoons
   dried leaf thyme
1 bay leaf
Salt
Freshly ground pepper
1 (3-inch) cinnamon stick, if desired
1 lb. button mushrooms, wiped

*To garnish:*
1 tablespoon fresh thyme leaves, if desired

1. Heat oil in a large saucepan. Add onions, celery, garlic and bacon; sauté over medium heat 5 minutes, stirring occasionally.
2. Stir in wine, tomatoes, thyme, bay leaf, salt, pepper and cinnamon stick, if desired. Bring to a boil; reduce heat.
3. Cut large mushrooms into halves or quarters; leave small mushrooms whole. Add mushrooms to saucepan.
4. Simmer 10 minutes. Cool in liquid; remove and discard bay leaf and cinnamon stick. Refrigerate at least 1 hour or up to 24 hours.
5. Drain mushrooms, discarding marinade. Place in a serving bowl; sprinkle with fresh thyme leaves, if desired. Makes 4 dinner salads or 4 starters.

# Lemon & Thyme Mushrooms

8 oz. large, flat mushrooms
1 small lemon
6 tablespoons olive oil
1 tablespoon fresh thyme leaves or 1 teaspoon
   dried leaf thyme
1 tablespoon chopped fresh parsley
Salt
Freshly ground pepper
1 small garlic clove, if desired, crushed

1. Slice mushrooms crosswise into long thin strips; arrange in a shallow serving dish.
2. Grate lemon peel into a small bowl; squeeze lemon juice into bowl.
3. Whisk in olive oil, thyme, parsley, salt, pepper and garlic, if desired.
4. Pour dressing over mushrooms. Refrigerate at least 1 hour or up to 24 hours. Makes 4 dinner salads or 4 starters.

### Variation
**Lemon & Thyme Mushrooms with Shrimp:** Stir 8 ounces deveined, peeled, cooked shrimp in salad before serving.

# Sweet & Sour Chinese Salad

2 tablespoons corn oil
1 tablespoon honey
1 tablespoon soy sauce
2 tablespoons lemon juice
4 oz. mushrooms, sliced
6 green onions, chopped
4 oz. bean sprouts (1 cup)
1/2 head Chinese cabbage, coarsely shredded

1. Combine oil, honey, soy sauce and lemon juice in a large bowl.
2. Stir mushrooms into soy-honey mixture until coated.
3. Stir in green onions and bean sprouts. Add Chinese cabbage; toss to coat with dressing. Serve with pork chops, spareribs or cold roast pork. Makes 4 dinner salads.

Top to bottom: Sweet & Sour Chinese Salad, Marinated Mushrooms

# Risotto Salad

2 tablespoons vegetable oil
4 bacon slices, chopped
1 medium onion, chopped
8 oz. chicken livers, chopped
1 garlic clove, if desired, crushed
1-1/4 cups uncooked long-grain white rice
2-1/2 cups chicken stock
1/2 teaspoon dried leaf oregano or dried leaf marjoram
Salt
Freshly ground pepper
1 (7-oz.) can whole-kernel corn, drained
1/2 cup Oil & Vinegar Dressing, page 112, or
　　prepared dressing

*To garnish:*
1 tablespoon chopped fresh parsley

*This chicken-liver risotto is cooked exactly as a hot risotto. While it is still hot, oil-and-vinegar dressing is stirred into the rice mixture to add extra flavor. Cool the risotto before serving.*

**1.** Heat oil in a large saucepan. Add bacon and onion; sauté 3 minutes.
**2.** Add chicken livers and garlic, if desired. Cook 2 minutes, stirring occasionally.
**3.** Stir in rice; cook 1 minute. Stir in chicken stock, oregano or marjoram, salt, pepper and corn. Bring to a boil; reduce heat.
**4.** Cover pan; simmer 15 to 20 minutes or until all stock is absorbed and rice is tender.
**5.** Transfer hot risotto to a bowl; stir in 1/2 of dressing. Cool to room temperature. Serve immediately, or cover and refrigerate up to 24 hours. Bring to room temperature before serving.
**6.** Immediately before serving, stir in remaining dressing; sprinkle with chopped parsley. Serve with a green salad. Makes 4 light main-dish servings.

**Variation**
Substitute long-grain brown rice for white rice. Use 3 cups of chicken stock; increase cooking time to 30 to 35 minutes. For perfect cooked rice, after all liquid has been absorbed and rice is tender, remove pan from heat. Do not remove lid; let stand a few minutes. The rice will fluff up in its own steam.

Left to right: Risotto Salad, Provençal Stuffed Eggs

# Provençal Potato Salad

1 (2-oz.) can anchovy fillets
1/2 teaspoon Italian seasoning
1 teaspoon chopped fresh parsley, if desired
3-3/4 cups thinly sliced peeled potatoes (about 1-1/4 lb.)
1 small onion, thinly sliced
2 small tomatoes, thinly sliced
1 tablespoon olive oil

1. Place anchovies with their oil in a small bowl. Add Italian seasoning and parsley, if desired; mash into a paste. Set aside.
2. Preheat oven to 375F (190C). Grease a 1-1/2-quart baking dish.
3. Arrange 1/3 of potatoes in bottom of dish. Cover with 1/2 of onion and 1/2 of tomatoes; spread lightly with 1/2 of anchovy paste. Repeat with 1/3 of potatoes and remaining 1/2 of onion, tomatoes and anchovy paste. Top with remaining 1/3 of potatoes. Brush top with oil.
4. Bake in preheated oven 1 to 1-1/4 hours or until top is golden and potatoes are tender. Cool to room temperature. Serve immediately, or cover and refrigerate up to 24 hours. Bring to room temperature before serving. Makes 4 to 6 dinner salads.

# Provençal Stuffed Eggs

16 pitted black olives
1 (2-oz.) can anchovy fillets
1 tablespoon capers
4 hard-cooked eggs

*To serve:*
Shredded lettuce
4 tomatoes, sliced
1 tablespoon chopped fresh parsley
2 tablespoons Oil & Vinegar Dressing, page 112, or prepared dressing

1. Place 12 olives in a medium bowl; reserve remaining olives. Add anchovies with their oil and capers to bowl; pound into a paste.
2. Cut eggs in half lengthwise. Remove yolks; mash yolks into anchovy mixture.
3. Divide egg-yolk mixture among egg-white halves. Cut reserved olives in half. Top each stuffed egg half with an olive half.
4. To serve, arrange lettuce on a platter. Arrange tomato slices in center; sprinkle tomatoes with parsley and dressing. Arrange stuffed eggs around edge of platter. Makes 4 starters.

# Stuffed Peppers

1 cup uncooked long-grain white rice
2 cups water
Salt
4 red, yellow or green bell peppers
2 small tomatoes, peeled, chopped
1/2 cup chopped walnuts
1/3 cup raisins
2 tablespoons chopped fresh parsley
1/4 cup Oil & Vinegar Dressing, page 112, or
    prepared dressing
Freshly ground black pepper
1/2 cup water or chicken stock

**1.** In a medium saucepan, combine rice, water and salt. Cover; bring to a boil. Reduce heat; simmer about 20 minutes or until all water has been absorbed and rice is tender.
**2.** While rice is cooking, cut bell peppers in half lengthwise; discard core and seeds.
**3.** When rice is cooked, stir in chopped tomatoes, walnuts, raisins, parsley, dressing, salt and black pepper.
**4.** Spoon rice mixture into bell-pepper halves; place stuffed peppers in a roasting pan or ovenproof dish. Pour water or stock around peppers. Cover pan with a lid or foil.
**5.** Bake in preheated oven about 45 minutes or until peppers are tender. Cool to room temperature. Serve immediately, or cover and refrigerate up to 24 hours. Bring to room temperature before serving. Makes 4 main-dish servings or 8 starters.

## Variations

**Stuffed Eggplant:** Halve 2 eggplants lengthwise; scoop out centers. Chop centers; place in a colander. Sprinkle lightly with salt. Sprinkle eggplant shells with salt; let stand upside-down 30 minutes to drain. Rinse shells and chopped centers; pat dry with paper towels. Combine rinsed chopped eggplant and rice mixture; spoon into eggplant shells. Bake in preheated oven 1 hour or until tender.
**Stuffed Zucchini:** Halve 4 zucchini lengthwise; scoop out centers. Combine chopped centers and rice mixture; spoon into zucchini. Bake in preheated oven 30 to 45 minutes or until tender.
**Stuffed Onions:** Peel 4 large onions; slice off root ends to make bottoms level. Place onions in a medium saucepan; cover with water. Bring to a boil; simmer 10 minutes. Drain; set aside to cool. Slice off tops; reserve tops for lids. Pull out centers; chop. Combine chopped onion and rice mixture; spoon into onions. Replace lids. Bake in preheated oven 45 minutes or until tender.
**Tomatoes:** Slice off tops of 8 small or 4 large tomatoes; reserve tops for lids. Scoop out pulp. Combine tomato pulp and rice mixture; spoon into tomatoes. Replace lids. Bake 15 to 20 minutes or until hot.

Stuffed Vegetables

# Chicken Salad Véronique

1/4 cup vegetable oil
1 garlic clove, if desired
4 boneless, skinless chicken-breast halves
1/2 cup sliced almonds

*Sour-Cream Dressing:*
2/3 cup dairy sour cream
1 tablespoon white vermouth or dry white wine
Salt
Freshly ground pepper

*To serve:*
Curly endive
8 oz. seedless green grapes

---

*This is a cold version of a classic hot French dish, Chicken Véronique. It is an excellent choice for a luncheon or buffet. It is attractive and can be prepared ahead.*

**1.** Heat oil in a large skillet; add garlic, if desired. Add chicken; sauté 10 minutes or until golden brown, turning once.
**2.** Remove chicken from skillet with tongs; drain on paper towels. Discard garlic. Add almonds to skillet; sauté, stirring constantly, until lightly browned. Remove from skillet; drain on paper towels. Cool chicken and almonds to room temperature. Reserve cooking oil for dressing; set aside to cool.
**3.** To make dressing, in a small bowl, combine sour cream, cooled cooking oil, vermouth or white wine, salt and pepper. Dressing, almonds and chicken can be refrigerated in separate containers up to 1 day.
**4.** To serve, arrange endive leaves on a serving plate; place cold chicken breasts on top.
**5.** Pour dressing over chicken; sprinkle with browned almonds and grapes. Makes 4 main-dish servings.

### Variation
To make serving easier, cut cooled chicken breasts into bite-size pieces. Fold chicken pieces, grapes and almonds into dressing. Spoon salad into a shallow serving bowl lined with lettuce leaves.

# Orchard Salad

Grated peel and juice of 2 small oranges
1 tablespoon chopped fresh mint or parsley
Salt
Freshly ground pepper
3 firm, medium pears
3 small apples
1/2 cup fresh blackberries
1/2 cup coarsely chopped almonds or other nuts

---

**1.** Place orange peel and orange juice in a medium bowl. Stir in mint or parsley, salt and pepper.
**2.** Quarter and core pears and apples. Cut each quarter crosswise into wedge-shaped slices. Add sliced pears and apples to orange-juice mixture; toss well.
**3.** Gently stir in blackberries and nuts. Serve with rich meats, such as pork and duck. Makes 4 to 6 dinner salads.

# Leek, Orange & Nut Salad

1 lb. leeks

*Orange Dressing:*
2 medium oranges
1/4 cup olive oil
Salt
Freshly ground pepper

*To garnish:*
1/2 cup chopped nuts

---

*If a milder flavor is preferred, blanch sliced leeks in boiling water 1 to 2 minutes before using.*

**1.** Cut off roots and green tops of leeks. Make a long, lengthwise cut in each leek, starting at green end. Pull open; plunge leeks, green ends first, into cold water to flush out any dirt from insides. Wash leeks carefully to remove all dirt between layers. Slice leeks into thin rounds. Separate into rings.
**2.** To make dressing, shred orange peel into long thin strips. Place orange-peel strips into a medium bowl. Squeeze orange juice into bowl; whisk in olive oil, salt and pepper.
**3.** When dressing is combined, stir in sliced leeks. Toss until leeks are coated with dressing.
**4.** Marinate 1 hour, or cover and refrigerate up to 8 hours to soften leeks. Serve with chicken or lamb. Sprinkle with nuts before serving. Makes 4 to 6 dinner salads.

# Chicken-Liver Ring

1 (1/4-oz.) envelope plus 1 teaspoon unflavored
  gelatin powder
2-1/2 cups chicken broth
1 teaspoon Worcestershire sauce
2 tablespoons dry sherry
1 bunch green onions, trimmed, sliced
2 tablespoons butter or margarine
1/2 lb. chicken livers, trimmed, coarsely chopped

*To garnish:*
1 carton radish sprouts

1. In a small saucepan, combine gelatin and 1/4 cup broth. Stir well; let stand 3 minutes. Stir over low heat until gelatin dissolves. Add remaining broth and Worcestershire sauce; stir until blended. Remove from heat; stir in sherry.

2. Rinse a 5-cup ring mold in cold water. Pour about 3/4 cup gelatin mixture into mold; set aside to cool to room temperature. Scatter about 1/2 of onions over gelatin mixture. Refrigerate until almost firm.

3. Melt butter or margarine in a small skillet. Add chicken livers; sauté 4 to 5 minutes or until livers are no longer pink. Remove livers with a slotted spoon; drain on paper towels. Cool completely.

4. Arrange cooled chicken livers and remaining onions over gelled gelatin mixture. Slowly pour remaining gelatin mixture into mold. Refrigerate until completely set.

5. To serve, run the tip of a sharp knife around edge of mold. Invert mold on a serving plate. Wet a dish towel with hot water; wring dry. Place hot towel around mold a few seconds. Remove towel and mold. Garnish with sprouts. Makes 4 to 6 main-dish servings.

Clockwise from top left: Orchard Salad; Chicken Salad
Véronique; Chicken-Liver Ring; Leek, Orange & Nut Salad

# Winter

## Leeks à la Grecque

1/2 cup water
1/2 cup white wine
2 tablespoons olive oil
Grated peel of 1 lemon
2 tablespoons lemon juice
1 shallot or small onion, thinly sliced
1 small celery stalk with leaves
1 parsley sprig
1/4 teaspoon dried leaf thyme
1 bay leaf
1/4 teaspoon salt
6 peppercorns
6 coriander seeds or 1/4 teaspoon ground coriander
1 lb. leeks

---

*If desired, leeks may be sliced into 3/4-inch pieces rather than left whole. Pieces will cook more quickly and are more suitable as a side dish.*

**1.** In a large saucepan, combine water, wine, olive oil, lemon peel, lemon juice, shallot or onion, celery, parsley, thyme, bay leaf, salt, peppercorns and coriander. Cover pan; bring to a boil. Simmer 10 minutes.
**2.** Cut off roots and green tops of leeks, so that each leek measures about 7 inches long.
**3.** Make a long, lengthwise cut in each leek, starting at green end. Pull open; plunge leeks, green ends first, into cold water to flush out any dirt from insides. Wash leeks carefully to remove all dirt between layers.
**4.** Place prepared leeks in simmering water. Cover and simmer 10 to 15 minutes or until leeks are tender.
**5.** Remove leeks from pan with a slotted spoon; place in a serving dish.
**6.** Boil cooking liquid until reduced to 1/2 cup. Pour reduced cooking liquid over leeks, removing herbs and spices, if desired. Let stand until cool. Serve immediately, or cover and refrigerate up to 24 hours. Makes 4 dinner salads or 4 starters.

## Moussaka Salad

1 (1-1/2-lb.) eggplant
1 tablespoon salt
About 1/2 cup vegetable oil
1 large onion, chopped
1-1/2 lb. lean ground lamb or beef
1 teaspoon tomato paste
Freshly ground pepper
1 garlic clove, if desired, crushed
1 large tomato, thinly sliced
3 eggs
1 tablespoon fresh marjoram or 1-1/2 teaspoons
  dried leaf marjoram

---

**1.** Cut eggplant into 1/8-inch slices. Place slices in a colander; sprinkle with salt. Stand colander on a plate; let drain 30 minutes.
**2.** Preheat oven to 350F (175C). Rinse eggplant slices; pat dry with paper towels.
**3.** Heat 3 tablespoons oil in a large skillet. Add rinsed eggplant slices, a few at a time. Sauté until golden brown on both sides, adding remaining eggplant and additional oil as necessary. Remove slices with a slotted spoon. Drain on paper towels.
**4.** Add onion to skillet; sauté 5 minutes. Add meat; sauté 5 to 10 minutes, stirring until lightly browned. Stir in tomato paste, salt, pepper and garlic, if desired.
**5.** Lightly grease a 1-quart casserole or 4 individual 1-cup casseroles. Arrange eggplant slices, overlapping, over bottom and side of dish or dishes, reserving enough to cover top or tops. Arrange tomato slices over eggplant slices on bottom.
**6.** Spoon meat mixture into eggplant-lined casserole. Beat eggs with marjoram, pepper and salt. Pour eggs over meat mixture; cover with remaining eggplant slices.
**7.** Bake in preheated oven 30 minutes for 1 large dish and 15 to 20 minutes for smaller dishes or until top is golden and egg mixture is set. Cool to room temperature. Serve immediately, or cover and refrigerate up to 24 hours.
**8.** Run a knife around edge to loosen moussaka; invert on a serving plate or individual salad plates. Remove mold or molds. Surround with endive leaves. Cut large moussaka into wedges to serve. Makes 4 dinner salads or 4 starters.

Top to bottom: Moussaka Salad, Leeks à la Grecque

# Red-Bean & Broccoli Salad

1 (15-oz.) can red kidney beans
8 oz. broccoli
1/2 cup Oil & Vinegar Dressing, page 112, or
  prepared dressing
2 celery stalks, thinly sliced
2 green onions, thinly sliced

1. Drain kidney beans; rinse with cold water.
2. Divide broccoli into flowerets; set aside.
3. Place rinsed beans in a medium bowl; stir in dressing. Add broccoli flowerets, celery and green onions; toss to coat with dressing.
4. Cover and refrigerate 3 to 4 hours to allow flavors to blend. Makes 4 dinner salads.

# Broccoli Niçoise

1 lb. broccoli
1 (6-1/2-oz.) can tuna, oil pack, drained, flaked
2 hard-cooked eggs
1 (2-oz.) can anchovy fillets, drained
8 small pitted black olives
1/2 cup Oil & Vinegar Dressing, page 112, or
  prepared dressing

1. Cut broccoli into small flowerets; cook in a little boiling, salted water 5 to 8 minutes or until crisp-tender. Drain; rinse with cold water to cool quickly.
2. When broccoli is cold, place on bottom of a shallow serving dish or platter. Arrange tuna on broccoli.
3. Cut hard-cooked eggs into wedges; place egg wedges, anchovies and olives on tuna. Salad can be covered and refrigerated 6 to 8 hours at this point.
4. To complete salad, pour dressing over salad. For a main-dish salad, serve with French bread. Makes 4 light main-dish servings or 6 starters.

Red-Bean & Broccoli Salad

Pickled-Herring Salad

# Pickled-Herring Salad

4 fresh herring, ready to cook
Salt
Freshly ground pepper
1 medium carrot, thinly sliced
1 medium onion, thinly sliced
1 apple, if desired, peeled, sliced
6 peppercorns
2 bay leaves
1/2 cup white-wine vinegar
1/2 cup water

---

**1.** Preheat oven to 350F (175C). Remove backbones from herring without removing tails. Press down on boned herring to flatten.
**2.** Sprinkle herring with salt and pepper; roll each herring, beginning at head end. Place rolled herrings in a shallow ovenproof dish, tails pointing upward.
**3.** Scatter carrot, onion and apple, if desired, over herring. Add peppercorns, bay leaves, vinegar and water. Cover with a lid or foil.
**4.** Bake in preheated oven about 20 minutes or until fish tests done. Cool to room temperature. Serve immediately, or cover and refrigerate up to 24 hours. Makes 4 starters.

# Sunchoke Salad

1-1/2 lb. sunchokes (Jerusalem artichokes)
Salt

*Dressing:*
Grated peel and juice of 1/2 lemon
1/4 cup olive oil
1 tablespoon fresh thyme leaves
1 tablespoon chopped fresh parsley
Freshly ground pepper

---

**1.** Place sunchokes and salt in a medium saucepan; cover with cold water. Cover pan; bring to a boil. Simmer about 15 minutes or until sunchokes are crisp-tender. Drain; cool. Peel cooled sunchokes.
**2.** To make dressing, in a small bowl, combine lemon peel, lemon juice, olive oil, thyme, parsley, salt and pepper.
**3.** Slice peeled sunchokes; place slices in a serving bowl. Pour dressing over sunchoke slices; stir to coat with dressing. Cover and refrigerate until chilled, or refrigerate up to 24 hours. Makes 4 dinner salads.

# Winter Root Salad

6 tablespoons orange juice
2 tablespoons white-wine vinegar
3 tablespoons vegetable oil
Salt
Freshly ground pepper
1/3 cup raisins
1 small celeriac, peeled
3 carrots, peeled

*Toss celeriac in dressing immediately after cutting to prevent browning.*

1. In a medium bowl, combine orange juice, vinegar and oil. Stir in salt, pepper and raisins.
2. Cut celeriac and carrots into julienne strips; add strips to orange dressing. Stir until coated with dressing.
3. Cover and refrigerate at least 1 hour or up to 24 hours before serving, stirring occasionally. Makes 4 dinner salads.

# Turnip & Watercress Salad

4 to 5 turnips
2 tablespoons lemon juice
Salt
Freshly ground pepper
1 large bunch watercress, coarse stalks removed
1 tablespoon Dijon-style mustard
1/2 cup Mayonnaise, page 112, or prepared mayonnaise

1. Peel turnips; coarsely shred into long thin strips with a shredder. Or, cut into julienne strips with a knife.
2. Place turnip strips in a medium bowl. Add lemon juice, salt and pepper. Toss until blended. Let stand about 30 minutes to soften turnips.
3. Coarsely chop watercress; add to turnips.
4. In a small bowl, blend mustard and mayonnaise. Add to salad; toss to coat turnip strips and watercress with dressing. Serve immediately. Makes 4 dinner salads.

Left to right: Winter Root Salad, Turnip & Watercress Salad,
Winter Leaf Salad, Christmas Coleslaw

# Winter Leaf Salad

1/2 head curly endive
1 large head Belgian endive
1 head radicchio
1 bunch watercress
Leaves from celery heart
1/4 cup Oil & Vinegar Dressing, page 112, or
    prepared dressing

1. Separate curly endive into individual leaves; tear into bite-size pieces. Place endive pieces in a salad bowl.
2. Slice Belgian endive crosswise into thin rings; add to salad bowl.
3. Separate radicchio; tear into bite-size pieces. Add radicchio pieces to salad bowl.
4. Cut off coarse watercress stalks; separate celery leaves. Add watercress and celery leaves to salad. Serve immediately, or cover and refrigerate up to 6 to 8 hours.
5. Immediately before serving, pour dressing over salad; toss until all leaves are coated with dressing. Makes 4 dinner salads.

# Christmas Coleslaw

1/4 head red cabbage
1/4 head white cabbage
2 red-skinned apples
1/2 cup chopped nuts
1/2 cup Mayonnaise, page 112, or prepared mayonnaise
2 tablespoons Oil & Vinegar Dressing, page 112, or
    prepared dressing

*To garnish:*
1 tablespoon chopped fresh parsley

1. Thinly shred both cabbages, discarding cores; place in a large bowl.
2. Cut apples into quarters; remove cores. Cut quarters into very thin slices; add to cabbage.
3. Add chopped nuts.
4. In a small bowl, combine mayonnaise and oil-and-vinegar dressing. Pour over cabbage salad; toss until salad is coated with dressing. Serve immediately, or cover and refrigerate 3 to 4 hours.
5. To serve, place salad in a serving bowl; sprinkle with parsley. Makes 4 to 6 dinner salads.

# Spinach-Noodle Salad

8 oz. spinach noodles
Salt
1/2 cup Oil & Vinegar Dressing, page 112, or
 prepared dressing
4 oz. mushrooms, thinly sliced
1 small garlic clove, if desired, crushed
4 oz. cooked ham, thinly sliced
1/3 cup grated Parmesan cheese (1 oz.)

1. Cook noodles in a large pan of boiling salted water according to package directions until tender. Do not overcook. Drain cooked noodles.
2. In a large bowl, combine dressing, mushrooms and garlic, if desired.
3. Add warm noodles; toss until coated with dressing.
4. Cut ham into strips the same width as noodles; add to salad. Toss to combine. Serve immediately, or cover and refrigerate up to 24 hours. Bring to room temperature before serving.
5. To serve, spoon into a serving bowl; sprinkle with Parmesan cheese. Makes 4 light main-dish servings or 6 to 8 starters.

## Variations
For larger main-dish servings, double the amount of ham. Or, substitute 1/2 cup Yogurt Dressing, page 79, and 2 tablespoons chopped fresh parsley for oil-and-vinegar dressing.

# Crab-&-Apple-Stuffed Avocados

1/4 cup Mayonnaise, page 112, or prepared mayonnaise
2 tablespoons ketchup
2 tablespoons lemon juice
Salt
Freshly ground pepper
1 apple
6 oz. cooked crabmeat, flaked
2 large ripe avocados

*To garnish:*
1 small head lettuce

1. In a medium bowl, combine mayonnaise, ketchup and lemon juice. Season with salt and pepper.
2. Cut apple into quarters; remove cores. Coarsely grate unpeeled apple into mayonnaise mixture. Stir to combine.
3. Stir in crabmeat.
4. Cut avocados in half; remove seeds. Divide filling among avocado halves. Serve immediately.
5. To serve, place lettuce leaves on a serving platter or 4 individual plates; place filled avocado halves on lettuce leaves. Makes 4 main-dish servings.

# Brussels Salad

8 oz. chestnuts
12 oz. Brussels sprouts
1/2 cup Oil & Vinegar Dressing, page 112, or
 prepared dressing

1. Preheat oven to 450F (230C). Slit chestnut shells with a sharp knife; place chestnuts on a baking sheet.
2. Bake on top rack in preheated oven about 15 minutes or until slits have opened.
3. While chestnuts are still warm, remove shells and inner skins. Coarsely chop shelled chestnuts.
4. Trim stalk and outer leaves from Brussels sprouts. Cut trimmed Brussels sprouts in half lengthwise. Place cut-side down on a board; shred very thinly.
5. Place shredded Brussels sprouts in a serving bowl; add chopped chestnuts. Pour dressing over salad; toss to coat with dressing. Serve immediately, or cover and refrigerate 4 to 6 hours. Serve with cold roast turkey or chicken. Makes 4 dinner salads.

Top to bottom: Spinach-Noodle Salad, Crab-&-Apple-Stuffed Avocados

# Tangerine-Flower Salad

4 large tangerines
1/2 cup chopped nuts
8 oz. cottage cheese (1 cup)
1/3 cup golden raisins
Salt
Freshly ground pepper

*To serve:*
1 small head lettuce

1. With a sharp pointed knife, cutting only through peel, make 4 shallow cuts beginning at blossom end of each tangerine. Cut almost to stem end. Pull back skin in 4 sections, leaving fruit intact. Peel skin back to make a case resembling petals of a flower, keeping skin joined at stem end; see illustration below.
2. Remove fruit; separate fruit into sections, removing white pith. Chop sections into small pieces; place in a medium bowl.
3. Stir in nuts, cottage cheese, raisins, salt and pepper.
4. Spoon filling into tangerine shells. Arrange lettuce leaves on 4 individual plates. Place filled tangerine shells on lettuce leaves. Serve immediately. Makes 4 dinner salads.

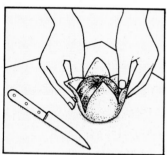

1/Pull back skin, along cuts, to make 4 sections.

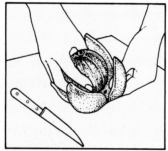

2/Remove fruit.

# Waldorf Salad

3 to 4 red-skinned apples
1 tablespoon lemon juice
4 celery stalks, thinly sliced crosswise
1/2 cup coarsely chopped walnuts
1/2 cup chopped dates, if desired
1/2 cup Mayonnaise, page 112, prepared mayonnaise, or Yogurt Dressing, page 113
Salt
Freshly ground pepper

*To garnish:*
Celery leaves
Apple slices, if desired, tossed in 1 tablespoon lemon juice

1. Quarter apples; remove cores. Chop apple quarters; place in a medium bowl. Add lemon juice; toss to prevent apples from browning.
2. Stir in celery, walnuts and dates, if desired.
3. Stir in mayonnaise or Yogurt Dressing. Season with salt and pepper.
4. Place salad in a serving dish. Garnish with celery leaves and apple slices, if desired. This salad is good with cold meats. Makes 4 dinner salads.

## Variation
For a main dish, serve salad with 4 cold roast-pork slices. Or, cube about 8 ounces cold roast pork; stir pork cubes into salad, adding additional dressing, if necessary.

# Pineapple & Cheese Boats

1 medium pineapple, about 2 lb.
8 oz. Cheddar cheese, cubed
1/2 cucumber, cut into cubes
1/2 cup sliced Brazil nuts
1/4 cup Oil & Vinegar Dressing, page 112, or prepared dressing
1 small head lettuce, shredded

*To garnish:*
1/3 cup shredded coconut, lightly toasted

1. Cut pineapple lengthwise into quarters, keeping top attached to each quarter. Cut pineapple away from peel; cut pineapple into cubes. Reserve shells.
2. In a large bowl, combine pineapple cubes, cheese, cucumber and nuts. Pour dressing over salad; toss until coated with dressing.
3. Arrange pineapple shells on a platter or individual plates. Place some lettuce on top of each pineapple shell; pile pineapple salad on lettuce.
4. Sprinkle with toasted coconut. Makes 4 light main-dish servings.

# Cauliflower Polonaise Salad

1 medium cauliflower
Salt
6 tablespoons Oil & Vinegar Dressing, page 112, or
   prepared dressing
2 hard-cooked eggs, finely chopped
2 tablespoons chopped fresh parsley
Freshly ground pepper

*Topping:*
1/4 cup butter or margarine
1 cup fresh bread crumbs
1 small garlic clove, if desired, crushed

1. Pour water 2 inches deep in a medium saucepan; bring to a boil. Divide cauliflower into flowerets; add cauliflowerets and salt to boiling water. Boil 2 minutes. Drain; let cool to room temperature.
2. Pour dressing into a medium bowl. Stir in hard-cooked eggs, parsley, salt and pepper. Add cooked cauliflowerets; toss until coated with dressing.
3. To make topping, melt butter or margarine in a large skillet; add bread crumbs and garlic, if desired. Sauté until golden brown, stirring frequently.
4. Cauliflower salad and topping can be prepared several hours ahead; refrigerate until served. To serve, place cauliflower salad in a shallow serving dish; sprinkle with topping. Makes 4 to 6 dinner salads.

Clockwise from top left: Cauliflower Polonaise Salad, Waldorf Salad, Pineapple & Cheese Boats, Tangerine-Flower Salad

# Pilaf & Curried-Chicken Salad

1 tablespoon vegetable oil
1 medium onion, chopped
1-1/4 cups uncooked long-grain white rice
2-1/2 cups water or chicken stock
1/3 cup raisins
1/3 cup chopped dried apricots
1/2 cup chopped walnuts
1 (3-inch) cinnamon stick or pinch of ground cinnamon
1 bay leaf
Salt
Freshly ground pepper
1/2 cup Oil & Vinegar Dressing, page 112, or
    prepared dressing
1-1/2 cups chopped cooked chicken
1/2 cup Curry Dressing, page 113

*To garnish:*
**Paprika**

---

**1.** To make pilaf, heat oil in a large saucepan. Add onion; sauté 5 minutes.
**2.** Add rice; cook 1 minute, stirring. Pour in water or stock; stir in raisins, apricots, walnuts, cinnamon, bay leaf, salt and pepper. Bring to a boil. Cover and simmer about 20 minutes or until rice is cooked and all water has been absorbed. Remove cinnamon stick and bay leaf.
**3.** Stir in dressing; while pilaf mixture is still hot, press into a 1-quart ring mold. Refrigerate until chilled or up to 24 hours.
**4.** In a medium bowl, combine chicken and Curry Dressing. Cover and refrigerate until chilled or up to 24 hours.
**5.** To serve, turn pilaf ring out on a large serving plate; remove mold. Fill center of ring with curried chicken. Sprinkle with paprika. Makes 4 main-dish servings.

Pilaf & Curried-Chicken Salad

# Gado Gado

1/4 head cabbage, shredded
1 cup cut fresh green beans
2 carrots, sliced
1/2 cauliflower, divided into flowerets
Salt
4 oz. bean sprouts (1 cup)

*Peanut Sauce:*
1/4 cup crunchy peanut butter
Juice of 1 lemon
1/4 cup water
Few drops of hot-pepper sauce
Freshly ground pepper

*To garnish:*
1/2 cup salted peanuts

---

*This is an Indonesian salad. It is normally served alone as a cold dish, but it can be served with a spicy chicken or fish curry. The peanut sauce should be thick and crunchy.*

**1.** Cook cabbage, beans, carrots and cauliflower separately in boiling salted water a few minutes or until crisp-tender. Rinse with cold water to cool quickly. Do not cook bean sprouts.
**2.** To make sauce, place peanut butter in a medium bowl. Gradually blend in lemon juice and water. Stir in hot-pepper sauce to taste; season with salt and pepper.
**3.** In a medium bowl, combine cooked vegetables and bean sprouts; arrange in a shallow serving dish. Vegetables can be prepared 2 to 3 hours ahead; cover and refrigerate. Sauce can be prepared 24 hours ahead; cover and refrigerate. Bring to room temperature before serving.
**4.** Pour peanut sauce over center of salad. Garnish with peanuts. Makes 4 to 6 dinner salads.

## Variation
For an authentic Indonesian flavor, substitute coconut milk for water in sauce. To make coconut milk, pour 1 cup boiling water over 1 cup shredded coconut in a medium bowl. Let stand 20 minutes. Pour through a sieve, pressing on coconut to extract all liquid. Extra coconut milk can be frozen in ice-cube trays for another use.

# Mussel Salad

4 to 5 dozen fresh mussels
2 tablespoons vegetable oil
2 shallots or 1 small onion, thinly sliced or chopped
1/2 cup dry white wine
Salt
Freshly ground pepper

*To serve:*
1 head lettuce, shredded
2 tablespoons olive oil
1 tablespoon lemon juice
2 tablespoons chopped fresh parsley

---

**1.** Discard any mussels that have broken shells or that do not close when tapped. Wash remaining mussels under cold running water.
**2.** Scrub each mussel; pull away beard and scrape off any barnacles with a sharp knife. Continue washing in running water until all mussels are thoroughly cleaned and water runs clear. Drain.
**3.** Heat oil in a large saucepan. Add shallots or onion; sauté 5 minutes or until lightly browned.
**4.** Pour in wine; add salt, pepper and mussels. Cover pan; bring to a boil. Cook 5 minutes, shaking pan occasionally, or until mussels open. Discard any that do not open.
**5.** Remove mussels, reserving liquid. Remove cooked mussels from shells. Boil cooking liquid until reduced to 1/4 cup; cool liquid.
**6.** Arrange shredded lettuce in a serving dish or individual dishes. Arrange cooled mussels on lettuce.
**7.** Stir olive oil, lemon juice and parsley into cooled cooking liquid; pour over mussels. Serve immediately. Makes 4 main-dish servings or 6 starters.

## Variation
If fresh mussels are not available, substitute 2 (8-3/4-ounce) jar mussels, drained, for fresh mussels. In a medium bowl, toss with 1/2 cup Oil & Vinegar Dressing with lemon peel, page 78, or prepared dressing; sprinkle with chopped parsley.

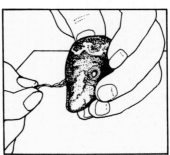

1/Pull away beards.

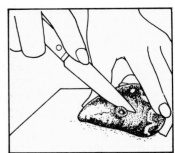

2/Scrape off any barnacles with a sharp knife.

# Guacamole Salad

4 tomatoes, peeled
2 tablespoons lemon juice
1 tablespoon grated onion
1 teaspoon chopped fresh coriander or 1/2 teaspoon ground coriander
1/4 teaspoon hot-pepper sauce
2 ripe avocados

*To garnish:*
1 small head lettuce
Cilantro sprigs
Corn chips

1. Dice tomatoes; place in a medium bowl.
2. Stir in lemon juice, onion, coriander and hot-pepper sauce.
3. Cut avocados in half; pit and peel avocados. Dice peeled avocados. Add to tomato mixture. Beat with a wooden spoon until partially blended but pieces of avocado and tomato still remain.
4. Arrange lettuce leaves on 4 individual plates. Spoon guacamole salad on lettuce; garnish with coriander sprigs. Serve immediately with corn chips. Makes 4 starters.

Clockwise from top left: Guacamole Salad, Gado Gado, Mussel Salad

# Vitello Tonnato

1 (2-lb.) boneless veal shoulder roast
1 onion, sliced
1 carrot, sliced
1 celery stalk, sliced
1 bay leaf
1 parsley sprig
Salt
Freshly ground pepper
2 tablespoons dry white wine or sherry

*Tuna Mayonnaise:*
2/3 cup Mayonnaise, page 112, or prepared mayonnaise
1/2 (6-1/2-oz.) can tuna, oil pack, undrained
1 tablespoon anchovy paste
1 teaspoon tomato paste
1 teaspoon lemon juice
Salt
Freshly ground pepper

*To garnish:*
1 (2-oz.) can anchovy fillets, drained
1 tablespoon capers
3 lemon slices, cut in half
Parsley sprigs

*This is a popular Italian dish.*

**1.** Place veal in a large saucepan. Add onion, carrot, celery, bay leaf, parsley, salt and pepper. Add enough cold water to almost cover veal; add wine or sherry.
**2.** Cover pan; bring to a boil. Reduce heat; simmer about 1-1/2 to 2 hours or until tender. Let cool in cooking liquid.
**3.** To make Tuna Mayonnaise, combine all ingredients in a blender or food processor fitted with a steel blade. Process until smooth. If mayonnaise is too thick, add some of cooled cooking liquid.
**4.** Thinly slice cooled veal. Spread each slice with 1 teaspoon of Tuna Mayonnaise; arrange slices, overlapping, on a serving platter. Cover with remaining mayonnaise.
**5.** Refrigerate several hours or overnight to firm mayonnaise.
**6.** To serve, garnish with anchovies, capers, lemon slices and parsley sprigs, as shown. This salad is ideal for a buffet lunch or dinner. Makes 4 to 6 main-dish servings.

# Turkey & Cranberry Salad

1 lb. cooked turkey, cut into 1/2-inch cubes
4 large celery stalks, thinly sliced crosswise
1 green bell pepper, diced
1/2 cup chopped walnuts
2/3 cup dairy sour cream
1/4 cup whole-berry cranberry sauce
1 tablespoon red-wine vinegar
Salt
Freshly ground black pepper

*To garnish:*
1 bunch watercress
8 to 10 walnut halves

**1.** Place turkey cubes in a medium bowl.
**2.** Stir in celery, bell pepper and walnuts.
**3.** In a small bowl, combine sour cream, cranberry sauce, vinegar, salt and pepper.
**4.** Pour cranberry mixture over turkey salad; toss until combined.
**5.** Spoon into a serving dish; garnish with watercress and walnut halves. Makes 4 main-dish servings.

# Ham & Pineapple Cornets

8 oz. cottage cheese (1 cup)
1 (8-oz.) can pineapple chunks, juice pack
1 small red bell pepper, finely chopped
1 celery stalk, chopped
Salt
Freshly ground black pepper
4 large or 8 small cooked-ham slices
Romaine lettuce leaves

**1.** To make filling, place cottage cheese in a medium bowl.
**2.** Drain pineapple; add to cottage cheese. Stir in bell pepper and celery. Season with salt and black pepper.
**3.** Divide filling among ham slices. Roll each slice into a cone shape; place each cone on a lettuce leaf, seam-side down. Arrange on a serving plate. Makes 4 light main-dish servings.

Top to bottom: Vitello Tonnato, Ham & Pineapple Cornets

# Salad Dressings

## Thousand Island Dressing

2/3 cup Mayonnaise, opposite, prepared
   mayonnaise, or dairy sour cream
2 tablespoons milk
1 tablespoon tomato paste
1 tablespoon finely chopped red bell pepper
1 tablespoon finely chopped green bell pepper
1 tablespoon finely chopped sweet pickle
1 hard-cooked egg, if desired, finely chopped

1. Spoon mayonnaise or sour cream into a small bowl.
Slowly beat in milk.
2. Stir in tomato paste until blended; stir in remaining
ingredients. Cover and refrigerate until served. Serve with
fish or vegetable salads. Makes about 1 cup.

## Oil & Vinegar Dressing

2 tablespoons wine vinegar or lemon juice
6 tablespoons oil (olive, soybean, walnut or peanut)
Pinch of dry mustard, if desired
Pinch of salt
Freshly ground black pepper

*A mixture of oils may be used, such as soybean oil blended
with a more exotic one, such as walnut oil. This recipe
makes enough dressing for 2 large salads.*

1. Combine all ingredients in a screw top jar; shake vigorously until blended. Shake again before using. Or, combine
ingredients in a small bowl; beat with a whisk until
blended.
2. Store in refrigerator up to 1 week. Makes about 2/3 cup.

### Variation
Add 1 or more of the following: 1 to 2 tablespoons
chopped fresh herbs; grated peel of 1/2 lemon or orange; 1
small peeled garlic clove, whole for a subtle flavor or
crushed for a stronger flavor; 1/4 to 1/2 teaspoon prepared
brown mustard.

## Mayonnaise

1 whole egg or 2 egg yolks
1/4 teaspoon dry mustard
1/4 teaspoon salt
1 tablespoon wine vinegar or lemon juice
1-1/4 cups olive oil, other vegetable oil,
   or a combination
1 tablespoon hot water

*Mayonnaise will keep, covered, in the refrigerator 2 days.*

**Using a blender:**
1. In a blender, combine egg or egg yolks, mustard, salt and
vinegar or lemon juice. Process at lowest speed until
blended.
2. With blender running at lowest speed, very slowly pour
in about 1/2 of oil. Mixture will begin to thicken. Add remaining oil in a slow steady stream.
3. With blender running, add water. Taste mayonnaise;
add a little more vinegar or lemon juice, if necessary.
Makes about 2 cups.

**By hand:**
1. Place a medium bowl on a folded damp cloth to keep it
steady while beating.
2. In bowl, combine egg or egg yolks, mustard, salt and 2
teaspoons vinegar or lemon juice. Using a wooden spoon,
small whisk or hand-held electric mixer, beat well.
3. Continue beating; beat in oil 1 drop at a time until 1/2 of
oil has been added. Mixture will begin to thicken.
4. Add remaining vinegar. Beating or whisking constantly,
add remaining oil in a thin, steady stream until mayonnaise is very thick. Add water; beat until blended. If
mayonnaise becomes too thick to add all of oil, whisk in
additional hot water; then whisk in remaining oil. Makes
about 2 cups.

### Variations
**Green Mayonnaise:** In a blender, combine 1-3/4 to 2 cups
mayonnaise and about 1 cup chopped, packed watercress,
sorrel or spinach, coarse stalks removed. Blend until
smooth.
**Anchovy Mayonnaise:** In a blender, combine 1-3/4 to 2
cups mayonnaise, 1 (2-ounce) can anchovy fillets with oil
and 1 tablespoon tomato paste. Blend until smooth.
**Garlic Mayonnaise:** In a blender, combine 1-3/4 to 2 cups
mayonnaise and 1 or 2 crushed garlic cloves. Blend until
smooth.

# Curry Dressing

1 tablespoon vegetable oil
1 small onion, chopped
1 tablespoon curry powder
2/3 cup chicken stock
1 tablespoon apricot jam
1 teaspoon lemon juice
2/3 cup Mayonnaise, opposite, or prepared mayonnaise
2/3 cup plain yogurt or dairy sour cream
Salt
Freshly ground pepper

1. Heat oil in a medium saucepan. Add onion; sauté over low heat 5 minutes or until softened. Do not brown.
2. Stir in curry powder; cook 2 minutes, stirring constantly.
3. Gradually stir in stock; bring to a boil. Stir in jam and lemon juice; bring to a simmer. Stirring constantly, simmer 5 minutes; set aside to cool.
4. Stir mayonnaise and yogurt or sour cream into cooled curry sauce. Season with salt and pepper. Serve with root vegetables or cold chicken salad. Makes about 2 cups.

# Yogurt Dressing

2/3 cup plain yogurt or dairy sour cream
1 tablespoon white-wine vinegar or lemon juice
Salt
Freshly ground pepper

1. In a small bowl, stir yogurt or sour cream until smooth.
2. Stir in vinegar or lemon juice. Season with salt and pepper; stir until blended.
3. Or, combine all ingredients in a blender or food processor fitted with a steel blade. Process until blended. Use immediately, or cover and refrigerate up to 1 week. Makes about 2/3 cup.

### Variations
**Herb-Yogurt Dressing:** Stir in 2 tablespoons chopped fresh watercress, parsley, chives, thyme, basil or tarragon.
**Yogurt & Blue-Cheese Dressing:** Stir in 2 tablespoons crumbled blue cheese.
**Cucumber & Mint Dressing:** Coarsely grate a 1-1/2-inch piece of unpeeled cucumber. Stir grated cucumber and 1/2 teaspoon dried mint or 1 teaspoon chopped fresh mint into dressing.

Top to bottom: Mayonnaise, Oil & Vinegar Dressing, Thousand Island Dressing, Curry Dressing, Yogurt Dressing

# Main Dishes

A main dish is the center of any meal, but is even more important to a special-occasion meal. A good example is stuffed turkey at Thanksgiving or glazed ham at Easter. When a host or hostess starts to plan a meal, the main dish is generally considered first. Then side dishes are selected that will complement and highlight the main dish without overshadowing it. Remember to contrast shapes, colors, textures and temperatures in a meal for added interest. Main dishes that combine several ingredients may only need a crisp, green salad and a loaf of crunchy bread to make a complete meal.

Recipes in this chapter have been selected to fit various categories. Some are quick and easy, requiring only minutes to prepare and cook. Others simmer slowly for hours to blend flavors and tenderize meat. Economy is also considered. Several recipes use chicken and less-tender cuts of meat. Many recipes are both elegant and economical. Some recipes are included for more expensive meats for those extra-special meals. Many recipes include suggestions for accompaniments and garnishes.

Most recipes serve four, however many can be doubled for additional servings or to make an extra dish for freezing. Adjust cooking times, as needed, if recipes are doubled.

## ADVANCE PREPARATION & FREEZING

Many main dishes freeze successfully, particularly stews and casseroles. Avoid freezing those with cream, egg yolks, hard-cooked eggs or potatoes. These ingredients don't freeze well. Most main dishes freeze well up to 2 to 3 months. If a dish is highly spiced, 2 to 3 weeks is long enough in the freezer. Frozen dishes can be reheated while still frozen, or first thawed in the refrigerator or microwave oven. Reheating must be done thoroughly; once the dish starts to bubble, bake 15 to 20 minutes. Food can be frozen in a foil-lined casserole. Remove food and foil once contents are frozen; wrap tightly. Meanwhile, the casserole dish can be used for other purposes. To reheat, place frozen food in original casserole dish. Other suitable freezer containers include plastic freezer containers, plastic freezer bags, freezer paper and heavy-duty foil. Remember to leave a 1-inch headspace in freezer containers to allow for food expansion.

Casseroles and stews are often more flavorful if made the day before serving. If a dish is prepared in advance, cook dish for all but the last 20 minutes. Refrigerate until needed. Before serving, bake at 325F (165C) or simmer on low heat 45 minutes to 1 hour.

## SLOW COOKERS & PRESSURE COOKERS

Slow cookers and pressure cookers can be convenient and economical. The slow cooker, after preliminary preparation, cooks food on low heat, usually taking 6 to 8 hours or longer. The advantages are that once under way, it needs no attention, and the amount of electricity used is minimal. It is ideal for the busy housewife or business woman who likes to come home to a hot evening meal. Small-size slow cookers are great for one or two persons.

A pressure cooker reduces cooking time because the increased pressure lets food cook at higher than usual temperatures. Using a pressure cooker is an efficient way to quickly cook less-tender meat cuts. It can be a wonderful time-saver for the creative but busy cook.

With both slow cookers and pressure cookers, it is essential to read the manufacturers' instructions carefully before using. Always follow them while cooking. With minor adjustments, made according to the manufacturers' directions, many recipes can be adapted for use with either a slow cooker or pressure cooker.

## MEAT

All types of meat are included—beef, lamb, pork, veal, ham and even oxtail. All can be turned into something special. Wines, sherry, Madeira, brandy and other types of alcohol are added to a number of recipes to enhance flavors and help tenderize meat. Many old favorites appear along with plenty of new ideas.

## POULTRY & GAME

This section presents a selection of exciting recipes suitable for family and friends. There is a wide variety of recipes using chicken, turkey, duck and Cornish hens. Many are fast and easy to prepare. Poultry is an ideal choice for an affordable and delicious main dish.

## FISH

Fish and shellfish are becoming more widely available throughout the country. Rapid transportation and a wide selection of frozen products mean that you no longer have to live by a seacoast to enjoy good seafood. Fish and shellfish are excellent choices for festive occasions because they can be prepared quickly. A good rule to follow is to cook fish 10 minutes per inch of thickness. Do not overcook fish or it may become dry and tasteless.

## FAVORITES FROM HOME & ABROAD

As an interesting contrast to the other sections, recipes included here are a mixture of special ideas. Here the French classics appear alongside dishes from Poland, Australia, New Zealand, Switzerland and the United States. Ingredients are often well-known, but used in surprising combinations.

## COOKING TERMS

**Beurre manié:** Paste made by blending flour and room-temperature butter. Small amounts of beurre manié can be beaten into hot liquids until desired thickness is obtained. The usual combination is 2 parts butter to 3 parts flour; exact proportions will vary.

**Bouquet garni:** Term used for an herb package containing 1 bay leaf, 2 parsley sprigs and thyme. If the herbs are fresh, they can serve as their own package. If dried herbs are used, they are usually wrapped in cheesecloth to make removal easy after the dish is cooked. Other ingredients, such as peppercorns or celery leaves, can be added, if desired.

**Deglazing:** Technique in which browned pan drippings are loosened and incorporated into sauce by heating the roasting pan, then stirring in wine, stock or other liquid. This adds a rich flavor and color to sauce.

**Degrease:** A method of removing fat from the surface of casseroles, pan drippings, stocks and stews by skimming the surface with a spoon or bulb baster or by chilling until fat hardens on the surface and can be lifted off. More complete removal of fat results from the chilling method. This method is particularly good for stews, soups and casseroles that improve in flavor when made in advance.

**Stock:** Stock is made by simmering meat, chicken or fish bones and trimmings with vegetables, herbs and water. Stock must be strained and degreased before using. Homemade stock can be frozen. If homemade stock is not available, use canned bouillon or broth. Bouillon cubes or granules are also available. Remember that prepared products may be higher in salt; adjust seasoning accordingly to avoid too salty a flavor.

# Beef Burgundy

2 tablespoons vegetable oil
1-1/2 lbs. beef-round steak, cut into 2" x 1" strips
2 onions, sliced
1 garlic clove, crushed
1-1/2 cups red wine
1 tablespoon tomato paste
1 bay leaf
2 teaspoons Worcestershire sauce
2/3 cup pitted prunes
Salt
Freshly ground pepper
1 tablespoon cornstarch
Water
4 oz. button mushrooms, halved

*To garnish:*
Grilled bacon rolls, see below
Parsley sprigs, if desired

1. Preheat oven to 325F (165C).
2. Heat oil in a large skillet over medium heat. Add beef strips; sauté until browned. Add onions and garlic; continue cooking a few minutes, stirring frequently. Transfer to a 3-quart casserole; set aside.
3. Add wine to skillet; bring to a boil. Stir in tomato paste, bay leaf, Worcestershire sauce and prunes. Season with salt and pepper. Pour wine mixture over browned beef strips. Cover casserole with foil or lid.
4. Bake in preheated oven 2 hours.
5. In a small bowl, blend cornstarch with a little cold water. Stir cornstarch mixture into hot casserole along with mushrooms and some water, if necessary. Discard bay leaf. Bake 15 minutes longer or until mushrooms are cooked. Serve hot, garnished with bacon rolls and parsley, if desired. Makes 4 servings.

---

To make *Bacon Rolls*, stretch bacon slices evenly on a board using the back of a knife. This will make bacon more even and easier to roll up. If you are worried about rolls unwinding during cooking, thread several on a metal skewer or push a wooden pick into each roll. Broil until crispy.

---

# Beef Carbonnade

3 tablespoons all-purpose flour
Salt
Freshly ground pepper
1-1/2 lbs. beef stew cubes
1/4 cup vegetable oil
2 large onions, thinly sliced
1 to 2 garlic cloves, crushed
1 cup dark beer or ale
1 cup beef stock
2 tablespoons ketchup or 1 tablespoon tomato paste
Pinch of ground mace or nutmeg
1 bay leaf
2 teaspoons brown sugar
2 teaspoons vinegar
1-1/2 teaspoons prepared brown mustard
3 to 4 carrots, cut into 3- to 4-inch sticks
4 oz. button mushrooms

*To garnish:*
Chopped fresh parsley, if desired

1. Preheat oven to 325F (165C).
2. In a plastic bag, combine flour, salt and pepper. Add beef cubes; shake to coat. Heat 3 tablespoons oil in a large skillet over medium heat. Add seasoned beef cubes; sauté until browned. With a slotted spoon, transfer to a 3-quart casserole.
3. In same skillet, heat remaining oil. Add onions and garlic; sauté until lightly colored. Stir in remaining seasoned flour; cook 1 minute, stirring constantly.
4. Gradually stir in beer or ale and stock; bring to a boil, stirring frequently. Stir in ketchup or tomato paste, mace or nutmeg, bay leaf, sugar, vinegar and mustard. Season to taste with salt and pepper. Pour beer mixture over browned beef cubes.
5. Add carrot sticks to casserole; stir well. Cover tightly with foil or lid; bake in preheated oven 1-1/4 hours.
6. Add mushrooms to hot casserole. Bake 25 to 30 minutes longer or until beef is tender. Discard bay leaf. Serve sprinkled with chopped parsley, if desired. Makes 4 servings.

Top to bottom: Beef Burgundy, Beef Carbonnade

# Boeuf à l'Orange

2 oranges
3 tablespoons vegetable oil
1-1/2 lbs. beef stew cubes
8 oz. small white onions
1 garlic clove, crushed
2 tablespoons all-purpose flour
1 cup beef stock
1 tablespoon tomato paste
3 tablespoons brandy
1 tablespoon molasses
Salt
Freshly ground pepper
4 oz. mushrooms, thickly sliced

*To garnish:*
Parsley sprigs
Orange wedges or slices

**1.** Preheat oven to 325F (165C).
**2.** With a vegetable peeler, remove peel from oranges; cut peel into julienne strips. Juice both oranges. Set julienned peel and juice aside.
**3.** Heat oil in a large skillet over medium heat. Add beef cubes; sauté until browned. With a slotted spoon, transfer to a 3-quart casserole.
**4.** Sauté onions and garlic in same fat until golden brown. With a slotted spoon, transfer to casserole.
**5.** Stir flour into fat in skillet; cook 1 minute, stirring constantly. Gradually stir in stock; bring to a boil. Add orange juice and strips of peel.
**6.** Stir tomato paste, brandy and molasses into sauce. Season with salt and pepper. Pour sauce over browned beef cubes. Cover casserole tightly with foil or lid.
**7.** Bake in preheated oven 2 hours.
**8.** Add mushrooms to hot casserole. Add extra stock, if necessary. Bake 30 minutes longer or until beef is tender.
**9.** To serve, garnish with parsley sprigs and orange wedges or slices. Makes 4 servings.

Clockwise from bottom: Fillet of Beef Dijon, Boeuf à l'Orange, Swiss Steak

# Swiss Steak

2 lbs. beef-round steak, cut into 8 serving pieces
Salt
Freshly ground pepper
2 tablespoons vegetable oil
1 (16-oz.) can tomatoes
2 onions, sliced
1 garlic clove, crushed
2 tablespoons all-purpose flour
1/2 cup red wine
1/2 cup beef stock
1 tablespoon tomato paste
2 tablespoons capers
1 tablespoon wine vinegar

*To garnish:*
Parsley sprigs, if desired

---

1. Preheat oven to 350F (175C).
2. Sprinkle beef with salt and pepper. Heat 1 tablespoon oil in a large skillet over medium heat. Add beef; sauté until browned. Transfer to a 3-quart casserole.
3. Drain tomatoes, reserving juice. Add drained tomatoes to casserole with beef. Add remaining oil to skillet. Add onions and garlic; sauté until lightly browned.
4. Stir in flour; cook 1 minute, stirring constantly. Stir in wine, stock and reserved tomato juice. Boil mixture 2 minutes, stirring frequently; add tomato paste, capers and vinegar. Season mixture with salt and pepper; pour over browned beef.
5. Cover casserole with foil or lid; bake in preheated oven 2 to 2-1/2 hours or until beef is tender.
6. Serve garnished with parsley, if desired. Makes 4 to 6 servings.

## Variation

Veal stew cubes make a good alternative to beef in this recipe. To change the flavor of this casserole, omit capers and add 4 ounces dried apricots. Alternatively, put pre-pared ingredients into a shallow casserole; cover with a layer of thinly sliced potatoes—about 1-1/2 pounds. Brush potatoes with melted butter; bake uncovered about 2 hours or until meat is tender, and potatoes are browned and crispy.

# Fillet of Beef Dijon

1 (1-1/2 to 1-3/4 lb.) beef-loin tenderloin roast
Salt
Freshly ground pepper
2 tablespoons butter or margarine
Juice of 1 orange
Juice of 1 lemon
1/4 cup beef stock
1 to 2 tablespoons wine vinegar
1 tablespoon Dijon-style mustard
2 tablespoons brandy
6 tablespoons half and half
2 teaspoons cornstarch
1 tablespoon finely chopped small sweet pickles, if desired

*To garnish:*
Sautéed button mushrooms
Sautéed bread crescents
Parsley sprigs

---

*Ask butcher for thick end of beef-loin tenderloin (rump end) and a thin piece of fat same size as roast to keep it moist during cooking. If you do not have the fat, rub roast with butter or margarine before roasting.*

1. Preheat oven to 400F (205C).
2. Trim roast; season with salt and pepper. If using fat as suggested, tie it evenly around roast with string. Place roast in a shallow roasting pan just large enough to hold it.
3. Roast in preheated oven about 35 minutes or to desired doneness, basting once with pan drippings. For well-cooked beef, increase cooking time by 10 to 15 minutes.
4. Transfer roast to a serving plate; remove string and fat. Cover roast with foil to keep warm.
5. Remove excess fat from pan drippings. In a small bowl, combine fruit juices, stock and vinegar, according to taste; use to deglaze roasting pan.
6. Bring deglazing mixture to a boil. Stir in mustard and brandy. In a small bowl, combine half and half and cornstarch; stir into hot mixture. Bring mixture to a simmer; cook until thickened, stirring frequently. Season with salt and pepper; add pickles, if desired. Pour sauce into a gravy boat or small pitcher.
7. Garnish roast with mushrooms, bread crescents and parsley; accompany with sauce. Makes 4 servings.

# Roast Beef with Ale

1 (3-lb.) beef-round rump roast
1-1/2 cups pale ale or beer
1 tablespoon vegetable oil
2 onions, sliced
1 garlic clove, crushed
Salt
Freshly ground pepper
2 bay leaves
1 tablespoon brown sugar
6 whole cloves
4 carrots, quartered
2 turnips, thickly sliced
1 tablespoon cornstarch
Water

*To garnish:*
Chopped fresh parsley

**1.** Preheat oven to 350F (175C).
**2.** Place roast in a glass dish just large enough to hold it; add ale or beer. Cover and refrigerate at least 24 hours (up to 48 hours); turn roast several times.
**3.** Drain roast, reserving marinade; pat dry with paper towels. Heat oil in a large skillet over medium heat. Add roast; sauté until well browned. Transfer to a large baking pan.
**4.** To fat remaining in skillet, add onions and garlic; sauté until lightly browned. Drain excess fat from skillet. Add reserved marinade; bring to a boil.
**5.** Add salt, pepper, bay leaves, sugar and cloves to hot marinade. Pour over roast. Cover pan tightly with foil or lid; bake in preheated oven 1-1/2 hours.
**6.** Add carrots and turnips to baking pan. Baste roast; replace cover. Bake about 1 hour longer or until beef is tender. Discard bay leaves.
**7.** Drain juices into a medium saucepan; skim off fat. In a small bowl, combine cornstarch with a little cold water. Stir cornstarch mixture into pan juices. Boil 1 minute or until thickened, stirring frequently. Season with salt and pepper. Pour sauce into a gravy boat or small pitcher.
**8.** Put beef on a warmed plate; surround by vegetables. Sprinkle with parsley. Serve sauce separately. Any leftovers are excellent served cold with salads. Makes 4 to 6 servings.

### Variation
Two pounds of beef stew cubes can be used for this dish. Marinate beef cubes in ale as for the roast; follow above directions but bake 1-1/2 to 2 hours. After juices have been thickened, pour them back over beef and vegetables before serving. All dishes made with beer are even better if made the day before serving. Before serving, reheat about 1 hour.

# Beef Rolls with Pecans

4 thin slices of beef-round steak, about 8" x 4"
*Stuffing:*
1/2 cup uncooked long-grain white rice
Salt
1-1/4 cups water
2 tablespoons vegetable oil
1 onion, chopped
1/2 teaspoon dried leaf thyme
1 tablespoon chopped fresh parsley or 1/2 teaspoon
    dried leaf parsley
1/3 cup chopped pecans
Freshly ground pepper
A little ground coriander
1 egg, lightly beaten

*Sauce:*
2 tablespoons vegetable oil
2 tablespoons all-purpose flour
1 cup beef stock
1/4 cup medium-dry sherry

*To garnish:*
1/4 cup dairy sour cream
A few pecan halves
Chopped fresh parsley

**1.** Preheat oven to 350F (175C). Pound steak slices between 2 sheets of plastic wrap or waxed paper until 1/4 inch thick.
**2.** For stuffing, in a medium saucepan over low heat, cook rice in 1-1/4 cups boiling salted water 12 to 14 minutes or until tender and water is absorbed.
**3.** Heat oil in a medium skillet over medium heat. Add onion; sauté until soft. Remove skillet from heat. Add thyme, parsley, pecans, salt, pepper, coriander and cooked rice. Cool rice mixture slightly; stir in beaten egg. Stuffing mixture should be fairly loose.
**4.** Divide stuffing among beaten beef slices. Roll each slice carefully to enclose stuffing. Secure each roll with wooden picks.
**5.** Heat oil in a large skillet over medium heat. Add beef rolls; sauté until browned. With tongs, transfer browned rolls to a shallow casserole or baking pan large enough to hold them in one layer.
**6.** Stir flour into juices left in skillet; cook 1 minute, stirring constantly. Gradually stir in stock and sherry. Bring sauce to a boil.
**7.** Season sauce with salt and pepper; pour over beef rolls. Cover pan with foil or lid. Bake in preheated oven about 1-1/4 hours or until beef is tender.
**8.** To serve, remove wooden picks from rolls; top each roll with a spoonful of sour cream, a few pecan halves and chopped parsley. Makes 4 servings.

Left to right: Beef Rolls with Pecans, Steak & Potato Dinner

## Steak & Potato Dinner

2 tablespoons vegetable oil
1-1/2 lbs. beef-round steak, cut into 1-1/2" x 1" strips
2 large onions, sliced
1 (16-oz.) can tomatoes
8 oz. carrots, sliced
1 green pepper, sliced
2 tablespoons all-purpose flour
1 cup beef stock
1 tablespoon prepared brown mustard
1 tablespoon Worcestershire sauce
1 tablespoon soy sauce
Salt
Freshly ground black pepper
1-1/2 lbs. potatoes, peeled, sliced (about 4-1/2 cups)

**1.** Preheat oven to 350F (175C).
**2.** Heat oil in a large skillet over medium heat. Add beef strips; sauté until well browned. With a slotted spoon, remove beef strips from skillet; set aside.
**3.** Add onions to fat remaining in skillet; sauté until golden brown. Drain tomatoes, reserving juice.
**4.** In a 3-quart casserole, layer browned beef strips, sautéed onions, carrots, green-pepper slices and drained tomatoes.
**5.** Stir flour into fat in skillet; cook 1 minute, stirring constantly. Gradually stir in stock and reserved tomato juice. Bring mixture to a boil; stir in mustard, Worcestershire sauce and soy sauce. Season mixture with salt and pepper.
**6.** Pour hot mixture over contents of casserole. Top with sliced potatoes.
**7.** Cover casserole with foil or lid. Bake in preheated oven 1-1/2 hours.
**8.** Remove cover from casserole. Increase oven heat to 400F (205C). Bake 45 minutes longer or until potatoes are tender and golden brown. Makes 4 servings.

# Deviled Meatballs

**Meatballs:**
1-1/4 lbs. lean ground beef
3/4 cup fresh breadcrumbs
1 small onion, finely chopped
Salt
Freshly ground pepper
1 tablespoon Worcestershire sauce
2 tablespoons vegetable oil

**Sauce:**
1 tablespoon all-purpose flour
1-1/2 teaspoons dry mustard
1-1/2 teaspoons Dijon-style mustard
1 tablespoon soy sauce
1 tablespoon Worcestershire sauce
1 tablespoon sweet chutney
1 cup beef stock
8 oz. carrots, cut into thin sticks
1 large cooking apple, peeled, cored, diced

**To garnish:**
Watercress or parsley

**1.** Preheat oven to 350F (175C).
**2.** In a medium bowl, combine ground beef, breadcrumbs, onion, salt, pepper and Worcestershire sauce. Shape into 16 equal balls.
**3.** Heat oil in a large skillet over medium heat. Add meatballs; sauté until browned. Remove from skillet; set aside. Pour off all but 1 tablespoon fat.
**4.** To make sauce, stir flour and dry mustard into fat remaining in skillet. Then stir in Dijon-style mustard, soy sauce, Worcestershire sauce, chutney and stock; bring mixture to a boil, stirring constantly. Season with salt and pepper.
**5.** Lay carrots and apples in a 2-1/2-quart casserole; arrange meatballs on top of carrots and apples. Pour sauce over meatballs. Cover casserole with foil or lid. Bake in preheated oven 45 minutes or until meatballs are done and carrots are tender.
**6.** To serve, remove any fat from surface of sauce. Stir casserole lightly; garnish with watercress or parsley. Spaghetti or noodles make a good accompaniment. Makes 4 servings.

Left to right: Deviled Meatballs, Spicy Oven Beef

# Curried Beef with Pineapple

2 tablespoons vegetable oil
1-1/2 lbs. beef stew cubes
1 (8-oz.) can crushed pineapple, juice pack
3 large onions
2 teaspoons curry powder
1 tablespoon tomato paste
1 (16-oz.) can tomatoes
1 tablespoon wine vinegar
2 tablespoons apricot jam
1/2 cup beef stock
Salt
Freshly ground pepper

*To garnish:*
Chopped fresh parsley

---

*This recipe has a mild curry flavor, suitable even for those who dislike curry. Lamb, pork or any kind of poultry can be used instead of beef. If using lamb or pork, cut cooking time to 1-1/2 to 1-3/4 hours. Turkey, cut into cubes, is also suitable and needs only 1 to 1-1/4 hours cooking. This dish is also good served with rice cooked with peppers, chopped toasted nuts, raisins and peas.*

1. Preheat oven to 325F (165C).
2. Heat oil in a large skillet over medium heat. Add beef cubes; sauté until evenly browned. Transfer to a 3-quart casserole.
3. Drain pineapple, reserving juice. Chop onions very finely, preferably in a food processor. Add chopped onions and pineapple to skillet along with remaining ingredients, including reserved pineapple juice. Bring mixture to a boil. Pour hot pineapple mixture over beef cubes; stir well. Cover casserole tightly with foil or lid.
4. Bake in preheated oven 2-1/2 hours or until beef is tender. Season to taste.
5. Garnish with chopped parsley. Serve with hot cooked rice or creamed potatoes. Makes 4 servings.

# Spicy Oven Beef

1-1/2 lbs. beef-round steak, cut into 4 serving pieces
Salt
Freshly ground pepper
1 teaspoon ground coriander
1 teaspoon ground ginger
2 tablespoons vegetable oil
16 small white onions
3 celery stalks, cut into 1-inch pieces
1/4 cup all-purpose flour
2 cups beef stock
1 tablespoon Worcestershire sauce
2 tablespoons whipping cream
3 to 4 tablespoons prepared horseradish

*To garnish:*
Celery leaves

---

1. Preheat oven to 325F (165C).
2. Sprinkle beef with salt, pepper, coriander and ginger; rub salt and spices into each piece. Heat oil in a large skillet over medium heat. Add beef; sauté until browned. Use a slotted spoon to transfer browned beef to a large casserole or baking pan.
3. Add onions and celery to fat remaining in skillet; sauté until soft. Stir in flour; cook 1 minute, stirring constantly. Gradually stir in stock. Bring mixture to a boil; add salt, pepper and Worcestershire sauce. Pour stock mixture over beef.
4. Cover casserole with foil or lid. Bake in preheated oven 2 hours or until beef is almost tender.
5. Stir in cream and horseradish. Bake 30 minutes longer. Garnish with celery leaves. Makes 4 servings.

# Beef-Noodle Casserole

6 oz. green noodles
1-1/2 lbs. lean ground beef
2 onions, chopped
1 to 2 garlic cloves, crushed
2 teaspoons cornstarch
1 (16-oz.) can tomatoes
1/2 cup beef stock
1 tablespoon soy sauce
1 tablespoon Worcestershire sauce
1 tablespoon tomato paste
1 teaspoon dried leaf oregano
Salt
Freshly ground pepper
2 tablespoons butter or margarine
1/4 cup all-purpose flour
1 cup milk
1/2 cup grated sharp Cheddar cheese (1-1/2 oz.)

---

**1.** Preheat oven to 400F (205C).
**2.** Cook noodles according to package directions until almost tender; drain noodles. Grease a shallow baking dish; set aside.
**3.** In a large skillet over medium heat, sauté ground beef with no extra fat until browned. Add onions and garlic; sauté 3 to 4 minutes.
**4.** In a small bowl, blend cornstarch with some juice from tomatoes. Stir cornstarch mixture into browned beef. Add tomatoes with rest of juice, stock, soy sauce, Worcestershire sauce, tomato paste, oregano, salt and pepper. Boil 2 minutes, stirring frequently.
**5.** Put half the noodles in greased baking dish. Cover with beef mixture; add remaining noodles.
**6.** Melt butter or margarine in a medium saucepan. Stir in flour; cook 1 minute. Gradually stir in milk. Boil 1 minute, stirring constantly. Season to taste. Pour over noodles.
**7.** Sprinkle cheese over noodles. Cover casserole with foil or lid. Bake in preheated oven 15 minutes. Uncover casserole; bake 10 to 15 minutes longer or until cheese topping is brown and crispy. Makes 4 to 5 servings.

## Variation

Four ounces of sliced mushrooms may be sautéed with the beef. Egg noodles or whole-wheat noodles may be used in place of green noodles.

# Gingered Beef

1/2 cup all-purpose flour
Salt
Freshly ground pepper
1-1/2 to 2 teaspoons ground ginger
1-1/2 lbs. beef stew cubes
3 tablespoons vegetable oil
1 tablespoon grated fresh gingerroot
1 garlic clove, crushed
2 onions, sliced
1 cup beef stock
1 cup canned tomatoes
2 tablespoons vinegar
1 tablespoon honey
1 tablespoon Worcestershire sauce
1 (15-oz.) can red kidney beans or white beans, drained

---

*This casserole has a rich tangy flavor which soon becomes a favorite, particularly because it is easy to prepare. It can be cooked in quantity and frozen up to 2 months—no longer because of its spiciness. For freezing, cook up to point of adding beans, but do not add them. Cool casserole rapidly; pack beef mixture into plastic containers or plastic freezer bags. To shape bags while filling, stand them in a bowl. Alternatively, line a casserole with foil. Add beef mixture; freeze until solid. Remove frozen beef mixture from casserole; wrap in foil and return to freezer. Remember, anything containing liquid will expand during freezing, so always allow at least 1 inch of headspace to prevent the container or bag from exploding during freezing. Thaw or partially thaw in refrigerator before cooking; add beans when ice melts. Cook 1 hour in a moderate oven (350F, 175C).*

**1.** Preheat oven to 325F (165C).
**2.** In a plastic bag, combine flour, salt, pepper and ground ginger to taste. Add beef cubes; shake to coat.
**3.** Heat oil in a large skillet over medium heat. Add seasoned beef cubes; sauté until browned. With a slotted spoon, transfer to a 2-quart casserole. Add gingerroot, garlic and onions to fat remaining in skillet; sauté until lightly browned. Stir in remaining seasoned flour; cook 1 minute, stirring constantly.
**4.** Gradually stir in stock, tomatoes, vinegar, honey and Worcestershire sauce; bring mixture to a boil. Pour hot mixture over browned beef; cover casserole with foil or lid. Bake in preheated oven 1-3/4 hours or until beef is almost tender.
**5.** Add drained beans; stir through casserole. Cover and bake 25 to 30 minutes longer. Serve with boiled potatoes and salad. Makes 4 servings.

# Biscuit-Topped Beef Bake

1-1/4 lbs. lean ground beef
1 large onion, sliced
2 carrots, diced
1-1/4 cups beef stock
1-1/2 tablespoons Angostura bitters
1 tablespoon tomato paste
Salt
Freshly ground pepper
2 teaspoons cornstarch
Water

*Biscuit topping:*
1-1/2 cups all-purpose flour
2 teaspoons baking powder
1/2 teaspoon salt
Freshly ground pepper
1/2 teaspoon Italian seasoning
1/4 cup butter or margarine
1/2 cup plus 2 tablespoons milk
Sesame seeds, if desired

**1.** Preheat oven to 350F (175C).
**2.** In a large skillet over medium heat, sauté beef with no extra fat, stirring constantly, until no longer pink. Add onion and carrots; cook 3 minutes. Drain off fat.
**3.** Add stock, bitters, tomato paste, salt and pepper to beef mixture; bring mixture to a boil. In a small bowl, blend cornstarch with a little cold water. Stir into beef mixture; cook until slightly thickened, stirring frequently.
**4.** Pour beef mixture into a 2-1/2-quart casserole. Cover with foil or lid. Bake in preheated oven 20 minutes.
**5.** To make biscuit topping, in a medium bowl, combine flour, baking powder, salt, pepper and Italian seasoning. Cut butter or margarine into dry ingredients until mixture resembles coarse crumbs. Add 1/2 cup milk; stir with a fork to make a soft dough. Stir only until combined.
**6.** Turn out dough on a lightly floured surface; knead about 10 times or until no longer sticky. Roll out dough to about 1/2 inch thick. Cut dough with a floured, round 1-1/2-inch cutter.
**7.** Remove casserole from oven. Increase oven heat to 400F (205C). Remove cover; arrange biscuits on top of casserole. Brush biscuits with 2 tablespoons milk; sprinkle with sesame seeds, if desired.
**8.** Bake, uncovered, 20 to 25 minutes or until biscuits are golden brown. Serve immediately. Makes 4 servings.

**Variation**
Ground pork, veal or turkey may be used in place of beef.

Top to bottom: Beef-Noodle Casserole, Biscuit-Topped Beef Bake

# Lamb Stew & Herbed Dumplings

2 lbs. lamb stew cubes
Salt
Freshly ground black pepper
2 tablespoons vegetable oil
1 onion, sliced
1 garlic clove, crushed
1 red bell pepper, sliced
1 tablespoon all-purpose flour
1/2 cup beef stock
1 cup cider or apple juice
1 teaspoon Italian seasoning
1 medium eggplant, cut into 2-inch cubes

*Dumplings:*
1 cup cake flour
2 teaspoons baking powder
1/2 teaspoon salt
1 teaspoon Italian seasoning
1 egg
Milk

1. Preheat oven to 350F (175C).
2. Season lamb cubes with salt and pepper. Heat oil in a large skillet over medium heat. Add lamb cubes; sauté until browned. With a slotted spoon, transfer to a 2-1/2-quart casserole.
3. Add onion, garlic and red pepper to fat remaining in skillet; sauté until onion is transparent.
4. Stir in flour; cook 1 minute, stirring constantly. Gradually stir in stock and cider or apple juice. Boil 2 minutes, stirring constantly. Remove from heat.
5. Season with salt and pepper. Add Italian seasoning and eggplant. Spoon eggplant mixture over browned lamb cubes. Cover casserole with foil or lid. Bake in preheated oven 1-1/4 hours or until lamb is almost tender.
6. To make dumplings, combine cake flour, baking powder, salt and Italian seasoning. Beat egg in measuring cup; add enough milk to make 1/2 cup. Stir egg mixture into dry ingredients. Add additional milk, if necessary, but keep batter stiff.
7. Skim excess fat from surface of casserole. Dip a tablespoon into hot water; drop dumplings by heaping tablespoonfuls on hot lamb mixture. Cover casserole; bake 10 to 15 minutes or until dumplings are cooked. Makes 4 to 6 servings.

# Lamb Chops with Apricots

4 lamb-loin double chops
Salt
Freshly ground pepper
1 tablespoon vegetable oil
1 onion, chopped
Juice of 1 orange
1/2 cup beef stock
1 tablespoon paprika
2/3 cup dried apricots (about 3 to 4 oz.)

*To garnish:*
Mint or parsley sprigs

*If loin double chops are not available, use large loin chops.*

1. Preheat oven to 350F (175C).
2. Trim chops; sprinkle with salt and pepper. Heat oil in a large skillet over medium heat. Add chops; sauté until evenly browned. Transfer to a shallow casserole.
3. Add onion to fat remaining in skillet; sauté until soft. Add orange juice, stock and paprika. Season with salt and pepper. Simmer 2 minutes.
4. Arrange apricots around browned lamb chops. Pour hot juice mixture over apricots and chops. Cover casserole with foil or lid. Bake in preheated oven 40 minutes or until lamb is tender.
5. To serve, garnish with mint or parsley. Makes 4 servings.

### Variations
Canned apricots can be used instead of dried ones. Allow 1 cup canned apricot halves (about 6 to 8 halves with their juice). Replace 1/4 cup of stock with apricot juice.
**Lamb Chops with Prunes:** Use 2/3 cups uncooked prunes; bake as above. Serve with Duchess Potatoes. To make *Duchess Potatoes*, beat mashed potatoes with beaten egg until smooth. Fill a piping bag fitted with a star nozzle. Pipe whirls of potato on greased baking sheets. To bake potatoes, place baking sheets on oven rack above casserole. Bake 30 minutes or until potatoes are lightly browned.

Top to bottom: Lamb Stew & Herbed Dumplings, Lamb Chops with Apricots

# Middle Eastern Lamb with Rice

2 oranges
1-1/2 lbs. lamb stew cubes
Salt
Freshly ground pepper
3 tablespoons vegetable oil
1 large onion, sliced
1 garlic clove, crushed
1-3/4 cups beef stock
1/2 cup raisins
1/4 teaspoon ground coriander
1 cup uncooked long-grain white rice

*To garnish:*
1/3 cup toasted slivered almonds (about 1-1/2 oz.)
Orange twists
Watercress

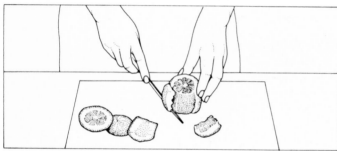

1/Cut away peel and bitter white pith.

2/Cut between membrane to remove sections.

**1.** Grease a 2-quart casserole; set aside. Preheat oven to 350F (175C).
**2.** Remove peel and pith from 1 orange with a sharp knife. Remove pith from inside of peel; discard pith. Cut peel into julienne strips. Section orange. Squeeze juice from second orange.
**3.** Sprinkle lamb cubes lightly with salt and pepper.
**4.** Heat oil in a large skillet over medium heat. Add lamb cubes; sauté until lightly browned. With a slotted spoon, remove browned lamb from skillet; set aside.
**5.** Add onion to fat remaining in skillet; sauté until lightly browned. Add julienned orange peel, orange juice, stock and raisins; bring mixture to a boil. Add coriander, salt and pepper.
**6.** Add rice and browned lamb to skillet; stir well. Spoon mixture into greased casserole. Cover casserole with foil or lid.
**7.** Bake in preheated oven 1 hour or until rice and lamb are tender.
**8.** To serve, add orange sections; stir lightly. Sprinkle top of casserole with slivered almonds; garnish with orange twists and watercress. Makes 4 servings.

### Variation
Substitute beef-sirloin cubes for lamb.

# Lamb & Tomato Casserole

2 tablespoons vegetable oil
6 lamb shoulder chops, trimmed
1 cup chopped onions
1 garlic clove, crushed
1 cup beef stock
1/4 cup pale dry sherry
1 teaspoon Worcestershire sauce
1/2 teaspoon dried leaf basil
2 cups chopped fresh tomatoes
Salt
Freshly ground pepper

*To garnish:*
Green-pepper rings

**1.** Preheat oven to 350F (175C).
**2.** Heat oil in large skillet over medium heat. Add lamb chops; sauté until browned. Using tongs, place chops in a single layer in a 2-quart shallow casserole.
**3.** Add onions and garlic to fat remaining in skillet; sauté until transparent. Add beef stock and sherry; bring mixture to a boil. Stir in Worcestershire sauce, basil and tomatoes. Season with salt and pepper. Spoon mixture over chops.
**4.** Cover casserole with foil or lid; bake in preheated oven 1 hour or until lamb is cooked. Spoon any fat from surface of casserole. To serve, garnish with green-pepper rings. Makes 4 to 6 servings.

Left to right: Middle Eastern Lamb with Rice, Lamb & Potato Casserole

# Lamb & Potato Casserole

2 tablespoons vegetable oil
1-1/2 lbs. lamb stew cubes
2 onions, sliced
2 carrots, sliced
1 tablespoon all-purpose flour
1/2 cup white wine
1 cup beef stock
1 tablespoon tomato paste
1 tablespoon brown sugar
Salt
Freshly ground pepper
1 to 1-1/2 teaspoons dried dill weed
1-1/2 lbs. potatoes, peeled, thinly sliced (about 4 cups)
1 tablespoon butter or margarine, melted

*Dill has a strong distinctive flavor; if you prefer a less-definite taste, use less dill.*

**1.** Preheat oven to 350F (175C).
**2.** Heat oil in a large skillet over medium heat. Add lamb cubes; sauté until browned. With a slotted spoon, transfer lamb cubes to a large casserole.
**3.** Add onions and carrots to fat remaining in skillet; sauté 2 minutes. Stir in flour; cook 1 minute, stirring frequently. Gradually stir in wine and stock. Bring mixture to a boil, stirring frequently. Remove skillet from heat.
**4.** Stir in tomato paste and sugar; season with salt and pepper. Spoon onion and carrot mixture over browned lamb. Stir in dill weed.
**5.** Arrange sliced potatoes evenly over contents of casserole. Brush potatoes with melted butter or margarine. Cover with foil or lid.
**6.** Bake in preheated oven 1-1/2 hours. Increase oven heat to 400F (205C). Remove cover from casserole; bake 30 minutes longer or until potatoes are tender and golden brown. Makes 4 servings.

# Leg of Lamb with Garlic & Rosemary

1 (4-lb.) leg of lamb
3 to 4 garlic cloves, slivered
Few rosemary sprigs or 1 tablespoon dried
   leaf rosemary
Salt
Freshly ground pepper
3/4 lb. small white onions
2 lbs. potatoes, peeled, diced (about 6 cups)
Water
1 cup beef stock, if desired

*To garnish:*
Fresh rosemary sprigs

1. Preheat oven to 350F (175C).
2. Make deep cuts over surface of lamb with a small pointed knife.
3. Stick garlic slivers and small pieces of rosemary into cuts. If dried rosemary is used, sprinkle it over lamb after spiking with garlic.
4. Place lamb in a roasting pan. Roast in preheated oven 1 hour.
5. In 2 medium saucepans, cook potatoes and onions separately in boiling water 10 to 15 minutes or until almost tender. Drain well; set aside.
6. Remove lamb from oven. Arrange precooked potatoes and onions around lamb; turn in pan drippings to coat. Sprinkle potatoes and onions with salt and pepper.
7. Roast lamb 45 to 60 minutes longer or until lamb reaches desired degree of doneness. Serve garnished with fresh rosemary. A sauce can be made by deglazing roasting pan with beef stock, if desired. Degrease sauce; serve in a gravy boat or small pitcher. Makes 6 to 8 servings.

Clockwise from bottom: Crispy Pork-Loin Roast, Leg of Lamb with Garlic & Rosemary, Lamb Chops with Fennel

# Lamb Chops with Fennel

4 thick lamb-shoulder arm chops
Salt
Freshly ground pepper
2 teaspoons ground coriander
1 tablespoon vegetable oil
1 onion, thinly sliced
2 fennel bulbs, chopped
1 cup beef stock
2 teaspoons cornstarch
Water

*Topping:*
3/4 cup fresh breadcrumbs
1/4 cup grated Cheddar cheese (1 oz.)
1 tablespoon grated Parmesan cheese

*To garnish:*
Fresh fennel or parsley sprigs

---

*If chops are small or thin, allow 2 per serving; decrease cooking time by 5 to 10 minutes.*

**1.** Preheat oven to 350F (175C).
**2.** Sprinkle lamb chops with salt, pepper and coriander. Heat oil in a large skillet over medium heat. Add chops; sauté until browned. With tongs, remove chops from skillet; set aside.
**3.** Add onion to fat remaining in skillet; sauté until soft. Drain any excess fat from skillet.
**4.** Place onion and fennel in a 9-inch-square baking pan; arrange browned chops over vegetables.
**5.** Pour stock into same skillet; bring to a boil. Pour hot stock over chops and vegetables. Cover pan with foil or lid.
**6.** Bake in preheated oven 45 to 55 minutes or until lamb is tender. Fennel should not be too soft.
**7.** Strain cooking juices into a medium saucepan; remove any fat from surface. In a small bowl, combine cornstarch and a little cold water. Stir cornstarch mixture into juices from pan; bring to a boil. Cook until thickened, stirring constantly. Pour thickened juices over vegetables and chops. Preheat broiler.
**8.** Combine breadcrumbs and cheeses; sprinkle cheese mixture over chops. Place lamb under preheated broiler; broil until topping is golden brown and crisp. Garnish with sprigs of fennel or parsley.

## Variation
Pork chops or pork shoulder steaks may be used in place of lamb chops. Fennel has a distinctive taste. If desired, it can be replaced with a mixture of sliced onions, potatoes and carrots. Use 2 onions, 1 pound potatoes and 2 carrots.

# Crispy Pork-Loin Roast

1 (2-1/2- to 3-lb.) pork-loin roast, chined or chopped
Salt
Freshly ground pepper

*Topping:*
1 cup fresh breadcrumbs
2 teaspoons chopped fresh sage or 1/2 teaspoon rubbed sage

*To garnish:*
Fresh mint or parsley sprigs

---

**1.** Preheat oven to 350F (175C).
**2.** Trim roast; sprinkle lightly with salt and pepper. Place in a roasting pan.
**3.** Roast in preheated oven about 1 hour.
**4.** Remove roast from oven; baste with pan drippings. In a small bowl, combine breadcrumbs and sage. Season crumb mixture with salt and pepper. Press crumb mixture over top of roast.
**5.** Increase oven heat to 400F (205C). Roast pork 30 minutes longer or until topping is crisp and lightly browned. Pork should reach an internal temperature of 170F (75C).
**6.** Serve roast sliced, or as a whole roast, surrounded by vegetables. Garnish with fresh mint or parsley. Makes 4 to 6 servings.

# Lasagna

1 lb. green lasagna noodles
Salt
Water
1 lb. ground beef or lamb
1 large onion, chopped
2 carrots, chopped
1 (16-oz.) can tomatoes
1/2 cup beef stock
1 tablespoon tomato paste
Freshly ground pepper
2 to 3 tablespoons chopped fresh basil or
   1-1/2 teaspoons dried leaf basil
6 tablespoons dairy sour cream
1 cup grated Cheddar cheese (about 4 oz.)
1 tablespoon grated Parmesan cheese

*To garnish:*
Tomato slices
Cucumber slices
Parsley sprigs

**1.** Cook lasagna noodles in boiling salted water according to package directions until just tender. Drain on paper towels. Preheat oven to 375F (190C). Grease a 9-inch-square baking pan; set aside.
**2.** With no extra fat added, sauté beef or lamb in a large, heavy saucepan over medium heat until no longer pink. Add onion and carrots; cook 2 minutes. Drain excess fat from saucepan.
**3.** Add tomatoes, stock, tomato paste and basil; bring to a boil. Simmer meat sauce 10 minutes or until thickened. Season with salt and pepper.
**4.** Place a layer of lasagna noodles in greased baking pan. Cover with half the meat sauce. Repeat layers of noodles and sauce, ending with noodles.
**5.** Spread sour cream over noodles. Combine cheeses; sprinkle over sour cream.
**6.** Bake in preheated oven 45 minutes or until top is golden and sauce is bubbling. Garnish with tomato, cucumber and parsley. Makes 6 servings.

**Variation**
Replace basil with oregano or marjoram; add 4 ounces chopped mushrooms with tomatoes.

Left to right: Lasagna, Lamb Marsala

# Lamb Marsala

1 (3- to 4-lb.) lamb-shoulder or lamb-leg roast, boneless
Salt
Freshly ground pepper

*Stuffing:*
2 tablespoons butter or margarine
1 onion, finely chopped
1 celery stalk, finely chopped
1-1/2 cups fresh breadcrumbs
1/3 cup chopped toasted almonds (1-1/2 oz.)
Grated peel of 1/2 lemon
1 egg, beaten

*Marsala sauce:*
3-1/2 tablespoons all-purpose flour
1 cup beef stock
1/4 cup Marsala
2 tablespoons lemon juice

*To garnish:*
Celery leaves
1/4 cup toasted flaked almonds

**1.** Preheat oven to 325F (165C).
**2.** Unroll lamb roast if it is rolled and tied; flatten if necessary. Sprinkle lightly with salt and pepper.
**3.** To make stuffing, melt butter or margarine in a large skillet over medium heat. Add onion and celery; sauté until soft. In a medium bowl, combine sautéed onion and celery with breadcrumbs, chopped almonds, lemon peel and egg. Season with salt and pepper.
**4.** Spread stuffing over flattened roast; roll lightly to enclose stuffing. Tie roast with string; place in a roasting pan.
**5.** Roast in preheated oven 1-1/2 to 2 hours or to desired doneness (35 to 40 minutes per pound for medium). Remove roast from pan; cover with foil to keep warm.
**6.** To make sauce, stir flour into pan juices; cook 1 minute, stirring constantly. Gradually stir in stock and Marsala; simmer 3 to 4 minutes.
**7.** Add lemon juice to hot Marsala sauce. Season with salt and pepper. Pour sauce into a gravy boat or small pitcher.
**8.** Remove string from roast. Cut roast into thick slices; arrange on a hot platter. Garnish with celery leaves; sprinkle with flaked almonds. Serve sauce separately. Makes 6 to 8 servings.

# Fruited Pork Tenderloin

2 pork-loin tenderloins, about 1-1/2 to 2 lbs. total
Salt
Freshly ground pepper
*Stuffing:*
1/3 cup pitted prunes, chopped
1 cup fresh breadcrumbs
1 small onion, finely chopped
1/2 teaspoon dried leaf thyme
1 egg yolk

*Sauce:*
2 tablespoons vegetable oil
1 onion, chopped
1/2 cup beef stock
1/2 cup white wine
2/3 cup pitted prunes
2 tablespoons brandy, if desired
3 to 4 tablespoons whipping cream, if desired

*To garnish:*
Fresh mint or parsley sprigs

1. Preheat oven to 350F (175C).
2. Split pork tenderloins halfway through lengthwise with a sharp knife; flatten slightly. Season tenderloins with salt and pepper.
3. To make stuffing, combine prunes, breadcrumbs, onion and thyme. Season mixture with salt and pepper; stir in egg yolk. Spread stuffing over 1 tenderloin; cover with second tenderloin. Tie into a roast with string.
4. Heat oil in a large skillet over medium heat; sauté roast until browned. Transfer to a shallow baking pan.
5. Add onion to fat remaining in skillet; sauté until lightly browned. Add stock, wine and prunes to skillet. Season with salt and pepper; bring mixture to a boil.
6. If desired, in a small saucepan, warm brandy. Pour warmed brandy over browned roast; ignite brandy carefully. When flames die, pour sauce over and around roast; cover pan with foil or lid.
7. Roast in preheated oven 45 to 60 minutes or until roast reaches an internal temperature of 170F (75C).
8. Remove string from roast; cut into slices. Place slices in a serving dish. Stir cream into cooking sauce, if desired. To serve, spoon prunes and cooking sauce over pork slices. Garnish with mint or parsley. Makes 4 servings.

# Pork Tenderloin Calvados

1-1/2 lbs. pork-loin tenderloin, cut into 3/4-inch slices
Salt
Freshly ground pepper
2 tablespoons butter or margarine
*Sauce:*
1 tablespoon butter or margarine
6 oz. mushrooms, sliced
3 tablespoons Calvados or other apple brandy
1/2 cup chicken stock
1/2 cup whipping cream
2 teaspoons cornstarch

*To garnish:*
1/3 cup toasted coarsely chopped hazelnuts
1 to 2 teaspoons chopped fresh thyme
1 tablespoon chopped fresh parsley

1. Preheat oven to 350F (175C).
2. Sprinkle pork slices lightly with salt and pepper. Melt 2 tablespoons butter or margarine in a large skillet over medium heat. Add pork slices; sauté until lightly browned. Transfer to a 2-quart casserole.
3. For sauce, add 1 tablespoon butter or margarine to skillet. Add mushrooms; sauté gently 2 to 3 minutes.
4. Add brandy, stock, salt and pepper; boil mixture 2 minutes.
5. Pour sauce mixture over pork; cover casserole with foil or lid. Bake in preheated oven 30 minutes or until pork is tender.
6. In a small bowl, combine cream and cornstarch; stir cornstarch mixture into hot casserole. Bake 5 to 10 minutes longer or until sauce is thickened.
7. Combine hazelnuts with thyme and parsley; sprinkle over casserole. Makes 4 servings.

**Variation**
Pork-loin tenderloin is now easily obtainable from larger supermarkets. It is a fairly expensive cut, but is solid meat, with no fat and no waste. However, if you cannot find pork-loin tenderloin, substitute boneless chicken or turkey breasts. Chicken breasts can be split in half if they are very thick, or cooked whole. Cut turkey breasts into slanting slices about 3/4 inch thick. Cook turkey or chicken in the same way as for pork.

Calvados is not always readily available. Brandy can be used instead or try using 2 tablespoons of any orange liqueur and 1 tablespoon lemon juice; this combination will alter the flavor but makes a tasty alternative.

Left to right: Fruited Pork Tenderloin, Pork Tenderloin Calvados

# Curried Veal with Apple Slices

2 tablespoons all-purpose flour
2 to 3 teaspoons curry powder
1-1/2 lbs. veal stew cubes
1/4 cup vegetable oil
1 cup chopped onions
1 green apple, peeled, cored, sliced
1 garlic clove, crushed
1 tablespoon brown sugar
2 tablespoons raisins
1-1/2 tablespoons Worcestershire sauce
1 tablespoon shredded coconut
1 cup water
Salt
Freshly ground pepper

1. In a plastic bag, combine flour and curry powder to taste. Add veal cubes; shake to coat.
2. Heat oil in large skillet over medium heat. Add seasoned veal cubes; sauté until lightly browned. Remove browned veal with slotted spoon; set aside.
3. Add onions, apple and garlic to fat remaining in skillet; sauté until slightly softened. Stir brown sugar, raisins, Worcestershire sauce, coconut and water into mixture in skillet; bring to a simmer. Return browned veal to skillet; cover skillet.
4. Simmer veal mixture 45 minutes or until veal is tender, stirring occasionally. Season with salt and pepper. Makes 4 servings.

# Veal in Madeira Sauce

2 tablespoons butter or margarine
1 tablespoon vegetable oil
1-1/2 lbs. veal stew cubes
8 small white onions
2 large carrots, diced
1 small red bell pepper, sliced
2 tablespoons all-purpose flour
1-1/2 cups chicken stock
1/4 cup Madeira
Salt
Freshly ground black pepper
4 oz. mushrooms, sliced
2 bay leaves

1. Preheat oven to 350F (175C).
2. Heat butter or margarine and oil in a large skillet over medium heat. Add veal cubes; sauté until lightly browned. With a slotted spoon, transfer browned veal cubes to a 2-1/2-quart casserole.
3. Add onions and carrots to fat remaining in skillet; sauté until vegetables begin to brown. Add red pepper; cook about 2 minutes.
4. Stir in flour; cook 1 minute. Gradually stir in stock and Madeira; bring to a boil. Season sauce with salt and pepper; add mushrooms and bay leaves. Pour hot sauce over browned veal.
5. Cover casserole tightly with foil or lid; bake in preheated oven 1-1/4 to 1-1/2 hours or until veal is tender.
6. Discard bay leaves; serve with hot cooked rice. Makes 4 servings.

# Veal in Wine & Cream Sauce

6 tablespoons butter or margarine
1-1/2 lbs. veal stew cubes
2 small onions
1 bouquet garni
1 cup white wine
1 cup chicken stock
Salt
Freshly ground pepper
1/4 cup all-purpose flour
1/4 cup whipping cream
2 tablespoons brandy

*To garnish:*
Sautéed button mushrooms
Sautéed button onions
Watercress

1. Preheat oven to 325F (165C).
2. Melt 3 tablespoons butter or margarine in a large skillet over medium heat. Add veal cubes; sauté until browned. Transfer browned veal to a 2-quart casserole; add onions and bouquet garni to casserole. Season with salt and pepper.
3. Add wine to skillet; bring to a boil. Pour hot wine over veal.
4. Cover casserole with foil or lid; bake in preheated oven 1 hour or until veal is tender.
5. Strain liquid from casserole into a medium saucepan; discard onions and bouquet garni. Boil liquid rapidly over high heat until reduced to 1-1/2 cups. Keep veal warm.
6. Cream remaining butter or margarine with flour; gradually whisk into hot sauce; cook until thickened, stirring constantly. Simmer 3 minutes. Season sauce with salt and pepper; add cream. Reheat sauce; do not boil.
7. In a small saucepan, warm brandy. Pour warmed brandy over veal; ignite brandy carefully. When flames die, pour sauce over veal; garnish with mushrooms, onions and watercress. Makes 4 servings.

Left to right: Veal in Wine & Cream Sauce, Veal Paprika

# Veal Paprika

2 tablespoons butter or margarine
2 tablespoons vegetable oil
1-1/2 lbs. veal stew cubes
2 large onions, sliced
1 tablespoon paprika
1/4 cup all-purpose flour
1 cup chicken stock
1 tablespoon tomato paste
1 tablespoon lemon juice
1 (16-oz.) can tomatoes
1/3 cup raisins
Salt
Freshly ground pepper

*To garnish:*
1 (2-inch) cucumber piece
4 to 6 tablespoons dairy sour cream

**1.** Preheat oven to 350F (175C).
**2.** Heat butter or margarine with 1 tablespoon oil in a large skillet over medium heat. Add veal cubes; sauté until browned. Transfer to a 2-quart casserole with a slotted spoon.
**3.** Add remainder of oil to skillet. Add onions; sauté until golden brown. Stir in paprika and flour; cook 1 minute, stirring constantly. Gradually stir in stock; bring to a boil.
**4.** Add tomato paste, lemon juice, tomatoes with their liquid and raisins; simmer 1 minute. Season sauce with salt and pepper; pour over browned veal.
**5.** Cover casserole tightly with foil or lid; bake in preheated oven 1-1/4 to 1-1/2 hours or until veal is tender.
**6.** Without peeling, coarsely grate or finely dice cucumber. Spoon sour cream over hot casserole; sprinkle with grated or diced cucumber. As an alternative topping, mix cucumber and sour cream; spoon over hot casserole. Makes 4 servings.

Main Dishes—Meats **139**

# Apple-Stuffed Veal Roast

1 (4-lb.) veal-shoulder roast, boneless
Salt
Freshly ground pepper

*Stuffing:*
About 3 tablespoons butter or margarine
2 celery stalks, finely chopped
1 small onion, chopped
2 oz. mushrooms, chopped
1 small apple, peeled, cored, finely chopped
1 cup fresh breadcrumbs
1 tablespoon chopped fresh parsley
1 teaspoon dried leaf thyme
Grated peel of 1 lemon
1 egg yolk

*Sauce:*
1 cup white wine or chicken stock
Juice of 1 small lemon
1 tablespoon cornstarch
Water

*To garnish:*
6 oz. button mushrooms, sautéed
Parsley sprigs
Lemon wedges

**1.** Preheat oven to 350F (175C).
**2.** Unroll roast; flatten if necessary. Sprinkle with salt and pepper.
**3.** To make stuffing, melt 2 tablespoons butter or margarine in a large skillet over medium heat. Add celery and onion; sauté until soft. Add mushrooms; cook 2 to 3 minutes.
**4.** Remove skillet from heat; add apple, breadcrumbs, parsley, thyme and half the lemon peel. Season mixture with salt and pepper; stir in egg yolk.
**5.** Spread stuffing over flattened roast; roll roast carefully to enclose stuffing. Tie roast with string.
**6.** Rub roast with butter or margarine. Place in a roasting pan.
**7.** Roast in preheated oven 1 hour. Baste with pan drippings; roast 1 to 1-1/2 hours longer or until roast is tender. Transfer roast to a warm serving dish.
**8.** Deglaze roasting pan with wine or stock. Add lemon juice and remaining lemon peel; season with salt and pepper.
**9.** In a small bowl, combine cornstarch with a little cold water; stir into pan juices. Boil sauce 2 minutes; season with salt and pepper. Pour sauce into a gravy boat or small pitcher.
**10.** To serve, slice roast; garnish with mushrooms, parsley and lemon wedges. Serve sauce separately. Makes 6 to 8 servings.

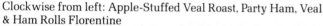

Clockwise from left: Apple-Stuffed Veal Roast, Party Ham, Veal & Ham Rolls Florentine

# Party Ham

1 cook-before-eating ham half (about 4 lbs.)
1 (16-oz.) can peach halves
2 tablespoons wine vinegar
1 tablespoon lemon juice
Whole cloves
1/3 cup packed brown sugar
1 tablespoon dry mustard
1/4 teaspoon grated nutmeg
2 to 3 teaspoons cornstarch, if desired
Water, if desired

*To garnish:*
Watercress

1. Preheat oven to 325F (165C).
2. Place ham in a roasting pan. Drain peaches; pour juice around ham. Add vinegar, lemon juice and about 8 cloves.
3. Cover roasting pan tightly with foil or lid. Bake in preheated oven 1-1/2 hours.
4. Remove ham from oven. Increase oven heat to 400F (205C). Carefully remove any skin from ham; score fat in a diamond pattern. Baste ham with pan juices. In a small bowl, combine sugar, mustard and nutmeg; spread sugar mixture over scored fat. If desired, stud ham with cloves. Bake 30 minutes longer. Ham should reach an internal temperature of 160F (70C).
5. Stud each peach half with 3 cloves; arrange around ham. Bake an additional 10 minutes.
6. Serve surrounded with peach halves. Garnish with watercress. Pan juices can be thickened with a mixture of 2 to 3 teaspoons cornstarch blended with a little cold water, if desired. Makes 6 to 8 servings.

# Hearty Oxtail Stew

1 large oxtail, cut up
1/2 cup all-purpose flour
Salt
Freshly ground pepper
2 tablespoons vegetable oil
2 large onions, sliced
2 celery stalks, sliced
2 large carrots, sliced
1 cup dark beer or ale
1 cup beef stock
1 tablespoon tomato paste
1 tablespoon brown sugar
1 tablespoon vinegar
2 bay leaves
1/4 teaspoon grated nutmeg

1. Preheat oven to 325F (165C).
2. Trim any excess fat from oxtail. Put flour in plastic bag; season with salt and pepper. Add oxtail pieces; shake to coat.
3. Heat oil in a large skillet over medium heat. Add oxtail pieces; sauté until browned. Transfer browned oxtail pieces to a large casserole or Dutch oven. Arrange vegetables around browned oxtail pieces.
4. Combine beer or ale, stock, tomato paste, sugar, vinegar, bay leaves and nutmeg in a medium saucepan. Bring mixture to a boil; season with salt and pepper. Pour over oxtail.
5. Cover casserole tightly with foil or lid; bake in preheated oven 3 hours or until oxtail is tender. Cool casserole slightly; place in refrigerator.
6. Next day, preheat oven to 325F (165C). Remove fat from top of casserole; discard bay leaves. Bake in preheated oven 1 hour before serving. Makes 4 servings.

# Veal & Ham Rolls Florentine

4 (4-oz.) veal cutlets
4 slices cooked ham
Salt
Freshly ground pepper
Grated nutmeg
1 (10-oz.) pkg. frozen leaf spinach, thawed
2 tablespoons butter or margarine
2 tablespoons vegetable oil
1 onion, sliced
1/3 cup all-purpose flour
1 cup chicken stock
1/2 cup dry white wine
1/4 cup half and half
4 oz. mushrooms, quartered, sliced

*To garnish:*
Parsley sprigs

1. Preheat oven to 350F (175C).
2. Lay cutlets on a flat surface. Cover each with a slice of ham; sprinkle with salt, pepper and nutmeg.
3. Squeeze excess water from spinach; divide into 4 equal portions. Place 1 portion of spinach on each cutlet. Roll each cutlet to enclose spinach; secure with wooden picks.
4. Heat oil in a large skillet over medium heat. Add veal rolls; sauté until lightly browned. Place in a baking dish large enough to hold rolls in 1 layer.
5. Add onion to fat remaining in skillet; sauté until soft. Stir in flour; cook 1 minute, stirring constantly. Gradually stir in stock and wine; bring to a boil.
6. Remove sauce from heat; add half and half and mushrooms. Pour hot sauce over veal rolls. Cover baking dish with foil or lid; bake in preheated oven 1 hour.
7. Remove wooden picks; garnish with parsley. Makes 4 servings.

> If the veal cutlets are over 1/4 inch thick or are cut unevenly, pound between 2 sheets of plastic wrap or waxed paper. Use a regular meat mallet if you have one; if not, the side of a sturdy saucer or the side of an empty champagne bottle make excellent substitutes.

# Medallions of Pork with Sesame Rounds

2 lbs. pork-loin tenderloin, cut into 3/4-inch slices
Salt
Freshly ground pepper
1/4 cup butter or margarine
1 tablespoon finely chopped onion
2 tablespoons all-purpose flour
1 cup milk
1/2 cup chicken stock
2 teaspoons lemon juice
2 teaspoons dried leaf tarragon or 4 teaspoons chopped
    fresh tarragon

*Sesame Rounds:*
1 cup all-purpose flour
1/4 teaspoon salt
2 tablespoons butter or margarine
2 tablespoons shortening
1 to 2 tablespoons ice water
1 egg yolk blended with 1 tablespoon water for glaze
Sesame seeds
Fresh tarragon or parsley

---

**1.** Preheat oven to 350F (175C).
**2.** Sprinkle slices of pork with salt and pepper.
**3.** Melt butter or margarine in a large skillet over medium heat. Add pork slices; sauté until lightly browned. With tongs, transfer browned pork to a shallow casserole.
**4.** Add onion to fat remaining in skillet; sauté until soft. Stir in flour; cook 1 minute, stirring constantly.
**5.** Gradually stir in milk and stock; bring mixture to a boil. Add lemon juice and tarragon. Season sauce with salt and pepper; pour over pork.
**6.** Cover casserole with foil or lid; bake in preheated oven 50 minutes or until pork is tender.
**7.** To make Sesame Rounds, preheat oven to 400F (205C). Grease a baking sheet; set aside.
**8.** In a medium bowl, combine flour and salt. Cut in butter or margarine and shortening until mixture resembles coarse crumbs. Stir ice water into flour mixture, 1 tablespoon at a time, until mixture begins to bind together. Gather dough into a ball; shape into flattened round.
**9.** Roll out dough on a lightly floured surface to 1/4-inch thick. Cut dough with floured 2- to 2-1/2-inch fluted round cutter. Place rounds on greased baking sheet about 1 inch apart. Prick rounds with a fork. Brush with glaze; sprinkle with sesame seeds.
**10.** Bake in preheated oven 10 to 12 minutes or until golden brown. Cool on a wire rack; reheat when required.
**11.** To serve, spoon pork and sauce into a serving dish; garnish with Sesame Rounds and fresh tarragon or parsley. Serve with Duchess Potatoes, page 129. Makes 4 servings.

**Variation**
Sliced turkey or chicken breasts can also be used for this recipe. If using poultry, cooking time can be decreased by 15 minutes. Try using fresh or dried rubbed sage instead of tarragon.

Medallions of Pork with Sesame Rounds

# Pork Chop Casserole

6 (1/4-inch-thick) center-cut pork chops
2 tablespoons vegetable oil
2 onions, cut into wedges
1 garlic clove, crushed
1 cup beer
1 cup beef stock
3 carrots, sliced
1 tablespoon Dijon-style mustard
2 teaspoons brown sugar
Salt
Freshly ground pepper
3 white-bread slices, crusts removed
1 egg, beaten
2 tablespoons milk

*To garnish:*
Chopped fresh parsley

---

**1.** Preheat oven to 350F (175C).
**2.** Heat oil in a medium skillet over medium heat. Add pork chops; sauté until browned. With tongs, transfer browned chops to a 2-quart casserole.
**3.** Add onions and garlic to oil remaining in skillet; sauté until onion is transparent. Gradually add beer and beef stock; bring mixture to a boil. Stir in carrots, mustard, sugar, salt and pepper. Pour mixture over pork chops.
**4.** Cover casserole with foil or lid; bake in preheated oven 1 hour. Cut bread into squares or triangles. In a flat bowl, beat together egg, milk, salt and pepper; dip bread triangles or squares into mixture.
**5.** Remove casserole from oven; stir lightly. Preheat broiler. Place egg-soaked bread on top of casserole. Broil until bread is crisp and lightly browned. Garnish with chopped parsley. Makes 4 to 6 servings.

Clockwise from top left: Pork Chop Casserole, Pork & Potato Bake, Oriental Pork Stew

# Oriental Pork Stew

1/4 cup butter or margarine
1-1/2 lbs. lean pork cubes
1 onion, finely chopped
4 celery stalks, thinly sliced
1 large red bell pepper, thinly sliced
1 to 2 garlic cloves, crushed
1 (8-oz.) can water chestnuts, drained, sliced if large
1/4 cup medium-dry sherry
2 tablespoons soy sauce
1 tablespoon lemon juice
About 3/4 cup beef stock
Salt
Freshly ground black pepper

*Topping:*
3 tablespoons butter or margarine
3/4 cup fresh breadcrumbs
1/3 cup chopped blanched almonds

*To garnish:*
Chopped fresh parsley

---

## Pork & Potato Bake

1 tablespoon vegetable oil
1-1/2 lbs. lean pork, cut into 1/2-inch strips
2 lbs. potatoes, thinly sliced (about 6 cups)
2 medium onions, thinly sliced
6 small sweet pickles, sliced
Salt
Freshly ground pepper
6 tablespoons dry white wine
1/2 cup half and half

*To garnish:*
Chopped fresh parsley

**1.** Preheat oven to 350F (175C). Grease a 2-1/2-quart casserole; set aside.
**2.** Heat oil in a large skillet over medium heat. Add pork strips; sauté until browned.
**3.** Layer potatoes in greased casserole with browned pork, onions and pickles. Season with salt and pepper.
**4.** Combine wine and half and half; pour over potatoes.
**5.** Cover casserole with foil or lid; bake in preheated oven 1 hour. Remove casserole cover; increase oven heat to 400F (205C).
**6.** Bake 30 to 40 minutes longer or until potatoes are golden brown on top. Garnish with parsley. Makes 4 servings.

### Variation
Any cut of lean pork can be used in this recipe, or substitute chicken or turkey breasts cut into 1/2-inch strips.

**1.** Preheat oven to 350F (175C).
**2.** Melt 2 tablespoons butter or margarine in a large skillet over medium heat. Add pork; sauté until browned. With a slotted spoon, transfer browned pork to a 2-quart casserole.
**3.** Add remaining butter or margarine to skillet. Add onion, celery, red pepper and garlic; cook over high heat 2 minutes, stirring frequently. Transfer vegetables to casserole containing browned pork. Stir in water chestnuts.
**4.** In a measuring cup, combine sherry, soy sauce and lemon juice; add enough stock to make 1 cup. Stir stock mixture into casserole; season with salt and pepper.
**5.** Cover casserole with foil or lid.
**6.** Bake in preheated oven 50 to 60 minutes or until pork is tender.
**7.** Meanwhile, melt butter or margarine for topping in a small skillet. Add breadcrumbs; sauté until lightly browned. Stir in nuts; cook until breadcrumbs are golden brown.
**8.** To serve, spoon nut topping over casserole; garnish with parsley. Makes 4 servings.

# Pork Tenderloin Véronique

2 pork-loin tenderloins, trimmed
24 green grapes, halved, seeded, if necessary
1/4 cup butter or margarine
Salt
Freshly ground pepper
1 onion, quartered
1 carrot, sliced
1 bay leaf
1/4 teaspoon dried leaf thyme
1/2 cup white wine
1/2 cup chicken stock
2 tablespoons butter or margarine
2 tablespoons all-purpose flour
1 egg yolk

1. Preheat oven to 350F (175C).
2. Cut tenderloins halfway through lengthwise; open out. Sandwich 24 grape halves together with 1/4 cup butter or margarine; arrange filled grapes down the center of 1 tenderloin. Place second tenderloin on top to form a roast; tie with string.
3. Place tenderloin roast in a shallow roasting pan. Arrange onion, carrot and bay leaf around roast; sprinkle with thyme. Pour wine and stock around roast. Roast in preheated oven 1-1/4 hours or until done. Pork should reach an internal temperature of 170F (80C).
4. Move roast to a warm serving platter; cover with foil to keep warm. Remove fat from cooking liquid. Strain liquid into a medium saucepan.
5. Cream flour and butter to make a beurre manié; gradually whisk flour mixture into strained cooking liquid. Cook over low heat, stirring constantly, until thickened. In a small bowl, beat egg yolk lightly; stir in some of hot sauce. Return mixture to saucepan; simmer sauce 2 to 3 minutes. Pour sauce over roast; garnish with remaining grape halves. Makes 4 servings.

# Ham Bake

1/4 cup butter or margarine
1/2 cup chopped onion
8 oz. mushrooms, sliced
3 tablespoons all-purpose flour
Salt
Freshly ground pepper
1/2 pint half and half (1 cup)
2 tablespoons pale dry sherry
1-1/2 to 2 cups cubed cooked ham
1 (5-oz.) can sliced water chestnuts, drained
1/4 cup shredded Swiss cheese (1 oz.)
1/2 cup fresh breadcrumbs

1. Preheat oven to 400F (205C). Grease a 2-quart casserole; set aside.
2. Melt 2 tablespoons butter or margarine in a large skillet. Add onion and mushrooms; sauté until onion is transparent.
3. Stir flour, salt and pepper into onion mixture. Stir in half and half and sherry; cook until mixture is thickened and bubbly, stirring frequently. Add ham and water chestnuts.
4. Spoon ham mixture into greased casserole; top with shredded cheese. Melt remaining 2 tablespoons butter or margarine in a small skillet. Stir in breadcrumbs; sprinkle buttered crumbs over casserole. Bake, uncovered, 25 minutes. Makes 4 servings.

---

Many people have a preference for rare, medium or well-done meat and would not consider eating meat any other way. The use of a meat thermometer ensures that meat will be cooked perfectly. Beef or lamb can be cooked to rare (140F, 60C), medium (160F, 70C) or well-done (170F, 75C). Both beef and lamb are more juicy and flavorful if not overcooked. Remove roasts from the oven when the internal temperature is 5 to 10 degrees below desired doneness. Roast will continue to cook a few minutes after it is removed from the oven.

Unlike beef or lamb, pork should not be served rare or medium-done. Cook fresh pork to an internal temperature of 170F (75C) for flavor and juiciness. Meat should be gray in color with no pink remaining. Although the parasite, trichina, is rarely found in pork today, it is easily destroyed by cooking. Usually trichina is destroyed at 140F (60C).

# Stuffed Pork Chops

*Stuffing:*
1 cup fresh breadcrumbs
1 teaspoon dried rubbed sage
1 small onion, finely chopped
3 tablespoons raisins
Finely grated peel of 1/2 lemon
2 tablespoons lightly beaten egg
Salt
Freshly ground pepper
4 extra-thick pork chops
1 cup apple juice or white wine

*To garnish:*
1 tablespoon finely chopped parsley

**1.** Preheat oven to 350F (175C).
**2.** For stuffing, combine breadcrumbs, sage, onion, raisins, lemon peel and egg. Season with salt and pepper; stir well.
**3.** Cut a slit in side of each pork chop to make a pocket for stuffing.
**4.** Stuff each pork chop; arrange stuffed chops in a shallow baking pan. Pour juice or wine around stuffed chops; bake in preheated oven 1 hour or until pork is tender. To serve, arrange on serving platter; sprinkle with parsley. Makes 4 servings.

**Variation**
If thick pork chops are not available, use 8 thin ones. Sandwich stuffing between 2 chops; fasten with wooden picks. If desired, the cooking liquid can be thickened with a little cornstarch blended with cold water.

Left to right: Pork Tenderloin Véronique, Stuffed Pork Chops

# Chicken Marengo

1 (3-lb.) broiler-fryer chicken, cut up
Salt
Freshly ground pepper
1/4 cup butter or margarine
2 tablespoons brandy
1 onion, sliced
1 to 2 garlic cloves, crushed
2 tablespoons all-purpose flour
1 (16-oz.) can tomatoes, pureed or very finely chopped
1/2 cup dry white wine
1 tablespoon tomato paste
4 oz. button mushrooms, halved

*To garnish:*
2 hard-cooked eggs, quartered
Black olives
4 crayfish or 8 large whole shrimp, if desired
2 tablespoons butter or margarine, if desired

1. Preheat oven to 350F (175C).
2. Season chicken with salt and pepper.
3. Melt 2 tablespoons butter or margarine in a large skillet over medium heat. Add chicken; sauté until browned. Transfer browned chicken to a 3-quart casserole.
4. In a small saucepan, warm brandy; pour warmed brandy over chicken. Ignite carefully; let burn until flame dies.
5. Add remaining butter or margarine to skillet. Add onion and garlic; sauté until lightly colored.
6. Stir flour into onions; cook 1 minute, stirring constantly. Gradually stir in tomatoes, wine and tomato paste; bring to a boil.
7. Season with salt and pepper. Add mushrooms; simmer 2 minutes. Pour over chicken. Cover casserole with foil or lid.
8. Bake in preheated oven 45 to 50 minutes or until chicken is tender.
9. Arrange chicken and sauce in a deep serving dish; garnish with hard-cooked eggs and olives. For additional garnish, if desired, lightly sauté crayfish or shrimp in butter or margarine. Makes 4 servings.

# Chicken with Artichoke Hearts

4 boneless chicken breasts
Salt
Freshly ground pepper
3 tablespoons butter or margarine
1 onion, sliced
1/2 cup dry white wine
1/2 cup chicken stock
1 (10-oz.) pkg. frozen artichoke hearts, thawed
2 tablespoons all-purpose flour
6 tablespoons half and half

*To garnish:*
Watercress

*A cut up broiler-fryer chicken may also be used for this recipe.*

1. Season chicken with salt and pepper. Heat butter or margarine in a large skillet over medium heat. Add seasoned chicken; sauté until browned. With tongs, remove chicken; set aside.
2. Add onion to fat remaining in skillet; sauté until soft but only lightly colored. Add wine and stock. Return chicken to skillet.
3. Cut each artichoke heart in half; add to skillet.
4. Cover and simmer 25 to 30 minutes or until chicken is tender. With a slotted spoon, remove chicken and artichokes to a warmed serving dish; cover with foil to keep warm.
5. In a small bowl, combine flour and half and half. Whisk flour mixture into skillet. Simmer sauce 3 to 4 minutes; pour over chicken and artichokes. Garnish with watercress. Makes 4 servings.

### Variation
This makes a hearty filling for a pie. Chill cooked mixture until cool. Coarsely chop chicken; return to sauce. Use pastry for a double-crust pie. Pour filling into a pastry-lined, 9-inch, deep-dish pie plate. Cover with top crust; brush with beaten egg. Bake in preheated 400F (205C) oven 45 minutes or until crust is golden.

Top to bottom: Chicken Marengo, Chicken with Artichoke Hearts

# Chicken Rossini

4 boneless chicken breasts
Salt
Freshly ground pepper
About 4 oz. firm liver pâté
3 tablespoons butter or margarine
6 oz. button mushrooms, sliced
3 tablespoons brandy
6 tablespoons chicken stock
4 slices bread
2 tablespoons butter or margarine
2 tablespoons vegetable oil
3 tablespoons half and half, if desired

*To garnish:*
Watercress

**1.** Remove skin from chicken breasts; pound to flatten. Sprinkle lightly with salt and pepper.
**2.** Cut pâté into 4 slices; wrap each slice with a chicken breast. Tie with string or secure with wooden picks.
**3.** Melt 3 tablespoons butter or margarine in a large skillet over medium heat. Add chicken; sauté until lightly browned. With tongs, set browned chicken aside.
**4.** Add mushrooms to fat remaining in skillet; sauté 1 minute. Add brandy and stock; bring to a boil. Season mushroom mixture with salt and pepper; return chicken to skillet.
**5.** Cover skillet with lid; simmer over low heat 20 to 25 minutes or until chicken is tender.
**6.** Cut bread into ovals the size of chicken rolls. Heat 2 tablespoon of butter or margarine and oil in a medium skillet. Sauté bread ovals in hot oil mixture until golden.
**7.** Place sautéed bread on a hot serving dish. Top each oval with a cooked chicken roll; remove string or wooden picks. Adjust seasoning in sauce. Add half and half, if desired; reheat, but do not boil. Spoon sauce over and around chicken. Garnish with watercress. Makes 4 servings.

Chicken Rossini

# Chicken Breasts with Apples & Cream

7 tablespoons butter or margarine
6 chicken-breast cutlets
2 apples, peeled, cored, sliced
2 tablespoons all-purpose flour
Salt
Freshly ground pepper
1 cup chicken stock
1/4 cup dry white wine
1/4 cup whipping cream

1. Melt 5 tablespoons butter or margarine in a large skillet over medium heat. Add cutlets; sauté 8 to 10 minutes or until chicken is tender and lightly browned, turning several times. Arrange cooked chicken in a serving dish; cover with foil to keep warm.
2. Add apples to fat remaining in skillet; cook until barely tender. Arrange apples around chicken.
3. Melt remaining 2 tablespoons butter or margarine in small saucepan. Blend in flour, salt and pepper. Gradually stir in stock; cook over medium heat until thickened, stirring constantly. Add wine; simmer 1 minute. Stir in cream; reheat sauce, but do not boil. Pour some sauce over chicken breasts. Serve additional sauce separately. Makes 4 to 6 servings.

# Baked Orange Chicken

1 cup orange juice
1 tablespoon dry vermouth
1 garlic clove, crushed
Salt
Freshly ground pepper
6 chicken-breast cutlets
1/2 cup orange marmalade

*To garnish:*
1 (11-oz.) can mandarin oranges, drained
Toasted slivered almonds

1. To make marinade, in a small bowl, combine orange juice, vermouth, garlic, salt and pepper. Place cutlets in a single layer in a 13" x 9" glass baking dish; pour marinade over. Cover and refrigerate several hours or overnight.
2. Preheat oven to 350F (175C).
3. Remove cover from pan; spoon some marmalade on top of each cutlet. Bake, uncovered, 30 minutes or until chicken is tender, basting occasionally with marinade.
4. Place chicken on serving platter. Strain juices into small pitcher or gravy boat; serve separately. Garnish chicken with mandarin oranges and almonds. Makes 4 to 6 servings.

# Chicken & Crab Rolls with Wild Rice

8 boneless skinless chicken-breast halves
Salt
Freshly ground pepper
1 (6-oz.) pkg. thawed frozen crabmeat
1/2 cup fresh bread crumbs
1 green onion, finely chopped
1/4 cup finely chopped celery
3 tablespoons butter or margarine
1/2 cup sliced mushrooms
1 green onion, sliced
1/4 cup brandy
1-1/4 cups chicken stock
2 cups hot cooked wild rice
1/2 cup shredded Monterey Jack cheese (2 oz.)
3/4 teaspoon cornstarch
2 tablespoons water

1. Place chicken between sheets of plastic wrap. Pound to 1/4 inch thick. Season with salt and pepper. Set aside.
2. In a medium bowl, combine crabmeat, bread crumbs, finely chopped green onion and celery. Divide mixture among pounded chicken pieces. Roll up to enclose stuffing. Secure with string or wooden picks.
3. Melt butter or margarine in a large skillet over medium heat. Add chicken rolls; sauté until browned. Remove chicken rolls; keep warm. Add mushrooms and sliced onion to skillet; sauté 2 minutes.
4. Return rolls to skillet. Add brandy and stock. Bring to a boil; reduce heat. Cover; simmer 20 minutes or until chicken is tender and juices run clear when pierced with a fork.
5. Spoon hot rice into a serving dish. Arrange chicken rolls over rice, reserving cooking liquid in skillet. Sprinkle rolls with cheese. Cover and keep warm.
6. In a small bowl, combine cornstarch and water. Stir cornstarch mixture into cooking liquid. Cook, stirring constantly, until slightly thickened. Spoon some sauce over chicken rolls. Serve remaining sauce separately. Makes 4 to 6 servings.

---

To make *chicken cutlets*, place boned chicken-breast halves on a work surface between sheets of waxed paper or plastic wrap. Using a meat mallet or cleaver, pound each breast until about 1/4 inch thick. To make turkey cutlets, cut boneless turkey breast into 1/2-inch diagonal slices before pounding. Chicken and turkey cutlets can be frozen on baking sheets, wrapped and stored up to 2 months.

# Chicken Patties with Mustard Sauce

1 lb. boneless chicken breasts, skinned
2 cups fresh breadcrumbs
1/2 cup butter or margarine
1/2 cup whipping cream
Salt
Freshly ground pepper
1/4 teaspoon ground nutmeg

*Mustard sauce:*
2 tablespoons butter or margarine
1 green onion, thinly sliced
2 tablespoons all-purpose flour
2 to 3 teaspoons Dijon-style mustard
1 cup chicken stock

1. In a food processor fitted with a steel blade, process chicken until coarsely chopped. Add 1 cup breadcrumbs, 1/4 cup butter or margarine, cream, salt, pepper and nutmeg; process until chicken is finely minced, stopping machine to scrape down sides. Chill chicken mixture at least 30 minutes.
2. Shape into 6 (1/2-inch-thick) patties. Dip patties into remaining 1 cup breadcrumbs, pressing to coat well.
3. Melt remaining 1/4 cup butter or margarine in a large skillet. Sauté patties 5 minutes on each side or until lightly browned and crisp.
4. To make mustard sauce, melt butter or margarine in a medium saucepan. Add onion; sauté until tender. Stir flour and mustard into saucepan; stir until blended. Gradually add stock, stirring constantly; cook until mixture is thickened and smooth.
5. Arrange chicken patties on a platter. Top with mustard sauce. Makes 4 to 6 servings.

# Beef & Game Casserole

1 to 2 Cornish hens, quartered
12 oz. beef stew cubes
Salt
Freshly ground pepper
2 tablespoons butter or margarine
1 tablespoon vegetable oil
8 oz. small white onions
1 tablespoon all-purpose flour
1-1/2 cups beef stock
1/2 cup red wine
4 oz. button mushrooms, trimmed, halved
1 bay leaf
2 to 3 tomatoes, peeled, quartered, if desired

*Caraway balls:*
2 cups fresh breadcrumbs
2 tablespoons vegetable oil
1/4 to 1/2 teaspoon caraway seeds
2 tablespoons lightly beaten egg
Vegetable oil for frying

1. Preheat oven to 350F (175C).
2. Season hens and beef cubes with salt and pepper.
3. Heat butter or margarine and oil in a large skillet over medium heat. Add hens; sauté until browned. Transfer to a 3-quart casserole or Dutch oven. Add beef cubes; sauté until browned. With a slotted spoon, transfer browned cubes to casserole with hens.
4. Add onions to fat remaining in skillet; sauté until soft. Stir in flour; cook 1 minute.
5. Gradually stir in stock and wine; bring to a boil. Add mushrooms, bay leaf and tomatoes, if desired. Pour hot mixture over beef and hens.
6. Cover casserole tightly with foil or lid. Bake in preheated oven 1-3/4 hours or until beef and hens are tender.
7. To make caraway balls, combine breadcrumbs, 2 tablespoons oil, caraway seeds, salt and pepper in a medium bowl. Stir in beaten egg. Shape mixture into 4 balls. Heat oil in a medium skillet; add caraway balls. Sauté 5 minutes or until golden brown.
8. Discard bay leaf from casserole; serve topped with caraway balls. Makes 4 servings.

# Glazed Roast

1 (4-lb.) pork-shoulder blade or venison roast, boneless
Salt
Freshly ground pepper

*Glaze:*
5 to 6 tablespoons dry sherry
3 tablespoons red-currant jelly
2 teaspoons lemon juice

*To garnish:*
Cooked artichokes
Watercress

1. Preheat oven to 325F (165C).
2. Season roast with salt and pepper; place in a roasting pan.
3. Roast in preheated oven 2-1/2 to 3 hours or until roast reaches an internal temperature of 170F (75C).
4. To make glaze, combine sherry, jelly and lemon juice in a small saucepan; place over low heat until jelly melts. Brush over roast 3 to 4 times during baking.
5. To serve, place roast on a warmed serving plate; remove string. Let roast stand 10 to 15 minutes before carving; garnish with artichokes and watercress. Makes 6 to 8 servings.

The term *game* refers to all wild animals used for food. This includes wild birds, small game, such as squirrels and rabbits, and large game, such as deer, elk and moose. Meat from deer is called venison. Game is not widely available unless friends or family members are hunters.

In general, game tends to have less fat than domestic animals. Marinating, basting with drippings or larding with bacon or pork fat are several ways of making game more moist and juicy. *Larding* is the insertion of long, thin strips of fat into meat with a special device called a *larding needle*.

Much of the gamey flavor of venison comes from the fat. If desired, remove most of the venison fat; substitute beef fat, pork fat or bacon.

Game birds have dark meat. Older game birds need long, slow braising. They are excellent in stews and casseroles. Young birds require shorter cooking times.

Left to right: Beef & Game Casserole, Glazed Roast

# Marinated Chicken

**1 (2-1/2- to 3-lb.) broiler-fryer chicken, quartered**

*Marinade:*
**1 onion, sliced**
**2 tablespoons vegetable oil**
**6 peppercorns**
**1 tablespoon lemon juice**
**1/2 cup red wine**

*Casserole:*
**2 tablespoons vegetable oil**
**2 onions, chopped**
**2 celery stalks, sliced**
**2 carrots, sliced**
**1-1/2 to 2 tablespoons all-purpose flour**
**1 cup beef stock**
**1 tablespoon red-currant jelly**
**2 bay leaves**
**Salt**
**Freshly ground pepper**

*Stuffing balls:*
**2 tablespoons butter or margarine**
**1 small onion, grated**
**2 celery stalks, finely chopped**
**Grated peel of 1/2 lemon**
**Pinch of grated nutmeg**
**2 cups fresh breadcrumbs**
**1 tablespoon chopped fresh parsley**
**1 egg yolk**

*To garnish:*
**Grilled bacon rolls**
**Parsley**

*The marinade will give chicken a mild game-bird flavor that is a delightful change from the usual baked chicken.*

**1.** Place chicken pieces in a glass or ceramic bowl; add marinade ingredients. Cover and refrigerate 3 hours.
**2.** Preheat oven to 325F (165C). Drain chicken; pat dry with paper towels. Strain marinade; discard onion and peppercorns. Heat oil in a large skillet over medium heat. Add chicken; sauté until brown. With tongs, transfer browned chicken to a large casserole or Dutch oven.
**3.** Add vegetables to fat remaining in skillet; sauté gently until golden brown, stirring occasionally. Sprinkle vegetables with flour; cook 1 minute, stirring constantly. Gradually stir in strained marinade, stock, jelly, bay leaves, salt and pepper. Pour mixture over chicken.
**4.** Cover casserole tightly with foil or lid. Bake in preheated oven 1-1/2 hours or until chicken is tender.
**5.** To make stuffing balls, grease an 8-inch-square baking pan; set aside. Heat butter or margarine in a large skillet. Add onion and celery; sauté gently until soft. Stir in remaining ingredients. Shape mixture into balls. Place in greased pan; bake 30 minutes. Bake stuffing during chicken's final 30 minutes of baking.
**6.** Remove bay leaves and any fat from surface of casserole. Spoon into a serving dish; top with baked stuffing balls. Garnish with bacon rolls and parsley. Makes 4 to 6 servings.

Marinated Chicken

# Duck with Red Cabbage

1 (5- to 6-lb.) duck, thawed, if frozen
Salt
Freshly ground pepper
8 oz. Italian sausages, halved

*Cabbage:*
2 tablespoons butter or margarine
2 onions, sliced
Bouquet garni
1/2 cup red wine
1/2 cup beef stock
2 tablespoons vinegar
1 head red cabbage, finely shredded
Salt
Freshly ground pepper

*To garnish:*
Parsley sprigs
Lemon wedges

1. Preheat oven to 350F (175C).
2. Remove giblets and neck from duck; reserve for other use. Remove excess fat from duck and discard. Prick skin all over to allow fat to escape during roasting. Place duck, breast-side up, on a rack in a shallow roasting pan. Sprinkle duck with salt and pepper.
3. Roast duck in preheated oven 1-1/2 hours. Arrange sausages around duck. Roast 30 to 40 minutes longer or until duck is done and sausages are cooked. Juices should run clear when duck is pierced between breast and thigh.
4. Prepare cabbage while duck is roasting. Melt butter or margarine in a large saucepan over medium heat. Add onions; sauté until soft.
5. Add bouquet garni, wine, stock and vinegar to saucepan; bring to a boil. Add cabbage; season with salt and pepper. Cover and cook over low heat 20 minutes or until cabbage is tender. Discard bouquet garni.
6. Cut duck into quarters. Arrange cabbage in a deep serving dish; top with duck and sausages. Garnish with parsley and lemon. Makes 4 servings.

# Duck with Plum Sauce

1 (5- to 6-lb.) duck, thawed, if frozen
Salt
Freshly ground pepper
Garlic powder
1 (1-lb.) can plums in syrup
2 teaspoons Worcestershire sauce
1 tablespoon wine vinegar

*To garnish:*
Watercress
Sautéed cherry tomatoes

1. Preheat oven to 350F (175C).
2. Remove giblets and neck from duck; reserve for other use. Remove excess fat from duck; discard. Prick skin all over to allow fat to escape during roasting. Place duck, breast-side up, in a shallow roasting pan. Sprinkle duck with salt, pepper and garlic powder.
3. Roast in preheated oven 1-1/2 hours.
4. Spoon off all fat from pan, leaving pan juices around duck.
5. Meanwhile, make plum sauce. Remove pits from plums. In a blender or a food processor fitted with a steel blade, puree plums with syrup until smooth. Blend in Worcestershire sauce, vinegar, salt and pepper.
6. Pour plum sauce over duck; bake 30 minutes longer or until duck is done. Juices should run clear when duck is pierced between breast and thigh.
7. Transfer duck to a serving dish; cover with foil to keep warm. Spoon fat off pan juices; adjust seasoning. Pour into a gravy boat or small pitcher. To serve, garnish duck with watercress and cherry tomatoes; accompany with sauce. Makes 4 servings.

# Turkey & Bean Bake

2 tablespoons butter or margarine
1 tablespoon vegetable oil
5 cups diced uncooked turkey
1 (15-oz.) can dried lima beans, drained
1 (15-oz.) can red kidney beans, drained
1 large onion, sliced
1 garlic clove, crushed
1 red bell pepper, chopped
1 tablespoon all-purpose flour
1/2 cup white wine
1 (16-oz.) can tomatoes
1/2 cup chicken stock
1 teaspoon ground ginger
1 tablespoon soy sauce
1 tablespoon Worcestershire sauce
Salt
Freshly ground black pepper

1. Preheat oven to 350F (175C).
2. Heat butter or margarine and oil in a large skillet over medium heat. Add turkey; sauté until lightly browned. With a slotted spoon, transfer browned turkey to a 3-quart casserole.
3. Add lima and kidney beans to turkey.
4. Add onion and garlic to fat remaining in skillet; sauté until onion is soft. Add red pepper; cook 2 minutes.
5. Stir in flour; cook 1 minute, stirring constantly. Stir in wine, tomatoes and stock; bring to a boil.
6. Add tomato mixture to turkey and beans. Stir in ginger, soy sauce and Worcestershire sauce. Season with salt and pepper. Cover casserole with foil or lid; bake in preheated oven 1 hour. Makes 6 servings.

# Duck with Orange Sauce

1 (5-to 6-lb.) duck, quartered
Salt
Freshly ground pepper
2 oranges
1 cup beef stock
Juice of 1/2 lemon
2 tablespoons orange marmalade
1 tablespoon cornstarch
1/4 cup port or red wine

*To garnish:*
Orange sections
Watercress

**1.** Preheat oven to 375F (190C).
**2.** Trim duck; remove excess fat. Prick skin all over with a fork to allow fat to escape during roasting. Sprinkle lightly with salt and pepper.
**3.** Place duck quarters, skin-side up, on a rack in a shallow roasting pan. Roast in preheated oven 1 hour or until duck is done. If skin is not crispy, place duck under broiler a few minutes.
**4.** With a vegetable peeler, remove peel from oranges. Cut peel into julienne strips. Or, coarsely grate peel from oranges. Juice both oranges. Set peel and juice aside.
**5.** Remove roasted duck to a warmed serving platter; cover with foil to keep warm. Remove fat from pan drippings. Deglaze roasting pan with stock. Stir orange juice and peel, lemon juice and marmalade into roasting pan.
**6.** Bring sauce to a boil; simmer until marmalade has melted. In a small bowl, combine cornstarch and port or wine. Stir cornstarch mixture into hot sauce. Cook until sauce is thickened, stirring constantly.
**7.** Spoon some sauce over duck; garnish with orange sections and watercress. Serve remaining sauce separately. Makes 4 servings.

Clockwise from top: Duck with Plum Sauce, Duck with Orange Sauce, Duck with Red Cabbage

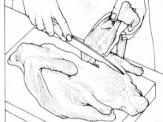

1/Cut in half, breast-side up.

2/Remove backbone.

3/Cut each half in two.

Clockwise from top left: Italian-Style Turkey, Turkey Fricassee, Chicken Véronique

# Italian-Style Turkey

**4 thick turkey-breast fillets**
**Salt**
**Freshly ground pepper**
**Garlic powder**
**2 tablespoons butter or margarine**
**1 (16-oz.) can tomatoes**
**1 tablespoon tomato paste**
**1/4 cup vermouth**
**2 teaspoons lemon juice**
**2 bay leaves**

*To garnish:*
**Parsley sprigs**
**Lemon slices**

**1.** Sprinkle turkey fillets with salt, pepper and garlic powder.
**2.** Melt butter or margarine in a large heavy saucepan over medium heat. Add fillets; sauté until lightly browned. Remove browned fillets; set aside.
**3.** In a blender or food processor fitted with a steel blade, puree canned tomatoes. Pour pureed tomatoes and tomato paste into saucepan; cook until tomatoes are reduced by almost half.
**4.** Add vermouth and lemon juice; bring mixture to a boil. Season with salt, pepper and garlic powder. Return fillets to saucepan; add bay leaves.
**5.** Cover and simmer over low heat 20 to 30 minutes or until turkey is tender.
**6.** To serve, discard bay leaves. Place turkey fillets on a deep serving platter; spoon sauce over fillets. Garnish with parsley and lemon slices. Serve with hot cooked rice or pasta. Makes 4 servings.

# Turkey Fricassee

5 cups diced uncooked turkey breast
2 onions, chopped
3 carrots, sliced
1 bay leaf
2 cups chicken stock
Salt
Freshly ground pepper
1/4 cup butter or margarine
4 oz. button mushrooms, sliced
1/3 cup all-purpose flour
1 egg yolk
3 tablespoons whipping cream
Juice of 1/2 small lemon

*To garnish:*
Grilled bacon rolls, page 118
Watercress

1. Place turkey, onions, carrots, bay leaf and stock in a large saucepan over medium heat.
2. Season turkey mixture with salt and pepper. Bring to a boil. Cover and simmer 15 minutes or until turkey and vegetables are done.
3. Strain cooking liquid from turkey; reserve. Discard vegetables and bay leaf. Keep turkey warm.
4. Melt butter or margarine in a medium saucepan. Add mushrooms; sauté 1 minute. Stir in flour; cook 1 minute, stirring constantly. Gradually stir in reserved cooking liquid; bring to a boil. Cook until thickened, stirring frequently.
5. In a small bowl, blend egg yolk with cream. Stir in a little of sauce; stir egg-yolk mixture into hot sauce. Reheat sauce, but do not boil. Adjust seasoning; stir in lemon juice.
6. Pour sauce over turkey; stir well. Garnish with bacon rolls and watercress.

**Variation:**
This recipe can be made equally well with veal or pork. Use veal cubes or lean pork cubes. Cook as above, increasing cooking time to 30 minutes or until meat is tender. Replace 1/2 cup stock with white wine, if desired. Tarragon or thyme may be added to the sauce for flavor.

# Chicken Véronique

4 chicken breasts
Salt
Freshly ground pepper
2 tablespoons butter or margarine
1 tablespoon vegetable oil
3 tablespoons all-purpose flour
1/2 cup white wine
1/2 cup chicken stock
Grated peel of 1/2 lemon
1 tablespoon lemon juice
1 bay leaf
1/2 cup whipping cream
1 egg yolk
4 oz. green grapes, halved, seeded

*To garnish:*
Green grapes or kiwifruit slices
Watercress

1. Preheat oven to 350F (175C).
2. Sprinkle chicken lightly with salt and pepper.
3. Heat butter or margarine and oil in a large skillet. Add chicken; sauté until lightly browned. With tongs, transfer browned chicken to a shallow casserole.
4. Stir flour into fat remaining in skillet; cook 2 minutes, stirring constantly. Stir in wine and stock; bring to a boil. Stir in lemon peel and juice. Season sauce with salt and pepper; pour over chicken. Add bay leaf.
5. Cover casserole with foil or lid. Bake in preheated oven 30 minutes. Place chicken breasts in a warmed serving dish.
6. In a medium saucepan, blend cream with egg yolk; gradually stir in sauce from casserole and grapes. Simmer over low heat 3 to 4 minutes, but do not boil.
7. Discard bay leaf; spoon sauce over chicken. Garnish with grapes or kiwifruit slices and watercress. Makes 4 servings.

# Lemon Chicken with Walnuts

1 (2-1/2- to 3-lb.) broiler-fryer chicken, quartered
Salt
Freshly ground pepper
3 tablespoons butter or margarine
2 tablespoons chopped green onion
1 tablespoon all-purpose flour
1 teaspoon ground ginger
1-1/2 cups beef stock
1 tablespoon molasses
Grated peel of 1 lemon
2 tablespoons lemon juice
1/2 cup chopped walnuts

*To garnish:*
Julienned lemon peel
Walnut halves
Parsley sprigs

1. Preheat oven to 350F (175C).
2. Season chicken with salt and pepper. Melt butter or margarine in a large skillet over medium heat. Add chicken; sauté until browned. With tongs, transfer browned chicken to a large casserole.
3. Add onion to fat remaining in skillet; sauté until soft. Stir in flour and ginger; cook 1 minute, stirring constantly. Gradually stir in stock; boil 1 minute.
4. Stir in molasses, lemon peel, lemon juice and chopped walnuts. Pour sauce over chicken; cover casserole with foil or lid.
5. Bake in preheated oven 1 hour or until chicken is done. Spoon any fat from surface of sauce.
6. Garnish with lemon peel, walnut halves and parsley. Makes 4 servings.

# Sausage-Stuffed Chicken Rolls

4 boneless chicken breasts
Salt
Freshly ground pepper
6 to 8 oz. smoked pork sausage
2 tablespoons butter or margarine
1 tablespoon oil
1 onion, sliced
3 tablespoons all-purpose flour
1 cup chicken stock
1/4 cup medium-dry sherry
4 oz. button mushrooms, thickly sliced
12 pimento-stuffed green olives, halved

*To garnish:*
Parsley sprigs

1. Preheat oven to 350F (175C). Remove skin from chicken; pound chicken lightly between 2 sheets of plastic wrap or waxed paper. Season with salt and pepper.
2. Trim ends from pork sausage; cut 4 (3-inch) pieces. Slice remainder of sausage; reserve for garnish. Place a 3-inch piece of sausage on each chicken breast; roll to enclose sausages. Secure with wooden picks.
3. Heat butter or margarine and oil in a large skillet over medium heat. Add chicken rolls; sauté until browned. With tongs, transfer chicken to a shallow casserole.
4. Add onion to fat remaining in skillet; sauté until lightly browned. Stir in flour; cook 1 minute, stirring frequently. Gradually stir in stock and sherry; bring to a boil. Add mushrooms and olives; season with salt and pepper. Pour sauce over chicken.
5. Cover casserole with foil or lid; bake 35 to 40 minutes or until chicken is tender. Garnish with reserved sausage and parsley. Makes 4 servings.

Left to right: Sausage-Stuffed Chicken Rolls, Turkey with Pâté Stuffing

# Turkey with Pâté Stuffing

1 (8- to 10-lb.) turkey

*Stuffing:*
2 tablespoons butter or margarine
1 onion, finely chopped
3 celery stalks, finely chopped
1 garlic clove, crushed, if desired
2 cups fresh breadcrumbs
4 oz. smooth liver pâté
1 teaspoon ground coriander
1 teaspoon Italian seasoning
Salt
Freshly ground pepper

*Sauce:*
1/2 cup red wine
8 oz. button mushrooms, chopped

*Buerre manié:*
2 tablespoons butter or margarine
3 tablespoons all-purpose flour

*To garnish:*
Homemade potato chips
Watercress

**1.** Debone turkey using illustrations below; do not remove leg and wing bones. Removal of bones makes turkey easier to carve. If desired, turkey can be stuffed without deboning.
**2.** To make stuffing, melt 2 tablespoons butter or margarine in a medium skillet over medium heat. Add onion, celery and garlic, if desired; sauté 2 to 3 minutes. Put sautéed vegetables into a large bowl; stir in remaining stuffing ingredients.
**3.** Place deboned turkey breast-side down; spread stuffing inside turkey; close back of turkey over stuffing. Fasten opening with small skewers or sew together with string.
**4.** Turn turkey over and reshape. Truss loosely. Place stuffed turkey on a roasting rack in a large roasting pan.
**5.** Roast in preheated oven 3-1/2 to 4 hours or until a thermometer inserted in inner thigh area reaches 180F (85C). Baste occasionally with pan drippings while roasting.
**6.** Remove turkey from roasting pan. Cover with foil to keep warm; set aside. Degrease pan drippings; add wine and mushrooms to roasting pan. Bring to a boil. In a small bowl, cream butter or margarine and flour together to make buerre manié, then whisk into sauce a little at a time. Boil 3 to 4 minutes, stirring frequently.
**7.** Place turkey on a serving platter; garnish with potato chips and watercress. Serve sauce separately in a gravy boat or small pitcher. Makes 8 servings.

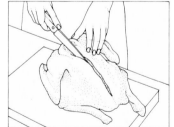

1/Remove tail. Cut along backbone with sharp knife.

2/Cut flesh and skin from ribs and first wing joint. Remove wing bone.

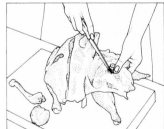

3/Remove flesh and skin from back to thigh.

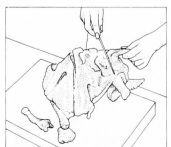

4/Remove flesh from thigh bone. Cut through joint; remove bone.

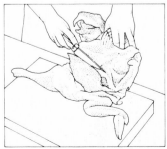

5/Carefully scrape flesh from one side of breast bone.

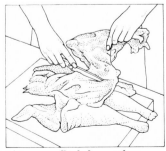

6/Remove flesh from other side of breast bone. Remove carcass.

# Duck with Cumberland Sauce

1 (5- to 6-lb.) duck, thawed, if frozen
Salt
Freshly ground pepper
Peel of 1 orange and 1 lemon
Juice of 2 oranges
Juice of 1/2 to 1 lemon
1/4 cup port
3 tablespoons red-currant jelly
2 tablespoons cornstarch
Water

*To garnish:*
Orange slices
Watercress

1. Preheat oven to 350F (175C).
2. Remove giblets and neck from duck; reserve for other use. Remove excess fat from duck and discard. Prick skin all over to allow fat to escape during roasting. Place duck, breast-side up, on a rack in a shallow roasting pan. Sprinkle duck with salt and pepper.
3. Roast duck in preheated oven 1 hour.
4. Meanwhile, cut fruit peels into julienne strips. Cook in boiling water 5 minutes; drain.
5. In a medium saucepan, heat fruit juices, port and jelly until jelly melts. Add two-thirds of cooked peel. Season with salt and pepper.
6. Spoon off fat from roasting pan, leaving pan juices. Baste duck with orange mixture. Roast duck 1 to 1-1/2 hours longer or until duck is done; baste occasionally with orange mixture. Juices should run clear when duck is pierced between breast and thigh.
7. Place roasted duck on a serving platter; cover with foil to keep warm. Strain pan juices into a saucepan. In a small bowl, combine cornstarch with a little water; stir cornstarch mixture into pan juices. Cook over medium heat until mixture boils and thickens. Serve sauce in a gravy boat or small pitcher.
8. Sprinkle duck with reserved peel; garnish with orange slices and watercress. Makes 4 servings.

---

The easiest way to remove peel from citrus without white pith is with a vegetable peeler; use as if peeling a potato. If a vegetable peeler is not available, use a small sharp knife to remove peel. Place on a flat surface, peel-side down, and cut off all white pith. Julienne strips are very narrow strips which can be easily cut with a large sharp knife.

# Stuffed Turkey Rolls

*Stuffing:*
1/4 cup butter or margarine
1/2 onion, finely chopped
1 celery stalk, finely chopped
1 cup fresh breadcrumbs
Grated peel of 1/2 orange
8 pimento-stuffed green olives, chopped

*Turkey Rolls:*
4 uncooked turkey-breast fillets
Salt
Freshly ground pepper
2 tablespoons butter or margarine
1 onion, thinly sliced
1 garlic clove, crushed
About 1/2 cup chicken stock
Juice of 1 orange
2 teaspoons all-purpose flour
Grated peel of 1/2 orange
1 (10-oz.) can cream-style corn

*To garnish:*
Orange slices
Pimento-stuffed green olives
Watercress

1. Preheat oven to 350F (175C).
2. For stuffing, melt butter or margarine in a heavy medium saucepan over medium heat. Add onion and celery; sauté until soft. Remove from heat; stir in breadcrumbs, orange peel, olives, salt and pepper.
3. Pound turkey fillets between 2 sheets of plastic wrap or waxed paper until 1/4 inch thick. Sprinkle lightly with salt and pepper.
4. Divide stuffing among beaten fillets; roll to enclose stuffing. Secure with wooden picks.
5. Melt butter or margarine in a large skillet over medium heat. Add turkey rolls; sauté until golden brown. With tongs, transfer browned rolls to a shallow casserole.
6. Add onion and garlic to fat remaining in skillet; sauté until golden brown.
7. Add enough stock to orange juice to make 1 cup.
8. Stir flour into onion mixture; cook 1 minute, stirring constantly. Gradually stir in juice and stock; bring to a boil. Stir in remaining orange peel and corn; bring back to a boil. Season sauce with salt and pepper; pour over turkey.
9. Cover casserole with foil or lid; bake in preheated oven 30 minutes.
10. Garnish with orange slices, olives and watercress. Makes 4 servings.

Top to bottom: Duck with Cumberland Sauce, Stuffed Turkey Rolls

Clockwise from top: Duck with Olives, Venison with Juniper Berries, Chicken Breasts with Apples

# Chicken Breasts with Apples

4 boneless chicken breasts
Salt
Freshly ground pepper
2 tablespoons butter or margarine
1 tablespoon vegetable oil
1 onion, chopped
1 tablespoon all-purpose flour
1 cup chicken stock
3 Golden Delicious apples, peeled, sliced

*To garnish:*
4 crisp-cooked bacon slices, crumbled

---

*For those who prefer dark meat, substitute 8 chicken thighs.*

1. Preheat oven to 350F (175C).
2. Season chicken with salt and pepper. Heat butter or margarine and oil in a large skillet over medium heat. Add chicken; sauté until browned. With tongs, transfer to a shallow casserole.
3. Add onion to fat remaining in skillet; sauté until lightly colored.
4. Stir flour into skillet; cook 1 minute, stirring constantly. Stir in stock; bring to a boil.
5. Add apples; season with salt and pepper. Pour sauce over chicken.
6. Cover casserole with foil or lid. Bake in preheated oven 35 minutes or until chicken is tender. Garnish with crumbled bacon. Makes 4 servings.

# Duck with Olives

2 duck breasts, halved
Salt
Freshly ground pepper
1 tablespoon vegetable oil
1 onion, thinly sliced
1 tablespoon all-purpose flour
1/2 cup chicken stock
6 tablespoons medium-dry sherry
2 tablespoons lemon juice
Grated peel of 1/2 lemon
12 to 16 pimento-stuffed green olives, halved

*To garnish:*
Lemon slices or wedges
Parsley sprigs, if desired

1. Preheat oven to 350F (175C).
2. Remove any excess fat from duck. Prick skin all over to allow fat to escape during cooking. Sprinkle duck with salt and pepper.
3. Heat oil in a large skillet over medium heat. Add duck; sauté until well browned. Transfer browned duck to a large casserole.
4. Discard all but 1 tablespoon fat from skillet. Add onion; sauté until soft. Stir in flour; cook 1 minute, stirring constantly.
5. Gradually stir in stock, sherry and lemon juice; boil 2 minutes. Add lemon peel and olives. Season sauce with salt and pepper; pour over duck.
6. Cover casserole with foil or lid; bake in preheated oven 40 to 50 minutes or until duck is tender, basting once during cooking.
7. Spoon excess fat from surface of casserole; garnish with lemon and parsley, if desired. Makes 4 servings.

## Variation
A whole duck can also be used if it is first cut into quarters. Use poultry shears, sharp kitchen scissors or a sharp knife to quarter duck.

# Venison with Juniper Berries

4 (6-oz.) venison steaks
Salt
Freshly ground pepper
2 tablespoons butter or margarine
Juice and grated peel of 1/2 lemon
12 juniper berries, crushed
1 cup beef stock
1 tablespoon wine vinegar
3 tablespoons whipping cream
1-1/2 teaspoons cornstarch

*To garnish:*
Carrot and celery sticks
Watercress, if desired

1. Preheat oven to 400F (205C).
2. Sprinkle venison with salt and pepper.
3. Melt butter or margarine in a large skillet. Add venison; sauté until browned. Transfer to a large shallow casserole.
4. Add lemon juice and peel, juniper berries, stock and vinegar to skillet. Boil rapidly 2 to 3 minutes, scraping any browned bits from skillet into sauce. Season with salt and pepper.
5. Pour sauce over venison; cover casserole with foil or lid. Bake in preheated oven 40 minutes or until venison is tender.
6. Drain sauce into a medium saucepan. Keep venison covered and warm. In a small bowl, blend cream with cornstarch; stir some sauce into cornstarch mixture. Stir mixture into pan; simmer 2 to 3 minutes.
7. Arrange venison in a deep serving dish; add sauce. Garnish with carrot and celery sticks and watercress, if desired.

## Variation
Substitute 4 (1-inch-thick) pieces of beef-round steak for venison.

# Country Roast Chicken

1 (4-lb.) roasting chicken
Salt
Freshly ground black pepper
2 onions, thickly sliced
1 garlic clove, crushed
1 red bell pepper, sliced
1 (16-oz.) can tomatoes
1/2 cup white wine or chicken stock
1 bay leaf
3 oz. sliced salami

*To garnish:*
Parsley sprigs

---

**1.** Preheat oven to 350F (175C).
**2.** Remove giblets and neck. Chop liver; reserve remaining giblets for other use. Season chicken with salt and pepper.
**3.** Place chicken in a large heavy casserole. Arrange onions, garlic, red pepper, chopped liver, tomatoes and wine or stock around chicken. Add bay leaf.
**4.** Chop 2 ounces of salami; reserve remainder for garnish. Add chopped salami to chicken. Cover casserole tightly with lid or foil.
**5.** Bake in preheated oven 1-1/2 hours or until chicken is tender.
**6.** Discard bay leaf; garnish with reserved salami and parsley. Makes 4 to 6 servings.

## Variation

Baked chicken with salami, peppers, tomatoes and garlic is a dish from the French countryside. Once it is prepared and in the oven, it can be forgotten until ready to serve. It goes well with boiled or creamed potatoes or cooked rice and a green vegetable or salad. Any leftover chicken can be served cold; the flavor is superb. To serve more people, a larger chicken or small turkey, 7 to 8 pounds, can be used; simply increase cooking time to 2-1/2 hours or until chicken or turkey is tender. If you do not have a large enough casserole, use a roasting pan covered tightly with foil. If desired, salami can be omitted or substitute crumbled crisp-cooked bacon.

# Cornish Hens with Cherries

2 Cornish hens, thawed, if frozen
Salt
Freshly ground pepper
2 tablespoons vegetable oil
6 oz. small white onions
2 tablespoons all-purpose flour
1 (16-oz.) can dark sweet cherries
About 1/2 cup beef stock
2 tablespoons wine vinegar
2 tablespoons brandy
1 teaspoon dried leaf thyme

*Fleurons:*
4 oz. puff pastry or 2 to 3 frozen patty shells, thawed
Milk or beaten egg

---

**1.** Halve Cornish hens; remove backbone, using a pair of poultry shears, kitchen scissors or a sharp knife. Sprinkle with salt and pepper.
**2.** Heat oil in a large skillet over medium heat. Add hen halves; sauté until browned. With tongs, transfer to a large casserole.
**3.** Add onions to fat remaining in skillet; sauté until lightly browned. Stir in flour; cook 1 minute, stirring constantly.
**4.** Drain juice from cherries; reserve juice. Add enough stock to cherry juice to make 1-1/2 cups. Gradually stir stock mixture into flour; bring to a boil. Add cherries. Season with salt and pepper.
**5.** Add vinegar, brandy and thyme to sauce; pour over hens. Cover casserole with foil or lid.
**6.** Bake in preheated oven 1 hour or until hens are tender.
**7.** To make pastry fleurons, preheat oven to 400F (205C). If baking at same time as Cornish hens, remove casserole when hens are done; increase oven heat to 400F (205C). Roll out puff pastry or patty shells on a lightly floured surface to 1/4 inch thick. Using a fluted pastry cutter, cut into 2-1/2-inch crescents. Place crescents on a ungreased baking sheet; brush with milk or beaten egg. Bake in preheated oven 10 to 15 minutes or until golden brown. Crescents can be made ahead; reheat when needed.
**8.** Garnish with baked fleurons. Makes 4 servings.

# Island Chicken

1 (2-1/2- to 3-lb.) broiler-fryer chicken, quartered
Salt
Freshly ground pepper
2 tablespoons butter or margarine
1 tablespoon vegetable oil
1 onion, sliced
1 garlic clove, crushed
2 celery stalks, sliced
2 tablespoons all-purpose flour
1 cup chicken stock
1/2 cup pineapple juice
Few strands of saffron or 1/4 teaspoon turmeric
1/2 teaspoon ground coriander
1/4 cup shredded coconut

*To garnish:*
Toasted shredded coconut
Parsley sprigs

1. Preheat oven to 350F (175C).
2. Season chicken with salt and pepper. Heat butter or margarine and oil in a large skillet over medium heat. Add chicken; sauté until well browned. With tongs, transfer browned chicken to a casserole.
3. Add onion, garlic and celery to fat remaining in skillet; sauté until soft. Stir in flour; cook 1 minute, stirring constantly.
4. Stir in stock and pineapple juice; bring to a boil. Stir in saffron or turmeric, coriander and coconut. Season sauce with salt and pepper; pour over chicken.
5. Cover casserole with foil or lid; bake in preheated oven 1 hour or until chicken is tender.
6. Spoon any excess fat from surface of casserole; garnish with toasted coconut and parsley. Makes 4 servings.

**Variation**
If fresh coconut is available, replace shredded coconut with 2 ounces freshly grated coconut. If desired, 1/2 cup coconut milk can replace 1/2 cup stock.

Clockwise from left: Country Roast Chicken, Cornish Hens with Cherries, Island Chicken

# Festive Pheasant with Chestnuts

2 (2- to 3-lb.) pheasants, cut up
Salt
Freshly ground pepper
2 tablespoons butter or margarine
1 tablespoon vegetable oil
8 to 12 oz. chestnuts, roasted or boiled, peeled
1 bay leaf
8 oz. small white onions
2 tablespoons all-purpose flour
1 cup dry white wine
1/2 cup chicken stock
1 tablespoon red-currant jelly
Julienned peel of 1 orange
Juice of 2 oranges
2 tablespoons brandy, if desired

*To garnish:*
**Orange slices**
**Watercress**

1. Preheat oven to 350F (175C).
2. Sprinkle pheasants with salt and pepper. Heat butter or margarine and oil in a large skillet over medium heat. Add pheasant pieces; sauté until browned. With tongs, transfer browned pheasant to a large casserole. Arrange chestnuts around pheasant. Add bay leaf.

3. Add onions to fat remaining in skillet; sauté until lightly colored. Use a slotted spoon to place sautéed onions over pheasants and chestnuts.
4. Stir flour into fat remaining in skillet; cook 1 minute, stirring constantly. Gradually stir in wine and stock; bring to a boil. Stir in jelly, orange peel and juice and brandy, if desired. Season with salt and pepper; pour sauce over pheasants.
5. Cover casserole tightly with foil or lid; bake in preheated oven 50 to 60 minutes or until pheasants are tender.
6. Discard bay leaf; serve pheasant pieces on a platter surrounded by onions and chestnuts. Spoon some sauce over pheasants; serve remaining sauce in a gravy boat or small pitcher. Garnish with orange slices and watercress. Makes 4 servings.

## Variation

Cornish hens are a good substitute if pheasants are not available. Canned chestnuts can be substituted for fresh ones; drain and rinse with cold water before using.

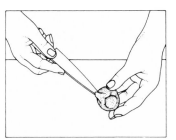

1/Pierce each chestnut; boil 25 minutes.

2/Use a sharp knife to peel.

Festive Pheasant with Chestnuts

# Cornish Hens Véronique

4 Cornish hens, thawed, if frozen
Salt
Freshly ground pepper
4 bacon slices
1 cup beef stock
2 tablespoons brandy
Juice of 1 orange
2 tablespoons medium-dry sherry
1 tablespoon cornstarch
4 to 6 oz. green grapes, halved, seeded

*To garnish:*
Orange slices, cut in half
Green grapes

**1.** Preheat oven to 350F (175C).
**2.** Sprinkle hens with salt and pepper. Place seasoned hens in a roasting pan. Cut bacon slices in half; lay 2 halves across each hen.
**3.** Roast in preheated oven 1-1/2 hours or until hens are tender.
**4.** Place roasted Cornish hens on a serving platter; cover with foil to keep warm.
**5.** Remove fat from pan drippings; deglaze pan with stock. Add brandy and orange juice. In a small bowl, combine sherry and cornstarch. Stir cornstarch mixture into pan. Bring to a boil, stirring constantly; add halved grapes. Simmer sauce 3 to 4 minutes; spoon over Cornish hens.
**6.** Garnish with orange slices and grapes. Makes 6 to 8 servings.

Cornish Hens Véronique

# Shrimp Veracruz-Style

1 lb. uncooked medium shrimp
1 large green pepper
3 tablespoons vegetable oil
1 small onion, chopped
5 small tomatoes, peeled, chopped (1-1/4 lbs.)
12 pimento-stuffed green olives
1-1/2 teaspoons capers
1 bay leaf
1/2 teaspoon sugar
1/2 teaspoon salt
Lime juice

---

**1.** Peel shrimp; devein. Set shrimp aside.
**2.** Cut green pepper into 1-1/2" x 1/2" strips. Heat 1 tablespoon oil in a large saucepan over medium heat. Add onion and pepper strips. Cook until onion is tender but not browned.
**3.** Add tomatoes, olives, capers, bay leaf, sugar and salt. Bring to a boil; reduce heat. Cover; simmer 20 minutes. Remove bay leaf from tomato sauce.
**4.** Heat remaining oil in a large skillet over medium heat. Add peeled shrimp. Cook about 3 minutes or until shrimp turn pink. Sprinkle a few drops of lime juice over shrimp.
**5.** Add cooked tomato sauce to shrimp. Cook 3 to 4 minutes, stirring constantly.
**6.** Serve hot shrimp mixture immediately. Makes 4 servings.

# Squid Provençal

3 lbs. fresh squid
2 tablespoons olive oil
2 onions, sliced
1 garlic clove, crushed
2 tablespoons all-purpose flour
1 tablespoon tomato paste
1 cup dry white wine or vermouth
1/2 cup chicken stock
1 tablespoon lemon juice
3 small tomatoes, peeled, sliced
Salt
Freshly ground black pepper
1/2 teaspoon paprika
Pinch of red (cayenne) pepper
Pinch of sugar
1 bay leaf

*To garnish:*
**Chopped fresh parsley**

---

**1.** Preheat oven to 325F (165C).
**2.** To prepare squid, pull gently to separate head from body and tentacles. Pull transparent pen from body. Remove speckled membrane, if desired. Wash cleaned squid; cut into rings. Remove beak from base of tentacles; cut tentacles into pieces. Discard head and ink sac.
**3.** Heat oil in a flameproof casserole. Add onions and garlic; sauté until lightly browned. Add squid; sauté until lightly colored.
**4.** Stir in flour; cook 2 minutes, stirring constantly. Stir in tomato paste, wine or vermouth, stock and lemon juice. Bring to a boil; add tomatoes, salt, black pepper, paprika, red pepper and sugar to taste. Add bay leaf; cover casserole with foil or lid.
**5.** Bake in preheated oven 45 minutes or until squid is tender. Discard bay leaf. Garnish with parsley. Makes 4 servings.

 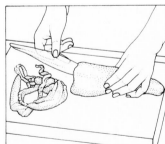

1/Pull head from body.     2/Remove pen and discard.

# Halibut Catalan

4 halibut fillets or steaks
6 tablespoons olive oil
Juice of 1 lemon
1 small onion, finely chopped
1 garlic clove, crushed
1 tablespoon all-purpose flour
8 oz. tomatoes, peeled, seeded, chopped
1 tablespoon tomato paste
1 cup dry white wine
Salt
Freshly ground pepper

*To garnish:*
1/2 cup finely chopped nuts
2 tablespoons chopped fresh parsley

*Around the Mediterranean, people love to cook white fish in thick sauces, highly flavored with tomatoes, onion and garlic. Halibut lends itself well to this flavor combination.*

**1.** Place fish in a large glass bowl or pan. Combine 1/4 cup oil and lemon juice; pour over fish. Cover and refrigerate 1 to 2 hours, turning occasionally.
**2.** Preheat oven to 350F (175C).
**3.** Heat remaining 2 tablespoons oil in a deep flameproof casserole. Add onion and garlic; sauté until golden brown. Stir flour into onions and garlic; cook 2 minutes, stirring constantly. Stir in tomatoes, tomato paste and wine. Slowly bring to a boil. Season with salt and pepper.
**4.** Add marinated fish to sauce; turn to coat.
**5.** Cover casserole with foil or lid; bake in preheated oven 10 to 15 minutes or until fish tests done.
**6.** Garnish casserole with nuts and parsley. Makes 4 servings.

Halibut Catalan

# Baked Haddock with Wine Sauce

1-1/2 lbs. haddock fillets, skinned
Salt
Freshly ground pepper
3 tomatoes, peeled, quartered, seeded
6 oz. mushrooms or apples, sliced
2 tablespoons butter or margarine
2 tablespoons all-purpose flour
1 cup white wine or apple juice
1 tablespoon chopped fresh chives or 1 teaspoon dried
  chives
1/4 teaspoon grated lemon peel
1 tablespoon lemon juice

1. Preheat oven to 350F (175C). Grease a shallow casserole; set aside.
2. Cut fish into 4 equal portions, sprinkle lightly with salt and pepper. Roll fillets; place in greased casserole. Arrange tomatoes and mushrooms or apples over fish.
3. Melt butter or margarine in a small saucepan. Stir in flour; cook 1 minute, stirring constantly. Gradually stir in wine or juice; bring to a boil. Add chives, lemon peel and juice. Season with salt and pepper.
4. Pour sauce over fish; cover casserole with foil or lid.
5. Bake in preheated oven 20 minutes or until fish tests done. Place fish on a serving dish; reduce sauce, if necessary, before pouring over fish. Makes 4 servings.

# Bouillabaisse

2-1/2 lbs. mixed fish and shellfish
6 tablespoons vegetable oil
2 large onions, thinly sliced
2 celery stalks, thinly sliced
2 carrots, diced
2 garlic cloves, crushed
1 lb. tomatoes, peeled, sliced
1 bouquet garni
Grated peel of 1/2 lemon
Juice of 1 lemon
Pinch of saffron or turmeric
Salt
Freshly ground pepper
About 1 cup white wine

*To garnish:*
Few whole shrimp or crayfish
Chopped fresh parsley, if desired

*A true bouillabaisse is made from at least 8 types of fish and shellfish, but many of the authentic types are only available in Mediterranean areas. Your fish market should help with a good selection if you explain your requirements. If you prefer more liquid in your stew, add 1 to 2 cups fish stock or chicken stock with the wine.*

Clockwise from top left: Baked Haddock with Wine Sauce, Salmon & Asparagus, Scallops & Mushrooms in Cream Sauce, Bouillabaisse

1. Clean fish, removing skin and any loose bones. Rinse fish in cold water; cut into 2-inch pieces. Peel all shrimp or crayfish except those used for garnish; rinse in cold water.
2. Heat oil in a large heavy saucepan over medium heat. Add onions, celery, carrots and garlic; sauté until soft but only lightly colored.
3. Add tomatoes, bouquet garni, lemon peel and juice and saffron or turmeric to saucepan; season vegetable mixture with salt and pepper. Bring to a boil. Reduce heat; simmer 10 minutes.
4. Lay fish over vegetables; add enough wine to almost cover fish. Simmer gently 2 to 3 minutes.
5. Add shellfish to saucepan; simmer an additional 4 to 6 minutes longer or until fish and shellfish are done. Do not overcook. Discard any mussels that do not open. Discard bouquet garni; adjust seasoning, if necessary.
6. Top with whole shrimp or crayfish and parsley, if desired. Serve with crusty bread. Makes 4 servings.

When fresh scallops are unavailable, use frozen ones. Be sure they are completely thawed before using.

1. If scallops are large, cut into 2 or 3 pieces.
2. Heat butter or margarine in a large skillet over medium heat. Add onion, celery and mushrooms; sauté until soft but not colored. Add scallops to vegetable mixture; sauté 1 to 2 minutes. Use a slotted spoon to remove scallops and vegetables from skillet; place in a flameproof casserole.
3. Stir flour into fat remaining in skillet; cook 2 minutes, stirring constantly. Gradually stir in wine, stock or water and lemon juice; bring to a boil. Simmer until slightly thickened and smooth, stirring frequently. Season with hot-pepper sauce, salt and pepper. Stir whipping cream or sour cream into sauce; pour over scallops and vegetables.
4. Preheat broiler.
5. Combine breadcrumbs and cheese; sprinkle over scallop mixture. Place casserole under preheated broiler until top is crisp and brown. Serve at once, garnished with cucumber and lemon slices. Makes 4 servings.

## Salmon & Asparagus

4 (1-inch-thick) salmon steaks
Salt
Freshly ground pepper
1 (12-oz.) can asparagus spears
2 teaspoons cornstarch
6 tablespoons whipping cream
2 teaspoons lemon juice

*To garnish:*
Lemon wedges

1. Preheat oven to 375F (190C). Grease a shallow baking pan large enough to hold salmon in a single layer.
2. Place salmon in greased baking pan; sprinkle with salt and pepper.
3. Bake salmon in preheated oven 10 minutes or until fish tests done.
4. Meanwhile, make sauce. Drain asparagus, reserving 6 tablespoons of liquid. Reserve 12 asparagus spears for garnish; coarsely chop remainder. Set chopped asparagus aside.
5. In a small saucepan, blend cornstarch with cream. Stir in reserved asparagus liquid and lemon juice. Cook mixture over low heat, stirring constantly, until slightly thickened and smooth. Season with salt and pepper. Gently stir in chopped asparagus; cook until hot.
6. Arrange baked salmon on a warmed serving plate. Spoon hot sauce over salmon. Garnish with reserved asparagus spears and lemon wedges. Makes 4 servings.

## Scallops & Mushrooms in Cream Sauce

10 to 12 sea scallops
3 tablespoons butter or margarine
1 large onion, finely chopped
2 to 3 celery stalks, thinly sliced
6 oz. button mushrooms, quartered or sliced
2 tablespoons all-purpose flour
1/2 cup white wine
1/2 cup chicken stock or water
1 tablespoon lemon juice
Few drops of hot-pepper sauce
Salt
Freshly ground black pepper
3 tablespoons whipping cream or dairy sour cream

*Crumb topping:*
1 cup fresh white breadcrumbs
1/4 cup grated Cheddar cheese (1 oz.)

*To garnish:*
Cucumber slices
Lemon slices

# Sole Paupiettes with Smoked Salmon

8 (3- to 4-oz.) sole fillets
Salt
Freshly ground pepper
4 oz. smoked salmon
3 tablespoons butter or margarine
1/4 cup all-purpose flour
1/2 cup dry white wine
1 cup milk
3 tablespoons half and half
1 tablespoon lemon juice

*To garnish:*
8 whole shrimp
Fresh parsley, fennel or dill, if desired

1. Preheat oven to 400F (205C). Grease a shallow baking dish.
2. Wipe sole fillets with a damp paper towel; sprinkle with salt and pepper. Divide smoked salmon into 8 pieces; lay 1 piece on skin-side of each fillet. Roll up loosely towards tail; place rolls in greased dish.
3. Melt butter or margarine in a medium saucepan. Stir in flour; cook 1 minute, stirring constantly. Gradually stir in wine and milk; boil 2 minutes. Season with salt and pepper; stir in half and half and lemon juice. Pour sauce over fish.
4. Cover dish with foil or lid; bake in preheated oven 10 minutes or until fish tests done. Do not overcook.
5. Garnish sole paupiettes with whole shrimp and parsley, fennel or dill, if desired. Makes 4 servings.

---

Sole fillets can be used with the skins on. If you prefer to remove them, it is simple to do. Place fillet on a wooden board or work surface, skin-side down. Using a sharp knife and beginning at the tail, carefully run the knife along towards the head, keeping blade slanting downwards, working away from you. The fillet will then lift away easily from skin. If you work from head to tail, flesh will crumble, break and not come away from skin in one piece. If the fish slips, sprinkle a little coarse salt on work surface before you begin; rinse fillets before cooking to remove any salt.

---

# Sole & Shrimp with Whiskey

4 (3- to 4-oz.) sole or flounder fillets
1/2 cup water or fish stock
1/2 cup white wine
4 peppercorns
1 bay leaf
Parsley sprig
Salt

*Shrimp topping:*
3 tablespoons butter or margarine
1 small onion, halved, sliced
1 large tomato, peeled, seeded, sliced
1/2 lb. peeled, deveined small shrimp
Salt
Freshly ground white pepper
2 to 3 tablespoons whiskey

*To garnish:*
Fresh dill, if desired

---

1. Preheat oven to 350F (175C). Grease a shallow baking dish.
2. Place fillets in a single layer in greased baking dish.
3. In a small saucepan, combine water or fish stock, wine, peppercorns, bay leaf, parsley and salt. Bring to a boil; pour over fillets. Cover fillets with a sheet of buttered waxed paper.
4. Poach in preheated oven 10 minutes or until fish tests done.
5. Meanwhile, make shrimp topping. Melt butter or margarine in a large skillet over medium heat. Add onion; sauté 3 to 4 minutes. Add tomatoes and shrimp; sauté 2 to 3 minutes or until shrimp turn pink, stirring frequently. Season with salt and white pepper. Pour whiskey into skillet. Heat mixture; ignite carefully.
6. Place poached fillets on a serving plate; discard poaching liquid or reserve for other use. When flame dies, spoon shrimp mixture over fillets; garnish with dill, if desired. Makes 4 servings.

# Turbot with Champagne

1/4 cup butter or margarine
3 shallots or 1 medium onion, finely chopped
1 bunch watercress
1 cup milk
Salt
Freshly ground white pepper
4 (4- to 6-oz.) turbot or other white-fish steaks
1 bay leaf
1 cup champagne

---

1. Preheat oven to 350F (175C). Grease a baking dish large enough to hold the fish in a single layer.
2. Melt butter or margarine in a heavy medium saucepan over medium heat. Add shallots or onion; sauté until soft. Reserve a few sprigs of watercress for garnish; finely chop remaining watercress. Add chopped watercress to skillet; sauté 2 minutes, stirring constantly.
3. Add milk; simmer 15 minutes. Season with salt and white pepper; allow to cool slightly.
4. While watercress mixture is simmering, bake fish. Place fish in a single layer in greased baking dish. Add bay leaf and champagne; season with salt and pepper. Cover baking dish with foil or lid; bake in preheated oven 10 minutes or until fish tests done.
5. Place fish on a warmed serving platter. Cover with foil to keep warm. Discard bay leaf.
6. In a blender or food processor fitted with a steel blade, puree cooking liquid and watercress mixture. Pour some sauce over fish; serve remaining sauce separately. Garnish fish with reserved watercress. Makes 4 servings.

Clockwise from top left: Mussel Kabobs, Turbot with Champagne, Sole & Shrimp with Whiskey

**Variation**
Any dry white wine can be substituted for the champagne. If turbot is not available, substitute halibut or another white fish.

# Mussel Kabobs

1/2 cup butter or margarine, melted
1/4 cup white wine
1 garlic clove, crushed
3 to 4 drops hot-pepper sauce
Salt
Freshly ground white pepper
24 mussels, cleaned, shucked
1 large green pepper, cut into 1-inch squares
1 large red bell pepper, cut into 1-inch squares
About 8 oz. ready-to-eat ham, cut in 1-inch chunks

---

1. Soak bamboo skewers in water 30 minutes. Preheat grill or broiler.
2. In a small saucepan over medium heat, combine butter or margarine, wine, garlic and hot-pepper sauce. Season mixture with salt and white pepper. Heat until hot.
3. Thread mussels, green and red peppers and ham on skewers, as shown below. Baste each kabob with butter mixture.
4. Place skewers on rack 4 inches from coals or high heat. Cook 2 minutes; baste with butter sauce and turn. Cook 2 minutes longer, basting once. Reheat sauce; serve separately. Makes 4 servings.

# Rainbow Trout with Brown Butter & Almonds

4 rainbow trout, cleaned
Salt
Freshly ground pepper
1/4 cup butter or margarine
1/2 cup coarsely chopped blanched almonds
2 tablespoons lemon juice

*Stuffing balls:*
1-1/2 cups fresh breadcrumbs
2 tablespoons grated onion
Grated peel of 1/2 lemon
1/4 cup finely chopped blanched almonds
1 tablespoon chopped fresh parsley
1 egg yolk

*To garnish:*
Parsley sprigs
Lemon wedges

1. Preheat oven to 400F (205C). Lightly grease a shallow baking dish. Season fish with salt and pepper. Place fish head-to-tail in a single layer in greased baking dish.
2. Melt butter or margarine in a small skillet. Add coarsely chopped almonds; sauté until almonds and butter or margarine are lightly browned. Remove skillet from heat. Stir in lemon juice; quickly pour mixture over fish.
3. For stuffing balls, in a medium bowl, combine breadcrumbs, onion, lemon peel, finely chopped almonds and parsley. Season with salt and pepper; stir in egg yolk.
4. Shape stuffing mixture into 8 balls; arrange around fish.
5. Cover dish with foil or lid; bake in preheated oven 20 minutes or until fish tests done. Do not overcook. Serve garnished with parsley and lemon wedges. Makes 4 servings.

# Moules Marinière

4 quarts fresh mussels
1/4 cup butter or margarine
2 onions, finely chopped
2 carrots, finely chopped
1 to 2 garlic cloves, crushed
1-1/2 cups white wine or apple juice
1 tablespoon lemon juice
Salt
Freshly ground pepper
2 bay leaves
4 teaspoons cornstarch
3 tablespoons whipping cream

*To garnish:*
Chopped fresh parsley

1. Scrub mussels with a brush to remove all dirt. Discard any that are broken or do not close when given a sharp tap. Pull away beards.
2. Melt butter or margarine in a large kettle. Add onions, carrots and garlic; sauté gently until soft but not browned.
3. Add wine or apple juice and lemon juice to kettle; bring mixture to a boil. Add salt, pepper and bay leaves.
4. Add mussels to kettle; stir well. Cover kettle tightly with foil or lid. Simmer 4 to 8 minutes or until mussels open. Discard bay leaves and any mussels that do not open.
5. Ladle mussels into 4 large serving bowls.
6. In a small bowl, blend cornstarch with cream; stir cornstarch mixture into cooking liquid in kettle. Bring slowly to a boil; stir constantly until slightly thickened.
7. Spoon sauce over mussels; sprinkle mussels with parsley. Serve with fresh crusty bread. Makes 4 servings.

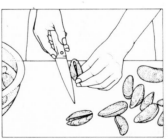 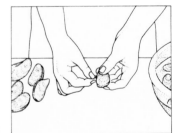

1/Check mussels by tapping to close.

2/Pull away hairy beard.

# Seafood Casserole

1-1/2 lbs. haddock or cod fillets, skinned
4 oz. peeled, deveined shrimp
3 to 4 sea scallops, quartered
1 (12-oz.) can whole-kernel corn, drained
1 to 2 canned red pimentos, sliced, if desired
3 tablespoons butter or margarine
1/4 cup all-purpose flour
1 cup milk
1 teaspoon Dijon-style mustard
1 tablespoon lemon juice
1/4 cup dairy sour cream
Salt
Freshly ground pepper

*To garnish:*
Whole shrimp

1. Preheat oven to 350F (175C).
2. Cut fish into 1-inch cubes. In a large, fairly shallow casserole, combine fish cubes, shrimp, scallops, corn and pimentos, if desired.
3. Melt butter or margarine in a medium saucepan. Stir in flour; cook 1 minute, stirring constantly. Stir in milk; bring to a boil. Remove from heat.
4. Stir mustard, lemon juice and sour cream into sauce; season with salt and pepper. Pour over fish, shellfish and corn.
5. Bake in preheated oven 20 minutes or until fish tests done.
6. Stir casserole gently before serving. Garnish with whole shrimp. Makes 6 servings

## Variation

Milk can be replaced by 1/2 cup each of apple juice or white wine and chicken stock. A quick fish stock can be made by simmering fish parts in 1 cup water, 1 sliced onion, 1 chopped carrot, 2 parsley sprigs and a bay leaf. Bring to a boil; then reduce heat and simmer gently 15 minutes. Strain and use in place of chicken stock.

Top to bottom: Moules Marinière, Rainbow Trout with Brown Butter & Almonds, Seafood Casserole

# Fish Paella

1/2 cup butter or margarine
1 tablespoon vegetable oil
1 large onion, sliced
1 to 2 garlic cloves, crushed
1 medium red bell pepper, thinly sliced
1 medium green pepper, thinly sliced
1 cup uncooked long-grain white rice
6 oz. mushrooms, thickly sliced
2 bay leaves
2 cups chicken stock or fish stock
Pinch of saffron or 1/2 teaspoon turmeric
Salt
Freshly ground black pepper
2 (4- to 5-oz.) sole fillets, cut into 1-inch pieces
4 to 6 oz. fresh, frozen or canned crabmeat, flaked
4 oz. peeled, deveined shrimp
4 to 8 crayfish
4 oz. frozen green peas, thawed
2 cups fresh mussels, cleaned, if desired

1. Preheat oven to 350F (175C). Grease a paella pan or a shallow 3-quart casserole; set aside.
2. Heat butter or margarine and oil in a medium skillet over medium heat. Add onion and garlic; sauté until soft. Add red and green peppers; cook 3 minutes. Place in greased paella pan or casserole.
3. Add rice, mushrooms and bay leaves.
4. Bring stock to a boil; add saffron or turmeric. Season with salt and pepper; pour over rice mixture.
5. Cover with foil or lid; bake in preheated oven 15 minutes.
6. Stir rice mixture; add sole, crabmeat, shrimp, crayfish, peas and mussels, if desired. Cover and bake 10 minutes longer or until mussels have opened. Discard bay leaves and any mussels that do not open. Makes 4 servings.

# Greek-Style Halibut

4 (1-inch-thick) halibut steaks
Salt
Freshly ground pepper
6 oz. button mushrooms, halved, if large
1 bay leaf
2 tablespoons vegetable oil
1 medium onion, chopped
2 carrots, diced
1 garlic clove, crushed
6 tablespoons white wine

*To garnish:*
Tomato slices
Chopped fresh parsley

1. Preheat oven to 375F (190C). Grease a shallow baking dish large enough to hold fish in a single layer.
2. Lay fish in greased dish; season with salt and pepper. Add mushrooms and bay leaf.
3. Heat oil in a medium skillet over medium heat. Add onion, carrots and garlic; sauté gently until onion and garlic are soft but not browned.
4. Add wine to skillet; boil 1 minute. Pour over fish.
5. Cover dish with foil or lid; bake in preheated oven 10 to 15 minutes or until fish tests done.
6. Discard bay leaf; garnish with tomato and parsley. Makes 4 servings.

# Scallop & Artichoke Medley

8 oz. Jerusalem artichokes (sunchokes)
Water
2 tablespoons lemon juice
1/4 cup butter or margarine
1 large onion, sliced
1 bay leaf
1/2 cup dry vermouth
1/2 cup water
12 sea scallops
Salt
Freshly ground pepper
2 tablespoons cornstarch
3 tablespoons whipping cream or dairy sour cream
1 to 2 canned red pimentos, sliced, if desired

*To garnish:*
Croutons
Parsley sprigs

1. Peel artichokes; slice into a medium bowl of cold water containing 1 tablespoon lemon juice.
2. Melt butter or margarine in a heavy medium saucepan. Add onion; sauté gently until soft. Drain sliced artichokes. Add to pan; sauté gently 3 to 4 minutes.
3. Add bay leaf, vermouth, remaining 1 tablespoon lemon juice and 1/2 cup water to pan; simmer 10 to 15 minutes or until artichokes are tender.
4. Cut scallops into 3 or 4 pieces; add to saucepan. Season with salt and pepper. Simmer scallops 1 to 2 minutes. Discard bay leaf.
5. Use a slotted spoon to place vegetables and scallops in a deep serving dish; keep warm.
6. In a small bowl, blend cornstarch with cream or sour cream; whisk cornstarch mixture into saucepan. Cook, stirring constantly until sauce is slightly thickened. Add strips of pimento, if desired. Pour sauce over scallops and vegetables.
7. Garnish with croutons and parsley. Makes 4 servings.

# Halibut in Crab Sauce

4 (1-inch thick) halibut steaks
Salt
Freshly ground pepper
2 tablespoons butter or margarine
1 tablespoon finely chopped onion
3 tablespoons all-purpose flour
1 cup milk
1 tablespoon lemon juice
1 teaspoon Angostura bitters
4 oz. fresh, frozen or canned crabmeat, flaked

*To garnish:*
Whole shrimp
Cucumber sticks

*Crabmeat in this recipe makes it a dish for special occasions. Any firm white fish can be substituted for halibut.*

**1.** Preheat oven to 350F (175C). Grease a shallow baking dish large enough to hold fish in a single layer.
**2.** Place fish steaks in greased baking dish; season with salt and pepper.
**3.** Melt butter or margarine in a skillet. Add onion; sauté gently until soft. Stir in flour; cook 1 minute, stirring constantly. Gradually stir in milk; bring to a boil.
**4.** Stir in lemon juice, bitters and crabmeat; season with salt and pepper. Pour sauce over fish.
**5.** Cover with foil or lid; bake in preheated oven 10 minutes or until fish tests done.
**6.** Arrange baked fish and sauce on a serving dish; garnish with whole shrimp and cucumber sticks. Makes 4 servings.

Clockwise from left: Fish Paella, Halibut in Crab Sauce, Greek-Style Halibut

# Trout with Tarragon

4 trout, ready to cook
1/2 cup dry white wine
2 tablespoons water
1 tablespoon finely chopped onion
1 lemon, thinly sliced
2 tablespoons chopped fresh parsley
2 tablespoons chopped fresh tarragon
1/2 cup whipping cream
Salt
Freshly ground pepper

1. Place trout in a large skillet with a lid. Add wine, water, onion, lemon and 1/2 of parsley and tarragon. Bring to a simmer. Cover and poach 10 to 12 minutes or until trout tests done.
2. Remove trout and lemon slices; arrange decoratively on a warmed serving plate; keep warm.
3. Add cream to skillet; increase heat. Cook until thickened, stirring constantly; season with salt and pepper. Spoon sauce over trout.
4. Sprinkle with remaining parsley and tarragon. Makes 4 servings.

# Honey-Baked Fish

2 mackerel or other fish (about 1 lb. each), ready to cook
2 tablespoons honey
1 carrot, cut into thin julienne strips
1 celery stalk, cut into julienne strips
1 (2-inch) piece gingerroot, cut into julienne strips
1 tablespoon wine vinegar
1 tablespoon soy sauce
Salt
Freshly ground pepper

1. Preheat oven to 375F (190C). Grease a piece of foil large enough to completely enclose fish. Place fish on greased foil. Brush fish with honey; sprinkle with carrot, celery, gingerroot, wine vinegar and soy sauce. Season with salt and pepper.
2. Fold over foil to completely enclose fish; seal edges. Place on a baking sheet.
3. Bake in preheated oven 8 to 10 minutes per inch of thickness of fish, measured at the thickest part, or until fish tests done.
4. Remove from foil to serve. Pour any cooking juices over fish. Makes 2 servings.

# Ocean Pie

1 lb. white fish, skinned, boned
1 cup milk
Salt
Freshly ground pepper
4 oz. shrimp, cooked, peeled, deveined
6 tablespoons butter or margarine
3 tablespoons all-purpose flour
1 tablespoon chopped fresh parsley
2 teaspoons grated lemon peel
4 cups chopped peeled potatoes (about 1-1/2 lb.)
1 cup shredded Cheddar cheese (4 oz.)

*To garnish:*
Lemon twists
Finely chopped fresh parsley

1. Preheat oven to 375F (190C). Place fish, milk, salt and pepper in a medium saucepan. Bring to a simmer. Cover and poach about 5 minutes or until fish tests done. Drain fish, reserving milk; flake fish into small pieces.
2. In a 1-1/2-quart casserole, combine flaked fish and shrimp.
3. Melt 3 tablespoons butter or margarine in a medium saucepan. Stir in flour; cook 1 minute, stirring. Gradually stir in reserved milk to make a smooth sauce. Boil 2 minutes, stirring. Stir in parsley and lemon peel; pour over fish mixture. Keep warm.
4. Meanwhile, cook potatoes in a pan of salted boiling water about 20 minutes or until tender. Drain and mash potatoes. Stir in remaining 3 tablespoons butter or margarine. Stir in 1/2 of cheese. Spoon potatoes around edge of fish mixture; sprinkle with remaining cheese.
5. Bake in preheated oven 20 to 25 minutes or until golden brown. Garnish with lemon twists and parsley. Makes 4 servings.

---

Do not overcook fish. It is already tender and cooks quickly. Cook only until firm and opaque. To test for doneness, cut into the center of the thickest part. It should be slightly opaque. One rule is to cook fresh or thawed fish 10 minutes per inch of thickness and to cook frozen fish 20 minutes per inch of thickness. However, this is only a general guide; cooking time will vary with the oven temperature and the shape and type of fish. Overcooked fish is tough and dry.

---

Left to right: Honey-Baked Fish, Ocean Pie

Left to right: Crab Gratinée, Sole & Lime Pinwheels

# Sole & Lime Pinwheels

6 tablespoons butter or margarine, room temperature
2 tablespoons chopped fresh chives
3/4 cup fresh bread crumbs
Grated peel of 1 lime
About 1/4 cup lime juice
Salt
Freshly ground pepper
8 skinless sole fillets

*To garnish:*
Lime twists
Fresh chives

1. Preheat broiler. Grease a shallow flameproof dish large enough to hold rolled fillets in 1 layer. In a small bowl, beat butter or margarine and chives until soft and creamy. Stir in bread crumbs, lime peel and enough lime juice to make a good spreading consistency for stuffing. Season with salt and pepper.
2. Spread sole fillets with equal amounts of stuffing. Roll up from wide end; secure rolls with wooden picks, using a small sharp-pointed knife to make an incision if necessary.
3. Place in greased dish; sprinkle with remaining lime juice.
4. Broil under preheated broiler 5 minutes. Turn over with tongs; broil 3 to 5 minutes or until fish tests done.
5. Garnish with lime twists and chives. Serve immediately. Makes 4 servings.

# Crab Gratinée

8 oz. cooked crabmeat
4 oz. shrimp, cooked, peeled, deveined
3 tablespoons butter or margarine
2 tablespoons all-purpose flour
1/2 cup dry white wine
1 tablespoon lemon juice
2 teaspoons chopped fresh parsley
2 tablespoons whipping cream
1/2 head Chinese cabbage, shredded
6 tablespoons dry bread crumbs

*To garnish:*
Dill or parsley sprigs

---

**1.** Pick over crabmeat. In a medium bowl, combine crabmeat and shrimp. Set aside.
**2.** Melt 1 tablespoon butter or margarine in a medium saucepan. Stir in flour; cook 1 minute, stirring constantly. Gradually stir in wine and lemon juice to make a smooth sauce. Bring to a boil; cook 1 minute, stirring. Remove from heat; stir in parsley and cream.
**3.** Preheat broiler. Melt remaining 2 tablespoons butter or margarine in another medium saucepan. Add Chinese cabbage; cook over medium heat 1 to 2 minutes or until softened. Divide equally among 4 flameproof dishes or scallop shells. Make a hollow in center of each cabbage portion.
**4.** Fill each hollow with an equal amount of crab mixture. Spoon sauce over cabbage and crab mixture. Sprinkle with bread crumbs.
**5.** Broil under preheated broiler 4 to 5 minutes or until golden. Garnish with dill or parsley. Serve immediately. Makes 4 servings.

 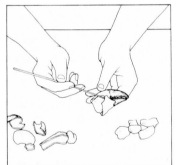

1/Using a knife and rolling pin, crack crab claws.

2/Remove crabmeat with a skewer or seafood fork.

# Marinated Fish Kabobs

2 tablespoons honey
1 tablespoon vegetable oil
2 tablespoons soy sauce
1/2 cup white wine
1 teaspoon grated gingerroot
2 tablespoons chopped fresh chives
1-1/4 to 1-1/2 lb. cod or other firm-textured fish fillets, about 1 inch thick

---

**1.** In a glass or stainless-steel bowl, combine honey, oil, soy sauce, wine, gingerroot and chives. Set aside.
**2.** Cut fish fillets into 1-inch cubes. Add to marinade. Stir until coated. Cover and refrigerate 1 hour.
**3.** Preheat broiler. Grease a broiler-pan rack. Thread marinated fish on metal skewers. Place kabobs on greased rack.
**4.** Broil under preheated broiler about 8 minutes or until fish tests done, brushing with marinade.
**5.** Serve immediately. Makes 4 servings.

# Grilled Hawaiian Chicken

1 (3- to 3-1/2-lb.) broiler-fryer chicken, cut up
Vegetable oil
Salt
Freshly ground pepper

*Pineapple glaze:*
1 (20-oz.) can sliced pineapple
2 tablespoons cornstarch
1/2 cup water
1/2 cup packed brown sugar
1/4 teaspoon salt
1/2 teaspoon Worcestershire sauce
1/4 cup white vinegar
2 tablespoons chili sauce
1/3 cup ketchup

---

1. Preheat grill.
2. Brush chicken pieces with oil; season with salt and pepper. Place on grill, skin-side down, 5 to 6 inches from source of heat. Grill over medium-hot coals 35 minutes, turning chicken occasionally with tongs.
3. Prepare pineapple glaze while chicken is cooking. To prepare glaze, drain pineapple juice into a small saucepan; reserve pineapple slices for garnish. In a small bowl, combine cornstarch and water. Gradually stir into pineapple juice. Cook over medium heat, stirring constantly, until smooth and thickened. Add brown sugar, salt, Worcestershire sauce, vinegar, chili sauce and ketchup. Stir well; simmer 3 to 4 minutes, stirring frequently.
4. Brush chicken with glaze; grill 10 to 15 minutes longer or until chicken is tender, turning chicken and brushing often with glaze.
5. Heat remaining glaze; pour into a gravy boat or small pitcher. If desired, grill pineapple slices 2 to 3 minutes on each side. Makes 4 servings.

# Leg of Lamb with Rice Stuffing

*Stuffing:*
2 tablespoons butter or margarine
1 onion, finely chopped
2 celery stalks, finely chopped
3 crisp-cooked bacon slices, crumbled
1/2 cup cooked rice
Pinch of ground allspice
Salt
Freshly ground pepper
1 (8-oz.) can apricot halves
1 cup cooked prunes
1 egg yolk
1 (4-1/2-lb.) lamb-leg roast, boneless
1 tablespoon butter or margarine, melted

*Sauce:*
1/2 cup dry white wine
1/2 cup beef stock
1-1/2 tablespoons cornstarch

*To garnish:*
Sliced zucchini, lightly cooked
Fresh rosemary or parsley sprigs

---

1. Preheat oven to 350F (175C).
2. For stuffing, melt butter or margarine in a large skillet over medium heat. Add onion and celery; sauté until lightly browned. Place sautéed mixture in a large bowl; add bacon, rice and allspice. Season with salt and pepper.
3. Drain apricots. Reserve 1/4 cup juice; set aside. Chop 4 apricots and 4 prunes; set aside remaining fruit. Add chopped fruit to stuffing; stir well. Add egg yolk; stir until mixture binds together.
4. Use stuffing to fill bone cavity of lamb; reshape roast, using a trussing needle and fine string or several skewers.
5. Brush surface of meat with melted butter or margarine; sprinkle with salt. Place on a rack in a roasting pan. Roast in preheated oven 2-1/4 to 3 hours or to desired doneness. Baste with pan drippings once or twice during cooking.
6. Remove string or skewers from lamb; place lamb on a serving dish. Deglaze roasting pan with wine; add stock. In a small bowl, combine cornstarch with reserved apricot juice. Stir cornstarch mixture into roasting pan; bring to a boil. Simmer 2 to 3 minutes or until slightly thickened. Season with salt and pepper. Remove fat from surface of sauce. Serve in a gravy boat.
7. Arrange remaining apricots and prunes, zucchini and herbs around roast. Serve with potatoes cooked in their skins, coated with butter or margarine and chopped parsley. Makes 6 to 8 servings.

Leg of Lamb with Rice Stuffing

# Flambéed Beef Stew

2 lbs. beef stew cubes
1 garlic clove, crushed
1 tablespoon chopped fresh parsley
1 teaspoon dried leaf thyme
1/2 cup dry red wine
2 tablespoons vegetable oil
1/4 cup brandy
2 onions, sliced
1-1/2 cups beef stock
1 bay leaf
Salt
Freshly ground pepper
2 carrots, sliced

*To garnish:*
Chopped fresh parsley

---

**1.** Place beef cubes in a glass or ceramic bowl. Add garlic, parsley, thyme and wine; stir well.
**2.** Cover and refrigerate about 2 hours, stirring at least once.
**3.** Drain beef, reserving marinade; pat beef dry with paper towels. Heat oil in a large skillet over medium heat. Add marinated beef cubes; sauté until browned. Warm brandy in a small saucepan; pour over beef cubes. Ignite brandy carefully. When flame dies, remove browned beef cubes to a large saucepan.
**4.** Add onions, reserved marinade, stock and bay leaf to saucepan. Season with salt and pepper.
**5.** Cover saucepan; simmer stew over low heat 2-1/2 to 3 hours or until beef is tender. Add carrots to stew after 1 hour.
**6.** To serve, discard bay leaf; sprinkle heavily with chopped parsley. Makes 5 to 6 servings.

## Variation
Chicken or turkey tastes very good when cooked in this way. Allow 1 chicken quarter or 2 smaller pieces of chicken or a turkey thigh per person, with or without bone. Cook for 1-1/4 to 1-1/2 hours or until meat is very tender. White wine may be used in place of red wine.

# Chicken Gumbo

3 tablespoons vegetable oil
1 (2-1/2- to 3-lb.) broiler-fryer chicken, cut up
2 tablespoons butter or margarine
1 large onion, sliced
1 garlic clove, crushed
1 green pepper, sliced
1 tablespoon all-purpose flour
1 (16-oz.) can tomatoes
1 cup chicken stock
1 (10-oz.) pkg. frozen okra or 12 oz. fresh okra, trimmed
2 tablespoons tomato paste
2 teaspoons Worcestershire sauce
Pinch of ground cloves
Pinch of chili powder
1/4 teaspoon dried leaf basil
Salt
Freshly ground black pepper
2 cups cooked long-grain white rice

*To garnish:*
2 tablespoons chopped fresh parsley

---

*Okra is an unusual ingredient which adds flavor and texture. It is used as a thickening agent in casseroles and stews. When available, fresh okra gives better results and color.*

**1.** Preheat oven to 350F (175C).
**2.** Heat oil in a large skillet over medium heat. Add chicken pieces; sauté until golden brown. Transfer to a 3-quart casserole.
**3.** Melt butter or margarine in a heavy, medium saucepan. Add onion, garlic and green pepper; sauté 2 minutes or until soft.
**4.** Stir flour into vegetable mixture; gradually stir in tomatoes and stock. Bring to a boil, stirring frequently.
**5.** Thickly slice okra; add to pan with tomato paste, Worcestershire sauce, cloves, chili powder, basil, salt and pepper. Simmer gently 5 minutes.
**6.** Pour okra mixture over chicken. Cover casserole with foil or lid; bake in preheated oven 1 hour or until tender.
**7.** To serve, spoon gumbo over hot cooked rice; garnish with fresh parsley. Makes 4 servings.

Jambalaya

# Jambalaya

2 tablespoons vegetable oil
2 tablespoons butter or margarine
1 lb. lean pork, cut into narrow strips
1 large onion, chopped
1 green pepper, sliced
1 red bell pepper, sliced
4 oz. mushrooms, thickly sliced
1 cup uncooked long-grain white rice
2 cups or more chicken stock
1/4 teaspoon ground allspice
4 oz. smoked sausage, sliced or chopped
Salt
Freshly ground black pepper
4 oz. peeled deveined shrimp

*To garnish:*
Few whole shrimp
Tomato wedges

**1.** Preheat oven to 350F (175C).
**2.** Heat oil and butter or margarine in a large heavy saucepan. Add pork strips; sauté until well browned. With a slotted spoon, transfer browned pork to a 3-quart casserole.
**3.** Add onion and green and red peppers to fat remaining in skillet; sauté 3 to 4 minutes.
**4.** Add mushrooms; sauté 1 minute. Stir in rice and 2 cups stock; bring to a boil.
**5.** Add allspice and smoked sausage; season with salt and pepper. Spoon seasoned rice mixture over pork; stir well. Cover casserole tightly with foil or lid. Bake in preheated oven 50 minutes.
**6.** Stir well; add shrimp and additional boiling stock, if necessary. Recover casserole; bake 10 minutes longer or until liquid has been absorbed and meat is tender.
**7.** To serve, garnish jambalaya with whole shrimp and tomato wedges. Makes 4 servings.

Left to right: Steak Bake with Mushrooms & Potatoes, Spicy Sweet & Sour Beef

# Steak Bake with Mushrooms & Potatoes

1/3 cup all-purpose flour
Salt
Freshly ground pepper
1-1/2 lbs. beef-round steak, cut into 4 serving pieces
1/4 cup butter or margarine
1 large onion, sliced
6 oz. mushrooms, sliced
3/4 cup beef stock
1 lb. potatoes, peeled, cut into 1-inch cubes (3 cups)
1/2 cup half and half

*To garnish:*
Chopped fresh parsley
Cooked carrot sticks

1. Preheat oven to 350F (175C).
2. Combine flour, salt and pepper in a plastic bag. Add beef; shake to coat. Melt 3 tablespoons butter or margarine in a large skillet over medium heat. Add seasoned beef; sauté until browned. With tongs, transfer browned beef to a shallow baking pan large enough to hold beef in a single layer.
3. Add remaining butter or margarine to skillet. Add onion; sauté until soft. Add mushrooms; cook 1 minute.
4. Add stock to skillet; bring to a boil. Season mushroom mixture with salt and pepper; pour over beef.
5. Cover baking pan with foil or lid. Bake in preheated oven 20 minutes.
6. Add potatoes to casserole. Cover and bake 40 minutes longer or until potatoes and steak are tender.
7. To serve, use a slotted spoon to place beef and potatoes in a deep serving dish. Add half and half to cooking liquid left in baking pan. Heat liquid and half and half to make sauce; do not boil. Pour over steak. Garnish with parsley and carrot. Makes 4 servings.

# Spicy Sweet & Sour Beef

1/4 teaspoon freshly grated nutmeg
1/2 teaspoon ground cinnamon
1 (3-1/2- to 4-lb.) beef-chuck cross-rib pot roast,
    boneless
8 whole cloves
1 large onion, sliced
1 garlic clove, crushed
2/3 cup packed brown sugar
1/2 cup wine vinegar
Salt
Freshly ground pepper
1/2 cup water
1 tablespoon cornstarch
Water

*To garnish:*
Cooked sliced zucchini, if desired

---

1. Combine nutmeg and cinnamon; rub over beef.
2. In a large glass or ceramic dish, combine cloves, onion, garlic, sugar, vinegar, salt, pepper and water; stir until sugar is dissolved. Add seasoned roast; turn to coat.
3. Cover and refrigerate 24 hours, turning several times.
4. To cook roast, preheat oven to 350F (175C). Place marinated roast and marinade in a large roasting pan. Cover pan with foil or lid. Bake in preheated oven 2-1/2 to 3 hours or until tender, basting once.
5. Place roast on a serving dish; cover with foil to keep warm. Discard cloves from cooking liquid.
6. Spoon fat from cooking liquid. In a small bowl, blend cornstarch with a little cold water; stir cornstarch mixture into cooking liquid in roasting pan. Bring to a boil, stirring constantly. Boil sauce rapidly 5 minutes or until slightly thickened and reduced in volume. Season sauce with salt and pepper. Pour some sauce over roast. Serve remaining sauce separately. Arrange zucchini around roast, if desired. Makes 8 to 10 servings.

# Chicken Cacciatore

3 tablespoons vegetable oil
1 (2-1/2- to 3-lb.) broiler-fryer chicken, cut up or
    4 chicken quarters
2 large onions, sliced
2 garlic cloves, crushed
1 (16-oz.) can tomatoes
2 tablespoons chopped fresh parsley or
    1 tablespoon dried leaf parsley
1 teaspoon dried leaf basil
1/2 cup red wine
1 tablespoon tomato paste, if desired
Salt
Freshly ground pepper

---

*This is a traditional Italian recipe in which chicken is flavored with garlic, tomatoes and basil.*

1. Heat oil in a large skillet over medium heat. Add chicken; sauté until browned. Remove chicken from skillet; set aside.
2. Add onions and garlic to fat remaining in skillet; sauté until golden brown. Add tomatoes with their juice, parsley, basil, wine and tomato paste, if desired. Bring tomato mixture to a boil; season with salt and pepper.
3. Return chicken to skillet. Cover and simmer over low heat 1 hour or until tender.
4. Serve with favorite pasta. Makes 4 servings.

# Boston Baked Beans

12 oz. pea beans or small white beans, soaked
4 oz. salt pork, cut into 1-inch pieces
2 large onions, sliced
1 teaspoon salt
1-1/2 teaspoons dry mustard
Freshly ground pepper
2 tablespoons molasses
2 tablespoons wine vinegar
8 whole cloves, tied in cheesecloth bag
1 tablespoon tomato paste or 2 tablespoons ketchup
Water

---

*Boston Baked Beans is an American favorite. To do the recipe justice, long slow cooking is essential. First, wash beans thoroughly in cold water, then soak overnight in fresh cold water. A fast method of soaking is to boil un-soaked beans in fresh cold water in a large saucepan 2 minutes. Remove saucepan from heat; cover pan and let beans stand in cooking water 1 hour. Drain beans; cook according to recipe.*

**1.** Preheat oven to 300F (150C).
**2.** Drain beans; place in a large heavy ovenproof casserole or bean pot.
**3.** Add salt pork to beans with onions, salt, mustard, pepper, molasses, vinegar, cloves and tomato paste or ketchup; stir well.
**4.** Add enough cold water to casserole to barely cover ingredients; cover casserole tightly with foil or lid. If lid is not a good fit, cover first with foil. Bake in preheated oven 5 to 6 hours or until beans are tender.
**5.** Check beans occasionally; add enough boiling water to keep beans covered during baking.
**6.** Discard bag containing cloves before serving. Makes 4 to 6 servings.

# Oven Beef Stew

1-1/2 lbs. beef stew cubes
1 cup red wine
Grated peel of 1/2 orange
Juice of 1 orange
1 garlic clove, crushed
1 bay leaf
2 tablespoons vegetable oil
1 onion, chopped
1 tablespoon all-purpose flour
1 cup beef stock
Salt
Freshly ground pepper
2 to 3 tablespoons brandy
4 oz. button mushrooms, sliced

***To garnish:***
**Baked puff-pastry triangles**
**Chopped fresh parsley**

---

**1.** In glass or ceramic bowl combine beef, wine, orange peel and juice, garlic and bay leaf. Cover and refrigerate 3 hours.
**2.** Preheat oven to 325F (165C).
**3.** Drain beef, reserving marinade. Heat oil in a large skillet over medium heat. Add beef cubes; sauté until well browned. With a slotted spoon, transfer browned beef to a 3-quart casserole.
**4.** Add onion to fat remaining in skillet; sauté until lightly browned. Stir flour into onion; cook 1 minute. Add marinade and stock to skillet; bring to a boil. Season sauce with salt and pepper.
**5.** Warm brandy; pour over browned beef. Ignite brandy carefully. When flame dies, pour sauce over beef.
**6.** Cover casserole with foil or lid. Bake in preheated oven 2 hours.
**7.** Add mushrooms to hot casserole; bake an additional 30 to 45 minutes or until beef is tender. Discard bay leaf.
**8.** Garnish with pastry triangles and parsley. Makes 4 servings.

**Variation**
For a different flavor, add 1 cup prunes or 1 sliced red bell pepper 1 hour before end of cooking time. For an interesting flavor, add 2 tablespoons chopped fresh herbs or 1 tablespoon dried Italian seasoning or any individual herb, such as oregano, marjoram or basil.

# Mexican Steak

1-1/2 lbs. beef-round steak, cut into 4 serving pieces
Salt
Freshly ground black pepper
3 tablespoons vegetable oil
1 onion, sliced
2 tablespoons all-purpose flour
1/2 teaspoon chili powder
1/4 teaspoon ground cumin
About 1-1/2 cups chicken stock
Hot-pepper sauce, if desired
1/2 cup canned whole-kernel corn, drained
1 avocado
Water
1 tablespoon lemon juice

**1.** Season beef with salt and pepper.
**2.** Heat oil in a large skillet over medium heat. Add beef; sauté until browned. With tongs, remove beef; set aside.
**3.** Add onion to fat remaining in skillet; sauté until soft. Stir in flour, chili powder and cumin; cook 2 minutes, stirring constantly. Stir in 1-1/2 cups stock; cook until slightly thickened. Season with salt, pepper and hot sauce, if desired.
**4.** Stir in corn. Return beef to skillet. Cover skillet; simmer 45 to 50 minutes or until beef is tender. Add additional stock, if necessary.
**5.** Peel and slice avocado. Place sliced avocado in a small bowl of water and lemon juice; set aside.
**6.** Arrange beef on a warmed serving dish. Add avocado to sauce; heat until warmed. Immediately spoon avocado and sauce over beef. Makes 4 servings.

Left to right: Mexican Steak, Oven Beef Stew

# New England Chicken

1 (2-1/2- to 3-lb.) broiler-fryer chicken, cut up
Salt
Freshly ground white pepper
1/4 cup butter or margarine
1/2 cup milk
1/4 teaspoon dried rubbed sage
1/4 teaspoon dried leaf basil
1 (8-oz.) can oysters, drained
1/2 cup whipping cream
2 teaspoons cornstarch

*To garnish:*
Watercress

*In New England, oysters are very plentiful in the fall. In other areas, fresh oysters may not be so easy to come by and may be expensive; however, canned oysters make a good alternative. If fresh oysters are available, use 1 cup shucked, drained fresh oysters.*

**1.** Preheat oven to 350F (175C).
**2.** Sprinkle chicken with salt and pepper. Melt butter or margarine in a large skillet over medium heat. Add chicken pieces; sauté until golden. Transfer to a 3-quart casserole.
**3.** Pour milk over chicken; sprinkle with sage and basil.
**4.** Cover casserole with foil or lid; bake in preheated oven 1 hour.
**5.** Add oysters to casserole. In a small bowl, blend cream with cornstarch; stir cornstarch mixture into hot casserole. Recover casserole; bake 15 to 20 minutes longer or until chicken is tender.
**6.** Arrange chicken on serving platter. Spoon sauce and oysters over chicken; garnish with watercress. Makes 4 servings.

# Australian Beef Curry

3 tablespoons vegetable oil
2 lbs. beef stew cubes
2 large onions, sliced
2 large cooking apples, peeled, cored, sliced
1 tablespoon curry powder
1 tablespoon all-purpose flour
1 cup beef stock
1 (16-oz.) can tomatoes
2/3 cup raisins
2 tablespoons wine vinegar
Salt

*To garnish:*
Hard-cooked eggs, sliced
Parsley sprigs
Homemade potato chips

Clockwise from left: New England Chicken, Greek-Style Oxtails, Australian Beef Curry.

**1.** Preheat oven to 350F (175C).
**2.** Heat oil in a large skillet over medium heat. Add beef cubes; sauté until brown. With a slotted spoon, transfer browned beef to a 3-quart casserole.
**3.** Add onions to fat remaining in skillet; sauté until soft. Add apples to skillet; cook 2 to 3 minutes.
**4.** Sprinkle curry powder and flour over onions and apples, stirring constantly. Stir in stock; bring to a boil.
**5.** Add tomatoes, raisins, vinegar and salt; spoon sauce over beef. Cover casserole with foil or lid.
**6.** Bake in preheated oven 2 hours. Stir casserole; bake an additional 15 to 30 minutes or until meat is tender.
**7.** To serve, spoon into a large serving dish. Garnish with hard-cooked egg, parsley and potato chips. Makes 4 to 5 servings.

# Greek-Style Oxtails

2 oxtails, cut up
3 tablespoons olive oil
1/4 cup brandy
1 onion, sliced
1 garlic clove, crushed
1 cup dry white wine
2 bay leaves
Grated peel of 1/2 orange
Juice of 1 orange
Salt
Freshly ground pepper
2 cups beef stock
8 oz. pitted black olives
1/4 cup butter or margarine
1/3 cup all-purpose flour

---

**1.** Preheat oven to 325F (165C).
**2.** Trim oxtails of excess fat. Heat oil in a large skillet over medium heat. Add oxtails; sauté until browned. Transfer to a 3-quart casserole.
**3.** Warm brandy in a small saucepan; pour warmed brandy over oxtails. Ignite carefully; shake until flame dies.
**4.** Add onion and garlic to fat remaining in skillet; sauté until golden brown. Add wine to skillet; bring to a boil.
**5.** Pour wine mixture over oxtails; add bay leaves and orange peel and juice. Season with salt and pepper.
**6.** Bring stock to a boil in same skillet; add enough boiling stock to barely cover oxtails.
**7.** Cover casserole; bake in preheated oven 3 hours.
**8.** Pour cooking liquid into a medium bowl. Discard bay leaves. Refrigerate oxtails and cooking liquid overnight.
**9.** Next day, lift layer of fat from cooking liquid; discard fat. Bring cooking liquid back to a boil in a medium saucepan; pour over oxtails. Add olives. Cover casserole; bake 1 to 1-1/2 hours longer or until oxtails are tender.
**10.** Cream butter and flour together to make a beurre manié.
**11.** Strain cooking liquid into a medium saucepan. Whisk beurre manié into cooking liquid over medium heat, a little at a time, until thickened; bring back to a boil. Season with salt and pepper.
**12.** Arrange oxtails and olives in a serving bowl; pour sauce over oxtails. Makes 6 to 8 servings.

---

Oxtail has a high proportion of bone and is generally rather fatty. The flavor is excellent; however, it needs long, slow cooking. It is thus ideal for casseroles and stews. If oxtails are frozen, they should be thawed before cooking. If cutting your own, use a sharp knife and meat cleaver or saw. Cut into pieces about 2 inches thick; then trim off any excess fat.

# Nasi Goreng

1-1/4 cups uncooked long-grain white rice
Salt
1/4 cup butter or margarine
1 lb. lean pork, cut into 1/4-inch-wide strips
2 onions, sliced
1 red bell pepper, chopped
1/2 cup green peas
1/4 cucumber, chopped
1 carrot, shredded
1/4 cup soy sauce
1 teaspoon curry powder
Pinch of five-spice powder
Freshly ground black pepper

*Omelet:*
1 egg
1 teaspoon cold water
Salt
Freshly ground black pepper
1 tablespoon butter or margarine

*To garnish:*
2 tomatoes, cut into wedges
Green-onion curls

*Nasi Goreng is an Indonesian dish. If kept warm and covered, it can stand up to 30 minutes before serving.*

**1.** In a medium saucepan, cook rice in boiling salted water according to package directions. Rice should be tender and water absorbed. Set aside.
**2.** Melt butter or margarine in a large skillet. Add pork; cook 5 to 8 minutes or until golden. Add onions; cook 10 minutes.
**3.** Add bell pepper, peas, cucumber and carrot to pork mixture; cook 5 minutes. Stir in soy sauce, curry powder, five-spice powder, salt and black pepper. Stir in cooked rice until combined and hot.
**4.** To make omelet, in a small bowl, beat egg with water, salt and pepper. Melt butter or margarine in a small skillet; add egg mixture. Cook gently until underside is golden. Turn and brown other side. Slide onto a plate; cut into 1/2-inch-wide strips.
**5.** Spoon rice mixture into a warmed serving dish; top with a lattice of omelet strips. Garnish with tomato wedges and green-onion curls. Makes 4 to 6 servings.

# French Onion Soup with Cheese Toast

1/4 cup butter or margarine
1 tablespoon vegetable oil
4 medium onions, thinly sliced
1/2 teaspoon sugar
2 tablespoons all-purpose flour
3-1/2 cups beef stock
Salt
Freshly ground pepper
4 thick bread slices
1 garlic clove, halved
1 cup shredded Gruyére cheese (4 oz.)
2 tablespoons brandy, if desired

**1.** Heat butter or margarine and oil in a large heavy saucepan. Add onions; cover. Cook over medium heat 20 minutes, stirring occasionally.
**2.** Stir in sugar. Cook, uncovered, until onions turn golden, stirring frequently.
**3.** Stir in flour; cook 1 minute. Gradually stir in stock. Season with salt and pepper. Bring to a boil; reduce heat. Simmer 20 minutes.
**4.** Preheat broiler. Rub bread slices with cut-side of garlic. Place seasoned bread on a baking sheet. Toast under preheated broiler. Turn over; sprinkle with cheese. Broil until golden and bubbly. Cut bread slices into thick strips.
**5.** Stir brandy into soup, if desired. Ladle hot soup into warmed soup bowls. Add toasted bread strips; serve immediately. Makes 4 servings.

Left to right: French Onion Soup with Cheese Toast, Nasi Goreng

# Lattice-Topped Meat Pie

**Meat Filling:**
2 tablespoons vegetable oil
2 bacon slices, diced
1 onion, chopped
1 garlic clove, crushed, if desired
1 celery stalk, chopped
1 large carrot, chopped
1 lb. lean ground beef
1 (8-oz.) can tomatoes, chopped
1/4 cup dry red wine or beef stock
Salt
Freshly ground pepper
Pinch of freshly grated nutmeg

**Lattice Topping:**
2-1/4 cups chopped, peeled potatoes (about 12 oz.)
1 large rutabaga or 3 parsnips, peeled
3 tablespoons butter or margarine
1/4 cup half and half or milk
1/4 cup shredded Cheddar cheese (1 oz.)
Salt
White pepper

**To garnish:**
Tomato slices
1 parsley sprig

1. To make filling, heat oil in a large saucepan. Add bacon, onion, garlic, celery and carrot; sauté over medium heat 5 minutes.
2. Stir in beef; cook about 10 minutes or until lightly browned. Drain off excess fat.
3. Stir in tomatoes, wine or stock, salt, pepper and nutmeg. Simmer over low heat about 15 minutes or until thickened. Spoon into an ovenproof dish.
4. To make topping, in a large saucepan, cook potatoes and rutabaga or parsnips in boiling salted water about 20 minutes or until tender.
5. Preheat oven to 425F (220C). Drain and mash cooked potatoes and rutabaga or parsnips. Beat in butter or margarine, half and half or milk, cheese, salt and white pepper until smooth. Spoon into a pastry bag fitted with a large star-shaped tip. Pipe a lattice over top of meat filling.
6. Bake in preheated oven 20 minutes or until lattice is golden and crisp. Garnish with tomato slices and parsley sprig. Makes 4 servings.

# Ham & Potato Gratin

1-1/2 cups thinly sliced peeled potatoes (8 oz.)
8 oz. sliced ham
2 onions, sliced
1-1/2 cups shredded Cheddar cheese (6 oz.)
Salt
Freshly ground pepper
1 teaspoon freshly grated nutmeg
2 eggs
1 cup milk
3 tablespoons whipping cream
2 tablespoons butter or margarine

**To garnish:**
Parsley sprigs or celery leaves

1. Preheat oven to 325F (165C). Grease a 1-1/2-quart casserole. Place alternate layers of potato, ham, onion and cheese in greased casserole, ending with ham. Season each layer with salt, pepper and nutmeg.
2. In a medium bowl, beat eggs, milk and cream until blended; pour over ham. Dot with butter or margarine.
3. Bake in preheated oven 1-1/2 hours or until potatoes are tender and topping is golden brown.
4. Garnish with parsley sprigs or celery leaves. Serve from baking dish. Serve with a vegetable salad. Makes 4 to 6 servings.

**Variations**
**Tongue & Potato Gratin:** Substitute 8 ounces sliced cooked tongue for ham.
**Bacon & Potato Gratin:** Substitute 8 slices crumbled crisp-cooked bacon for ham.

Top to bottom: Lattice-Topped Meat Pie, Ham & Potato Gratin

# Spicy Moroccan Chicken

1/4 cup honey
1 teaspoon curry powder
1/2 teaspoon freshly ground pepper
1 teaspoon salt
Pinch of ground allspice
1 (3-1/4-lb.) roasting chicken, cut into serving pieces
1 lemon, thinly sliced
1 cup water
1/4 cup butter or margarine
1 cup chicken stock
1/4 cup raisins
Chopped fresh parsley

1. In a small bowl, combine 2 tablespoons honey, curry powder, pepper, salt and allspice. Spread over chicken pieces; place coated chicken in a glass or stainless-steel bowl. Cover and refrigerate overnight.
2. Drain any liquid from chicken into a medium saucepan. Add lemon slices and water; cook 10 minutes over low heat.
3. Melt butter or margarine and remaining 2 tablespoons honey in a large flameproof casserole. Add marinated chicken pieces; cook about 15 to 20 minutes or until chicken is a deep golden brown on all sides.
4. Add hot lemon mixture, stock and raisins to casserole. Bring to a boil; reduce heat. Cover and simmer 30 to 35 minutes or until chicken is tender.
5. Sprinkle with chopped parsley; serve hot with warm pita bread. Makes 4 servings.

# Chicken Stew with Bacon Dumplings

2 to 3 tablespoons vegetable oil
1 (3-1/2- to 4-lb.) roasting chicken, cut into serving pieces
1 large garlic clove, crushed
12 to 16 small white onions
2 tablespoons all-purpose flour
2-1/2 cups chicken stock
1 bay leaf
1-1/2 teaspoons Italian seasoning
Salt
Freshly ground pepper
8 oz. small mushrooms, trimmed

*Bacon Dumplings:*
1 cup all-purpose flour
1 teaspoon baking powder
1/2 teaspoon Italian seasoning
1/2 teaspoon salt
1 small onion, finely chopped
4 bacon slices, crisp-cooked, crumbled
2 tablespoons vegetable oil
1/2 cup milk

*To garnish:*
Freshly chopped parsley

1. Heat oil in a Dutch oven. Add chicken pieces; cook until browned on all sides. Remove chicken with tongs; set aside.
2. Add garlic and onions to fat remaining in pan; sauté until onions are golden. Remove onions with slotted spoon; set aside.
3. Stir flour into pan drippings; cook 1 minute, stirring. Gradually stir in stock; cook, stirring constantly, until mixture thickens and comes to a boil. Stir in bay leaf, Italian seasoning, salt and pepper. Return chicken and onions to pan. Cover and cook over low heat 30 to 35 minutes or until chicken is tender.
4. To make dumplings, in a medium bowl, combine flour, baking powder, Italian seasoning and salt. Stir in onion and bacon. In a small bowl, combine oil and milk; stir into flour mixture until blended.
5. Remove and discard bay leaf from stew. Stir in mushrooms. Drop dumplings by tablespoonfuls onto hot stew. Lower heat; simmer, uncovered, 10 minutes. Cover and simmer 10 to 12 minutes or until dumplings are cooked. Sprinkle with parsley; serve from pan. Makes 4 servings.

**Variation**
**Parsley & Lemon Dumplings:** Substitute 1-1/2 tablespoons freshly chopped parsley, 1 teaspoon grated lemon peel and 1 tablespoon lemon juice for Italian seasoning and bacon.

# Chicken Catalan

6 tablespoon olive oil
6 chicken-breast halves, with wings attached, if desired
3 onions, sliced
2 garlic cloves, crushed
2-1/2 cups uncooked long-grain white rice
2 tablespoons tomato paste
3/4 teaspoon ground turmeric
5 cups hot chicken stock
1 teaspoon paprika
Salt
Freshly ground black pepper
4 oz. cooked Italian sausage, skinned, cut into
   bite-sized pieces
1 green bell pepper, sliced
1 red bell pepper, sliced
1/2 cup pimento-stuffed olives
1 tablespoon chopped fresh parsley

**1.** Heat 3 tablespoons oil in a large flameproof casserole. Add chicken; cook about 15 minutes or until lightly browned on both sides. Remove with a slotted spoon; keep warm.
**2.** Add onions and garlic to pan juices; cook 2 to 3 minutes or until softened.
**3.** Add remaining oil and rice to casserole; cook until rice turns a light golden color, stirring.
**4.** Stir in tomato paste, turmeric, stock, paprika, salt and black pepper. Bring to a boil; add browned chicken, sausage and bell peppers, pressing them into rice mixture. Reduce heat; simmer, covered, about 30 minutes or until rice is tender, stirring occasionally.
**5.** Stir in olives; cook 2 to 3 minutes to warm through. Sprinkle with parsley; serve from casserole. Makes 6 servings.

Left to right: Chicken Stew with Bacon Dumplings, Chicken Catalan

# Chicken & Sausage Pot Pies

3/4 lb. bulk Italian sausage
1/2 teaspoon rubbed sage or Italian seasoning
1 tablespoon prepared mustard
2 tablespoons butter or margarine
1 lb. chicken cutlets, trimmed, cut into cubes
8 oz. mushrooms, sliced (about 3-1/4 cups)
1 large onion, chopped
1 garlic clove, crushed
2 tablespoons all-purpose flour
1 cup chicken stock
1/2 cup dry white wine or dry sherry
Salt
Freshly ground pepper

*Biscuit Topping:*
1-1/2 cups all-purpose flour
2 teaspoons baking powder
1/2 teaspoon Italian seasoning
1/4 teaspoon salt
1/4 cup butter or margarine
7 tablespoons milk
1 egg yolk beaten with 1 tablespoon milk for glaze

---

**1.** In a medium bowl, combine sausage, sage or Italian seasoning and mustard. Shape mixture into 12 (1-1/2-inch) balls; set aside.
**2.** Melt butter or margarine in a large skillet. Add chicken; cook over medium heat until lightly browned. Remove chicken with a slotted spoon; set aside. Add sausage balls to skillet; cook until browned on all sides. Remove with a slotted spoon; set aside. Drain off all but 2 tablespoons fat from skillet.
**3.** Add mushrooms, onion and garlic to skillet; sauté until onion is transparent. Sprinkle flour over mushroom mixture; cook 1 minute, stirring. Gradually stir in stock and wine or sherry; cook, stirring, until sauce is thickened and comes to a boil. Return chicken and sausage to skillet. Season with salt and pepper. Simmer 5 minutes, stirring occasionally.
**4.** Preheat oven to 425F (220C). To make Biscuit Topping, in a medium bowl, combine flour, baking powder, Italian seasoning and salt. With a pastry blender or 2 knives, cut in butter or margarine until mixture resembles coarse crumbs. Stir in milk to make a soft dough. Knead in bowl 8 to 10 strokes.
**5.** On a lightly floured surface, roll out dough to about 1/2 inch thick. Cut with a floured 2-inch round cutter.
**6.** Spoon chicken-sausage mixture into 4 (1-3/4- to 2-cup) casseroles. Arrange biscuits, slightly overlapping, on top. Brush biscuit tops with egg glaze.
**7.** Bake 20 to 25 minutes or until biscuits are golden brown. Makes 4 servings.

**Variation**
**Sesame Topping:** Make topping as above. Glaze and sprinkle with sesame seeds. Bake as above.

# Liver & Bacon with Wine Sauce

4 bacon slices, halved
1/4 cup all-purpose flour
Salt
Freshly ground pepper
1 lb. calves' liver, thinly sliced
1/4 cup dry red wine
1/2 cup beef stock
1/4 cup lemon juice
2 teaspoons cornstarch, if desired
Water, if desired

*To garnish:*
Chopped fresh parsley
Lemon twists

---

**1.** In a large heavy skillet, sauté bacon with no added fat until crisp. Remove with a slotted spoon; drain on paper towels.
**2.** In a shallow bowl, combine flour, salt and pepper. Coat liver with seasoned flour. Add coated liver to skillet; cook about 5 minutes or until browned on both sides. Gradually stir in wine, stock and lemon juice. Cover and simmer 10 to 15 minutes or until liver is tender.
**3.** If desired, in a small bowl, blend cornstarch with a little water. Stir cornstarch mixture into cooking liquid. Cook until thickened, stirring.
**4.** Garnish with chopped parsley and lemon twists. Top with drained bacon. Serve hot with cooked carrots or other vegetables. Makes 4 servings.

Top to bottom: Chicken & Sausage Pot Pies, Liver & Bacon with Wine Sauce

# Pork & Mango Curry

3 tablespoons all-purpose flour
1-1/2 lb. pork tenderloin, cut into 1-inch cubes
2 tablespoons vegetable oil
1 onion, thickly sliced
2 small green or red bell peppers, sliced
1 teaspoon ground turmeric
1 teaspoon salt
1 tablespoon curry powder
1 teaspoon ground cumin
1 teaspoon ground ginger
1/2 teaspoon ground chilies
5 medium tomatoes, peeled, seeded, chopped
2 teaspoons tomato paste
1-1/2 cups chicken stock
1-1/2 lb. small new potatoes, scrubbed or peeled
    (about 8 to 12)
1 (15-oz.) can mango slices, drained, or
    2 large mangoes, peeled, stoned, sliced

1. Place flour in a plastic bag. Add pork cubes; toss to coat. Heat oil in a large flameproof casserole. Add coated pork; sauté about 5 minutes or until golden. Add onion and bell peppers; cook 3 minutes.
2. Stir in turmeric, salt, curry powder, cumin, ginger and ground chilies. Cook 1 minute, stirring constantly.
3. Stir in tomatoes, tomato paste and stock. Add potatoes; cover and cook 15 minutes over low heat, stirring occasionally. Add mango slices; cook 5 minutes or until potatoes are tender.
4. Serve curry with a selection of accompaniments, such as hot cooked rice, sliced bananas dipped in lemon juice, shredded coconut, mango chutney, poppadums, chopped cucumber in plain yogurt, or a crisp green salad. For information about poppadums, see comments in recipe for Tropical Curried-Chicken Salad, page 38. Makes 4 to 6 servings.

# Stir-Fried Beef & Vegetables

12 oz. beef round steak
1/4 cup vegetable oil
3 carrots, cut into julienne strips
1 red or yellow bell pepper, sliced
1 bunch green onions, sliced into 1-inch lengths
1 (10-oz.) can miniature corn-on-the-cob, drained
1 garlic clove, crushed
1 teaspoon cornstarch
6 tablespoons red wine or apple cider
2 tablespoons soy sauce
1/2 cup beef stock
Salt
Freshly ground black pepper
1/2 (10-oz.) pkg. frozen green peas, thawed
4 oz. bean sprouts (1 cup)

*To serve:*
Cooked green noodles or white rice

*To garnish:*
1 green onion cut into julienne strips.

1. Slice beef into thin strips across grain. Heat 2 tablespoons oil in a large skillet or wok over high heat. Add beef strips; stir-fry 2 to 3 minutes. Remove cooked beef with a slotted spoon; keep warm.
2. Add remaining oil to skillet or wok; heat until hot. When hot, add carrots, bell pepper, green onions, corn and garlic. Stir-fry over high heat 3 to 4 minutes.
3. In a small bowl, blend cornstarch and wine or cider. Stir cornstarch mixture, soy sauce and stock into vegetable mixture. Bring to a boil, stirring constantly. Season with salt and black pepper.
4. Add cooked beef, peas and bean sprouts; cook 2 minutes to heat through.
5. Arrange green noodles or rice on a serving plate. Spoon beef mixture over noodles or rice. Garnish with green onion. Makes 4 servings.

Left to right: Pork & Mango Curry with accompaniments, Eggplant Moussaka, Stir-Fried Beef & Vegetables

# Eggplant Moussaka

6 tablespoons vegetable oil
1 onion, chopped
12 oz. lean ground beef
2 teaspoons tomato paste
1 (8-oz.) can tomato sauce
Salt
Freshly ground pepper
2 medium eggplants, thinly sliced
8 oz. plain yogurt (1 cup)
2 eggs, beaten
3 tablespoons grated Parmesan cheese

**1.** Preheat oven to 375F (190C). Grease a 2-quart casserole. Heat 2 tablespoons oil in a medium saucepan. Add onion; cook about 5 minutes or until softened.
**2.** Add beef; cook about 5 minutes or until lightly browned, stirring to break up beef. Drain off excess fat. Stir in tomato paste and tomato sauce. Season with salt and pepper. Simmer over a low heat 5 minutes.
**3.** Meanwhile, heat remaining oil in a large skillet. Add eggplant slices; cook until lightly browned. Drain on paper towels.
**4.** Place alternate layers of beef mixture and cooked eggplant slices in greased casserole, beginning and ending with eggplant slices.
**5.** In a small bowl, beat yogurt, eggs, salt and pepper. Spoon over moussaka; sprinkle with Parmesan cheese.
**6.** Bake in preheated oven 30 minutes or until top is golden and mixture is bubbly. Serve hot with a tossed salad and French bread. Makes 4 servings.

# Potato-Topped Pork Bake

2 tablespoons vegetable oil
1 onion, sliced
1 lb. pork tenderloin, cut into 1-inch cubes
1 (1-lb.) can tomatoes
4 small leeks, white parts only, sliced
4 small zucchini, sliced
1 teaspoon finely chopped fresh basil
Salt
Freshly ground pepper
3 cups thinly sliced peeled potatoes (1 lb.)
1 cup shredded Cheddar cheese (4 oz.)

*To garnish:*
Parsley sprigs

**1.** Preheat oven to 350 (175C). Heat oil in a 2-quart flame-proof casserole. Add onion and pork; cook, stirring, about 10 minutes or until browned.
**2.** Stir in tomatoes with their juice, leeks, zucchini, basil, salt and pepper. Remove from heat; layer potatoes over meat mixture. Cover casserole.
**3.** Bake in preheated oven 30 minutes. Sprinkle potatoes with cheese; bake, uncovered, 20 minutes or until potatoes are tender and cheese is melted. Garnish with parsley sprigs. Makes 4 servings.

Left to right: Potato-Topped Pork Bake, Sweet & Sour Pork Balls with Bean-Sprout Salad

# Sweet & Sour Pork Balls

1-1/4 lb. lean ground pork
1 cup fresh bread crumbs
1/2 small onion, finely chopped
1/2 teaspoon rubbed sage
1 large egg yolk, beaten
Salt
Freshly ground pepper
2 tablespoons vegetable oil

*Sweet & Sour Sauce:*
1 (1-lb.) can apricot halves in light syrup
2 tablespoons cornstarch
1/4 cup soy sauce
1/4 cup ketchup
1/2 cup chicken stock
1 small green bell pepper, chopped
1 small red bell pepper, chopped
1 tablespoon chopped gingerroot

1. In a medium bowl, combine pork, bread crumbs, onion, sage, egg yolk, salt and pepper. Shape into 24 small balls.
2. Heat oil in a large heavy skillet. Add pork balls; sauté over medium heat about 15 minutes or until browned, turning occasionally. Remove with a slotted spoon; drain on paper towels. Keep warm.
3. To make sauce, drain apricots, reserving syrup. In a medium saucepan, combine cornstarch and reserved syrup. Stir in soy sauce, ketchup and stock. Bring to a boil, stirring constantly.
4. Reduce heat; stir in bell peppers and gingerroot; simmer 5 minutes.
5. Add pork balls, coating with sauce; simmer about 5 minutes, stirring frequently.
6. Slice apricots; gently stir into pork mixture. Serve immediately with cooked rice and Bean-Sprout Salad; see box. Makes 4 servings.

---

**Bean-Sprout Salad:** In a medium salad bowl, combine 1-1/2 cups bean sprouts and 2 cups sliced mushrooms. To make dressing, in a small bowl, whisk together 3 tablespoons olive oil, 1/4 cup fresh orange juice, 1 tablespoon lemon peel, salt and freshly ground pepper. Pour dressing over salad; toss to combine.

---

# Chili con Carne

3 tablespoons vegetable oil
2 onions, chopped
1 garlic clove, crushed
1 lb. lean ground beef
2 teaspoons dried leaf oregano
1 teaspoon ground cumin
2 teaspoons chili powder
1 teaspoon paprika
Salt
Freshly ground pepper
1 (1-lb.) can tomatoes
1/2 cup beef stock
6 oz. chorizo sausage, skinned, coarsely chopped
1 (15-oz.) can red kidney beans, drained

---

*This is a speedy but extra-tasty version of classic chili con carne. It has a hot spicy taste that comes not only from the chili powder but also from chorizo sausage. Mexican chorizo sausage can be bought at most good delicatessens and is easily recognizable by its bright red color. It is pork sausage flavored with hot red pepper. If it is difficult to find, use any cured sausage with a hot spicy flavor. Flavor of chili improves when it is made a day ahead and reheated.*

1. Heat oil in a large saucepan. Add onions and garlic; cook 5 to 10 minutes or until softened.
2. Add beef; cook about 10 minutes or until lightly browned, stirring to break up beef. Stir in oregano, cumin, chili powder, paprika, salt and pepper. Cook over medium heat 2 to 3 minutes.
3. Coarsely chop tomatoes; stir chopped tomatoes and their juice into beef mixture. Stir in stock. Cook, uncovered, over medium heat 10 to 15 minutes.
4. Stir in chorizo sausage and beans; cook 10 minutes.
5. Serve hot with cooked rice or warm tortillas. Makes 4 servings.

# Light Meals & Snacks

In order to eat well, it is not necessary to spend hours in the kitchen. Even during the week, it is possible to prepare delicious meals and snacks. Today there are several labor-saving pieces of equipment, convenience-style foods and many beautiful styles of freezer-to-oven-to-table cookware that save on valuable cleanup time. It is possible to have delicious, home-cooked meals in a fraction of the time it used to take. For this chapter, recipes were chosen that are delicious, nutritious and easy to prepare. With these goals in mind, you'll see that the preparation time in each of these recipes is kept to a minimum.

Preparing quick, tasty and nutritious light meals and snacks does not necessarily demand a large supply of frozen, dried or canned convenience foods. Just the opposite, it involves judiciously using a few convenience foods with fresh ingredients to save time, add flavor or reduce the workload. A well-stocked, but not heavily-stocked pantry, can prove to be a lifesaver when unexpected guests call, when a meal for four suddenly has to expand to serve six and when quick, but interesting, snacks are required.

Foods to have on hand fall into three main categories: dried and packaged products, canned goods and those foods that must be refrigerated or frozen.

## DRIED & PACKAGED PRODUCTS

Keep a wide variety of dried herbs, spices and seasonings on hand. They can literally lift a dish from the ordinary to the luxury class. Remember to keep your supply fresh. If your herbs and spices are several months old, you might want to replace them. Bouillon cubes are helpful, especially if you haven't the time to make stock. Remember that bouillon cubes are salted; make adjustments in your recipe.

A good selection of dried fruits and nuts will always come in handy. They can be used as basic ingredients, or as garnishes to add an interesting touch. Currants, raisins, walnuts, almonds and pecans are a good selection to have on hand. If nuts are not used quickly, store them in the refrigerator or freezer. This prevents the fats they contain from becoming rancid and giving the nuts an off flavor.

A well-stocked pantry will also include a good selection of rice, hot and cold cereals, flour, pasta, cornmeal, sugar and other ingredients for baking. Choose a few quick mixes for breads, cakes or brownies. A package of nonfat dried milk will be useful for emergencies. A favorite dried-soup mix, sauce mix or seasoning packet may be one of your standbys. Beyond that, the choice is yours. Dried vegetables, such as onions, instant potatoes, dried peas and dried beans, keep well and are useful. A pressure cooker will save time when cooking dried peas and beans.

## CANNED GOODS

These can really be a bonus when time is short. Include a good selection of condensed soups, chicken stock and beef stock. Canned stocks are excellent substitutes for homemade stock when time is short.

A few cans of fish and shellfish, such as sardines, anchovies, crab, shrimp, mussels and tuna, should be on hand. These are useful in hors d'oeuvres, salads, soups, or gratin-type dishes. Canned pâté, ham, corned beef and chicken are indispensable for a quick meal or snack. In addition to canned seafood and meats, canned vegetables and fruits, such as beans, corn, mushrooms, apricots, pears and peaches, all have a well-earned place. Don't forget canned milk for soups and sauces.

Without question, one of the most useful groups of canned goods is the wide array of tomato products, such as canned tomatoes, tomato paste and tomato sauce. These are always in season and do not have to be peeled or chopped.

Remember to keep a supply of special ingredients, such as olives, capers, chutneys or pickles. These can be used to add flavor and as garnishes. Keep a supply of sweets—for example, jams, syrups and dessert sauces.

A good selection of oils, vinegars and salad dressings will make serving a variety of salads easier. Of course, wines, spirits and liqueurs add a flavor all their own. Use the same wine for cooking that you do for drinking.

Some foods to have on hand

## REFRIGERATED & FROZEN FOODS

A refrigerator and freezer are high on the list of kitchen essentials. A refrigerator can be stocked with eggs; milk; butter or margarine; bacon; a selection of hard and soft cheeses; a carton or two of fruit juice; a few fresh oranges, lemons and other fruits and milk.

The range of prepared foods that is available in the supermarket is extensive, and the choice of which to buy is an individual one. However, there are some foods particularly useful for preparing recipes in this chapter. These include frozen fish and shellfish, a good-quality ground beef, cut-up chicken and ready-made beef patties. In addition, include a good selection of home- or commercially-frozen vegetables and fruits.

In the pastry section, some ready-made crepes stacked between foil or freezer paper and frozen puff pastry will be timesavers. These will simplify meal planning and preparation.

For quick desserts, one or two favorite dessert sauces, some ice cream, frozen cakes or cookies will add the finishing touch to a meal.

Other items to keep on hand, if space permits, are lemon peel, lemon juice and chopped herbs. Store only those items you use regularly. Inventory your refrigerator and freezer on a regular basis to determine what needs to be used.

When cooking food that is to be frozen, reheating prepared dishes, or defrosting frozen foods, it is important to follow food-safety rules. Remember that freezing does not destroy bacteria in foods. When the food is thawed, any bacteria that is present will start to grow again. Some foods, such as poultry, pork, sausage and shellfish, need to be handled with care since these are more susceptible to spoilage. Leftovers should always be stored in the refrigerator and not at room temperature. Most frozen foods should be thawed in the refrigerator rather than at room temperature. When reheating foods that have been made ahead or frozen, reheat thoroughly. Use most leftovers within 24 hours. If in doubt about the freshness of a food, do not eat it.

## A NUTRITIOUS EATING PLAN

If snacks are planned that provide part of the daily nutrient requirements, eating snacks need not play havoc with good eating habits. A balanced and varied diet should provide all the nutrients needed for health. Eating a healthy diet does not mean buying expensive foods from health-food stores. The supermarket is the source for ingredients used in this book. These recipes have been developed so that you can choose a varied and nutritious range of foods. They can be part of a sensible overall eating plan.

Current nutritional recommendations on which to base your plan include:

1. Eating lean cuts of meat and trimming away fat before cooking.
2. Eating more fish and poultry.
3. Eating less than five eggs per week. This reduces cholesterol intake.
4. Replacing high-fat foods with low-fat alternatives. For example, substitute skimmed milk for whole milk or low-fat cheeses for high-fat cheeses.
5. Eating a wide selection of fruit and vegetables. Eat at least 4 servings daily.
6. Eating more cereals, especially whole-grain varieties.
7. Cutting down on all fats.
8. Trying to eat less salt and refined sugar.

## HELPFUL HINTS

Despite the help of convenience foods and modern equipment, there are still moments in a cook's life when there is simply not enough time. However, there are some helpful ideas that the cook can use for spicing up the simplest meals so that they need never become humdrum. These include:

● Add flavor to a stuffing mix, if you don't have time to make one from scratch, by adding herbs and substituting fruit juice for half of the water. Good flavor combinations include sage and onion with apple juice or orange juice and thyme and lemon with grapefruit juice.

● Add a spoonful of cream to a sauce or to pan juices to produce that swirl of luxury on sautéed or broiled foods.

● Make delicious and unusual short-crust pastry by adding additional ingredients. Good ones to try include chopped nuts, grated fruit peels, ground spices, dried leaf herbs, wheat germ, chopped cooked bacon, cooked chopped onion, dried coconut and fruit juices, depending on whether the crust is for a sweet or savory pie.

● Savory rice dishes taste all the more delicious if you substitute fruit juice or stock for some of the cooking water. *Coconut Rice* also makes a delicious accompaniment to a curry or spiced dish. Add approximately 2 tablespoons cream of coconut to 1-1/4 cups rice; cook in the usual way.

● A good choice of marinades helps tenderize and adds flavor to economical meat cuts prior to cooking. Use this *Meat Marinade* for kabob cubes or man-size pot roasts. In a medium bowl, combine 2 tablespoons vinegar, 1 tablespoon olive oil, 1/2 teaspoon honey, 1/2 teaspoon dried leaf marjoram and 1/4 cup apple juice. Add meat; marinate at least 4 hours. Or, cover and refrigerate overnight.

● Keep flavored butters in the refrigerator or freezer for topping broiled or sautéed meats and fish, and poached fish. Use flavored butters to top baked potatoes and sandwiches. Herbs, such as parsley, chives, thyme and tarragon, are versatile, or try onion butter, blue-cheese butter, mint butter and lemon butter.

● Salads needn't be made of only lettuce, tomato and cucumber. Combine an imaginative selection of everyday, as well as exotic, fruits and vegetables with fish, meats, eggs, cheese and, more importantly, a tasty dressing. Keep a variety of salad dressings on hand. Store in the refrigerator, and simply shake to use.

● Basic mayonnaise can be flavored with curry, mint, lemon, garlic or chilies for interesting additions to salads and sandwiches.

● Canned and packaged soups offer tremendous advantages to the busy cook. Use them instead of stock for stews, casseroles, chowders and sauces. Or, add cream, sherry, herbs or a topping of croutons, onion rings or paprika for a quick, flavorful soup.

## GARNISHES

Remember to serve food with style by adding attractive garnishes and table settings. Mix and match foods with the following garnish ideas.

● Chopped herbs or herb sprigs
● Tomato slices or hard-cooked-egg slices
● Lemon slices, twists, butterflies or wedges
● Cucumber slices
● A dusting of spices or coconut
● Chopped, halved or whole nuts, olives, or dried fruit
● A border of shredded lettuce or Chinese cabbage
● Crispy croutons
● A golden-brown border of piped, then broiled, mashed potatoes
● A spoonful or swirl of sour cream, whipped cream or yogurt
● An aspic glaze with colorful vegetable pieces
● Hollowed-out fruit and vegetable shells
● Toasted French bread, baked choux buns or freshly cooked fluffy dumplings
● Shredded cheese or toasted bread crumbs
● Toast fingers or triangles
● Green-onion curls, carrot scrolls or decorative vegetable shapes for an Oriental effect
● Pleated and grilled bacon slices, page 63
● Julienne strips of fruit peel, such as orange, lemon or lime

# Stuffed French Bread

1 large French-bread loaf
2 tablespoons butter or margarine, room temperature

*Coleslaw:*
1/4 head cabbage, shredded
1/2 small onion, finely chopped
1 small carrot, grated
1 celery stalk, chopped
3 tablespoons raisins
2 tablespoons coarsely chopped walnuts
3 to 4 tablespoons mayonnaise

*Filling:*
2 lettuce leaves, shredded
3 bologna slices, rolled
3 salami slices, rolled into cornets
2 oz. smoked cheese, sliced
2 oz. blue cheese, sliced
1 hard-cooked egg, sliced
1 large tomato, sliced

1. Split loaf in half horizontally. Thinly spread butter or margarine on cut sides of loaf.
2. To make coleslaw, in a medium bowl, combine cabbage, onion, carrot, celery, raisins and walnuts. Stir in enough mayonnaise to bind ingredients.
3. Spread coleslaw along length of bottom half of loaf; top with lettuce, bologna, salami, smoked cheese, blue cheese, hard-cooked egg and tomato, arranging attractively.
4. Press loaf halves firmly together; cut vertically into 3 sections to serve. Makes 3 servings.

**Variation**
For an Oriental-flavored coleslaw, substitute shredded Chinese cabbage for regular cabbage, bean sprouts for celery and water chestnuts for onions. Continue as above.

# Greek Pita-Pocket Sandwiches

4 pita-bread rounds

*Greek Salad*
1 cup finely chopped cooked lamb
2 oz. mushrooms, thinly sliced (about 1 cup)
1 small bunch green onions, chopped
2 lettuce leaves, shredded
2 tomatoes, peeled, seeded, chopped
4 black olives, pitted, sliced
2 to 3 tablespoons plain yogurt
Salt
Freshly ground pepper
3/4 cup shredded Monterey Jack cheese (3 oz.)

1. Preheat broiler. Cut off 1 to 2 inches from top of each pita round. Carefully open to form a pocket.
2. To make Greek Salad, in a medium bowl, combine lamb, mushrooms, green onions, lettuce, tomatoes, olives, yogurt, salt and pepper.
3. Spoon Greek Salad into pita pockets. Place filled sandwiches on a baking sheet. Sprinkle cheese on sandwiches.
4. Broil under preheated broiler 5 to 6 minutes or until cheese melts. Serve immediately. Makes 4 servings.

**Variation**
**West Indies Pita-Pocket Sandwiches:** In a medium bowl, combine 1/2 cup diced cooked chicken, 1/4 cup finely chopped pineapple, 1/4 cup finely chopped green bell pepper, 1 small sliced banana, 1/4 cup chopped toasted almonds, 2 to 3 tablespoons mayonnaise, salt and freshly ground black pepper. Use to fill pita rounds.

Top to bottom: Greek Pita-Pocket Sandwiches; Pork, Beef & Chicken Saté with Peanut Sauce, page 262

# Salami & Mozzarella Snacks

4 thick homemade-style bread slices
4 oz. salami, thinly sliced
4 tomatoes, peeled, sliced
Freshly ground black pepper
1 green or yellow bell pepper, sliced
8 thin mozzarella-cheese slices
1/2 teaspoon Italian seasoning

*To garnish:*
4 to 8 small black olives
Parsley sprigs

1. Preheat broiler. Place bread on a broiler-pan rack. Toast on 1 side under preheated broiler.
2. Turn bread slices over; cover with salami and tomatoes. Season with black pepper. Top with bell pepper and cheese. Sprinkle each with 1/8 teaspoon Italian seasoning.
3. Broil under preheated broiler about 10 minutes or until cheese melts.
4. Top with olives; garnish with parsley. Serve hot. Makes 4 servings.

Left to right: Salami & Mozzarella Snacks, Bean & Egg Snacks, Baked Ham & Cheese Loaf

# Bean & Egg Snacks

1 (1-lb.) can pork and beans with tomato sauce
1 to 2 teaspoons chili powder
1 canned pimento, finely chopped
1/2 teaspoon Worcestershire sauce
1/4 cup butter or margarine
6 eggs, beaten
Salt
Freshly ground pepper
4 slices hot buttered toast
1 tomato, thinly sliced

*To garnish:*
Cilantro sprigs

**1.** In a medium saucepan, combine beans, chili powder, pimento and Worcestershire sauce. Stir over medium heat until hot.
**2.** Melt butter or margarine in a large skillet. Add eggs, salt and pepper. Cook over low heat until lightly scrambled.
**3.** Spoon scrambled eggs around edges of toast; see photo.
**4.** Spoon bean mixture into center of eggs. Top with tomato slices; garnish with cilantro. Serve immediately. Makes 4 servings.

# Baked Ham & Cheese Loaf

1 large French-bread loaf
1/4 cup butter or margarine, room temperature
1 garlic clove, crushed
8 slices Monterey Jack cheese
8 cooked ham slices
8 salami-with-peppercorns slices
2 tomatoes, thinly sliced

**1.** Preheat oven to 375F (190C). Make 8 diagonal cuts at equal distances along length of loaf, cutting almost through loaf.
**2.** In a small bowl, cream butter or margarine and garlic; spread on cut sides of bread. Place buttered bread on a piece of foil large enough to completely wrap it.
**3.** Place 1 slice each of cheese, ham, salami and tomato in each cut. Press gently together to re-form loaf. Wrap loaf loosely with foil.
**4.** Bake in preheated oven 10 to 15 minutes.
**5.** Open top of foil; bake 5 minutes or until cheese melts. Pull apart or cut between filled sections to serve. Makes 4 servings.

1/Spread creamed garlic butter or margarine on cut sides of bread.

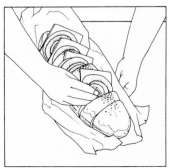

2/Place 1 slice each of cheese, ham, salami and tomato in each cut.

# Smorrebrod

4 pumpernickel-bread slices
1/4 cup butter or margarine, room temperature
4 lettuce leaves
4 salami slices
2 tablespoons grated cabbage
1 tablespoon grated carrot
2 green onions, finely chopped
4 hard-cooked eggs, chopped
1/4 cup mayonnaise
Salt
Freshly ground pepper
1 teaspoon capers
1 bratwurst, broiled, sliced
1 teaspoon mango chutney
1 teaspoon chopped raisins
1 tomato, sliced
2 tablespoons radish sprouts

*To serve more people, double or triple this recipe.*

**1.** Spread bread generously with butter or margarine; top each slice with a lettuce leaf.
**2.** Top 2 bread slices with 2 salami slices each. In a medium bowl, combine cabbage, carrot, green onions, 2 hard-cooked eggs, 2 tablespoons mayonnaise, salt and pepper. Spoon mixture on top of salami; garnish with capers.
**3.** Top remaining 2 bread slices with bratwurst. In a medium bowl, combine remaining 2 hard-cooked eggs with remaining 2 tablespoons mayonnaise, chutney, raisins, salt and pepper. Spoon mixture on bratwurst. Arrange slices of tomato over chutney-egg mixture. Garnish with radish sprouts.
**4.** Serve 1 salami sandwich and 1 sausage sandwich per person. Makes 2 servings.

# Spicy Club Sandwiches

1/2 cup diced cooked chicken
1/4 cup mayonnaise
1 teaspoon mild curry powder
1 tablespoon raisins
4 Canadian-bacon slices
8 whole-wheat-bread slices, crusts removed, toasted
4 white-bread slices, crusts removed, toasted
1/4 cup butter or margarine, room temperature
4 lettuce leaves
About 16 thin cucumber slices
1 small green bell pepper, sliced
2 tomatoes, thinly sliced
1 tablespoon chopped fresh parsley

**1.** In a medium bowl, combine chicken, mayonnaise, curry powder and raisins.
**2.** Cook bacon in a medium skillet over low heat until hot. Keep warm.
**3.** Spread 1 side of whole-wheat bread and both sides of white bread with butter or margarine.
**4.** Spread chicken mixture over buttered sides of 4 whole-wheat-bread slices. Top each with a buttered white-bread slice.
**5.** Cover each white-bread slice with a lettuce leaf, 4 cucumber slices and 1/4 of bell pepper.
**6.** Top each sandwich with a final whole-wheat-bread slice, buttered-side down. Cover with tomato slices and a bacon slice. Sprinkle tomato with chopped parsley. Serve immediately with a knife and fork. Makes 4 servings.

# New Yorkers

8 rye-bread slices
1 (8-oz.) pkg. cream cheese, room temperature
4 smoked-salmon slices
1 red onion, sliced into rings
16 fresh parsley sprigs
Freshly ground pepper

**1.** Spread bread generously with cream cheese.
**2.** Cut each salmon slice in half; roll each half into a small cornet. Place a salmon cornet on top of each bread slice.
**3.** Top salmon with a few onion rings and 2 parsley sprigs. Sprinkle with a little pepper. Makes 4 servings.

Clockwise from left: Beef & Cheese Roll, Smorrebrod,
Spicy Club Sandwich

# Beef & Cheese Rolls

4 large soft sesame rolls
6 tablespoons butter or margarine, room temperature
1/2 cup finely chopped cold roast beef
1/4 cup mayonnaise
1 tablespoon chopped fresh chives
1 to 2 teaspoons prepared horseradish
4 lettuce leaves
4 oz. sharp Cheddar cheese, thinly sliced
1 tomato, thinly sliced
2 tablespoons chutney
1 medium leek, white part only, thinly sliced
1 teaspoon grated lemon peel
1 tablespoon raisins

1. Cut 3 horizontal slits in each roll, cutting almost completely through. Spread bread layers with butter or margarine.
2. In a medium bowl, combine beef, 1/2 of mayonnaise, chives and horseradish to taste.
3. Place a lettuce leaf on bottom layer of each buttered roll; top each lettuce leaf with 1/4 of beef filling.
4. Fill middle layer of rolls with cheese, tomato and chutney.
5. Separate sliced leek into rings. In a small bowl, combine leek, lemon peel, remaining 2 tablespoons mayonnaise and raisins. Use to fill top layer of rolls. Press top of each roll down lightly before serving. Makes 4 servings.

# Bacon & Cheese Sandwiches

8 thin white-bread slices, crusts removed
1 to 2 teaspoons prepared coarse mustard
4 oz. Gruyère cheese, sliced
8 bacon slices, crisp-cooked
2 tomatoes, thinly sliced
3 tablespoons butter or margarine, melted

1. Preheat oven to 450F (230C). Spread 1/2 of bread slices with mustard to taste. Top each with an equal amount of cheese, bacon and tomato slices. Cover with remaining bread slices, pressing down well.
2. Place sandwiches on a baking sheet; brush tops lightly with about 1/2 of butter or margarine.
3. Bake in preheated oven about 5 minutes or until lightly browned.
4. Using a spatula, turn sandwiches over; brush with remaining butter or margarine. Bake 3 to 5 minutes or until lightly browned. Cut diagonally in half to serve. Makes 4 servings.

# French-Bread Pizzas

1 large French-bread loaf
3 tablespoons tomato paste
1 (8-oz.) can tomatoes, drained, chopped
1 teaspoon dried leaf oregano or dried leaf marjoram
Salt
Freshly ground pepper
1 cup shredded mozzarella cheese (4 oz.)
2 (2-oz.) cans anchovy fillets in oil, drained

*To garnish:*
8 black olives

1. Preheat broiler. Slice French bread in half horizontally. Cut each half in half crosswise. Place on a baking sheet.
2. Broil under preheated broiler until golden brown.
3. Spread toasted bread with tomato paste. Top with tomatoes, oregano or marjoram, salt, pepper and cheese.
4. Arrange anchovy fillets in a lattice pattern over cheese; garnish with olives.
5. Broil under preheated broiler about 10 minutes or until golden and bubbly.
6. Cut into thick slices. Serve hot. Makes 4 servings.

### Variation
Substitute 2 cups chopped cooked ham and pimento-stuffed olives for anchovies and black olives. Sprinkle ham over tomato base; top with cheese. Garnish with a few sliced olives. Cook as above.

To prevent soggy sandwiches, spread soft butter, margarine, or soft cheese on the bread before adding the filling. Use toasted bread or crisp rolls for sandwiches that are made ahead. Add moist ingredients, such as tomato slices, immediately before serving. If the sandwich is for a packed lunch, wrap tomato slices separately.

To prevent sandwiches from drying out, wrap tightly with plastic wrap, or use plastic sandwich bags.

Many sandwiches can be frozen. However, hard-cooked eggs and mayonnaise do not freeze well. Hard-cooked egg whites become rubbery when frozen; mayonnaise separates.

Left to right: Broiled Asparagus & Cheese Sandwiches, French-Bread Pizzas

# Broiled Asparagus & Cheese Sandwiches

4 whole-wheat-bread slices
3 tablespoons butter or margarine, room temperature
4 tomatoes, sliced
Salt
Freshly ground pepper
12 cooked asparagus spears
1 cup shredded Cheddar cheese (4 oz.)

**1.** Preheat broiler. Place bread slices on a baking sheet. Broil under preheated broiler until golden on 1 side.
**2.** Turn bread slices over; spread generously with butter or margarine.
**3.** Top with tomato slices. Sprinkle with salt and pepper. Arrange asparagus on tomatoes. Top with cheese.
**4.** Broil under preheated broiler 4 to 5 minutes or until cheese melts. Serve immediately. Makes 4 servings.

# Pumpernickel Party Snacks

1 (8-oz.) pkg. cream cheese, room temperature
1 tablespoon brandy
Freshly ground pepper
2 tablespoons finely chopped walnuts or almonds
36 pumpernickel or rye cocktail rounds

*To garnish:*
Black-grape halves or walnut halves

1. In a medium bowl, combine cream cheese, brandy, pepper and chopped nuts.
2. Spread 2/3 of rounds evenly with cheese mixture, reserving a little for securing garnish.
3. Assemble each sandwich, using 2 cheese-topped rounds and 1 plain round, placing plain round on top; see photo opposite.
4. Place a small amount of cheese mixture on top of each sandwich. Press a grape half or walnut half into cheese mixture.

---

Many sandwiches can be made ahead and frozen until needed. Most traditional fillings can be used. However, hard-cooked eggs and mayonnaise do not freeze well. Hard-cooked egg whites become rubbery when frozen; mayonnaise separates. Sandwiches that are packed frozen for a picnic will thaw in time for lunch.

Vary the types of breads, spreads and fillings to make sandwiches more interesting. Choose breads and fillings that complement each other. For example, robust, sturdy bread goes well with sausages and cheese. Choose a bread with a more delicate flavor and texture for chicken-salad sandwiches. Seasoned butters make excellent spreads, or try one of the many mustards on the market. Let your imagination take charge!

---

# Salami & Pita Specials

4 pita-bread rounds
2 to 3 cups shredded lettuce
1 medium onion, chopped
Olive oil
6 oz. feta cheese or mozzarella cheese, cubed
4 oz. salami, thinly sliced
1/4 cup pitted black olives, chopped
Freshly ground pepper

1. Preheat oven to 350F (175C). Wrap pita bread loosely in foil. Heat in preheated oven 5 minutes.
2. Cut each pita to form a pocket.
3. Fill pockets with a layer of lettuce and a little chopped onion. Drizzle a little olive oil over lettuce and onion.
4. Add some cheese, salami and olives to each pocket. Season with pepper. Work quickly so bread does not cool.
5. Serve while bread is still warm. Makes 4 sandwiches.

# Smoked-Salmon Rarebit

2 cups shredded Swiss cheese (8 oz.)
2 eggs, separated
1 teaspoon prepared brown mustard
Freshly ground pepper
3 tablespoons milk
3 oz. smoked-salmon trimmings, finely chopped
4 whole-wheat-bread slices

*To garnish:*
Lemon slices
Fresh parsley sprigs

1. Preheat broiler. In a medium bowl, combine cheese, egg yolks, mustard, pepper, milk and smoked salmon.
2. In a medium bowl, beat egg whites until stiff but not dry. Fold beaten egg whites into cheese mixture.
3. Toast bread on 1 side only.
4. Divide cheese mixture among 4 bread slices, spreading evenly on untoasted side of bread.
5. Broil under preheated broiler until cheese topping puffs and is golden brown.
6. Serve hot. Makes 4 servings.

Clockwise from top: Pumpernickel Party Snacks, Smoked-Salmon Rarebit, Salami & Pita Specials

# Fishermen's Sticks

12 fish sticks
Butter or margarine, melted
6 long crusty rolls
Ketchup
2 small pkgs. potato chips, coarsely crushed
3 tomatoes, cut into thin wedges

---

*This makes an excellent party snack for older children. The rolls look appetizing and are easy to eat. I have yet to meet a child who does not like fish sticks!*

1. Preheat broiler. Brush fish sticks with butter or margarine. Place under preheated broiler. Broil 8 to 10 minutes, turning once. Keep warm.
2. Preheat oven to 375F (190C). Split rolls lengthwise; do not cut all the way through. Brush inside each roll with butter or margarine. Place buttered rolls on a baking sheet. Bake in preheated oven 5 minutes.
3. Spread buttered surface of warm rolls with ketchup. Fill each roll with a layer of potato chips, 2 broiled fish sticks and tomato wedges. Serve immediately. Makes 6 servings.

---

Avocados, sometimes called alligator pears, originally came from Central America. To choose avocados, look for ones that are firm and free from cuts and bruises. The avocado should yield slightly when pressed. If it is too hard, it may rot rather than ripen. Ripen avocados at room temperature for two to three days. After cutting the avocado, sprinkle with lime or lemon juice to prevent browning. If you are only using half of the avocado, sprinkle the remaining half with lime or lemon juice; refrigerate with the seed still in place.

# Baked Sardine Toasts

2 eggs
1 tablespoon Worcestershire sauce
Salt
Freshly ground pepper
4 bread slices
2 (7-oz.) cans sardines in oil
Grated peel of 1/2 lemon
8 oz. cream cheese with chives
2 tablespoons mayonnaise
1 small onion, finely chopped

---

1. Preheat oven to 375F (190C). Grease a baking sheet. In a medium bowl, beat eggs, Worcestershire sauce, salt and pepper.
2. Dip both sides of bread slices into egg mixture. Place dipped bread on greased baking sheet. Bake in preheated oven 5 minutes.
3. Drain oil from sardines; mash sardines with lemon peel and pepper. Spread evenly over each slice of baked bread.
4. In a medium bowl, beat cream cheese with a wooden spoon to soften; beat in mayonnaise and onion. Spread cheese mixture evenly over sardine mixture.
5. Bake in preheated oven 15 minutes or until topping is golden. Serve immediately. Makes 4 servings.

# Avocado & Shrimp Rolls

4 whole-wheat rolls
Butter or margarine, room temperature
1 ripe avocado, halved
Juice of 1 lemon
Salt
Freshly ground black pepper
6 oz. deveined, peeled, cooked shrimp
1/4 cup mayonnaise
Red (cayenne) pepper
Lettuce leaves

---

1. Cut each roll in half crosswise.
2. Spread 1 cut surface of each layer with butter or margarine.
3. Cut avocado into thin slices. In a small bowl, toss avocado slices in lemon juice. Season with salt and black pepper.
4. In a medium bowl, combine shrimp, mayonnaise, a little red pepper, salt and pepper.
5. Divide avocado slices, shrimp mixture and lettuce among roll bottoms. Sandwich together with roll tops. Makes 4 servings.

# Smoked-Haddock Triangles

1 lb. smoked haddock
Milk
1 bay leaf
Freshly ground pepper
About 1/2 cup mayonnaise
Grated peel of 1 lemon
8 white-bread slices
4 whole-wheat-bread slices
Butter, room temperature
Chopped fresh parsley

*To garnish:*
Small lemon fans

**1.** Place fish in a shallow pan. Add enough milk to half cover; add bay leaf and pepper. Simmer until fish is tender.
**2.** Drain fish, discarding milk and bay leaf. Discard any skin and bone; flake flesh. Cool.
**3.** In a small bowl, combine flaked fish with enough mayonnaise to bind. Stir in lemon peel.
**4.** Spread 1 side of each white-bread slice and both sides of whole-wheat-bread slices evenly with butter or margarine.
**5.** For each sandwich, spread 1/8 of fish mixture on buttered side of 1 white-bread slice and 1 whole-wheat-bread slice. Place whole-wheat-bread slice over topping on white bread. Top with an untopped white-bread slice, buttered-side down. Repeat to make 4 sandwiches.
**6.** Cut off crusts; cut each sandwich into 4 triangles.
**7.** Spread tops of each triangle lightly with mayonnaise; sprinkle with chopped parsley.
**8.** Garnish triangles with lemon fans. Makes 16 triangles.

Left to right: Baked Sardine Toasts, Smoked-Haddock Triangles

# Beef & Coleslaw Sandwich

3 hot toast slices
Butter or margarine, room temperature
10 to 12 thin cucumber slices
2 tablespoons coleslaw
Prepared horseradish
2 rare roast-beef slices

*To garnish:*
Radish slices
Pickled onion
Sweet pickle

1. Spread 1 side of each toast slice with butter or margarine.
2. Top 1 buttered side of toast with a layer of cucumber and coleslaw, reserving 1 cucumber slice for garnish. Spread buttered side of 1 piece of toast with horseradish. Place horseradish-side up on first layer.
3. Arrange beef slices on horseradish; place third slice of toast on top, buttered-side down.
4. Cut sandwich in half diagonally; garnish 1 sandwich half with radish slices and reserved cucumber slice; garnish remaining half with pickle and onion. Makes 1 serving.

# Blue-Cheese Special

2 whole-wheat-bread slices
Butter or margarine, room temperature
1/2 cup crumbled blue cheese (2 oz.)
2 crisp-cooked bacon slices, crumbled
1 tablespoon mayonnaise
Freshly ground pepper

1. Preheat broiler. Spread 1 side of both bread slices with butter or margarine.
2. Place 1 bread slice, buttered-side down, on a broiler-pan rack.
3. In a small bowl, combine blue cheese, bacon, mayonnaise and pepper.
4. Spread cheese mixture evenly over bread slice on rack. Top with remaining slice, buttered-side up. Press bread gently together.
5. Broil sandwich under preheated broiler 4 to 5 minutes, turning sandwich once.
6. Serve immediately. Makes 1 sandwich.

# Pâté Beehives

14 whole-wheat-bread slices
12 oz. liver pâté
Butter or margarine, melted
1/4 cup chopped fresh parsley
1/4 cup chopped toasted nuts
2 pimento-stuffed olives, sliced

*These attractive sandwiches are made of 3 layers of bread each. Each layer is a different diameter. You should be able to get 1 (2-1/2-inch) circle from 1 slice of bread, 2 (2-inch) circles from 1 slice and 4 (1-1/2-inch) circles from 1 slice.*

1. Cut 8 (2-1/2-inch) bread circles, 8 (2-inch) bread circles and 8 (1-1/2-inch) bread circles.
2. Spread large circles with 2/3 of pâté; spread medium circles with remaining pâté.
3. To assemble beehives, place a medium circle on top of each large circle; top with a small circle. See illustration below.
4. Smooth edges, using a round-bladed knife. Refrigerate 20 minutes.
5. Brush beehives with melted butter or margarine. Roll 4 beehives in chopped parsley; roll remaining beehives in toasted nuts.
6. Top each coated beehive with an olive slice. Makes 8 sandwiches.

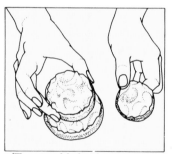 

1/To assemble beehives, place a medium circle on top of each large circle; top with a small circle.

2/Smooth edges, using a round-bladed knife.

Left to right: Beef & Coleslaw Sandwich, Pâté Beehives

Left to right: Chicken & Almond Rounds, Toasted Ham & Cheese Sandwich, Toasted Tuna & Egg Sandwich, Toasted Chicken Sandwich

# Chicken & Almond Rounds

16 whole-wheat-bread slices
Butter or margarine, room temperature
3/4 cup finely chopped cooked chicken
2 tablespoons dairy sour cream
1/4 cup chopped toasted almonds
Salt
Freshly ground pepper
About 1/4 cup red-currant jelly

1. Cut 1 (3-1/2-inch) circle from each bread slice using a fluted pastry cutter.
2. Cut a 1-inch center from 1/2 of circles to make rings.
3. Spread 1 side of each circle and ring with butter or margarine.
4. In a small bowl, combine chicken, sour cream, almonds, salt and pepper.
5. Spread circles with chicken mixture; top with rings.
6. Place 1 teaspoon jelly into center of each sandwich. Makes 8 sandwiches.

# Toasted Ham & Cheese Sandwich

2 white-bread slices
Butter or margarine, room temperature
Prepared brown mustard
1/2 cup shredded Cheddar cheese (2 oz.)
1 ham slice (2 oz.)
Freshly ground pepper

1. Preheat broiler. Spread 1 side of both slices of bread thinly with butter or margarine; spread unbuttered side with a thin layer of mustard.
2. Place 1 bread slice, buttered-side down, on a broiler-pan rack.
3. Place 1/2 of cheese on bread on rack. Top with ham, remaining cheese and pepper.
4. Top with remaining bread, buttered-side up. Press sandwich gently together.
5. Broil sandwich under preheated broiler 4 to 5 minutes, turning sandwich once.
6. Serve immediately. Makes 1 sandwich.

# Toasted Tuna & Egg Sandwich

2 white-bread slices
Butter or margarine, room temperature
1 hard-cooked egg, chopped
1 green onion, chopped
Salt
Freshly ground pepper
2 tablespoons tuna
2 tablespoons mayonnaise

---

**1.** Preheat broiler. Spread both sides of bread with butter or margarine.
**2.** Place 1 bread slice on a broiler-pan rack.
**3.** In a small bowl, combine egg, onion, salt, pepper, tuna and mayonnaise.
**4.** Spread egg mixture evenly over bread on rack; top with remaining slice. Press sandwich gently together.
**5.** Broil sandwich under preheated broiler 4 to 5 minutes, turning sandwich once.
**6.** Serve immediately. Makes 1 sandwich.

# Toasted Chicken Sandwich

2 whole-wheat-bread slices
Butter or margarine, room temperature
1/2 cup chopped cooked chicken
1 tablespoon mayonnaise
2 tablespoons corn relish
1 tablespoon finely chopped celery
Salt
Freshly ground pepper

---

**1.** Preheat broiler. Spread both sides of bread with butter or margarine.
**2.** Place 1 bread slice on a broiler-pan rack.
**3.** In a small bowl, combine chicken, mayonnaise, corn relish, celery, salt and pepper.
**4.** Spread chicken mixture evenly over bread on rack. Top with remaining slice. Press sandwich gently together.
**5.** Broil sandwich under preheated broiler 4 to 5 minutes, turning sandwich once.
**6.** Serve immediately. Makes 1 sandwich.

# Frankfurter & Onion Delight

1 tablespoon vegetable oil
1 small onion, peeled, cut into thin rings
2 white-bread slices
Butter or margarine, room temperature
1 frankfurter, cut into thin slices
1 tablespoon chopped pickle
Freshly ground pepper

1. Preheat broiler. Heat oil in a small skillet. Add onion; sauté until tender and lightly golden.
2. Spread 1 side of both bread slices with butter or margarine.
3. Place 1 slice of bread, buttered-side down, on a broiler-pan rack.
4. In a small bowl, combine cooked onion, frankfurter, pickle and pepper.
5. Spread frankfurter mixture evenly over bread on rack. Top with remaining slice, buttered-side up. Press sandwich gently together.
6. Broil sandwich under preheated broiler 4 to 5 minutes, turning sandwich once.
7. Serve immediately. Makes 1 sandwich.

# Cheesy-Potato Burgers

4 (4-oz.) ground beef patties
Vegetable oil
2 hamburger buns
1/4 cup ketchup
Salt
Freshly ground pepper
1 cup mashed potatoes
1 cup shredded Cheddar cheese (4 oz.)

1. Preheat broiler. Place beef patties on a broiler-pan rack. Broil under preheated broiler 3 minutes per side or to desired doneness.
2. Separate buns in half. Lightly toast buns.
3. Spread buns with ketchup; top each with a broiled hamburger. Season with salt and pepper.
4. Preheat oven to 375F (190C). In a small bowl, combine mashed potatoes and cheese. Spread potato mixture over hamburgers.
5. Bake in preheated oven 15 minutes or until potato topping is golden.
6. Serve hot. Makes 4 servings.

# Steak & Egg Toast

2 tablespoons butter or margarine
1 beef cube steak, about 4 oz.
Salt
Freshly ground pepper
2 bread slices
1 or 2 teaspoons vegetable oil
1 egg
Prepared brown mustard

*To garnish:*
Watercress

*A perfect sandwich to choose when you are on your own. This is an excellent way to pamper yourself.*

1. Melt butter or margarine in a skillet. Add steak; sauté about 3 minutes on each side for medium done or to desired doneness.
2. Season steak with salt and pepper. Keep warm.
3. Cut crusts from bread; toast until golden.
4. In a small skillet, heat enough oil to keep egg from sticking. Add egg; cook until set.
5. Spread 1 toast slice with mustard. Top with steak, fried egg and remaining toast.
6. Garnish with watercress; serve immediately. Makes 1 sandwich.

### Variation
Substitute any thin, tender beef steak for cube steak. Some markets sell a breakfast steak that is ideal.

Clockwise from top: Cheesy-Potato Burgers, Steak & Egg Toast, Frankfurter & Onion Delight

Many school children and workers take packed lunches every day. Sandwiches are convenient for packing and eating. But sandwiches take time to make. Freezer sandwiches are ideal. They can be made any time and then frozen. Placed directly into a lunch box, frozen sandwiches will be thawed and fresh at lunch time. If desired, freeze only the fillings; make sandwiches as needed.

Most traditional fillings can be used except for hard-cooked egg whites and mayonnaise. Here are two rather unusual fillings.

## Curried-Beef & Banana Sandwiches

12 oz. corned beef, minced
1-1/2 teaspoons prepared brown mustard
1/2 cup banana-flavored or plain yogurt
1/4 teaspoon curry powder
Salt
Butter, room temperature
20 bread slices

1. In a medium bowl, combine corned beef, mustard, yogurt, curry powder and salt. Butter bread.
2. Spread filling over 1/2 of buttered bread slices; top with remaining bread slices. Makes 10 sandwiches.

### Variation
Wrap sandwiches individually in foil or freezer paper; label. Freeze up to 1 month. Thaw in refrigerator or pack frozen for lunch.

## Smoked-Fish Sandwiches

12 oz. kippers or other smoked fish, minced
Grated peel and juice of 1 lemon
1 small apple, peeled, minced
Salt
Freshly ground pepper
Butter, room temperature
20 whole-wheat-bread slices

1. In a medium bowl, combine kippers or other smoked fish, lemon peel, lemon juice and apple. Season to taste with salt and pepper.
2. Lightly butter bread; spread 1/2 of buttered bread slices with filling. Top with remaining bread slices.
**To freeze:** Wrap sandwiches individually in foil or freezer paper; label. Freeze up to 1 month. Thaw in refrigerator or pack frozen for lunch. Makes 10 sandwiches.

## Family Sandwich

*Egg Filling:*
2 tablespoons butter or margarine
3 eggs
2 tablespoons milk
Salt
Freshly ground pepper
3 green onions, finely chopped

*Chicken Filling:*
3/4 cup minced cooked chicken
1 celery stalk, thinly sliced
1/4 teaspoon curry powder
2 to 3 tablespoons mayonnaise-style salad dressing

*Cheese Filling:*
1 cup finely shredded Cheddar cheese (4 oz.)
2 tomatoes, peeled, finely chopped
1 tablespoon mayonnaise-style salad dressing
1 (7-inch) round loaf whole-wheat bread
Butter, room temperature

*To garnish:*
Lettuce leaves

*This is a good way to use up leftover meat or cheese. Take the filled loaf on a picnic or eat for a light lunch or supper at home. Fillings can be varied according to your needs.*

1. To make egg filling, melt butter or margarine in a medium skillet over medium heat. In a medium bowl, beat eggs with a whisk; beat in milk, salt and pepper until blended. Add egg mixture to skillet; cook until scrambled, stirring constantly. Stir in onions; cool.
2. To make chicken filling, in a medium bowl, combine chicken, celery and curry powder. Add salad dressing until of spreading consistency.
3. To make cheese filling, in a medium bowl, combine cheese, tomatoes and salad dressing.
4. Slice loaf horizontally into 4 layers. Spread each cut surface with butter. Spread each filling over 1 layer. Reassemble loaf.
5. To serve, slice filled loaf vertically. Serve with lettuce leaves. Makes 4 to 6 servings.

# Lamb Pita Pockets

## Marinade:
2 tablespoons vegetable oil
2 tablespoons red wine
1/4 teaspoon chili powder
1/4 teaspoon ground coriander
1 bouquet garni
Salt
Freshly ground pepper
12 oz. lean lamb, cut in thin slices
1 medium onion, thinly sliced
2 teaspoons sesame seeds

## To serve:
4 pita breads
Shredded Chinese cabbage or lettuce
Tomato slices
Cucumber slices

**1.** To make marinade, in a large bowl, combine oil, wine, chili powder, coriander, bouquet garni, salt and pepper. Add lamb, onion and sesame seeds; stir well. Cover and refrigerate 4 hours or overnight, stirring occasionally.
**2.** Transfer lamb and marinade to a saucepan over medium heat. Cook gently 25 to 30 minutes or until lamb and onion are tender. Add a little water, if necessary. Discard bouquet garni.
**3.** Make a short cut along edge of pita breads; open to make pockets. Fill with hot meat mixture. Add Chinese cabbage or lettuce, tomato and cucumber to each sandwich. Serve warm. Makes 4 sandwiches.

Left to right: Family Sandwich, Lamb Pita Pockets

# Fish Paprika

6 tablespoons butter or margarine
2 large onions, sliced
3 canned pimentos, chopped
4 (4- to 6-oz.) pieces hake, haddock or whiting,
  thawed if frozen
Salt
Freshly ground pepper
8 oz. plain yogurt (1 cup)
2 teaspoons paprika

*To garnish:*
Plain croutons
Parsley sprigs

1. Preheat oven to 375F (190C). Grease a shallow baking dish large enough to hold fish in 1 layer. Melt 1/4 cup of butter or margarine in a medium skillet. Add onions; sauté about 5 minutes or until softened. Stir in pimentos.
2. Spoon 1/2 of onion mixture into greased dish. Top with fish; season fish with salt and pepper. Dot with remaining 2 tablespoons butter or margarine.
3. Bake in preheated oven, uncovered, 10 minutes. Top with remaining onion mixture. In a small bowl, combine yogurt and paprika; pour over fish. Bake 5 to 10 minutes or until fish tests done.
4. Garnish with croutons and parsley sprigs. Serve immediately. Makes 4 servings.

# Herbed-Cheese Pasta

6 oz. green or white noodles
1 (3-oz.) pkg. cream cheese with herbs and garlic,
  room temperature
4 eggs, beaten
8 bacon slices, chopped
1 small onion, chopped
8 oz. mushrooms, sliced (about 3-1/4 cups)

*To garnish:*
1 tablespoon chopped fresh parsley
1 tomato, cut into wedges

1. Cook pasta in boiling salted water in a large saucepan according to package directions until tender. Do not overcook. Drain thoroughly; return to saucepan.
2. In a small bowl, beat cream cheese and eggs until combined; set aside.
3. In a medium skillet, cook bacon with no added fat until crisp and golden. Discard all but about 1 tablespoon fat. Stir in onion and mushrooms; cook 5 minutes.
4. Stir egg mixture and bacon mixture into cooked pasta. Stir over low heat until mixture thickens slightly.
5. Spoon into a warmed serving dish; sprinkle with parsley. Top with tomato wedges. Serve immediately. Makes 4 servings.

# Tuna-Stuffed Tomatoes

4 large tomatoes
2 tablespoons butter or margarine
1 onion, chopped
1 (6-1/2-oz.) can tuna packed in oil, drained, flaked
1-1/2 cups fresh bread crumbs
1 tablespoon chopped fresh parsley
1 egg, beaten
Salt
Freshly ground pepper
1 (2-oz.) can anchovy fillets in oil

*To garnish:*
8 small black olives
Cilantro sprigs

1. Preheat oven to 350F (175C). Cut a thin slice from top of each tomato. Scoop out pulp; reserve pulp, discarding seeds.
2. Melt butter or margarine in a medium saucepan. Add onion; sauté 5 minutes. Remove from heat; stir in reserved tomato pulp, tuna, bread crumbs, parsley, egg, salt and pepper.
3. Spoon mixture into prepared tomatoes.
4. Drain anchovies, reserving oil; arrange anchovies over top of tomatoes. Place in an ovenproof dish; drizzle with anchovy oil.
5. Bake in preheated oven about 20 minutes or until heated through. Garnish with black olives and cilantro. Serve hot with crusty bread. Makes 4 servings.

Top to bottom: Tuna-Stuffed Tomatoes, Fish Paprika

# Spicy Beef Stir-Fry

10 oz. roast beef, cut into thin strips
6 tablespoons orange juice
1 tablespoon lemon juice
2 tablespoons black-bean sauce or 2 tablespoons
    concentrated beef stock
2 tablespoons chili powder
1 teaspoon cornstarch
Salt
Freshly ground black pepper
3 tablespoons vegetable oil
1 large red bell pepper, sliced
1 onion, sliced
1 (10-oz.) pkg. frozen green peas

1. In a medium glass or stainless-steel bowl, combine beef, orange juice, lemon juice, black-bean sauce or beef stock, chili powder, cornstarch, salt and black pepper. Cover and marinate 1 hour.
2. Heat oil in a large skillet or wok; add bell pepper and onion. Stir-fry over high heat 2 to 3 minutes.
3. Add marinated beef and marinade mixture; stir-fry 2 minutes. Add peas; stir-fry 1 minute.
4. Serve hot with Chinese noodles. Makes 4 servings.

# Beef Patties with Chasseur Sauce

*Chasseur Sauce:*
2 tablespoons vegetable oil
1 bacon slice, chopped
1 small celery stalk, chopped
1 small carrot, chopped
2 tablespoons all-purpose flour
1/2 cup beef stock
1/2 cup dry white wine
1 teaspoon tomato paste
1 teaspoon Dijon-style mustard
2 large tomatoes, peeled, seeded, chopped
Salt
Freshly ground pepper
2 tablespoons butter or margarine
4 oz. button mushrooms, chopped
1 small onion, chopped
2 tablespoons sherry or brandy, if desired
4 (4- to 6-oz.) beef patties

*To serve:*
4 thick bread slices, toasted
1 tablespoon chopped fresh parsley

1. To make sauce, heat oil in a medium saucepan. Add bacon, celery and carrot; sauté about 5 minutes or until vegetables are softened.

Left to right: Beef Patties with Chasseur Sauce, Crispy Beef & Bean Bundles

2. Stir in flour. Cook, stirring constantly, over low heat about 15 minutes or until flour is a rich brown color. Gradually stir in stock and wine. Stir in tomato paste, mustard and tomatoes. Cook over a medium heat 5 minutes.
3. Press sauce through a fine sieve. Reheat; season with salt and pepper.
4. Preheat broiler. Melt butter or margarine in a medium saucepan. Add mushrooms and onion; cook about 5 minutes or until softened. Stir into sauce with sherry or brandy, if desired. Keep warm.
5. Place beef patties on a broiler-pan rack. Broil under preheated broiler 5 to 8 minutes on each side, depending on size and desired degree of doneness.
6. To serve, place a bread slice on each of 4 individual plates. Top each bread slice with a broiled patty; spoon sauce over patties. Sprinkle with parsley; serve with broiled tomatoes. Makes 4 servings.

# Crispy Beef & Bean Bundles

8 oz. lean ground beef
2 oz. mushrooms, sliced
1 (15-oz.) can refried beans
1 teaspoon chili powder
Salt
Freshly ground pepper
8 (6- to 8-inch) flour tortillas
2 tablespoons butter or margarine
1 tablespoon vegetable oil

*To garnish:*
**Red- and green-bell-pepper rings**

1. In a large skillet, cook beef with no added fat over medium heat. Stirring to break up beef, cook about 5 minutes or until lightly browned.
2. Stir in mushrooms; cook 5 minutes. Remove from heat; drain off excess fat. Stir in beans, chili powder, salt and pepper.

3. Spoon beef-and-bean mixture equally into center of each tortilla. Fold opposite sides of each tortilla over filling slightly overlapping at center. Fold remaining 2 sides in to enclose filling completely. Press down gently to seal.
4. Heat butter and oil in a large skillet. Add filled tortillas; cook over medium heat until crisp and golden on both sides. Drain on paper towels.
5. Arrange on a platter; garnish with bell-pepper rings. Makes 4 servings.

1/Fold opposite sides of each tortilla over filling, slightly overlapping at center.

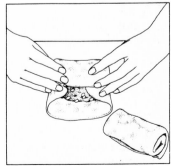

2/Fold remaining 2 sides in to enclose filling completely.

# Baked Eggs Mornay

4-1/2 cups chopped, peeled potatoes (about 1-1/2 lb.)
2 tablespoons butter or margarine
Salt
White pepper
4 hard-cooked eggs, halved

*Sauce:*
3 tablespoons butter or margarine
3 tablespoons all-purpose flour
1 cup milk
1/2 teaspoon prepared mustard
3/4 cup shredded Cheddar cheese (3 oz.)
1 tablespoon chopped fresh chives
Salt
White pepper

*To garnish:*
Parsley sprigs

---

1. Grease 4 (2-cup) flameproof dishes or a shallow 2-quart flameproof dish. In a large saucepan, cook potatoes in boiling salted water about 20 minutes or until tender. Drain and mash potatoes. Stir in butter or margarine, salt and white pepper.
2. Spoon mashed potatoes into a pastry bag fitted with a large star-shaped tip. Pipe potatoes around edges of individual greased dishes or large greased dish.
3. Preheat broiler. Divide hard-cooked eggs among individual dishes or place in large dish.
4. To make sauce, melt butter or margarine in a medium saucepan. Stir in flour; cook 1 minute, stirring. Gradually stir in milk. Bring to a boil; cook 2 to 3 minutes, stirring. Stir in mustard, cheese, chives, salt and white pepper. Spoon sauce over eggs.
5. Broil under preheated broiler 5 to 10 minutes or until golden and bubbly. Serve immediately. Makes 4 servings.

# Dilled Crabmeat Soufflé

3 tablespoons butter or margarine
3 tablespoons all-purpose flour
1 cup milk
1/4 cup whipping cream
Salt
White pepper
1/2 teaspoon dry mustard
4 eggs, separated
2 (6-1/2-oz.) cans crabmeat, drained
2 tablespoons chopped fresh dill or 2 teaspoons dried dill weed

---

1. Preheat oven to 375F (190C). Grease a 7-inch soufflé dish. Melt butter or margarine in a medium saucepan. Stir in flour; cook 1 minute, stirring. Gradually stir in milk; cook, stirring constantly, until sauce is thickened and comes to a boil. Stir in cream, salt, white pepper and mustard. Remove from heat.
2. Beat in egg yolks, 1 at a time, beating throughly after each addition. Pick over crabmeat. Fold in crabmeat and dill.
3. In a medium bowl, beat egg whites until stiff but not dry. Fold beaten egg whites into crabmeat mixture. Pour into greased soufflé dish.
4. Bake in preheated oven 40 to 45 minutes or until puffed and golden brown. Serve immediately with a tossed salad. Makes 3 to 4 servings.

# Dutch-Cheese Fondue

1 cup dry white wine or apple cider
1 garlic clove, crushed
1/2 teaspoon freshly grated nutmeg
4 cups shredded Gouda cheese or Edam cheese (1 lb.)
1 tablespoon cornstarch
Salt
White pepper
2 to 3 tablespoons kirsch
1 large French-bread loaf, cubed

---

1. Heat wine or cider, garlic and nutmeg in a fondue pot or heavy saucepan until hot but not boiling.
2. In a medium bowl, combine cheese and cornstarch. Stir into wine mixture, a little at a time. Stir over very low heat until thick and creamy.
3. Season with salt and white pepper; stir in kirsch to taste.
4. Serve hot fondue with French bread. Makes 4 servings.

# Deviled Spanish Pizza

*Sauce:*
1 (1-lb.) can tomatoes, drained, chopped
1 small onion, chopped
2 tablespoons tomato paste
2 teaspoons dried leaf oregano
Salt
Freshly ground pepper

*Dough:*
1-1/2 cups self-rising flour
Freshly ground pepper
1/4 cup milk
1/4 cup olive oil

*Topping:*
6 oz. mozzarella cheese, sliced
4 oz. salami, sliced
1 tablespoon grated Parmesan cheese
4 to 6 pimento-stuffed olives, sliced

**1.** Preheat oven to 400F (205C). Grease a baking sheet. To make sauce, place tomatoes, onion, tomato paste and oregano in a medium saucepan. Cook over medium heat 15 to 20 minutes or until thick, stirring occasionally.
**2.** To make dough, in a medium bowl, combine flour and pepper. Stir in milk and olive oil to form a soft dough.
**3.** On a lightly floured surface, knead dough until smooth. Roll out dough to a 10-inch circle. Place on greased baking sheet. Spoon sauce over dough circle to within 1 inch of edge.
**4.** Top with mozzarella cheese, salami, Parmesan cheese and olives.
**5.** Bake in preheated oven 30 minutes or until crust is golden brown.
**6.** Cut into wedges. Serve hot with a tossed green salad. Makes 2 servings.

Top to bottom: Deviled Spanish Pizza, Dutch-Cheese Fondue

# Spanish-Style Omelet

2 tablespoons butter or margarine
1 large onion, sliced
4 bacon slices, chopped
2 cups diced cooked potatoes (about 12 oz.)
1 red bell pepper, chopped
1 green bell pepper, chopped
4 eggs, beaten
Salt
Freshly ground pepper
1 teaspoon dried leaf marjoram
1/2 cup shredded Cheddar cheese (2 oz.)
6 pimento-stuffed olives, sliced
1 teaspoon paprika

1. Preheat broiler. Melt butter or margarine in a large heavy skillet. Add onion and bacon; sauté until bacon is crisp and lightly browned.
2. Add potatoes and bell peppers; cook 2 minutes. In a medium bowl, beat eggs with salt, pepper and marjoram. Pour over potato mixture; cook over low heat until mixture is almost set. Sprinkle with cheese, olives and paprika.
3. Broil under preheated broiler about 3 minutes or until cheese melts.
4. Serve hot with warm crusty bread and a vegetable salad. Makes 4 servings.

# Pickled-Herring Salad

1 (12-oz.) jar pickled herrings, drained
3 dill pickles, thinly sliced
2 red-skinned apples, cored, sliced into rings
1 bunch green onions, chopped
1/2 cup dairy sour cream
1/2 teaspoon dried dill weed

1. Cut herrings into thin strips; place in a medium bowl.
2. Add dill pickles, apples, green onions, sour cream and dill; stir until combined.
3. Spoon into a chilled serving dish; serve with warm crusty bread. Makes 4 servings.

# Camembert Puffs

8 individual wedges Camembert cheese, well-chilled
2 tablespoons all-purpose flour
2 eggs, beaten
1-1/2 cups fresh white-bread crumbs
Vegetable oil for deep-frying

*To serve:*
1/2 cup gooseberry, damson or cherry conserve, chilled

1. Dust cheese wedges with flour. Dip floured wedges into beaten egg; coat with bread crumbs. Set aside.
2. Heat oil in a deep saucepan to 375F (190C) or until a 1-inch bread cube turns golden brown in 40 seconds. Add coated cheese wedges to hot oil. Deep-fry 3 to 4 minutes or until crisp and golden.
3. Drain on paper towels. Serve immediately with fruit conserve. Makes 4 servings.

# Cheese & Walnut Croquettes with Watercress Dip

1 cup finely chopped walnuts
1-1/2 cups fresh bread crumbs
1/2 small onion, grated
1/2 cup shredded Edam cheese (2 oz.)
1 tablespoon chopped fresh parsley
Salt
Freshly ground pepper
1 egg, beaten
1 to 2 tablespoons milk
2 tablespoons vegetable oil

*Watercress Dip:*
1 bunch watercress, finely chopped
1/2 cup dairy sour cream
1 teaspoon Italian seasoning
Pinch of freshly grated nutmeg
Salt
White pepper

1. In a medium bowl, combine walnuts, bread crumbs, onion, cheese, parsley, salt and pepper. Stir in egg and 1 tablespoon milk. Stir in additional milk, if necessary. Shape mixture into 12 equal croquettes.
2. Heat oil in a large skillet. Add croquettes; sauté over medium heat about 10 minutes or until browned on all sides. Drain on paper towels.
3. To make dip, blend watercress, sour cream, Italian seasoning, nutmeg, salt and white pepper. Spoon into a small serving bowl.
4. Serve warm croquettes with dip. Makes 4 servings.

Clockwise from left: Spanish-Style Omelet, Pickled-Herring Salad, Camembert Puffs with fruit conserve

# Cottage-Cheese Pancakes

*Spreads:*
2 (3-oz.) pkgs. cream cheese, room temperature
6 tablespoons dairy sour cream
1 (2-oz.) jar red lumpfish caviar
Fresh chopped chives
1 (3-3/4-oz.) can sardines packed in oil, drained
1 tablespoon lemon juice
Paprika

*Pancakes:*
1/4 cup all-purpose flour
1/4 teaspoon salt
2 tablespoons butter or margarine, melted
3/4 cup cream-style cottage cheese
3 eggs, separated
Butter or margarine for cooking

---

*Serve these small, savory pancakes as an appetizer.*

**1.** To make spreads, in a blender or food processor fitted with a steel blade, process 1 package cream cheese, 3 tablespoons sour cream and caviar until smooth. Spoon into a small serving dish; sprinkle with chopped chives.
**2.** In a blender or food processor fitted with a steel blade, process remaining package of cream cheese, remaining 3 tablespoons sour cream, sardines and lemon juice until smooth. Spoon into a small serving dish; sprinkle with paprika.
**3.** To make pancakes, in a medium bowl, combine flour and salt. In a small bowl, combine butter or margarine, cottage cheese and egg yolks. Stir cottage-cheese mixture into flour mixture until blended.
**4.** In a medium bowl, beat egg whites until stiff but not dry; fold beaten egg whites into batter.
**5.** Heat 1 to 2 tablespoons butter or margarine in a large skillet. Drop batter by rounded tablespoonfuls into skillet, spacing pancakes well apart. Cook over medium heat 2 to 3 minutes. Turn pancakes over with a wide spatula; cook 2 to 3 minutes or until golden brown. Remove from skillet; keep warm. Repeat with additional butter or margarine and remaining batter.
**6.** Serve spreads with warm pancakes. Makes 12 to 14 small pancakes.

# Tropical Kabobs

5 all-beef frankfurters
1 (15-oz.) can pineapple chunks in natural juice
2 green bell peppers, cut into 1-inch pieces
1 tablespoon soy sauce
1 teaspoon vegetable oil
1 teaspoon grated gingerroot
Salt
Freshly ground pepper
2 teaspoons cornstarch
Water

---

**1.** Preheat broiler. Score frankfurters diagonally along 1 side; cut each scored frankfurter into 4 pieces.
**2.** Drain pineapple chunks, reserving juice.
**3.** Thread frankfurters on 4 skewers, alternating with pineapple chunks and bell-pepper pieces. Place kabobs on a broiler-pan rack.
**4.** In a small saucepan, combine reserved pineapple juice, soy sauce, oil, gingerroot, salt and pepper Brush kabobs with a little of pineapple mixture.
**5.** Broil under preheated broiler until hot and bubbly, basting occasionally with sauce.
**6.** In a small bowl, combine cornstarch and a little water; stir mixture into remaining sauce. Boil, stirring constantly, until thickened.
**7.** Serve hot kabobs with sauce. Serve with hot cooked rice or cooked noodles. Makes 4 servings.

Left to right: Tropical Kabobs, Cottage-Cheese Pancakes with Spreads, Stuffed Onions

# Cheesy Stuffed Onions

4 large Spanish onions, peeled
Salt
8 oz. lean ground beef
2 garlic cloves, crushed
1/2 cup pine nuts
1 teaspoon Italian seasoning
Freshly ground pepper
1 cup fresh bread crumbs
3/4 cup shredded Cheddar cheese (3 oz.)
1 egg, beaten
1/2 cup plain yogurt

**1.** Boil onions in a large saucepan of salted boiling water 10 minutes. Drain, reserving about 1/2 cup of cooking liquid.
**2.** Scoop out centers of onions with a small knife or spoon; reserve for another dish. Set hollowed-out onions aside.
**3.** Preheat oven to 375F (190C). In a medium skillet, cook beef with no added fat over medium heat. Cook, stirring constantly, until lightly browned. Add garlic, pine nuts, Italian seasoning, salt and pepper. Cook 5 minutes. Remove from heat; stir in bread crumbs, cheese and egg until blended.
**4.** Fill onions with beef mixture; place filled onions in an ovenproof dish large enough to hold them in 1 layer. Pour reserved cooking liquid around stuffed onions. Cover with a lid or foil.
**5.** Bake in preheated oven 30 minutes. Uncover; bake 30 minutes or until tender.
**6.** Serve hot with yogurt. Makes 4 servings.

Clockwise from left: Fish & Egg Puff, Potato & Fish Bake,
Seafood Crepes

# Potato & Fish Bake

3 cups chopped peeled potatoes (about 1 lb.)
Salt
2 tablespoons butter or margarine
White pepper
1 cup shredded Cheddar cheese (4 oz.)
4 (4-oz.) pieces cod or other fish
1 cup wine
1 shallot, chopped
1 bay leaf
2 tablespoons all-purpose flour
2 tablespoons butter or margarine, room temperature

*To garnish:*
Lemon wedges
Parsley sprigs

1. Grease 4 large scallop shells or 4 individual baking
dishes. Cook potatoes in a large saucepan of boiling salted
water about 20 minutes or until tender. Drain and mash
potatoes. Stir in butter or margarine, salt and white
pepper. Stir in 1/2 of cheese. Spoon into a pastry bag fitted
with a large star-shaped tip. Pipe swirls of potato mixture
around edges of greased scallop shells or individual dishes.
Set aside.
2. Preheat oven to 350F (175C). Arrange fish in a baking
dish. Add wine, shallot, bay leaf and enough water to
cover fish. Cover with a lid or foil.
3. Bake fish in preheated oven 8 to 10 minutes or until fish
tests done. Remove fish from cooking liquid, reserving
liquid. Let fish cool slightly. Flake fish; set aside.
4. Preheat broiler. Strain reserved cooking liquid into a
medium saucepan; boil until reduced to 1 cup. In a small
bowl, blend flour and butter or margarine into a paste.
Whisk paste into hot liquid. Cook until thickened. Stir
flaked fish into sauce. Season with salt and white pepper.
Spoon sauce mixture into center of piped potatoes in scallop shells or dishes; sprinkle with remaining cheese.
5. Broil under preheated broiler 5 minutes or until potatoes
are golden and sauce is bubbly.
6. Garnish with lemon wedges and parsley sprigs. Makes 4
servings.

# Seafood Crepes

*Crepe Batter:*
1-1/4 cups all-purpose flour
3 eggs
1-1/2 cups milk
1/3 cup butter or margarine, melted
Butter or margarine for cooking

*Filling:*
1/4 cup butter or margarine
1/4 cup all-purpose flour
1/2 cup dry white wine
1-1/2 cups fish or chicken stock
1 tablespoon tomato paste
Salt
Freshly ground pepper
1/4 cup whipping cream
1 tablespoon chopped fresh parsley
1 (4-1/4-oz.) can shrimp, drained
1 (8-3/4-oz.) jar mussels, drained, chopped
1 (6-1/2-oz.) can crabmeat, drained, flaked
1 teaspoon lemon juice

*Using a blender to make the crepe batter saves time.*

**1.** Place flour, eggs and milk in a blender or food processor fitted with a steel blade; process until smooth, scraping down bowl sides as necessary. Pour melted butter slowly into batter with machine motor running; process until combined. Pour batter into a large measuring cup or small pitcher. Cover and refrigerate 1 hour.
**2.** To cook crepes, melt 1 tablespoon butter or margarine in a 6- or 7-inch skillet or crepe pan. Pour in just enough batter to cover bottom of pan in a thin layer. Cook over medium heat 1-1/2 minutes or until small bubbles begin to form on surface of crepe. Turn crepe; cook 1-1/2 minutes. Remove to a flat plate; repeat process with remaining batter. Add additional butter or margarine to skillet as necessary.
**3.** To make filling, melt butter or margarine in a medium saucepan. Stir in flour; cook 1 minute, stirring. Gradually stir in wine and stock. Bring to a boil; cook 2 to 3 minutes, stirring. Stir in tomato paste, salt and pepper. Cook over low heat 10 minutes. Stir in cream and 1/2 of parsley.
**4.** Preheat oven to 350F (175C). Grease a 13" x 9" baking pan. In a medium bowl, combine shrimp, mussels and crabmeat; stir in 1/2 of sauce. Fill 15 crepes with an equal amount of filling; roll up. Place filled crepes, seam-side down, in greased pan.
**5.** Stir lemon juice into remaining sauce; pour over crepes.
**6.** Bake in preheated oven 10 to 15 minutes or until heated through.
**7.** Sprinkle with remaining parsley; serve hot. Makes 5 servings of 3 crepes each.

# Fish & Egg Puffs

1/2 (17-1/4-oz.) pkg. frozen puff pastry
    (1 sheet), thawed
4 small flounder, sole, haddock or halibut fillets
2 hard-cooked eggs, sliced
1/2 cup condensed cream of mushroom soup, undiluted
1 teaspoon lemon juice
4 teaspoons capers, drained, chopped
1 tablespoon chopped chives
Salt
Freshly ground pepper
1 egg yolk beaten with 1 tablespoon water for glaze

**1.** Preheat oven to 425F (220C). Unfold pastry; lay flat on a lightly floured surface. Roll out pastry with a lightly floured rolling pin to a 13-inch square. Cut off 2 (1-inch) strips down length and width of pastry to make a 12-inch square. Reserve pastry strips for decorations. Cut pastry into 4 (6-inch) squares; place on ungreased baking sheet.
**2.** Place 1 fish fillet in center of each pastry square. Top with 2 or 3 egg slices. In a small bowl, combine soup, lemon juice, capers, chives, salt and pepper; spoon soup mixture over eggs.
**3.** Brush pastry edges with egg glaze. Bring opposite corners of pastry together in center to enclose filling. Pinch pastry edges to seal. Poke small hole in center of each puff to allow steam to escape. Cut reserved pastry strips into decorative shapes. Brush decorations with egg glaze; attach to puffs. Brush puffs all over with egg glaze.
**4.** Bake in preheated oven 20 to 25 minutes or until puffed and golden brown. Serve hot with tossed green salad or sliced tomatoes. Makes 4 servings.

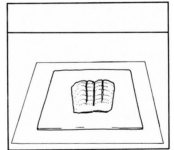

1/Place 1 fish fillet in center of each pastry square.

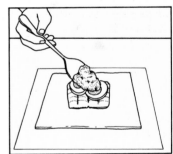

2/Spoon soup mixture over eggs.

3/Bring opposite corners of pastry together in center to enclose filling.

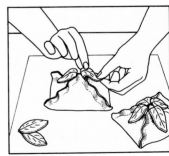

4/Attach decorations to puffs.

# Stuffed Peppers

4 large green bell peppers
1 tablespoon vegetable oil
1 large onion, chopped
4 oz. button mushrooms, sliced
1/4 cup chopped almonds or pecans
1/3 cup dried apricots, soaked overnight,
    drained, chopped
1 cup cooked long-grain white rice
1 egg, slightly beaten
Worcestershire sauce
Salt
Freshly ground black pepper

*Sauce:*
2 tablespoons butter or margarine
2 tablespoons all-purpose flour
1 cup milk
1 teaspoon prepared brown mustard
1 cup shredded Cheddar cheese (4 oz.)
Salt
Freshly ground pepper

1. Preheat oven to 350F (175C). Cut off stem end of each bell pepper. Remove and discard seeds and inner pith. If peppers do not stand straight, trim to level bottoms.
2. Heat oil in a large skillet over medium heat. Add onion; sauté 5 minutes or until onion is softened.
3. Add mushrooms, nuts and apricots; cook 3 minutes. Stir in rice and egg. Season with Worcestershire sauce, salt and pepper.
4. Fill bell peppers with rice mixture; stand filled peppers upright in a baking dish large enough to hold them in a single layer.
5. To make sauce, melt butter or margarine in a medium saucepan. Stir in flour; cook 1 minute, stirring constantly. Gradually stir in milk. Bring to a boil; cook until smooth and thickened, stirring constantly. Stir in mustard and half of cheese. Season with salt and pepper. Pour sauce around filled peppers. Sprinkle filled peppers with remaining cheese. Cover with foil.
6. Bake in preheated oven about 1 hour or until peppers are tender. Makes 4 servings.

**Variation**
Fill bell peppers with freshly made Savory Hamburger Mix, page 252. Pipe mashed potatoes on top. Substitute a tomato sauce for cheese sauce. Cook as above.

# Pizza Omelet

2 tablespoons vegetable oil
1 small onion, finely chopped
1-1/2 cups diced, peeled, parboiled potatoes (8 oz.)
1/2 green bell pepper, diced
1 large tomato, peeled, seeded, chopped
6 pimento-stuffed green olives, chopped
6 eggs
Salt
Freshly ground black pepper

*To serve:*
1 tablespoon vegetable oil
1 tablespoon butter
3/4 cup shredded sharp Cheddar cheese (3 oz.)
4 anchovy fillets, halved lengthwise
4 pimento-stuffed green olives, halved

*Spanish Omelet, full of interesting vegetables and flavors, makes a super snack. Here it is used as a base for a cheese topping that makes it into a meal. Eat the plain omelet, cold, cut into small wedges as a cocktail snack.*

1. Preheat broiler. Heat oil in a 9-inch, nonstick, flame-proof skillet. Add onion; sauté gently until softened. Add potatoes, bell pepper, tomato and chopped olives; cook 5 minutes, stirring gently.
2. In a medium bowl, beat eggs; season with salt and pepper. Pour egg mixture over vegetable mixture in skillet. Cook about 5 minutes or until eggs are set on bottom.
3. Place skillet under preheated broiler. Cook until top is set and lightly browned.
4. Top warm omelet with cheese; place under preheated broiler until cheese is melted. Garnish with anchovy strips and olives. Serve immediately with hot garlic bread and a salad. Makes 4 servings.

Top to bottom: Stuffed Peppers, Pizza Omelet

# Seafood & White-Wine Fondue

1 (12-oz.) white-fish fillet
3/4 cup all-purpose flour
1/2 teaspoon baking powder
Salt
1 egg
1/2 cup water
Vegetable oil for deep-frying

*Fondue:*
5 tablespoons butter or margarine
1/2 cup all-purpose flour
1 cup chicken stock
1-1/2 cups dry white wine
Salt
Freshly ground pepper
1/2 cup whipping cream
3 egg yolks

*To dip:*
6 oz. deveined, peeled, cooked shrimp
8 oz. shelled cooked mussels

1. Cut fish fillet into 1-inch squares.
2. Sift flour, baking powder and salt into a medium bowl. Add egg and 1/2 of water; beat until smooth. Beat in remaining water.
3. Fill a deep pan 1/3 full of oil. Heat to 375F (190C), or until a 1-inch bread cube turns golden brown in 50 seconds. Dip fish pieces into batter. Carefully add coated fish to hot oil; fry 3 minutes or until crisp and golden. Drain on paper towels.
4. If prepared in advance, heat fried fish in a 375F (190C) oven to crisp.
5. To make fondue, melt butter in a medium saucepan; stir in flour. Cook 1 minute constantly.
6. Gradually stir in chicken stock and wine until sauce is smooth and thickened. Season with salt and pepper.
7. Transfer wine mixture to a fondue pot or chafing dish; place over a low flame.
8. In a small bowl, beat cream and egg yolks. Gradually stir cream mixture into hot wine mixture. Do not allow to boil.
9. Divide crispy fish pieces, shrimp and mussels among 4 individual plates.
10. To eat, dip fish, shrimp and mussels into hot fondue. Accompany with chunks of hot French bread. Makes 4 servings.

# Beer & Gouda Fondue

1 garlic clove, crushed
1 cup dark beer
3-1/2 cups shredded Gouda cheese (14 oz.)
1 tablespoon all-purpose flour
Freshly ground pepper
1 teaspoon caraway seeds

*To dip:*
1 French-bread loaf, cut into 1-inch cubes

Left to right: Beer & Gouda Fondue with French bread, Seafood & White-Wine Fondue

*This fondue is quite thick. Do not use too high a heat when melting cheese.*

**1.** Rub inside a fondue pot with garlic; discard garlic.
**2.** Pour beer into seasoned fondue pot. Heat over low heat until beer starts to boil.
**3.** In a medium bowl, combine cheese and flour. Stir cheese mixture into hot beer until smooth.
**4.** Season with pepper. Stir in caraway seeds.
**5.** Keep warm over a low flame. Serve with bread cubes. Makes 4 servings.

## Cottage-Cheese & Chive Fondue

8 oz. dry cottage cheese (1 cup)
1 cup shredded Swiss cheese (8 oz.)
1-1/2 tablespoons all-purpose flour
1 cup white wine or unsweetened apple juice
1 tablespoon Worcestershire sauce
2 teaspoons prepared brown mustard
2 tablespoons chopped fresh chives
Salt
Freshly ground pepper

***To dip:***
1 French-bread loaf, cut into 1-inch cubes

**1.** Press cottage cheese through a sieve. In a medium bowl, combine sieved cottage cheese, Swiss cheese and flour.
**2.** Pour wine or juice into fondue pot. Heat until wine or juice starts to boil.
**3.** Stir cheese mixture into hot wine or juice until smooth.
**4.** Stir in Worcestershire sauce, mustard and chives. Season with salt and pepper.
**5.** Keep warm over a low flame. Serve with bread cubes. Makes 4 servings.

## Crab Fondue

1 garlic clove, crushed
1 cup dry white wine
2-1/2 cups shredded mild Cheddar cheese (10 oz.)
1 tablespoon all-purpose flour
Salt
Freshly ground pepper
6 oz. white crabmeat, flaked

***To dip:***
Puff-pastry crescents or cheese straws

**1.** Rub inside a fondue pot with garlic; discard garlic.
**2.** Pour white wine into seasoned fondue pot. Heat until wine starts to boil.
**3.** In a medium bowl, combine cheese and flour. Stir cheese mixture into hot wine until smooth.
**4.** Season with salt and pepper. Stir in crabmeat.
**5.** Keep warm over a low flame. Serve with crescents or cheese straws. Makes 4 servings.

# Cannelloni with Tomato Sauce

*Sauce:*
2 (15-oz.) cans tomatoes, chopped
1 onion, finely chopped
2 tablespoons tomato paste
1 teaspoon Italian seasoning
1 red bell pepper, finely chopped
1/2 cup red wine
1/2 cup chicken stock
2 teaspoons red-currant jelly
Salt
Freshly ground black pepper

*Filling:*
1 (10-oz.) pkg. frozen chopped spinach, cooked, drained
1/2 cup cottage cheese
2 tablespoons dry bread crumbs
Freshly grated nutmeg
8 cannelloni tubes
Grated Parmesan cheese

---

*Filling cooked cannelloni tubes can be quite difficult. In this recipe, uncooked pasta is filled. Sauce is made thinner than usual; extra liquid is absorbed by pasta during cooking. If desired, pasta can be precooked, following directions on package. Use slightly less liquid in sauce. Double recipe, if desired.*

**1.** To make sauce, in a large saucepan over medium heat, combine all sauce ingredients. Bring to a boil. Reduce heat; cover. Simmer 20 minutes, stirring occasionally. Cool slightly.
**2.** To make filling, in a medium bowl, combine spinach, cottage cheese, bread crumbs and nutmeg. Spoon filling into uncooked cannelloni tubes.
**3.** Spread half of sauce in a shallow freezer-to-oven dish, large enough to hold cannelloni without touching. Arrange stuffed cannelloni in a single layer, not touching and with sauce under and between them.
**4.** Cover completely with remaining sauce. Refrigerate overnight.
**5.** Preheat oven to 375F (190C).
**6.** Bake about 40 minutes or until cannelloni are tender and sauce is bubbling. Sprinkle with Parmesan cheese. Serve extra cheese in a separate dish. Makes 4 servings.

# Spaghetti Layer Bake

2 tablespoons vegetable oil
1 large onion, chopped
1 lb. tomatoes, peeled, chopped
4 oz. mushrooms, chopped
1 tablespoon tomato paste
1 teaspoon dried leaf oregano
Salt
Freshly ground pepper
8 oz. ground beef or pork
1 garlic clove, crushed
6 oz. spaghetti

*Topping:*
2 tablespoons butter
2 tablespoons all-purpose flour
1 cup milk
1 egg, slightly beaten
1 teaspoon dry mustard
3/4 cup shredded sharp Cheddar cheese (3 oz.)

---

**1.** Preheat oven to 375F (190C). Heat 1 tablespoon oil in a large saucepan over medium heat. Add onion; sauté until soft. Add tomatoes, mushrooms, tomato paste, oregano, salt and pepper. Cook 5 minutes.
**2.** To make meatballs, in a medium bowl, combine meat, garlic, salt and pepper. With floured hands, shape mixture into 16 meatballs.
**3.** Heat remaining oil in a large skillet over medium heat. Add meatballs; sauté until lightly browned on all sides. As meatballs brown, remove from skillet; drain on paper towels.
**4.** Cook spaghetti according to package directions until barely tender. Drain cooked spaghetti; add to tomato mixture.
**5.** Place 1/2 of spaghetti mixture into a deep 1-1/2-quart freezer-to-oven dish. Top with meatballs; cover with remaining spaghetti mixture.
**6.** To make topping, melt butter in a saucepan over medium heat. Stir in flour; cook 1 minute, stirring constantly. Gradually stir in milk. Bring to a boil, stirring constantly; cook until thickened and smooth. Cool slightly. Beat in egg, mustard and cheese. Stir until blended and cheese is melted. Season with salt and pepper.
**7.** Pour topping over spaghetti.
**8.** Bake in preheated oven 1 to 1-1/4 hours or until hot and bubbling. Topping should be set and browned. Serve with a green salad or vegetables. Makes 4 servings.

# Meat Loaf

1 cup minced cooked roast beef or lamb
1/2 cup minced cooked ham
1 small onion, minced
4 parsley sprigs, minced
1-1/2 cups fresh bread crumbs
1 egg
1 teaspoon Worcestershire sauce
1 teaspoon salt
Freshly ground pepper

*This meat loaf is also delicious cold in sandwiches or with salad. Serve hot with ratatouille and steamed new potatoes.*

1. Grease a 3-cup metal bowl or mold; set aside. In a large bowl, combine all ingredients.
2. Pack meat mixture into greased bowl or mold. Cover with buttered waxed paper and foil; seal well.
3. Place bowl or mold in a large saucepan. Add enough boiling water to saucepan to cover two-thirds of bowl or mold. Cover; steam over medium heat 2 hours. Remove bowl or mold from water. Cool slightly. Remove from bowl or mold.
4. Serve hot. Or refrigerate until chilled. Cut in slices to serve. Makes 4 servings.

Left to right: Spaghetti Layer Bake, Meat Loaf

# Ham Quiche

**Basic pastry, page 251**

*Filling:*
1-1/2 cups diced cooked ham
1 onion, chopped
1 large tomato, diced
2 tablespoons chopped fresh mixed herbs,
 any combination
1 cup shredded Swiss or Gruyère cheese (4 oz.)
3 eggs
1 cup half and half

**1.** Prepare Basic Pastry through step 3, page 251.
**2.** Preheat oven to 375F (190C).
**3.** In a medium bowl, combine ham, onion, tomato and herbs. Sprinkle half of cheese in bottom of cooled pastry shell. Spoon ham mixture over cheese. In a medium bowl, beat eggs; beat in half and half until blended. Pour egg mixture into pastry shell; sprinkle remaining cheese on top.
**4.** Bake in preheated oven 40 to 50 minutes or until center is set.
**5.** Serve warm. Cut into wedges to serve. Makes 4 to 6 servings.

Left to right: Ham Quiche, Chicken & Asparagus Turnovers

# Spinach & Bacon Quiche

*Basic Pastry:*
1-1/2 cups sifted all-purpose flour
1/2 teaspoon salt
1/2 cup butter, margarine or vegetable shortening
1 egg, slightly beaten
2 to 3 tablespoons iced water

*Filling:*
2 tablespoons butter or margarine
1 medium onion, chopped
1 (10-oz.) pkg. frozen chopped spinach,
  thawed, drained
Salt
Freshly ground pepper
Freshly grated nutmeg
6 crisp-cooked bacon slices, crumbled
1 cup finely shredded Swiss or Gruyère cheese (4 oz.)
3 eggs
1 cup half and half

1. Preheat oven to 400F (205C).
2. To make pastry, in a medium bowl, combine flour and salt. With a pastry blender or 2 knives, cut in butter, margarine or shortening until mixture resembles coarse crumbs. In a small bowl, blend egg and 2 tablespoons water. Sprinkle egg mixture over flour mixture, tossing with a fork until mixture begins to stick together. Add remaining water, if necessary. Gather pastry into a ball.
3. Roll out pastry on a lightly floured surface to 1/8 inch thick. Line a 9-inch flan pan with a removable bottom with pastry. Prick pastry with fork. Line pastry with foil; fill with pie weights or dried beans. Bake in preheated oven 10 minutes. Remove foil and pie weights or beans; bake 5 minutes longer. Cool on a wire rack.
4. Reduce oven temperature to 375F (190C). Melt butter or margarine in a medium skillet over medium heat. Add onion; sauté until transparent. Stir in spinach. Season with salt, pepper and nutmeg. Set aside to cool.
5. Sprinkle bacon and 1/2 of cheese in bottom of cooled pastry shell. Spoon spinach mixture over cheese. In a small bowl, beat eggs with a whisk; beat in half and half until blended; pour into pastry. Top with remaining cheese.
6. Bake in preheated oven 40 to 50 minutes or until center is set.
7. Serve warm. Cut into wedges to serve. Makes 4 to 6 servings.

# Chicken & Asparagus Turnovers

*Pastry:*
2-1/4 cups all-purpose flour
1 teaspoon baking powder
1 teaspoon salt
3/4 cup vegetable shortening
6 tablespoons iced water

*Filling:*
1 (8-oz.) can cut asparagus
Milk
1 tablespoon butter or margarine
1 tablespoon all-purpose flour
1-1/2 cups diced cooked chicken
Salt
Freshly ground pepper
1 egg yolk beaten with 1 tablespoon milk for glaze

1. To prepare pastry, in a medium bowl, combine flour, baking powder and salt. Cut in shortening with pastry blender or 2 knives until mixture resembles coarse crumbs.
2. Sprinkle crumb mixture with water; toss with a fork until mixture begins to stick together. Gather pastry into a ball. Divide pastry into 4 equal pieces.
3. To prepare filling, drain asparagus, reserving liquid. Add enough milk to liquid to measure 2/3 cup; set aside.
4. Melt butter or margarine in a small saucepan over low heat. Stir in flour; cook 1 minute. Gradually stir in milk mixture; cook until sauce is thickened, stirring constantly. Set aside to cool. Stir in drained asparagus, chicken, salt and pepper.
5. Preheat oven to 400F (205C). Roll out each pastry piece on a lightly floured surface to a 7-inch circle. Spoon 1/4 of filling onto center of each pastry circle. Brush pastry edges with water; fold pastry over filling to make half-moons. Flute pastry edges to seal. Prick tops lightly with a fork.
6. Place turnovers on an ungreased baking sheet. Brush tops with egg-yolk glaze. Bake turnovers 20 to 25 minutes or until tops are golden brown. Serve warm. Makes 4 servings.

## Variation
Prepare pastry as directed above. Melt 2 tablespoons butter or margarine in a medium saucepan. Add 1 chopped onion; sauté until transparent. Add 1/2 pound lean ground beef; sauté until no longer pink. Drain off fat. Stir in 1 large diced, cooked potato. Season with 1 tablespoon chopped fresh dill or 1 teaspoon dried dill weed, salt and pepper. Fill turnovers and bake as above.

# Sausage & Rice

2 tablespoons butter or margarine
1 tablespoon vegetable oil
1 large onion, chopped
1 cup uncooked long-grain white rice
2-1/4 cups chicken stock
1/4 cup whole-kernel corn
1/4 cup raisins
8 oz. Polish sausage, sliced
Salt
Freshly ground pepper

*To serve:*
2 small sweet pickles, chopped
1 hard-cooked egg, chopped

1. Heat butter or margarine and oil in a medium saucepan over medium heat. Add onion; sauté 5 minutes or until softened.
2. Stir in rice and stock; bring to a boil. Cover; simmer about 25 minutes or until rice is tender and stock has been absorbed. Stir occasionally.
3. Stir in corn, raisins, sausage, salt and pepper.
4. Stir in pickles; sprinkle with chopped egg. Serve with a green salad. Makes 4 servings.

# Savory Hamburger Mix

3 lb. lean ground beef
2 large onions, chopped
3 tablespoons bread crumbs
1/2 teaspoon Italian seasoning
2 teaspoons salt
Freshly ground pepper
1/2 cup beef stock

1. In a large skillet over medium heat, sauté beef, without added fat, 2 minutes. Add onions; sauté until beef is browned and onion is tender. Stir frequently to separate beef.
2. Add bread crumbs, Italian seasoning, salt and pepper. Cool slightly.
3. Use as a filling for Stuffed Peppers, page 244. Mixture can also be added to tomato sauce for a meat-and-tomato spaghetti sauce.

# Spanish Rice

2/3 cup uncooked long-grain white rice
2 tablespoons vegetable oil
1 large onion, sliced
8 oz. tomatoes, peeled, quartered
1 cup chopped cooked roast beef
2 oz. mushrooms, chopped
2 tablespoons tomato paste
1/2 teaspoon dried leaf oregano
Salt
Freshly ground pepper
1/2 cup shredded Cheddar cheese (2 oz.)

1. Cook rice according to package directions until barely tender.
2. Preheat oven to 375F (190C). Grease a baking dish. Heat oil in a large skillet over medium heat. Add onion; sauté until lightly browned. Stir in tomatoes, beef and mushrooms; cook 5 minutes.
3. Stir in tomato paste, oregano, cooked rice, salt and pepper. Spoon into greased dish; sprinkle cheese on top.
4. Bake in preheated oven about 20 minutes or until heated through. Serve with a green salad. Makes 4 servings.

**Variation**
Substitute any cooked meat or smoked sausage for roast beef.

# Chicken Stir-Fry

1 red bell pepper, cut into strips
1 cauliflower, broken into cauliflowerets
2 celery stalks, cut into 1/4-inch slices
6 green onions, cut into 3/4-inch lengths
2 small zucchini, cut into 1/4-inch slices
2 tablespoons butter or margarine
1 tablespoon vegetable oil
4 boneless chicken breasts, skinned, cut into strips
4 oz. button mushrooms, halved

*To serve:*
2 tablespoons butter or margarine
1 tablespoon vegetable oil
2 teaspoons cornstarch
1 teaspoon sugar
2 teaspoons soy sauce
1/4 teaspoon dried leaf thyme
Salt
Freshly ground black pepper
Hot cooked rice or noodles

*The secret of this dish is to keep the vegetables very crisp. This is a good opportunity to use up small amounts of raw vegetables; vary mixture accordingly.*

**1.** Bring a saucepan of lightly salted water to a boil. Add bell pepper, cauliflowerets, celery, green onions and zucchini; bring to a boil. Drain immediately; cool blanched vegetables in iced water. Drain thoroughly.
**2.** Heat butter or margarine and oil in a large skillet over medium heat. Add chicken; sauté 3 minutes. Add mushrooms; sauté 1 minute.
**3.** Add drained vegetables; stir-fry until hot. In a small bowl, combine cornstarch, sugar, soy sauce and thyme; add to skillet or wok. Cook until thickened, stirring constantly. Season with salt and pepper. Serve with hot cooked rice or noodles. Makes 4 servings.

Left to right: Spanish Rice, Chicken Stir-Fry

# Indonesian Lamb Kabobs

1/2 cup plain yogurt
1 teaspoon ground ginger
1 garlic clove, crushed
1/4 teaspoon ground cumin
1/4 teaspoon ground coriander
2 tablespoons lemon juice
1 tablespoon vegetable oil
Salt
Freshly ground pepper
1 lb. lamb for stew, cut into 1-inch cubes
2 medium onions
1 green bell pepper, cut into 8 pieces
1 red bell pepper, cut into 8 pieces
12 medium button mushrooms

*To serve:*
Cooked saffron rice

---

1. In a medium, glass or stainless-steel bowl, combine yogurt, ginger, garlic, cumin, coriander, lemon juice, oil, salt and pepper. Stir in lamb until coated. Cover and refrigerate 2 to 3 hours or up to 24 hours.
2. Preheat broiler. Blanch onions in boiling water 3 minutes; drain. When cool, quarter onions.
3. Remove lamb from marinade with a slotted spoon; thread on 4 skewers, alternating with onion quarters, bell-pepper pieces and mushrooms. Place kabobs on a broiler-pan rack; brush with marinade.
4. Broil under preheated broiler 15 to 20 minutes or until lamb is cooked to desired doneness. Baste frequently with marinade during cooking. Serve with hot cooked rice. Makes 4 servings.

# Beef, Apricot & Apple Kabobs

1 lb. beef round steak, thinly sliced
2 tablespoons butter or margarine
1 onion, chopped
2 cups fresh bread crumbs
1/2 teaspoon dried leaf thyme
2 tablespoons chopped fresh parsley
Salt
Freshly ground pepper
2 teaspoons lemon juice
1 egg, beaten
1 (1-lb.) can apricot halves, drained, or 12 fresh
   apricots, pitted, halved
3 green apples, cored, cut into 8 pieces
4 bay leaves
2 cups barbecue sauce

---

1. Cut beef into 12 strips about 1-1/2 inches wide.
2. Melt butter or margarine in a medium skillet. Add onion; sauté 5 minutes. Remove from heat; stir in bread crumbs, thyme, parsley, salt and pepper. Stir in lemon juice and egg. Divide mixture evenly among beef strips; roll up, enclosing stuffing.
3. Thread stuffed beef rolls on 4 skewers, alternating with apricots, apples and bay leaves. Brush with barbecue sauce. Place on a broiler-pan rack.
4. Broil under preheated broiler 20 to 25 minutes or until golden brown, turning frequently and basting with barbecue sauce.
5. Serve hot with any remaining barbecue sauce. Makes 4 servings.

# Stroganoff-Topped Toast

1 lb. rare roast beef
Salt
Freshly ground black pepper
2 tablespoons butter or margarine
2 tablespoons finely chopped onion
6 oz. button mushrooms, sliced (about 2-1/2 cups)
5 tablespoons mayonnaise
5 tablespoons dairy sour cream
Pinch of red (cayenne) pepper
1 tablespoon chopped fresh chives

*To serve:*
Curly endive or watercress
8 whole-wheat-bread slices or rye-bread slices, toasted
Chopped chives

---

1. Slice beef across grain into fairly thick slices. Cut slices into small strips. Season with salt and black pepper.
2. Melt butter or margarine in a medium skillet. Add onion; sauté 2 minutes. Add mushrooms; cook 2 minutes. Remove from heat; stir in mayonnaise, sour cream, red pepper and 1 tablespoon chives.
3. Stir beef into stroganoff mixture; cook over low heat about 1 minute or until hot. Do not boil.
4. To serve, arrange endive or watercress on 4 individual plates; place 2 toast slices on each plate. Spoon stroganoff over toast. Garnish with chopped chives. Serve immediately. Makes 4 servings.

Clockwise from left: Indonesian Lamb Kabobs; Beef, Apricot & Apple Kabobs; Stroganoff-Topped Toast

# Ham & Mushroom Gougère

1 tablespoon vegetable oil
1 onion, chopped
4 oz. mushrooms, sliced (about 1-3/4 cups)
2 cups chopped cooked ham (about 8 oz.)
Freshly ground pepper
6 tablespoons butter or margarine
3/4 cup water
3/4 cup all-purpose flour
3 eggs
2 tablespoons fresh bread crumbs
3/4 cup shredded Cheddar cheese (3 oz.)
1 tablespoon chopped fresh chives

1. Preheat oven to 425F (220C). Grease an oval 12" x 7" x 3" baking dish. Heat oil in a medium skillet. Add onion and mushrooms; cook about 5 minutes or until softened. Add ham and pepper. Set aside.
2. Heat butter or margarine and water in a medium, heavy saucepan until mixture boils. Add flour, all at once. With a wooden spoon, beat over medium heat until mixture is smooth and forms a ball that leaves side of saucepan.
3. Cool slightly; beat in eggs, 1 at a time, beating well after each addition.
4. Spread 1/2 of this choux paste over base of greased dish; spoon remaining choux paste around edge of dish. The layer of choux paste will not be very thick. Spoon ham mixture into center. Sprinkle evenly with bread crumbs.
5. Bake in preheated oven 25 minutes or until puffed and golden brown. Sprinkle ham mixture with cheese; bake 5 to 10 minutes or until cheese melts and dough is firm.
6. Sprinkle with chives; serve immediately. Makes 4 servings.

## Variation

For two people, halve quantities, using two eggs; reduce cooking time to about 25 minutes.

# Pasta with Creamy Ham & Cheese Sauce

8 oz. pasta shells (about 2 cups)
Salt
2 tablespoons butter or margarine
4 oz. mushrooms, sliced (about 1-3/4 cups)
1-1/2 cups chopped cooked ham (about 6 oz.)
1/2 cup whipping cream
1-1/2 cups shredded Cheddar cheese (6 oz.)
Freshly ground pepper
1 tablespoon chopped fresh parsley

*To garnish:*
6 to 8 black olives
2 tablespoons grated Parmesan cheese

1. Cook pasta shells in a large saucepan of salted boiling water according to package directions until tender. Do not overcook. Drain thoroughly.
2. Preheat oven to 350F (175C). Melt butter or margarine in a large saucepan. Add mushrooms and ham; cook about 5 minutes or until mushrooms are softened. Add drained pasta; toss over low heat to warm through.
3. In a medium bowl, combine cream, cheese, salt, pepper and parsley. Stir into pasta mixture; stir over low heat until pasta is coated and sauce is slightly thickened.
4. Spoon into a warmed serving dish. Garnish with black olives; sprinkle with Parmesan cheese. Serve hot with a green salad. Makes 4 servings.

# Mushroom Puffs

1/2 (17-1/4-oz.) pkg. frozen puff pastry
   (1 sheet), thawed
6 oz. mushrooms, chopped (about 2-1/2 cups)
Lemon juice
2 teaspoons finely chopped fresh parsley
1 teaspoon chopped chives
Vegetable oil for deep-frying

*Blue-Cheese Sauce:*
4 oz. blue cheese, crumbled
2/3 cup plain yogurt or dairy sour cream
2 tablespoons milk
1 tablespoon chopped fresh chives
Salt
White pepper

*To garnish:*
Lemon slices
Fresh parsley sprigs

1. Unfold pastry; lay flat on a lightly floured surface. With a lightly floured rolling pin, roll out pastry to a 12-inch square. Cut into 16 (3-inch) squares.
2. In a medium bowl, combine mushrooms, lemon juice, parsley and chives. Brush edges of each pastry square lightly with water. Spoon 1 tablespoon mushroom mixture on center of 1/2 of pastry squares. Top each with 1 of remaining pastry squares. Pinch edges to seal tightly.
3. Heat oil in a deep saucepan or deep-fat fryer to 350F (175C) or until a 1-inch bread cube turns golden brown in 65 seconds. Drop 3 to 4 mushroom parcels into hot oil; fry 2 to 3 minutes. Turn parcels over; fry 2 to 3 minutes or until golden brown. Remove with a slotted spoon; drain on paper towels. Keep warm. Repeat with remaining mushroom parcels.
4. To make sauce, in a blender, process cheese, yogurt or sour cream and milk until smooth. Add chives; process until finely chopped. Season with salt and white pepper. Spoon sauce into a small serving bowl.
5. Arrange mushroom puffs on a warmed serving plate. Garnish with lemon slices and parsley sprigs. Serve warm with sauce. Makes 8 servings of 2 puffs each.

Left to right: Mushroom Puffs with Blue-Cheese Sauce, Ham & Mushroom Gougère

Mushrooms & Ham with toast, Bacon-Stuffed Potato

# Mushrooms & Ham

1/2 cup butter or margarine, room temperature
8 oz. button mushrooms
2 cups finely chopped cooked ham (about 8 oz.)
1/4 cup Madeira
1/4 cup whipping cream
1 cup shredded sharp Cheddar cheese (4 oz.)
1 teaspoon Italian seasoning
4 white-bread slices, crusts removed
Paprika

*To garnish:*
Parsley sprigs

*This dish is a specialty of an award-winning restaurant near Amersham in Buckinghamshire, England. The secret of its success lies in choosing the smallest mushrooms available and using a rich Madeira.*

1. Preheat broiler. Melt 1/4 cup butter or margarine in a medium saucepan. Add mushrooms; sauté about 4 minutes or until softened. Add ham; cook 2 minutes.
2. Stir in Madeira; boil 1 minute to reduce slightly. Stir in cream; simmer 2 minutes.
3. Spoon mixture into a large shallow flameproof dish or 4 individual flameproof dishes; sprinkle with cheese.
4. Broil under preheated broiler until bubbly. Sprinkle with paprika; garnish with parsley. Keep hot.
5. In a small bowl, blend remaining 1/4 cup butter or margarine and Italian seasoning. Spread herb mixture on both sides of bread. Place herbed bread on a baking sheet. Toast bread under preheated broiler on both sides until golden. Cut each slice in half lengthwise; serve with hot mushroom mixture. Makes 4 servings.

# Bacon-Stuffed Potatoes

**4 large baking potatoes**
**8 bacon slices, chopped**
**4 oz. mushrooms, sliced (about 1-3/4 cups)**
**1/2 cup dairy sour cream**
**Salt**
**Freshly ground pepper**
**2 tablespoons chopped fresh chives**

*To garnish:*
**4 bacon slices**

**1.** Preheat oven to 375F (190C). Prick potatoes. Place pricked potatoes on a baking sheet.
**2.** Bake potatoes in preheated oven 1 hour or until tender.
**3.** Meanwhile, in a medium skillet, cook bacon with no added fat until crisp and golden. Drain off all but 2 tablespoons fat. Add mushrooms to bacon; cook 5 minutes.
**4.** Slice off tops of baked potatoes; scoop out potatoes into a medium bowl, reserving potato skins. Stir mushroom mixture, 1/4 cup sour cream, salt and pepper into potatoes. Fold in 1 tablespoon chives. Spoon mixture into reserved potato skins. Place stuffed potatoes on a baking sheet.
**5.** Bake 10 minutes. Keep warm.
**6.** Preheat broiler. To make bacon garnishes, pleat bacon onto a skewer. Broil under preheated broiler until golden.
**7.** Spoon remaining sour cream over baked stuffed potatoes. Top each potato with a broiled bacon slice and remaining chives. Makes 4 servings.

# Individual Boeuf en Croûte

4 (1/2-inch-thick) beef-loin tenderloin steaks
1/2 cup red wine
Salt
Freshly ground pepper
1 garlic clove, crushed
1/4 cup butter or margarine
3 oz. mushrooms, chopped
1 (17-1/2-oz.) pkg. puff pastry, thawed, if frozen
3 oz. liver pâté, cut into 4 slices
1 egg, beaten

1. Place steaks in a shallow dish. Add wine, salt, pepper and garlic.
2. Cover; refrigerate overnight.
3. Pat steaks dry with paper towels.
4. Melt butter or margarine in a skillet. Add steaks; sauté 1 to 2 minutes on each side. Cool steaks.
5. Preheat oven to 400F (205C). Grease a baking sheet.
6. Add mushrooms to fat remaining in skillet; cook 2 to 3 minutes. Drain mushrooms.
7. Cut each pastry sheet in half. On a lightly floured surface, roll out each half to a piece large enough to enclose 1 steak.
8. Put a cooled steak in center of each pastry piece. Top with 1/4 of mushrooms and a pâté slice.
9. Brush pastry edges with beaten egg. Wrap pastry around steak. Trim off excess pastry; reserve. Pinch edges to seal. Repeat with remaining pastry, steaks, mushrooms and pâté.
10. Place on greased baking sheet; brush with egg to glaze.
11. Roll out pastry trimmings; cut small leaves for decoration. Arrange leaves on pastry; brush with egg.
12. Bake in preheated oven 25 minutes or until pastry is puffed and golden.
13. Serve hot or cold. Makes 4 servings.

# Spaghetti al Cartoccio

8 oz. spaghetti
1/4 cup butter or margarine
2 garlic cloves, minced
1/2 lb. uncooked shrimp, peeled, deveined
1/2 pint whipping cream (1 cup)
1/4 lb. smoked-salmon trimmings, coarsely chopped
4 anchovy fillets, drained, chopped
1 (8-3/4-oz.) jar mussels, drained
1/2 cup grated Parmesan cheese
Freshly ground pepper

*This pasta dish can be served as a first course or as a light main dish accompanied by a salad.*

1. Cook spaghetti in lightly salted boiling water about 10 minutes or until almost tender. Drain well; return to saucepan. Set aside.
2. Melt butter or margarine in a medium saucepan. Add garlic and shrimp; cook 2 minutes. Stir in cream, smoked salmon, anchovies and mussels. Stirring gently, cook 2 to 3 minutes or until heated through. Remove from heat; stir in cheese and pepper. Pour sauce over spaghetti; toss to combine.
3. Preheat oven to 400F (205C). Cut 2 large sheets of parchment paper; place in a double layer on a 15" x 10" jelly-roll pan. Crinkle papers around outer edges; turn up slightly to make a large bag. Spoon spaghetti into bag. Pull opposite sides of paper over spaghetti; staple closed. Pull remaining sides of paper over; staple closed.
4. Bake in preheated oven 12 to 15 minutes or until paper is puffed.
5. Place on a serving plate. Carefully remove staples; open to release the wonderful aroma. Serve immediately from paper dish. Makes 8 first-course servings or 4 light main-dish servings.

Top to bottom: Spaghetti al Cartoccio, Individual Boeuf en Croûte

# Beef & Rice Koulabiac

1 tablespoon butter or margarine
1 medium onion, finely chopped
8 oz. lean ground beef
1 garlic clove, crushed
3/4 cup cooked white rice
Salt
Freshly ground pepper
2 tablespoons sherry
2 tablespoons whipping cream
2 tablespoons chopped fresh parsley
1 hard-cooked egg, finely chopped
1 (17-1/2-oz.) pkg. puff pastry, thawed, if frozen
1 egg, beaten

*Egg Sauce:*
2 hard-cooked eggs
1 teaspoon prepared brown mustard
Juice of 1/2 lemon
1/2 cup olive oil
1 tablespoon chopped fresh chives

1. Melt butter or margarine in a large skillet. Add onion; sauté 2 to 3 minutes.
2. Add meat; sauté 5 minutes or until no longer pink. Drain off excess fat.
3. Stir in garlic, cooked rice, salt, pepper, sherry and cream. Cook 1 minute, stirring constantly.
4. Stir in parsley and chopped hard-cooked egg; cool.
5. Overlap 2 sheets of puff pastry into 1 sheet, brushing edge with water. On a lightly floured surface, roll out pastry to a 14-inch square.
6. Spoon meat mixture into center of pastry.
7. Brush pastry edges with beaten egg. Fold corners of pastry to center. Pinch pastry edges together to seal, completely enclosing filling.
8. Place on greased baking sheet; refrigerate 20 minutes.
9. Preheat oven to 425F (220C). Brush pastry with beaten egg to glaze. Bake in preheated oven 30 to 35 minutes or until pastry is puffed and golden.
10. To make sauce, separate hard-cooked eggs. Sieve yolks; chop whites finely. In a small bowl, combine sieved yolks, mustard and lemon juice. Gradually beat in olive oil; season with salt and pepper. Stir in chopped egg whites and chives.
11. Serve sauce with hot koulabiac. Makes 4 servings.

# Chicken Crepes

2 tablespoons butter or margarine
2 tablespoons all-purpose flour
1 cup milk
1 cup shredded Swiss cheese (4 oz.)
Salt
Freshly ground pepper
1 cup chopped cooked chicken
1/4 cup chopped walnuts, almonds or pecans
1 tablespoon chopped fresh parsley
8 crepes, page 19

1. Melt butter or margarine in a medium saucepan over medium heat. Stir in flour; cook 1 minute, stirring constantly. Slowly stir in milk; cook until slightly thickened, stirring constantly. Stir in cheese until melted. Season with salt and pepper. Stir in chicken, nuts and parsley.
2. Preheat oven to 350F (175C). Grease a 13" x 9" baking dish.
3. Spoon 1-1/2 tablespoons chicken mixture onto each crepe. Fold crepe over filling. Place filled crepes, seam-side down, in greased baking dish.
4. Cover with foil. Bake in preheated oven 15 to 20 minutes or until heated through.
5. Serve immediately. Makes 4 servings, 2 crepes each.

# Pork, Beef & Chicken Saté

12 oz. lean boneless pork
12 oz. beef round steak
12 oz. boneless chicken breasts, skinned
6 tablespoons vegetable oil
6 tablespoons soy sauce
1 garlic clove, crushed
1 tablespoon curry powder
1-1/2 tablespoons sugar

*Peanut Sauce:*
2 tablespoons vegetable oil
1 onion, finely chopped
1 garlic clove, crushed
1 teaspoon chili powder
1 teaspoon ground coriander
1/4 teaspoon ground cumin
1/2 cup peanut butter
1 cup coconut milk or chicken stock
2 tablespoons light-brown sugar
1 tablespoon soy sauce
1 tablespoon lemon juice

1. Cut pork, beef and chicken into 1/2-inch cubes; place each meat in a separate medium, glass or stainless-steel bowl.
2. In another medium bowl, combine oil, soy sauce, garlic, curry powder and sugar. Pour 1/3 of marinade over each meat. Cover and refrigerate at least 4 hours or up to 24 hours.
3. Preheat broiler. To make sauce, heat oil in a medium saucepan. Stir in onion, garlic, chili powder, coriander and cumin; cook 2 minutes. Stir in peanut butter, coconut milk or stock, brown sugar, soy sauce and lemon juice. Bring to a boil. Reduce heat; Simmer 10 minutes or until creamy. Set aside to cool.
4. Thread marinated meats on 12 small skewers, using 4 for each type of meat. If using wooden skewers, soak in cold water 30 minutes before using. Brush kabobs with a little peanut sauce. Place on a broiler-pan rack.
5. Broil under preheated broiler 6 to 8 minutes or until browned on all sides. Pork should be well-done. Serve hot with remaining peanut sauce. Makes 4 servings.

# Frankfurter & Beans in Bundles

1 tablespoon vegetable oil
4 frankfurters
1 (8-oz.) pkg. refrigerator crescent-roll dough
1 egg, beaten
1 (15-oz.) can baked beans in tomato sauce
2 tablespoons grated Parmesan cheese

1. Preheat oven to 375F (190C). Grease a baking sheet.
2. Heat oil in a skillet. Add frankfurters; sauté 3 to 4 minutes, turning from time to time. Drain on paper towels.
3. Separate dough into 4 rectangles; press to seal perforations. On a lightly floured surface, roll each rectangle to a 8" x 6" rectangle. Or, roll rectangles large enough to cover frankfurters and beans.
4. Brush edges of pastry rectangles with beaten egg.
5. Lay a sautéed frankfurter on each pastry rectangle; add about 1/3 cup beans. Fold pastry over frankfurters and beans; pinch pastry edges together to seal.
6. Place on greased baking sheet; brush with beaten egg to glaze. Sprinkle with Parmesan cheese.
7. Bake in preheated oven 20 minutes or until golden brown. Makes 4 servings.

Top to bottom: Chicken Crepes, Beef & Rice Koulabiac with Egg Sauce

## Garlic Chicken in Cabbage Leaves

1/4 cup butter or margarine, room temperature
3 tablespoons chopped fresh parsley
2 large garlic cloves, crushed
Salt
Freshly ground pepper
4 chicken drumsticks, boned
8 large cabbage leaves
About 1/2 cup white wine

1. In a small bowl, combine butter or margarine, 2 tablespoons parsley, garlic, salt and pepper.
2. Spoon 1/4 of flavored butter or margarine into cavity of each drumstick. Wrap in plastic wrap; refrigerate 1 hour to firm filling.
3. Preheat oven to 350F (175C). Cut away tough stalk from each cabbage leaf. Place in boiling water; blanch 1 minute. Place in a bowl of cold water.
4. Drain blanched cabbage leaves on paper towels.
5. Wrap each chilled drumstick in 2 cabbage leaves. Place in a shallow ovenproof dish.
6. Pour 1/2 cup wine over cabbage rolls. Season with salt, pepper and remaining parsley. Cover dish with foil.
7. Bake in preheated oven 40 minutes or until chicken is tender when pierced with a skewer, adding additional wine if necessary.
8. Uncover dish; serve immediately. Makes 4 servings.

## Duck with Apricot & Cherry Sauce

4 duck quarters, 10 to 12 oz. each
Salt
Freshly ground pepper
1 (7-oz.) can apricot halves in light syrup
1 (15-oz.) can dark sweet cherries, drained

1. Preheat oven to 400F (205C).
2. Prick duck quarters all over with a fork or skewer. Sprinkle with salt and pepper.
3. Place seasoned duck on a roasting rack in a roasting pan.
4. Bake in preheated oven 40 minutes. Allow duck to cool slightly.
5. In a blender or food processor fitted with a steel blade, process apricots and syrup until blended.
6. Stir cherries into apricot puree.
7. Place each baked duck quarter in center of a foil square large enough to completely enclose it, shiny-side up. Pull up foil edges.
8. Spoon fruit sauce over duck. Pinch foil edges together to seal.
9. Bake in preheated oven 20 to 25 minutes. Open one package to test that duck is tender.
10. Serve hot. Makes 4 servings.

## Baked Pork & Red-Cabbage Rolls

4 pork chops, trimmed
1/4 cup applesauce
1 tablespoon chopped fresh sage or 1 teaspoon
   dried leaf sage
Salt
Freshly ground pepper
8 large red-cabbage leaves
2/3 cup unsweetened apple juice

*To garnish:*
Raw apple slices tossed in lemon juice, if desired

1. Preheat broiler. Place pork chops on a broiler-pan rack. Broil 3 minutes per side. Cool slightly.
2. Spread 1 side of each broiled pork chop with applesauce. Sprinkle with sage, salt and pepper.
3. Cut any tough stalk from cabbage leaves. Place in boiling water; blanch 2 minutes. Place in a bowl of cold water.
4. Drain blanched cabbage leaves on paper towels.
5. Preheat oven to 350F (175C). Wrap each pork chop in 2 cabbage leaves. Place in a shallow ovenproof dish.
6. Pour over apple juice. Cover dish with foil.
7. Bake in preheated oven 1 hour or until pork chops are tender when pierced with a knife.
8. Garnish with apple slices, if desired. Makes 4 servings.

Top to bottom: Baked Pork & Red-Cabbage Rolls, Duck with Apricot & Cherry Sauce

# Stuffed Onions

4 large onions, peeled
Water
6 bacon slices, chopped
3 tablespoons chopped fresh parsley
1/4 cup fresh bread crumbs
1 egg, beaten
2 tablespoons grated Parmesan cheese
Salt
Freshly ground pepper

*To serve:*
Seasoned tomato sauce or mushroom sauce

**1.** Preheat oven to 375F (190C). Grease a baking dish large enough to hold onions in 1 layer.
**2.** Carefully hollow out onions, using a grapefruit knife, leaving shells about 1/2 inch thick; reserve onion pieces.
**3.** Place onions in a large saucepan. Add enough water to cover; bring to a boil. Boil 6 minutes.
**4.** Finely chop pieces from onion centers.
**5.** Place bacon in a skillet over medium heat. Sauté until fat starts to run. Add chopped onions; sauté 3 minutes.
**6.** In a medium bowl, combine cooked onion mixture, parsley, bread crumbs, egg, cheese, salt and pepper.
**7.** Spoon stuffing mixture into each onion shell.
**8.** Place onions in greased baking dish; cover with foil.
**9.** Bake in preheated oven 1 hour or until onions are tender when pierced with a fork.
**10.** Serve with a simple tomato or mushroom sauce, if desired. Makes 4 servings.

Top to bottom: Mustard Baked Trout, Sole & Spinach Rolls with Lemon Sauce

# Mustard Baked Trout

4 trout, ready for cooking
Vegetable oil
3 tablespoons butter or margarine
1 small onion, finely chopped
1 garlic clove, crushed
3 tablespoons all-purpose flour
1/2 cup milk
1/2 cup chicken stock
1 tablespoon prepared horseradish mustard
Salt
Freshly ground pepper

*To garnish:*
Chopped parsley

---

1. Preheat oven to 375F (190C). Fillet trout, if desired.
2. Cut 4 rectangular pieces of foil, each large enough to completely enclose a trout. Brush each foil piece with oil. Pull up foil edges; lay a trout along center of each foil piece.
3. To make sauce, in a medium saucepan, melt butter or margarine. Add onion; sauté 3 minutes. Stir in garlic and flour; cook 1 minute.
4. Gradually stir in milk and stock.
5. Bring to a boil; stir in mustard, salt and pepper. Simmer sauce 5 minutes, stirring frequently.
6. Spoon sauce over each trout.
7. Pull edges of foil up and over trout, folding edges together to seal. Place foil packages on a baking sheet.
8. Bake in preheated oven 25 minutes or until fish tests done. Check for doneness by carefully opening 1 package.
9. To serve, carefully fold back foil. Garnish with chopped parsley, if desired. Serve immediately. Makes 4 servings.

# Sole & Spinach Rolls

4 large sole fillets, skinned
12 anchovy fillets
Freshly ground pepper
2 tablespoons chopped fresh parsley
Grated peel of 1/2 lemon
12 medium fresh spinach leaves
6 tablespoons butter or margarine, melted

*Lemon Sauce:*
1/2 cup mayonnaise
3 tablespoons whipping cream
Grated peel of 1 lemon

---

1. On a work surface, lay sole fillets out flat.
2. Arrange 3 anchovy fillets on each sole fillet. Sprinkle with pepper, parsley and lemon peel.
3. Roll up fillets. Secure with wooden picks; refrigerate 30 minutes.
4. Preheat oven to 400F (205C). Grease a baking dish large enough to hold rolled fillets in 1 layer.
5. Place spinach in boiling water. Blanch 30 seconds. Place in a bowl of iced water. Drain on paper towels. On a work surface, spread out blanched leaves.
6. Remove wooden picks from each rolled fillet; roll each fillet in 3 spinach leaves.
7. Place sole-and-spinach rolls in greased baking dish. Spoon over melted butter or margarine.
8. Cover dish. Bake in preheated oven 15 minutes or until fish tests done.
9. To make sauce, place mayonnaise, cream and lemon peel in the top of a double boiler over simmering water. Stir until heated. Serve sauce separately with cooked fish. Makes 4 servings.

# Breads

Nothing gives a feeling a warm and homey feeling more than the smell of baking bread. Yet many people think that baking bread is too difficult to attempt. They couldn't be more wrong! Like other areas of cooking, it's helpful to have some basic information about ingredients and techniques before starting to bake. However, these techniques are not difficult to master. Breads can be divided into two major categories by the type of *leavening agent* used in making the bread. These categories are quick breads and yeasts.

## QUICK BREADS

Quick breads are leavened by baking powder or baking soda. In addition, air beaten in during preparation and steam from liquid ingredients add additional leavening. Quick breads include muffins, corn bread, biscuits, scones and pancakes. The method used for most quick breads is the *muffin method*. In this method, all dry ingredients are added to a bowl. All liquid ingredients, such as eggs, vegetable oil or milk, are combined and added to the dry ingredients at the same time. The mixture is stirred only until the dry ingredients are moistened. Overmixing results in a heavy product. Biscuits and some other quick breads are made by the *biscuit method*. This is similar to pastry, because the fat is cut into the dry ingredients. However, more liquid is used to give a softer dough.

## YEAST BREADS

Traditional breads, dinner rolls, sweet rolls and coffeecakes are included in this section. Dried yeast has been used for the recipes as it is the most commonly available form. All recipes call for dissolving yeast and a small amount of sugar in a warm liquid and allowing it to stand until foamy. This is called *proofing*. This gives the yeast a good start before adding it to the other ingredients. It also lets you check if the yeast is active. Discard any yeast that does not start to grow during proofing. Don't waste other ingredients; start with a fresh package of yeast!

Dissolve dry yeast in liquid that is between 105F to 115F (40C to 45C). Use a thermometer until you can judge the temperature accurately. Too low a temperature will make the yeast grow slowly. High temperatures will kill it.

Yeast dough is kneaded to develop the *gluten*, the protein strands that trap the gas produced by the yeast and give the baked product its shape. Kneading can be done by hand or with a heavy-duty mixer with a dough hook.

Let your yeast dough rise in a warm, not hot, place that is free from drafts. The ideal temperature is about 80F to 85F (25C to 30C).

## BASIC INGREDIENTS

Breads are made of several basic ingredients. The major ingredient is flour. Flour forms the structure of the bread when the gluten it contains combines with liquid. Eggs add color, flavor and nutrients. Fat makes a product more tender by separating the strands of gluten. Fat used in breads include vegetable shortening, butter, margarine and vegetable oil. Liquids include water, potato water, milk and fruit juices.

Other bread ingredients include leavening agents, such as baking powder, baking soda or yeast. Leavening agents produce a gas that causes the bread to rise. This gives a light product with an open texture. The amount of yeast, baking soda or baking powder will determine the volume and structure of the final product. Baking powder starts to act when liquid is added to the dry ingredients. Baking soda requires an acid ingredient, such as buttermilk, to start producing gas. Steam formed during baking or air beaten into egg whites or from creaming also help to leaven some breads.

Salt and some type of flavoring are usually added to baked products. Salt is important in yeast breads because it helps control the action of the yeast. In addition, sugar, honey, molasses, a fruit puree, spices, nuts or raisins might be added to create a special product. Herbs or cheese are often added to savory breads to add interesting flavors.

Vienna Rolls, page 286

# Quick Griddle Scone

2 cups self-rising flour
1/4 cup sugar
1/4 cup shortening, butter or margarine
1/2 cup currants
1 egg
6 to 8 tablespoons milk

*To serve:*
Butter or margarine

1. In a medium bowl, combine flour and sugar. With a pastry blender or 2 knives, cut in shortening, butter or margarine until mixture resembles coarse crumbs. Stir in currants.
2. In a small bowl, beat egg and 6 tablespoons milk until blended. Stir egg mixture into flour-currant mixture with a fork to make a soft, non-sticky, dough, adding more milk if necessary.
3. On a lightly floured surface, knead dough 8 to 10 strokes. Pat out dough to an 8-inch circle.
4. Heat a griddle or large skillet over medium heat. When hot, brush griddle or skillet with vegetable oil. Place scone on hot oiled griddle or skillet. Reduce heat; cook 10 minutes. Check bottom of scone frequently. Reduce heat again to prevent burning, if necessary. Carefully turn over scone with a large flat spatula. Cook 8 to 10 minutes or until golden brown.
5. Using spatula, slide baked scone onto a serving plate; cut into wedges. Serve warm with butter or margarine. Makes 4 to 6 servings.

# Scones

2 cups sifted all-purpose flour
1 tablespoon baking powder
2 tablespoons sugar
1/2 teaspoon salt
1/4 cup shortening, butter or margarine
2 eggs
About 1/3 cup milk or half and half

*To serve:*
Butter or margarine

1. Preheat oven to 425F (220C). Grease 2 baking sheets.
2. In a medium bowl, combine flour, baking powder, sugar and salt. With a pastry blender or 2 knives, cut in shortening, butter or margarine until mixture resembles coarse crumbs.
3. In a small bowl, beat eggs and 1/3 cup milk or half and half until blended. Stir egg mixture into flour mixture with a fork to make a soft, non-sticky dough, adding more milk or half and half if necessary.
4. On a lightly floured surface, knead dough 8 to 10 strokes. Roll out dough to 1/2 inch thick. Cut dough with a floured 2- to 2-1/2-inch fluted biscuit cutter. Place on greased baking sheets 1-1/2 to 2 inches apart. Brush tops with milk.
5. Bake in preheated oven 12 to 15 minutes or until golden brown. Remove from baking sheets; serve warm of butter or margarine. Makes 14 to 18 scones.

## Variations
**Whole-Wheat Scones:** Substitute whole-wheat flour for 1 cup all-purpose flour. Add 1 to 2 tablespoons more milk.
**Spicy Scones:** Add 2 teaspoons pumpkin-pie spice to flour mixture. Substitute brown sugar for granulated sugar.
**Cheese Scones:** Add 2/3 cup shredded sharp Cheddar cheese (3 ounces), 1 teaspoon dry mustard and a pinch of red (cayenne) pepper to flour mixture. Omit sugar.
**Fruit Scones:** Add 1/3 cup currants or raisins to flour mixture.
**Yogurt & Honey Scones:** Substitute plain yogurt for milk. Substitute 3 tablespoons honey for sugar. Blend eggs, yogurt and honey together; add to flour mixture. Brush dough circles with milk; sprinkle with brown sugar before baking.

Clockwise from top left: Quick Griddle Scone, Scones with variations

Honey-Nut Loaf

# Banana-Raisin Bread

1/2 cup butter or margarine, room temperature
3/4 cup firmly packed light-brown sugar
2 eggs
1 teaspoon vanilla extract
1-3/4 cups all-purpose flour
1-1/2 teaspoons baking powder
1/2 teaspoon baking soda
1/2 teaspoon salt
1/4 teaspoon freshly grated nutmeg
2 large ripe bananas, mashed (about 1 cup)
1/2 cup raisins, chopped

1. Preheat oven to 350F (175C). Grease a 9" x 5" loaf pan.
2. In a medium bowl, beat butter or margarine and brown sugar 5 to 8 minutes or until light and fluffy. Beat in eggs and vanilla.
3. Sift flour, baking powder, baking soda, salt and nutmeg into a medium bowl. Stir flour mixture into egg mixture alternately with mashed bananas, stirring until combined. Fold in chopped raisins. Pour into greased pan; smooth top.
4. Bake in preheated oven 55 to 60 minutes or until a wooden pick inserted in center comes out clean.
5. Cool in pan on a wire rack 10 minutes. Remove from pan; cool completely on wire rack. Wrap in plastic wrap; store in a cool place 1 to 2 days before serving. Makes 1 loaf.

# Honey-Nut Loaf

1/2 cup butter or margarine, room temperature
2/3 cup firmly packed light-brown sugar
2 eggs
1-1/2 cups all-purpose flour
2 teaspoons baking powder
2 teaspoons ground cinnamon
1/2 teaspoon salt
1/2 cup milk
1 cup finely chopped, almonds, hazelnuts, walnuts or pecans

*For decoration:*
2 tablespoons honey, warmed
Assorted whole nuts

1. Preheat oven to 350F (175C). Grease an 8" x 4" loaf pan.
2. In a medium bowl, beat butter or margarine and brown sugar 5 to 8 minutes or until light and fluffy. Add eggs; beat until blended. Sift flour, baking powder, cinnamon and salt into a medium bowl. Stir flour mixture into egg mixture alternately with milk, stirring until combined. Fold in chopped nuts. Pour batter into greased pan; smooth top.
3. Bake in preheated oven 55 to 60 minutes or until a wooden pick inserted in center comes out clean. Cool in pan on a wire rack 10 minutes. Remove from pan; cool completely on rack.
4. Brush top of bread lightly with honey. Arrange a nut cluster in center of glazed bread. Brush nuts with honey. Makes 1 loaf.

# Whole-Wheat Soda Bread

1-1/2 cups whole-wheat flour
1-1/2 cups all-purpose flour
1 tablespoon sugar
1 teaspoon salt
1 teaspoon baking soda
1/4 cup butter or margarine
1 tablespoon white vinegar
1 cup milk

**1.** Preheat oven to 375F (190C). Grease a round 8-inch baking pan; set aside.
**2.** In a medium bowl, combine flours, sugar, salt and baking soda. Using 2 knives or a pastry blender, cut in butter or margarine until mixture resembles coarse crumbs. Stir vinegar into milk; add to flour mixture, stirring to make a soft dough.
**3.** Turn out dough onto a lightly floured surface; knead 8 to 10 times or until smooth. Shape into a round flat loaf. Place dough in prepared pan; cut a deep cross on top of bread.
**4.** Bake in preheated oven 45 to 50 minutes or until golden brown. Remove from pan. Cool on a wire rack 5 minutes.
**5.** Serve warm or cool completely on wire rack. Makes 1 loaf.

Left to right: Banana-Raisin Bread; Cherry Turnovers, page 344

# Coconut Bread

2 cups flaked or shredded coconut
1-3/4 cups milk
2-1/2 cups all-purpose flour
2-1/2 teaspoons baking powder
1 teaspoon ground cinnamon
1/2 teaspoon salt
1/4 teaspoon ground cloves
1-1/3 cups sugar

---

**1.** In a medium bowl, combine coconut and milk. Let stand at room temperature 30 minutes.
**2.** Preheat oven to 350F (175C). Grease a 9" x 5" loaf pan.
**3.** Sift flour, baking powder, cinnamon, salt and cloves into a large bowl. Stir in sugar. Make a well in center of dry ingredients. Pour in coconut mixture; stir with a wooden spoon until dry ingredients are barely moistened. Pour into greased pan; smooth top.
**4.** Bake in preheated oven 65 to 70 minutes or until a wooden pick inserted in center comes out clean. Cool in pan on a wire rack 10 minutes. Remove from pan; cool completely on rack. Makes 1 loaf.

# Date & Lemon Loaf

3/4 cup butter or margarine
1/2 cup firmly packed light-brown sugar
1/3 cup honey
1 (8-oz.) pkg. pitted dates, chopped
3 eggs, beaten
2 teaspoons grated lemon peel
1-3/4 cups all-purpose flour
1 teaspoon baking powder
1 teaspoon baking soda
1/2 teaspoon salt

*Topping:*
3 tablespoons all-purpose flour
1 tablespoon sugar
1 tablespoon butter or margarine

---

**1.** In a medium saucepan over low heat, combine butter or margarine, brown sugar and honey. Cook, stirring, until butter or margarine melts and sugar dissolves. Remove pan from heat; stir in dates. Let cool.
**2.** Preheat oven to 350F (175C). Grease a 9" x 5" loaf pan.
**3.** Stir eggs into cooled date mixture until blended.
**4.** In a medium bowl, combine lemon peel, flour, baking powder, baking soda and salt. Make a well in center of dry ingredients. Pour in date mixture; stir until dry ingredients are barely moistened. Pour into greased pan; smooth top.
**5.** To make topping, in a small bowl, combine flour and sugar. With a pastry blender or 2 knives, cut in butter or margarine until mixture resembles fine crumbs. Sprinkle crumbs on top of batter.
**6.** Bake in preheated oven 50 to 55 minutes or until a wooden pick inserted in center comes out clean. Cool in pan on a wire rack 5 to 10 minutes. Remove from pan; cool completely on rack. Makes 1 loaf.

Left to right: Sticky Gingerbread Bars, page 313; Date & Lemon Loaf

# Southern Cornsticks

3/4 cup all-purpose flour
2 cups white cornmeal
1-1/2 teaspoons baking powder
1/2 teaspoon baking soda
1/2 teaspoon salt
1 teaspoon sugar
2 eggs, beaten
1/4 cup vegetable oil
2 cups buttermilk

1. Preheat oven to 450F (230C). Heat a heavy cornstick pan in preheated oven.
2. In a medium bowl, combine flour, cornmeal, baking powder, baking soda, salt and sugar.
3. In a small bowl, combine eggs, oil and buttermilk. Pour egg mixture into flour mixture; stir until dry ingredients are barely moistened.
4. Grease hot cornstick pan. Spoon batter into greased pan, filling about 2/3 full; reserve any remaining batter.
5. Bake in preheated oven about 15 minutes or until golden brown. Remove cornsticks from pan. Bake remaining batter if necessary, greasing pan again. Serve hot. Makes 12 large cornsticks.

## Variation

Pour batter into a greased 8-inch round cake pan. Bake in preheated oven about 20 minutes or until golden brown.

# Double Corn Bread

1 cup sifted all-purpose flour
1 cup yellow cornmeal
3 tablespoons sugar
4 teaspoons baking powder
1 teaspoon salt
1 egg
1 cup milk
1/4 cup butter or margarine, melted
1 (8-oz.) can cream-style corn

*To serve:*
Butter or margarine

1. Preheat oven to 425F (220C). Grease an 8- or 9-inch-square baking pan.
2. In a medium bowl, combine flour, cornmeal, sugar, baking powder and salt. In a small bowl, blend egg, milk and butter or margarine.
3. Make a well in center of dry ingredients. Add egg mixture and corn. Stir until dry ingredients are barely moistened. Pour into greased pan.
4. Bake in preheated oven 20 to 25 minutes or until golden brown. Cut into squares; serve hot with butter or margarine. Makes 9 servings.

# Blueberry Muffins

2 cups all-purpose flour
1/2 cup granulated sugar
2-1/2 teaspoons baking powder
2 teaspoons grated lemon peel
1/2 teaspoon salt
1/4 teaspoon freshly grated nutmeg
1/3 cup vegetable oil
1 egg
1 cup milk
1 cup fresh or thawed, frozen blueberries
Brown sugar

1. Preheat oven to 400F (205C). Grease a 12-cup muffin pan or line muffin cups with paper cupcake liners.
2. In a medium bowl, combine flour, granulated sugar, baking powder, lemon peel, salt and nutmeg. In a small bowl, blend oil, egg and milk. Make a well in center of dry ingredients; stir in egg mixture until dry ingredients are barely moistened. Fold in blueberries.
3. Spoon batter into prepared muffin cups, filling cups about two-thirds full. Sprinkle tops with brown sugar.
4. Bake in preheated oven 20 to 25 minutes or until a wooden pick inserted in center of a muffin comes out clean. Remove from pan; serve hot. Makes 12 muffins.

# Grandma's Biscuits

2 cups all-purpose flour
1 tablespoon baking powder
1 teaspoon salt
5 tablespoons vegetable shortening, butter or margarine
3/4 cup milk

*To serve:*
Butter or margarine

1. Preheat oven to 450F (230C).
2. Sift flour, baking powder and salt into a large bowl. With a pastry blender or 2 knives, cut in shortening, butter or margarine until mixture resembles coarse crumbs. Stir milk into flour mixture with a fork to make a soft dough.
3. On a lightly floured surface, knead dough 10 strokes. Roll out dough to 1/2 inch thick. Cut dough with a floured 2- to 2-1/2-inch-round cutter.
4. Place biscuits on an ungreased baking sheet about 1 inch apart for crusty biscuits or close together for soft biscuits.
5. Bake in preheated oven 12 to 15 minutes or until golden brown. Remove from baking sheet; serve hot with butter or margarine. Makes 12 biscuits.

# Silver-Dollar Pancakes

1-1/2 cups sifted all-purpose flour
2 tablespoons sugar
2 teaspoons baking powder
1/2 teaspoon salt
1 egg, beaten
1/4 cup vegetable oil
1-1/4 cups milk

*To serve:*
Butter, margarine, preserves or jam

1. In a large bowl, combine flour, sugar, baking powder and salt. In a small bowl, beat egg, oil and milk until blended. Stir egg mixture into flour mixture until dry ingredients are barely moistened.
2. Heat a griddle or large skillet over medium heat. Brush hot griddle or skillet with vegetable oil.
3. Drop batter by tablespoons onto hot oiled griddle or skillet, a few at a time. Cook over medium heat until bubbles appear on top of pancake and edges are browned. Turn pancakes with a wide spatula; cook until bottom is golden. Remove cooked pancakes; keep warm. Repeat with remaining batter.
4. Serve warm pancakes with butter, margarine, preserves or jam. Makes 18 to 24 small pancakes.

Left to right: Silver-Dollar Pancakes; Walnut Brownies, page 315; Raisin-Bran Muffins

# Cinnamon-Apple Muffins

2 cups all-purpose flour
1/3 cup firmly packed light-brown sugar
1 tablespoon baking powder
1 teaspoon salt
1 teaspoon ground cinnamon
1/2 teaspoon freshly grated nutmeg
3/4 cup milk
2 eggs
3 tablespoons vegetable oil
1 tablespoon lemon juice
1 cup finely chopped, peeled, tart apple (1 large apple)

---

**1.** Preheat oven to 400F (205C). Grease a 12-cup muffin pan or line cups with paper cupcake liners.
**2.** In a large bowl, combine flour, brown sugar, baking powder, salt, cinnamon and nutmeg.
**3.** In a small bowl, beat milk, eggs, oil and lemon juice until blended. Make a well in center of dry ingredients; stir in milk mixture until dry ingredients are barely moistened. Fold in chopped apple. Spoon batter into prepared muffin cups, filling cups about two-thirds full.
**4.** Bake in preheated oven 20 to 25 minutes or until a wooden pick inserted in center of a muffin comes out clean. Remove from pan. Serve warm or cool completely on a wire rack. Makes 12 muffins.

# Raisin-Bran Muffins

1/4 cup vegetable oil
1/2 cup firmly packed light-brown sugar
1 egg
1 cup milk
1 cup all-purpose flour
1 cup unprocessed bran
1 tablespoon baking powder
1/2 teaspoon baking soda
1/2 teaspoon salt
1/2 cup raisins

---

**1.** Preheat oven to 400F (205C). Grease a 12-cup muffin pan or line muffin cups with paper cupcake liners.
**2.** In a medium bowl, beat oil, brown sugar, egg and milk until blended. In another medium bowl, combine flour, bran, baking powder, baking soda and salt. Stir flour mixture into milk mixture until combined. Fold in raisins.
**3.** Spoon batter into prepared muffin cups, filling cups about two-thirds full.
**4.** Bake in preheated oven 18 to 22 minutes or until a wooden pick inserted in center of a muffin comes out clean. Remove from pan. Serve warm or cool completely on a wire rack. Makes 12 muffins.

# Cool-Rise White Bread

2 (1/4-oz.) pkgs. active dry yeast (2 tablespoons)
1/3 cup plus 1 teaspoon sugar
1-1/2 cups warm water (110F, 45C)
1/2 cup butter or margarine
2 teaspoons salt
1/2 cup milk, scalded
About 6-1/2 cups all-purpose flour or bread flour
1 egg beaten with 1 tablespoon milk for glaze

1. In a large bowl, dissolve yeast and 1 teaspoon sugar in warm water. Let stand 5 to 10 minutes or until foamy.
2. Stir remaining sugar, butter or margarine and salt into hot milk until butter or margarine melts. Cool to room temperature.
3. Stir cooled milk mixture into yeast mixture until blended. Add 5 cups flour; stir until combined. Stir in enough remaining flour to make a soft dough that comes away from side of bowl.
4. On a lightly floured surface, knead in enough remaining flour to make a stiff dough. Knead 8 to 10 minutes or until smooth and elastic.
5. Cover dough with plastic wrap and a dry towel. Let rest 20 minutes.
6. Grease 2 (9" x 5") loaf pans. Divide dough in half. Shape each piece into a loaf; place in greased pans. Brush tops lightly with vegetable oil.
7. Cover loaves loosely with plastic wrap. Refrigerate at least 2 hours or overnight.
8. Preheat oven to 375F (190C). Let loaves stand at room temperature 20 minutes before baking. Brush tops of loaves with egg glaze.
9. Bake in preheated oven 35 to 40 minutes or until bread sounds hollow when tapped on bottom. Remove from pans; cool completely on a wire rack. Makes 2 loaves.

# Harvest-Time Bread

1/3 recipe White Bread, page 284
1 egg beaten with 1 tablespoon milk for glaze
2 currants

1. Prepare dough as directed through step 6, page 284. Grease a baking sheet. Cut dough into 3 equal pieces.
2. To make basic wheat sheaf, on a lightly floured surface, roll out 1 piece of dough about 12 inches long, 10 inches across top, making top rounded, and 8 inches across bottom. Place on greased baking sheet. Brush dough all over with egg glaze.
3. Cut second piece of dough into 4 equal pieces. Cut each piece into 6 pieces, making 24 small pieces.
4. Roll small pieces into 5-inch strips. Set 3 strips aside. Vertically place remaining 21 strips next to each other on bottom 1/3 of wheat sheaf to form stalks. Brush strips with egg glaze. Twist 2 reserved strips together to form tie; place horizontally across wheat sheaf along top edge of stalks. Brush with egg glaze. Shape remaining strip into a small oval field mouse; place in stalks. Use currants for eyes.
5. Roll out remaining piece of dough to a 16" x 8" rectangle. Cut dough lengthwise into 8 (1-inch-wide) strips. Cut strips on sharp diagonals, making small diamond-shaped pieces.
6. Attach a row of diamonds to outside edge of sheaf, starting at bottom left above tie. Fill in with remaining diamonds, working from top to bottom. Overlap diamonds, brushing with glaze as you go. Fill in top 2/3 of wheat sheaf completely with diamonds to make wheat heads.
7. Cover with a dry towel; let rise in a warm place, free from drafts, 15 to 20 minutes.
8. Preheat oven to 375F (190C). Brush sheaf all over with egg glaze.
9. Bake in preheated oven 30 to 35 minutes or until deep golden brown. Cool on baking sheet on a wire rack 10 minutes. Carefully slide sheaf from baking sheet to wire rack; cool completely on rack. Makes 1 wheat sheaf.

Harvest-Time Bread

# Homemade Buns

1 (1/4-oz.) pkg. active dry yeast (1 tablespoon)
1 teaspoon sugar
1/2 cup warm water (110F, 45C)
1/4 cup vegetable shortening
2 teaspoons salt
1/2 cup milk, scalded
About 3-1/4 cups all-purpose flour

1. In a large bowl, combine yeast, sugar and water. Stir until dissolved. Let stand 5 to 10 minutes or until foamy.

2. Add shortening and salt to hot milk, stirring until melted. Cool to lukewarm.

3. Stir cooled milk mixture into yeast mixture. Stir in 2-1/2 to 3 cups flour or enough flour to make a soft dough.

4. Turn out dough on a lightly floured surface; knead in enough remaining flour to make a stiff dough. Knead until dough is smooth and elastic, 8 to 10 minutes.

5. Clean and grease bowl. Place dough in greased bowl; turn to coat. Cover with a clean towel. Let rise in a warm place, free from drafts, until doubled in bulk, 1 to 1-1/2 hours. Grease 2 baking sheets.

6. Punch down dough. Cut dough into 8 equal pieces. Shape each piece into a ball. Flatten each ball with palm of your hand into a round bun 4 inches in diameter. Place buns on greased baking sheets. Cover; let rise 25 minutes or until doubled in bulk.

7. Preheat oven to 425F (220C). Dust buns lightly with flour. Bake in preheated oven 12 to 15 minutes or until golden brown. Remove from baking sheets; serve warm. Makes 8 buns.

### Variations

**Quick Supper Pizzas:** Slice buns in half. Toast lightly; spread with butter. Top with smoked sausages slices and tomato slices. Sprinkle with shredded Cheddar cheese; place under a preheated broiler until cheese is melted and lightly browned. Serve hot.

This recipe can also be used to make 12 small rolls. Serve rolls warm for breakfast, or split and fill like pita pockets.

1/Stir in enough flour to make a soft dough.

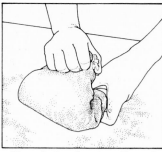
2/Knead dough on a floured surface.

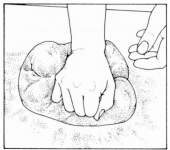
3/Push dough away with heel of your hand.

4/Cut dough into 8 pieces. Shape into balls.

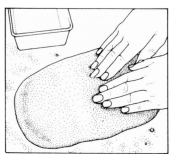
1/Shape dough into a rectangle as wide as your loaf pan is long.

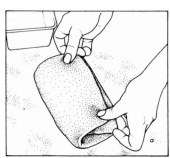
2/Fold dough into thirds to fit loaf pan. Press edges to seal.

# Sesame-Whole-Wheat Bread

2 (1/4-oz.) pkgs. active dry yeast (2 tablespoons)
1 tablespoon granulated sugar
1/4 cup warm water (110F, 45C)
1/3 cup butter or margarine
1/3 cup molasses
1/4 cup packed dark-brown sugar
1 tablespoon salt
2-1/4 cups milk, scalded
3-1/2 cups whole-wheat flour
4 cups all-purpose flour
Sesame seeds or poppy seeds

---

*Double recipe, if desired.*

**1.** In a large bowl, combine yeast, granulated sugar and water. Stir until dissolved. Let stand 5 to 10 minutes or until foamy.
**2.** Add butter or margarine, molasses, brown sugar and salt to hot milk, stirring until blended. Cool to lukewarm.
**3.** Stir cooled milk mixture into yeast. Beat in 2 cups whole-wheat flour and 2 cups all-purpose flour. Stir in remaining whole-wheat flour and 1-1/2 cups all-purpose flour or enough remaining all-purpose flour to make a soft dough.
**4.** Turn out dough onto a lightly floured surface; knead in enough remaining all-purpose flour to make a stiff dough. Knead until smooth and elastic, 8 to 10 minutes.
**5.** Clean and grease bowl. Place dough in greased bowl; turn to coat. Cover with a clean towel. Let rise in a warm place, free from drafts, until doubled in bulk. Grease 2 (9" x 5") loaf pans; set aside.
**6.** Punch down dough. Divide dough in half. Shape each half into a loaf; place in prepared pans. Cover; let rise until doubled.
**7.** Preheat oven to 375F (190C). Brush tops of loaves with water; sprinkle with sesame or poppy seeds. Bake 35 to 40 minutes or until browned. Remove from pans. Cool on a wire rack. Makes 2 loaves.

Top to bottom: Sesame-Whole-Wheat Bread, Homemade Buns, Quick Supper Pizzas

# White Bread

3 (1/4-oz.) pkgs. active dry yeast (3 tablespoons)
1/4 cup plus 2 teaspoons sugar
1-1/2 cups warm water (110F, 45C)
1/3 cup butter or margarine
4 teaspoons salt
2 cups milk, scalded
8-1/2 to 9 cups all-purpose flour or bread flour
1 egg yolk beaten with 1 tablespoon milk for glaze

1. In a large bowl, dissolve yeast and 2 teaspoons sugar in warm water. Let stand 5 to 10 minutes or until foamy.
2. Add remaining sugar, butter or margarine and salt to hot milk; stir until butter or margarine melts. Cool to room temperature.
3. Stir cooled milk mixture into yeast mixture until blended. Stir in 6 cups flour until combined. Stir in enough remaining flour to make a soft dough that comes away from side of bowl.
4. On a lightly floured surface, knead in enough remaining flour to make a stiff dough. Knead 8 to 10 minutes or until smooth and elastic.
5. Clean and grease bowl. Place dough in greased bowl, turning to coat all sides. Cover with a slightly damp towel. Let rise in a warm place, free from drafts, until doubled in bulk, 1 to 1-1/2 hours.
6. Grease 3 (9" x 5") loaf pans. Punch down dough; divide dough into 3 equal pieces. Shape each piece into a loaf, pinching and tucking ends under. Place loaves in greased pans. Cover with a dry towel; let rise until doubled in bulk.
7. Preheat oven to 375F (190C). Brush tops of loaves with egg-yolk glaze.
8. Bake in preheated oven 35 to 40 minutes or until bread sounds hollow when tapped on bottom. Remove from pans; cool on wire racks. Makes 3 loaves.

## Variations

**Buttered Split Loaves:** Prepare dough; let rise as directed above. Punch down dough; divide into 3 equal pieces. Shape loaves; place in greased 9" x 5" loaf pans. Cover and let rise until doubled in bulk. Split top of each loaf lengthwise with a sharp razor blade. Pour 2 tablespoons melted butter or margarine into each split. Brush remainder of loaf top with egg-yolk glaze; bake.
**Free-Form Loaves:** Prepare dough; let rise as directed above. Grease baking sheets. Punch down dough; divide into 3 equal pieces. Shape each piece into an 11-inch round or oval loaf. Place loaves on greased baking sheets. Cut several diagonal slashes on top of each loaf with a sharp razor blade or sharp knife. Cover and let rise until doubled. Brush with egg-yolk glaze; bake according to directions above.

1/To knead, bring dough toward you.

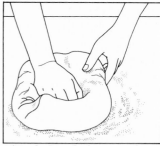

2/Push dough down and away from you.

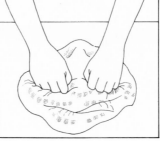

3/Punch down dough to remove air.

4/Cut several diagonal slashes on top of loaf.

# Poppy-Seed Braid

1 (1/4-oz.) pkg. active dry yeast (1 tablespoon)
1 tablespoon plus 1 teaspoon sugar
1-1/4 cups warm water (110F, 45C)
1-1/2 teaspoons salt
2 tablespoons butter or margarine, melted, cooled
About 3-1/4 cups all-purpose flour or bread flour
1 egg yolk beaten with 1 tablespoon milk for glaze
Poppy seeds

1. In a large bowl, dissolve yeast and 1 teaspoon sugar in warm water. Let stand 5 to 10 minutes or until foamy.
2. Add remaining sugar, salt and butter or margarine to yeast mixture; stir until blended. Stir in 2-1/2 cups flour until combined. Stir in enough remaining flour to make a soft dough that comes away from side of bowl.
3. On a lightly floured surface, knead in enough remaining flour to make a stiff dough. Continue kneading 8 to 10 minutes or until smooth and elastic.
4. Clean and grease bowl. Place dough in greased bowl, turning to coat all sides. Cover with a slightly damp towel. Let rise in a warm place, free from drafts, until doubled in bulk, about 1 hour.
5. Grease a baking sheet. Punch down dough; divide into 3 equal pieces. Shape each piece into a 18-inch-long rope. Braid ropes together to form a loaf, pinching and tucking ends under. Place loaf on greased baking sheet. Cover with a dry towel; let rise until almost doubled in bulk.
6. Preheat oven to 375F (190C). Brush bread with egg-yolk glaze; sprinkle with poppy seeds.
7. Bake in preheated oven 35 to 40 minutes or until bread sounds hollow when tapped on bottom. Remove from baking sheet; cool on a wire rack. Makes 1 loaf.

# Whole-Wheat Bread

1 (1/4-oz.) pkg. active dry yeast (1 tablespoon)
1 teaspoon granulated sugar
1-1/4 cups warm water (110F, 45C)
1/4 cup firmly packed dark-brown sugar
2 tablespoons butter or margarine, melted, cooled
1-1/2 teaspoons salt
2 cups whole-wheat flour
About 1-1/4 cups all-purpose flour or bread flour
Milk or water
Cracked wheat or oat flakes

**1.** In a large bowl, dissolve yeast and 1 teaspoon granulated sugar in warm water. Let stand 5 to 10 minutes or until foamy.
**2.** Stir brown sugar, butter or margarine and salt into yeast mixture until blended. Stir in whole-wheat flour and 3/4 cup all-purpose flour or bread flour until blended. Stir in enough remaining all-purpose flour or bread flour to make a soft dough that comes away from side of bowl.
**3.** On a lightly floured surface, knead in enough remaining all-purpose flour or bread flour to make a stiff dough. Knead 8 to 10 minutes or until smooth and elastic.
**4.** Clean and grease bowl. Place dough in greased bowl, turning to coat all sides. Cover with a slightly damp towel. Let rise in a warm place, free from drafts, until doubled in bulk, about 1 hour.
**5.** Grease a baking sheet. Punch down dough; shape into a round loaf, pinching and tucking side under. Cut a deep cross on top of loaf with a sharp razor blade. Cover with a dry towel; let rise until almost doubled in bulk.
**6.** Preheat oven to 400F (205C). Brush top of bread with milk or water; sprinkle with cracked wheat or oat flakes. Bake in preheated oven 30 to 35 minutes or until bread sounds hollow when tapped on bottom. Remove from baking sheet; cool on a wire rack. Makes 1 loaf.

**Variations**
**Traditional Loaf:** Prepare dough; let rise as directed above. Grease a 9" x 5" loaf pan. Punch down dough; shape into a loaf, pinching and tucking ends under. Place in greased pan. Cover and let rise until doubled. Bake as directed above.
**Rolls:** Prepare dough; let rise as directed above. Grease a 12-cup muffin pan or a 13" x 9" baking pan. Punch down dough; shape into 12 equal balls, pinching and tucking sides under. Place balls, seam-side down, in greased muffin cups, or arrange balls in greased baking pan, allowing room for expansion. Cover and let dough in muffin cups rise 20 to 30 minutes; let rolls in pan rise 50 to 60 minutes. Bake in preheated 400F (205C) oven 15 to 20 minutes or until rolls sound hollow when tapped on bottom.

Top to bottom: Poppy-Seed Braid, Free-Form White Bread, Whole-Wheat Bread

# Vienna Rolls

1 (1/4-oz.) pkg. active dry yeast (1 tablespoon)
3 tablespoons plus 1 teaspoon sugar
1/2 cup warm water (110F, 45C)
1/4 cup butter or margarine
1-1/2 teaspoons salt
3/4 cup milk, scalded
About 3-1/4 cups all-purpose flour or bread flour
1 egg yolk beaten with 1 tablespoon milk for glaze
Poppy seeds, if desired

---

1. In a large bowl, dissolve yeast and 1 teaspoon sugar in warm water. Let stand 5 to 10 minutes or until foamy.
2. Stir remaining sugar, butter or margarine and salt into hot milk until butter or margarine melts. Cool to room temperature.
3. Stir cooled milk mixture into yeast mixture until blended. Stir in 2-1/2 cups flour until combined. Stir in enough remaining flour to make a soft dough that comes away from side of bowl.
4. On a lightly floured surface, knead in enough remaining flour to make a stiff dough. Knead 8 to 10 minutes or until smooth and elastic.
5. Clean and grease bowl. Place dough in greased bowl, turning to coat all sides. Cover with a slightly damp towel. Let rise in a warm place, free from drafts, until doubled in bulk, about 1 hour.
6. Lightly grease baking sheets. Punch down dough; cut dough into 16 equal pieces. Shape each piece into desired shape; see below. Place shaped rolls 2 to 3 inches apart on greased baking sheets. Cover with a dry towel; let rise until almost doubled in bulk.
7. Preheat oven to 400F (205C). Brush rolls with egg-yolk glaze; sprinkle with poppy seeds, if desired.
8. Bake in preheated oven 18 to 20 minutes or until golden brown. Remove from baking sheets; cool on wire racks. Serve warm. Makes 16 rolls.

**Cloverleaf:** Cut each piece of dough into 3 small pieces. Shape each piece into a ball, pinching and tucking sides under. Place balls in sets of 3, barely touching each other, on greased baking sheets.

**Knots:** Shape each piece of dough into an 8-inch-long rope. Tie in a knot.

**Figure 8:** Shape each piece of dough into an 8-inch-long rope. Curl opposite ends toward center to make a figure 8.

**Ovals:** Shape each piece of dough into a small oval loaf. Cut 2 or 3 diagonal slashes on top of roll with a sharp razor blade.

**Braid:** Divide each piece of dough into 3 equal pieces. Shape each piece into an 8-inch-long rope. Braid ropes; tuck ends under.

**Snails:** Shape each piece of dough into an 8-inch-long rope. Coil rope into a snail shape.

**Cottage:** Divide each piece of dough into 2 pieces, making 1 piece slightly larger than the other. Shape both pieces into balls, pinching and tucking sides under. Place large ball on greased baking sheet; top with small ball. Using the handle of a small wooden spoon, poke hole in center of small ball down through large ball to baking sheet.

Vienna Rolls

# Currant Bread

1 (1/4-oz.) pkg. active dry yeast (1 tablespoon)
3 tablespoons plus 1 teaspoon sugar
1/4 cup warm water (110F, 45C)
2 tablespoons butter or margarine
1 teaspoon salt
1 cup milk, scalded
About 3-1/4 cups all-purpose flour or bread flour
1 cup currants
Honey

1. In a large bowl, dissolve yeast and 1 teaspoon sugar in warm water. Let stand 5 to 10 minutes or until foamy.
2. Stir remaining sugar, butter or margarine and salt into hot milk until butter or margarine melts. Cool to room temperature.
3. Stir cooled milk mixture into yeast mixture until blended. Stir in 2 cups flour and currants until combined. Stir in enough remaining flour to make a soft dough that comes away from side of bowl.
4. On a lightly floured surface, knead in enough remaining flour to make a stiff dough. Knead 8 to 10 minutes or until smooth and elastic.
5. Clean and grease bowl. Place dough in greased bowl, turning to coat all sides. Cover with a slightly damp towel. Let rise in a warm place, free from drafts, until doubled in bulk, about 1 hour.
6. Grease a 9" x 5" loaf pan. Punch down dough. Shape dough into a loaf, pinching and tucking ends under. Place in greased pan. Cover with a dry towel; let rise until doubled in bulk.
7. Preheat oven to 375F (190C). Brush top of bread with water.
8. Bake in preheated oven 35 to 40 minutes or until bread sounds hollow when tapped on bottom. Remove bread from pan; brush top with honey while still warm. Cool on a wire rack. Makes 1 loaf.

# Whole-Wheat & Rye Twists

2 (1/4-oz.) pkgs. active dry yeast (2 tablespoons)
1/4 cup plus 1 teaspoon firmly packed
   dark-brown sugar
2 cups warm water (110F, 45C)
1/4 cup butter or margarine, melted, cooled
1 tablespoon salt
4 cups whole-wheat flour
2 cups medium rye flour
1 egg white beaten with 1 tablespoon water for glaze

1. In a large bowl, dissolve yeast and 1 teaspoon brown sugar in warm water. Let stand 5 to 10 minutes or until foamy.
2. Stir remaining brown sugar, butter or margarine and salt into yeast mixture until blended. Stir whole-wheat flour and rye flour together until blended. Add 4-1/2 cups of flour mixture; stir until combined. Stir in enough remaining flour mixture to make a soft dough that comes away from side of bowl.
3. On a lightly floured surface, knead in enough remaining flour mixture to make a stiff dough. Knead 8 to 10 minutes or until smooth and elastic.
4. Clean and grease bowl. Place dough in greased bowl, turning to coat all sides. Cover with a slightly damp towel. Let rise in a warm place, free from drafts, until doubled in bulk, about 1-1/4 hours.
5. Grease 2 baking sheets. Punch down dough; cut into 2 equal pieces. Cut each piece in half. Shape pieces into 16-inch-long ropes. Twist 2 ropes together; tuck ends under. Repeat with remaining 2 ropes. Place loaves on greased baking sheets. Cover with a dry towel; let rise until doubled in bulk.
6. Preheat oven to 400F (205C). Brush loaves with egg-white glaze.
7. Bake in preheated oven 35 to 40 minutes or until bread sounds hollow when tapped on bottom. Remove from baking sheets; cool completely on a wire rack. Makes 2 loaves.

Left to right: Currant Bread, Whole-Wheat & Rye Twist, Cheese & Herb Bread, Buttermilk Cottage Loaf

# Cheese & Herb Bread

2 tablespoons butter or margarine
1 small onion, finely chopped
1 (1/4-oz.) pkg. active dry yeast (1 tablespoon)
2 tablespoons plus 1 teaspoon sugar
1-1/4 cups warm water (110F, 45C)
1-1/2 teaspoons salt
1 teaspoon dry mustard
1 tablespoon chopped mixed fresh herbs or
   1 teaspoon Italian seasoning
2 cups whole-wheat flour
1-1/4 cups shredded sharp Cheddar cheese (6 oz.)
About 1-1/4 cups all-purpose flour or bread flour

---

**1.** Melt butter or margarine in a small skillet over medium heat. Add onion; sauté until golden. Let cool.
**2.** In a large bowl, dissolve yeast and 1 teaspoon sugar in warm water. Let stand 5 to 10 minutes or until foamy.
**3.** Stir remaining sugar, salt, mustard, herbs or Italian seasoning and cooled onion into yeast mixture until combined. Stir in whole-wheat flour and 1 cup Cheddar cheese until combined. Stir in enough all-purpose flour or bread flour to make a soft dough that comes away from side of bowl.
**4.** On a lightly floured surface, knead in enough remaining all-purpose flour or bread flour to make a stiff dough. Knead 8 to 10 minutes or until smooth and elastic.
**5.** Clean and grease bowl. Place dough in greased bowl, turning to coat all sides. Cover with a slightly damp towel. Let rise in a warm place, free from drafts, until doubled in bulk, about 1 hour.
**6.** Grease a 9" x 5" loaf pan. Punch down dough; shape into a loaf, pinching and tucking ends under. Place in greased pan. Cover with a dry towel; let rise until doubled in bulk.
**7.** Preheat oven to 375F (190C). Brush top of bread with water; sprinkle with remaining 1/4 cup Cheddar cheese.
**8.** Bake in preheated oven 35 to 40 minutes or until bread sounds hollow when tapped on bottom. Remove from pan; cool completely on a wire rack. Makes 1 loaf.

# Buttermilk Cottage Loaf

1 cup buttermilk
1/3 cup butter or margarine, room temperature
1 (1/4-oz.) pkg. active dry yeast (1 tablespoon)
1/4 cup plus 1 teaspoon sugar
3/4 cup warm water (110F, 45C)
2 teaspoons salt
1/2 teaspoon baking soda
About 5 cups all-purpose flour or bread flour
1 egg yolk beaten with 1 tablespoon milk for glaze

---

**1.** In a small saucepan over low heat, heat buttermilk and butter or margarine, stirring, until butter or margarine melts. Cool to room temperature.
**2.** In a large bowl, dissolve yeast and 1 teaspoon sugar in warm water. Let stand 5 to 10 minutes or until foamy.
**3.** Stir cooled buttermilk mixture, remaining sugar and salt into yeast mixture until blended. Add baking soda and 3-1/2 cups flour; stir until combined. Stir in enough remaining flour to make a soft dough that comes away from side of bowl.
**4.** On a lightly floured surface, knead in enough remaining flour to make a stiff dough. Knead 8 to 10 minutes or until smooth and elastic.
**5.** Clean and grease bowl. Place dough in greased bowl, turning to coat all sides. Cover with a slightly damp towel. Let rise in a warm place, free from drafts, until doubled in bulk, 1 to 1-1/2 hours.
**6.** Grease a baking sheet. Punch down dough; divide into 2 pieces, making 1 piece 2/3 of dough. Shape large piece of dough into a slightly flattened ball; place on greased baking sheet. Shape small piece of dough into a ball; place on top of large piece of dough. Flour a wooden spoon handle; poke through center of small ball down through large ball to baking sheet. Cover with a dry towel; let rise until doubled in bulk. Brush with egg-yolk glaze.
**7.** Preheat oven to 400F (205C).
**8.** Bake in preheated oven 40 to 45 minutes or until bread sounds hollow when tapped on bottom. Remove from baking sheet and cool completely on a wire rack. Makes 1 large loaf.

# Rum Savarin

1 (1/4-oz.) pkg. active dry yeast (1 tablespoon)
2 tablespoons plus 1 teaspoon sugar
1/3 cup warm milk (110F, 45C)
2 cups sifted all-purpose flour
1/2 teaspoon salt
3 eggs, beaten
1/3 cup butter or margarine, melted, cooled

*Rum Syrup:*
1/2 cup sugar
1 cup water
1/3 to 1/2 cup dark rum

*To serve:*
2 cups sweetened whipped cream
Sliced strawberries, bananas, raspberries or peaches

**1.** Grease an 8- or 9-inch ring mold or savarin mold. In a medium bowl, dissolve yeast and 1 teaspoon sugar in warm milk. Let stand 5 to 10 minutes or until foamy.
**2.** Stir remaining sugar, 1 cup flour and salt into yeast mixture until combined. Add remaining flour, eggs and butter or margarine; beat vigorously with a wooden spoon 2 to 3 minutes or until batter is smooth.
**3.** Spoon batter into greased mold, spreading evenly.
**4.** Cover with a slightly damp towel. Let rise in a warm place, free from drafts, until dough almost reaches rim of pan, about 1 hour.
**5.** Preheat oven to 375F (190C).
**6.** Bake in preheated oven 25 to 30 minutes or until top is golden brown. Remove from pan; cool on a wire rack.
**7.** To make syrup, combine sugar and water in a medium saucepan over medium heat; stir until sugar is dissolved. Boil 5 minutes or until syrupy, without stirring. Cool slightly. Stir in rum.
**8.** Place cooled savarin in a deep serving dish; prick all over with a fork. Slowly pour warm syrup over savarin; let stand until syrup has been absorbed.
**9.** To serve, spoon whipped cream into center; fill with fruit. Makes 8 to 10 servings.

Apple-Filled Doughnuts

# Apple-Filled Doughnuts

1 (1/4-oz.) pkg. active dry yeast (1 tablespoon)
3 tablespoons plus 1 teaspoon sugar
3/4 cup warm milk (110F, 45C)
1/4 cup butter or margarine, melted, cooled
1 egg, beaten
1 teaspoon salt
About 3 cups all-purpose flour flour
1 cup chunk-style applesauce
Vegetable oil for deep-frying
2 teaspoons ground cinnamon mixed with 1/3 cup sugar

---

**1.** In a large bowl, dissolve yeast and 1 teaspoon sugar in warm milk. Let stand 5 to 10 minutes or until foamy.
**2.** Stir remaining sugar, butter or margarine, egg and salt into yeast mixture until blended. Add 2-1/4 cups flour; stir until combined. Stir in enough remaining flour to make a soft dough that comes away from side of bowl.
**3.** On a lightly floured surface, knead in enough flour to make a stiff dough. Knead 8 to 10 minutes or until smooth and elastic.
**4.** Clean and grease bowl. Place dough in greased bowl, turning to coat all sides. Cover with a slightly damp towel. Let rise in a warm place, free from drafts, until doubled in bulk, about 1 hour.
**5.** Grease 2 baking sheets. Punch down dough; cut into 24 equal pieces. On a lightly floured surface, roll out each piece of dough to a 4-inch circle. Place 1 teaspoon applesauce in center of each circle. Brush edges of dough lightly with water. Gather edges; draw up to enclose filling completely. Pinch to seal. Place filled balls, seam-side down, on greased baking sheets about 2 inches apart. Cover with a dry towel; let rise 30 minutes.
**6.** Heat oil in a deep-fat fryer to 350F (175C) or until a 1-inch bread cube turns golden brown in 50 seconds. Carefully drop doughnuts, a few at a time, into hot oil. Deep-fry until doughnuts are puffed and golden brown. Remove with a slotted spoon; drain on paper towels. Repeat with remaining doughnuts.
**7.** Place cinnamon-sugar mixture in a medium bowl. Add warm doughnuts, a few at a time; toss to coat with sugar mixture. Makes 24 doughnuts.

# Sesame-Seed Breadsticks

2 (1/4-oz.) pkgs. active dry yeast (2 tablespoons)
1 tablespoon sugar
1-1/2 cups warm water (110F, 45C)
1/4 cup vegetable oil
2 teaspoons salt
About 3-1/2 cups all-purpose flour or bread flour
1 egg white beaten with 1 tablespoon water for glaze
About 1/2 cup raw sesame seeds

---

**1.** In a large bowl, dissolve yeast and 1 teaspoon sugar in warm water. Let stand 5 to 10 minutes or until foamy.
**2.** Stir remaining sugar, oil, salt and 1/2 cup flour into yeast mixture until well blended. Add about 2-1/2 cups flour; beat vigorously with a wooden spoon until dough is soft and shiny and comes away from side of bowl.
**3.** On a lightly floured surface, knead in enough remaining flour to make a stiff dough. Knead 8 to 10 minutes or until smooth and elastic.
**4.** Cover dough with a dry towel; let rest 15 minutes.
**5.** Preheat oven to 350F (175C). Grease 2 baking sheets. Shape dough into a 24-inch-long rope; cut into 24 (1-inch) pieces. Roll each piece into a 12-inch stick.
**6.** Brush breadsticks with egg-white glaze; sprinkle with sesame seeds. Place breadsticks about 1-1/2 inches apart on greased baking sheets.
**7.** Bake in preheated oven 30 to 35 minutes or until golden brown. Remove from baking sheets; cool on wire racks. Serve warm or let cool completely. Makes 24 breadsticks.

# Parkerhouse Rolls

1 (1/4-oz.) pkg. active dry yeast (1 tablespoon)
3 tablespoons plus 1 teaspoon sugar
1/2 cup warm water (110F, 45C)
1/4 cup butter or margarine
1 teaspoon salt
1/2 cup milk, scalded
1 egg
About 3-1/4 cups all-purpose flour
About 1/4 cup butter or margarine, melted

1. In a large bowl, dissolve yeast and 1 teaspoon sugar in warm water. Let stand 5 to 10 minutes or until foamy.
2. Stir remaining sugar, 1/4 cup butter or margarine and salt into hot milk until butter or margarine melts. Cool to room temperature.
3. Stir cooled milk mixture and egg into yeast mixture until blended. Add 2-1/2 cups flour; stir until combined. Stir in enough remaining flour to make a soft dough that comes away from side of bowl.
4. On a lightly floured surface, knead in enough remaining flour to make a stiff dough. Knead 8 to 10 minutes or until smooth and elastic.
5. Clean and grease bowl. Place dough in greased bowl, turning to coat all sides. Cover with a slightly damp towel. Let rise in a warm place, free from drafts, until doubled in bulk, about 1 hour.
6. Grease a 15" x 10" jelly-roll pan. Punch down dough. Divide dough in half; roll out 1 piece of dough to about 1/2 inch thick. Cut with a floured 2-1/2- to 3-inch plain cookie cutter. Repeat with remaining piece of dough. Gather dough scraps; reroll. Cut as many circles as possible.
7. Brush circles with melted butter or margarine. Press handle of a wooden spoon across each circle, slightly off center, to make a crease. Fold circles almost in half along crease with smaller portion on top; press edges lightly together. Place rolls fairly close together in greased pan. Cover with a dry towel; let rise until almost doubled in bulk.
8. Preheat oven to 400F (205C). Brush rolls with melted butter or margarine.
9. Bake in preheated oven 15 to 20 minutes or until rolls are golden brown. Remove from baking sheets; serve warm. Makes 16 to 20 rolls.

# Almond-Filled Loaf

1 (1/4-oz.) pkg. active dry yeast (1 tablespoon)
1/4 cup plus 1 teaspoon sugar
1/2 cup warm milk (110F, 45C)
1/4 cup butter or margarine, melted, cooled
1/2 teaspoon salt
1 egg, beaten
About 2-1/3 cups all-purpose flour
1 egg yolk beaten with 1 tablespoon milk for glaze

*Filling:*
3/4 cup finely ground blanched almonds
1/3 cup sugar
1 egg white, beaten
1 tablespoon milk
1/2 teaspoon almond extract
1/4 cup chopped red candied cherries
2 tablespoons raisins

Icing:
1 cup powdered sugar, sifted
1 to 2 tablespoons hot water

To decorate:
1 to 2 tablespoons toasted sliced or slivered almonds
Red candied cherries, quartered

1. In a large bowl, dissolve yeast and 1 teaspoon sugar in warm milk. Let stand 5 to 10 minutes or until foamy.
2. Stir remaining sugar, butter or margarine, salt and egg into yeast mixture until blended. Stir in 1-3/4 cups flour until combined. Stir in enough remaining flour to make a soft dough that comes away from side of bowl.
3. On a lightly floured surface, knead in enough remaining flour to make a stiff dough. Knead 8 to 10 minutes or until smooth and elastic.
4. Clean and grease bowl. Place dough in greased bowl, turning to coat all sides. Cover with a slightly damp towel. Let rise in a warm place, free from drafts, until doubled in bulk, about 1 hour.
5. To make filling, in a small bowl, blend ground almonds and sugar. Stir in egg white, milk and almond extract until thoroughly blended. Set aside.
6. Grease a 9" x 5" loaf pan. Punch down dough. On a lightly floured surface, roll out dough to a 12" x 9" rectangle. Spread almond mixture over dough to within 1/4 inch of edges. Sprinkle chopped cherries and raisins over almond mixture. Roll, jelly-roll style, starting at 1 short end. Pinch ends to seal. Place filled loaf, seam-side down, in greased pan. Cover with a dry towel; let rise until doubled in bulk.
7. Preheat oven to 375F (190C). Brush top of loaf with egg-yolk glaze.
8. Bake in preheated oven 35 to 40 minutes or until top is deep golden brown and loaf sounds hollow when tapped on bottom. Remove from pan; cool on a wire rack.
9. To make icing, in a small bowl, stir powdered sugar and 1 tablespoon water until smooth, adding more water if necessary. Spoon icing on top of loaf; decorate loaf with toasted almonds and cherries quarters. Let stand until icing is set. Makes 1 loaf.

# Fruity Raisin Buns

2 teaspoons active dry yeast
2 tablespoons plus 1 teaspoon granulated sugar
1/2 cup warm milk (110F, 45C)
1 egg, beaten
2 tablespoons butter or margarine, room temperature
1/2 teaspoon salt
1-1/2 cups all-purpose flour
1/2 cup raisins
2 tablespoons chopped candied orange peel or
  lemon peel
1 egg yolk beaten with 1 tablespoon milk for glaze
Crystal sugar or crushed sugar cubes

**1.** In a large bowl, dissolve yeast and 1 teaspoon granulated sugar in warm milk. Let stand 5 to 10 minutes or until foamy.
**2.** Stir remaining granulated sugar, egg, butter or margarine and salt into yeast mixture; stir until blended. Add flour; beat with a wooden spoon 2 minutes. Stir in raisins and candied peel until combined.
**3.** Cover with a slightly damp towel. Let rise in a warm place, free from drafts, until doubled in bulk, about 1 hour.
**4.** Grease 2 baking sheets. Stir down dough with a wooden spoon. Drop by heaping tablespoons 2 to 3 inches apart on greased baking sheets. Brush buns with egg-yolk glaze; sprinkle with coarse sugar. Cover loosely with a dry towel; let rise until almost doubled in bulk.
**5.** Preheat oven to 400F (205C).
**6.** Bake buns in preheated oven 12 to 15 minutes or until golden brown. Remove from baking sheets; cool on wire racks. Serve warm with butter or margarine. Makes 14 buns.

Left to right: Fruity Raisin Buns, Almond-Filled Loaf

# Danish Pastries

1 (1/4-oz.) pkg. active dry yeast (1 tablespoon)
2 tablespoons plus 1 teaspoon sugar
1/4 cup warm water (110F, 45C)
3/4 cup butter or margarine
1/2 teaspoon salt
1/2 cup milk, scalded
1 egg
1 egg yolk
1/2 teaspoon ground mace
About 2-1/2 cups all-purpose flour
2 tablespoons all-purpose flour

*Spice Filling:*
1/4 cup butter or margarine, room temperature
2 tablespoons sugar
1 teaspoon ground cinnamon
1/4 cup currants

*Almond Filling:*
1/3 cup finely ground almonds
2 tablespoons sugar
1 tablespoon egg white
1 egg yolk beaten with 1 tablespoon milk for glaze

*Icing:*
1 cup powdered sugar, sifted
1-1/2 tablespoons warm water

---

**1.** In a medium bowl, dissolve yeast and 1 teaspoon sugar in warm water. Let stand 5 to 10 minutes or until foamy.
**2.** Stir remaining sugar, 1/4 cup butter or margarine and salt into hot milk until butter or margarine melts. Cool to room temperature. Stir cooled milk mixture, egg and egg yolk into yeast mixture until combined.
**3.** Add mace and 1-3/4 cups flour; stir until combined. Stir in enough remaining flour to make a soft dough that comes away from side of bowl.
**4.** On a lightly floured surface, knead in enough remaining flour to make a stiff dough. Knead 8 to 10 minutes or until smooth and elastic.
**5.** Cover dough with a dry towel; let rest 30 minutes.
**6.** In a small bowl, blend remaining 1/2 cup butter or margarine with 2 tablespoons flour; shape into a 5" x 4" rectangle. Refrigerate until almost firm.
**7.** On a lightly floured surface, roll out dough to a 15" x 5" rectangle. Place chilled block of butter or margarine lengthwise in center of dough. Fold 1/3 of dough over butter or margarine. Fold remaining dough over dough-covered butter or margarine. Press edges to seal.
**8.** Roll out dough to a 15" x 5" rectangle; fold in thirds. Wrap in plastic wrap or waxed paper; refrigerate 20 minutes.
**9.** Repeat rolling and folding dough 2 times, for a total of 3 times. Wrap and refrigerate dough 20 minutes after second rolling and folding. Wrap and refrigerate dough 30 minutes after last folding and rolling.

**10.** To make spice filling, in a small bowl, beat butter or margarine, sugar and cinnamon until smooth. Fold in currants.
**11.** To make almond filling, in a small bowl, stir almonds, sugar and egg white until blended.
**12.** Cut dough in half. Refrigerate 1/2 until needed. Roll out dough half to a 16" x 8" rectangle. Spread spice filling over dough; cut in half lengthwise. Roll 1 piece jelly-roll style, starting from short end. Cut into 4 equal slices. Place slices, cut-side down, on ungreased baking sheets. Brush with egg-yolk glaze. Fold remaining spice-filling-covered dough crosswise into thirds; cut into 4 equal strips from folded edge to folded edge. Twist ends of each strip in opposite directions; place on baking sheet. Brush with egg-yolk glaze.
**13.** Roll out reserved dough to a 16" x 8" rectangle. Cut into 8 (4-inch) squares. Shape almond filling into 8 flattened balls. Place 1 ball in center of each square. Cut squares diagonally from each corner in toward center almost to almond ball. Fold points in toward center to enclose filling; press down lightly to seal. Place on baking sheet. Brush with egg-yolk glaze. Cover pastries with a dry towel; let rise 30 to 40 minutes.
**14.** Preheat oven to 425F (220C). Brush pastries with egg-yolk glaze again.
**15.** Bake in preheated oven 10 to 12 minutes or until golden brown. Remove from baking sheets; cool on wire racks.
**16.** To make icing, in a small bowl, combine powdered sugar and water until smooth. Drizzle over pastries; let stand until set. Makes 16 pastries.

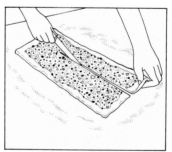
1/Spread spice filling over dough. Cut in half lengthwise.

2/Cut into 4 equal slices.

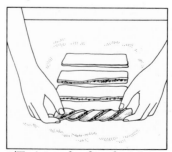
3/Twist ends of each strip in opposite directions.

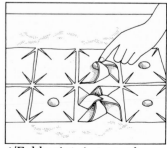
4/Fold points in toward center to enclose filling.

# Cinnamon Rolls

1 (1/4-oz.) pkg. active dry yeast (1 tablespoon)
1/4 cup plus 1 teaspoon sugar
1 cup warm milk (110F, 45C)
1 teaspoon salt
6 tablespoons butter or margarine, melted, cooled
2 eggs, beaten
About 4 cups all-purpose flour
2 tablespoons butter or margarine, melted, cooled

*Filling:*
1/2 cup firmly packed light-brown sugar
2 teaspoons ground cinnamon
3/4 cup raisins or currants

*Glaze:*
2 cups sifted powdered sugar
1/2 teaspoon vanilla extract
3 tablespoons milk or water

**1.** In a large bowl, dissolve yeast and 1 teaspoon sugar in warm milk. Let stand 5 to 10 minutes or until foamy.
**2.** Stir remaining sugar, salt, 6 tablespoons butter or margarine and eggs into yeast mixture until blended. Add 3 cups flour; stir until combined. Stir in enough remaining flour to make a soft dough that comes away from side of bowl.

**3.** On a lightly floured surface, knead in enough remaining flour to make a stiff dough. Knead 8 to 10 minutes or until smooth and elastic.
**4.** Clean and grease bowl. Place dough in greased bowl, turning to coat all sides. Cover with a slightly damp towel. Let rise in a warm place, free from drafts, until doubled in bulk.
**5.** Grease a 13" x 9" baking pan. Punch down dough. On a lightly floured surface, roll out dough to an 18" x 12" rectangle. Brush with 2 tablespoons melted butter or margarine.
**6.** To make filling, in a small bowl, combine brown sugar, cinnamon and raisins or currants; sprinkle over dough.
**7.** Roll up dough, jelly-roll style, starting at 1 long end. Pinch seam to seal. Cut dough into 15 equal slices. Arrange slices, cut-side down, in greased pan, allowing room for expansion. Cover with a dry towel; let rise until almost doubled in bulk.
**8.** Preheat oven to 375F (190C).
**9.** Bake in preheated oven 25 to 30 minutes or until top is golden brown. Cool in pan on a wire rack.
**10.** To make glaze, in a small bowl, combine powdered sugar, vanilla and milk or water. Spread glaze over warm rolls in pan. Let stand until glaze is set. To serve, pull rolls apart with 2 forks; remove from pan. Makes 15 rolls.

Danish Pastries

# Panettone

1/2 cup butter or margarine, room temperature
1/4 cup plus 1 teaspoon sugar
3 eggs
1 teaspoon salt
1 tablespoon grated lemon peel
1 (1/4-oz.) pkg. active dry yeast (1 tablespoon)
1/3 cup warm milk (110F, 45C)
About 3 cups all-purpose flour
3/4 cup raisins
1/2 cup chopped mixed candied fruit
1 egg yolk beaten with 1 tablespoon milk for glaze

---

1. In a large bowl, beat butter or margarine and 1/4 cup sugar 8 to 10 minutes or until light and fluffy. Beat in eggs, 1 at a time, beating well after each addition. Beat in salt and lemon peel until blended.
2. In a small bowl, dissolve yeast and remaining sugar in warm milk. Let stand 5 to 10 minutes or until foamy.
3. Stir egg mixture into yeast mixture until blended. Add 2 cups flour, raisins and mixed fruit; stir until combined. Stir in enough remaining flour to make a soft dough that comes away from side of bowl.
4. On a lightly floured surface, knead in enough remaining flour to make a stiff dough. Knead 8 to 10 minutes or until smooth and elastic.
5. Clean and grease bowl. Place dough in greased bowl, turning to coat all sides. Cover with a slightly damp towel. Let rise in a warm place, free from drafts, until doubled in bulk, about 1-1/2 hours.
6. Grease an 8-inch springform pan or deep cake pan. Punch down dough; shape into a round loaf, pinching and tucking sides under. Place shaped dough, seam-side down, in greased pan. Cover with a dry towel; let rise until doubled in bulk.
7. Preheat oven to 400F (205C). Brush loaf top with egg-yolk glaze.
8. Bake in preheated oven 10 minutes. Reduce oven temperature to 350F (175C); bake 30 to 35 minutes or until top is deep golden brown and loaf sounds hollow when tapped on bottom. Remove from pan; cool completely on a wire rack. Slice and serve with butter or margarine. Makes 1 loaf.

# Hungarian Coffeecake

1 (1/4-oz.) pkg. active dry yeast (1 tablespoon)
3 tablespoons plus 1 teaspoon sugar
1/2 cup warm milk (110F, 45C)
1/4 cup butter or margarine, melted, cooled
1/2 teaspoon salt
1 egg, beaten
About 2-1/4 cups all-purpose flour
1 teaspoon ground cinnamon
1/4 cup sugar
1/4 cup finely chopped walnuts, pecans or almonds
1/4 cup raisins, chopped

*Icing:*
1 cup sifted powdered sugar
1 to 2 tablespoons milk

---

1. In a large bowl, dissolve yeast and 1 teaspoon sugar in warm milk. Let stand 5 to 10 minutes or until foamy.
2. Stir in remaining sugar, 2 tablespoons butter or margarine, salt and egg until blended. Stir in 1-3/4 cups flour until combined. Stir in enough remaining flour to make a soft dough that comes away from side of bowl.
3. On a lightly floured surface, knead in enough remaining flour to make a stiff dough. Knead 8 to 10 minutes or until smooth and elastic.
4. Clean and grease bowl. Place dough in greased bowl, turning to coat all sides. Cover with a slightly damp towel. Let rise in a warm place, free from drafts, until doubled in bulk, about 1 hour.
5. In a small bowl, combine cinnamon, 1/4 cup sugar, nuts and raisins. Set aside.
6. Grease an 8-inch springform pan or deep cake pan. Punch down dough; cut into 16 equal pieces. Shape each piece into a ball, pinching and tucking sides under. Dip balls in remaining 2 tablespoons melted butter or margarine; roll in sugar-nut mixture. Place 1/2 of coated balls in bottom of greased pan, allowing room for expansion. Place remaining balls on top to make a second layer. Drizzle remaining butter or margarine over top layer; sprinkle with remaining sugar-nut mixture. Cover with a dry towel; let rise until doubled in bulk.
7. Preheat oven to 375F (190C).
8. Bake in preheated oven 30 to 35 minutes or until coffeecake is a deep golden brown and top is firm. Cool in pan on a wire rack 15 minutes. Remove side of pan; slide coffeecake carefully onto rack. Let cool completely.
9. To make icing, in a small bowl, combine powdered sugar and 1 tablespoon milk until smooth and a good pouring consistency, adding more milk if necessary. Drizzle icing over top of coffeecake; let stand until set. Makes 1 coffeecake.

# Oatmeal Batter Bread

1 (1/4-oz.) pkg. active dry yeast (1 tablespoon)
1 teaspoon sugar
1 cup warm milk (110F, 45C)
3 tablespoons dark molasses
1/2 cup butter or margarine, room temperature
1-1/2 teaspoons salt
2 eggs
About 3 cups all-purpose flour
1 cup quick-cooking rolled oats
About 2 tablespoons butter or margarine, melted

1. In a large bowl, dissolve yeast and 1 teaspoon sugar in warm milk. Let stand 5 to 10 minutes or until foamy.
2. Add molasses, 1/2 cup butter or margarine, salt, eggs and 1 cup flour to yeast mixture. Beat with an electric mixer on low speed 1 minute or until blended. Increase speed to medium; beat 2 minutes, scraping side of bowl.
3. Add rolled oats and 1-1/2 cups flour. Stir vigorously with a wooden spoon to make a smooth, elastic batter. Stir in enough remaining flour to make a stiff batter that comes away from side of bowl.
4. Cover with a slightly damp towel. Let rise in a warm place, free from drafts, until doubled in bulk, about 1 hour.
5. Grease a 2-quart casserole. Stir down dough with a wooden spoon; scrape into greased casserole with a rubber spatula. Cover with a dry towel; let rise until doubled in bulk.
6. Preheat oven to 375F (190C).
7. Bake in preheated oven 40 to 45 minutes or until top is golden brown and bread sounds hollow when tapped on bottom. Brush top of bread with melted butter or margarine. Remove from casserole; cool completely on a wire rack. Makes 1 loaf.

Left to right: Panettone, Hungarian Coffeecake

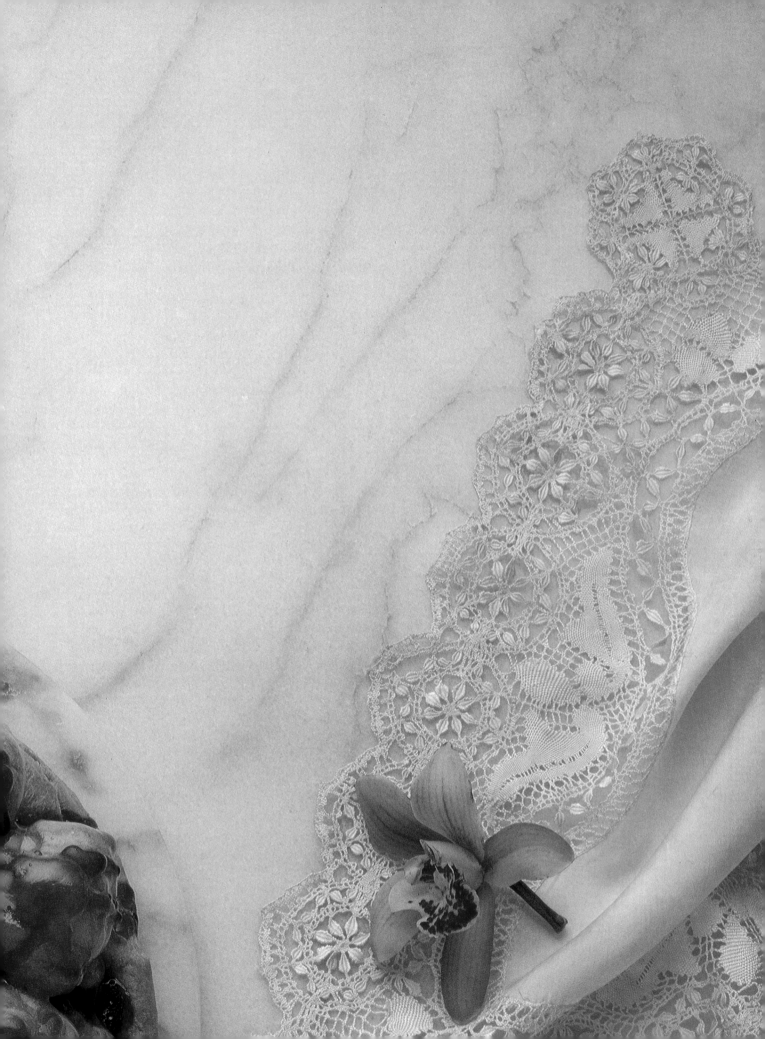

# Desserts

Desserts are the perfect way to end a meal. Why not invite friends over for a dessert party? You're sure to find a dessert for even the most discriminating palate! Although there is a theme to each section, many basic mixtures, including pastry, meringue and custards, are found in more than one section.

## CAKES

Cakes are made by several methods depending on the type of cake and the ingredients.

**One-bowl cakes,** such as *Iced Orange Squares,* are made by combining all the ingredients in one bowl and beating with an electric mixer. This is a fast and easy method.

The **conventional method** of making cakes is to cream the shortening and sugar until the mixture is light and fluffy. This incorporates air into the mixture and will result in a light, fine-grained product. In addition, baking powder, and sometimes baking soda, is added for additional leavening. Sometimes the eggs are separated and the whites are beaten and folded in.

**Sponge cakes** do not contain baking powder for leavening. They are leavened by the air that is beaten into the eggs which are usually warmed over hot water. *Strawberry-Cream Cake,* is an example of a sponge cake. It is important to beat the eggs or eggs and sugar, depending on the recipe, until the mixture is light and fluffy. Underbeating will result in a heavy cake. It is not until you can leave a trail in the mixture when you lift the beaters that the mixture is ready to fold in the flour. Room-temperature eggs will beat to a greater volume and make a lighter cake. Fold in the flour without removing the air beaten into the egg mixture.

**To fold in** means to use a large metal spoon or a spatula to combine two or more ingredients, such as cake batter and beaten egg whites. Spoon the beaten egg whites onto the cake batter. To fold, bring the spatula or spoon down through egg whites and cake batter, across the bottom and back up the opposite side against bowl. Repeat until no egg-white streaks remain. Do not overfold or the air beaten into the egg whites will be lost.

**Creaming,** the method in which fat and sugar are beaten to a light creamy texture, forms the basis of many rich, flavorful cakes and cookies. Since it gives the best flavor, butter is often used for creamed cakes. However, margarine and vegetable shortening also produce excellent cakes. In fact, because vegetable shortening is softer and more pliable, it enables you to incorporate more air into the product for a lighter texture. Butter or margarine should be at room temperature before using. If your kitchen is cold, warm utensils in hot water and dry before using. Creaming will be much easier with warm utensils.

## COOKIES

There are several types of cookies—bar, dropped, rolled, molded, pressed and refrigerator cookies.

*Bar cookies,* made from soft dough, are quick and easy to make. Spread the dough in a baking pan. Cut baked cookies into bars to serve. Some bar cookies have more than one layer. Sometimes a rich, firm dough is pressed into the pan, and a topping is added later. *Walnut Brownies,* are an example of a bar cookie.

*Dropped cookies,* also made from a soft dough, are dropped by teaspoons onto a baking sheet. Use a rubber spatula or another spoon to push the dough off the spoon. *Whole-Wheat Raisin Drops,* are dropped cookies.

*Refrigerator cookies* are sliced cookies. The firm cookie dough is shaped into a roll, wrapped tightly and refrigerated until chilled. To bake, the chilled dough is cut into thin slices. This is a time-saver, because the cookie dough can be made ahead.

*Molded cookies* are other examples of cookies made from firm cookie dough. Molded cookies are pressed into cookie molds or shaped by hand. *Cinnamon Jumbles,* are molded cookies.

*Pressed cookies* are formed with a cookie press or pastry bag. These cookies take more time to shape than dropped or bar cookies. The dough must be soft enough to go through the cookie press or pastry bag, but firm enough to hold its shape while baking. *Coffee Kisses* are an example of pressed cookies.

## PIES & PASTRIES

All types of pastries are included in this section—flaky pie crusts, rich puff pastry, choux paste and crumb crusts. Each recipe includes detailed instructions.

**Cutting in** is the technique used to combine a solid fat and a flour mixture. Use a pastry blender or two knives to cut through the mixture until it resembles coarse crumbs. To achieve good results when making pie crusts, handle the dough as little as possible. Overworking results in a tough crust. The dough should be moist enough to form a ball, but it should not be sticky.

*Puff pastry* is time-consuming but well worth the effort. When rolling and folding the pastry, keep the corners as square as possible to form lots of airy layers. Refrigerate until chilled between rollings. A hot summer day is not the best time to make this pastry; it needs to remain cool during rolling and folding.

*Choux paste* is a versatile pastry that forms the base for many elegant desserts, such as *Paris Brest.* Choux paste needs a medium-high oven temperature to rise and set. For larger cream puffs, reduce the oven temperature after ten or fifteen minutes of baking to bake the pastry completely without burning.

## QUICK & EASY

As the name implies, this section includes desserts that can be put together simply and easily. Some are made from fresh whipped cream with added flavorings, such as *Strawberry & Cointreau Cream, Scottish Honey Crunch* and *Creamy Toffee Crunch.*

Fresh and canned fruits are easy to prepare and can be served in a variety of ways. For example, canned apricots accompany toasted pound cake for *Apricot Toasts.*

Liqueurs and wine blend successfully with fruits to give delicious results, as in *Banana Flambé* and *Cherries in Red Wine.*

Gelatin-based desserts are always quick and easy to make although it takes time for them to set. Several gelatin desserts are included. Many recipes use ingredients you can keep on hand to make an interesting dessert for unexpected guests.

## SPECIAL OCCASIONS

Many recipes in this section include the preparation of custards, for which the basic ingredients are eggs and milk or cream. *Crème Brûlée* is a rich spoonable custard with a caramel crust. *Crème Caramel,* a firm custard with a caramel topping, is

Examples of designs made by piping whipped cream with a star tip.

baked and then unmolded. Stirred custard is the base for *Floating Islands*. A rich egg custard is baked around apples for *French Apple Tart*.

Fresh fruit always makes a good dessert, especially if it is prepared with imagination. *Pineapple & Kirsch Roll*, for example, is spectacular with a fresh pineapple. Fruits can also be made into mousses, fools and whips. Two examples are *Gooseberry Fool* and *Berry Whip*.

Soft cheeses, such as cream cheese, ricotta cheese or cottage cheese, are good for making cheesecakes, but try *Paskha* or *Coeur à la Crème* for unusual variations.

This section also includes a variety of pastries, from shortcrust and frozen puff pastry, to rich sweet pastries and strudel.

Egg white is used in a variety of ways: baked into meringues, poached in milk for *Floating Islands* or simply beaten to add lightness to mousses and fools.

## ELEGANT DESSERTS

Some of these desserts require extra time to prepare, assemble and decorate. However, this is time well spent because the results are spectacular. Some are quite inexpensive, using basic ingredients with perhaps a special seasonal fruit. Good examples are *Nectarine-Meringue Torte* and *Kiwifruit Pavlova*, both variations of meringue decorated with whipped cream and exotic fruit. If the fruit suggested in the recipe is not available, experiment with other flavors. Most fresh fruits can be used, or use well-drained canned fruit.

Liqueurs and spirits are used frequently to enhance and complement the flavor of the desserts and to add sparkle.

## FAVORITE DESSERTS

This section includes some traditional favorites, such as *Apple Crisp, Peach Cobbler, Crepes Suzette*

and *Christmas Pudding*. There are also some new ideas for using basic ingredients. *Sweet Noodle Pudding* uses pasta as an alternative to rice in a rich egg custard. *Steamed Chocolate Pudding* with *Chocolate Sauce* will be a success with chocolate lovers. *Lemon Sponge Pudding* separates as it bakes to give a golden sponge top with a tangy lemon sauce beneath.

## FROZEN DESSERTS

Frozen desserts are always a bonus when you are faced with unexpected guests or if extra time is needed to prepare a main course. This section contains recipes that are served frozen and those that are softened in the refrigerator or at room temperature before serving. All ice creams, ices and sorbets will scoop better if allowed to soften slightly. The exact time will depend on the mixture, but it will probably be from 15 minutes to one hour in the average refrigerator. If the mixture is frozen in a shaped mold, such as *Coffee-Ice-Cream Bombe*, the dessert is unmolded on a serving plate and returned to the freezer to firm up before decorating. *Frozen Zabaglione* and *Chocolate-Rum Cake* can be served straight from the freezer. The ingredients in these recipes keep the mixtures from freezing solid.

## EQUIPMENT

Some recipes in this book call for specialized equipment such as a bombe mold, melon baller or flan pan. The right equipment makes dessert preparation easier. If you plan to make recipes that call for these items regularly, you may want to invest in them. However, there are substitutes. If you do not have an ice-cream scoop or a melon baller, use a spoon. Cake pans with removable bottoms can double as flan pans. Metal or ceramic bowls make excellent substitutes for bombe molds or steamed-pudding molds. Pages 304 and 305 show examples of some equipment used in dessert preparation.

1. Soufflé dish, 2. Springform pan, 3. Metal fluted flan pan,
4. Porcelain flan pan, 5. Ramekins, 6. Bombe mold with lid,
7. Charlotte mold, 8. Cloth pastry bag, 9. Paper pastry bag,
10. Pastry tips, 11. Cherry pitter, 12. Citrus zester, 13. Melon
baller, 14. Small spatula, 15. Coeur à la crème molds and
16. Copper molds

# Molasses Crinkles

3/4 cup butter or margarine, room temperature
1 cup sugar
1/4 cup molasses
1 egg
2-1/4 cups all-purpose flour
2 teaspoons baking soda
1-1/2 teaspoons ground ginger
1 teaspoon ground cinnamon
1/2 teaspoon ground cloves
1/2 teaspoon salt
Sugar

**1.** Preheat oven to 375F (190C). Grease 2 baking sheets.
**2.** In a medium bowl, beat butter or margarine and 1 cup sugar 5 to 8 minutes or until light and fluffy. Beat in molasses and egg until blended. Sift flour, baking soda, ginger, cinnamon, cloves and salt over sugar mixture. Stir with a wooden spoon to make a stiff dough.
**3.** Shape dough into walnut-sized balls; roll in sugar to coat. Place about 2-1/2 inches apart on greased baking sheets.
**4.** Bake in preheated oven 12 to 14 minutes. Remove from baking sheets; cool on wire racks. Makes about 30 cookies.

### Variation
Add 1-1/2 cups chopped raisins to cookie dough. Shape and bake as directed above. Makes about 36 cookies.

# Macadamia-Chip Cookies

1/2 cup butter or margarine, room temperature
1/2 cup granulated sugar
1/2 cup firmly packed light-brown sugar
1 tablespoon light or dark corn syrup
1 egg
1 teaspoon vanilla extract
1-1/4 cups all-purpose flour
1/2 teaspoon baking soda
1/2 teaspoon salt
1 cup semisweet chocolate pieces
1/2 cup coarsely chopped macadamia nuts

**1.** Preheat oven to 375F (190C). Lightly grease 2 or 3 baking sheets.
**2.** In a medium bowl, beat butter or margarine and sugars 5 to 8 minutes or until light and fluffy. Beat in corn syrup, egg and vanilla until blended.
**3.** In a small bowl, combine flour, baking soda and salt. Add to sugar mixture; stir with a wooden spoon until blended. Stir in chocolate pieces and nuts.
**4.** Drop mixture by rounded teaspoons about 1-1/2 inches apart on greased baking sheets.
**5.** Bake in preheated oven 9 to 11 minutes or until golden brown. Remove from baking sheets; cool on wire racks. Makes 36 to 42 cookies.

# Snickerdoodles

1/2 cup butter or margarine, room temperature
3/4 cup sugar
1 egg
1 teaspoon vanilla extract
1-1/2 cups all-purpose flour
1 teaspoon baking powder
1/2 teaspoon baking soda
1/4 teaspoon salt
2 teaspoons ground cinnamon mixed with
   2 tablespoons sugar

**1.** Preheat oven to 375F (190C).
**2.** In a medium bowl, beat butter or margarine and sugar 5 to 8 minutes or until light and fluffy. Beat in egg and vanilla until blended.
**3.** Sift flour, baking powder, baking soda and salt over sugar mixture. Stir with a wooden spoon to make a stiff dough.
**4.** Shape dough into walnut-sized balls; roll in cinnamon-sugar mixture to coat. Place balls about 2 inches apart on ungreased baking sheets.
**5.** Bake in preheated oven 10 to 12 minutes or until lightly browned. Remove from baking sheets; cool on wire racks. Makes about 36 cookies.

Clockwise from center left: Snickerdoodles, Macadamia-Chip Cookies, Molasses Crinkles

# Whole-Wheat Raisin Drops

1 cup whole-wheat flour
1 cup all-purpose flour
1 teaspoon baking powder
1/2 teaspoon salt
1/2 teaspoon ground cinnamon
1/4 teaspoon freshly grated nutmeg
3/4 cup butter or margarine, room temperature
1 cup sugar
2 eggs
1 cup raisins

1. Preheat oven to 375F (190C). Grease 2 baking sheets.
2. In a small bowl, combine flours, baking powder, salt, cinnamon and nutmeg; set aside.
3. In a medium bowl, beat butter or margarine and sugar 5 to 8 minutes or until light and fluffy. Beat in eggs until blended. Add flour mixture; stir with a wooden spoon until combined. Stir in raisins.
4. Drop mixture by rounded teaspoons about 1-1/2 inches apart on greased baking sheets.
5. Bake in preheated oven 12 to 15 minutes or until golden brown. Remove from baking sheets; cool on wire racks. Makes about 36 cookies.

# Crunchy Peanut Cookies

1/2 cup butter or margarine, room temperature
3/4 cup firmly packed light-brown sugar
1/2 cup granulated sugar
2 eggs
1/2 cup crunchy peanut butter
1-3/4 cups all-purpose flour
1/2 teaspoon baking powder
1/2 teaspoon baking soda
1/2 teaspoon salt

1. In a medium bowl, beat butter or margarine and sugars 5 to 8 minutes or until light and fluffy. Beat in eggs and peanut butter until blended.
2. Sift flour, baking powder, baking soda and salt over peanut-butter mixture; stir with a wooden spoon until blended. Cover bowl with plastic wrap; refrigerate 1 hour.
3. Preheat oven to 375F (190C). Grease 2 or 3 baking sheets.
4. Shape dough into 1-inch balls; place about 1-1/2 inches apart on greased baking sheets. Flatten each ball in a crisscross pattern with prongs of a fork dipped in sugar.
5. Bake in preheated oven 10 to 12 minutes or until golden brown. Remove from baking sheets; cool on wire racks. Makes about 48 cookies.

**Variation**
Stir in 1/2 cup finely chopped peanuts with flour mixture.

Left to right: Whole-Wheat Raisin Drops, Crunchy Peanut Cookies, Shortbread, Hazelnut-Chip Cookies

# Shortbread

1/2 cup butter or margarine, room temperature
1/3 cup superfine sugar
1/4 cup ground blanched almonds
1/4 cup finely chopped candied orange peel
  or lemon peel
1-1/4 cups all-purpose flour
About 2 tablespoons granulated sugar

**1.** Preheat oven to 325F (165C). Grease a 9- or 10-inch fluted quiche pan or tart pan with a removable bottom.
**2.** In a medium bowl, beat butter or margarine and superfine sugar 5 to 8 minutes or until light and fluffy. Stir in almonds and candied peel. Add flour; stir with a wooden spoon to make a soft dough. Knead dough in bowl 8 to 10 strokes.
**3.** Pat out dough evenly in bottom of greased pan, carefully pressing dough into fluted ridges. Smooth top of dough with back of a spoon; prick with a fork.
**4.** Bake in preheated oven 30 to 35 minutes or until golden. Cool in pan on a wire rack 10 minutes. Sprinkle with granulated sugar. Remove from pan; cool completely on wire rack. Cut into 8 to 10 wedges. Makes 8 to 10 cookies.

# Hazelnut-Chip Cookies

1/2 cup butter or margarine, room temperature
3/4 cup firmly packed light-brown sugar
2 tablespoons molasses
1 egg
2 cups all-purpose flour
1 teaspoon baking powder
1 teaspoon ground cinnamon
1/3 cup finely chopped toasted hazelnuts or almonds
1 oz. semisweet chocolate, chopped

**1.** In a medium bowl, beat butter or margarine and brown sugar 5 to 8 minutes or until light and fluffy. Beat in molasses and egg until blended.
**2.** In a small bowl, combine flour, baking powder and cinnamon. Add flour mixture to sugar mixture; stir with a wooden spoon until blended. Stir in nuts and chocolate.
**3.** Shape dough into a 2-inch-thick roll. Wrap in waxed paper or plastic wrap; refrigerate 2 to 3 hours or until firm.
**4.** Preheat oven to 375F (190C). Grease 2 or 3 baking sheets. Cut dough into 3/8-inch-thick slices. Place cookies about 1 inch apart on greased baking sheets.
**5.** Bake in preheated oven 10 to 12 minutes or until lightly browned. Remove from baking sheets; cool on wire racks. Makes 36 to 42 cookies.

# Almond Macaroons

3/4 cup ground blanched almonds
1/2 cup sugar
3 egg whites
1/2 teaspoon almond extract
20 whole almonds

**1.** Preheat oven to 350F (175C). Line 2 baking sheets with parchment paper.
**2.** In a medium bowl, combine ground almonds and sugar; set aside.
**3.** In a medium bowl, beat egg whites until stiff but not dry. Fold beaten egg whites and almond extract into sugar mixture.
**4.** Spoon mixture into a pastry bag fitted with a number 6 plain tip. Pipe 20 mounds of mixture about 1-1/2 inches apart on parchment-lined baking sheets. Place 1 whole almond in center of each cookie.
**5.** Bake in preheated oven 20 to 25 minutes or until golden. Cool on baking sheets on wire racks 1 minute. Peel cookies off paper; cool on wire racks. Makes about 20 cookies.

# Florentines

1/4 cup butter or margarine
1/3 cup firmly packed light-brown sugar
2 tablespoons light corn syrup
1/4 cup chopped red candied cherries
1/4 cup chopped walnuts, pecans, almonds or hazelnuts
1/4 cup currants
1/4 cup chopped mixed candied fruit
3 tablespoons all-purpose flour
1/3 cup sliced or slivered almonds
2 teaspoons lemon juice
4 oz. semisweet chocolate, melted, cooled

**1.** Preheat oven to 350F (175C). Line 2 baking sheets with foil.
**2.** In a small saucepan over low heat, combine butter or margarine, brown sugar and corn syrup. Cook, stirring, until butter or margarine melts and sugar dissolves. Remove from heat.
**3.** Stir in candied cherries, chopped nuts, currants, mixed fruit, flour, sliced or slivered almonds and lemon juice until combined.
**4.** Drop mixture by teaspoons about 2-1/2 inches apart on lined baking sheets. Flatten each cookie with back of a spoon.
**5.** Bake in preheated oven 8 to 10 minutes or until golden brown. Cool on baking sheets on wire racks 1 minute. Carefully remove cookies from foil; cool completely on wire racks.
**6.** Spread chocolate over flat side of cookies, making wavy lines in chocolate with a fork. Let stand until chocolate is set. Makes 18 to 24 cookies.

Top to bottom: Almond Macaroons, Florentines

# Nutty Coconut-Oatmeal Cookies

1/2 cup butter or margarine
2 tablespoons light corn syrup
3 tablespoons water
1 cup all-purpose flour
3/4 cup flaked or shredded coconut
3/4 cup quick-cooking rolled oats
2/3 cup sugar
1/3 cup finely chopped walnuts, pecans or almonds
1 teaspoon baking soda

1. Preheat oven to 350F (175C). Grease 2 baking sheets.
2. In a small saucepan over low heat, combine butter or margarine, corn syrup and water. Cook, stirring, until butter or margarine melts. Let cool.
3. In a medium bowl, combine flour, coconut, rolled oats, sugar, nuts and baking soda. Stir in cooled corn-syrup mixture until combined.
4. Shape mixture into 1-inch balls; place about 2 inches apart on greased baking sheets. Flatten each ball slightly.
5. Bake in preheated oven 12 to 14 minutes or until golden brown. Cool on baking sheets on wire racks 1 minute. Remove from baking sheets; cool completely on wire racks. Makes about 36 cookies.

# Muesli Bars

3 tablespoons honey
1/2 cup butter or margarine
1/3 cup firmly packed light-brown sugar
1/3 cup chopped almonds
1 cup quick-cooking rolled oats
1/3 cup flaked or shredded coconut
1/3 cup sesame seeds
4 oz. semisweet chocolate, melted, cooled, if desired

1. Preheat oven to 350F (175C). Grease an 11" x 7" baking pan.
2. In a medium saucepan over low heat, combine honey, butter or margarine and brown sugar. Cook, stirring, until butter or margarine melts and sugar dissolves. Remove pan from heat.
3. Stir in almonds, rolled oats, coconut and sesame seeds until combined. Press mixture evenly into greased pan with back of a spoon.
4. Bake in preheated oven 15 to 18 minutes or until golden. Cool in pan on a wire rack 10 minutes. Score into 18 bars. Cool completely in pan on wire rack. Cut into bars; remove from pan. Dip bars into chocolate, if desired. Let stand until chocolate is set. Makes 18 bars.

Top to bottom: Nutty Coconut-Oatmeal Cookies, Muesli Bars

## Dried-Fruit Bars

1 (8-oz.) pkg. mixed dried fruit, chopped
  (about 1-1/3 cups)
2/3 cup orange juice
1 cup water
1 cup all-purpose flour
3/4 cup semolina flour
1/2 cup sugar
3/4 cup butter or margarine
About 2 tablespoons sugar

---

1. In a medium saucepan over medium heat, combine dried fruit, orange juice and water. Bring to a boil. Reduce heat. Cover and simmer 30 minutes, stirring occasionally. Let cool.
2. Preheat oven to 375F (190C). Grease an 11" x 7" baking pan.
3. In a medium bowl, combine flours and 1/2 cup sugar. With a pastry blender or 2 knives, cut in butter or margarine until mixture resembles fine crumbs.
4. Press 1/2 of crumb mixture in bottom of greased pan. Spread cooled fruit mixture over crumb layer. Sprinkle remaining crumb mixture over fruit mixture; press down lightly with your fingertips.
5. Bake in preheated oven 30 to 35 minutes or until top is golden brown. Sprinkle top lightly with sugar. Cool completely in pan on a wire rack. Cut into bars; remove from pan. Makes 18 to 24 bars.

## Lacy Ginger Wafers

1/4 cup butter or margarine
1/4 cup sugar
1/3 cup light corn syrup
2 teaspoons lemon juice
1/2 cup all-purpose flour
1 teaspoon ground ginger

---

1. Preheat oven to 350F (175C). Line 3 baking sheets with foil.

2. In a small saucepan over low heat, combine butter or margarine, sugar and corn syrup. Cook, stirring, until butter or margarine melts and sugar dissolves. Remove from heat.
3. Stir in lemon juice, flour and ginger until blended. Let cool.
4. Drop mixture by level teaspoons about 2-1/2 inches apart on lined baking sheets.
5. Bake, 1 sheet at a time, in preheated oven 9 to 11 minutes or until golden brown. Cool on baking sheet on a wire rack 2 to 3 minutes. Peel cookies off foil; cool on wire rack. Repeat with remaining cookies. Makes 24 to 26 cookies.

## Currant & Spice Wheels

1 cup butter or margarine, room temperature
1 cup firmly packed light-brown sugar
1 egg
2-1/3 cups all-purpose flour
2 tablespoons ground almonds
1 teaspoon pumpkin-pie spice
1/2 teaspoon baking soda
1/4 cup currants
1 egg white beaten with 1 tablespoon water for glaze
1/4 cup granulated sugar

---

1. In a medium bowl, beat butter or margarine and brown sugar 5 to 8 minutes or until light and fluffy. Beat in egg until blended. In a medium bowl, combine flour, almonds, pumpkin-pie spice and baking soda. Add to sugar mixture; stir until combined. Stir in currants.
2. Divide dough in half. Wrap each piece of dough in waxed paper or plastic wrap; refrigerate 1 hour.
3. Preheat oven to 375F (190C). Grease 2 or 3 baking sheets. On a lightly floured surface, roll out 1 piece of dough to a 12" x 8" rectangle. Brush dough with egg-white glaze; sprinkle with 2 tablespoons granulated sugar. Cut dough into 24 (8" x 1/2") strips. Starting from short end, roll up each strip, jelly-roll style; place, cut-side down, about 1 inch apart on greased baking sheets. Flatten each cookie slightly with your fingertips. Repeat with remaining dough.
4. Bake in preheated oven 12 to 15 minutes or until golden brown. Remove from baking sheets; cool on wire racks. Makes 48 cookies.

# Sticky Gingerbread Bars

2 cups all-purpose flour
1 tablespoon ground ginger
1 teaspoon ground cinnamon
1 teaspoon baking soda
1/2 teaspoon salt
1/2 cup butter or margarine
1/2 cup molasses
1/2 cup dark corn syrup
1/4 cup firmly packed dark-brown sugar
3/4 cup milk
2 eggs, beaten

**1.** Preheat oven to 350F (175C). Grease and flour an 8- or 9-inch-square baking pan.
**2.** Sift flour, ginger, cinnnamon, baking soda and salt into a medium bowl; set aside.
**3.** In a medium saucepan over low heat, combine butter or margarine, molasses, corn syrup, brown sugar and milk. Cook, stirring, until butter or margarine melts and sugar dissolves. Remove from heat; stir in eggs until blended.
**4.** Add molasses mixture to flour-spice mixture; stir until blended. Pour into prepared pan.
**5.** Bake in preheated oven 50 to 55 minutes or until a wooden pick inserted in center comes out clean. Cool in pan on a wire rack 15 minutes. Remove from pan; cool completely on wire rack. Cut into bars. Makes 16 bars.

Left to right: Currant & Spice Wheels, Dried-Fruit Bars

# Cinnamon Jumbles

1/2 cup butter or margarine, room temperature
3/4 cup sugar
1 egg
1-1/2 cups all-purpose flour
1 teaspoon baking powder
1/2 teaspoon baking soda
1/2 teaspoon salt
1-1/4 teaspoons ground cinnamon
2 tablespoons sugar

1. In a medium bowl, beat butter or margarine and 3/4 cup sugar 5 to 8 minutes or until light and fluffy. Beat in egg until blended.
2. Sift flour, baking powder, baking soda, salt and 1/4 teaspoon cinnamon over sugar mixture. Stir with a wooden spoon until blended. Cover bowl; refrigerate 2 hours.
3. Preheat oven to 350F (175C). Grease 2 baking sheets. Divide dough into 24 walnut-sized pieces. Shape each piece into a 5- to 6-inch-long rope. Shape ropes into S shapes, circles and knots. Place about 2 inches apart on greased baking sheets.
4. In a small bowl, combine remaining cinnamon and 2 tablespoons sugar; sprinkle over cookies.
5. Bake in preheated oven 13 to 15 minutes or until golden brown. Remove from baking sheets; cool on wire racks. Makes 24 cookies.

**Variation**
Roll each cookie rope in cinnamon-sugar mixture before shaping.

# Coffee Kisses

*Cookies:*
1/2 cup butter or margarine, room temperature
1/2 cup sugar
1 egg
1 teaspoon instant coffee powder
2 tablespoons warm water
1-1/2 cups all-purpose flour

*Icing:*
1/4 cup butter or margarine, room temperature
1 cup powdered sugar, sifted
1 tablespoon strong black coffee
Powdered sugar

Left to right: Coffee Kisses, Cinnamon Jumbles

1. Preheat oven to 375F (190C).
2. To make cookies, in a medium bowl, beat butter or margarine and sugar 5 to 8 minutes or until light and fluffy. Beat in egg until blended. In a small bowl, dissolve coffee in warm water. Beat coffee mixture into sugar mixture until combined. Add flour to sugar mixture; stir with a wooden spoon until blended.
3. Spoon dough into a pastry bag fitted with a large number 6 open-star tip. Pipe dough into small stars about 1 inch apart on ungreased baking sheets.
4. Bake in preheated oven 9 to 11 minutes or until golden. Remove from baking sheets; cool on wire racks.
5. To make icing, in a medium bowl, beat butter or margarine, powdered sugar and coffee until smooth and icing is a good spreading consistency. Mound icing over bottoms of 1/2 of cookies. Top with remaining cookies. Dust with powdered sugar immediately before serving. Makes about 16 filled cookies.

# Walnut Brownies

2 oz. unsweetened chocolate, broken into pieces
1/3 cup butter or margarine
1 cup sugar
2 eggs, beaten
1 teaspoon vanilla extract
2/3 cup all-purpose flour
1/2 teaspoon baking powder
1/2 teaspoon salt
1/2 cup chopped walnuts

**1.** Preheat oven to 350F (175C). Grease an 8- or 9-inch-square baking pan.
**2.** In a medium saucepan over very low heat, combine chocolate and butter or margarine. Cook, stirring, until mixture melts. Remove pan from heat.
**3.** Stir in sugar until blended. Stir in eggs and vanilla until blended. In a small bowl, combine flour, baking powder and salt. Add to chocolate mixture; stir with a wooden spoon until blended. Fold in walnuts. Pour into greased pan; smooth top.
**4.** Bake in preheated oven 25 to 30 minutes. Cool completely in pan on a wire rack. Cut into squares; remove from pan. Makes 16 brownies.

# Coffee Layer Cake

*Cake:*
3/4 cup butter or margarine, room temperature
1 cup sugar
3 eggs
1-3/4 cups all-purpose flour
2 teaspoons baking powder
1/2 teaspoon salt
1 tablespoon instant coffee powder
2/3 cup warm milk

*Icing:*
1/4 cup butter or margarine, room temperature
2-1/2 cups sifted powdered sugar
2 tablespoons strong black coffee

---

**1.** Preheat oven to 350F (175C). Grease and flour 2 (8-inch) round cake pans.
**2.** To make cake, in a medium bowl, beat butter or margarine and sugar 5 to 8 minutes or until light and fluffy. Beat in eggs, 1 at a time, beating well after each addition.
**3.** Sift flour, baking powder and salt into a medium bowl. Dissolve coffee in milk. Add flour mixture to sugar mixture alternately with milk; beat until blended. Pour batter into prepared pans; smooth tops.
**4.** Bake in preheated oven 30 to 35 minutes or until a wooden pick inserted in center comes out clean. Cool in pans on a wire rack 5 minutes. Remove from pans; cool completely on wire rack.
**5.** To make icing, in a medium bowl, beat butter or margarine, powdered sugar and coffee until icing is smooth and a good consistency for spreading.
**6.** Place 1 cooled layer, bottom-side up, on a serving plate; spread with 1/2 of icing. Top with remaining layer, bottom-side down. Spread remaining icing over top of cake, swirling icing with a small spatula. Makes 6 to 8 servings.

# Chocolate-Rose Cake

*Cake:*
3/4 cup butter or margarine, room temperature
1 cup sugar
1 teaspoon vanilla extract
3 eggs
1-1/4 cups all-purpose flour
1 teaspoon baking powder
1/2 teaspoon salt
1/3 cup milk
2 tablespoons unsweetened cocoa powder
2 tablespoons boiling water
3 to 4 drops red food coloring

*Fudge Icing:*
2 oz. unsweetened chocolate, coarsely chopped
1/4 cup butter or margarine
2 cups sifted powdered sugar
2 tablespoons milk

---

**1.** Preheat oven to 350F (175C). Grease and flour an 11" x 7" baking pan.
**2.** To make cake, in a medium bowl, beat butter or margarine and sugar 5 to 8 minutes or until light and fluffy. Beat in vanilla. Beat in eggs, 1 at a time, beating well after each addition.
**3.** Sift flour, baking powder and salt into a medium bowl. Add flour mixture to sugar mixture alternately with milk; beat until blended.
**4.** Pour 1/2 of batter into another bowl. In a small bowl, dissolve cocoa in boiling water; stir into 1/2 of batter. Tint remaining batter with red food coloring.
**5.** Place alternate spoonfuls of chocolate and pink batters in prepared pan. Swirl through batters with tip of a knife to create a marbled effect.
**6.** Bake in preheated oven 25 to 30 minutes or until a wooden pick inserted in center comes out clean. Cool in pan on a wire rack.
**7.** To make icing, place chocolate and butter or margarine in top of a double boiler over simmering water. Cook, stirring, until chocolate is melted. Remove top from simmering water; stir in powdered sugar and milk until icing is smooth and glossy.
**8.** Spread icing over cooled cake in pan, swirling icing with a small spatula. Let stand until icing is set. Cut iced cake into 24 bars; remove from pan. Makes 24 bars.

Top to bottom: Coffee Layer Cake, Chocolate-Rose Cake

# Raisin Spice Cake

1/2 cup butter or margarine, room temperature
1 cup granulated sugar
1 egg
1 tablespoon grated orange peel
1-1/2 cups sifted all-purpose flour
1-1/2 teaspoons baking powder
1 teaspoon ground cinnamon
1/2 teaspoon ground allspice
1/2 teaspoon freshly grated nutmeg
1/4 teaspoon salt
2/3 cup orange juice
1 cup raisins
Powdered sugar

**1.** Preheat oven to 350F (175C). Grease an 8- or 9-inch-square baking pan. Line bottom of pan with waxed paper; grease paper.
**2.** In a medium bowl, beat butter or margarine and granulated sugar 8 to 10 minutes or until light and fluffy. Beat in egg and orange peel until blended.
**3.** Sift flour, baking powder, cinnamon, allspice, nutmeg and salt into a medium bowl. Add flour mixture to sugar mixture alternately with orange juice; beat until blended. Fold in raisins. Pour into prepared pan; smooth top.
**4.** Bake in preheated oven 35 to 40 minutes or until a wooden pick inserted in center comes out clean. Cool in pan on a wire rack 10 minutes. Remove from pan; cool completely on wire rack.
**5.** Place cake on a serving plate. Sift powdered sugar over top of cake immediately before serving. Makes 9 servings.

Left to right: Citrus Sunshine Cake, Vanilla Ring Cake

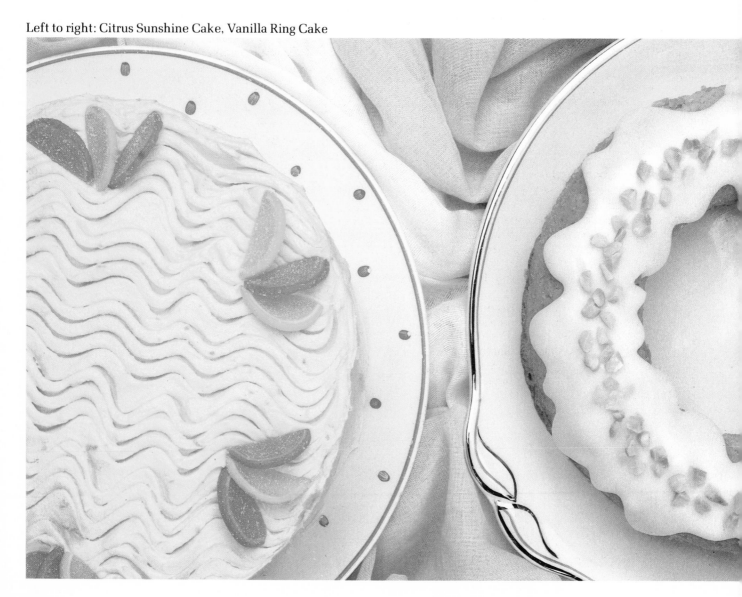

# Citrus Sunshine Cake

*Cake:*
2/3 cup butter or margarine, room temperature
1-1/3 cups sugar
3 eggs
1/4 cup lemon juice
1 tablespoon grated lemon peel
2 teaspoons grated orange peel
2 cups all-purpose flour
2-1/2 teaspoons baking powder
3/4 teaspoon salt
1/2 cup milk

*Frosting:*
6 tablespoons butter or margarine, room temperature
4 cups sifted powdered sugar
3 to 4 tablespoons orange juice
1 teaspoon grated orange peel
Few drops red and yellow food coloring

*To decorate:*
Sugar-coated orange and lemon jelly slices

1. Preheat oven to 350F (175C). Grease and flour 2 (8- or 9-inch) round cake pans.
2. To make cake, in a medium bowl, beat butter or margarine and sugar 5 to 8 minutes or until light and fluffy. Beat in eggs, 1 at a time, beating well after each addition. Beat in lemon juice, lemon peel and orange peel until blended.
3. Sift flour, baking powder and salt into a medium bowl. Add flour mixture to sugar mixture alternately with milk; beat until blended. Pour batter into prepared pans; smooth tops.
4. Bake in preheated oven 35 to 40 minutes or until a wooden pick inserted in center comes out clean. Cool in pans on a wire rack 5 minutes. Remove from pans; cool completely on wire rack.
5. To make frosting, in a medium bowl, beat butter or margarine until creamy. Add powdered sugar, 3 tablespoons orange juice and orange peel; beat until frosting is smooth and a good consistency for spreading, adding more orange juice if necessary. Tint frosting with a few drops red and yellow food coloring.
6. Place 1 cooled cake layer, bottom-side up, on a serving plate. Spread with 1/3 of frosting. Top with second cake layer, bottom-side down. Spread remaining frosting around side and over top of cake, smoothing frosting with a small spatula. Make wavy lines on top of cake with prongs of a fork. Decorate with orange and lemon jelly slices. Makes 6 to 8 servings.

# Vanilla Ring Cake

*Cake:*
1/2 cup butter or margarine, room temperature
1/3 cup sugar
1/4 cup mild-flavored honey
2 eggs
1 teaspoon vanilla extract
1-1/4 cups all-purpose flour
2 teaspoons baking powder
1/2 teaspoon salt

*Icing:*
1 cup powdered sugar, sifted
1/2 teaspoon vanilla extract
About 2 tablespoons milk
1 to 2 tablespoons chopped toasted almonds

1. Preheat oven to 350F (175C). Grease and flour an 8- or 9-inch (5-1/2- to 6-1/2-cup) ring mold.
2. To make cake, in a medium bowl, beat butter or margarine, sugar and honey 5 to 8 minutes or until light and fluffy. Beat in eggs and vanilla until blended.
3. Sift flour, baking powder and salt into a small bowl. Add to sugar mixture; beat until blended. Spread batter in prepared pan; smooth top.
4. Bake in preheated oven 25 to 30 minutes or until a wooden pick inserted in center comes out clean. Cool in pan on a wire rack 10 minutes. Remove from pan; cool completely on wire rack.
5. To make icing, in a small bowl, beat powdered sugar, vanilla and 2 tablespoons milk until smooth, adding more milk if necessary.
6. Place cooled cake on a serving plate; spoon icing over top. Sprinkle with chopped almonds. Let stand until icing is set. Makes 6 to 8 servings.

# Devil's Food Cake

*Cake:*
1/2 cup unsweetened cocoa powder
3/4 cup boiling water
3/4 cup butter or margarine, room temperature
1-1/4 cups sugar
4 eggs
1 teaspoon vanilla extract
2 cups all-purpose flour
1-1/4 teaspoons baking soda
1/2 teaspoon salt

*Frosting:*
1/2 cup butter or margarine, room temperature
4 cups powdered sugar, sifted
4 oz. unsweetened chocolate, melted, cooled
3 to 4 tablespoons milk or half and half
2 teaspoons vanilla extract

**1.** Preheat oven to 350F (175C). Grease and flour 2 (8-inch) round cake pans.
**2.** To make cake, in a medium bowl, stir cocoa into boiling water until completely dissolved. Let cool.
**3.** Using an electric mixer, beat in butter or margarine, sugar, eggs, vanilla, flour, baking soda and salt. Beat at low speed about 1 minute or until blended. Increase speed to high; beat 3 minutes, scraping down side of bowl occasionally. Pour batter into prepared pans; smooth tops.
**4.** Bake in preheated oven 30 to 35 minutes or until a wooden pick inserted in center comes out clean. Cool in pans on a wire rack 5 minutes. Remove from pans; cool completely on wire rack.
**5.** To make frosting, in a medium bowl, beat butter or margarine until creamy. Gradually beat in powdered sugar, chocolate, milk or half and half and vanilla. Beat until frosting is smooth and a good consistency for spreading.
**6.** Place 1 cooled layer, bottom-side up, on a serving plate; spread with a thin layer of frosting. Top with remaining layer, bottom-side down. Spread remaining frosting around side and over top of cake, swirling frosting with a small spatula. Makes 6 to 8 servings.

# Easy Orange Layer Cake

*Cake:*
1/2 cup butter or margarine, room temperature
1-1/4 cups sugar
3 eggs
Grated peel of 1 orange
2 cups all-purpose flour
1 tablespoon baking powder
1/2 teaspoon salt
1/2 cup milk
1/2 cup orange juice

*Filling & Topping:*
2 seedless oranges
1 cup ricotta or small-curd cottage cheese
1/4 cup granulated sugar
1/4 teaspoon almond extract
Superfine sugar

**1.** Preheat oven to 350F (175C). Grease and flour 2 (8-inch) round cake pans.
**2.** To make cake, in a medium bowl, beat butter or margarine and sugar 5 to 8 minutes or until light and fluffy. Beat in eggs and orange peel until blended.
**3.** Sift flour, baking powder and salt into a medium bowl. Add flour mixture to sugar mixture alternately with milk and orange juice; beat until blended. Pour batter into prepared pans; smooth tops.
**4.** Bake in preheated oven 30 to 35 minutes or until a wooden pick inserted in center comes out clean. Cool in pans on a wire rack 5 minutes. Remove from pans; cool completely on wire rack.
**5.** To make filling and topping, peel oranges, removing bitter white pith. Cut 1 orange into sections; set aside for decoration. Chop remaining orange; set aside.
**6.** In a blender or food processor fitted with a steel blade, process ricotta cheese or cottage cheese, granulated sugar and almond extract until smooth. Pour into a bowl. Fold in chopped orange.
**7.** Place 1 cake layer, bottom-side up, on a serving plate; spread with orange-cheese filling. Top with remaining cake layer, bottom-side down. Sprinkle with superfine sugar; decorate with reserved orange sections. Refrigerate until served. Makes 6 to 8 servings.

Top to bottom: Easy Orange Layer Cake, Devil's Food Cake

# Mocha & Praline Gâteau

*Cake:*
4 oz. semisweet chocolate
1 teaspoon instant coffee powder
1/4 cup water
5 eggs
2/3 cup sugar
1 cup cake flour, sifted

*Buttercream:*
1/2 cup butter or margarine, room temperature
4 oz. unsweetened chocolate, melted, cooled
2 egg yolks
4 cups powdered sugar, sifted
2 to 3 tablespoons coffee-flavored liqueur

*Praline:*
1/2 cup sugar
1/3 cup whole blanched almonds

*To decorate:*
Chocolate curls

---

1. Preheat oven to 350F (175C). Grease 2 (8-inch) round cake pans. Line bottoms of pans with waxed paper. Grease and flour paper and sides of pans.
2. To prepare cake, in a small heavy saucepan over low heat, heat chocolate, coffee and water; stir until chocolate melts and mixture is smooth. Let cool.
3. Place eggs in a large bowl set over a pan of barely simmering water. Let stand 5 minutes or until warm to the touch. Beat eggs until fluffy. Gradually beat in sugar; beat about 10 minutes or until mixture is thickened. Remove bowl from pan.
4. Add flour to egg mixture alternately with cooled chocolate mixture; beat until blended. Pour batter into prepared pans; smooth tops.
5. Bake in preheated oven 25 to 30 minutes or until center springs back when lightly pressed. Cool in pans on a wire rack 10 minutes. Remove from pans; peel off lining paper. Cool completely on wire rack.
6. To make buttercream, in a medium bowl, beat butter or margarine, chocolate and egg yolks until blended. Gradually beat in powdered sugar and liqueur; beat until frosting is fluffy and a good consistency for spreading. Spoon 2/3 cup frosting into a pastry bag fitted with a small star tip. Refrigerate frosting until ready to use.
7. Line a baking sheet with foil; grease foil. To make praline, place sugar in a small heavy skillet over low heat. Cook, stirring, until sugar is caramel-colored. Stir in almonds to coat. Cook until sugar is deep golden brown. Pour caramel mixture onto foil-lined baking sheet. Let stand until hard.
8. Break praline into small pieces; process in a food processor fitted with a steel blade until crushed. Or, place praline between 2 sheets of waxed paper; crush by striking with a rolling pin. Set aside.
9. Cut cooled cake layers in half horizontally. Place 1 layer on a serving plate; spread with a thin layer of buttercream. Top with another layer; spread with buttercream. Repeat with remaining layers and buttercream. Spread a thin layer of buttercream around side and over top of cake. Press crushed praline lightly around side of cake. Pipe reserved buttercream decoratively around top edge of cake; decorate with chocolate curls. Makes 6 to 8 servings.

# Yogurt & Honey Cake

*Cake:*
4 eggs
1 cup sugar
8 oz. lemon-flavored yogurt (1 cup)
1-3/4 cups all-purpose flour
1 tablespoon baking powder
3/4 teaspoon salt
1/4 teaspoon baking soda

*Topping:*
1/3 cup honey
1/4 cup water
1 (3-inch) cinnamon stick
1 (2-inch) lemon-peel strip
2 to 3 tablespoons toasted sliced almonds

---

1. Preheat oven to 375F (190C). Grease and flour a 13" x 9" baking pan.
2. To make cake, in a large bowl, beat eggs and sugar until thick and lemon-colored. Beat in yogurt until blended.
3. Sift flour, baking powder, salt and baking soda into a medium bowl. Gradually beat flour mixture into sugar mixture, beating until barely blended. Pour batter into prepared pan; smooth top.
4. Bake in preheated oven 30 to 35 minutes or until a wooden pick inserted in center comes out clean. Cool completely in pan on a wire rack.
5. To make topping, in a small saucepan over medium heat, heat honey, water, cinnamon stick and lemon peel. Bring to a boil. Reduce heat; simmer 5 minutes, stirring occasionally.
6. With a fork or metal skewer, make holes in top of cake in pan. Remove and discard cinnamon stick and lemon peel from syrup; spoon hot syrup over top of cake. Sprinkle almonds over glazed cake; let stand until topping is set. Cut into 24 bars; remove from pan. Makes 24 bars.

# Strawberry-Cream Cake

*Cake:*
**4 eggs**
**3/4 cup sugar**
**1 teaspoon grated lemon peel**
**3/4 cup all-purpose flour, sifted**
**1/4 cup unsalted butter, melted, cooled**

*Filling & Decoration:*
**1/2 pint whipping cream (1 cup)**
**1 teaspoon vanilla extract**
**2 tablespoons powdered sugar**
**1 pint fresh strawberries, washed, hulled**
**3 tablespoons red-currant jelly, melted, cooled**

**1.** Preheat oven to 350F (175C). Grease 2 (8-inch) round cake pans. Line bottoms of pans with waxed paper. Grease and flour paper and sides of pans.

**2.** To make cake, place eggs in a large bowl set over a pan of barely simmering water. Let stand 5 minutes or until warm to the touch. Beat eggs until fluffy. Gradually beat in sugar; beat about 10 minutes or until mixture is thickened and falls from beaters in glossy ribbons. Beat in lemon peel.

**3.** Remove bowl from pan of water. Spoon flour over egg mixture; fold in gently. Fold in butter only until streaks disappear. Pour batter into prepared pans; smooth tops.

**4.** Bake in preheated oven 20 to 25 minutes or until cakes spring back when lightly pressed. Cool in pans on a wire rack 5 minutes. Remove from pans; cool completely on wire rack.

**5.** To prepare filling, in a medium bowl, beat cream until soft peaks form. Beat in vanilla and powdered sugar. Spoon 3/4 cup whipped-cream mixture into a pastry bag fitted with a medium star tip; set aside.

**6.** Set aside 12 to 14 strawberries for decoration. Slice remaining strawberries; fold into remaining cream mixture.

**7.** Place 1 cake layer, bottom-side up, on a serving plate; spread with strawberry-cream mixture. Top with remaining cake layer, bottom-side down. Cut reserved strawberries in half. Arrange strawberries, cut-side down, on top of cake; brush with melted jelly. Pipe reserved whipped-cream mixture into rosettes around edge of cake. Refrigerate until served. Makes 6 to 8 servings.

Left to right: Mocha & Praline Gâteau, Strawberry-Cream Cake

# Chocolate Ripple Cake

3/4 cup butter or margarine, room temperature
1-1/2 cups granulated sugar
4 eggs
1 teaspoon almond extract
2-1/2 cups all-purpose flour
2-1/2 teaspoons baking powder
1 teaspoon salt
1 cup milk
4 oz. semisweet chocolate, melted, cooled
1/3 cup finely ground blanched almonds
Powdered sugar

1. Preheat oven to 350F (175C). Grease and flour a 12-cup Bundt pan.
2. In a large bowl, beat butter or margarine and granulated sugar 5 to 8 minutes or until light and fluffy. Beat in eggs, 1 at a time, beating well after each addition. Beat in almond extract.
3. Sift flour, baking powder and salt into a medium bowl. Add flour mixture to sugar mixture alternately with milk; beat until thoroughly blended.
4. Pour 1/2 of batter into another bowl. Stir chocolate into 1 bowl of batter; beat until blended. Fold in ground almonds.
5. Pour 1/2 of plain batter into prepared pan. Pour 1/2 of chocolate batter in a zigzag fashion over top. Pour remaining plain batter carefully over chocolate batter. Pour remaining chocolate batter in zigzag fashion over plain batter. Gently tap bottom of pan on counter 3 or 4 times.
6. Bake in preheated oven 55 to 60 minutes or until a wooden pick inserted in center comes out clean. Cool in pan on a wire rack 10 minutes. Remove from pan; cool completely on wire rack. Place cooled cake on a serving plate; sift powdered sugar over cake immediately before serving. Makes 14 to 18 servings.

# Brandy Gâteau

*Cake:*
1/2 cup butter or margarine, room temperature
3/4 cup sugar
3 eggs, separated
1 teaspoon brandy extract
1-1/4 cups cake flour
2 teaspoons baking powder
1/4 teaspoon salt

*Topping & Filling:*
1 recipe Lacy Ginger Wafers, page 312
1 pint whipping cream (2 cups)
3 tablespoons powdered sugar
3 tablespoons brandy

1. Preheat oven to 350F (175C). Grease 2 (8-inch) round cake pans. Line bottoms of pans with waxed paper. Grease and flour paper and sides of pans.
2. In a medium bowl, beat butter or margarine and sugar 5 to 8 minutes or until light and fluffy. Beat in egg yolks, 1 at a time, beating well after each addition. Beat in brandy extract.
3. Sift flour, baking powder and salt over sugar mixture; fold in.
4. In a medium bowl, beat egg whites until stiff but not dry. Fold beaten egg whites into batter. Spread batter evenly in prepared pans; smooth tops.
5. Bake in preheated oven 30 to 35 minutes or until centers spring back when lightly pressed. Cool in pans on a wire rack 5 minutes. Remove from pans; cool completely on wire rack.
6. For topping and filling, make and bake Lacy Ginger Wafers as directed on page 312. Remove 6 wafers from baking sheet immediately; roll wafers, 1 at a time, around a wooden-spoon handle to make cone shapes. Remove cones from spoon handle; cool on a wire rack. Cool remaining wafers on wire rack; break into small pieces when cool.
7. In a medium bowl, beat cream until soft peaks form. Beat in powdered sugar and brandy. Spoon about 1 cup whipped-cream mixture into a pastry bag fitted with a medium rosette tip; set aside.
8. Place 1 cake layer, bottom-side up, on a serving plate; spread with 1/3 of remaining whipped-cream mixture. Sprinkle 2 tablespoons broken wafers over cream mixture. Top with remaining cake layer, bottom-side down. Spread remaining cream mixture around side and top of cake. Press remaining broken wafers onto side of cake.
9. Pipe reserved cream mixture into wafer cones; place on top of cake like spokes of a wheel. Pipe rosettes around edge and in center. Refrigerate until served. Makes 6 to 8 servings.

# Lemon Pound Cake

1 cup butter or margarine, room temperature
1-1/2 cups granulated sugar
6 eggs
Grated peel and juice of 2 lemons
1-1/2 cups sifted all-purpose flour
1 tablespoon baking powder
1 teaspoon salt
3/4 cup milk
Powdered sugar

1. Preheat oven to 350F (175C). Grease and flour a 12-cup Bundt pan.
2. In a large bowl, beat butter or margarine and granulated sugar 5 to 8 minutes or until light and fluffy. Beat in eggs, 1 at a time, beating well after each addition.
3. Beat in lemon peel and lemon juice until blended.
4. Sift flour, baking powder and salt into a medium bowl. Add flour mixture to sugar mixture alternately with milk; beat until blended. Pour batter into prepared pan; smooth top.
5. Bake in preheated oven 55 to 60 minutes or until a wooden pick inserted in center comes out clean. Cool in pan on a wire rack 10 minutes. Remove from pan; cool completely on wire rack.
6. Place cake on a serving plate. Sift powdered sugar over top immediately before serving. Makes 12 to 18 servings.

Orange-Meringue Gâteau

# Orange-Meringue Gâteau

*Cake:*
2 eggs, separated
3 tablespoons orange juice
1/2 cup sugar
1 tablespoon grated orange peel
3/4 cup sifted cake flour
1/2 teaspoon baking powder
2 tablespoons sweet sherry

*Meringue Layers:*
2 egg whites
1/3 cup superfine sugar
1/2 teaspoon almond extract
1/2 cup ground toasted almonds
1 oz. semisweet chocolate, melted, cooled

*Filling & Decoration:*
1-1/2 cups whipping cream
3 to 4 tablespoons powdered sugar
1 (15-oz.) can mandarin-orange sections, drained

**1.** Preheat oven to 350F (175C). Grease and flour an 8-inch-round cake pan.
**2.** To prepare cake, in a medium bowl, beat egg yolks and orange juice until foamy. Beat in sugar until thickened and lemon-colored. Fold in grated orange peel.
**3.** Sift flour and baking powder over egg-yolk mixture; fold in.
**4.** In a medium bowl, beat egg whites until stiff but not dry. Fold beaten egg whites into egg-yolk mixture. Pour batter into prepared pan; smooth top.
**5.** Bake in preheated oven 25 to 30 minutes or until a wooden pick inserted in center comes out clean. Cool in pan on a wire rack 10 minutes. Remove from pan; cool completely on wire rack.
**6.** Place cake on a flat plate. With a fork or skewer, make holes in top of cake; sprinkle with sherry. Set aside.
**7.** Preheat oven to 300F (150C). To make meringue layers, line a large baking sheet with parchment paper. Draw 2 (8-inch) circles on parchment paper. In a medium bowl, beat egg whites until stiff but not dry. Gradually beat in sugar; beat until stiff and glossy. Beat in almond extract. Fold ground almonds into beaten egg whites. Spread meringue evenly over circles, keeping meringue inside of circles.
**8.** Bake in preheated oven 30 to 35 minutes or until layers are firm and lightly browned. Remove from oven; score 1 layer into 8 equal wedges. Cool both layers on baking sheet on a wire rack 10 minutes. Carefully remove layers from paper; cool completely on wire rack.
**9.** Place scored layer on a flat surface; cut into wedges. Spoon melted chocolate into a pastry bag fitted with a small plain writing tip. Pipe chocolate in a wavy line over each wedge. Set wedges aside.
**10.** To make filling, in a medium bowl, beat cream until soft peaks form. Beat in powdered sugar.
**11.** Place unscored meringue layer on a serving plate; spread with 1/3 of whipped-cream mixture. Cover with 1/2 of oranges; top with cake. Cover cake layer with 1/3 of whipped-cream mixture. Spoon remaining whipped-cream mixture into a pastry bag fitted with a medium star tip.
**12.** Pipe whipped-cream mixture in 8 spokes on top of cake, starting at center and working toward outer edge. Pipe whipped-cream stars around edge of cake. Reserve 1 orange section; place remaining orange sections between spokes of whipped cream.
**13.** Place meringue wedges along spokes of whipped cream, pressing 1 long side of wedge down slightly. Overlap wedges at cake center. Pipe a swirl of whipped-cream mixture in center; decorate swirl with reserved orange section. Refrigerate until served. Makes 8 servings.

# Petits Fours

*Cake:*
**4 eggs**
**3/4 cup sugar**
**1 teaspoon vanilla extract**
**3/4 cup cake flour**
**1/2 teaspoon salt**
**3 tablespoons butter, melted**

*Topping:*
**1 (12-oz.) jar apricot jam or preserves**
**1/4 cup water**
**10 oz. marzipan, tinted yellow, page 332**

*Icing:*
**1 (16-oz.) pkg. powdered sugar**
**1/4 cup water**
**3 tablespoons light corn syrup**
**Red, green and yellow food coloring**

*For decoration:*
**Nuts, candied cherries, small jelly candies,**
**sprinkles and silver dragees**

**1.** Preheat oven to 350F (175C). Grease a 13" x 9" baking pan. Line bottom of pan with waxed paper; grease paper. Dust paper and sides of pan with flour.

**2.** Combine eggs and sugar in a large bowl set over a pan of barely simmering water. Let stand about 5 minutes or until warm to the touch. Beat eggs and sugar about 8 minutes or until thick and lemon-colored and mixture has doubled in volume. Remove from pan; beat in vanilla.

**3.** Sift flour and salt over beaten egg mixture, folding in while sifting. Fold in butter only until streaks disappear. Pour batter into prepared pan; smooth top.

**4.** Bake in preheated oven 20 to 25 minutes or until center springs back when lightly pressed. Cool in pan on a wire rack 10 minutes. Remove from pan; peel off lining paper. Cool completely on wire rack.

**5.** To make topping, press apricot jam through a fine strainer into a small saucepan; stir in water. Cook, stirring, 2 to 3 minutes or until mixture is smooth. Cool slightly.

**6.** Roll out marzipan between 2 sheets of waxed paper to a 13" x 9" rectangle.

**7.** Brush top of cake with melted apricot jam. Remove 1 sheet of waxed paper from marzipan. Invert marzipan onto top of cake; peel off waxed paper. Trim edges even with cake. Cut cake into 1-1/2-inch squares, rectangles, circles or triangles.

**8.** To make icing, combine powdered sugar, 1/4 cup water and corn syrup in top of a double boiler set over simmering water. Cook, stirring constantly, until sugar dissolves and mixture is smooth. Divide icing into several bowls; tint with food coloring as desired.

**9.** Brush cut surface of cakes with apricot jam. Place coated cakes on a wire rack set over a jelly-roll pan, using a separate rack for each icing color. Spoon icing over cakes, covering marzipan and sides completely. Let stand until icing is set. Scrape up excess icing from pan; reheat if necessary. Again spoon icing over cakes. Let stand until icing is set. Decorate as desired with nuts, candied cherries, small candies, sprinkles or dragees. Makes 36 to 42 petits fours.

# Double-Chocolate Cupcakes

*Cupcakes:*
1/2 cup butter or margarine, room temperature
3/4 cup sugar
2 eggs
1 teaspoon vanilla extract
2 oz. unsweetened chocolate, melted, cooled
1 cup all-purpose flour
1-1/2 teaspoons baking powder
1/2 teaspoon salt
1/3 cup milk

*Glaze:*
4 to 5 oz. semisweet chocolate
1 tablespoon shortening

1. Preheat oven to 375F (190C). Grease or line a 12-cup muffin pan with paper cupcake liners.
2. To make cupcakes, in a medium bowl, beat butter or margarine and sugar 5 to 8 minutes or until light and fluffy. Beat in eggs until blended. Beat in vanilla and chocolate until combined.
3. Sift flour, baking powder and salt into a medium bowl. Add flour mixture to sugar mixture alternately with milk; beat until blended.
4. Spoon batter into prepared muffin cups, filling cups about half full.
5. Bake in preheated oven 18 to 22 minutes or until tops spring back when lightly pressed. Cool in pan on a wire rack 5 minutes. Remove from pan; cool completely on wire rack.
6. To make glaze, in a small heavy saucepan over very low heat, melt chocolate and shortening, stirring until smooth. Cool slightly. Spoon melted chocolate mixture over top of each cooled cupcake. Let stand until chocolate is set. Makes 12 cupcakes.

# Chocolate & Praline Fancies

*Cake:*
3 eggs
3/4 cup sugar
1 teaspoon vanilla extract
1 cup sifted cake flour
1/2 teaspoon baking powder
1/4 teaspoon salt

*Hazelnut Praline:*
3/4 cup sugar
3/4 cup hazelnuts

*Icing:*
2 tablespoons unsweetened cocoa powder
3 tablespoons hot water
1/2 cup butter or margarine, room temperature
4 cups powdered sugar, sifted
1 teaspoon vanilla extract
3 tablespoons milk

1. Preheat oven to 350F (175C). Grease an 8-inch-square baking pan. Line bottom and sides of pan with waxed paper; grease paper.
2. To make cake, in a medium bowl, beat eggs until foamy. Gradually beat in sugar; beat until mixture is thickened and lemon-colored. Beat in vanilla.
3. Sift flour, baking powder and salt into a medium bowl. Beat flour mixture into egg mixture, beating only until blended. Pour batter into prepared pan; smooth top.
4. Bake in preheated oven 30 to 35 minutes or until center springs back when lightly pressed. Cool in pan on a wire rack 5 minutes. Remove from pan, peel off lining paper. Cool completely on wire rack.
5. Line a baking sheet with foil; grease foil. To make praline, place sugar in a medium heavy skillet over low heat. Cook, stirring, until sugar is melted and caramel-colored. Stir in hazelnuts to coat. Cook until sugar is deep golden brown. Remove from heat. Grease a teaspoon; with greased teaspoon, lift out 25 nuts, 1 at a time. Place nuts at 1 end of foil-lined baking sheet. Pour remaining nut mixture onto opposite end of baking sheet. Let stand until hard. Set nuts aside for decoration.
6. Break remaining praline into small pieces; process in a food processor fitted with a steel blade until crushed. Or, place praline between 2 sheets of waxed paper; crush by striking with a rolling pin. Spread crushed praline on sheet of waxed paper; set aside.
7. To make icing, in a small bowl, dissolve cocoa in hot water; cool. In a medium bowl, combine butter or margarine, powdered sugar, vanilla, cooled cocoa mixture and 2 tablespoons milk; beat until smooth. Spoon 3/4 to 1 cup icing into a pastry bag fitted with a small star tip; set aside.
8. Beat enough remaining milk into remaining icing to make a good consistency for spreading. Cut cooled cake into 25 (1-1/2-inch) squares. Spread a thin layer of icing around sides of cake squares; roll frosted sides in crushed praline to coat. Spread a little icing on top; place squares on a serving plate. Pipe reserved icing decoratively on top of squares. Place a reserved whole hazelnut in center of each square. Makes 25 squares.

# Chocolate Toffee Bars

### Shortbread:
3/4 cup butter or margarine, room temperature
1/2 cup sugar
1-1/2 cups all-purpose flour

### Topping:
1/2 cup butter or margarine
1/4 cup sugar
2 tablespoons light corn syrup
2/3 cup sweetened condensed milk
4 oz. semisweet chocolate
1 tablespoon shortening

**1.** Preheat oven to 325F (160C). Lightly grease an 8- or 9-inch square baking pan.
**2.** To make shortbread, in a medium bowl, beat butter or margarine and sugar 5 to 8 minutes or until light and fluffy. Stir in flour to make a smooth dough. Knead dough in bowl 8 to 10 strokes. Pat out dough evenly in bottom of greased pan. Prick dough with a fork.
**3.** Bake in preheated oven 35 to 40 minutes or until golden. Cool in pan on a wire rack.
**4.** To make topping, in a medium saucepan over low heat, combine butter or margarine, sugar, corn syrup and condensed milk. Cook, stirring, until mixture comes to a boil. Boil 5 to 7 minutes or until mixture is toffee-colored and thickened, stirring occasionally. Cool slightly. Spread over cooled shortbread in pan. Let stand until cool.
**5.** In a small heavy saucepan over very low heat, melt chocolate and shortening. Cook, stirring until smooth. Cool slightly. Spread chocolate over cooled toffee. Let stand until chocolate is set. Cut into bars; remove from pan. Makes 20 bars.

Clockwise from top left: Double-Chocolate Cupcakes, Chocolate & Praline Fancies, Chocolate Toffee Bars

# Upside-Down Peach Cake

*Topping*:
1/4 cup butter or margarine
1/2 cup firmly packed light-brown sugar
1 maraschino cherry
1 (29-oz.) can peach slices, well drained

*Cake*:
1/3 cup butter or margarine, room temperature
1 cup sugar
1 egg
3/4 teaspoon almond extract
1-1/2 cups cake flour
2 teaspoons baking powder
1/2 teaspoon salt
2/3 cup milk

**1.** Preheat oven to 350F (175C). To make topping, place 1/4 cup butter or margarine in a 9-inch-square baking pan; place in preheated oven until butter or margarine melts. Stir in brown sugar. Place cherry in center of brown sugar mixture. Arrange peach slices in rows around cherry.
**2.** To make cake, in a medium bowl, beat butter or margarine and sugar 5 to 8 minutes or until light and fluffy. Beat in egg and almond extract until blended.
**3.** Sift flour, baking powder and salt into a medium bowl. Add flour mixture to sugar mixture alternately with milk; beat until blended. Spread batter evenly over fruit in pan.
**4.** Bake in preheated oven 40 to 45 minutes or until a wooden pick inserted in center comes out clean. Cool in pan on a wire rack 2 minutes.
**5.** Place a serving plate over pan; invert cake onto plate. Leave pan in place 2 to 3 minutes. Remove pan carefully. Serve warm. Makes 9 to 12 servings.

1/Spread sides of cake circles with apricot jam.

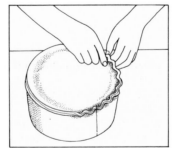
2/Flute to make a decorative border.

# Marzipan-Covered Cake

*Cake*:
1/2 cup butter or margarine, room temperature
1-1/4 cups sugar
3 eggs
1 teaspoon vanilla extract
2 cups all-purpose flour
1 tablespoon baking powder
1/2 teaspoon salt
1 cup milk
Few drops red food coloring

*Filling & Decoration*:
1/2 cup apricot jam, melted, cooled
2 (7-oz.) pkgs. marzipan, tinted yellow, box below
Sugar-coated marzipan fruit, if desired

**1.** Preheat oven to 350F (175C). Grease and flour 2 (8-inch) round cake pans.
**2.** To make cake, in a medium bowl, beat butter or margarine, sugar, eggs, vanilla, flour, baking powder, salt and milk with electric mixer at low speed 1 minute or until blended.
**3.** Increase speed to high; beat 3 minutes, scraping down side of bowl occasionally. Pour 1/2 of batter into 1 prepared pan. Tint remaining batter pink with a few drops of red food coloring. Stir until thoroughly blended.
**4.** Pour pink batter into second prepared pan. Smooth tops.
**5.** Bake in preheated oven 30 to 35 minutes or until a wooden pick inserted in center comes out clean. Cool in pans on a wire rack 5 minutes. Remove from pans; cool completely on wire rack.
**6.** To make checkered effect, cut a 4-inch circle from center of each cake. Remove 4-inch circles. Spread sides of cake circles with apricot jam. Place plain ring on a serving plate; place pink center in plain ring. Place plain center in pink ring. See illustration opposite.
**7.** Spread bottom layer with apricot jam; top with remaining layer. Spread top and side of cake with apricot jam.
**8.** Place 1/2 of marzipan between 2 sheets of waxed paper; roll out to a 24" x 3" rectangle. Place around side of cake, extending marzipan about 1/2 inch above top edge of cake. Roll out remaining marzipan to a 9-inch circle; place on top of cake, turning edge up. Pinch edges together; flute to make a decorative border.
**9.** Brush bottoms of marzipan fruit with apricot jam; place around top edge of cake in a decorative pattern, if desired. Makes 8 to 10 servings.

> To tint marzipan, knead marzipan on a sheet of waxed paper until soft and pliable. Add about 8 drops of yellow food coloring for 2 (7-ounce) packages; knead until thoroughly blended.

Left to right: Marzipan-Covered Cake, Iced Orange Squares

# Iced Orange Squares

*Cake:*
**3/4 cup butter or margarine, room temperature**
**1-1/4 cups sugar**
**3 eggs**
**2-1/2 cups all-purpose flour**
**1-1/2 teaspoons baking soda**
**1-1/4 cups orange juice**
**1 tablespoon grated orange peel**

*Icing:*
**1-1/4 cups powdered sugar, sifted**
**3 tablespoons orange juice**

**1.** Preheat oven to 350F (175C). Grease and flour a 13" x 9" baking pan.
**2.** To make cake, in large bowl, beat butter or margarine, sugar, eggs, flour, baking soda, orange juice and orange peel with an electric mixer at low speed 1 minute or until blended. Increase speed to high; beat 3 minutes, scraping down side of bowl occasionally. Pour batter into prepared pan; smooth top.
**3.** Bake in preheated oven 45 to 50 minutes or until a wooden pick inserted in center comes out clean. Cool in pan on a wire rack 15 minutes.
**4.** To make icing, in a small bowl, beat powdered sugar and orange juice until smooth. Spoon icing over top of warm cake in pan. Cool iced cake completely in pan on wire rack. Cut into squares; remove from pan. Makes 18 to 24 squares.

# Simnel Cake

1 cup butter or margarine, room temperature
1 cup sugar
3 eggs
1 cup dark raisins
1 cup golden raisins
1 cup currants
1/2 cup coarsely chopped red candied cherries
1/2 cup chopped mixed candied fruit
3 tablespoons dark rum or sweet sherry
3 tablespoons orange juice
2 cups sifted all-purpose flour
1 teaspoon baking powder
1 teaspoon ground cinnamon
1 teaspoon ground allspice
2 (7-oz.) pkgs. marzipan
1 egg yolk beaten with 1 tablespoon milk for glaze

*To decorate:*
Sugared flowers, if desired
Ribbons, if desired

1. Preheat oven to 325F (165C). Grease an 8-inch spring-form pan or deep cake pan. Line bottom and side of pan with waxed paper; grease paper.
2. In a large bowl, beat butter or margarine and sugar 5 to 8 minutes or until light and fluffy. Beat in eggs, 1 at a time, beating well after each addition. Stir in raisins, currants, cherries, mixed fruit, rum or sherry and orange juice until combined.
3. Sift flour, baking powder, cinnamon and allspice over fruit mixture; fold in.
4. Place 1 package of marzipan between 2 sheets of waxed paper; roll out to an 8-inch circle.
5. Spoon 1/2 of cake batter into prepared pan. Place marzipan circle over batter. Spoon remaining cake batter over marzipan; smooth top.
6. Bake in preheated oven 2 hours 30 minutes to 3 hours or until cake center springs back when lightly pressed. Remove from oven; cool completely in pan on a wire rack.
7. Increase oven temperature to 425F (220C). Remove cooled cake from pan, peel off lining paper. Place cake on a small baking sheet. Place remaining marzipan between 2 sheets of waxed paper; roll out to an 8-inch circle. Brush top of cake with egg-yolk glaze. Place marzipan circle on top of cake; flute edge. Score marzipan in a lattice pattern with a blunt knife. Brush lightly with egg-yolk glaze.
8. Bake in preheated oven 10 to 12 minutes or until marzipan is lightly browned. Remove cake from baking sheet; cool completely on wire rack.
9. Place cake on a serving plate. Decorate with flowers and ribbons, if desired. Makes 16 to 24 servings.

Simnel Cake

Left to right: Carrot Layer Cake; Lacy Brandy Wafers,
page 312

# Carrot Layer Cake

**Cake:**
1 cup vegetable oil
1 cup firmly packed light-brown sugar
1/2 cup granulated sugar
3 eggs
2-1/4 cups all-purpose flour
2 teaspoons baking soda
1 teaspoon ground cinnamon
1/2 teaspoon freshly grated nutmeg
1/2 teaspoon ground cloves
1/2 teaspoon salt
1-3/4 to 2 cups grated carrots (about 4 medium carrots)
3/4 cup chopped walnuts or pecans

**Cream-Cheese Frosting:**
1 (8-oz.) pkg. cream cheese, room temperature
2 to 3 tablespoons lemon juice
3-1/2 cups sifted powdered sugar
About 1/3 cup finely chopped walnuts or pecans

**1.** Preheat oven to 350F (175C). Grease and flour 2 (9-inch) round cake pans.
**2.** To make cake, in a large bowl, beat oil, sugars and eggs until well blended. Sift flour, baking soda, cinnamon, nutmeg, cloves and salt over sugar mixture. Beat until thoroughly blended. Fold in carrots and nuts. Pour batter into prepared pans; smooth tops.
**3.** Bake in preheated oven 35 to 40 minutes or until a wooden pick inserted in center comes out clean. Cool in pans on a wire rack 10 minutes. Remove from pans; cool completely on wire racks.
**4.** To make frosting, in a medium bowl, beat cream cheese until light and fluffy. Beat in lemon juice and powdered sugar; beat until smooth and frosting is a good consistency for spreading.
**5.** Place 1 cooled layer, bottom-side up, on a serving plate; spread with a thin layer of frosting. Top with remaining layer, bottom-side down. Spread remaining frosting around side and over top of cake. Sprinkle side and top edge of frosted cake with nuts. Refrigerate until served. Makes 8 to 10 servings.

# Glazed Fruitcake

*Cake:*
3/4 cup butter or margarine, room temperature
1 cup sugar
3 eggs
1/3 cup chopped blanched almonds
1/4 cup chopped red candied cherries
1/4 cup chopped crystallized ginger
1/4 cup chopped candied pineapple
1/3 cup chopped dried apricots
1/4 cup finely ground blanched almonds
1-3/4 cups all-purpose flour
1 teaspoon baking powder

*Topping:*
1/4 cup apricot jam
1 tablespoon water
2 tablespoons chopped red candied cherries
2 tablespoons chopped candied orange peel
2 tablespoons chopped blanched almonds

**1.** Preheat oven to 300F (150C). Grease a deep 8-inch-round cake pan or springform pan. Line bottom and side of pan with waxed paper. Grease paper.
**2.** To make cake, in a large bowl, beat butter or margarine and sugar 5 to 8 minutes or until light and fluffy. Beat in eggs, 1 at a time, beating well after each addition.
**3.** Stir in chopped almonds, candied cherries, crystallized ginger, candied pineapple and dried apricots until combined. Fold in ground almonds.
**4.** Sift flour and baking powder over fruit mixture; fold in. Spoon into prepared pan; smooth top.
**5.** Bake in preheated oven 2 hours 30 minutes or until a wooden pick inserted in center comes out clean. Cool in pan on a wire rack 30 minutes. Remove from pan; peel off lining paper. Cool completely on wire rack.
**6.** To make topping, press apricot jam through a sieve into a small saucepan. Cook, stirring, until jam is melted. Stir in water, candied cherries, candied orange peel and almonds. Spread warm mixture over top of cooled cake. Let stand until set. Cut into wedges to serve. Makes 12 to 14 servings.

# Dundee Cake

*Cake:*
1/2 cup butter or margarine, room temperature
1 cup firmly packed dark-brown sugar
4 eggs
Grated peel of 1 orange
Grated peel of 1 lemon
1 cup currants
1-1/2 cups dark raisins
1-1/2 cups golden raisins
1/3 cup red candied cherries, quartered
1/2 cup chopped mixed candied fruit
2 cups all-purpose flour
1 teaspoon ground allspice
1 teaspoon ground cinnamon
1/4 teaspoon ground nutmeg
1/2 teaspoon baking powder

*To decorate:*
Whole blanched almonds

**1.** Preheat oven to 325F (165C). Grease a deep 8-inch-round cake pan or springform pan. Line bottom and side of pan with waxed paper. Grease paper.
**2.** To make cake, in a large bowl, beat butter or margarine and brown sugar 5 to 8 minutes or until light and fluffy. Beat in eggs, 1 at a time, beating well after each addition. Fold in orange peel, lemon peel, currants, raisins, candied cherries and mixed fruit until combined.
**3.** Sift flour, allspice, cinnamon, nutmeg and baking powder over fruit mixture; fold in. Spoon mixture into prepared pan; smooth top. Decorate top of cake with whole almonds.
**4.** Bake in preheated oven 2 hours 30 minutes to 2 hours 45 minutes or until a wooden pick inserted in center comes out clean. Cool in pan on a wire rack 30 minutes. Remove from pan; peel off lining paper. Cool completely on wire rack. Wrap cooled cake in waxed paper; then wrap with foil. Store in a cool place up to 2 months. Cut into wedges to serve. Makes 12 to 14 servings.

1/To line pan side, cut parchment paper 1 inch longer than inside of pan and 2 inches higher than pan is deep. Snip bottom edge as shown.

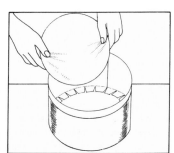

2/Place paper strip around side so snipped edge lies flat. Cut a circle to fit bottom of pan. Place circle over bottom of pan.

Clockwise from top left: Dark Fruitcake, Glazed
Fruitcake, Dundee Cake

# Dark Fruitcake

1 cup butter or margarine, room temperature
1-1/4 cups firmly packed dark-brown sugar
2 eggs
1 cup currants
3/4 cup golden raisins
3/4 cup dark raisins
2-1/3 cups all-purpose flour
2 teaspoons baking powder
1 teaspoon ground cinnamon
1/2 teaspoon ground allspice
2/3 cup dark beer

**1.** Preheat oven to 300F (150C). Grease a deep 8-inch-round cake pan or springform pan. Line bottom and sides of pan with parchment paper, extending paper 1 inch above rim of pan. See opposite page.
**2.** In a large bowl, beat butter or margarine and brown sugar 5 to 8 minutes or until light and fluffy. Beat in eggs, 1 at a time, beating well after each addition. Stir in currants and raisins with a wooden spoon.
**3.** Sift flour, baking powder, cinnamon and allspice into a medium bowl. Add flour mixture to sugar mixture alternately with beer; stir with a wooden spoon until blended. Spoon mixture into prepared pan; smooth top.
**4.** Bake in preheated oven 2 hours 30 minutes or until a wooden pick inserted in center comes out clean.
**5.** Cool completely in pan on a wire rack. Remove from pan; peel off lining paper. Wrap cooled cake in waxed paper; then wrap with foil. Store 2 or 3 days in a cool place before serving. Cut into wedges to serve. Makes 10 to 12 servings.

# Farmhouse Fruitcake

3/4 cup butter or margarine, room temperature
1 cup granulated sugar
3 eggs
2 cups raisins or currants or a combination
1/2 cup chopped mixed candied fruit
2 cups all-purpose flour
2 teaspoons baking powder
1 teaspoon ground cinnamon
1/2 teaspoon ground allspice
1/2 cup milk
Crystal sugar or crushed sugar cubes

---

**1.** Preheat oven to 325F (165C). Grease an 8-inch spring-form pan or deep cake pan. Line bottom and side of pan with waxed paper; grease paper.
**2.** In a large bowl, beat butter or margarine and granulated sugar 5 to 8 minutes or until light and fluffy. Beat in eggs. Stir in raisins or currants and mixed fruit until combined.
**3.** Sift flour, baking powder, cinnamon and allspice into a medium bowl. Add flour mixture to fruit mixture alternately with milk; stir until blended. Spoon mixture into prepared pan; smooth top. Sprinkle with coarse sugar.
**4.** Bake in preheated oven 2 hours or until a wooden pick inserted in center comes out clean. Cool in pan on a wire rack 15 minutes. Remove from pan; peel off lining paper. Cool completely on wire rack. Makes 10 to 12 servings.

Left to right: Christmas-Candle Cake, Farmhouse Fruitcake

# Applesauce-Date Cake

1/4 cup butter or margarine, room temperature
1/2 cup granulated sugar
1 egg
1 teaspoon vanilla extract
1 cup applesauce
1-1/4 cups all-purpose flour
1 teaspoon baking soda
1/2 teaspoon baking powder
1/2 teaspoon ground cinnamon
1/4 teaspoon ground cloves
1/4 teaspoon freshly grated nutmeg
1 cup snipped dates
1/2 cup chopped walnuts or pecans, if desired
Powdered sugar

---

**1.** Preheat oven to 350F (175C). Grease and flour a 9-inch-square baking pan.
**2.** In a medium bowl, beat butter or margarine and sugar 5 to 8 minutes or until light and fluffy. Beat in egg and vanilla until blended. Stir in applesauce until combined.
**3.** Sift flour, baking soda, baking powder, cinnamon, cloves and nutmeg over applesauce mixture; fold in. Fold in dates and chopped nuts, if desired. Pour batter into prepared pan; smooth top.
**4.** Bake in preheated oven 25 to 30 minutes or until center springs back when lightly pressed. Cool in pan on a wire rack. Cut into squares. Sift powdered sugar over squares immediately before serving. Makes 9 servings.

# Christmas-Candle Cake

*Cake:*
3/4 cup butter or margarine, room temperature
1 cup firmly packed light-brown sugar
4 eggs
Grated peel of 1 lemon
2 tablespoons brandy
2 cups currants
1-1/3 cups golden raisins
3/4 cup dark raisins
1/3 cup red candied cherries, halved
1/3 cup chopped mixed candied fruit
1/3 cup chopped blanched almonds
1-3/4 cups all-purpose flour
1/2 cup ground almonds
1 teaspoon ground cinnamon
1/2 teaspoon freshly grated nutmeg
1/2 teaspoon ground allspice

*Topping:*
1/3 cup apricot jam, melted, cooled
2 (7-oz.) pkgs. marzipan

*Icing:*
3 egg whites
1/2 teaspoon cream of tartar
1 (16-oz.) pkg. powdered sugar, sifted

*To decorate:*
1 (7-oz.) pkg. marzipan
Red, yellow and green food coloring

1. Preheat oven to 325F (165C). Grease an 8-inch spring-form pan or deep cake pan. Line bottom and side of pan with waxed paper; grease paper.
2. To make cake, in a large bowl, beat butter or margarine and brown sugar 5 to 8 minutes or until light and fluffy. Beat in eggs and lemon peel; beat until blended. Beat in brandy.
3. Stir in currants, raisins, candied cherries, mixed fruit and chopped almonds until combined. Sift flour, ground almonds, cinnamon, nutmeg and allspice over fruit mixture; stir with a wooden spoon until combined. Spoon mixture into prepared pan; smooth top.
4. Bake in preheated oven 3 hours to 3 hours 30 minutes or until a wooden pick inserted in center comes out clean. Cool completely in pan on a wire rack. Remove from pan; peel off lining paper. Wrap in waxed paper. Overwrap in foil; store in airtight container in a cool place at least 1 month before serving.
5. When ready to serve, brush top and side of cake with melted jam. Roll out 1 package of marzipan between 2 sheets of waxed paper to a 9-inch circle. Center marzipan circle on top of cake; press edges of marzipan on side of cake. Roll out second package of marzipan to a strip 25 inches long and about 2 inches wide. Brush strip with jam, wrap around side of cake, jam-side in. Press edges of marzipan around top edge of cake to make a smooth edge. Place cake on a serving plate.
6. To make icing, in a large bowl, beat egg whites and cream of tartar until soft peaks form. Gradually beat in powdered sugar. Beat until icing stands in sharp peaks when beaters are lifted. Cover bowl with a damp cloth to prevent icing from drying out while using.
7. Spread a thin layer of icing around side and over top of cake, covering marzipan completely. Let stand until icing is firm. Spread with a second layer of icing; let stand until firm. Spread with a third layer of icing, making icing as smooth as possible. Let stand until icing is completely dry.
8. To decorate, divide package of marzipan into small pieces. Tint some pieces red, some green and 1 small piece yellow, page 332. Roll out each tinted piece of marzipan separately between 2 sheets of waxed paper. Cut candle from red marzipan; brush 1 side with melted jam. Starting about 1-1/2 inches from edge of cake, place candle in center, jam-side down. Use remaining red marzipan to make holly berries.
9. Cut holly leaves from green marzipan; brush 1 side with jam; arrange decoratively on top of cake, jam-side down. Decorate leaves with red holly berries. Roll out yellow marzipan; shape into a flame for candle. Brush 1 side with melted jam; attach to top of candle, jam-side down. Tie red and green ribbons around cake, if desired. Makes 16 to 24 servings.

# Creamy Fruit Tart

1 recipe Quick Puff Pastry, Currant & Spice Pastries, page 343

*Filling & Decoration:*
2 tablespoons cornstarch
1/4 cup granulated sugar
1 cup milk
1 egg yolk, beaten
1 teaspoon vanilla extract
3/4 cup whipping cream
1 tablespoon powdered sugar
Strawberries, raspberries, red seedless grapes, sliced bananas and thinly sliced peaches
3 tablespoons apricot jam

1. Make, roll and chill pastry as directed through step 4, page 343.
2. Preheat oven to 425F (220C).
3. On a lightly floured surface, roll out pastry to a 12" x 8" rectangle. Fold pastry in half lengthwise. Cut a 1-inch strip from folded pastry, cutting 1 continuous piece around 3 open edges. Do not cut along folded edge. Unfold large piece of pastry; roll out to a 12" x 8" rectangle.
4. Place pastry rectangle on ungreased baking sheet; prick with a fork. Brush edges lightly with water. Open the 1-inch pastry strip; place around edge of pastry rectangle. Press edges of pastry together to seal. To flute edges, place your fingertip on rim of pastry. Place floured knife against pastry, pointed-end down; draw knife up against pastry edge with quick slanting strokes. Repeat at 1/2-inch intervals all the way around.
5. Bake in preheated oven 20 to 25 minutes or until golden brown. Remove from baking sheet; cool on a wire rack.
6. To make filling, in a small saucepan, whisk cornstarch, granulated sugar and milk until smooth. Cook over low heat, stirring constantly, until mixture is thickened and comes to a boil. Remove from heat. Stir 1/4 cup hot mixture into egg yolk until blended. Return mixture to saucepan; cook, stirring, until thickened. Do not boil.
7. Pour into a large bowl; stir in vanilla. Place a piece of waxed paper over surface of filling to prevent a skin from forming. Cool 30 minutes. Refrigerate 2 to 3 hours.
8. In a medium bowl, beat cream until soft peaks form. Beat in powdered sugar. Stir chilled filling until smooth. Fold in whipped-cream mixture.
9. Spread custard-cream mixture in bottom of cooled pastry shell. Arrange fruit over filling in diagonal rows.
10. Press apricot jam through a fine sieve into a small saucepan. Cook over low heat, stirring, until jam is melted. Cool slightly. Brush melted jam over fruit. Let stand until set. Serve immediately or refrigerate until served. Cut into slices to serve. Makes 6 to 8 servings.

# Chocolate Chiffon Pie

*Crust:*
1 cup chocolate-cookie crumbs
1/4 cup finely chopped almonds
1/4 cup butter or margarine, melted

*Filling:*
1 cup milk
1 cup granulated sugar
2 eggs, separated
1/4 teaspoon salt
1 (1/4-oz.) envelope unflavored gelatin (1 tablespoon)
4 oz. unsweetened chocolate, coarsely chopped
1 teaspoon vanilla extract or 1/2 teaspoon almond extract
1/2 pint whipping cream (1 cup)
2 tablespoons powdered sugar

1. Preheat oven to 375F (190C). To make crust, in a small bowl, combine cookie crumbs, almonds and butter or margarine. Press crumb mixture over bottom and up side of a 9-inch pie pan.
2. Bake in preheated oven 8 minutes. Cool in pan on a wire rack.
3. To make filling, in a medium saucepan, whisk milk, granulated sugar, egg yolks and salt until blended. Sprinkle gelatin over milk mixture; let stand 3 minutes. Stir in chocolate.
4. Cook over low heat, stirring constantly, until chocolate melts and gelatin dissolves. Remove from heat; stir in vanilla or almond extract.
5. Pour chocolate mixture into a large bowl; beat with an electric mixer on high speed 1 to 2 minutes or until mixture is syrupy. Refrigerate 30 to 40 minutes or until almost firm.
6. Beat chilled chocolate mixture with an electric mixer at high speed 2 minutes or until fluffy. In a medium bowl, beat cream until soft peaks form. Beat in powdered sugar. Remove 1 cup whipped-cream mixture; refrigerate. Fold remaining whipped-cream mixture into chocolate mixture.
7. In a medium bowl, beat egg whites until stiff peaks form. Fold beaten egg whites into chocolate mixture. Pour into cooled crust; smooth top. Refrigerate 2 to 3 hours or until set. To serve, decorate top of pie with reserved whipped cream. Cut into wedges to serve. Makes 6 to 8 servings.

Creamy Fruit Tart

# Apricot & Raisin Envelopes

**1 recipe Quick Puff Pastry, Currant & Spice Pastries,**
**opposite**

*Filling:*
**1/2 cup dried apricots, coarsely chopped**
**1/2 cup raisins**
**1-1/4 cups water**
**1/4 cup sugar**
**1/3 cup ground almonds**
**2 tablespoons milk**
**Sugar**

**1.** Prepare, roll and chill pastry as directed through step 4, opposite.
**2.** To make filling, in a medium saucepan, combine apricots, raisins, water and sugar. Bring to a boil over medium heat. Reduce heat. Cover and simmer 20 minutes, stirring occasionally. Remove from heat; stir in almonds. Let cool.
**3.** Preheat oven to 425F (220C). On a lightly floured surface, roll out chilled pastry to a 16" x 12" rectangle. Cut pastry into 12 (4-inch) squares.
**4.** Place 1 tablespoon filling in center of pastry squares. Brush edges of pastry lightly with water. Bring opposite corners in toward center; pinch edges to seal. Place filled envelopes, seam-side up, about 1-1/2 inches apart on ungreased baking sheets. Brush envelopes with milk; sprinkle with sugar.
**5.** Bake in preheated oven 20 to 25 minutes or until pastry is crisp and golden brown. Remove from baking sheets; cool on wire racks. Makes 12 pastries.

Clockwise from bottom left: Currant & Spice Pastries, Apricot & Raisin Envelopes, Mincemeat & Apple Tart

# Mincemeat & Apple Tart

*Pastry:*
2-1/4 cups all-purpose flour
1 teaspoon salt
6 tablespoons vegetable shortening
6 tablespoons butter or margarine
1 egg
3 to 4 tablespoons iced water

*Filling:*
2 tart apples, peeled, cored
2 teaspoons grated orange peel
1 (16-oz.) jar prepared mincemeat (about 1-2/3 cups)
Powdered sugar

---

**1.** To make pastry, in a medium bowl, combine flour and salt. With a pastry blender or 2 knives, cut in shortening and butter or margarine until mixture resembles coarse crumbs. In a small bowl, beat egg and 3 tablespoons water. Sprinkle over flour mixture; toss with a fork until mixture binds together, adding more water if necessary. Shape into a flattened ball. Wrap; refrigerate 30 minutes.
**2.** To make filling, grate apples into a medium bowl. Stir in orange peel and mincemeat until blended.
**3.** Preheat oven to 400F (205C). On a lightly floured surface, roll out 2/3 of pastry to a 1/4-inch-thick rectangle. Use pastry to line an 11" x 7" baking pan; press into corners and up sides of pan. Trim pastry even with rim of pan.
**4.** Spread mincemeat filling evenly in bottom of pastry-lined pan. Roll out remaining 1/3 of pastry; cut into 10 (8" x 1/2") strips. Holding strips by ends, twist ends in opposite directions. Arrange twists in a lattice pattern over filling. Trim strips even with pastry rim. Dampen ends of strips; press down lightly onto pastry rim to seal.
**5.** Bake in preheated oven 35 to 40 minutes or until pastry is golden. Cool in pan on a wire rack. Sift powdered sugar over cooled tart. Cut into squares. Makes 8 servings.

1/Stir with end of a blunt knife to make a soft, lumpy dough.

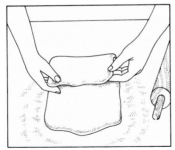

2/Fold into thirds.

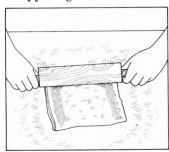

3/With a rolling pin, press edges together to seal.

# Currant & Spice Pastries

*Quick Puff Pastry:*
1-2/3 cups all-purpose flour
1/2 teaspoon salt
3/4 cup butter, chilled
2 teaspoons lemon juice
1/2 cup iced water

*Filling:*
2 tablespoons butter or margarine, melted
1 cup currants
2 tablespoons finely chopped candied orange peel
   or lemon peel
1/4 cup firmly packed light-brown sugar
1 teaspoon ground cinnamon
1/2 teaspoon freshly grated nutmeg
1/2 teaspoon ground allspice
1 egg white beaten with 1 tablespoon water for glaze
Granulated sugar

---

**1.** To make pastry, in a medium bowl, combine flour and salt. Cut butter into small cubes; add to flour. Toss with a fork until cubes are coated. Add lemon juice and water; stir with end of a blunt knife to make a soft, lumpy dough. Do not use a fork or dough will not be the right consistency. Knead in bowl 8 to 10 strokes or until dough binds together. Shape into a 5-inch square. Wrap in plastic wrap or waxed paper; refrigerate 30 minutes. See illustration opposite.
**2.** On a lightly floured surface, roll out chilled dough to a 15" x 5" rectangle. Fold into thirds. With a rolling pin, press edges together to seal; see illustration. Give dough a quarter turn; roll out again to a 15" x 5" rectangle. Fold into thirds. Wrap and refrigerate 20 minutes.
**3.** Repeat rolling and folding dough 2 times for a total of 3 times. Wrap and refrigerate dough 20 minutes after second rolling and folding, 30 minutes after last rolling and folding.
**4.** Preheat oven to 425F (220C). To make filling, in a small bowl, combine butter or margarine, currants, candied peel, brown sugar, cinnamon, nutmeg and allspice. Set aside.
**5.** On a lightly floured surface, roll out chilled dough to 1/4 inch thick. Cut dough into 12 rounds with a floured plain 4-inch cookie cutter. Spoon a heaping tablespoon of currant mixture in center of each pastry round. Brush edges of pastry lightly with water. Gather edges of pastry; draw up to enclose filling completely. Pinch edges to seal.
**6.** Place filled pastry rounds, seam-side down, about 2 inches apart on ungreased baking sheets. Flatten rounds with heel of your hand. Cut 3 parallel slits in center of each pastry round. Brush tops with egg-white glaze; sprinkle with sugar.
**7.** Bake in preheated oven 20 to 25 minutes or until pastry is crisp and golden brown. Remove from baking sheets; cool on wire racks. Makes 12 pastries.

# Pear & Hazelnut Tart

**Pastry:**
1 cup all-purpose flour
1/3 cup finely ground hazelnuts
2 tablespoons sugar
6 tablespoons butter or margarine
1 egg yolk
1 tablespoon iced water

**Filling:**
2 to 3 medium pears, peeled, cored
1/3 cup sugar
3 tablespoons all-purpose flour
1 cup milk
1 egg
1 egg yolk
3 tablespoons brandy, if desired

**1.** Preheat oven to 425F (220C). To make pastry, in a medium bowl, combine flour, hazelnuts and sugar. With a pastry blender or 2 knives, cut in butter or margarine until mixture resembles coarse crumbs. In a small bowl, blend egg yolk and water; sprinkle over flour mixture. Toss with a fork until mixture binds together. Shape into a flattened ball.
**2.** On a lightly floured surface, roll out pastry to an 11-inch circle. Use pastry to line a 9-inch quiche pan or tart pan with a removable bottom. Press pastry into fluted sides of pan. Trim pastry edge even with rim of pan.
**3.** To make filling, thinly slice pears. Arrange pear slices, cut-side down, in pastry-lined pan in a circular pattern. Sprinkle pears with 2 tablespoons sugar.
**4.** Bake in preheated oven 15 to 18 minutes or until pastry is golden and pears are lightly browned. Remove from oven. Reduce oven temperature to 375F (190C).
**5.** In a small bowl, whisk remaining sugar, flour, milk, egg, egg yolk and brandy, if desired, until blended. Pour over partially-baked pears. Bake 30 to 35 minutes or until center is set. Cool in pan on a wire rack. Remove from pan; serve warm or chilled. Cut into wedges to serve. Makes 6 to 8 servings.

# Old-Fashioned Custard Pie

1 recipe 9-inch pastry, Apple & Orange Tart, page 351
1 tablespoon butter or margarine, room temperature

**Filling:**
1-1/2 cups half and half
1 cup milk
2/3 cup sugar
4 eggs
1-1/2 teaspoons vanilla extract
1/2 teaspoon salt
1/4 teaspoon freshly grated nutmeg

**To decorate:**
Sweetened whipped cream
Chocolate curls

**1.** Preheat oven to 425F (220C). Make pastry as directed through step 1, page 351. On a lightly floured surface, roll out pastry to an 11-inch circle. Use pastry to line a 9-inch pie pan. Trim pastry edge to within 1 inch beyond rim of pan. Fold edge under and flute. Brush pastry bottom and side with butter or margarine. Refrigerate while preparing filling.
**2.** To make filling, in a large bowl, whisk half and half, milk, sugar, eggs, vanilla, salt and nutmeg until blended.
**3.** Pull out center oven rack; place chilled pastry-lined pan on rack. Carefully pour custard filling into pastry shell; carefully push oven rack back into oven.
**4.** Bake in preheated oven 25 to 30 minutes or until filling is set. Remove from oven; cool on a wire rack. Refrigerate until served. To serve, decorate top of pie with whipped cream and shaved chocolate. Cut into wedges. Makes 6 to 8 servings.

# Cherry Turnovers

**Filling:**
3/4 lb. fresh or thawed frozen dark sweet cherries, pitted
1/4 cup sugar
2 tablespoons water

**Pastry:**
1-1/3 cups all-purpose flour
1/4 teaspoon salt
1/3 cup vegetable shortening
1/3 cup butter or margarine
2 to 3 tablespoons iced water
About 2 tablespoons milk
Sugar

**1.** To make filling, in a small saucepan over low heat, cook cherries, sugar and water, stirring occasionally, 5 to 7 minutes or until cherries are softened. Let cool.
**2.** To make pastry, in a medium bowl, combine flour and salt. With a pastry blender or 2 knives, cut in shortening and butter or margarine until mixture resembles coarse crumbs. Sprinkle with 2 tablespoons water; toss with a fork until mixture binds together, adding more water if necessary. Shape into a flattened ball.
**3.** Preheat oven to 400F (205C). On a lightly floured surface, roll out pastry to 3/8 inch thick. Cut pastry into 12 rounds with a floured plain 3-1/2- to 4-inch cookie cutter.
**4.** Spoon 2 or 3 cooled cherries, without juice, in center of pastry rounds. Brush edges of pastry lightly with water. Bring edges together over filling, enclosing completely. Pinch and flute seams.
**5.** Place filled turnovers, seam-side up, on ungreased baking sheets. Brush with milk; sprinkle with sugar.
**6.** Bake in preheated oven 20 to 25 minutes or until golden brown. Remove from baking sheets; cool on wire racks. Makes 12 pastries.

**Variation**
Substitute 1 cup cherry pie filling for fresh cherries. Omit step 1.

Pear & Hazelnut Tart

# Lemon Meringue Pie

1 recipe 9-inch pastry, Apple & Orange Tart, page 351

*Filling:*
1-1/2 cups warm water
1 cup sugar
5 tablespoons cornstarch
1/4 teaspoon salt
Grated peel and juice of 2 large lemons
4 egg yolks, beaten
2 tablespoons butter or margarine

*Meringue Topping:*
4 egg whites
1/4 teaspoon cream of tartar
1/2 cup sugar

---

1. Preheat oven to 425F (220C). Make pastry as directed through step 1, page 351. Line a 9-inch pie pan with pastry. Trim pastry edge to 1 inch beyond rim of pan. Fold edge under and flute. Line pastry with foil; fill with pie weights or dried beans.

2. Bake in preheated oven 8 minutes. Remove foil and pie weights or beans. Reduce oven temperature to 375F (190C); bake 5 to 7 minutes or until pastry is golden. Cool completely in pan on a wire rack.
3. To make filling, in a medium saucepan, whisk water, sugar, cornstarch and salt until blended and smooth. Stir in lemon peel and lemon juice. Cook over low heat, stirring constantly, until mixture is thickened and comes to a boil. Remove from heat.
4. Stir 1/2 cup hot mixture into egg yolks until blended. Return mixture to saucepan; cook, stirring constantly, until mixture is thickened. Do not boil. Remove from heat; stir in butter or margarine. Pour into cooled crust; set aside.
5. Preheat oven to 400F (205C).
6. To make meringue topping, in a medium bowl, beat egg whites and cream of tartar until soft peaks form. Beat in sugar, 2 tablespoons at a time; beat until stiff peaks form. Continue beating until sugar is dissolved. Spread meringue over lemon filling to pastry edge. Do not leave any space between meringue and edge of pastry. Swirl meringue decoratively with back of a spoon.
7. Bake in preheated oven 8 to 10 minutes or until meringue is lightly browned. Cool on a wire rack. Refrigerate until served. Cut into wedges to serve. Makes 6 to 8 servings.

# Cherry Basket

1 recipe Puff Pastry, Custard Mille Feuilles,
   opposite

*Filling:*
1-1/2 cups whipping cream
3 tablespoons powdered sugar
2 tablespoons kirsch
1 lb. fresh or thawed frozen dark sweet cherries, pitted
2 to 3 tablespoons slivered almonds

1. Make pastry as directed through step 6, opposite.
2. Preheat oven to 425F (220C).
3. Divide chilled pastry into 3 equal pieces. On a lightly floured surface, roll out each pastry piece to a 8-inch circle. Cut out 2 (4-inch) circles from centers of 2 (8-inch) circles with a floured cookie cutter. Cut 4-inch circles into 8 pastry leaves.

4. Place pastry circle, 2 pastry rings and pastry leaves on ungreased baking sheets.
5. Bake in preheated oven 15 to 18 minutes or until puffed and golden brown. Remove from baking sheets; cool on wire racks.
6. To make filling, in a medium bowl, beat cream until soft peaks form. Beat in powdered sugar and kirsch. Spoon about 3/4 cup whipped-cream mixture into a pastry bag fitted with a rosette tip; set aside.
7. Place pastry circle on a flat serving plate; spread with 1/3 of remaining whipped-cream mixture. Scatter 1/2 of cherries over whipped-cream mixture. Top with 1 pastry ring; spread with whipped-cream mixture. Set aside a few cherries for decoration. Scatter remaining cherries over whipped-cream mixture; top with remaining pastry ring. Spread remaining whipped-cream mixture over top. Sprinkle with almonds. Pipe reserved cream mixture in rosettes around top edge of pastry ring. Decorate with pastry leaves and reserved cherries.
8. Serve immediately or refrigerate up to 4 hours. Cut into wedges to serve. Makes 6 servings.

Left to right: Cherry Basket, Custard Mille Feuilles

# Custard Mille Feuilles

**Puff Pastry:**
1-3/4 cups sifted all-purpose flour
1/2 teaspoon salt
1 cup butter
2 teaspoons lemon juice
About 1/2 cup iced water

**Filling:**
1/4 cup all-purpose flour
1/4 cup granulated sugar
1-1/4 cups milk
1 egg or 2 egg yolks, beaten
1 teaspoon vanilla extract
2 tablespoons butter or margarine
1/2 cup strawberry jam or raspberry jam
Powdered sugar

**1.** To make pastry, in a medium bowl, combine flour and salt. Cut 1/4 cup butter into small cubes; add to flour mixture. Toss with a fork until cubes are coated. Add lemon juice and water; stir with end of a blunt knife to make a soft dough. Do not use a fork or dough will not be the right consistency.

**2.** Knead dough on a lightly floured surface about 3 minutes or until smooth and silky. Shape dough into a 5-inch square. Wrap in waxed paper or plastic wrap; refrigerate 30 minutes.

**3.** Place remaining butter on a flat plate; shape into a 5" x 4" rectangle. Freeze until almost hard.

**4.** On a lightly floured surface, roll out chilled pastry to a 15" x 5" rectangle. Place chilled butter lengthwise on center of pastry. Fold 1/3 of pastry over butter. Fold remaining pastry over pastry-covered butter. Press edges of pastry to seal.

**5.** Give pastry a quarter turn; flatten slightly with a rolling pin. Roll out pastry to a 15" x 5" rectangle; fold into thirds. Wrap and refrigerate 20 minutes.

**6.** Roll and fold pastry 3 more times, for a total of 4 times. Wrap and refrigerate pastry 20 minutes after second and third rolling and folding, 30 minutes after last rolling and folding.

**7.** Preheat oven to 425F (220C). Roll out pastry to a 15" x 12" rectangle. Cut pastry into 3 (12" x 5") strips. Place pastry strips on ungreased baking sheets.

**8.** Bake in preheated oven 15 to 18 minutes or until puffed and golden brown. Remove from baking sheets; cool on wire racks.

**9.** To make filling, in a medium saucepan, whisk flour, granulated sugar and milk until smooth. Cook over low heat, stirring constantly, until mixture is thickened and comes to a boil. Remove from heat. Beat 1/4 cup hot mixture into egg or egg yolks until blended. Return to saucepan; cook, stirring, until thickened. Do not boil.

**10.** Pour hot filling into a medium bowl; stir in vanilla and butter or margarine. Cover surface of filling with waxed paper to prevent skin from forming. Cool 30 minutes; refrigerate until chilled.

**11.** Place 1 cooled pastry strip on a flat serving plate; spread with 1/2 of jam. Spread 1/2 of chilled filling over jam; top with second pastry strip. Spread with remaining jam and filling. Top with last pastry strip; sift powdered sugar over top. Refrigerate up to 4 hours. Cut into pieces to serve. Makes 6 servings.

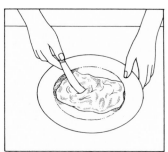

1/Shape remaining butter into a 5" x 4" rectangle.

2/Place chilled butter lengthwise on center on pastry.

# Beignets with Cherry Sauce

1 lb. fresh or thawed frozen dark sweet cherries, pitted
1/2 cup sugar
1/2 cup dry red wine
3 tablespoons water
2 tablespoons red-currant jelly
1 (3-inch) cinnamon stick
1 recipe Choux Paste, Cream Puffs, opposite
Vegetable oil for deep-frying
Sugar

**1.** In a medium saucepan over low heat, combine cherries, sugar, wine, water, jelly and cinnamon stick. Bring to a boil.
**2.** Reduce heat; simmer 20 minutes, stirring occasionally. Discard cinnamon stick. Let cool.
**3.** Make choux paste as directed in steps 2 and 3, opposite. Heat 2 to 3 inches vegetable oil in a deep-fat fryer to 350F (175C) or until a 1-inch bread cube turns golden brown in 65 seconds. Drop heaping teaspoons of dough into hot oil, a few teaspoons at a time. Deep-fry about 2 minutes or until puffed and golden. Remove with a slotted spoon; drain on paper towels. Repeat with remaining dough.
**4.** Place drained beignets on a serving plate; spoon cooled sauce over. Sprinkle with sugar. Makes 6 to 8 servings.

Clockwise from bottom left: Chocolate Eclairs, Beignets with Cherry Sauce, Cream Puffs

# Cream Puffs

*Choux Paste:*
1 cup water
1/2 cup butter or margarine
2 tablespoons sugar
1/4 teaspoon salt
1 cup all-purpose flour
4 eggs

*Filling & Decoration:*
1/2 cup sugar
1/4 cup all-purpose flour
1/4 teaspoon salt
1-1/2 cups milk
2 eggs, beaten
1 teaspoon vanilla extract
2 tablespoons butter or margarine
2 oz. semisweet chocolate, melted, cooled
Powdered sugar

1. Preheat oven to 375F (190C). Grease 2 baking sheets.
2. To make choux paste, in a medium saucepan over medium heat, combine water, butter or margarine, sugar and salt. Bring to a boil. Add flour all at once. Stir with a wooden spoon until dough forms a ball and comes away from side of pan. Let cool slightly.
3. Beat in eggs, 1 at a time, beating well after each addition.
4. Drop dough by heaping tablespoons about 3 inches apart on greased baking sheets to make 12 mounds.
5. Bake in preheated oven 40 to 45 minutes or until puffed and golden brown.
6. Remove from baking sheets; cut a small slit in side of each cream puff to allow steam to escape. Cool completely on wire racks.
7. To make filling, in a medium saucepan, combine sugar, flour and salt. Stir in milk until mixture is smooth.
8. Cook over low heat, stirring constantly, until mixture comes to a boil and begins to thicken. Remove from heat. Stir 1/2 cup hot mixture into eggs until blended. Return mixture to saucepan. Cook, stirring, until thickened. Do not boil. Cool 5 minutes.
9. Stir in vanilla and butter or margarine. Place a sheet of waxed paper over surface of cream filling to prevent a skin from forming. Cool 30 minutes. Refrigerate 2 to 3 hours or until chilled.
10. Split puffs; remove and discard soft interiors. Spoon chilled filling into shells; press tops down lightly.
11. Spoon melted chocolate into a pastry bag fitted with a small plain writing tip. Pipe chocolate in a zigzag line over filled cream puffs. Sift powdered sugar over top immediately before serving. Makes 12 large cream puffs.

## Variation
**Chocolate Eclairs:** Spoon choux paste into a pastry bag fitted with a large plain writing tip. Pipe dough into 4-inch lengths about 2 inches apart on greased baking sheets. Bake in preheated oven 30 to 35 minutes. Fill cooled eclairs with cream filling or sweetened whipped cream. In a small heavy saucepan over very low heat, melt 4 ounces semisweet chocolate; stir until smooth. Cool slightly. Spread melted chocolate over tops of eclairs. Let stand until chocolate is set. Makes 14 to 16 eclairs.

# Paris Brest

1 recipe Choux Paste, Cream Puffs, opposite
1/3 cup slivered or sliced blanched almonds

*Filling & Decoration:*
1/2 pint whipping cream (1 cup)
1 teaspoon almond extract
2 tablespoons powdered sugar
Powdered sugar

1. Preheat oven to 375F (190C). Prepare choux paste as directed in steps 2 and 3, opposite.
2. Line a baking sheet with parchment paper. Draw an 8-inch circle on parchment paper. Spoon dough into a pastry bag fitted with a 3/4-inch plain writing tip. Pipe mixture into a 1-1/4-inch-wide ring inside circle on lined baking sheet. Sprinkle almonds over ring.
3. Bake in preheated oven 35 to 40 minutes or until puffed and golden brown. Remove from baking sheet; peel off paper. Cool on a wire rack.
4. To make filling, in a medium bowl, beat cream until soft peaks form. Beat in almond extract and 2 tablespoons powdered sugar.
5. Split cooled choux ring in half horizontally; remove and discard soft interior. Fill bottom of ring with whipped cream. Replace top; sift powdered sugar over filled ring. Refrigerate until served. Cut into pieces to serve. Makes 6 to 8 servings.

# Crunchy Cheese Tart

**Crust:**
1/4 cup butter or margarine, melted
1 cup vanilla-wafer crumbs
1/4 cup finely chopped walnuts or pecans

**Filling:**
2 (8-oz.) pkgs. cream cheese, room temperature
1/3 cup sugar
2 eggs
2 teaspoons grated lemon peel
2 tablespoons lemon juice

**To decorate:**
Sliced fresh fruit, such as strawberries or kiwifruit

**1.** Preheat oven to 375F (190C). In a small bowl, combine butter or margarine, crumbs and nuts until blended. Press crumb mixture over bottom and up side of a 9-inch fluted quiche pan or flan pan with a removable bottom.
**2.** Bake in preheated oven 8 minutes. Cool in pan on a wire rack.
**3.** To make filling, in a medium bowl, beat cream cheese, sugar, eggs, lemon peel and lemon juice until blended. Pour cream-cheese mixture into cooled crust.
**4.** Bake in preheated oven 30 to 35 minutes or until filling is set. Cool in pan on a wire rack. To serve, remove from pan; place on a serving plate. Decorate top with sliced fruit. Refrigerate until served. Cut into wedges to serve. Makes 6 to 8 servings.

Clockwise from left: Crunchy Cheese Tart, Cherry Strudel, Apple & Orange Tart

# Apple & Orange Tart

*Pastry:*
1-1/3 cups all-purpose flour
2 tablespoons sugar
6 tablespoons butter or margarine, room temperature
1 egg, beaten
1 tablespoon iced water

*Filling:*
Grated peel and juice of 1 small orange
1 lb. medium, tart apples, peeled, thinly sliced
    (about 3 apples)
1/4 cup sugar
2 eggs
1 cup half and half

1. To make pastry, in a medium bowl, combine flour, sugar, butter or margarine, egg and water. Beat with an electric mixer at low speed until blended. Knead dough in bowl 8 to 10 strokes or until smooth. Shape dough into a flattened ball. Wrap in plastic wrap or waxed paper; refrigerate 1 hour.

2. Preheat oven to 425F (220C). On a lightly floured surface, roll out dough to a 3/8-inch-thick circle. Use pastry to line a 10-inch fluted quiche or tart pan with a removable bottom. Trim edge even with pan. Line pastry with foil; fill with pie weights or dried beans.

3. Bake in preheated oven 10 minutes. Remove foil and pie weights or beans; let cool on a wire rack. Reduce oven temperature to 375F (190C).

4. To make filling, in a medium bowl, combine orange peel, orange juice and apple slices; toss to coat with juice. Arrange apple slices in concentric circles in bottom of cooled pastry-lined pan.

5. In a small bowl, beat sugar, eggs and half and half until blended. Pour over apples.

6. Bake in preheated oven 30 to 35 minutes or until filling is set. Cool completely in pan on a wire rack. Serve at room temperature or refrigerate until chilled. Cut into wedges to serve. Makes 8 to 10 servings.

# Cherry Strudel

1/2 (1-lb.) pkg. filo dough, thawed if frozen
1/2 cup butter or margarine, melted
1/2 cup dry sponge-cake crumbs

*Filling:*
1 lb. fresh or thawed frozen dark sweet cherries, pitted
1/2 cup raisins
1/3 cup finely ground almonds
1/3 cup granulated sugar
1/2 teaspoon ground cinnamon
Powdered sugar

1. Preheat oven to 375F (190C). Grease a baking sheet. Unfold filo dough; place on a slightly damp towel. Cover with a second damp towel. Remove 1 filo sheet; place on a dry towel. Brush with butter or margarine; sprinkle with 1 tablespoon cake crumbs. Top with a second filo sheet; brush with butter or margarine. Sprinkle with 1 tablespoon cake crumbs. Repeat with remaining dough, butter or margarine and cake crumbs.

2. To make filling, in a medium bowl, combine cherries, raisins, almonds, granulated sugar and cinnamon. Spoon filling over filo in a 2-inch strip 1-1/2 inches in from both short ends and 1 long side.

3. Roll up strudel, jelly-roll style, starting from long side close to filling and using towel as a guide; lift and roll strudel. Tuck ends in; brush strudel with butter or margarine. Lift strudel gently with towel; place, seam-side down, on greased baking sheet, removing towel.

4. Bake in preheated oven 30 to 35 minutes or until golden brown. Cool on baking sheet on a wire rack. Sift powdered sugar over top. Serve warm or at room temperature. Cut into slices to serve. Makes 6 to 8 servings.

# Cranberry-Apple Tart

*Filling:*
2 cups fresh or frozen cranberries
1 cup sugar
2 tablespoons cornstarch
2-1/2 cups peeled, diced tart apples
1 teaspoon grated lemon peel
1/2 teaspoon ground cinnamon
1/4 teaspoon ground nutmeg

*Pastry:*
1-1/2 cups all-purpose flour
2 tablespoons sugar
1/2 teaspoon salt
1/2 cup butter or margarine
3 to 4 tablespoons iced water

*To serve:*
Sweetened whipped cream or ice cream, if desired

---

**1.** To make filling, in a large saucepan, combine cranberries, sugar, cornstarch, apples, lemon peel, cinnamon and nutmeg. Stirring occasionally, cook over low heat until cranberries begin to pop and mixture thickens. Cool slightly.
**2.** Preheat oven to 400F (205C).
**3.** To make pastry, in a medium bowl, combine flour, sugar and salt. With a pastry blender or 2 knives, cut in butter or margarine until mixture resembles coarse crumbs. Sprinkle with water; toss with a fork until mixture holds together. Gather dough; shape into a ball.
**4.** On a lightly floured surface, roll out dough to a 12-inch circle. Use to line a 10-inch tart pan with removable bottom. Trim pastry edge even with rim of pan. Spoon cooled cranberry mixture into pastry-lined pan.
**5.** Bake in preheated oven 25 to 35 minutes or until crust is golden. Cool on a wire rack.
**6.** Serve warm with sweetened whipped cream or ice cream, if desired. Makes 6 to 8 servings.

# Apple-Mincemeat Tart

1-3/4 cups peeled chopped tart apples (2 large apples)
2 tablespoons water
1 (9-oz.) pkg. condensed mincemeat
1 (17-1/2-oz.) pkg. frozen puff pastry, thawed
1 egg yolk beaten with 1 tablespoon milk for glaze
3 or 4 tablespoons honey

*To serve:*
Vanilla ice cream or sweetened whipped cream

---

**1.** In a large saucepan, combine apples and water. Bring to a boil. Cover; simmer 10 to 12 minutes or until apples are tender. Remove from heat; stir in mincemeat. Cool to room temperature.
**2.** Preheat oven to 425F (220C). Unfold 1 pastry sheet onto a lightly floured surface. Roll out pastry to an 11" x 9" rectangle. Repeat with second pastry sheet.
**3.** Place 1 pastry sheet on ungreased baking sheet. Spread mincemeat filling over pastry to within 3/4 inch of each edge. Brush pastry edges with water. Fold second pastry sheet in half lengthwise. With a floured sharp knife, cut pastry every 1/2 inch, cutting across pastry through fold to within 3/4 inch of outside edge. Place over mincemeat filling with fold at center; unfold pastry.
**4.** Press pastry edges together to seal. Using back of a flat-bladed knife, flute pastry edges as shown below. Brush pastry with egg-yolk glaze. Bake 25 to 30 minutes or until pastry is puffed and golden brown.
**5.** Remove from baking sheet; cool on a wire rack. Brush top of pastry with honey while still warm. Serve warm with vanilla ice cream or sweetened whipped cream. Makes 8 to 10 servings.

### Variation
**Cranberry-Mincemeat Tart:** Substitute 1-1/2 cups fresh or frozen cranberries for apples. In a medium saucepan, combine cranberries, 1/2 cup water, 1/2 cup sugar and 2 teaspoons grated orange peel. Cook 5 to 7 minutes or until skins pop. Add mincemeat to undrained cooked cranberries. Continue as above.

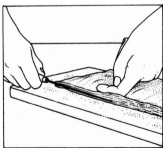

1/Using back of a knife, make several shallow, horizontal cuts in sealed pastry edge.

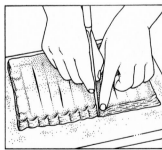

2/Using back of a flat-bladed knife, indent pastry at regular intervals to flute.

# Honey Tart

**Pastry, page 354**

*Filling:*
1/2 cup honey
1/2 cup light corn syrup
1/2 cup ground almonds
2 eggs
1/2 cup whipping cream
2 cups fresh bread crumbs

**1.** On a lightly floured surface, roll out pastry to an 11-inch circle. Use to line a 9-inch flan pan with a removable bottom. Prick pastry with a fork; refrigerate until needed. Gather pastry scraps to make a lattice top.

**2.** Preheat oven to 375F (190C).

**3.** To make filling, in a medium bowl, combine honey, corn syrup, almonds, eggs, cream and bread crumbs until blended. Pour into pastry-lined pan.

**4.** On a lightly floured surface, roll out pastry scraps to 1/8 inch thick. Cut 8 (9" x 1/2") strips. Arrange strips in a lattice pattern over filling. Brush ends of pastry strips with water; press firmly to edge of pastry shell to seal.

**5.** Bake 30 to 35 minutes or until filling is set. Cool completely in pan on a wire rack. Makes 6 to 8 servings.

Left to right: Apple-Mincemeat Tart, Honey Tart

# Glazed-Lemon Tart

**Pastry:**
1-1/2 cups all-purpose flour
3 tablespoons sugar
1/2 teaspoon salt
1/2 cup butter or margarine
1 egg
2 to 3 tablespoons iced water

**Filling:**
3 eggs
3/4 cup sugar
1/4 cup butter or margarine, melted
Grated peel and juice of 3 lemons

**To decorate:**
1/4 cup sugar
1 cup water
1 lemon, thinly sliced

Left to right: Fresh Grape Tart, Glazed-Lemon Tart, French Apple Tart

**1.** To make pastry, in a medium bowl, combine flour, sugar and salt. With a pastry blender or 2 knives, cut in butter or margarine until mixture resembles coarse crumbs. In a small bowl, beat egg with 2 tablespoons water. Sprinkle egg mixture over flour; toss with a fork until pastry holds together. Add remaining water, if necessary. Shape pastry into a ball.
**2.** On a lightly floured surface, roll out pastry to an 11-inch circle. Line a 9-inch quiche pan or flan pan with a removable bottom. Trim pastry edge even with rim of pan. Refrigerate 30 minutes.
**3.** Preheat oven to 375F (190C). To make filling, in a medium bowl, combine eggs, sugar, butter or margarine, grated lemon peel and lemon juice until blended. Set aside.
**4.** Prick chilled pastry with a fork. Line pastry with foil; fill foil with pie weights or dried beans.
**5.** Bake in preheated oven 10 minutes. Remove foil and pie weights or beans; bake 5 minutes longer. Pour filling into baked pastry. Bake 25 to 30 minutes or until filling is set. Cool on a wire rack.
**6.** To decorate, place sugar and water in a small heavy saucepan over low heat. Boil 2 minutes. Add lemon slices; boil until syrup is almost gone. Remove lemon slices with a slotted spoon; place on a flat plate. Let stand until cool. Cut cooled lemon slices in half; arrange around inside edge of tart. Makes 6 to 8 servings.

# French Apple Tart

*Pastry:*
1-1/2 cups all-purpose flour
2 tablespoons sugar
1/2 teaspoon salt
1/2 cup butter or margarine
3 or 4 tablespoons iced water

*Filling:*
4 tart apples, peeled, cored, halved
2 tablespoons cornstarch
5 tablespoons sugar
1-1/2 cups milk
3 egg yolks, beaten
1 teaspoon vanilla extract
1/4 cup butter

1. To make pastry, in a medium bowl, combine flour, sugar and salt. With a pastry blender or 2 knives, cut in butter or margarine until mixture resembles coarse crumbs. Sprinkle with 3 tablespoons water; toss with a fork until mixture holds together. Add remaining water, if necessary.

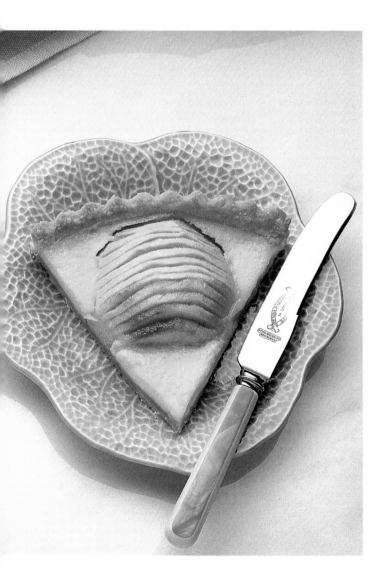

2. On a lightly floured surface, roll out dough to a 12-inch circle. Use to line a 10-inch quiche pan or flan pan with removable bottom. Refrigerate 30 minutes.
3. Place an apple half, cut-side down, on a flat surface; make narrow slashes to create an apple fan, see photo. Repeat with remaining apples. Arrange apples, flat-side down, in bottom of pastry-lined pan.
4. Preheat oven to 375F (190C). In a medium saucepan, blend cornstarch, 1/4 cup sugar and milk until smooth. Cook over low heat until thickened, stirring constantly. Stir 1/4 cup hot custard into egg yolks until blended. Return mixture to saucepan; cook until thickened. Stir in vanilla.
5. Pour custard around apples. Sprinkle remaining 1 tablespoon sugar over apples; dot with butter.
6. Bake in preheated oven 50 to 60 minutes or until custard is set. Cool on a wire rack. Makes 8 servings.

# Fresh Grape Tart

*Pastry:*
1-1/2 cups all-purpose flour
2 tablespoons sugar
1/2 teaspoon salt
1/2 cup butter or margarine
3 or 4 tablespoons iced water

*Filling:*
3/4 lb. seedless green grapes
1/2 lb. seedless red or black grapes

*Glaze:*
1/4 cup apricot jam
1 tablespoon sweet sherry

*To serve:*
Sweetened whipped cream, if desired

1. Preheat oven to 425F (220C). To make pastry, in a medium bowl, combine flour, sugar and salt. With a pastry blender or 2 knives, cut in butter or margarine until mixture resembles coarse crumbs. Sprinkle with 3 tablespoons water; toss with a fork until mixture holds together. Add remaining water, if necessary. Shape pastry into a ball.
2. On a lightly floured surface, roll out dough to a 12-inch circle. Use to line a 10-inch quiche pan or flan pan with removable bottom. Prick pastry with fork; line with foil. Fill foil with pie weights or dried beans. Bake 10 minutes. Remove foil and pie weights or beans; bake 5 minutes longer or until golden brown. Cool completely on a wire rack. Reduce oven temperature to 400F (205C).
3. Arrange grapes in alternating circles in bottom of cooled crust, beginning with green grapes.
4. Bake 12 to 15 minutes. Cool on a wire rack.
5. Press jam through a sieve into a small saucepan. Cook over low heat until jam is melted, stirring constantly. Cool slightly; stir in sherry. Brush glaze over grapes; let stand until set.
6. Serve at room temperature or chilled, with sweetened whipped cream, if desired. Makes 6 to 8 servings.

# Lemon-Pineapple Mold

1 (20-oz.) can pineapple chunks (juice pack)
2 cups boiling water
1 (6-oz.) pkg. lemon-flavored gelatin
1/2 cup fresh orange juice

1. Lightly oil a decorative 4-cup mold; invert onto paper towels to drain.
2. Drain pineapple chunks, reserving juice.
3. Pour boiling water into a large bowl. Stir in gelatin until dissolved. Stir in reserved pineapple juice and orange juice.
4. Refrigerate until mixture has consistency of unbeaten egg whites.
5. Fold drained pineapple chunks into partially set gelatin mixture. Pour into oiled mold. Refrigerate 6 hours or until firm. To serve, invert onto a serving plate; remove mold. Makes 4 to 6 servings.

# Quick Creamy Delight

36 (2-1/2-inch) vanilla cookies
About 1 cup milk
1 (6-oz.) pkg. miniature chocolate pieces
2 tablespoons orange-flavored liqueur
1 (12-oz.) carton frozen whipped topping, thawed

*To decorate:*
Chocolate curls

*The cookies and topping blend together as this dessert stands. This is an easy way to impress guests; they won't believe how simple this is to make.*

1. Arrange 1/4 of cookies in bottom of a 1-1/2-quart casserole or serving dish, dipping each cookie in milk before placing in casserole or dish. Sprinkle with 1/4 of chocolate pieces.
2. Stir liqueur into whipped topping until blended. Spread 1/4 of flavored whipped topping over cookies. Repeat layers of dipped cookies, chocolate pieces and whipped topping, ending with whipped topping. There should be 4 layers of each.
3. Refrigerate 8 hours or overnight. Decorate with chocolate curls. Makes 6 to 8 servings.

**Variation**:
Substitute chocolate-chip cookies or chocolate chocolate-chip cookies for vanilla cookies and chocolate pieces.

# Strawberry & Cointreau Cream

8 oz. strawberries, hulled
2 tablespoons sugar
1 to 2 tablespoons Cointreau
1/2 pint whipping cream (1 cup)

1. Slice 4 to 6 strawberries for decoration; set aside. Place remaining strawberries and sugar in a medium bowl; crush with a potato masher.
2. Pour Cointreau and cream into a medium bowl; whip until stiff peaks form. Fold strawberry mixture into whipped-cream mixture.
3. Spoon into individual dessert dishes; top with strawberry slices. Refrigerate until served. Makes 4 servings.

# Blackberry Fluff

1 (17-oz.) can blackberries
1-1/2 teaspoons grated orange peel
1 (1/4-oz.) envelope unflavored gelatin (1 tablespoon)
1/2 cup orange juice
2 egg whites
1/4 cup sugar

*To decorate:*
Whipped cream
Orange-peel strips

1. Drain blackberries, reserving syrup. In a blender or food processor fitted with a steel blade, process blackberries and orange peel until pureed. Press mixture through a sieve to remove seeds; set aside.
2. In a small saucepan, combine gelatin and reserved blackberry syrup. Stir well; let stand 3 minutes. Stir over low heat until gelatin dissolves. Remove from heat; stir in orange juice and sieved blackberries. Refrigerate until mixture mounds when dropped from a spoon.
3. In a medium bowl, beat egg whites until soft peaks form. Gradually beat in sugar; continue beating until stiff and glossy. Fold beaten egg-white mixture into partially set blackberry mixture.
4. Spoon mixture into 4 dessert dishes. Refrigerate 2 to 3 hours or until set.
5. To serve, decorate with whipped cream and orange peel. Makes 4 servings.

Clockwise from top: Lemon-Pineapple Mold, Strawberry & Cointreau Cream, Blackberry Fluff

# Scottish Honey Crunch

3 tablespoons regular rolled oats
6 tablespoons honey
Grated peel and juice of 1/2 orange
2 tablespoons whisky
1-1/4 cups whipping cream

*To decorate:*
Orange slices

---

1. Spread oats on a baking sheet; toast under a broiler until golden brown. Set aside to cool.
2. Combine honey, orange peel, orange juice, whisky and cream in a medium bowl. Beat with an electric mixer until soft peaks form.
3. Stir in toasted oats; spoon into individual glasses. Decorate with orange slices. Makes 4 to 6 servings.

# Pineapple & Kirsch Roll

1 medium pineapple
1 pint whipping cream (2 cups)
1 cup coarsely crushed macaroons
2 tablespoons kirsch

*To decorate:*
Angelica leaves

---

1. Remove green top from pineapple, cut top in half lengthwise, reserving half for decoration. Peel pineapple, removing eyes with a knife point. Slice pineapple; cut each slice in half. Blot slices dry with paper towels. Remove core.
2. Whip cream until stiff peaks form; reserve 1/3 of whipped cream. Stir macaroons into remaining whipped cream.
3. Sandwich halved pineapple slices and macaroon cream; place flat-side down on an oval serving plate. Continue to alternate macaroon cream and pineapple until all pineapple and macaroon cream are gone.
4. Stir kirsch into reserved whipped cream; use to frost filled pineapple. With a spatula, swirl cream frosting to resemble pineapple peel; decorate with angelica leaves. Place reserved pineapple top at 1 end as shown. Refrigerate until served. Makes 4 to 6 servings.

Left to right: Pineapple & Kirsch Roll, Rhubarb Mallow, Scandinavian Raspberry Flummery

# Rhubarb Mallow

1 (16-oz.) pkg. frozen rhubarb, thawed
1 cup water
1-1/4 cups sugar
1 (1/4-oz.) envelope unflavored gelatin (1 tablespoon)
1/4 cup lemon juice
1/2 cup whipping cream
1/2 cup miniature marshmallows

1. In a medium saucepan, combine rhubarb and 1/2 cup water; bring to a boil. Stir in sugar. Cover; simmer 15 to 20 minutes or until tender. Set aside to cool.
2. In a small saucepan, combine gelatin and remaining water. Stir well; let stand 3 minutes. Stir over low heat until gelatin dissolves. Remove from heat; stir in lemon juice. In a large bowl, stir gelatin mixture into cooled rhubarb mixture. Refrigerate until mixture has consistency of unbeaten egg whites.
3. In a medium bowl, beat cream until soft peaks form. Fold whipped cream into partially set rhubarb mixture. Fold in marshmallows. Spoon into individual dessert dishes. Refrigerate several hours or until set. Makes 4 to 6 servings.

# Scandinavian Raspberry Flummery

1 lb. fresh raspberries
About 1 cup water
3/4 cup sugar
1/4 cup semolina

1. Reserve 12 raspberries for decoration. Place remaining raspberries, 1 cup water and 1/2 cup sugar in a medium saucepan. Simmer 5 minutes or until soft. Press mixture through a sieve to remove seeds. Pour into a 2-cup measuring cup; add enough water to make 2 cups.
2. Rinse saucepan to remove any seeds; add raspberry mixture to cleaned saucepan. Bring to a boil; stir in remaining sugar and semolina. Simmer 10 minutes, stirring frequently.
3. Spoon partially set raspberry mixture into a large bowl. With an electric mixer, beat mixture 5 minutes or until light and fluffy. Serve warm in individual dessert dishes. Decorate with reserved raspberries. Makes 4 servings.

# Butterscotch Mousse

1/4 cup cornstarch
3/4 cup packed dark-brown sugar
2 cups milk
2 tablespoons butter or margarine
1 teaspoon vanilla extract
2 egg whites

*To decorate:*
**Whipped cream**
**Chocolate coffee-bean candies**

1. In a medium saucepan, combine cornstarch and brown sugar. Slowly stir in milk. Cook over low heat until thickened, stirring constantly.
2. Cool slightly; stir in butter or margarine and vanilla.
3. In a medium bowl, beat egg whites until stiff but not dry. Fold beaten egg whites into butterscotch mixture. Pour into a serving dish; refrigerate several hours.
4. To serve, decorate with whipped cream and candy. Makes 8 servings.

---

**Chocolate Curls**
**The easy way**—Use a vegetable peeler; pull peeler across a chocolate block to make curls.
**The professional way**—Spread melted chocolate on a cool, dry, hard surface. If possible, use a marble slab for this, because it cools chocolate quickly. Smooth chocolate's surface, if necessary; let harden. Holding the long cutting edge of a large sharp knife at a 45-degree angle, push knife away from you, separating chocolate from work surface. The chocolate will roll and form curls as knife edge moves along under it.

---

# Spiced-Apple Swirl

1-1/4 cups whipping cream
16 oz. plain yogurt (2 cups)
Grated peel of 1 lemon
1 cup apple butter

*To serve:*
**Thin crisp cookies**

---

1. In a medium bowl, whip cream until soft peaks form. Spoon yogurt into a large bowl, fold in lemon peel and whipped cream. Spoon into 8 individual dishes.
2. Top each dish with 2 tablespoons apple butter. With the tip of a knife, swirl apple butter through mixture.
3. Refrigerate until chilled. Serve with thin crisp cookies. Makes 8 servings.

Left to right: Spiced-Apple Swirl, Chestnut Cream, Creamy Toffee Crunch

# Creamy Toffee Crunch

**4 chocolate-covered toffee bars**
**1 egg white**
**1/2 pint whipping cream (1 cup)**

*To decorate:*
**Orange-peel twists**

---

**1.** Place toffee bars in a strong plastic bag. Hold open end of bag securely; coarsely crush toffee bars by pounding with a rolling pin or wooden mallet.
**2.** In a small bowl, beat egg white until stiff but not dry. In a medium bowl, whip cream until stiff peaks form. Fold beaten egg white into whipped cream.
**3.** Stir in crushed toffee bars.
**4.** Spoon mixture into 4 dessert dishes.
**5.** Refrigerate several hours. Decorate with orange-peel twists. Makes 4 servings.

# Chestnut Cream

**3/4 cup whipping cream**
**2 tablespoons rum or brandy**
**1 (8-oz.) can sweetened chestnut puree**

*To decorate:*
**Chocolate curls, opposite**

---

**1.** In a medium bowl, whip cream and rum or brandy until stiff peaks form.
**2.** Gradually fold in chestnut puree. Spoon mixture into a pastry bag fitted with a large star tip.
**3.** Pipe chestnut mixture into 4 dessert dishes. Refrigerate until served.
**4.** Decorate each dessert with chocolate curls. Makes 4 servings.

# Apricot Toasts

1 pound-cake loaf
1/2 cup apricot jam
2 tablespoons sugar
1/2 teaspoon ground cinnamon
16 canned apricot halves, drained

*To decorate:*
Whipped cream
1 tablespoon chopped pistachios or toasted almonds

---

1. Preheat broiler. Cut 4 (3/4-inch-thick) cake slices; reserve remaining cake for another use.
2. Spread each cake slice with 2 tablespoons apricot jam. In a small bowl, combine sugar and cinnamon. Sprinkle sugar mixture over jam.
3. Broil cake slices under preheated broiler until sugar melts and is lightly browned. Top each broiled cake slice with 4 apricot halves. Decorate with whipped cream and nuts. Serve immediately. Makes 4 servings.

Clockwise from top: Beignets with Strawberry Sauce, Layered Chocolate Crunch, Apricot Toasts

# Crunchy Nut Squares

1 cup all-purpose flour
1/2 cup granulated sugar
1 teaspoon ground cinnamon
1/2 teaspoon baking powder
1/2 cup butter or margarine
1 egg, separated
1/4 cup firmly packed brown sugar
1/2 cup chopped almonds, walnuts, pecans or hazelnuts

---

1. Preheat oven to 350F (175C). Grease a 9-inch-square baking pan.
2. In a medium bowl, combine flour, granulated sugar, cinnamon and baking powder. With a pastry blender or 2 knives, cut in butter or margarine until mixture resembles coarse crumbs. With a fork, stir in egg yolk until dough binds together. Press dough onto bottom of prepared pan.
3. Beat egg white until foamy; brush over top of dough. Combine brown sugar and nuts; sprinkle over dough.
4. Bake 20 to 25 minutes or until firm. Cool in pan on a wire rack 10 minutes. Cut into squares while still warm. Cool completely in pan. Makes 16 squares.

# Beignets with Strawberry Sauce

*Strawberry Sauce:*
1/4 cup granulated sugar
1 cup water
2 teaspoons cornstarch
2 tablespoons brandy
1 tablespoon lemon juice
1-1/2 to 2 cups coarsely chopped strawberries
1/2 cup red currants, if desired

*Choux Paste:*
1/2 cup water
1/4 cup butter or margarine
2 tablespoons granulated sugar
1/2 cup all-purpose flour
2 eggs
Vegetable oil for deep-frying
Powdered sugar

1. To make Strawberry Sauce, combine sugar and water in a medium saucepan over medium heat. Bring to a boil, stirring until sugar is dissolved. Boil rapidly, without stirring, 3 minutes or until syrupy. Remove from heat. In a small bowl, blend cornstarch, brandy and lemon juice until smooth. Stir into hot syrup; return pan to heat. Cook until mixture comes to a boil, stirring constantly. Stir in strawberries and red currants, if desired. Simmer 5 to 6 minutes. Cool to room temperature.
2. To make choux paste, combine water, butter or margarine and sugar in a medium saucepan over low heat. Bring to a boil; stir until butter or margarine is melted. Add flour all at once, stirring vigorously with a wooden spoon until dough forms a ball and comes away from side of pan. Stir 1 minute or until smooth. Remove from heat. Beat in eggs, 1 at a time, beating well after each addition. Spoon dough into a pastry bag fitted with a large star tip.
3. Heat 1-1/2 to 2 inches oil in a deep-fat fryer to 375F (190C) or until a 1-inch bread cube turns golden brown in 50 seconds. Pipe a 1-1/2-inch-long piece of choux paste into hot oil. Use a wet knife to cut choux paste from pastry tip. Deep-fry 3 or 4 beignets at a time. Deep-fry 1 to 2 minutes on each side or until golden brown. Remove beignets with a slotted spoon; drain on paper towels.
4. Sprinkle warm beignets with powdered sugar. Serve with Strawberry Sauce. Makes 4 to 6 servings.

# Layered Chocolate Crunch

2 cups chocolate-cookie crumbs
2 teaspoons instant coffee powder
1-1/2 cups whipping cream

*To decorate:*
Chocolate lace, page 386

1. Set aside 1 cup cookie crumbs. In a small bowl, combine remaining cookie crumbs and coffee powder.
2. In a medium bowl, whip cream until soft peaks form; reserve 1/2 cup whipped cream for decoration. Fold coffee mixture into remaining whipped cream.
3. Spoon coffee-and-cream mixture into 6 dessert dishes. Sprinkle reserved cookie crumbs evenly over desserts. Top each dessert with a spoonful of reserved whipped cream. Refrigerate several hours.
4. Decorate with chocolate lace immediately before serving. Makes 6 servings.

**Variation**
Omit coffee powder. Spoon half of crumb-and-cream mixture into serving dishes. Top each with 1 tablespoon strawberry or other jam. Top with remaining crumb-and-cream mixture.

# Cherries in Red Wine

1 lb. dark sweet cherries, pitted
1 cup light red wine
1/4 cup sugar
1/2 teaspoon ground cinnamon
2 teaspoons cornstarch
1/4 cup red-currant jelly

1. Combine cherries, wine, sugar and cinnamon in a medium saucepan. Bring to a boil.
2. In a small bowl, combine cornstarch and red-currant jelly. Stir into hot cherry mixture. Simmer 1 minute, stirring constantly. Cover; cool 5 minutes.
3. Serve warm or cold with vanilla ice cream. If a thicker sauce is desired, remove cherries with a slotted spoon; boil liquid until reduced in volume. Makes 4 servings.

# Banana Flambé

1/4 cup butter or margarine
6 medium bananas, peeled, cut in half lengthwise
1/3 cup packed light-brown sugar
1/4 cup brandy

*To decorate:*
Sliced almonds, toasted

1. Melt butter or margarine in a large skillet. Add bananas; sauté until golden and barely tender.
2. Sprinkle with sugar; stir carefully until bananas are coated. Stir in brandy.
3. Bring to a boil. Immediately ignite brandy; shake skillet until flames die. Decorate with toasted sliced almonds. Makes 6 servings.

**Variation**
**Peach Flambé:** Substitute 4 to 6 peeled, halved and pitted fresh peaches for bananas.

# Brandied Peaches

4 ripe peaches
Lemon juice
2 tablespoons sugar
1/4 cup brandy

1. Dip peaches in boiling water about 20 seconds. Dip immediately in cold water; peel. In a serving bowl, toss peeled peaches in lemon juice.
2. In a small bowl, stir sugar and brandy until sugar dissolves. Prick peaches with a fork or skewer. Pour brandy mixture over peaches.
3. Cover and refrigerate several hours to blend flavors. Makes 4 servings.

Clockwise from top left: Banana Flambé, Brandied Peaches, Cherries in Red Wine, Blackberry & Apple Compote

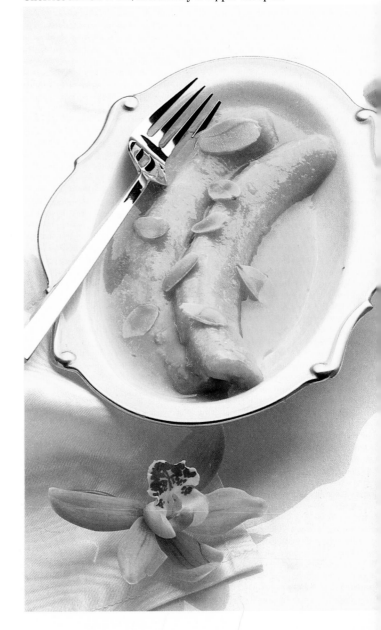

# Blackberry & Apple Compote

1-1/2 to 1-3/4 lb. apples, peeled, cored
1 teaspoon lemon juice
6 tablespoons sugar
1 cup water
8 oz. blackberries, thawed, if frozen
2 tablespoons brandy

*To serve:*
Ice cream or whipping cream, if desired

**1.** Thickly slice apples. Combine sliced apples, lemon juice, sugar and water in a large saucepan. Simmer 5 to 7 minutes or until tender.
**2.** Remove cooked apples with a slotted spoon, reserving cooking liquid. Spoon cooked apple and blackberries into a serving dish.
**3.** Boil cooking liquid until slightly syrupy. Cool slightly; stir in brandy. Pour over fruit; refrigerate until chilled.
**4.** Serve with ice cream or whipping cream, if desired. Makes 4 to 6 servings.

**Variation**
**Pear & Raspberry Compote:** Substitute peeled, cored and sliced pears and raspberries for apples and blackberries. If desired, substitute kirsch for brandy.

# Paskha

1-1/2 lb. cream-style cottage cheese (3 cups)
1/2 cup unsalted butter, room temperature
2 egg yolks
1/2 cup sugar
1/2 teaspoon rose water
2/3 cup dairy sour cream
1/2 cup chopped toasted blanched almonds
1/3 cup raisins
1/3 cup chopped mixed candied fruit
1/3 cup red candied cherries, quartered

*To decorate:*
Red candied-cherry halves
Angelica
Candied orange wedges, if desired

1. Place a sieve over a medium bowl. Add cottage cheese; drain 1 hour. Discard liquid in bowl; press cottage cheese through sieve into bowl. Set aside.
2. Dampen a piece of doubled cheesecloth large enough to line a 5-cup paskha mold or a 6-inch-diameter, 6-inch-deep clean clay flowerpot with a hole in bottom. Line mold or flowerpot with damp cheesecloth.
3. In a large bowl, beat butter, egg yolks and sugar until sugar is dissolved and mixture thickens. Beat in sieved cottage cheese and rose water until smooth. Fold in sour cream, almonds, raisins, candied fruit and quartered candied cherries.
4. Spoon cheese mixture into lined mold; smooth top. Fold ends of cheesecloth over top of mold. Place filled mold on a rack in a shallow pan. Place a small flat plate on top of mold; place a 2-pound weight or a 29 ounce can on plate. Refrigerate 24 hours or longer.
5. Remove weight; uncover top of paskha. Unmold onto a serving plate; carefully remove mold and cheesecloth. Smooth top and side of paskha with a small metal spatula.
6. Decorate with candied-cherry halves, angelica and candied orange wedges, if desired. Refrigerate until served. Makes 8 to 10 servings.

# Raisin Cheesecake

2 (8-oz.) pkgs. cream cheese, room temperature
3/4 cup whipping cream
1/3 cup granulated sugar
2 eggs
2 tablespoons grated lemon peel
1 tablespoon lemon juice
1/2 cup raisins
1/4 cup cornstarch
Pastry, page 354, baked in a 9-inch springform pan
Powdered sugar

1. Preheat oven to 375F (190C).
2. In a large bowl, beat cream cheese, cream, granulated sugar, eggs, lemon peel and lemon juice until blended and creamy. In a small bowl, toss raisins with cornstarch; fold into cheese mixture.
3. Pour cheese mixture into baked pastry shell; smooth top. Bake in preheated oven 40 minutes. Turn off oven; leave cheesecake in oven, with oven door slightly ajar, until cool. Refrigerate until served.
4. To serve, remove cheesecake from pan; place on a serving plate. Dust top with powdered sugar; score in a lattice pattern with a blunt knife. Makes 8 to 10 servings.

### Variation
**Peach or Apricot Cheesecake:** Substitute 1 (8-ounce) can sliced peaches or apricot halves, drained and chopped, for raisins. Beat in cornstarch with cream cheese.

Top to bottom: Paskha, Raisin Cheesecake

# Crème Caramel with Strawberries

**Caramel Syrup:**
1/2 cup sugar
2 tablespoons water

**Custard:**
4 eggs
4 egg yolks
1/3 cup sugar
3-1/2 cups milk, scalded
1 tablespoon finely grated orange peel

**To serve:**
1 pint strawberries, washed

---

**1.** Preheat oven to 325F (165C). Grease an 8-inch cake pan or 6-cup ring mold.
**2.** To make caramel syrup, place sugar and water in a small heavy saucepan over low heat; cook until syrup is golden brown, stirring constantly. Set aside to cool slightly. Pour syrup into bottom of prepared pan or mold, tilting from side to side to coat bottom thoroughly. Set aside.
**3.** To make custard, in a large bowl, beat eggs, egg yolks and sugar until blended. Gradually beat in milk. Stir in orange peel. Pour mixture into syrup-lined pan.
**4.** Set cake pan in a shallow baking dish; pour in enough boiling water to come to within 1/2 inch of cake rim.
**5.** Bake 75 to 85 minutes or until tip of a knife inserted slightly off center comes out clean.
**6.** Remove custard from water bath; cool to room temperature. Serve at room temperature or refrigerate until served.
**7.** To serve, run a knife blade around inside edge of pan. Invert custard onto a serving plate, letting syrup run down side of custard. Remove pan. Serve with strawberries. Makes 6 to 8 servings.

**Variation**
Substitute sections from 3 oranges for strawberries. To section oranges, use a sharp knife to cut peel and bitter white pith from each orange. To free the sections, cut between the flesh and membrane at either side of each section.

---

To test a baked custard, such as Crème Caramel, for doneness, insert a knife blade in custard, slightly off center. The knife blade should come out clean. After cooking, always remove the custard from the water bath before cooling. Cool to room temperature or refrigerate before unmolding.

---

# Coeur à la Crème

1/2 pint whipping cream (1 cup)
2 (8-oz.) pkgs. cream cheese, room temperature
1 egg white
2 tablespoons sugar

---

**1.** Rinse 6 perforated heart-shaped molds. Dampen enough double cheesecloth to line molds and to fold over top of filling.
**2.** In a medium bowl, beat cream until thickened. Beat in cream cheese until smooth. In a small bowl, beat egg white until soft peaks form. Gradually beat in sugar; beat until stiff and glossy. Fold beaten egg-white mixture into cheese mixture.
**3.** Spoon mixture into prepared molds; press down lightly. Fold ends of cheesecloth over filling. Place molds on a rack in a shallow pan. Refrigerator overnight to drain.
**4.** To serve, uncover top of molds. Invert onto individual serving plates; carefully remove molds and cheesecloth. Makes 6 servings.

**Crème Caramel with Strawberries**

# Crème Brûlée

1 pint whipping cream (2 cups)
1 teaspoon cornstarch
1/4 cup granulated sugar
4 egg yolks, slightly beaten
1 teaspoon vanilla extract
1/2 cup firmly packed dark-brown sugar

*Crème Brûlée is a rich smooth custard with a hard caramel glaze.*

1. In a medium saucepan, blend 1/2 cup cream and cornstarch until smooth. Stir in remaining 1-1/2 cups cream and granulated sugar. Cook over low heat until tiny bubbles form around edge of pan, stirring constantly. Remove from heat.
2. Slowly stir 1/2 cup hot mixture into beaten egg yolks until blended. Return to saucepan; cook until mixture is thickened and coats back of a spoon, stirring constantly. Do not boil. Cool slightly. Stir in vanilla.
3. Pour custard into 4 (5- or 6-oz.) ramekins; cool to room temperature. When cool, refrigerate 2 to 3 hours or until set.
4. Preheat broiler. Sprinkle 2 tablespoons brown sugar on top of each ramekin, covering custard completely. Place ramekins 2 to 3 inches from preheated broiler 2 to 3 minutes or until sugar is melted. Watch carefully to prevent burning. Refrigerate 1 to 2 hours or until caramel is hard.
5. Immediately before serving, crack caramel by tapping with back of a spoon. Makes 4 servings.

# Chocolate-Mint Mousse

5 oz. semisweet chocolate, broken into pieces
4 eggs
1/2 cup sugar
3 tablespoons crème de menthe
3/4 cup whipping cream

1. Melt chocolate in the top of a double boiler over boiling water, stirring until smooth. Set aside to cool.
2. In a medium bowl, combine 1 egg, sugar and crème de menthe. Separate remaining eggs. Add egg yolks to sugar mixture; stir to blend. Set bowl over, but not in, a pan of simmering water. Beat with a whisk 5 minutes or until mixture is foamy. Remove bowl from heat; beat 5 minutes longer or until mixture is thick. Fold in melted chocolate. Set aside to cool.
3. In a small bowl, whip cream until soft peaks form. Fold whipped cream into cooled chocolate mixture.
4. In a medium bowl, beat egg whites until stiff but not dry. Fold beaten egg whites into chocolate mixture.
5. Spoon into individual dessert dishes; refrigerate 3 to 4 hours or until thoroughly chilled. Makes 4 to 6 servings.

# Layered Orange Cream

1 (3-1/4-oz.) pkg. vanilla pudding-and-pie-filling mix
2 teaspoons unflavored gelatin powder
3-1/4 cups milk
3 tablespoons orange-flavored liqueur
1/2 pint whipping cream (1 cup)
1 tablespoon powdered sugar
1 (16-oz.) can mandarin oranges, drained

1. In a medium saucepan, combine pudding-and-pie-filling mix and gelatin. Gradually stir in milk; continue stirring until blended. Over low heat, cook until mixture thickens and comes to a boil, stirring constantly.
2. Pour into a large bowl. Place a sheet of waxed paper over surface of pudding to prevent a skin from forming. Cool completely. Stir in liqueur.
3. In a medium bowl, whip cream until soft peaks form. Add powdered sugar; beat until stiff peaks form. Reserve about 2/3 cup whipped cream; refrigerate. Fold remaining whipped cream into pudding. Refrigerate 3 to 4 hours or until thoroughly chilled.
4. To serve, spoon 3 or 4 tablespoons orange cream into 4 dessert dishes. Reserve 4 orange sections for decoration. Spoon remaining orange sections over orange cream. Top with remaining orange cream. Decorate each dessert with a dollop of reserved whipped cream and an orange section.
5. Refrigerate until served. Makes 4 servings.

# Lemon-Wine Syllabub

1/2 cup white wine or sherry
1/2 cup sugar
2 teaspoons grated lemon peel
2 tablespoons lemon juice
1-1/4 cups whipping cream
*To decorate:*
Julienned lemon peel
Lemon-peel twists

*Serve this dish as soon as it is chilled; otherwise, it will separate.*

**1.** In a medium glass bowl, combine wine or sherry, sugar, lemon peel and lemon juice. Let stand 1 hour.
**2.** Add cream to wine mixture; beat until soft peaks form.
**3.** Spoon beaten cream mixture into wine or sherbet glasses; decorate with julienned lemon peel and lemon-peel twists. Refrigerate 1 hour or until chilled. Makes 4 to 6 servings.

# Berry Whip

1 (17-oz.) can blackberries or blueberries
1 (1/4-oz.) envelope unflavored gelatin (1 tablespoon)
3 tablespoons cold water
2 tablespoons fruit-flavored brandy
1/2 pint whipping cream (1 cup)
2 egg whites
1/4 cup sugar

**1.** Drain berries, reserving syrup. Reserve 12 berries for decoration.
**2.** In a blender or food processor fitted with a steel blade, process remaining berries until pureed. Press puree through a sieve to remove seeds; set aside.
**3.** In a small saucepan, combine gelatin and reserved syrup. Stir well; let stand 3 minutes. Stir over low heat until gelatin dissolves. Remove from heat; stir in water, brandy and sieved berries.
**4.** Pour berry mixture into a medium bowl; refrigerate until mixture mounds when dropped from a spoon, 30 to 45 minutes.
**5.** In a medium bowl, whip cream until stiff peaks form. Fold whipped cream into partially set berry mixture.
**6.** In a medium bowl, beat egg whites until soft peaks form. Gradually beat in sugar until stiff and glossy. Fold beaten egg-white mixture into berry mixture.
**7.** Spoon mixture into 6 wine or sherbet glasses. Refrigerate 1 to 2 hours or until firm. To serve, decorate with reserved berries. Makes 6 servings.

Top to bottom: Lemon-Wine Syllabub, Berry Whip

# Gooseberry Fool

**2 cups canned, sweetened gooseberries, drained**
**1/2 cup sugar**
**3/4 cup whipping cream**
**1 egg white**

**1.** In a blender or food processor fitted with a steel blade, process gooseberries until pureed. Press puree through a sieve to remove seeds. Stir in 6 tablespoons sugar. Refrigerate until chilled.
**2.** In a medium bowl, whip cream until stiff peaks form.
**3.** In a small bowl, beat egg white until soft peaks form. Gradually beat in remaining 2 tablespoons sugar; beat until stiff and glossy. Fold beaten egg-white mixture into whipped cream. Fold gooseberry puree into cream mixture.
**4.** Spoon into 4 wine or sherbet glasses. Refrigerate until chilled. Makes 4 servings.

### Variations
If desired, spoon a few canned gooseberries into glasses before adding the fool.

**Mango Fool:** Substitute a large peeled mango for gooseberries. Puree mango with 3 tablespoons sugar and 1 teaspoon lime or lemon juice. Continue as for Gooseberry Fool. If desired, spoon some chopped mango into glasses before spooning in fool. Or, place some chopped fruit on top of fool.

---

Use this recipe as a basic guide for almost any fruit fool. Cook firm fruit before pureeing; puree soft fruit without cooking. Sieve to remove seeds, if necessary. Use about 1/2 cup sweetened puree for 1 egg white and 3/4 cup whipping cream. Sweeten to taste.

---

Top to bottom: Gooseberry Fool, Mango Fool

# Cherry & Cream-Cheese Strudel

**2 (8-oz.) pkgs. cream cheese, room temperature**
**3/4 cup granulated sugar**
**1/4 teaspoon ground cinnamon**
**2 egg yolks**
**1 (17-oz.) can pitted dark sweet cherries, drained**
**8 oz. filo dough, thawed if frozen**
**1/2 cup butter or margarine, melted**
**3/4 cup finely ground almonds**
**Powdered sugar**

---

**1.** In a medium bowl, beat cream cheese, granulated sugar, cinnamon and egg yolks until light and fluffy. Fold in cherries; set aside.
**2.** Preheat oven to 375F (190C). Grease a baking sheet.
**3.** Unfold filo leaves; place on a slightly damp towel. Cover with another damp towel. Remove 1 leaf; place on a clean dry towel. Brush leaf with butter or margarine; sprinkle with 1 tablespoon almonds. Place second leaf directly over first leaf. Brush with butter; sprinkle with 1 tablespoon almonds. Repeat with remaining leaves.
**4.** Spread cherry-cheese mixture over leaves in a 2- to 3-inch strip 1-1/2 inches from ends and along 1 long edge.
**5.** Using towel, roll up strudel, jelly-roll style, patting roll to keep shape. Tuck in ends; brush strudel with butter or margarine. Place seam-side down on greased baking sheet.
**6.** Bake in preheated oven 30 to 35 minutes or until golden brown. Cool on baking sheet 5 minutes. Sprinkle with powdered sugar.
**7.** Serve warm or at room temperature. Makes 10 to 12 servings.

---

The custard for Floating Islands can also be used as a *Custard Sauce*.

# Floating Islands

**2 egg whites**
**2/3 cup sugar**
**2 cups milk**
**2 tablespoons sugar**
**3 eggs**
**1 tablespoon cornstarch**
**1/4 teaspoon vanilla extract**

*To decorate:*
**1/4 cup whole almonds**
**3 tablespoons sugar**

---

**1.** In a medium bowl, beat egg whites until soft peaks form. Gradually beat in 2/3 cup sugar; beat until stiff and glossy.
**2.** In a large saucepan, combine milk and 2 tablespoons sugar; heat until simmering. Shape beaten egg-white mixture into egg shapes, as shown below. Place 4 egg shapes at a time on hot milk mixture. Simmer 3 minutes. Drain on a clean towel. Repeat with remaining egg-white mixture.
**3.** In a medium bowl, beat eggs and cornstarch until smooth. Stir in hot milk mixture and vanilla. Strain into a medium saucepan; cook until thick enough to coat back of a spoon, stirring constantly. Cool slightly; pour into a serving dish.
**4.** To make topping for decoration, butter a baking sheet. In a small saucepan, combine almonds and 3 tablespoons sugar. Cook over low heat until sugar caramelizes. Pour caramel mixture onto buttered baking sheet; cool. When cool and hard, place mixture on a cutting board; coarsely chop with a large heavy knife.
**5.** Place cooked meringues on cooled custard. Sprinkle with chopped caramel mixture; serve immediately. Makes 4 to 6 servings.

 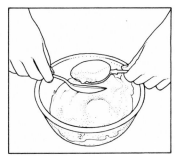

1/To shape meringue islands, use 2 tablespoons as shown.

2/Pass meringue between tablespoons to form a smooth egg shape.

# White-Chocolate Mousse

**6 oz. white chocolate, broken into pieces**
**2 tablespoons unsalted butter**
**3 eggs, separated**
**2 tablespoons light rum**
**1/2 pint whipping cream (1 cup)**
**1/4 cup powdered sugar**

*To decorate:*
**Kiwifruit slices**

**1.** Melt chocolate and butter in top of a double boiler over simmering water. Stir until smooth. Pour chocolate mixture into a large bowl; cool slightly. Beat in egg yolks until thoroughly blended. Cool to room temperature. Stir in rum.
**2.** In a medium bowl, whip cream until soft peaks form. Add powdered sugar; beat until stiff peaks form. Fold into chocolate mixture.
**3.** In a medium bowl, beat egg whites until stiff but not dry. Fold into chocolate mixture.
**4.** Spoon into wine or sherbet glasses. Refrigerate several hours or until set. Decorate with kiwifruit slices. Makes 6 to 8 servings.

**Variation**
**Dark-Chocolate Mousse:** Substitute semisweet chocolate and dark rum for white chocolate and light rum. Proceed as above. Decorate with orange sections or strawberries.

Floating Islands

# Pear & Orange Compote

**6 small pears, peeled, cored, quartered**
**Water**
**3/4 cup sugar**
**2 large oranges**

**1**. In a large saucepan, combine pears, 2/3 cup water and 1/3 cup sugar. Simmer 10 minutes or until pears are tender. Drain; reserve syrup.
**2**. With a vegetable peeler or small knife, cut peel from 1 orange. Cut peel into julienne strips. Place julienned peel in a small saucepan; cover with water. Bring to a boil. Rinse blanched peel in cold water; drain.
**3**. Cut away bitter white pith from orange. Remove peel and bitter pith from other orange. Slice both oranges. Oil a baking sheet; set aside.
**4**. To make caramel topping, place remaining sugar in a small saucepan over medium heat. Without stirring, cook until mixture turns light caramel. Pour immediately onto oiled baking sheet. When caramel is set, break into chips.
**5**. Place sliced oranges and cooked pears in a serving dish. Pour reserved syrup over fruit; refrigerate until chilled.
**6**. Immediately before serving, sprinkle with blanched orange peel and caramel chips. Makes 4 to 6 servings.

### Variation
**Tangerine Compote:** Prepare caramel chips as above. Remove peel and pith from 12 firm-skinned tangerines. Place 1/3 cup sugar and 2/3 cup water in a small saucepan over low heat; stir until sugar dissolves. Simmer 5 minutes. Cool syrup. Arrange peeled tangerines in a serving dish; add cooled syrup. Sprinkle with 3/4 of the caramel chips; refrigerate 2 to 3 hours. Add remaining caramel chips immediately before serving.

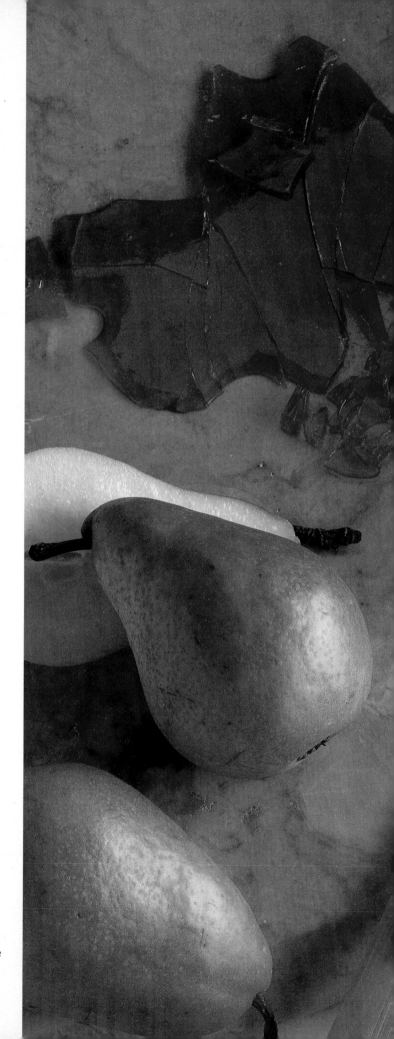

Top to bottom: Pear & Orange Compote, Tangerine Compote

# Tangy Lime Mousse

1 (1/4-oz.) envelope unflavored gelatin (1 tablespoon)
1/4 cup cold water
1 cup milk
1/3 cup fresh lime juice
1 tablespoon cornstarch
2 teaspoons grated lime peel
3 eggs, separated
3/4 cup sugar
1 or 2 drops green food coloring, if desired

*To decorate:*
Lime slices

1. In a medium saucepan, combine gelatin and water. Stir well; let stand 3 minutes. Stir over low heat until gelatin dissolves; set aside to cool.
2. Stir in milk, lime juice, cornstarch and lime peel until blended. Stirring constantly, cook until mixture is thickened and coats back of a spoon. Cool slightly.
3. In a medium bowl, beat egg yolks and sugar until thick and lemon-colored. Beat in warm lime mixture until thoroughly blended. Add 1 or 2 drops food coloring, if desired. Set mixture aside to cool.
4. Beat egg whites until stiff but not dry. Fold beaten egg whites into cooled lime mixture. Cover and refrigerate 2 to 3 hours or until set.
5. To serve, spoon into 4 dessert dishes. Decorate with lime slices. Makes 4 servings.

# Ambrosia

2 bananas
2 navel oranges
2 tablespoons superfine sugar
1-1/2 cups shredded coconut

1. Slice bananas into a serving dish. Peel and section oranges.
2. Add orange sections, sugar and coconut to bananas; stir gently. Refrigerate until thoroughly chilled.
3. Makes 4 servings.

# Peppermint Pears

2/3 cup sugar
1 cup water
1 tablespoon lemon juice
8 small pears with stems attached
3 tablespoons crème de menthe
Few drops green food coloring

*To decorate:*
Mint sprigs

1. In a medium saucepan, combine sugar, water and lemon juice. Stir over low heat until sugar dissolves.
2. Peel pears, leaving stems attached. Level base of each pear, if necessary. Using a small pointed knife, carefully scoop out seeds from base so pears remain whole.
3. Add crème de menthe and food coloring to sugar syrup. Bring to a boil. Place pears upright in saucepan. Cover; simmer 20 to 25 minutes or until pears are tender.
4. Place pears in a serving dish. Boil syrup rapidly until thickened. Spoon thickened syrup over pears. Refrigerate several hours, spooning syrup over pears occasionally.
5. Decorate with mint sprigs. Makes 4 servings.

# Red-Fruit Salad

2/3 cup sugar
1 cup water
Peel of 1/2 lemon, in 1 or 2 pieces
Juice of 1/2 lemon
2 lb. mixed red fruits, such as red currants, raspberries, strawberries, cherries and plums, ready for eating

1. In a medium saucepan, combine sugar, water and lemon peel. Stir over low heat until sugar dissolves. Boil 10 minutes. Cool; remove lemon peel. Stir in lemon juice.
2. Slice or halve strawberries; slice plums.
3. Place prepared fruit in a serving dish; cover with lemon syrup. Refrigerate until served. Makes 6 to 8 servings.

**Variation**
**Green-Fruit Salad:** Substitute green fruit for red ones. Use a combination of melons, grapes, pears, apples, bananas, kiwifruit and green plums.

Clockwise from top right: Peppermint Pears, Tangy Lime Mousse, Green-Fruit Salad

# Raspberry Soufflé

2 (10-oz.) pkgs. frozen raspberries, thawed
1/4 cup water
1 (1/4-oz.) envelope unflavored gelatin (1 tablespoon)
1 tablespoon lemon juice
3 eggs, separated
1/2 cup sugar
1/2 pint whipping cream (1 cup)

*To decorate:*
Sweetened whipped cream

1. Cut a piece of foil large enough to fit around a 1-quart soufflé dish. Fold foil in half lengthwise; grease on 1 side. Wrap around dish, greased-side in, with collar standing 3 inches above rim. Secure collar with straight pins or wooden picks, if necessary.
2. Reserve 4 to 6 raspberries for decoration. In a blender or food processor fitted with a steel blade, process remaining raspberries until pureed. Press puree through a sieve to remove seeds; set puree aside.
3. In a small saucepan, combine water and gelatin. Stir well; let stand 3 minutes. Stir over low heat until gelatin dissolves. Stir in lemon juice; set aside to cool.
4. In a medium bowl, beat egg yolks and sugar until thick and lemon-colored. Stir in raspberry puree and cooled gelatin mixture. Refrigerate 30 minutes or until mixture mounds when dropped from a spoon.
5. In a medium bowl, whip cream until stiff peaks form; fold sweetened whipped cream into partially set raspberry mixture. In a medium bowl, beat egg whites until stiff but not dry; fold beaten egg whites into raspberry mixture. Spoon mixture into prepared soufflé dish. Refrigerate 3 to 4 hours or until set.
6. To serve, carefully remove collar. Decorate soufflé with sweetened whipped cream and reserved raspberries. Makes 6 to 8 servings.

# Sweet Shortbread Treats

1 cup all-purpose flour
1/4 cup powdered sugar, sifted
1/4 teaspoon salt
1/2 cup butter or margarine
1/2 teaspoon vanilla extract

*To decorate:*
1 cup sweetened whipped cream
Raspberries or blackberries

1. Preheat oven to 325F (165C).
2. In a medium bowl, combine flour, powdered sugar and salt. With a pastry blender or 2 knives, cut in butter or margarine until mixture resembles coarse crumbs. Stir in vanilla until blended. Gather dough; shape into a ball.
3. On a lightly floured surface, roll out dough until 1/8 inch thick. Cut out 4 (4-inch) circles. Place circles on an ungreased baking sheet; flute edges.
4. Bake in preheated oven 20 to 25 minutes or until golden brown. Remove from baking sheet; cool on a wire rack.
5. To serve, top each shortbread with whipped cream and berries. Makes 4 servings.

# Nut-Topped Cheesecake

*Crust:*
1 cup graham-cracker crumbs
1/4 cup ground hazelnuts or almonds
3 tablespoons brown sugar
1/4 cup butter or margarine, melted

*Filling:*
1/4 cup milk
1 (1/4-oz.) envelope unflavored gelatin (1 tablespoon)
2 (8-oz.) pkgs. cream cheese, room temperature
1/2 cup sugar
1 teaspoon vanilla extract or almond extract
8 oz. plain or vanilla-flavored yogurt (1 cup)
1/2 pint whipping cream (1 cup)
1/2 cup toasted chopped almonds or hazelnuts

1. Grease a 9-inch springform pan. To make crust, in a medium bowl, combine cracker crumbs, nuts and brown sugar. Stir in butter or margarine until blended. Press crumb mixture into bottom of prepared pan. Refrigerate 30 minutes.
2. To make filling, in a small saucepan, combine milk and gelatin. Stir well; let stand 3 minutes. Stir over low heat until gelatin dissolves; set aside to cool.
3. In a large bowl, beat cream cheese, sugar and vanilla until light and fluffy. Beat in cooled gelatin mixture until blended. Stir in yogurt. Refrigerate 15 minutes.
4. In a medium bowl, beat cream until stiff peaks form. Fold whipped cream into refrigerated cheese mixture. Pour into crust-lined pan; smooth top. Refrigerate 3 to 4 hours or until set.
5. Before serving, sprinkle chopped nuts over top of cheesecake; press down lightly. Run tip of a knife around edge of pan. Remove side of pan. Place cake on a serving plate. Makes 8 to 10 servings.

Clockwise from top left: Nut-Topped Cheesecake, Raspberry Soufflé, Sweet Shortbread Treat

# Strawberry Gâteau

*Cake:*
4 eggs
1/2 cup sugar
3/4 cup sifted all-purpose flour
3 tablespoons butter or margarine, melted

*Strawberry-Cream Filling:*
1 pint strawberries, washed, hulled
1/2 pint whipping cream (1 cup)
2 tablespoons powdered sugar
1/4 cup amaretto liqueur

*Glaze:*
1/3 cup red-currant jelly
1 tablespoon water

1. Preheat oven to 375F (190C). Grease a round, deep 8-inch pan. Line bottom of pan with waxed paper. Grease and flour paper and side of pan.
2. To make cake, combine eggs and sugar in a large bowl over a pan of simmering water. Let stand 5 minutes or until eggs are barely warm. Beat 8 minutes or until mixture is thick and lemon-colored. Remove bowl from pan; beat until mixture is cool.
3. Sift flour over egg mixture; fold in flour. Fold in butter or margarine until no streaks remain. Pour into prepared pan; smooth top.
4. Bake in preheated oven 18 to 20 minutes or until center springs back when lightly pressed. Cool in pan on a wire rack 10 minutes. Remove cake from pan; peel off paper. Cool completely on rack. Cut cake into 3 layers.
5. Set aside 12 to 14 strawberries for decoration. To make filling, in a small bowl, mash remaining strawberries; set aside.
6. In a medium bowl, whip cream until soft peaks form. Beat in powdered sugar; beat until stiff peaks form. Spoon about 3/4 cup whipped cream into a pastry bag fitted with an open star tip. Refrigerate filled pastry bag. Fold mashed strawberries into remaining whipped cream.
7. Place 1 cake layer on a serving plate, sprinkle with 2 tablespoons amaretto. Spread with 1/2 of strawberry cream. Repeat with second layer, using remaining strawberry cream. Place third layer on top. Cut reserved strawberries in half; arrange on top of cake, cut-side down.
8. To make glaze, combine jelly and water in a small saucepan over low heat. Stir until jelly melts; cool. Brush cooled glaze over strawberries. Pipe reserved whipped cream around edge of cake. Refrigerate until served. Makes 8 servings.

**Variation**
**Marzipan-Strawberry Gâteau:** See photo. Sprinkle a flat surface with powdered sugar. Roll out 7 ounces marzipan on a sugared surface to a strip large enough to cover side of cake. Brush 1 side of marzipan strip with 1/4 cup melted red-currant jelly. Carefully press marzipan, jelly-side in, around side of filled cake.

# Strawberry Malakoff

1 cup unsalted butter, room temperature
3/4 cup sugar
1 cup ground blanched almonds
1 teaspoon almond extract
1-1/2 cups whipping cream
1-1/2 pints strawberries, washed, hulled, patted dry
2 tablespoons orange-flavored liqueur
2 tablespoons water
7 ladyfingers, split, or other long cookies

1. Butter a 2-quart charlotte mold or soufflé dish. Line bottom of mold with waxed paper; butter paper.
2. In a large bowl, beat butter and sugar until light and fluffy. Fold in ground almonds and almond extract. In a medium bowl, whip cream until stiff peaks form. Fold whipped cream into butter mixture.
3. Reserve 8 to 10 strawberries for decoration. Coarsely chop remaining strawberries; fold into butter mixture.
4. In a small bowl, blend liqueur and water. Brush flat side of cookies with liqueur mixture. Line mold with brushed cookies, rounded-side out. Fold any remaining liqueur into butter mixture. Spoon mixture into center of mold; press down lightly. Cover; refrigerate several hours.
5. To serve, let stand at room temperature 5 minutes. Wet a clean towel in hot water; wring dry. Wrap around outside of mold 30 seconds; remove towel. Invert mold onto serving plate; remove mold. Peel off paper. Slice reserved strawberries; arrange around tops of cookies. Makes 10 to 12 servings.

**Variation**
Fruit and liqueur may be varied according to taste. Substitute fresh raspberries and framboise or blackberries and kirsch for strawberries and orange-flavored liqueur.

Top to bottom: Strawberry Malakoff, Marzipan-Strawberry Gâteau

# Cream-Filled Cinnamon Gâteau

*Cake:*
1-1/2 cups butter or margarine, room temperature
2 cups sugar
2 eggs
2-1/4 cups all-purpose flour, sifted
2 tablespoons ground cinnamon

*Cream Filling:*
2 pints whipping cream (4 cups)
4 to 6 tablespoons powdered sugar
2 to 3 tablespoons kirsch

*To decorate:*
Powdered sugar
Cherries

---

**1.** Cut out 14 (9-inch) parchment-paper circles. Turn 2 (9-inch) round cake pans upside down; grease bottom surface. Place 1 parchment circle on greased surface of each pan. Lightly grease parchment paper. Set aside.
**2.** Preheat oven to 375F (190C).
**3.** To make cake, in a large bowl, beat butter or margarine and sugar until light and fluffy. Beat in eggs, 1 at a time, beating well after each addition. Sift flour and cinnamon over butter mixture; fold in. Spread about 1/3 cup batter onto each prepared parchment circle, starting from center and spreading batter toward outside edge. Place pans on a baking sheet.
**4.** Bake in preheated oven 10 minutes. Cool layers on pans 2 minutes. Invert cake layers onto a wire rack. Carefully peel off paper; cool completely. Repeat with remaining batter to make a total of 14 layers. Layers are very fragile; do not stack.
**5.** To make filling, in a large bowl, whip cream until soft peaks form. Beat in powdered sugar and kirsch; beat until stiff peaks form. Spoon 2/3 cup whipped-cream mixture into a pastry bag fitted with a rosette tip; refrigerate.
**6.** Carefully place 1 cake layer on a serving plate; spread with a thin layer of remaining whipped-cream mixture. Repeat with remaining cake layers and whipped-cream mixture. Dust center top of cake with powdered sugar. Pipe reserved whipped-cream mixture in a circle on top of cake; decorate with cherries. Refrigerate until served. Makes 12 to 14 servings.

# Brandy Alexander Pie

*Sweet Pastry:*
1-1/3 cups all-purpose flour
2 tablespoons sugar
1/2 teaspoon salt
1/2 cup butter or margarine
3 or 4 tablespoons iced water

*Filling:*
1 (1/4-oz.) envelope unflavored gelatin (1 tablespoon)
3/4 cup sugar
1/2 cup water
3 eggs, separated
1/4 teaspoon ground nutmeg
1/4 cup brandy
1/4 cup crème de cacao
1/2 pint whipping cream (1 cup)

*To decorate:*
Sweetened whipped cream
Chocolate curls, page 360

---

**1.** Preheat oven to 425F (220C). To make pastry, in a medium bowl, combine flour, sugar and salt. With a pastry blender or 2 knives, cut in butter or margarine until mixture resembles coarse crumbs. Sprinkle with 3 tablespoons water; toss with a fork until mixture holds together. Add remaining water, if necessary. Shape into a ball.
**2.** On a lightly floured surface, roll out dough to a 12-inch circle. Line a 9-inch pie pan with pastry. Trim pastry edge; flute. Prick pastry with a fork. Line with foil; fill foil with pie weights or dried beans.
**3.** Bake in preheated oven 10 minutes. Remove foil and pie weights or beans; bake 5 minutes longer or until pastry is golden. Cool completely on a wire rack.
**4.** To make filling, combine gelatin, 1/2 cup sugar and water in a medium saucepan until blended. Stir over low heat until gelatin and sugar are dissolved. Remove from heat.
**5.** In a small bowl, beat egg yolks and nutmeg. Stir 1/4 cup gelatin mixture into beaten egg yolks until blended. Return mixture to saucepan; cook over low heat until mixture is thickened, stirring constantly.
**6.** Pour custard into a large bowl; cool slightly. Stir in brandy and crème de cacao. Place waxed paper over top of custard to prevent film from forming. Refrigerate custard until mixture mounds when dropped from a spoon.
**7.** In a medium bowl, whip cream until stiff peaks form. Fold whipped cream into thickened custard. In a medium bowl, beat egg whites until soft peaks form. Beat in remaining 1/4 cup sugar until stiff and glossy. Fold beaten egg-white mixture into custard mixture. Pour into cooled crust; smooth top. Refrigerate 3 to 4 hours or until set.
**8.** To serve, decorate top of pie with sweetened whipped cream and chocolate curls. Makes 6 to 8 servings.

# Pecan Pie

**Pastry:**
1-1/3 cups all-purpose flour
1 tablespoon sugar
1/2 teaspoon salt
1/2 cup butter or margarine
3 or 4 tablespoons iced water

**Filling:**
1-1/2 cups pecan halves
1 cup dark corn syrup
1/3 cup granulated sugar
1/3 cup firmly packed light-brown sugar
1/4 cup butter or margarine
3 eggs
1 teaspoon vanilla extract

**1.** Preheat oven to 350F (175C).
**2.** To make pastry, in a medium bowl, combine flour, sugar and salt. With a pastry blender or 2 knives, cut in butter or margarine until mixture resembles coarse crumbs. Sprinkle with 3 tablespoons water. Toss with a fork until mixture holds together. Shape into a ball.
**3.** On a lightly floured surface, roll out dough to a 12-inch circle. Line a 9-inch pie pan with pastry. Trim pastry edge; flute.
**4.** To make filling, arrange pecan halves in bottom of pastry-lined pan. Combine syrup, sugars and butter or margarine in a small saucepan over low heat. Stir until sugar is dissolved and butter or margarine is melted. Remove from heat.
**5.** In a medium bowl, beat eggs and vanilla until blended. Stir in syrup mixture. Slowly pour mixture over pecans. Bake in preheated oven 50 to 60 minutes or until tip of knife inserted in center comes out clean. Cool on a wire rack. Serve warm. Makes 6 to 8 servings.

Cream-Filled Cinnamon Gâteau

# Mocha Pots de Crème

3 oz. semisweet chocolate
1 tablespoon instant coffee powder
1/4 cup sugar
1-1/2 cups whipping cream
4 egg yolks, slightly beaten
1 to 2 tablespoons coffee-flavored liqueur

*To decorate:*
**Sweetened whipped cream**
**Crystallized violets**

**1.** Combine chocolate, coffee powder, sugar and cream in a heavy saucepan over low heat. Stir until chocolate is melted and coffee is dissolved. Remove from heat.
**2.** Stir about 6 tablespoons hot chocolate mixture, 1 tablespoon at a time, into egg yolks until blended. Return mixture to saucepan. Stirring constantly, cook until mixture is thickened and coats back of a spoon. Cool slightly; stir in liqueur.
**3.** Pour mixture into demitasse cups or other small dessert dishes. Refrigerate several hours or until set.
**4.** To serve, decorate each serving with a rosette of sweetened whipped cream and a crystallized violet. Makes 6 to 8 servings.

Left to right: Cream-Filled Nut Roll, Mocha Pots de Crème

# Cream-Filled Nut Roll

*Cake:*
**1/2 cup sugar**
**3 eggs**
**2/3 cup ground toasted hazelnuts or almonds**
**2 tablespoons whole-wheat flour**
**Superfine sugar**

*Filling:*
**1/2 pint whipping cream (1 cup)**
**2 tablespoons powdered sugar**
**1 teaspoon vanilla extract**
**1/2 pint fresh raspberries or blackberries**

**1.** Preheat oven to 400F (205C). Grease a 13" x 9" baking pan. Line pan with waxed paper; grease paper.

**2.** To make cake, combine 1/2 cup sugar and eggs in a medium bowl; set bowl over a pan of simmering water. Let stand 5 minutes or until eggs are barely warm. Beat 8 minutes or until mixture is thick and lemon-colored. Remove bowl from heat; beat until mixture is cool. Fold in ground nuts and flour. Spread mixture in prepared pan.

**3.** Bake in preheated oven 10 to 12 minutes or until cake springs back when touched. Sprinkle a thin towel with 2 tablespoons superfine sugar. Invert cake onto sugared towel. Remove pan; peel off paper. Roll up cake in sugared towel, jelly-roll style. Cool rolled cake, seam-side down, on a wire rack.

**4.** To make filling, in a medium bowl, whip cream until soft peaks form. Beat in sugar and vanilla until stiff peaks form. Spoon 3/4 cup whipped-cream mixture into a pastry bag fitted with an open star tip; refrigerate.

**5.** Unroll cake; spread remaining whipped-cream mixture over cake to within 1/2 inch of outside edges. Set aside 6 berries for decoration. Scatter remaining berries over cream filling. Carefully roll cake to enclose filling.

**6.** Place filled cake, seam-side down, on a flat serving plate. Sprinkle lightly with superfine sugar. Decorate with reserved whipped cream and reserved berries. Refrigerate until served. Makes 6 servings.

1/Invert cake onto sugared towel. Remove pan; peel off paper.

2/Roll up cake in sugared towel, jelly-roll style.

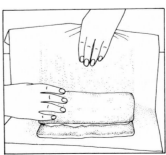

3/Carefully roll cake to enclose filling.

# Ginger & Cream Bavarian

1/2 cup sugar
1 (1/4-oz.) envelope unflavored gelatin (1 tablespoon)
3 eggs, separated
1-1/2 cups milk
2 tablespoons orange juice
1/2 pint whipping cream (1 cup)
1/4 cup orange-flavored liqueur
1/3 cup coarsely chopped stem ginger
  preserved in syrup

**To decorate:**
Sweetened whipped cream
Orange-peel strips

1. Stir sugar and gelatin together in a medium saucepan. In a medium bowl, beat egg yolks, milk and orange juice until blended. Slowly stir into gelatin mixture. Over low heat, stir until mixture thickens and coats back of a spoon. Pour into a large bowl; cool to room temperature. Refrigerate until mixture mounds when dropped from a spoon.
2. In a medium bowl, whip cream until soft peaks form. Add liqueur; beat until stiff peaks form. Fold whipped-cream mixture into partially set gelatin mixture.
3. In a medium bowl, beat egg whites until stiff but not dry. Fold beaten egg whites into gelatin mixture. Fold in preserved ginger.
4. Rinse a 1-1/2-quart charlotte or decorative mold with water. Spoon bavarian mixture into rinsed mold; smooth top. Refrigerate 3 to 4 hours or until set.
5. To serve, invert on a serving plate; remove mold. Pipe whipped cream around bottom and top of bavarian; decorate with orange-peel strips. Makes 6 servings.

# Cream-Filled Chocolate Roll

**Cake:**
6 oz. semisweet chocolate
3 tablespoons water
5 eggs, separated
1/2 cup granulated sugar
1/4 cup sifted all-purpose flour
Powdered sugar

**Filling:**
1-1/2 cups whipping cream
2 tablespoons powdered sugar
1 teaspoon vanilla extract

**To decorate:**
Chocolate lace, see illustration opposite

*The texture of this cake is similar to a mousse; therefore, it will crack when rolled.*

1. Preheat oven to 350F (175C). Grease a 15" x 10" jelly-roll pan. Line greased pan with waxed paper; grease paper.
2. In a small saucepan, stir chocolate and water over low heat until chocolate is melted and mixture is smooth. Set aside to cool.

3. In a large bowl, beat egg yolks and granulated sugar 10 minutes or until thick and lemon-colored. Stir in cooled chocolate mixture until blended. Fold in flour.
4. In a medium bowl, beat egg whites until stiff but not dry; fold into chocolate mixture. Pour into prepared pan; spread evenly.
5. Bake in preheated oven 18 to 20 minutes or until firm. Cover baked cake with a damp towel. Cool on a wire rack until completely cool.
6. Lightly sprinkle a dry towel with powdered sugar. Invert cooled cake onto sugared towel; peel off paper.
7. To make filling, in a medium bowl, whip cream until soft peaks form. Beat in powdered sugar and vanilla; beat until stiff peaks form. Spoon 1-1/2 cups whipped cream into a pastry bag fitted with an open star tip; refrigerate.
8. Spread remaining whipped cream over cake to within 1/2 inch of edges. Using towel, roll up cake, jelly-roll style. Place filled cake on a serving plate, seam-side down. Cake will crack when rolled. Pipe reserved whipped cream over cake. Decorate with chocolate lace. Refrigerate until served. Makes 6 to 8 servings.

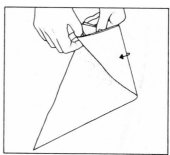

1/Fold a 10-inch square of parchment paper in half diagonally. Holding long side of triangle away from you, bring left corner to middle corner.

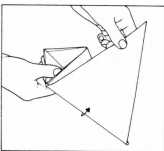

2/Bring other corner around cone, pulling it tight to form a sharp tip.

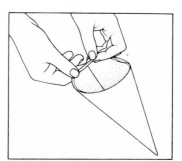

3/Fasten pastry bag by tucking corners inside; make a double fold.

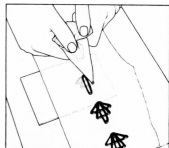

4/Fill pastry bag with melted chocolate. Cut off tip of bag. Place design under a sheet of waxed paper. Trace design to form chocolate lace. When chocolate is firm, remove from paper.

Top to bottom: Ginger & Cream Bavarian, Cream-Filled Chocolate Roll

# Gâteau Pithiviers

1/2 cup granulated sugar
1 cup ground almonds
1/4 cup butter, room temperature
2 egg yolks
2 tablespoons dark rum
1 (17-1/2-oz.) pkg. frozen puff pastry, thawed
Powdered sugar

1. Preheat oven to 400F (205C). In a medium bowl, beat granulated sugar, almonds, butter, egg yolks and rum until blended; set aside.
2. On a lightly floured surface, flatten each pastry sheet. Cut out 1 (9-1/2-inch) circle from each pastry sheet.
3. Place 1 pastry circle on an ungreased baking sheet. Spread filling over pastry to within 3/4 inch of edge. Brush pastry edge with water.
4. Make 8 crescent-shaped cuts in top of remaining pastry sheet. Start at center and cut to within 1 inch of pastry edge, as shown. Place pastry over filling; lightly press edges together to seal. Crimp and flute pastry edge.
5. Bake in preheated oven 20 minutes. Remove from oven; dust top with powdered sugar. Bake 5 to 10 minutes longer or until sugar is melted. Cool on baking sheet 5 minutes. Remove from baking sheet; cool completely on a wire rack. Makes 6 to 8 servings.

1/Make 8 crescent-shaped cuts in top pastry sheet.

Left to right: Gâteau Saint Honoré, Gâteau Pithiviers

# Gâteau Saint Honoré

*Pastry Base:*
2/3 cup all-purpose flour, sifted
2 tablespoons sugar
1/4 cup butter

*Pastry Cream:*
2 tablespoons all-purpose flour
2 tablespoons cornstarch
1/4 cup sugar
1-1/4 cups milk
2 egg yolks, slightly beaten
1/2 teaspoon vanilla extract

*Choux Paste:*
1/2 cup water
2 teaspoons sugar
Pinch salt
1/4 cup butter
1/2 cup all-purpose flour, sifted
2 eggs

*Caramel:*
1 cup sugar
1/2 cup water

*Whipped-Cream Filling:*
1 cup whipping cream
1 tablespoon powdered sugar
1 to 2 tablespoons sweet sherry

*To decorate:*
Chopped pistachios

**1.** Preheat oven to 350F (175C). Grease a baking sheet. To make pastry base, in a medium bowl, combine flour and sugar. With a pastry blender or 2 knives, cut in butter until mixture resembles coarse crumbs. Shape into a ball. On a lightly floured surface, roll out dough to a 9-inch circle. Prick well with a fork. Place on greased baking sheet. Bake in preheated oven 20 minutes or until golden. Remove from baking sheet; cool on a wire rack.

**2.** To make pastry cream, in a medium saucepan, blend flour, cornstarch and sugar. Stir in milk until blended. Stir over low heat until thickened and smooth. Stir about 3 tablespoons hot milk mixture into egg yolks until blended. Pour back into saucepan; cook until thickened, stirring constantly. Do not boil. Remove from heat; stir in vanilla. Place a sheet of waxed paper over pastry cream to prevent film from forming. Cool to room temperature. Refrigerate until needed.

**3.** Preheat oven to 400F (205C). Grease a baking sheet. To make choux paste, combine water, sugar, salt and butter in a medium saucepan. Bring to a boil. Add flour all at once; stir with a wooden spoon until dough forms a ball and comes away from side of pan. Remove from heat. Beat in eggs, 1 at a time, beating well after each addition. Beat until smooth. Spoon dough into a pastry bag fitted with a plain tip. Pipe out 12 to 14 small balls onto greased baking sheet. With remaining choux paste, pipe out an 8-inch ring. Bake in preheated oven 20 to 25 minutes or until golden. Remove from baking sheet; cool on a wire rack.

**4.** To complete gâteau, place pastry base on a serving plate. Cut cooled ring in half crosswise; place bottom of ring on top of baked pastry base. Spoon chilled pastry cream into ring bottom; cover with ring top.

**5.** To prepare caramel, place sugar and water in a small saucepan over low heat. Stir until syrup caramelizes. Remove from heat.

**6.** Dip each choux ball into caramel; place on outside edge of choux ring. Spoon any remaining caramel over balls.

**7.** To make whipped-cream filling, in a medium bowl, whip cream until soft peaks form. Beat in powdered sugar and sherry to taste; beat until stiff peaks form. Fill center of ring with filling. Sprinkle with pistachios; refrigerate until served. Makes 6 to 8 servings.

# Nectarine-Meringue Torte

**6 egg whites**
**1/4 teaspoon cream of tartar**
**1-1/2 cups superfine sugar**
**1/3 cup ground toasted almonds or hazelnuts**
**1 pint whipping cream (2 cups)**
**3 to 4 tablespoons powdered sugar**
**5 or 6 nectarines, sliced**

**1.** Preheat oven to 250F (95C). Line a large baking sheet with parchment paper. Draw 3 (9-inch) circles on paper-lined baking sheet. Use 2 baking sheets, if necessary.
**2.** In a mixer bowl, beat egg whites and cream of tartar with an electric mixer at high speed until soft peaks form. Gradually beat in superfine sugar; beat until stiff and glossy. Fold in nuts.
**3.** Spoon meringue into a pastry bag fitted with a large plain tip. Pipe out meringue into 3 spirals. Start at center of each circle drawn on parchment paper; continue piping until each circle is complete.
**4.** Bake in preheated oven 2 hours or until meringues are crisp and dry. Cool completely on baking sheet on a wire rack. Carefully peel off paper.
**5.** In a medium bowl, whip cream until soft peaks form. Beat in powdered sugar; beat until stiff peaks form. Place 1 meringue layer on a flat serving plate; spread with 1/3 of whipped cream. Arrange 1/3 of nectarine slices on cream.
**6.** Place second meringue layer on a flat surface; spread with second 1/3 of whipped cream; top with second 1/3 of nectarine slices. Carefully place second covered meringue layer on top of first layer. Top with remaining layer; arrange remaining nectarine slices in center of top layer.
**7.** Spoon dollops of remaining whipped cream around nectarine slices. Serve immediately. Makes 10 to 12 servings.

**Variation**
Substitute another fruit for nectarines. Raspberries are excellent served this way.

Meringues are simple to make if a few basic rules are followed.

Bowls and whisks or beaters must be clean and free from grease. Grease prevents egg whites from beating to their full volume. Since egg yolks contain fat, be sure that egg whites do not contain any yolk.

A pinch of salt or a squeeze of lemon juice or cream of tartar will help stabilize beaten egg whites.

Beat egg whites until stiff but not dry. Overbeaten egg whites lose volume and deflate when folded into other ingredients. Beat in about 1 tablespoon sugar at a time, beating well between each addition. Beat until the meringue is thick, white and glossy. After egg whites are beaten, fold in any extra ingredients, such as ground nuts.

Meringues are usually baked in a slow oven one to three hours.

Store hard meringues in a cool dry place. Wrapped in foil or stored in a rigid plastic container, hard meringues will keep at least a week.

Nectarine-Meringue Torte

# Coffee-Cream & Meringue Sandwiches

**4 egg whites**
**1-1/4 cups sugar**
**1/2 cup hazelnuts or almonds, finely ground**
**1-1/4 cups whipping cream**
**2 teaspoons instant coffee powder,**
    **dissolved in 1 teaspoon boiling water**

*To decorate:*
**Chocolate curls**

1. Preheat oven to 250F (120C). Line 2 baking sheets with parchment paper.
2. In a mixer bowl, beat egg whites with an electric mixer at high speed until soft peaks form. Gradually beat in sugar; beat until stiff and glossy. Fold in nuts.
3. Spoon 16 oval shapes of meringue onto paper-lined baking sheets. Bake in preheated oven 2 hours or until dry. When done, meringues will lift easily from paper. Remove from paper; cool on a wire rack.
4. In a medium bowl, whip cream until stiff peaks form. Fold in coffee mixture. Spread coffee cream on half of meringues; top with remaining meringues. Decorate with chocolate curls. Makes 8 servings.

# Baked Stuffed Peaches

**1 cup sponge-cake crumbs**
**3/4 cup almonds, finely ground**
**Grated peel and juice of 1 medium orange**
**4 large ripe peaches or nectarines, halved**
**2 tablespoons sugar**
**2 tablespoons butter or margarine**
**1/2 cup sweet white wine**

1. Preheat oven to 350F (175C). Butter a baking dish large enough to hold peach or nectarine halves in 1 layer.
2. In a medium bowl, blend cake crumbs, almonds, orange peel and orange juice into a paste.
3. Spoon some almond mixture on top of each peach half. Or, fill a pastry bag fitted with an open star tip with almond mixture. Pipe mixture over peach or nectarine halves.
4. Place filled peaches or nectarines in buttered baking dish in a single layer. Sprinkle with sugar; dot with butter or margarine.
5. Pour wine around fruit; bake in preheated oven 15 to 20 minutes or until fruit is almost tender and topping is lightly browned. Serve immediately. Makes 4 servings.

# Kiwifruit Pavlova

**4 egg whites**
**1-1/4 cups sugar**
**1 teaspoon vanilla extract**
**1 teaspoon lemon juice**
**2 teaspoons cornstarch**
**1 pint whipping cream (2 cups), whipped**
**6 kiwifruit, peeled, sliced**

*This classic dessert from Australia is similar to a meringue. However, cornstarch, lemon juice and vanilla extract are added to the beaten egg whites. The additional ingredients and the shorter cooking time produce a crisp exterior and a soft chewy center.*

1. Preheat oven to 300F (150C). Line a baking sheet with parchment paper. Draw a 9-inch circle on parchment paper.
2. In a large bowl, beat egg whites until stiff but not dry. Gradually beat in sugar, 1 tablespoon at a time. Beat until mixture is thick and glossy.
3. Fold in vanilla, lemon juice and cornstarch. Spoon mixture inside circle on parchment paper. Hollow center; make outside edge slightly higher.
4. Bake in preheated oven 1 hour. Cool on a wire rack. Remove paper. Place meringue on a flat serving plate.
5. Fill center with whipped cream. Top cream with kiwifruit slices. Makes 8 servings.

**Variation**
Substitute other fresh fruits for kiwifruit. Try a combination of strawberry, pineapple and mango or canned or fresh lychees, decorated with tiny mint leaves.

Clockwise from top: Kiwifruit Pavlova, Coffee-Cream & Meringue Sandwiches, Baked Stuffed Peaches

# Crepes Suzette

*Crepes:*
1/2 cup all-purpose flour
2 tablespoons sugar
2 eggs
2/3 cup milk
2 tablespoons butter or margarine, melted
2 tablespoons cognac, if desired
Butter or margarine for cooking

*Orange Butter:*
1/2 cup butter or margarine
1/3 cup sugar
Grated peel and juice of 1 large orange
1/4 cup orange-flavored liqueur
1 tablespoon brandy

**1.** Sift flour and sugar into a medium bowl. In a small bowl, beat eggs and milk until blended. Gradually stir into flour mixture; beat until smooth. Beat in melted butter or margarine. Stir in cognac, if desired.
**2.** Pour batter into a pitcher. Cover and refrigerate 1 hour.
**3.** Melt about 1 teaspoon butter or margarine in a 6- or 7-inch crepe pan or skillet. Stir batter; pour about 2 tablespoons batter into crepe pan. Swirl pan so batter makes a thin layer in bottom of pan. Cook over medium heat 1 to 1-1/2 minutes or until small bubbles begin to form on surface of crepe.
**4.** Turn crepe over; cook 1 to 1-1/2 minutes or until bottom is golden brown. Slide crepe onto a flat plate. Repeat with remaining batter, making 12 crepes.
**5.** To make Orange Butter, melt butter or margarine in a medium saucepan. Stir in sugar, orange peel and orange juice until blended. Cook until sugar dissolves.
**6.** Fold crepes in quarters. Pour warm Orange Butter into a chafing dish or shallow flameproof serving dish. Arrange folded crepes in dish; spoon Orange Butter over crepes.
**7.** Heat liqueur and brandy in a small pan over low heat. Pour warmed liqueur and brandy over crepes; ignite carefully. Shake pan until flames die. Serve immediately. Makes 6 servings.

# Orange Cake with Rum-&-Raisin Filling

*Cake:*
5 eggs, separated
3/4 cup sugar
1 tablespoon grated orange peel
1 tablespoon orange juice
1 tablespoon dark rum
1 cup cake flour
1/2 cup ground almonds
1/2 teaspoon salt

*Filling:*
1/3 cup raisins
3 tablespoons dark rum
1/2 pint whipping cream (1 cup)
2 tablespoons powdered sugar

*To decorate:*
Powdered sugar
Orange sections

**1.** Preheat oven to 350F (175C). Grease and flour an 8-inch springform pan. To make cake, in a large bowl, beat egg yolks and sugar until thick and lemon-colored. Stir in orange peel, orange juice and rum. Fold in flour, ground almonds and salt.
**2.** In a medium bowl, beat egg whites until stiff but not dry. Fold beaten egg whites into batter.
**3.** Pour mixture into prepared pan. Bake in preheated oven 40 to 45 minutes or until a wooden pick inserted in center comes out clean. Cool cake in pan on a wire rack 10 minutes. Remove from pan; cool completely on wire rack. Cut cake into 2 layers.
**4.** To make filling, chop raisins; place in a small bowl. Stir in rum; set aside.
**5.** In a medium bowl, whip cream until soft peaks form. Beat in powdered sugar; beat until stiff peaks form. Spoon 3/4 cup whipped cream into a pastry bag fitted with an open star tip; refrigerate. Fold raisin-and-rum mixture into remaining whipped cream.
**6.** Place 1 cake layer on a serving plate, cut-side down; spread raisin mixture on top. Cover with remaining cake layer, cut-side down. Dust with powdered sugar. Pipe reserved whipped cream on top of cake; decorate with orange sections. Refrigerate until served. Makes 8 servings.

# Traditional Baked Cheesecake

*Crust:*
**1-1/4 cups graham-cracker crumbs**
**2 tablespoons sugar**
**1/4 cup butter or margarine, melted**

*Cheese Filling:*
**4 (8-oz.) pkgs. cream cheese, room temperature**
**1 cup sugar**
**2 eggs**
**1/4 cup all-purpose flour**
**Grated peel of 1 lemon**
**1 cup dairy sour cream**

*To decorate:*
**Fresh strawberries or other fruit**

**1.** Preheat oven to 350F (175C). Grease a 9-inch springform pan. To make crust, in a small bowl, combine cracker crumbs and sugar. Stir in butter or margarine. Press crumbs onto bottom of greased pan. Bake 10 minutes. Remove from oven; cool on a wire rack. Increase oven temperature to 400F (205C).
**2.** To make filling, in a large bowl, beat cream cheese and sugar until smooth. Beat in eggs, flour and lemon peel until blended. Stir in sour cream. Pour cheese mixture over bottom crust; smooth top.
**3.** Bake in preheated oven 45 to 50 minutes or until center is set. Turn off oven; leave cheesecake in oven, with oven door slightly ajar, 3 hours. Remove from oven; cool completely in pan on a wire rack. Refrigerate until served.
**4.** To serve, run tip of a knife around inside edge of pan. Release and remove pan side. Place cheesecake on a serving plate. Decorate top of cake with strawberries or other fruit. Makes 12 to 14 servings.

Top to bottom: Traditional Baked Cheesecake, Orange Cake with Rum-&-Raisin Filling

# Bread & Butter Pudding

2 tablespoons butter or margarine, room temperature
4 slices day-old white bread, crusts removed
1/4 cup apricot jam
1/2 cup raisins
2 eggs
2 tablespoons sugar
2 cups milk
Ground cinnamon

1. Butter a shallow 1-1/2-quart casserole. Spread butter or margarine on bread. Spread each buttered slice with apricot jam; cut bread diagonally into 4 triangles.
2. Arrange 1/2 the triangles in bottom of buttered casserole; sprinkle with 1/2 the raisins. Top with remaining triangles and raisins.
3. In a medium bowl, beat eggs, sugar and milk until blended. Pour over bread and raisins; let stand at room temperature 1 hour.
4. Preheat oven to 350F (175C). Place casserole in a roasting pan. Add enough boiling water to come halfway up sides of casserole.
5. Bake 50 to 60 minutes or until a knife tip inserted slightly off center comes out clean. Remove from roasting pan; cool on a wire rack 5 to 10 minutes.
6. Sprinkle with cinnamon; serve warm. Makes 4 to 6 servings.

# Baked Pears in White Wine

6 tablespoons orange marmalade
6 tablespoons coarsely crushed macaroons
6 large ripe pears, peeled, halved, cored
1 cup sweet white wine
3 tablespoons butter or margarine

1. Preheat oven to 350F (175C). Grease a shallow oven-proof dish large enough to hold pears in a single layer.
2. In a small bowl, blend marmalade and macaroons. Place pear halves in greased dish, cut-side up. Fill pears with marmalade mixture.
3. Pour wine around pears. Dot filled pears with butter or margarine.
4. Bake in preheated oven 20 to 30 minutes or until tender when tested with a wooden pick.
5. Serve warm or at room temperature. Makes 6 servings.

# Spiced Bread Pudding

8 slices day-old whole-wheat bread, crumbled
1-3/4 cups milk
1/4 cup butter or margarine
1/4 cup firmly packed dark-brown sugar
1/3 cup raisins
1/3 cup currants
1 teaspoon ground cinnamon
1 teaspoon ground ginger
1/2 teaspoon ground nutmeg
2 eggs, beaten
Dark-brown sugar

1. Preheat oven to 350F (175C). Grease an 11" x 7" baking dish.
2. Place bread in a medium bowl; set aside. In a small saucepan, combine milk, butter or margarine and 1/4 cup brown sugar. Stir over medium heat until mixture comes to a boil and butter or margarine melts.
3. Stir hot milk mixture into bread. Let stand 15 minutes, stirring occasionally. Stir in raisins, currants, cinnamon, ginger, nutmeg and eggs. Pour into greased dish.
4. Bake 40 to 45 minutes or until a knife tip inserted slightly off center comes out clean. Sprinkle with brown sugar while still hot.
5. Cut into squares; serve immediately. Makes 6 to 8 servings.

Clockwise from top left: Spiced Bread Pudding, Bread & Butter Pudding, Baked Pears in White Wine

# Harvest Apple Pie

Double recipe Pastry, page 383

6 to 7 medium, tart apples, peeled, sliced
1 tablespoon lemon juice
4 teaspoons cornstarch
1 teaspoon grated lemon peel
1 teaspoon ground cinnamon
1/4 teaspoon ground nutmeg
1/4 teaspoon ground allspice
1/2 to 3/4 cup sugar
2 tablespoons butter or margarine, diced
Milk
Sugar

*To serve:*
Sharp Cheddar cheese

---

**1.** Preheat oven to 425F (220C). Make pastry as directed in step 2. On a lightly floured surface, roll out 1/2 of pastry to a 12-inch circle. Use to line a 9- or 10-inch pie pan. Do not trim pastry edge.
**2.** Place apples in a large bowl; sprinkle with lemon juice. In a small bowl, combine cornstarch, lemon peel, cinnamon, nutmeg and allspice. Add sugar to taste, depending on tartness of apples. Sprinkle sugar mixture over apples; toss to coat.
**3.** Arrange apple slices in pastry-lined pan, mounding apples in center. Dot with butter or margarine.
**4.** On a lightly floured surface, roll out remaining pastry to an 11- or 12-inch circle. Carefully place pastry over apples. Trim pastry edges to 1 inch beyond rim of pie pan. Fold overhang under to build up edge; press edges together to seal. Pinch folded edge up to form high edge; flute.
**5.** Cut 3 or 4 slits in center of top crust to allow steam to escape. Brush crust with milk; sprinkle with sugar.
**6.** Bake in preheated oven 45 to 50 minutes or until crust is golden and apples are tender. Cool on a wire rack.
**7.** Serve warm or cold with cheese. Makes 6 to 8 servings.

# Banana Puffs with Walnut-Rum Sauce

1/2 (17-1/2-oz.) pkg. frozen puff pastry, thawed
4 medium, firm-ripe bananas, peeled
1 egg white, slightly beaten
1 tablespoon sugar

*Walnut-Rum Sauce:*
2/3 cup water
1/3 cup packed light-brown sugar
1/4 cup butter or margarine
1/4 cup chopped walnuts
2 tablespoons dark rum

---

**1.** Cut pastry into 4 pieces. On a lightly floured surface, roll out each piece until large enough to cover a banana.
**2.** Wrap bananas in pastry. Brush edges with water; seal. Cut away excess pastry; reserve.
**3.** Roll trimmings from each banana-filled pastry to a narrow 10-inch strip. Wrap a pastry strip around each pastry; form into a bow.
**4.** Rinse a baking sheet with water. Place pastries on damp baking sheet. Brush with egg white; sprinkle with sugar. Bake in a preheated oven 20 to 25 minutes or until puffed and golden.
**5.** To make sauce, in a medium saucepan over low heat, combine water and brown sugar. Stir until sugar dissolves. Boil rapidly about 5 minutes or until slightly syrupy. Remove from heat; stir in remaining ingredients. Stir until butter or margarine melts.
**6.** Serve sauce immediately with warm banana puffs. Makes 4 servings.

# Layered Apple Bake

1 lb. cooking apples, peeled, cored, sliced (4 medium)
Grated peel and juice of 1/2 lemon
3/4 cup sugar
1 egg, beaten
1/2 cup butter or margarine
4 cups fresh white-bread crumbs

*To serve:*
Vanilla ice cream

---

**1.** In a medium saucepan, combine apples, lemon peel and lemon juice. Simmer until soft. Stir in 1/2 cup sugar. Cool slightly; beat in egg and 2 tablespoons butter or margarine. Cool.
**2.** Preheat oven to 425F (220C). In a medium skillet, melt remaining butter or margarine. Stir in bread crumbs and remaining sugar.
**3.** Press 1/2 the crumb mixture on bottom of a 9-inch oven-proof dish. Spread apple mixture over crumbs; top with remaining crumb mixture. Press down gently.
**4.** Bake in preheated oven 30 minutes. Cool on a wire rack 5 minutes; turn out on a serving plate.
**5.** Serve warm with vanilla ice cream. Makes 6 servings.

# Plum Dumplings

**8 firm red plums**
**8 teaspoons sugar**
**Pastry, page 383**
**Milk**
**Sugar**

*To serve:*
**Whipped cream**

1. Split each plum enough to remove and discard pits; remove pits. Fill cavity with 1 teaspoon sugar; set plums aside. Grease a baking sheet.

2. Preheat oven to 400F (205C). Make pastry as directed in step 2, page 383. Divide pastry into 8 pieces.

3. On a lightly floured surface, roll out each pastry piece into a square large enough to cover a plum. Place a sugar-filled plum in center of each pastry square. Draw corners of pastry to center, see photo. Trim off excess pastry. Brush edges with water; seal.

4. On a lightly floured surface, roll out pastry trimmings; cut out pastry leaves. Decorate each dumpling with pastry leaves made from trimmings.

5. Place dumplings on greased baking sheet. Brush with milk; sprinkle with sugar.

6. Bake in preheated oven 20 to 25 minutes or until crisp and golden on outside and tender in center when pierced with a wooden pick.

7. Serve immediately with whipped cream. Makes 4 servings.

Clockwise from top left: Custard Sauce, page 372; Plum Dumplings; Banana Puffs with Walnut-Rum Sauce

# Almond & Pear Crepes

8 Crepes, page 394

*Filling:*
1 (16-oz.) can sliced pears
1/2 cup butter or margarine, room temperature
1/2 cup powdered sugar, sifted
1/3 cup finely ground blanched almonds

1. Prepare crepes according to recipe on page 394. Place small sheets of waxed paper between extra crepes; wrap in foil. Freeze for another use.
2. Drain pears, reserving syrup. Coarsely chop pears; set aside.
3. In a small bowl, beat butter or margarine and powdered sugar until light and fluffy. Fold in almonds and chopped pears.
4. Preheat broiler. Grease a shallow, flameproof baking dish. Fold each crepe in quarters. Spoon a little pear filling into 1 quarter of each crepe. Place filled crepes in a single layer in greased dish. Spoon a little reserved pear syrup over each crepe.
5. Place dish under preheated broiler, 3 to 4 inches from source of heat; broil 3 to 4 minutes or until crepes are lightly browned.
6. Serve immediately. Makes 4 servings.

Left to right: Almond & Pear Crepes, Raspberry Clafoutis

# Raspberry Clafoutis

3 eggs
1/4 cup granulated sugar
1/2 cup sifted all-purpose flour
Pinch salt
1-1/4 cups milk
3 tablespoons butter or margarine, melted
1 (10-oz.) pkg. frozen raspberries, thawed, drained
Superfine sugar

*Clafoutis, a thick fruit pancake, is baked in the oven and served warm. It originates from the Limousin area in France. It is traditionally made with black cherries.*

**1.** Preheat oven to 400F (205C). Grease a 9-inch au gratin dish.
**2.** In a medium bowl, beat eggs and sugar 5 minutes or until pale and foamy. Fold in flour and salt. Stir in milk and butter or margarine to make a smooth batter.
**3.** Pour 1/2 of batter into prepared dish. Bake 15 minutes.
**4.** Arrange raspberries on baked batter; carefully pour remaining batter around fruit.
**5.** Bake 35 minutes longer or until top is golden.
**6.** Sprinkle with superfine sugar; serve immediately. Makes 4 to 6 servings.

# Strawberry-&-Cream-Filled Crepes

Crepes, page 394
1 pint fresh strawberries, washed, hulled
1/2 pint whipping cream (1 cup)
2 tablespoons powdered sugar
1 teaspoon vanilla extract
1/2 cup strawberry jam

**1.** Make crepes according to recipe, page 394. Keep crepes warm in a low oven.
**2.** Slice 6 to 8 strawberries; reserve for decoration. Coarsely chop remaining strawberries; set aside.
**3.** In a medium bowl, whip cream until soft peaks form. Add powdered sugar and vanilla; beat until stiff peaks form. Fold chopped strawberries into whipped-cream mixture.
**4.** Spread each crepe with 1 to 2 teaspoons strawberry jam. Spoon a heaping tablespoon strawberry cream down center of each crepe; fold sides over filling.
**5.** Place 2 crepes, seam-side down, on dessert plates. Top with remaining strawberry cream and sliced strawberries. Serve filled crepes immediately. Makes 6 servings.

# Apricot & Almond Pudding

1 (16-oz.) can apricot halves, well drained
6 tablespoons butter or margarine, room temperature
1/2 cup sugar
2 eggs
1/2 teaspoon almond extract
1 cup sifted all-purpose flour
1-1/2 teaspoons baking powder
1/3 cup ground blanched almonds
1/4 cup milk
6 whole blanched almonds

**1.** Grease a 1-quart heatproof bowl or pudding mold. Reserve 6 apricot halves. Chop remaining apricots.
**2.** In a medium bowl, beat butter or margarine and sugar until light and fluffy. Beat in eggs and almond extract until blended.
**3.** In a small bowl, combine flour, baking powder and ground almonds; fold into butter mixture. Stir in milk until blended; fold in chopped apricots.
**4.** Place 1 almond in cavity of each reserved apricot half. Arrange apricots, cut-side down, in bottom of greased bowl or mold. Spoon batter carefully over apricots. Cover with a double thickness of greased waxed paper. Wrap in foil; secure with kitchen string.
**5.** Place bowl on a trivet in a large saucepan. Add enough boiling water to come 3/4 up side of bowl or mold. Cover; steam 2 hours, adding boiling water as necessary. Remove pudding from saucepan. Cool slightly.
**6.** To serve, unwrap; invert pudding on a serving plate. Remove mold or bowl. Serve warm. Makes 6 servings.

Left to right: Apricot & Almond Pudding, Almond & Fig Pudding

# Raisin-Bread Pudding

2-1/2 cups milk
1/2 cup sugar
3 tablespoons butter or margarine
3 eggs, slightly beaten
1 teaspoon vanilla extract
12 slices raisin bread
1/3 cup raisins
1 teaspoon ground cinnamon
1/4 teaspoon ground nutmeg

*To serve:*
Custard Sauce, page 372

---

1. Preheat oven to 350F (175C). Lightly grease a 1-1/2-quart casserole. In a medium saucepan, combine milk, sugar and butter or margarine. Cook over low heat until butter or margarine melts, sugar dissolves and tiny bubbles form around edge of pan. Remove from heat.
2. Stir 1/4 cup hot milk mixture into eggs until well blended. Return mixture to saucepan, stirring until thoroughly blended. Stir in vanilla.
3. Remove crusts from bread, if desired. Cut bread into small cubes. In a medium bowl, combine bread cubes, raisins, cinnamon and nutmeg. Stir milk mixture into bread mixture. Spoon into greased casserole. Place casserole in a roasting pan; add enough boiling water to come halfway up side of casserole.
4. Bake 50 to 60 minutes or until tip of a knife inserted slightly off center comes out clean. Remove from roasting pan; cool on a wire rack 5 to 10 minutes.
5. Serve warm or at room temperature with custard sauce. Makes 4 to 6 servings.

# Apple Crisp

6 medium, tart apples, peeled, cored, sliced
2 tablespoons lemon juice
1/4 cup sugar

*Topping:*
1/2 cup all-purpose flour
1/2 cup regular rolled oats
1/2 cup firmly packed brown sugar
1/4 cup granulated sugar
1 teaspoon ground cinnamon
1/4 teaspoon ground nutmeg
6 tablespoons butter or margarine

*To serve:*
Ice cream or sweetened whipped cream

---

1. Preheat oven to 375F (190C).
2. Place apples in a large bowl; sprinkle with lemon juice and sugar. Toss to coat. Arrange apples in an ungreased deep 9-inch pie plate or 2-quart casserole.
3. To make topping, in a medium bowl, combine flour, oats, brown sugar, granulated sugar, cinnamon and nutmeg. With a pastry blender or 2 knives, cut in butter or margarine until mixture resembles coarse crumbs. Sprinkle crumbs over apples.
4. Bake 25 to 30 minutes or until apples are tender and topping is lightly browned. Cool on a wire rack 5 to 10 minutes.
5. Serve warm with ice cream or sweetened whipped cream. Makes 4 to 6 servings.

# Almond & Fig Pudding

1/2 cup butter or margarine, room temperature
1/3 cup sugar
2 eggs
1 tablespoon grated lemon peel
1 cup sifted all-purpose flour
1-1/2 teaspoons baking powder
1/3 cup milk
1/2 (7-oz.) pkg. marzipan, diced
1 (17-oz.) can figs, drained, cut in half

---

1. Grease a 1-quart heatproof bowl or pudding mold. In a medium bowl, beat butter or margarine and sugar until light and fluffy. Beat in eggs and lemon peel until blended. In a small bowl, blend flour and baking powder; fold into sugar mixture. Stir in milk until blended. Stir in marzipan.
2. Place 6 fig halves, cut-side down, in bottom of greased bowl or mold. Spoon 1/2 the batter over figs. Top with remaining figs; spoon remaining batter over figs.
3. Cover with a double thickness of greased waxed paper. Wrap in foil; secure with kitchen string. Place bowl or mold on a trivet in a large saucepan. Add enough boiling water to come 3/4 up side of mold or bowl. Cover; steam 2 hours, adding boiling water as necessary. Remove pudding from saucepan. Cool slightly.
4. To serve, unwrap; invert pudding on a serving plate. Remove mold or bowl. Serve warm. Makes 6 servings.

# Indian Pudding

1/2 cup yellow cornmeal
1 qt. milk (4 cups)
1/2 cup molasses
1/4 cup firmly packed brown sugar
3 tablespoons butter or margarine
1 teaspoon ground cinnamon
1/2 teaspoon ground ginger
1/2 teaspoon salt
2 eggs
1/2 cup chopped almonds

1. Preheat oven to 350F (175C). Grease a 1-quart casserole or baking dish. Place cornmeal in top of double boiler. In a medium saucepan, scald 3 cups milk. Pour scalded milk over cornmeal, stirring constantly.
2. Cook over pan of simmering water about 20 minutes, stirring constantly. Stir in molasses, brown sugar, butter or margarine, cinnamon, ginger and salt until blended. Cook 5 minutes, stirring constantly. Set aside.
3. In a medium bowl, beat eggs with remaining 1 cup milk until blended. Stir into cornmeal mixture.
4. Pour mixture into greased casserole. Place casserole in a roasting pan. Add enough boiling water to come halfway up side of casserole.
5. Bake 60 to 70 minutes or until tip of a knife inserted slightly off center comes out clean. Remove from roasting pan; cool on a wire rack 5 minutes.
6. Sprinkle with almonds; serve warm. Makes 6 servings.

# Christmas Pudding

3/4 cup dark raisins
3/4 cup golden raisins
3/4 cup currants
1/2 cup finely chopped mixed candied fruit
1/4 cup finely chopped red candied cherries
Grated peel and juice of 1 orange
3/4 cup dark beer or ale
1-1/4 cups all-purpose flour
1 teaspoon baking powder
1 teaspoon ground cinnamon
1/2 teaspoon ground nutmeg
1/4 teaspoon ground cloves
2 cups fresh bread crumbs
1 cup firmly packed brown sugar
3/4 cup shredded suet
1 tart apple, peeled, cored, grated
1 carrot, grated
1/2 cup chopped toasted blanched almonds
3 eggs
2 tablespoons molasses

*To serve:*
1/4 cup brandy, cognac or dark rum, if desired

1. In a medium bowl, combine raisins, currants, mixed candied fruit, candied cherries and orange peel. Stir in beer or ale; let stand 30 minutes.
2. Grease 2 (1-quart) pudding molds or heatproof bowls.
3. In a large bowl, combine flour, baking powder, cinnamon, nutmeg and cloves. With a wooden spoon, stir in bread crumbs, brown sugar, suet, apple, carrot and almonds until blended. In a small bowl, blend eggs, orange juice and molasses. Stir egg mixture and fruit mixture into dry ingredients. Stir until blended.
4. Divide mixture equally between greased molds or bowls. Cover with a double thickness of greased waxed paper. Wrap in foil; secure with kitchen string. Place covered molds or bowls on a rack in a large kettle. Add enough boiling water to come 3/4 up side of molds or bowls. Cover; steam 4 hours, adding more boiling water as necessary.
5. Remove molds or bowls; cool covered puddings completely on a wire rack. Recover molds with clean waxed paper and foil. Store in a cool place until ready to serve.
6. To serve, steam puddings as directed above about 1 hour. Cool slightly; uncover puddings. Invert on serving plates; remove molds or bowls.
7. If desired, warm brandy in a small saucepan; pour over pudding. Carefully ignite brandy; serve while flaming. Makes 12 to 14 servings.

Christmas Pudding

# Peach Cobbler

1/3 cup sugar
1 tablespoon cornstarch
1/2 teaspoon ground cinnamon
5 to 6 medium peaches, peeled
    sliced (about 2 lb.)
1 tablespoon lemon juice

*Topping:*
1 cup all-purpose flour
2 tablespoons sugar
1-1/2 teaspoons baking powder
1/2 teaspoon salt
1/4 cup butter or margarine
1/2 cup milk
Ground cinnamon

**1.** Preheat oven to 400F (205C). In a large saucepan, combine sugar, cornstarch and cinnamon. Stir in peaches and lemon juice until coated. Cook over low heat until mixture comes to a boil and thickens, stirring gently. Pour peach mixture into an ungreased 2-quart casserole.
**2.** To make topping, in a medium bowl, combine flour, sugar, baking powder and salt. With a pastry blender or 2 knives, cut in butter or margarine until mixture resembles coarse crumbs. Stir in milk until blended.
**3.** Drop dough by heaping tablespoons on top of hot peach mixture, making 6 mounds of dough. Sprinkle cinnamon over dough. Bake 25 to 30 minutes or until topping is lightly browned.
**4.** Serve warm. Makes 6 servings.

Holly leaves and berries are poisonous; do not eat.

# Christmas Tart

Pastry, page 354
6 tablespoons butter or margarine
2 eggs, slightly beaten
1/4 cup sugar
2/3 cup chopped mixed candied fruit

**1.** Preheat oven to 350F (175C). Make pastry through step 1. On a lightly floured surface, roll out pastry to an 11-inch circle. Use to line a 9-inch quiche pan or flan pan with removable bottom. Pastry should come only halfway up side of pan.
**2.** To make filling, in a small saucepan, combine butter or margarine, eggs and sugar. Cook over medium heat until mixture comes to a boil, stirring constantly. Remove from heat immediately; stir in candied fruit. Pour mixture into pastry-lined pan; smooth top.
**3.** Bake 30 to 35 minutes or until center is set and pastry is golden brown. Cool in pan on a wire rack.
**4.** Makes 6 servings.

# Lemon Sponge Pudding

1/4 cup butter or margarine, room temperature
1/2 cup sugar
3 eggs, separated
1/4 cup all-purpose flour, sifted
Grated peel and juice of 1 lemon
3/4 cup milk

**1.** Preheat oven to 350F (175C). Grease a 1-1/2-quart casserole. In a medium bowl, beat butter or margarine and sugar until light and fluffy. Beat in egg yolks, 1 at a time, beating well after each addition.
**2.** Fold in flour, lemon peel and lemon juice. Beat in milk until blended. In a medium bowl, beat egg whites until stiff peaks form. Fold into batter. Pour mixture into greased casserole; smooth top. Place casserole in a roasting pan; add enough boiling water to come halfway up side of casserole.
**3.** Bake 35 to 40 minutes or until top is golden brown. Remove from roasting pan; cool on a wire rack 5 minutes.
**4.** Serve warm or at room temperature. Makes 4 to 6 servings.

Clockwise from left: Sweet Noodle Pudding, Christmas Tart, Upside-Down Plum Pie

# Sweet Noodle Pudding

3 cups medium egg noodles (4 oz.)
1/4 cup butter or margarine, melted
2 eggs, separated
1/2 cup plus 2 tablespoons sugar
1 teaspoon vanilla extract
1/2 cup dairy sour cream
1/2 cup small-curd cottage cheese
1 cup milk
1/2 teaspoon ground cinnamon

---

**1.** Preheat oven to 375F (190C). Grease a 1-1/2-quart baking dish.
**2.** In a large saucepan, cook noodles according to package directions until almost tender. Drain well; place in greased baking dish. Stir in butter or margarine.
**3.** In a medium bowl, beat egg yolks, 1/2 cup sugar, vanilla, sour cream and cottage cheese until smooth and blended. Gradually stir in milk.
**4.** In a medium bowl, beat egg whites until stiff but not dry. Fold beaten egg whites into cheese mixture. Pour cheese mixture over noodles; stir gently. In a small bowl, combine remaining 2 tablespoons sugar and cinnamon; sprinkle over noodles.
**5.** Bake 40 to 45 minutes or until center is set.
**6.** Serve warm. Makes 4 to 6 servings.

# Upside-Down Plum Pie

1-1/4 cups all-purpose flour
1/3 cup ground almonds
1/2 cup sugar
1/2 cup plus 2 tablespoons butter or margarine
1 egg yolk
1 to 2 tablespoons iced water
6 to 7 small red plums, halved, pitted (about 1-1/4 lb.)

---

**1.** In a medium bowl, combine flour, almonds and 1/4 cup sugar. With a pastry blender or 2 knives, cut in 1/2 cup butter or margarine until mixture resembles coarse crumbs.
**2.** In a small bowl, blend egg yolk with 1 tablespoon water; sprinkle over flour mixture. Toss with a fork until mixture holds together. Add remaining water, if necessary. Shape into a ball; wrap in plastic wrap. Refrigerate 30 minutes.
**3.** Preheat oven to 375F (190C). Melt remaining 2 tablespoons butter or margarine in a pie pan in preheated oven. Stir in remaining 1/4 cup sugar; cook until sugar dissolves and syrup is caramel in color. Remove from heat. Place plums, cut-side up, in bottom of pie pan.
**4.** On a lightly floured surface, roll out dough to a 10-inch circle. Place over plums, tucking edges in around edge of pan.
**5.** Bake 35 to 45 minutes or until pastry is golden brown. Cool in pan on a wire rack 5 minutes.
**6.** Invert onto a serving plate; serve warm. Makes 6 to 8 servings.

# Prune & Almond Custard

1 cup pitted prunes
Water
About 20 whole almonds
3 eggs, separated
1/2 cup sugar
2/3 cup whipping cream
2/3 cup half and half
1/4 cup butter or margarine
1 tablespoon port
Few drops of almond extract

---

*This dessert is interesting because of the contrast in flavors and textures. The top is a puffy meringue, the middle is a smooth custard and the bottom layer is the prunes and crunchy almonds. Meringue top will collapse when chilled.*

**1.** Place prunes in a medium saucepan; cover with water. Simmer 10 minutes or until tender. Cool in cooking liquid. Drain and discard cooking liquid. Place an almond in center of each prune. Grease a 1-1/2-quart casserole.
**2.** Preheat oven to 350F (175C). Arrange stuffed prunes in a single layer in greased casserole.
**3.** In a medium bowl, beat egg yolks and sugar until thick and pale. In a medium saucepan, heat whipping cream, half and half and butter or margarine until butter or margarine melts. Beat hot cream mixture into egg mixture. Stir in port and almond extract.
**4.** Beat egg whites until stiff but not dry. Fold beaten egg whites into egg mixture.
**5.** Pour egg mixture over prunes. Place casserole in a roasting pan. Add enough boiling water to come halfway up side of casserole.
**6.** Bake in preheated oven about 1 hour. After 30 minutes, if top is getting too brown, reduce oven temperature to 325F (165C).
**7.** Serve at room temperature or refrigerate until chilled. Makes 4 servings.

# Steamed Chocolate Pudding

1/2 cup butter or margarine, room temperature
1 cup sugar
2 eggs
1-1/3 cups all-purpose flour
1/3 cup unsweetened cocoa powder
1-1/2 teaspoons baking powder
1/3 cup milk

*Chocolate Sauce:*
3 oz. semisweet chocolate, broken into pieces
1/4 cup light corn syrup
2 tablespoons butter or margarine
2 tablespoons water
1/2 teaspoon vanilla extract

1. Grease a 1-1/2-quart pudding mold or heatproof bowl. In a medium bowl, beat butter or margarine and sugar until light and fluffy. Beat in eggs, 1 at a time, beating well after each addition. Sift flour, cocoa powder and baking powder over creamed mixture; fold in. Stir in milk until well blended.
2. Spoon into greased mold or bowl. Cover with a double thickness of greased waxed paper. Wrap in foil; secure with kitchen string.
3. Place covered pudding on a trivet in a large saucepan. Add enough boiling water to come halfway up side of mold or bowl. Cover; steam 1-1/2 hours, adding more boiling water as necessary.
4. Remove mold; cool covered pudding on a wire rack 5 minutes. Uncover; invert on a serving plate. Remove mold or bowl.
5. To make Chocolate Sauce, in a medium saucepan, combine chocolate, corn syrup and butter or margarine. Cook over low heat until chocolate melts, stirring constantly. Stir in water and vanilla until blended. Pour sauce over pudding; serve immediately. Makes 6 to 8 servings.

Left to right: Upside-Down Toffee-Apple Pie, Pineapple Upside-Down Cake

# Upside-Down Toffee-Apple Pie

1-3/4 cups all-purpose flour
2 teaspoons baking powder
1 teaspoon salt
3/4 cup vegetable shortening
5 to 6 tablespoons water
1/4 cup butter or margarine
2/3 cup firmly packed brown sugar
3 or 4 medium, tart apples, peeled, cored,
   thinly sliced (1-1/2 lb.)

1. Sift flour, baking powder and salt into a medium bowl. With a pastry blender or 2 knives, cut in shortening. Add 5 tablespoons water; stir to make a stiff dough. Add remaining water, if necessary. Cover; refrigerate 1 hour.
2. Preheat oven to 350F (175C). In a small bowl, blend butter or margarine and 1/3 cup brown sugar. Spread over bottom and up side of a 9-inch pie pan.
3. Divide pastry in half. On a lightly floured surface, roll out 1/2 of pastry; place in prepared pie pan. Do not trim pastry edges. Arrange 1/2 of apples in pastry-lined pan. Sprinkle apples with remaining 1/3 cup brown sugar. Top with remaining apples. Fold pastry edges in towards center.
4. On a lightly floured surface, roll out remaining pastry. Brush pastry with water; place over apples, brushed-side down. Tuck in edges.
5. Bake in preheated oven 60 to 65 minutes or until pastry is golden and apples are tender. Cool on a wire rack 5 minutes.
6. Invert on a serving plate; remove pan. Serve immediately. Makes 8 servings.

# Pineapple Upside-Down Cake

1/4 cup butter or margarine
1/2 cup firmly packed brown sugar
6 slices canned pineapple, well drained
6 candied or maraschino cherries
1-1/4 cups all-purpose flour
1 cup granulated sugar
2 teaspoons baking powder
1/2 teaspoon salt
1 egg
6 tablespoons vegetable shortening
3/4 cup milk
1 teaspoon vanilla extract

*To serve:*
Sweetened whipped cream, if desired

**1.** Preheat oven to 350F (175C). Place butter or margarine in a 9-inch cake pan. Place pan in oven until butter or margarine melts. Stir brown sugar into melted butter or margarine.
**2.** Arrange pineapple slices in a single layer in butter-sugar mixture. Place 1 cherry, cut-side up, in center of each pineapple slice.
**3.** To make cake, sift flour, granulated sugar, baking powder and salt into a large mixer bowl. Add egg, shortening, milk and vanilla; beat at low speed until blended. Increase speed to high; beat 3 minutes. Pour batter evenly over pineapple slices; smooth top.
**4.** Bake 40 to 45 minutes or until a wooden pick inserted in center of cake comes out clean. Cool in pan on a wire rack 2 minutes. Invert cake on a serving plate; leave pan over cake 3 to 4 minutes. Carefully remove pan.
**5.** Serve warm or cold with sweetened whipped cream, if desired. Makes 6 servings.

# Frozen Zabaglione

**6 egg yolks**
**6 tablespoons sugar**
**6 tablespoons Marsala**
**2/3 cup whipping cream**

*To decorate:*
**Whipped cream**
**Toasted nuts or angelica leaves**

1. In a large heatproof bowl, combine egg yolks, sugar and Marsala. Place over a pan of simmering water; beat 10 minutes or until thick and pale.
2. Remove from heat; beat 5 minutes or until cool.
3. In a small bowl, whip cream until soft peaks form. Fold whipped cream into cooled egg mixture.
4. Spoon mixture into an ice-cream container. Freeze in an ice-cream maker according to manufacturer's directions. Decorate with whipped cream, nuts or angelica leaves.
5. For special occasions, make lemon baskets as illustrated. Fill with softened zabaglione. Place in freezer until firm. Makes 6 to 8 servings.

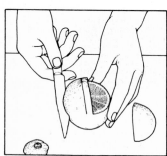

1/Using a sharp knife, form a handle.

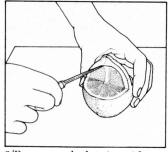

2/Remove pulp, leaving pith and peel intact.

# Lemon Ice Cream

**Grated peel of 2 lemons**
**Juice of 3 lemons**
**3/4 cup sugar**
**1-1/4 cups whipping cream**
**1 cup milk**

*To decorate:*
**Angelica leaves, if desired**

1. In a medium bowl, combine lemon peel, lemon juice and sugar. Add cream; whip until soft peaks form.
2. Slowly beat in milk. Pour into an ice-cream container. Freeze in an ice-cream maker according to manufacturer's directions.
3. Serve ice cream in dessert dishes. Decorate with angelica leaves, if desired. Makes 8 servings.

# Strawberry Ice

**1/2 cup sugar**
**1 cup water**
**1-1/2 teaspoons lemon juice**
**2 cups fresh or frozen strawberries, pureed**

1. In a medium saucepan, combine sugar and water. Stir over low heat until sugar dissolves. Boil 3 minutes. Cool.
2. Stir in lemon juice and strawberries. Pour into an ice-cream container. Freeze in an ice-cream maker according to manufacturer's directions.
3. To serve, make small scoops with a melon baller. Makes 4 servings.

**Variation**
Substitute any soft fruit or fruit puree for strawberries. As a general guide, use 1 cup unsweetened fruit puree; follow directions above. For an attractive presentation, serve 2 or 3 different flavors. Decorate with a medley of fresh fruit. For example, serve pear, strawberry and raspberry ices with pear slices and 1 or 2 raspberries and strawberries. Or, spoon a little fruit liqueur over top of ices before serving.

Clockwise from top left: Strawberry Ice, Frozen Zabaglione in lemon baskets, Lemon Ice Cream

# Praline Ice Cream

*Praline:*
1/2 cup sugar
3/4 cup unblanched almonds

*Custard Base:*
1-1/4 cups half and half
1 egg
2 egg yolks
1/2 cup sugar
1-1/4 cups whipping cream

1. To make praline, grease a baking sheet. Place sugar and almonds in a saucepan over medium heat until sugar caramelizes. Do not stir. Pour mixture onto greased baking sheet; cool until hard. Grate hard praline with a rotary grater; set aside.
2. In a small saucepan over low heat, bring half and half to a simmer.
3. In a medium, heatproof bowl, beat egg, egg yolks and sugar. Stir in hot half and half; place bowl over a pan of hot water. Cook about 20 minutes or until custard is thick enough to coat back of a spoon, stirring constantly. Cool to room temperature. Refrigerate until cold.
4. In a medium bowl, whip cream until stiff peaks form. Fold into refrigerated custard with 3/4 of praline. Spoon into an ice-cream container. Freeze in an ice-cream maker according to manufacturer's directions.
5. To serve, scoop spoonfuls into a serving dish; sprinkle with remaining praline. Makes 6 servings.

# Chestnut Log

8 oz. semisweet chocolate pieces
3/4 cup butter or margarine
2 cups chestnut puree (about 16 oz.)
2 eggs
1 cup sugar
2 tablespoons brandy

*To decorate:*
Semisweet chocolate, melted
Marrons glacés, if desired

1. In a heatproof bowl over hot water, melt 1/2 of chocolate pieces and butter or margarine. Remove from heat; beat in chestnut puree.
2. In a medium bowl, beat eggs and sugar until thick and pale. Beat into chocolate mixture. Stir in brandy and remaining chocolate pieces.
3. Line a 9" x 5" loaf pan with foil or plastic wrap. Spoon chocolate mixture into lined pan. Freeze until almost firm. Remove from pan. Place frozen mixture on a large piece of foil; roll into a log shape. Return to freezer until firm.
4. To serve, place chocolate log on a serving plate. Decorate with melted chocolate and marrons glacés, if desired. Soften at room temperature 15 to 30 minutes before serving. Makes 10 to 12 servings.

# Chocolate-Rum Cake

1/2 cup butter or margarine, room temperature
8 oz. semisweet chocolate
1/2 cup sugar
3 eggs
2/3 cup maraschino cherries
1 cup coarsely chopped pecans, almonds or walnuts
2 tablespoons dark rum
1/2 (11-oz.) pkg. tea cookies, broken into pieces

1. Grease a 9" x 5" loaf pan. Line pan with waxed paper; grease paper.
2. In a small saucepan over low heat, melt butter or margarine and chocolate until smooth, stirring constantly. Cool.
3. In a medium bowl, beat sugar and eggs until thick and lemon-colored. Gradually stir in cooled chocolate mixture. Stir in cherries, nuts, rum and cookies. Spoon mixture into prepared pan; cover with waxed paper. Freeze several hours or until firm.
4. To serve, invert on a serving plate; remove pan and paper. Place in refrigerator 30 minutes to soften. Makes 12 to 14 servings.

# Mississippi Mud Pie

### Crumb Crust:
1-1/2 cups chocolate wafer crumbs
1/4 cup butter or margarine, melted

### Filling:
1 qt. mocha or coffee ice cream (4 cups)
1 pint double-chocolate ice cream (2 cups)
3 tablespoons coffee-flavored liqueur

### Chocolate Sauce:
4 oz. unsweetened chocolate, broken into pieces
1 cup milk or half and half
1/2 cup sugar
1/3 cup light corn syrup
3 tablespoons butter or margarine
1 teaspoon vanilla extract

### To decorate:
Sweetened whipped cream
Grated chocolate

*This is a simple ice-cream pie served with a warm chocolate sauce.*

**1.** To make crust, in a medium bowl, combine crumbs and butter or margarine until blended. Press crumbs on bottom and up side of a 9-inch pie pan. Freeze until firm.

**2.** To make filling, in a large bowl, combine mocha ice cream and chocolate ice cream; let stand at room temperature about 15 minutes to soften. Stir in coffee-flavored liqueur until blended. Spoon ice-cream mixture into frozen crust; smooth top. Place in freezer until ice cream is firm.

**3.** To make sauce, in a medium saucepan over low heat, combine chocolate, milk or half and half, sugar and corn syrup. Cook until chocolate is melted, stirring constantly. Remove from heat; stir in butter or margarine and vanilla. Pour warm sauce into a serving pitcher.

**4.** Decorate frozen pie with sweetened whipped cream and grated chocolate. Serve with warm Chocolate Sauce. Makes 8 to 10 servings.

Clockwise from top left: Chestnut Log, Praline Ice Cream, Chocolate-Rum Cake

# Coffee-Ice-Cream Bombe

1 qt. coffee ice cream (4 cups)
1 pint French-vanilla ice cream (2 cups)
1/2 cup toasted hazelnuts or almonds, finely chopped

*To decorate:*
1/2 pint whipping cream (1 cup)
Chocolate coffee-bean candies or toasted nuts

---

**1.** Place a 1-1/4- or 1-1/2-quart bombe mold or metal bowl in freezer overnight.
**2.** Reserve 1 cup coffee ice cream for top of mold. Soften remaining coffee ice cream, if necessary.
**3.** With back of a large spoon, spread coffee ice cream evenly around side and bottom of chilled mold or bowl. Return mold or bowl and remaining ice cream to freezer until firm.
**4.** In a medium bowl, soften vanilla ice cream; stir in nuts. Pack vanilla-ice-cream mixture in center of coffee-ice-cream-lined mold or bowl, leaving a 1-inch space at top. Freeze again until solid.
**5.** Soften reserved coffee ice cream; use to fill mold to top. Cover with an oiled circle of waxed paper and a lid. Freeze until firm.
**6.** To decorate, whip cream until stiff peaks form. Spoon whipped cream into a pastry bag fitted with an open star tip. Refrigerate pastry bag while unmolding bombe.
**7.** To serve, invert bombe on a serving plate. Wet a dish towel with hot water; wring dry. Wrap towel around mold a few seconds. Carefully remove mold.
**8.** Decorate bombe with whipped cream. Pipe whipped cream into 2 rows of shell designs across bombe, intersecting rows at top. Pipe stars around base of bombe; pipe a large star where rows of shells meet. Arrange coffee-bean candies or toasted nuts along whipped-cream shells.
**9.** Serve immediately. Makes 6 to 8 servings.

Coffee-Ice-Cream Bombe

# Frozen Lemon Pie

*Crust:*
3 cups graham-cracker crumbs
1/2 cup butter or margarine, melted

*Filling:*
8 eggs, separated
Grated peel of 3 lemons
1 cup lemon juice
1 (14-oz. can) sweetened condensed milk
1/2 cup sugar

*To decorate:*
Whipped cream
Finely shredded lemon peel

---

**1.** To make crust, in a medium bowl, combine graham-cracker crumbs and butter or margarine. Line bottoms and sides of 2 (9-inch) pie pans with crumb mixture. Refrigerate until firm.
**2.** To make filling, in a large bowl, beat egg yolks until pale. Stir in lemon peel, lemon juice and condensed milk.
**3.** In a large bowl, beat egg whites until soft peaks form; gradually beat in sugar. Beat until stiff and glossy. Fold beaten egg-white mixture into lemon mixture. Divide filling between chilled crusts.
**4.** Freeze until firm. When frozen, wrap pies tightly with plastic wrap and then foil; label. Freeze up to 1 month.
**5.** Decorate top with small dollops of whipped cream and lemon peel. Makes 2 (9-inch) pies.

# Chocolate & Orange Cups

4 oz. semisweet chocolate, melted
1/2 cup whipping cream
2 tablespoons orange-flavored yogurt
2 tablespoons orange-juice concentrate, thawed

*To decorate:*
Candied orange-peel strips

---

**1.** Working 1 at a time, pour a little melted chocolate into 6 foil baking cups. Carefully brush a thin layer of chocolate up sides of cups.
**2.** Refrigerate until firm; then repeat step 1 using remaining chocolate. Refrigerate until firm again. Carefully peel away foil cups. Place chocolate cups on a baking sheet; freeze.
**3.** To make filling, in a medium bowl, whip cream until stiff peaks form. Fold in yogurt and orange-juice concentrate. Spoon into frozen chocolate cups; swirl tops.
**4.** Decorate each cup with candied orange-peel strips. Freeze until served. Makes 6 servings.

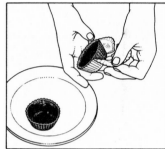
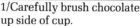

1/Carefully brush chocolate up side of cup.

2/When firm, carefully peel away foil cup.

Chocolate & Orange Cups

Snappy Ginger Sundaes

# Snappy Ginger Sundaes

*Ginger Horns:*
1/4 cup butter or margarine
1/4 cup superfine sugar
2 tablespoons light corn syrup
1/2 cup sifted all-purpose flour
1/2 teaspoon ground ginger
1 tablespoon ginger-flavored brandy or
  syrup from preserved ginger

*Filling:*
3/4 cup whipping cream
1 tablespoon powdered sugar
1 qt. vanilla ice cream, or praline ice cream, page 412
Stem ginger preserved in syrup, chopped

1. Preheat oven to 350F (175C). Grease 2 baking sheets.
2. To make Ginger Horns, in a small saucepan, combine butter or margarine, superfine sugar and corn syrup. Stir over low heat until butter or margarine is melted. Remove from heat; stir in flour, ground ginger and brandy or ginger syrup until blended.

3. Using 1 level teaspoon of batter for each cookie, form 3 cookies 3 inches apart on each greased baking sheet. Do not put more than 3 cookies on 1 baking sheet.
4. Place 1 baking sheet at a time in oven; bake 5 to 6 minutes or until cookies are golden brown. Cool on baking sheet 10 seconds. Remove cookies carefully with a wide flat spatula; roll each cookie around a metal pastry horn. Cool completely on a wire rack. When cool, remove metal horn. Repeat to make about 18 cookies.
5. To make filling, in a medium bowl, beat cream until soft peaks form. Beat in powdered sugar; beat until stiff peaks form. Spoon whipped-cream mixture into a pastry bag fitted with an open star tip. Pipe whipped cream into Ginger Horns.
6. Spoon ice cream into 6 tall glasses. Add 2 or 3 filled Ginger Horns; decorate with preserved ginger. Serve immediately. Makes 6 servings.

# Mocha-Marshmallow Bombe

1/3 cup dark raisins
1/4 cup golden raisins
1/4 cup currants
1/3 cup pitted, dark sweet cherries, cut into quarters
1/3 cup chopped toasted blanched almonds
3 tablespoons sweet sherry
22 large marshmallows (2-3/4 cups)
2/3 cup milk
1 tablespoon instant coffee powder
1 tablespoon unsweetened cocoa powder
1/2 pint whipping cream (1 cup)
2 tablespoons powdered sugar

---

1. In a medium bowl, combine raisins, currants, cherries and almonds. Stir in sherry. Let stand at room temperature 1 hour.
2. In a medium saucepan, combine marshmallows, milk, coffee powder and cocoa powder. Cook over low heat until marshmallows are melted, stirring constantly. Set aside to cool.
3. In a medium bowl, whip cream until soft peaks form. Beat in powdered sugar; beat until stiff peaks form. Fold in cooled marshmallow mixture. Fold in fruit mixture. Pour into a 6-cup mold; smooth top. Freeze until firm.
4. To serve, invert on a serving plate. Wet a dish towel with hot water; wring dry. Place hot towel around mold a few seconds. Remove mold. Place in refrigerator 20 to 30 minutes to soften before serving. Makes 6 to 8 servings.

### Variation
Soften 1 quart of good-quality mocha or coffee ice cream. Stir sherried fruit mixture from step 1 into ice cream. Pack into a 1-quart mold. Freeze until firm.

# Nut Tortoni

2 egg whites
1/4 cup sugar
1-1/4 cups whipping cream
1/4 cup amaretto liqueur
1-1/2 cups toasted blanched almonds, coarsely chopped

---

1. In a medium bowl, beat egg whites until soft peaks form. Gradually beat in sugar, 1 tablespoon at a time, until mixture is stiff and glossy.
2. In a medium bowl, whip cream until stiff peaks form. Fold whipped cream into egg-white mixture. Fold in amaretto liqueur and 1/2 of almonds.
3. Spoon mixture into a 9" x 5" loaf pan. Cover and freeze.
4. Invert on a serving plate. Wet a dish towel with hot water; wring dry. Wrap hot towel around pan a few seconds. Remove pan. Press remaining almonds over loaf until completely covered. Freeze again until served. Makes 6 to 8 servings.

# Lemon Loaf

1 cup butter or margarine, room temperature
2 cups powdered sugar
Grated peel and juice of 2 large lemons
2 eggs, separated
2/3 cup whipping cream
2 tablespoons Marsala or medium sherry
1 (1-lb.) pound-cake loaf, cut into 3/8-inch slices

*To decorate:*
Whipped cream
Grated lemon peel

---

1. In a medium bowl, cream butter or margarine, 1-3/4 cups powdered sugar and lemon peel until light and fluffy. Beat in egg yolks, 1 at a time. Beat in 1/2 of lemon juice.
2. In a medium bowl, whip cream until soft peaks form. Fold whipped cream into lemon butter. In a medium bowl, beat egg whites until stiff peaks form. Fold beaten egg whites into lemon mixture.
3. In a small bowl, combine remaining lemon juice and Marsala or sherry. Cover bottom of a 9" x 5" loaf pan with cake slices; sprinkle with a little of Marsala or sherry mixture. Spoon in 1/3 of lemon mixture. Repeat layers, ending with cake. There should be 3 layers of lemon mixture and 4 layers of cake. Freeze until served.
4. To serve, invert on a serving plate; remove pan. Decorate with whipped-cream rosettes and grated lemon peel. Allow to soften in refrigerator 30 minutes before serving. Makes 8 servings.

Top to bottom: Mocha-Marshmallow Bombe, Nut Tortoni

# Chocolate

Smooth, luscious chocolate, one of the world's great luxuries, can be used to create a great variety of delights. In this section, we cover the whole field of tempting chocolate morsels, from impressive cakes to simple treats, such as candies and cookies.

There is a selection of delicious, easily made puddings, sauces and desserts. These are chocolate treats you can whip up in a hurry to impress family and friends. Try the eye-catching *Fruit Split* with a chocolate sauce, or *Apricot & Chocolate Dream*, so easy and so good!

This section also includes the more exotic and impressive chocolate desserts. There are cheesecakes, pies, soufflés and ice creams that would make a grand finale to any dinner party. Impress your guests with *Soufflé Monte Carlo*, or *Ginger Charlotte Russe*. Thrill them with the elegance of *Chocolate Hearts*, or spoil them with classic *Cream Puffs with Chocolate Sauce*. Try mouthwatering *Chocolate Fudge*, or the *Coconut-Topped Pyramids*.

Around the World gives you a taste of chocolate treats from other countries. Old favorites, such as *Bûche de Noel* and *Truffles*, are included. We also show that classic desserts can be adapted to make the most of chocolate. Even the great Australian dessert, *Pavlova*, can be enhanced by the addition of chocolate.

## TYPES OF CHOCOLATE

The major difference in the types of chocolate is in the amounts of *chocolate liquor*, *cocoa butter*, sugar and other flavorings that the chocolate contains. After the cacao beans are fermented, dried, roasted and hulled, *chocolate liquor* is the finished product. It contains approximately 50 percent cocoa butter. To make unsweetened cocoa powder, some of this cocoa butter is removed. Additional cocoa butter is blended with chocolate liquor to make fine chocolates. The quality and specific formula for a type of chocolate will vary from one brand to another. There is a wide price range in chocolates; buy the one dictated by your taste and budget.

### Unsweetened Chocolate

This is also known as bitter or baking chocolate. Bitter chocolate contains no sugar; it may replace a proportion of the chocolate used in some recipes for a stronger, slightly bitter flavor.

### Bittersweet Chocolate

This is a slightly sweet chocolate that is widely used in baking, desserts and candy. This is also sometimes called sweet chocolate. The amount of sugar will depend on the brand.

### Sweet Cooking Chocolate

This is a special blend of chocolate that includes sugar. It is used most often for German Chocolate Cake.

### Milk Chocolate

Milk chocolate has a mild chocolate flavor and is the type preferred by most Americans. In addition to sugar, chocolate liquor, cocoa butter and flavorings, dried milk is added during processing.

### White Chocolate

White chocolate is not legally chocolate since it contains no chocolate liquor, but only cocoa butter. It also contains sugar, flavorings and dried milk. White chocolate has a higher sugar content than dark chocolate and is usually considered more of a candy than a cooking chocolate. However, it can be used in cooking and is included in a few recipes here. Great care should be taken when cooking with white chocolate. It is difficult to melt; it softens very slowly and is apt to become grainy.

### Confectionery Coating

This is often called artificial chocolate or compound chocolate since some or all of the cocoa butter has been replaced by other fats, such as coconut oil or palm oil. Sometimes part of the chocolate liquor is replaced by other flavoring agents. This chocolate is economical and easy to use. It is suitable for dipping, cake frostings and chocolate decorations.

# CHOCOLATE DECORATIONS

## Chocolate Squares, Triangles & Wedges

Melt 4 ounces chocolate; see box below. Using a long flexible spatula, spread melted chocolate 1/8-inch thick on waxed paper or foil. Let set. When set, trim the edges of the chocolate. Using a ruler, mark out even-sized squares or rectangles. Cut with a thin sharp knife. Cut squares diagonally to make triangles; cut rectangles diagonally to make wedges. Carefully lift onto a flat plate or board lined with parchment paper. Handle as little as possible to prevent melting.

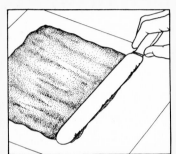

1/Using a long, flexible spatula, spread melted chocolate 1/8-inch thick on waxed paper or foil.

2/Using a ruler, mark out squares or rectangles. Cut with a thin sharp knife.

---

### Melting Chocolate

There are several methods to successfully melt chocolate. Always grate or chop chocolate into pieces before melting. Excess heat causes chocolate to become dry and grainy.

To use a double boiler, place chocolate pieces in the top of a double boiler over barely simmering water. Stir until smooth. Do not get any water drops in the chocolate or it will *seize*, or become hard and grainy. Chocolate that has seized can be saved by stirring in a few teaspoons vegetable shortening, a little at a time.

To use a microwave oven, place chocolate pieces in a small microwave-safe dish. Cook 30 seconds. Check chocolate; chocolate may still look solid but actually be melted. Repeat as many times as needed to almost melt chocolate. Stir until smooth. This method works best with larger amounts of chocolate.

To use a saucepan, melt chocolate pieces in a heavy saucepan over very low heat. Stir until smooth. This method is most successful when additional ingredients, such as butter or margarine, are heated with the chocolate.

## Chocolate Leaves

Melt 2 ounces chocolate; see box below. Stir until smooth; cool to 92F to 100F (35C) or until it has a smooth, glossy appearance. Follow the illustrations below.

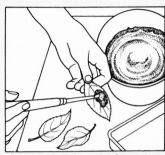

1/Using a brush, spread melted chocolate on underside of dry, clean leaves.

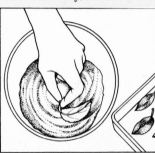

2/Or, dip underside of leaves in melted chocolate. Place on waxed paper to set.

3/When chocolate is firm, carefully peel away leaf, starting at the stem.

## Chocolate Curls

Hold a bar of room-temperature chocolate over a plate. Draw the blade of a vegetable peeler along the thin edge of the bar; let the curls fall onto the plate.

## Grated Chocolate

Chill chocolate for about 15 minutes. Using the size grater desired, grate chocolate finely or coarsely onto a plate. Hold

the chilled chocolate with a small piece of foil to prevent your fingers from melting the chocolate. Remove foil as the chocolate piece gets smaller.

## Chopped Chocolate

Break room-temperature chocolate into squares. Place on a chopping board. With a sharp, heavy knife, chop squares into pieces of desired size.

## Chocolate Cut-Out Shapes

Melt 4 ounces chocolate; see page 423. Using a long flexible spatula, spread melted chocolate 1/8-inch thick on waxed paper or foil. Let set. Stamp out shapes using small cookie or canapé cutters. Leftover chocolate can be melted and used again.

## Chocolate Scrolls

Melt unsweetened or semisweet chocolate; see page 423. Using a long flexible spatula, spread melted chocolate to a thickness of about 1/8 inch on a cool work surface. Cool until set. Push a long heavy knife or heavy metal spatula under the chocolate at a slight angle. Shorter scrolls are formed by pushing the blunt end of a spatula under chocolate.

## Chocolate Bark

Spread melted chocolate as above; cool until set. Place a long sharp knife on the surface of chocolate; hold the tip of knife securely. Holding the knife at a slight angle, push knife slightly into the chocolate. Scrape in a quarter circle to produce long thin chocolate curls, keeping knife point at the same location. With practice, very long curls can be made.

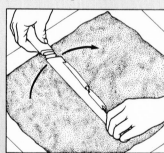

## STORING & CHILLING CHOCOLATE

Store chocolate in a cool, dry place. During hot weather all chocolate used for decorations may need to be placed in the refrigerator to set. Chocolate absorbs odors very easily. If you keep chocolate in the refrigerator or freezer for any length of time, wrap it tightly. The grayish-white film or *bloom* that you sometimes see on chocolate is the result of cocoa butter or sugar crystals rising to the surface after exposure to varying temperatures. It does not affect the flavor and disappears when the chocolate is melted.

## PIPED DECORATIONS

**Rosettes**—Use a star or special rosette tip. With tip close to cake surface, pipe icing in a complete circle, ending in the center. Finish off quickly to leave a small raised point.

**Stars**—Use a star tip. With pastry bag upright and tip close to cake surface, pipe out icing to size of star desired; quickly pull away with a down and then up movement.

**Shells**—Use a special shell tip or star tip. Pressing lightly on bag and with tip close to cake surface, move the tip away from and then toward you, pressing out more icing for the fat part of the shell.

**Scrolls**—Use a star tip. With tip close to cake surface, make a question mark with icing, beginning with a thick head and gradually releasing the pressure to make a long tail. Make a second scroll on the tail of the first to form a chain, or reverse design to make double scrolls.

**Ropes**—Use a plain tip. Pipe icing with a steady pressure to make even ropes and lines.

**Ribbons**—Use a flat serrated-ribbon tip to make basket designs, ribbons or edgings. To make woven baskets, use a ribbon tip and a plain tip.

## To make a parchment-paper pastry bag

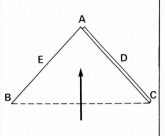

1/Fold a 10-inch square of parchment paper in half to form a triangle.

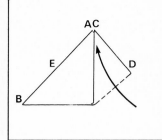

2/Place triangle on a flat surface. Fold point C to point A; crease well.

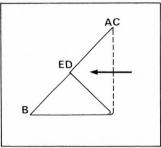

3/Fold point D to point E; crease well.

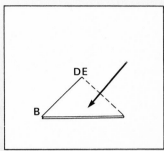

4/Fold point AC to point B; crease well.

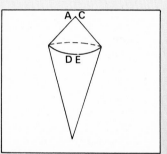

5/Hold bag where points D and E meet. Shape into a cone; fold point AC inside bag.

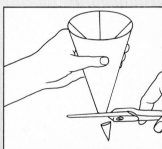

6/Barely cut off tip of cone. Do not fill bag more than half full.

---

### Piping Whipped Cream

Whipped cream for piping can be sweetened or unsweetened. The whipped cream should be stiff enough to hold its shape. Too soft a cream will flatten and not be attractive. Do not overbeat the cream or it will turn into butter and be grainy.

To pipe whipped cream, spoon into a cloth or plastic pastry bag or a parchment-paper pastry bag; see illustrations above. Attach the tip to the pastry bag with a coupling if you want to change tips. Be sure to put the tip or coupling in place before filling the bag! Force the cream out by exerting pressure with your fingers and palm of one hand, while guiding the tip with the other hand.

Sometimes piping will cause the cream to be buttery and uneven. If this happens, discard cream; wash and dry the bag and start again.

# Soufflé Monte Carlo

1 tablespoon instant coffee powder
1 tablespoon boiling water
1 (1/4-oz.) envelope unflavored gelatin (1 tablespoon)
1/2 cup granulated sugar
4 eggs, separated
1/2 cup cold water
1-3/4 cups whipping cream
3 tablespoons powdered sugar
1 cup almond-macaroon crumbs
1/4 cup coffee-flavored liqueur
4 oz. semisweet chocolate, finely chopped
Chocolate coffee-bean candies

*To decorate:*
Chocolate scrolls, page 424

1. Wrap a 3-inch foil collar around outside of a 1-quart glass soufflé dish. Secure collar with a small piece of tape.
2. In a small bowl, dissolve coffee in boiling water. Combine gelatin and granulated sugar in top of a double boiler. Whisk egg yolks and cold water into dissolved coffee until blended. Whisk egg mixture into gelatin mixture until blended.
3. Place over a pan of simmering water. Cook, stirring constantly, until mixture thickens and coats back of a spoon. Pour cooked coffee mixture into a large bowl. Let cool 15 minutes, stirring occasionally. Cover surface with a sheet of waxed paper to prevent a skin from forming; refrigerate until cooled.
4. In a medium bowl, beat cream until soft peaks form. Beat in powdered sugar. Spoon 2/3 cup whipped-cream mixture into a pastry bag fitted with a star or rosette tip; refrigerate. Fold remaining whipped-cream mixture into cooled coffee mixture. Refrigerate 30 minutes.
5. In a small bowl, combine cookie crumbs and liqueur; let stand until liqueur is absorbed. Stir in chocolate.
6. In a large bowl, beat egg whites until stiff but not dry. Fold beaten egg whites into chilled coffee cream.
7. Sprinkle a layer of crumb mixture into bottom of prepared soufflé dish. Top with a layer of coffee cream. Repeat to make 3 layers of each, ending with coffee cream. Refrigerate 3 hours or until set.
8. Carefully remove foil collar from soufflé dish. Pipe reserved whipped-cream mixture in rosettes on top of soufflé. Decorate with coffee-bean candies and chocolate scrolls. Refrigerate until served. Makes 6 to 8 servings.

# Chocolate-Mint Soufflé

2 tablespoons sugar
1/4 cup butter or margarine
1/4 cup all-purpose flour
1 cup milk
1/4 cup sugar
3 oz. semisweet or sweet chocolate, chopped
4 egg yolks
2 tablespoons white or green crème de menthe
5 egg whites

*Sauce:*
2/3 cup whipping cream
2 oz. semisweet chocolate, chopped
1 egg yolk, beaten
2 tablespoons white or green crème de menthe

1. Butter a 1-1/2-quart 7-inch soufflé dish. Sprinkle with about 2 tablespoons sugar; shake out excess.
2. Melt butter or margarine in a medium saucepan over medium heat. Whisk in flour to make a smooth roux. Cook, stirring, 1 minute. Gradually whisk in milk; cook, stirring constantly, until mixture thickens and comes to a boil. Whisk in 1/4 cup sugar. Add chocolate; stir until chocolate melts. Remove from heat.
3. In a small bowl, slightly beat egg yolks. Stir 1/4 cup hot sauce into egg yolks until blended. Return mixture to saucepan; stir well. Cook, stirring, until thickened. Do not boil. Pour into a large bowl; stir in crème de menthe. Cover surface with a sheet of waxed paper to prevent a skin from forming; refrigerate until cooled.
4. Preheat oven to 350F (175C). In a large bowl, beat egg whites until stiff but not dry. Fold beaten egg whites into cooled chocolate mixture. Pour mixture into prepared dish.
5. Bake in preheated oven 40 to 50 minutes or until puffed and a skewer inserted in center comes out clean.
6. While soufflé is baking, make sauce. To make sauce, in a small saucepan over low heat, combine cream and chocolate. Cook, stirring, until chocolate melts and mixture is smooth. Remove from heat. Whisk in egg yolk and crème de menthe until smooth. Pour into a small serving pitcher.
7. Remove soufflé from oven; serve immediately with sauce. Makes 6 servings.

Left to right: Soufflé Monte Carlo, Chocolate-Mint Soufflé

# Ginger Charlotte Russe

*Topping:*
1 teaspoon unflavored gelatin powder
5 tablespoons water
5 tablespoons ginger wine or ginger brandy
1/2 maraschino cherry
5 candied orange slices or 5 canned mandarin-orange
   sections, drained
1 thin strip angelica, about 2 inches long
About 8 whole ladyfingers, split lengthwise

*Bavarian:*
1 (1/4-oz.) envelope unflavored gelatin (1 tablespoon)
1/3 cup granulated sugar
1 cup milk
2 oz. semisweet chocolate, chopped
2 eggs, separated
1/4 cup ginger wine or ginger brandy
1-1/4 cups whipping cream
2 tablespoons powdered sugar

*To decorate:*
1 (3-foot) ribbon, if desired

Left to right: Ginger Charlotte Russe, Chocolate-Pear Cake, Mandarin-Yogurt Dessert

1. To make topping, in a small saucepan, combine gelatin and water. Stir well; let stand 3 minutes. Stir over low heat until gelatin dissolves; cool slightly. Stir in wine or brandy.
2. Pour half of gelatin mixture into bottom of a 2-quart, 6-inch-diameter charlotte mold. Place cherry, rounded-side down, in bottom of mold. Arrange candied orange slices or orange sections around cherry to resemble a flower. Use strip of angelica for stem. Refrigerate 30 minutes or until gelatin is firm.
3. Pour remaining dissolved gelatin mixture into mold; refrigerate 10 to 15 minutes or until almost set. Line mold with ladyfingers, pushing bottom ends of ladyfingers into almost-set gelatin. Refrigerate until gelatin is firm.
4. To make bavarian, in a medium saucepan, combine gelatin and granulated sugar. Stir in milk. Cook over low heat, stirring, until gelatin dissolves. Stir in chocolate; cook until mixture thickens and coats back of a spoon. Remove pan from heat.
5. In a small bowl, slightly beat egg yolks. Stir 1/4 cup hot chocolate mixture into beaten egg yolks until blended. Return mixture to saucepan; stir well. Cook, stirring, until mixture is thickened. Do not boil.
6. Pour into a medium bowl. Stir in wine or brandy. Cover surface with a sheet of waxed paper to prevent a skin from forming. Refrigerate until mixture mounds when dropped from a spoon.
7. In a medium bowl, beat cream until soft peaks form. Beat in powdered sugar. Spoon 1/3 of whipped-cream mixture into a pastry bag fitted with a star or rosette tip; refrigerate. Fold remaining whipped-cream mixture into chilled chocolate mixture.

8. In a medium bowl, beat egg whites until stiff but not dry. Fold beaten egg whites into chocolate-cream mixture. Spoon mixture into lined charlotte mold; smooth top. Refrigerate several hours or until set.
9. To unmold, dip bottom of mold into hot water; invert onto a serving plate. Remove mold. Pipe chilled whipped-cream mixture in small rosettes on top of each ladyfinger. Refrigerate until served. Tie with ribbon immediately before serving, if desired. Makes 6 to 8 servings.

3. In a medium bowl, combine cooled gelatin mixture and yogurt. Gradually stir in melted chocolate until blended. Stir in reserved chopped orange sections, grated chocolate and liqueur until combined.

4. Pour mixture into a 2-1/2-cup decorative mold. Refrigerate 2 to 3 hours or until set.

5. To unmold, run tip of a knife around edge of mold to loosen. Rinse a towel under hot running water; wring dry. Wrap hot towel around mold; let stand 1 minute. Invert mold onto a serving plate; remove mold.

6. To serve, in a small bowl, beat cream until soft peaks form. Beat in powdered sugar. Spoon whipped-cream mixture into a pastry bag fitted with a star or rosette tip. Pipe a large rosette in center of molded mixture. Pipe small rosettes around base. Decorate top with reserved orange section and chocolate leaf. Refrigerate until served. Makes 6 servings.

## Chocolate-Pear Cake

*Topping:*
1/4 cup butter or margarine
1/3 cup firmly packed dark-brown sugar
1 (29-oz.) can pear halves, well drained
6 maraschino cherries or red candied cherries

*Cake:*
1/3 cup butter or margarine, room temperature
3/4 cup sugar
2 eggs
1 cup all-purpose flour
1/4 cup unsweetened cocoa powder
1 teaspoon baking powder
1/2 teaspoon salt
1/3 cup milk

*To decorate:*
Sliced almonds, if desired

1. Preheat oven to 350F (175C). Place butter or margarine in a deep 8-inch-round cake pan. Melt butter or margarine in preheated oven. Remove from oven. Sprinkle brown sugar over melted butter or margarine. Arrange 6 pear halves, cut-side down, on top of sugar. Slide 1 cherry under cavity of each pear half. Chop remaining pears; set aside.

2. To make cake, in a medium bowl, beat butter or margarine, sugar, eggs, flour, cocoa, baking powder, salt and milk with an electric mixer at low speed 1 minute or until blended.

3. Increase speed to medium; beat 2 minutes, scraping down side of bowl occasionally. Fold in reserved chopped pears. Carefully spoon batter over pear halves; smooth top.

4. Bake in preheated oven 45 to 50 minutes or until a wooden pick inserted in center comes out clean. Cool in pan on wire rack 2 minutes. Invert onto a serving plate; leave pan in place 3 minutes. Carefully remove pan. Serve warm or at room temperature. Decorate with sliced almonds, if desired. Makes 6 to 8 servings.

## Mandarin-Yogurt Dessert

1 (11-oz.) can mandarin-orange sections
1 (1/4-oz.) envelope unflavored gelatin (1 tablespoon)
8 oz. plain yogurt or vanilla-flavored yogurt (1 cup)
3 oz. semisweet chocolate, melted, cooled
1 oz. semisweet chocolate, finely grated
2 tablespoons orange-flavored liqueur
1/2 cup whipping cream
1 tablespoon powdered sugar

*To decorate:*
Chocolate leaf, page 423

1. Drain oranges, reserving syrup. Set 1 orange section aside for decoration. Coarsely chop remaining orange sections; set aside.

2. In a small saucepan, combine gelatin and reserved orange syrup. Stir well; let stand 3 minutes. Stir over low heat until gelatin dissolves; set aside to cool.

# Banana Bavarian

1 (3-oz.) pkg. lemon-flavored gelatin
1 cup boiling water
2 small bananas
1/4 cup granulated sugar
1 (1/4-oz.) envelope unflavored gelatin (1 tablespoon)
1-1/4 cups milk
3 eggs, separated
1 teaspoon grated lemon peel
1 teaspoon vanilla extract
1/2 pint whipping cream (1 cup)
2 tablespoons powdered sugar
4 oz. semisweet or bittersweet chocolate, coarsely
    chopped

1. In a medium bowl, dissolve lemon gelatin in boiling water. Pour 1/2 cup gelatin into bottom of an 8" x 4" loaf pan. Refrigerate 30 minutes or until firm. Thinly slice bananas; add to remaining lemon gelatin, stirring gently until banana slices are coated.

2. Remove banana slices with a slotted spoon; arrange in 3 lengthwise rows over set gelatin, slightly overlapping slices. Repeat with remaining banana slices. Spoon remaining lemon gelatin over banana slices; refrigerate until firm.

3. In a medium saucepan, combine granulated sugar and unflavored gelatin; stir in milk until smooth. Cook over low heat, stirring, until mixture thickens and coats back of a spoon. Remove from heat.

4. In a small bowl, slightly beat egg yolks. Stir 1/4 cup hot milk mixture into beaten egg yolks until blended. Return mixture to saucepan; stir well. Cook, stirring, until thickened. Do not boil. Pour into a large bowl.

5. Stir in lemon peel and vanilla until blended. Cover surface of custard with a sheet of waxed paper to prevent a skin from forming. Refrigerate about 45 minutes or until mixture mounds when dropped from a spoon.

6. In a medium bowl, beat cream until soft peaks form. Beat in powdered sugar. Fold 1/2 of whipped-cream mixture into chilled custard. Refrigerate remaining whipped-cream mixture.

7. In a medium bowl, beat egg whites until stiff but not dry. Fold beaten egg whites into custard mixture. Spoon custard-egg-white mixture over banana layer; smooth top. Refrigerate 3 to 4 hours or until set.

Left to right: Banana Bavarian, Steamed Fudge Pudding

**8.** Run tip of a knife around edge of pan to loosen dessert. Dip pan into hot water 30 seconds. Invert onto a serving plate; carefully remove pan.

**9.** Spread 1/2 of reserved whipped-cream mixture around sides of bavarian, smoothing cream with a long spatula. Spoon remaining reserved whipped-cream mixture into a pastry bag fitted with a small open-star tip; refrigerate.

**10.** Melt chocolate in a small heavy saucepan over very low heat; stir until smooth. Cool slightly. Spread chocolate on a sheet of foil to a 12" x 8" rectangle. Let stand until chocolate is set. Cut chocolate into 2" x 1" rectangles. Arrange chocolate rectangles lengthwise, slightly overlapping, around sides of bavarian, pressing rectangles gently into whipped cream. Pipe chilled whipped-cream mixture decoratively around top edge of chocolate rectangles. Refrigerate until served. Makes 8 to 10 servings.

# Steamed Fudge Pudding

*Pudding:*
1/4 cup butter or margarine, room temperature
3/4 cup sugar
1 egg
1 cup self-rising flour
1/4 cup unsweetened cocoa powder
1/4 cup milk

*Custard Sauce:*
1 tablespoon cornstarch
1/3 cup sugar
1/4 teaspoon salt
2 cups milk
3 egg yolks, beaten
1 teaspoon vanilla extract

*To decorate:*
Grated chocolate, if desired

**1.** Grease a 1-quart heatproof bowl or pudding mold. Cut a double thickness of foil large enough to cover top of bowl or mold and extend 2 inches down sides; grease 1 side.

**2.** To make pudding, in a medium bowl, beat butter or margarine and sugar until light and fluffy. Beat in egg until blended. Sift flour and cocoa into a medium bowl. Add flour mixture to sugar mixture alternately with milk; beat until blended.

**3.** Spoon into greased bowl or mold; smooth top. Cover bowl with foil, greased-side down; secure with kitchen string.

**4.** Place bowl or mold on a rack in a large deep pan. Pour in enough boiling water to come two-thirds of way up side of bowl or mold. Cover pan; steam pudding 1-1/4 to 1-1/2 hours or until a wooden pick inserted in center of pudding comes out clean, adding more boiling water as necessary to maintain water level. Remove pudding from pan; uncover. Let stand 5 minutes. Invert pudding onto a serving dish; remove bowl or mold.

**5.** To make custard sauce, in top of a double boiler, combine cornstarch, sugar and salt. Gradually stir in milk until smooth. Cook over a pan of simmering water, stirring, until sugar dissolves and mixture is slightly thickened. Remove from heat. Stir 6 tablespoons hot milk mixture into beaten egg yolks until thoroughly blended. Return mixture to pan; stir well. Cook, stirring, until mixture thickens and coats back of a spoon. Remove from heat; stir in vanilla.

**6.** Serve sauce warm or refrigerate until cooled. To serve, pour 1/2 of sauce over pudding; serve remaining sauce separately. Sprinkle pudding with chocolate, if desired. Makes 4 to 6 servings.

# Apricot & Chocolate Cheesecake

1 (11-1/2-oz.) pkg. creme-filled chocolate rolls (8 small rolls)
1 (1-lb.) can apricot halves
2 (8-oz.) pkgs. cream cheese, room temperature
1/3 cup granulated sugar
1 tablespoon lemon juice
2 eggs, separated
1 (1/4-oz.) envelope unflavored gelatin (1 tablespoon)
1/2 cup whipping cream
1 tablespoon powdered sugar

*To decorate:*
1 oz. semisweet chocolate, chopped
1 teaspoon vegetable shortening

---

1. Cut rolls into 1/2-inch-thick slices; use slices to line side and bottom of a 10-inch serving dish or glass pie dish.
2. Drain apricots, reserving 1/4 cup syrup. Set 4 apricots aside for decoration. In a blender or food processor fitted with a steel blade, process remaining apricots until pureed.
3. In a large bowl, beat cream cheese, granulated sugar and lemon juice until fluffy. Beat in egg yolks until blended. Beat in pureed apricots until blended.
4. In a small saucepan, combine gelatin and reserved apricot syrup. Stir well; let stand 3 minutes. Stir over low heat until gelatin dissolves; let cool.
5. Stir cooled gelatin mixture into cream-cheese mixture. Refrigerate about 30 minutes or until mixture is thickened.
6. In a medium bowl, beat cream until soft peaks form. Beat in powdered sugar. Fold 1/2 of whipped-cream mixture into cream-cheese mixture. Spoon remaining whipped-cream mixture into a pastry bag fitted with a star or rosette tip; refrigerate.
7. In a medium bowl, beat egg whites until stiff but not dry. Fold beaten egg whites into cream-cheese mixture. Pour cream-cheese mixture into cake-lined dish; smooth top. Refrigerate several hours or until set.
8. To decorate, in a small saucepan over low heat, melt chocolate and shortening; stir until smooth. Remove from heat; let cool. Spoon chocolate into a pastry bag fitted with a small plain writing tip. Pipe chocolate in parallel lines about 1 inch apart on top of cheesecake. Draw point of a sharp knife across piped lines in alternate directions to create a feathered effect.
9. Pipe chilled whipped-cream mixture in small rosettes around edge of cheesecake. Cut reserved apricots in half. Cut each apricot half into a fan shape; place between rosettes. Refrigerate until served. Makes 8 to 10 servings.

# Chocolate Chiffon Pie

*Pastry:*
1-1/2 cups all-purpose flour
2 tablespoons sugar
1/4 teaspoon salt
1/2 cup butter or margarine
1 egg yolk
2 to 2-1/2 tablespoons iced water

*Filling:*
1/2 cup half and half
1/2 cup sugar
1 (1/4-oz.) envelope unflavored gelatin (1 tablespoon)
1/2 cup water
2 eggs, separated
2 oz. unsweetened chocolate, chopped

*To decorate:*
Powdered sugar
2 oz. semisweet or sweet chocolate, finely grated

---

1. Preheat oven to 425F (220C). To make pastry, in a medium bowl, combine flour, sugar and salt. With a pastry blender or 2 knives, cut in butter or margarine until mixture resembles coarse crumbs. In a small bowl, beat egg yolk and 2 tablespoons water until blended. Sprinkle over flour; toss with a fork until mixture binds together, adding additional water if necessary. Knead dough in bowl 8 to 10 strokes or until smooth.
2. On a lightly floured surface, roll out pastry to an 11-inch circle. Use pastry to line a 9-inch quiche pan or tart pan with a removable bottom. Trim pastry even with rim of pan. Prick bottom of pastry with a fork. Line pastry with foil; fill with pie weights or dried beans.
3. Bake in preheated oven 10 minutes. Remove foil and pie weights or beans; reduce oven temperature to 375F (190C). Bake 5 to 8 minutes or until golden. Cool completely in pan on a wire rack.
4. To make filling, in a medium saucepan, whisk half and half, sugar, gelatin, water and egg yolks until thoroughly blended. Stir in chocolate. Cook over low heat, stirring constantly, until chocolate melts and gelatin dissolves. Pour into a medium bowl.
5. Beat chocolate mixture with an electric mixer at high speed 1 minute. Refrigerate 45 minutes or until thickened.
6. In a medium bowl, beat egg whites until stiff but not dry. Beat chocolate mixture on high speed 2 minutes or until fluffy. Fold beaten egg whites into beaten chocolate mixture. Pour into cooled pastry shell; smooth top. Refrigerate 2 to 3 hours or until set.
7. To serve, remove pie from pan; place on a serving plate. Sift powdered sugar over top; top with rows of chocolate. Makes 6 to 8 servings.

Left to right: Chocolate Chiffon Pie, Apricot & Chocolate
Cheesecake, Hot Chocolate Trifle

# Hot Chocolate Trifle

1 (11-1/2-oz.) pkg. jelly-filled rolls (8 small rolls)
1/4 cup sweet sherry
2 eggs
1 egg yolk
1/3 cup sugar
1 teaspoon vanilla extract
1-1/4 cups milk, scalded
2 oz. semisweet chocolate, melted

*To decorate:*
1/4 cup chopped red candied cherries
1/4 cup chopped walnuts, pecans or almonds

**1.** Grease a 1-quart ovenproof serving bowl. Cut rolls into
1/2-inch-thick slices; use slices to line bottom and side of
bowl. Cut remaining jelly-roll slices into cubes. Add cubed
jelly-roll slices to bowl. Sprinkle sherry over cake; set
aside.
**2.** In a medium bowl, beat eggs, egg yolk, sugar and vanilla
until blended. Gradually beat in hot milk and chocolate
until combined. Pour custard through a fine sieve over
cake in bowl. Let stand 30 minutes.
**3.** Preheat oven to 350F (175C). Place bowl in a deep pan.
Pour in enough boiling water to come halfway up side of
bowl.
**4.** Bake in preheated oven 1 hour 15 minutes or until custard is set. Remove bowl from pan; cool slightly on a wire
rack.
**5.** Sprinkle with cherries and nuts immediately before
serving. Serve warm or refrigerate until chilled. Makes 6
servings.

# Chocolate-Pecan Pots

1/2 cup pecan halves
1 (8-oz.) pkg. cream cheese, room temperature
1 tablespoon milk
1 tablespoon honey
2 teaspoons grated lemon peel
1 tablespoon lemon juice
1/3 cup chopped pitted dates
4 oz. semisweet chocolate
1 tablespoon butter or margarine

**1.** Set 4 pecan halves aside for decoration. Chop remaining pecans.

**2.** In a medium bowl, beat cream cheese until fluffy. Beat in milk, honey, lemon peel and lemon juice until blended. Fold in chopped pecans and dates.
**3.** Grate 2 ounces chocolate; fold into cream-cheese mixture. Spoon chocolate mixture into 4 (1/2-cup) ramekins; smooth tops.
**4.** Melt remaining 2 ounces chocolate and butter or margarine in a small saucepan over low heat; stir until smooth. Cool slightly.
**5.** Spoon a little melted chocolate over top of each dish; spread evenly. Place a reserved pecan half in center of each dish. Refrigerate 1 hour or until served. Makes 4 servings.

Strawberry-Cheesecake Boxes

# Chocolate Mousse

5 oz. semisweet chocolate, coarsely chopped
2 tablespoons strong black coffee
4 eggs, separated
1 tablespoon orange-flavored liqueur
1/2 pint whipping cream (1 cup)
2 tablespoons powdered sugar
Shaved chocolate, page 423

1. Melt chocolate in a medium heavy saucepan over very low heat; stir until smooth. Stir in coffee until blended. Remove from heat.
2. In a small bowl, slightly beat egg yolks. Stir in 3 tablespoons chocolate mixture until blended. Return mixture to pan.
3. Cook over low heat, stirring, 1 minute. Pour chocolate mixture into a medium bowl. Stir in liqueur; refrigerate until cool.
4. In a medium bowl, beat cream until soft peaks form. Beat in powdered sugar. Reserve 3/4 cup whipped-cream mixture for decoration; cover and refrigerate. Fold remaining whipped-cream mixture into cooled chocolate mixture.
5. In a medium bowl, beat egg whites until stiff but not dry. Fold beaten egg whites into chocolate-cream mixture. Spoon mixture into 6 to 8 individual ramekins, champagne glasses or a large serving bowl. Refrigerate at least 3 hours or overnight. To serve, spoon a dollop of reserved whipped-cream mixture on top of each serving; sprinkle with shaved chocolate. Makes 6 to 8 servings.

# Strawberry-Cheesecake Boxes

*Cake:*
2 eggs
1/3 cup sugar
1/2 teaspoon vanilla extract
1/2 cup sifted cake flour

*Filling:*
1 (3-oz.) pkg. strawberry-flavored gelatin
1/2 teaspoon unflavored gelatin powder
1 cup boiling water
1 tablespoon lemon juice
1 (8-oz.) pkg. cream cheese, room temperature
1/2 pint whipping cream (1 cup)
2 tablespoons powdered sugar
4 to 5 tablespoons red-currant jelly, melted, cooled

*To decorate:*
10 oz. semisweet or sweet chocolate, chopped
8 fresh strawberries, washed, hulled

1. Preheat oven to 375F (190C). Grease an 8-inch-square baking pan. Line bottom of pan with waxed paper; grease paper.
2. To make cake, in a medium bowl, beat eggs and sugar 10 to 12 minutes or until thick and lemon-colored. Mixture should fall in thick ribbons when beaters are lifted. Beat in vanilla.
3. Sift flour over egg mixture; fold in. Pour batter into prepared pan; smooth top.
4. Bake in preheated oven 18 to 20 minutes or until center springs back when lightly pressed. Cool in pan on a wire rack 5 minutes. Remove from pan; peel off lining paper. Cool completely on wire rack.
5. To make filling, line an 8-inch-square pan with waxed paper. In a small bowl, combine strawberry-flavored gelatin and unflavored gelatin. Stir in boiling water until gelatins dissolve. Stir in lemon juice. Refrigerate 30 to 40 minutes or until gelatin is syrupy.
6. In a large bowl, beat cream cheese until fluffy. Gradually beat in chilled gelatin mixture until blended. Refrigerate 30 minutes or until thickened.
7. In a medium bowl, beat cream until soft peaks form. Beat in powdered sugar. Spoon about 2/3 cup whipped-cream mixture into a pastry bag fitted with a star or rosette tip; refrigerate. Fold remaining whipped-cream mixture into cream-cheese mixture. Pour mixture into prepared pan. Refrigerate 3 hours or until set.
8. Place cooled cake on a flat surface; brush top lightly with jelly. Invert strawberry cheesecake on top of cake; peel off paper. Trim filling even with cake edges, if necessary. Cut into 16 (2-inch) squares.
9. To decorate, tape 2 waxed-paper or parchment-paper pieces together, making an area larger than a 16-inch square. Draw a 16-inch square on paper. Melt chocolate in a small heavy saucepan over very low heat; stir until smooth. Let cool slightly. Spread melted chocolate inside square. When chocolate is almost set, with a sharp knife, score into 64 (2-inch) squares. Let stand until completely set. Cut chocolate with a sharp knife along scored lines.
10. Brush sides of each cheesecake-topped cake square lightly with jelly. Press 4 chocolate squares onto sides of each cake square.
11. Pipe chilled whipped-cream mixture in a rosette in center of each square. Cut strawberries in half; place a strawberry half on each rosette. Place on a serving plate; refrigerate until served or up to 4 hours. Makes 16 servings.

# Chocolate Bread Pudding

2 tablespoons butter or margarine, room temperature
5 white-bread slices, crusts removed
1 teaspoon ground cinnamon
2-1/4 cups milk
1 teaspoon instant coffee powder
2 oz. semisweet chocolate, chopped
3 eggs
1/3 cup sugar
1 oz. semisweet chocolate, grated

1. Grease a 1-1/2- to 2-quart casserole.
2. Spread butter or margarine on 1 side of bread slices; sprinkle with cinnamon. Cut slices into 4 triangles; place triangles in greased casserole.
3. In a medium saucepan over low heat, combine milk, coffee and chopped chocolate. Cook, stirring, until chocolate melts. Remove from heat.
4. In a medium bowl, beat eggs and sugar until thick and lemon-colored.
5. Pour hot milk mixture into egg mixture in a slow steady stream, beating constantly. Pour milk mixture over bread in casserole; let stand at room temperature 30 minutes.
6. Preheat oven to 350F (175C). Place casserole in a deep roasting pan; pour in enough boiling water to come halfway up side of casserole.
7. Bake in preheated oven 1 hour. Sprinkle grated chocolate over top of pudding; bake 10 minutes or until pudding is set. Serve warm or chilled. Makes 4 to 6 servings.

# Crowning Glory

8 oz. semisweet chocolate, coarsely chopped
1/4 cup butter or margarine
2 eggs
3 tablespoons dark rum
1-2/3 cups vanilla-wafer or chocolate-cookie crumbs
    (35 to 40 cookies)
1/3 cup chopped toasted hazelnuts or almonds
1/3 cup red candied cherries, quartered
1/2 cup whipping cream
1 tablespoon powdered sugar
6 maraschino cherries

*Serve this rich confection in small slices. This is a good summertime dessert; no baking is required!*

1. Generously grease a 3-cup ring mold. Melt chocolate and butter or margarine in a medium heavy saucepan over very low heat. Stir until smooth.
2. In a medium bowl, beat eggs until blended. Whisk in 4 to 5 tablespoons melted chocolate mixture. Beat in remaining chocolate mixture until blended.
3. Beat in rum until blended. Stir in cookie crumbs, nuts and candied cherries until combined. Pour into greased mold; smooth top. Refrigerate 3 hours or until firm.
4. In a medium bowl, beat cream until soft peaks form. Beat in powdered sugar. Spoon whipped-cream mixture into a pastry bag fitted with a medium rosette or star tip; refrigerate.
5. To serve, dip mold in hot water 20 seconds. Invert onto a serving plate. Remove mold. Pipe 6 whipped-cream rosettes on top of mold; decorate with maraschino cherries. Refrigerate until served. Makes 6 to 8 servings.

# Rum & Raisin Mousse

1/3 cup raisins
1/4 cup rum
4 oz. semisweet chocolate, broken into pieces
2 eggs, separated
1-1/4 cups whipping cream

1. In a small bowl, combine raisins and rum. Cover and let stand 8 hours or overnight.
2. Melt chocolate in a small saucepan over very low heat; stir until smooth. Cool slightly.
3. Beat in egg yolks. Stir in raisins and rum.
4. In a medium bowl, beat cream until almost stiff. Spoon 1/2 cup whipped cream into a pastry bag fitted with a star or rosette tip; refrigerate. Fold remaining whipped cream into chocolate mixture.
5. In a medium bowl, beat egg whites until stiff but not dry. Fold beaten egg whites into chocolate mixture.
6. Spoon mixture into a 2-cup freezer-to-table serving dish; freeze about 2 hours or until barely firm. If frozen firm, soften in refrigerator before serving.
7. Pipe chilled whipped cream in a shell border around edge of mousse. Makes 4 servings.

Left to right: Rum & Raisin Mousse, Chocolate Bread Pudding,
Chocolate Hearts

# Chocolate Hearts

3 oz. semisweet chocolate, chopped
1 (8-oz.) pkg. cream cheese, room temperature
2 tablespoons granulated sugar
2 teaspoons grated orange peel
1/3 cup orange juice
1 teaspoon unflavored gelatin powder
1/2 cup whipping cream
1 teaspoon powdered sugar

*To serve:*
1 recipe Quick Chocolate Sauce, page 459, or sweetened
    whipped cream
Small chocolate hearts, page 424
Fresh orange sections

1. Dampen 4 pieces of double cheesecloth large enough to line 4 individual coeur a la crème molds or heart-shaped molds. Line molds with damp cheesecloth. Melt chocolate in a small heavy saucepan over very low heat; stir until smooth. Let cool slightly.
2. In a medium bowl, beat cream cheese and granulated sugar until fluffy. Beat in orange peel. Gradually beat in cooled chocolate.
3. In a small saucepan, combine orange juice and gelatin. Stir well; let stand 3 minutes. Stir over low heat until gelatin dissolves; let cool.
4. Stir cooled gelatin into chocolate mixture until thoroughly blended. Refrigerate 20 minutes or until thickened.
5. In a medium bowl, beat cream until soft peaks form. Beat in powdered sugar. Fold whipped-cream mixture into chocolate mixture.
6. Spoon chocolate mixture into lined molds; smooth tops. Fold ends of cheesecloth over top of chocolate mixture. Place mold in a baking pan. Refrigerate 2 hours.
7. Unfold ends of cheesecloth; invert molds onto 4 serving plates. Remove cheesecloth. Spread each heart with a thin layer of chocolate sauce, or decorate with sweetened whipped cream and chocolate hearts. Serve with fresh orange sections. Makes 4 servings.

# Cream Puffs with Chocolate Sauce

*Choux Paste:*
1/2 cup butter or margarine
1 cup water
1 tablespoon sugar
1/4 teaspoon salt
1 cup sifted all-purpose flour
4 eggs

*Filling:*
2 tablespoons cornstarch
6 tablespoons granulated sugar
1 tablespoon unsweetened cocoa powder
1 cup milk
3 egg yolks, beaten
3/4 cup whipping cream
1 teaspoon vanilla extract
2 tablespoons powdered sugar

*To serve:*
1 recipe Special Chocolate Sauce, page 459

**1.** Preheat oven to 400F (205C). Grease 2 baking sheets.
**2.** To make choux paste, in a medium saucepan over medium heat, combine butter or margarine, water, sugar and salt; bring to a boil. Stir in flour, all at once, with a wooden spoon until dough forms a ball and comes away from side of pan. Cool slightly.
**3.** Beat in eggs, 1 at a time, beating well after each addition.
**4.** Spoon dough into a pastry bag fitted with a large plain tip. Pipe 24 small balls about 2 inches apart on greased baking sheets.
**5.** Bake in preheated oven 25 to 30 minutes or until puffed and golden brown. Remove from baking sheets; cut a small slit in side of each cream puff to let steam escape. Cool completely on wire racks.
**6.** To make filling, in a medium saucepan, combine cornstarch, granulated sugar and cocoa. Stir in milk until blended. Cook, stirring, until mixture thickens and comes to a boil. Remove from heat. Stir 1/4 cup hot mixture into egg yolks until blended. Return mixture to saucepan; stir well. Cook, stirring, until mixture thickens. Do not boil.
**7.** Pour custard into a large bowl. Cover surface with a sheet of waxed paper to prevent a skin from forming. Refrigerate 2 to 3 hours or until completely chilled.
**8.** In a medium bowl, beat cream until soft peaks form. Beat in vanilla and powdered sugar. Fold whipped-cream mixture into chilled custard.
**9.** Cut tops off cream puffs. Remove and discard any soft dough from insides. Spoon filling into a pastry bag fitted with a large plain tip; pipe filling into bottom half of cream puffs. Replace tops.
**10.** Place filled cream puffs on a serving plate. Pour a little chocolate sauce over cream puffs; serve remaining sauce separately. Makes 24 cream puffs.

# Chocolate & Almond Pastry

1-1/2 cups sponge-cake crumbs
2/3 cup finely chopped almonds
1/4 cup granulated sugar
1/3 cup unsweetened cocoa powder
1/4 cup prepared mincemeat
1/3 cup butter or margarine, room temperature
1 egg, beaten
1/2 (17-1/4-oz. pkg.) frozen puff pastry, thawed (1 sheet)
About 3 tablespoons milk
About 2 tablespoons powdered sugar

**1.** Preheat oven to 425F (220C).
**2.** In a medium bowl, combine cake crumbs, almonds, granulated sugar, cocoa, mincemeat, butter or margarine and egg. Beat with a wooden spoon until thoroughly blended; set aside.
**3.** On a lightly floured surface, unfold pastry. Roll out pastry to a 13" x 11" rectangle. Place on an ungreased baking sheet. With a blunt knife, score 2 straight lines lengthwise 3 inches in from each long side of pastry.
**4.** Spread chocolate-crumb mixture in a 4-inch-wide strip lengthwise down center of pastry between scored lines to within 1/2 inch of lines.
**5.** Cut pastry diagonally at 1/2-inch intervals on sides of filling from scored lines to edge of pastry. Brush pastry strips lightly with milk. Fold ends of pastry over filling. Alternately fold pastry strips over filling overlapping strips in center. Brush pastry with milk; sprinkle with powdered sugar.
**6.** Bake in preheated oven 25 to 30 minutes or until pastry is puffed and golden brown. Remove from baking sheet; cool completely on a wire rack. Slice to serve. Makes 8 to 10 servings.

Left to right: Cream Puffs with Chocolate Sauce, Chocolate & Almond Pastry

# Trifle Cake

**Cake:**
3/4 cup butter or margarine, room temperature
1-1/3 cups sugar
3 eggs
1 teaspoon vanilla extract
1-1/4 cups cake flour
1/2 cup unsweetened cocoa powder
1-1/4 teaspoons baking soda
1/2 teaspoon salt
3/4 cup milk

**Topping:**
1/4 cup sweet sherry
4 to 6 tablespoons strawberry jam or preserves
2/3 cup whipping cream
1 tablespoon powdered sugar

**To decorate:**
4 or 5 strawberries, sliced
About 30 small almond macaroons

---

**1.** Preheat oven to 350F (175C). Generously grease a deep 8-inch-round cake pan or springform pan.
**2.** In a medium bowl, beat butter or margarine and sugar until light and fluffy. Beat in eggs and vanilla until blended.
**3.** Sift flour, cocoa, baking soda and salt into a medium bowl. Add flour mixture to sugar mixture alternately with milk; beat until blended. Pour batter into greased pan; smooth top.
**4.** Bake in preheated oven 55 to 60 minutes or until a wooden pick inserted in center comes out clean. Cool in pan on a wire rack 5 minutes. Remove from pan; cool completely on wire rack.
**5.** Place cake, top-side up, on a serving plate. Prick top all over with prongs of a fork. Sprinkle 3 tablespoons sherry over top of cake; let stand 1 hour. Spread jam or preserves over top of cake.
**6.** In a medium bowl, beat cream until soft peaks form. Beat in powdered sugar and remaining 1 tablespoon sherry. Spread whipped-cream mixture over top of cake. Decorate with strawberries and macaroons. Refrigerate until served. Makes 6 to 8 servings.

**Variation**
Substitute raspberry, blackberry or other jam for strawberry jam.

# Fruit Split

3 oz. semisweet chocolate, broken into pieces
2 tablespoons butter or margarine
2 tablespoons corn syrup
1/4 cup half and half
Juice of 1 lemon
4 small bananas, peeled, halved lengthwise
1/2 cup fresh or canned pineapple chunks, drained
2 kiwifruit, peeled, sliced
8 black grapes, halved, seeded
4 scoops Chunky-Fudge Ice Cream, page 443, or other ice cream, if desired
1/3 cup pine nuts

---

**1.** In a small saucepan over low heat, combine chocolate, butter or margarine and corn syrup; stir until mixture is smooth. Cool slightly.
**2.** Stir in half and half until smooth. Set aside.
**3.** Squeeze lemon juice over banana halves; place 2 banana halves, rounded-side up, in each individual serving dish.
**4.** Divide remaining fruit equally among dishes. Top each dish with a scoop of ice cream, if desired.
**5.** Drizzle warm chocolate sauce over fruit and ice cream. Sprinkle with pine nuts; serve immediately. Pass remaining sauce separately. Makes 4 servings.

**Variation**
Substitute other fruits for fruit listed above. Sliced strawberries and peaches make a colorful and delicious combination.

Top to bottom: Trifle Cake, Fruit Split

# Peach & Caramel Parfait

1/2 cup sugar
1/4 cup water
1/2 cup half and half
1 tablespoon unsweetened cocoa powder
4 large fresh ripe peaches or 8 canned peach halves,
    drained
1 pint butter-pecan ice cream

*To decorate:*
3/4 cup whipping cream
1/4 cup chopped toasted nuts
4 maraschino cherries
4 chocolate wedges, page 423, if desired

1. In a small saucepan over medium heat, stir sugar and water until sugar dissolves. Boil, without stirring, until mixture is a deep golden brown. Remove from heat.
2. While sugar is caramelizing, in a small saucepan over medium heat, blend half and half and cocoa. Bring to a boil. Carefully pour boiling mixture into caramelized sugar. Stir rapidly until caramel is dissolved. Return to heat, if necessary. Let cool.
3. If using fresh peaches, place peaches in a heatproof bowl; cover with boiling water. Let stand 1 minute; plunge peaches into cold water to prevent cooking. Peel off skins. Halve peeled peaches; remove and discard seeds. Cut peaches into quarters.
4. Place alternate layers of peach quarters and scoops of ice cream in 4 tall glasses, ending with a scoop of ice cream. Divide cooled caramel sauce among desserts.
5. To decorate, in a medium bowl, whip cream until soft peaks form. Spoon whipped cream into a pastry bag fitted with a star or rosette tip. Pipe a large rosette of whipped cream on each dessert. Sprinkle with nuts; top each with a cherry. Insert a chocolate wedge beside each cherry, if desired. Serve immediately. Makes 4 servings.

Top to bottom: Peach & Caramel Parfaits, Pineapple with Coconut Sauce

# Pineapple with Coconut Sauce

1 fresh medium pineapple, peeled, cored, sliced into 8
  rings
1 tablespoon honey
Juice of 1 lemon
2 tablespoons light rum
2 tablespoons butter or margarine

*Coconut Sauce:*
2 tablespoons unsweetened cocoa powder
3 tablespoons honey
1/2 cup water
1 tablespoon light rum
2 tablespoons cream of coconut
2 tablespoons half and half
1/2 cup shredded coconut, if desired

---

**1.** Place pineapple rings in a large shallow dish. In a small
bowl, combine honey, lemon juice and rum; pour over
pineapple. Cover and refrigerate overnight.
**2.** Drain pineapple; reserve marinade. Melt butter or margarine in a large skillet over low heat. Add pineapple; heat
through. Do not brown. Transfer to a heated serving dish;
keep warm.
**3.** To make sauce, in a medium saucepan over medium
heat, combine reserved marinade, cocoa, honey, water and
rum. When hot, stir in cream of coconut and half and half,
a little at a time. Stir until smooth.
**4.** Arrange 2 slices of warm pineapple on each of 4 individual plates. Pour warm sauce over each serving; sprinkle
with coconut, if desired. Makes 4 servings.

# Chocolate-Cookie Ice Cream

1 pint whipping cream (2 cups)
1/2 cup sugar
1 teaspoon vanilla extract
2 cups chocolate-cookie crumbs (about 38 (2-1/4-inch)
  cookies)
1/2 cup chopped toasted hazelnuts
4 oz. semisweet or sweet chocolate, coarsely chopped

---

**1.** In a medium bowl, beat cream, sugar and vanilla until
blended.
**2.** Pour into an ice-cream container. Freeze in an ice-cream
maker according to manufacturer's directions until almost
firm.
**3.** Add cookie crumbs, hazelnuts and chocolate to partially
frozen ice cream. Freeze until firm. Makes about 1-1/2
quarts or 6 to 8 servings.

# Chunky-Fudge Ice Cream

*Fudge:*
2 tablespoons butter or margarine
2 oz. semisweet chocolate, broken into pieces
1 tablespoon milk
1 cup powdered sugar, sifted
1 teaspoon vanilla extract

*Chocolate Ice Cream*
1/2 cup water
1/2 cup firmly packed light-brown sugar
2 tablespoons unsweetened cocoa powder
4 egg yolks, beaten
1-1/2 cups half and half or whipping cream
1 teaspoon vanilla extract
1/4 cup chopped toasted almonds

---

**1.** Line an 8-inch-square pan with waxed paper. To make
fudge, in a small saucepan over low heat, combine butter
or margarine, chocolate and milk; stir until smooth. Beat
in powdered sugar until smooth. Stir in vanilla. Spoon
chocolate mixture into lined pan. Refrigerate about 20
minutes or until set.
**2.** When chocolate mixture is set, invert on a flat surface.
Remove paper; coarsely chop. Set aside.
**3.** To make ice cream, in a small saucepan over medium
heat, combine water and sugar. Stir until sugar dissolves.
Boil 5 minutes, without stirring. Beat in cocoa.
**4.** Pour hot syrup in a steady stream into yolks, beating
constantly. Continue beating until cool. Mixture should be
light and creamy.
**5.** Beat half and half into cooled egg-yolk mixture. Stir in
vanilla. Pour mixture into an ice-cream container. Freeze
in an ice-cream maker according to manufacturer's directions until almost firm.
**6.** Stir chopped fudge and almonds into partially frozen ice
cream. Freeze until firm. Makes about 2 quarts or 6 to 8
servings.

# Pears with Chocolate-Maple Sauce

3/4 cup sugar
6 cups water
1 (3-inch) cinnamon stick
4 large ripe pears, peeled
1-1/2 cups chocolate-cake crumbs
1/4 cup chopped walnuts
3 maraschino cherries, chopped
1 to 2 tablespoons maraschino-cherry syrup

*Sauce:*
1/2 cup maple syrup
1 tablespoon unsweetened cocoa powder

*To decorate:*
Chocolate leaves, page 423, if desired

---

**1.** Preheat oven to 350F (175C). In a large saucepan over medium heat, combine sugar and water. Cook, stirring, until sugar dissolves. Add cinnamon and pears; cover and simmer about 20 minutes or until pears are barely tender when pierced with a skewer at widest part of pear. Cool in sugar syrup.
**2.** Cut a slice from blossom end of cooled pears so they will stand upright. Cut off about 1 inch of pear at stem to form a top; reserve tops. Scoop out core with a teaspoon or melon baller.
**3.** In a small bowl, combine cake crumbs, walnuts and cherries; stir in enough cherry syrup to make a stiff paste. Spoon mixture into pear cavities. Replace tops.
**4.** To make sauce, in a small saucepan over medium heat, blend syrup and cocoa. Bring to a boil, stirring constantly. Pour a little sauce into individual serving dishes; place a filled pear in middle of sauce. Decorate with chocolate leaves, if desired. Makes 4 servings.

Left to right: Pears with Chocolate-Maple Sauce, Lemon Crunch, Apricot-Chocolate Delight

# Lemon Crunch

1 teaspoon unflavored gelatin powder
Grated peel and juice of 2 lemons
1/2 pint whipping cream (1 cup)
5 tablespoons superfine sugar
1 cup chocolate-cookie crumbs (about 18 (2-1/4 inch) cookies)
1/3 cup chopped toasted almonds

*To decorate:*
Shaved chocolate or chocolate curls, page 423

**1.** In a small saucepan, combine gelatin and lemon juice. Stir well; let stand 3 minutes. Stir over low heat until gelatin dissolves; let cool.
**2.** In a medium bowl, beat cream until soft peaks form. Beat in sugar. Fold in cooled gelatin mixture and lemon peel until blended. Refrigerate 1 to 2 hours or until mixture mounds when dropped from a spoon.
**3.** In a small bowl, combine cookie crumbs and almonds. Spoon alternate layers of crumb mixture and lemon cream into a serving bowl, ending with a layer of lemon cream. Refrigerate until served. Decorate with chocolate before serving. Makes 4 servings.

# Apricot-Chocolate Delight

16 oz. plain or vanilla-flavored yogurt (2 cups)
1/2 cup muesli, page 470
1/2 cup chopped toasted hazelnuts
2 tablespoons honey
1 (8-oz.) pkg. dried apricots, finely chopped (about
   1-2/3 cups)
4 oz. semisweet chocolate, chopped
2 tablespoons butter or margarine

*To decorate:*
Chocolate curls, page 423

1. In a medium bowl, combine yogurt, muesli and hazelnuts. Stir in honey. Fold in apricots. Cover and refrigerate 30 minutes.
2. Melt chocolate and butter or margarine in a small heavy saucepan over very low heat; stir until smooth. Cool to room temperature.
3. Place a heaping tablespoon yogurt mixture in bottom of each of 4 individual serving glasses or parfait dishes. Top each dish with 2 to 3 teaspoons melted chocolate, swirling chocolate to outside edge of glass.
4. Spoon remaining yogurt and chocolate alternately into each glass, ending with chocolate. Refrigerate until served. Decorate with chocolate curls before serving. Makes 4 servings.

# Chocolate-Banana Pie

**Crust:**

1-1/2 cups vanilla-cookie crumbs or chocolate-cookie crumbs (about 33 cookies)

5 tablespoons butter or margarine, melted

**Filling:**

4 medium bananas

1 (14-oz.) can sweetened condensed milk

2 teaspoons grated lemon peel

1 (1/4-oz.) envelope unflavored gelatin (1 tablespoon)

About 1/4 cup lemon juice

3/4 cup water

4 oz. semisweet chocolate, chopped

2 tablespoons butter or margarine

**1.** Preheat oven to 375F (190C). In a small bowl, combine cookie crumbs and melted butter or margarine. Press crumbs on bottom and up side of an 8-inch fluted quiche pan or pie pan.

**2.** Bake in preheated oven 10 minutes. Cool on a wire rack.

**3.** Cut 2 bananas into pieces. Reserve remaining bananas for topping. In a blender or food processor fitted with a steel blade, process banana pieces and 2/3 cup condensed milk until bananas are pureed. Pour into a medium bowl; stir in lemon peel.

**4.** In a small saucepan, combine gelatin, 2 tablespoons lemon juice and water. Stir well; let stand 3 minutes. Stir over low heat until gelatin dissolves; cool slightly. Stir cooled gelatin into banana puree. Spoon banana puree into cooled crust; smooth top. Refrigerate 1 hour or until set.

**5.** In a medium saucepan over low heat, combine remaining condensed milk, chocolate and butter or margarine. Cook, stirring, until chocolate melts and mixture is smooth. Cool slightly.

**6.** Pour chocolate mixture over chilled pie, covering banana filling completely. Refrigerate 2 hours or until set.

**7.** To serve, slice remaining bananas. In a small bowl, toss slices with lemon juice to coat. Arrange slices around edge of pie. Refrigerate until served. Makes 6 servings.

Clockwise from left: Chocolate-Banana Pie, Chocolate Syllabub, Raspberry & Lychee Delight

# Chocolate Syllabub

1/3 cup sweet sherry
1 tablespoon brandy
1/4 cup chocolate-flavored drink mix
1/2 pint whipping cream (1 cup)
2 tablespoons powdered sugar
4 oz. semisweet or sweet chocolate, finely grated
2 egg whites

*To decorate:*
Grated semisweet or sweet chocolate

1. In a small bowl, combine sherry and brandy. Stir in drink mix until dissolved and mixture is smooth.
2. In a medium bowl, beat cream until soft peaks form. Beat in powdered sugar. Fold chocolate into whipped-cream mixture. Fold in sherry mixture.
3. In a medium bowl, beat egg whites until stiff but not dry. Fold beaten egg whites into chocolate-cream mixture.
4. Spoon mixture into 4 tall wine glasses. Refrigerate 1 to 2 hours or until served. Decorate with grated chocolate. Serve with cookies, if desired. Makes 4 servings.

# Raspberry & Lychee Delight

1/4 cup butter or margarine
2-1/2 cups fresh bread crumbs
2 tablespoons light-brown sugar
1 teaspoon ground cinnamon
Grated peel of 1 orange
5 oz. semisweet chocolate, finely grated
1-1/2 cups fresh raspberries
1 (20-oz.) can lychees, well drained, chopped

1. Melt butter or margarine in a medium skillet. Add bread crumbs; cook, stirring, until crisp and golden brown. Cool to room temperature.
2. In a medium bowl, combine cooled bread crumbs, brown sugar, cinnamon, orange peel and 1/3 of chocolate.
3. Set 12 raspberries aside for decoration. Spoon a layer of crumb mixture in bottom of a 3-cup glass serving dish. Top with a layer of raspberries and lychees. Repeat with remaining crumb mixture, raspberries and lychees. Sprinkle with remaining chocolate, covering top completely. Decorate with reserved raspberries. Refrigerate until served. Makes 4 to 6 servings.

# Cocoa Layer Cake

3/4 cup butter or margarine, room temperature
1-1/4 cups sugar
4 eggs
1 teaspoon vanilla extract
1-1/2 cups cake flour
1/2 cup unsweetened cocoa powder
1-1/4 teaspoons baking soda
1/2 teaspoon salt
1/2 cup milk

1. Preheat oven to 350F (175C). Grease and flour 2 (8-inch) round cake pans.
2. In a large bowl, beat butter or margarine and sugar 5 to 8 minutes or until light and fluffy. Beat in eggs and vanilla until blended.
3. Sift flour, cocoa, baking soda and salt into a medium bowl. Add flour mixture to egg mixture alternately with milk; beat until blended. Pour batter into prepared pans; smooth tops.
4. Bake in preheated oven 25 to 35 minutes or until centers spring back when lightly pressed. Cool in pans on wire racks 5 minutes. Remove from pans; cool completely on wire racks. Fill and frost as desired. Makes 2 layers.

# Chocolate Buttercream

2 tablespoons unsweetened cocoa powder
2 tablespoons boiling water
1/2 cup butter or margarine, room temperature
2 cups powdered sugar, sifted
1 tablespoon half and half

1. In a small bowl, blend cocoa and boiling water into a smooth paste.
2. In a medium bowl, beat butter or margarine until creamy. Beat in 1/2 of powdered sugar until light and fluffy. Beat in cocoa paste, remaining powdered sugar and half and half until fluffy and icing is a good consistency for spreading. Makes about 1-1/2 cups.

# Mocha Dessert Cups

5 oz. semisweet chocolate, coarsely chopped
1/4 cup butter or margarine, room temperature
1/4 cup sugar
2/3 cup milk
1 egg
1 teaspoon instant coffee powder
2 cups small almond macaroons
2 tablespoons coffee-flavored liqueur

*To decorate:*
1/4 cup whipping cream, lightly whipped, if desired

---

*This is a simple dessert that can be made ahead of time and refrigerated. Serve with small whipped-cream-filled almond macaroons, if desired.*

**1.** Melt chocolate in a small heavy saucepan over very low heat; stir until smooth. Let cool.
**2.** In a medium bowl, beat butter or margarine and sugar until light and fluffy. Beat in cooled chocolate until blended. Set aside.
**3.** In a small bowl, whisk milk and egg until blended. Pour through a fine sieve into a small saucepan; stir in coffee. Cook over low heat, stirring constantly, until sauce thickens and coats back of a spoon. Do not boil. Cool slightly.
**4.** Gradually pour warm custard into chocolate mixture, beating constantly. Refrigerate 2 hours or until thickened.
**5.** Place almond macaroons in a medium bowl; sprinkle with coffee liqueur. Let stand 30 minutes.
**6.** Spoon 1/2 of chilled chocolate mixture into 4 individual serving dishes. Place liqueur-soaked macaroons over mixture. Spoon remaining chocolate mixture evenly over macaroons. Refrigerate 2 hours. To serve, decorate each dessert with 1 tablespoon cream, if desired. Makes 4 servings.

# Chocolate Crepes with Rum & Raisin Sauce

*Crepes:*
1/2 cup all-purpose flour
1/4 cup unsweetened cocoa powder
1/4 cup sugar
2 eggs
1 cup milk
2 tablespoons butter or margarine, melted
Butter or margarine for cooking

*Rum & Raisin Sauce:*
3 oz. semisweet or sweet chocolate, coarsely chopped
3/4 cup half and half
2 tablespoons dark rum
1/3 cup raisins
Powdered sugar

---

**1.** To make crepes, sift flour and cocoa into a medium bowl; stir in sugar.
**2.** In a small bowl, beat eggs and milk until blended. Beat egg mixture into flour mixture with a whisk until blended. Gradually beat in butter or margarine. Or, combine all ingredients in a blender or food processor fitted with a steel blade; process until batter is smooth.
**3.** Pour crepe batter into a pitcher; refrigerate 1 hour.
**4.** Melt 1 teaspoon butter or margarine in a 6- or 7-inch crepe pan or skillet over medium heat. Stir crepe batter. Pour 2 to 3 tablespoons batter into skillet, or enough batter to make a thin layer. Tilt pan from side to side to spread batter evenly. Cook 1 minute or until tiny bubbles form on surface of crepe. Turn crepe; cook 1 minute.
**5.** Remove crepe; place on a flat plate. Repeat with remaining batter, adding more butter or margarine to pan as necessary.
**6.** To make sauce, in a small heavy saucepan over low heat, combine chocolate and half and half. Cook, stirring, until chocolate melts and mixture is smooth. Remove from heat; stir in rum and raisins.
**7.** Fold each crepe into quarters. Place 4 folded crepes on each serving plate. Sift powdered sugar over crepes; spoon some sauce over each serving. Serve remaining sauce separately. Makes 4 to 6 servings or 16 to 24 crepes.

**Variation**
**Whiskey & Walnut Sauce:** Substitute 2 tablespoons rye whiskey for rum. Substitute 1/3 cup chopped walnuts for raisins.

Clockwise from left: Chocolate Soufflé Omelet, Chocolate Crepes
with Rum & Raisin Sauce, Cream-filled macaroons, Mocha
Dessert Cups

# Chocolate Soufflé Omelet

2 eggs, separated
3 tablespoons chocolate-flavored drink mix
2 tablespoons milk
2 teaspoons grated orange peel, if desired
1 tablespoon butter or margarine

*To serve:*
Orange marmalade or Special Chocolate Sauce, page 459

*To decorate:*
Julienned orange peel or grated chocolate

**1.** In a medium bowl, beat egg yolks, drink mix and milk
until blended. Fold in orange peel, if desired.
**2.** In a medium bowl, beat egg whites until stiff but not
dry. Fold beaten egg whites into chocolate mixture. Preheat broiler.
**3.** Melt butter or margarine in an 8-inch ovenproof skillet
or omelet pan over medium heat until bubbly. Pour in
chocolate mixture; spread evenly with a long flat spatula.
**4.** Cook until underside of omelet is set. Cook under preheated broiler, about 3 inches from heat, until top is almost
firm.
**5.** Spoon marmalade or Special Chocolate Sauce over 1/2
of omelet; fold omelet in half. With a spatula, slide filled
omelet onto a serving plate. Decorate with orange peel or
grated chocolate. Serve immediately. Makes 2 servings.

# Coconut-Nougat Squares

Edible rice paper
1 cup granulated sugar
1 cup firmly packed dark-brown sugar
2/3 cup water
2 egg whites
1 cup toasted flaked or shredded coconut
1/2 cup red candied cherries, chopped
4 oz. semisweet chocolate, chopped

1. Wipe bottom of an 8-inch-square pan with a damp cloth. Cut 2 sheets of rice paper to fit bottom of pan. Line pan bottom with 1 sheet of rice paper, pressing paper onto damp surface of pan.
2. In a medium saucepan over low heat, stir sugars and water until sugar dissolves and mixture comes to a boil. Boil rapidly until mixture reaches the soft-crack stage 270F to 290F (132C to 143C) on a candy thermometer. Remove from heat.
3. In a medium bowl, beat egg whites until stiff but not dry. Gradually pour in hot sugar syrup in a slow steady stream, beating constantly. Beat until stiff and glossy. Fold in coconut and cherries.
4. Pour mixture into lined pan; spread evenly. Cover with remaining sheet of rice paper. Cover rice paper with waxed paper or foil. Place another 8-inch-square pan on top of paper or foil, bottom-side down. Place a 2-pound can or other heavy weight in pan.
5. Refrigerate at least 24 hours. Remove weighted pan and waxed paper or foil; run a knife tip around edge of pan; carefully ease nougat out of pan. Place on a flat work surface; cut into 25 squares.
6. Melt chocolate in a small heavy saucepan over very low heat; stir until smooth. Let cool slightly. Dip squares halfway into melted chocolate. Place on waxed paper or foil; let stand until chocolate is set. Makes 25 squares.

# Chocolate & Nut Squares

1 cup all-purpose flour
2 tablespoons unsweetened cocoa powder
1 (3-3/8-oz.) pkg. instant vanilla pudding
1/4 cup sugar
3/4 cup butter or margarine

*Topping:*
2 tablespoons apricot jam, melted, cooled
6 tablespoons butter or margarine
1/2 cup firmly packed light-brown sugar
1 tablespoon honey
1 oz. semisweet chocolate, chopped
1 cup finely chopped toasted almonds

1. Preheat oven to 300F (150C). Line an 8-inch-square pan with waxed paper or foil; grease paper or foil.
2. Sift flour, cocoa and pudding mix into a medium bowl. Stir in sugar. With a pastry blender or 2 knives, cut in butter or margarine until mixture resembles coarse crumbs. Knead dough in bowl until smooth. Press mixture into bottom of lined pan; prick lightly with a fork.
3. Bake in preheated oven 1 hour 15 minutes or until center is firm when lightly pressed. Cool completely in pan on a wire rack.
4. To make topping, brush jam over cooled cake. In a medium saucepan over medium heat, stir butter or margarine, brown sugar and honey until mixture comes to a boil. Boil 3 minutes, stirring constantly.
5. Remove from heat; stir in chocolate until melted. Stir in nuts. Spread nut mixture over cake; let stand 15 minutes. Score into 25 squares. Cool until topping is firm.
6. Remove from pan; peel off paper or foil. Cut into squares. Makes 25 squares.

**Variation**
Spread 4 ounces melted semisweet chocolate over nut topping; let stand until set.

Top to bottom: Chocolate & Nut Squares, Coconut-Nougat Squares

Clockwise from left: Chocolate Stars, Caramel Crunch Cookies, Chocolate Fudge

# Chocolate Fudge

1/4 cup butter or margarine
4 oz. unsweetened chocolate, chopped
1/3 cup evaporated milk or whipping cream
1 teaspoon vanilla extract
1 (16-oz.) box powdered sugar
1/2 cup chopped nuts, if desired

*To decorate:*
4 oz. semisweet chocolate, chopped

1. Butter an 8-inch-square pan.
2. Combine butter or margarine, chocolate and evaporated milk or whipping cream in top of a double boiler set over a pan of simmering water. Cook, stirring, until chocolate melts and mixture is smooth. Stir in vanilla. Remove top of double boiler from heat.
3. Sift powdered sugar into a medium bowl; make a well in center. Slowly beat warm chocolate mixture into sugar, beating until mixture is blended and all of powdered sugar has been incorporated. Fold in chopped nuts, if desired.
4. Pour into prepared pan; spread evenly. Refrigerate about 2 hours or until set.
5. To decorate, melt chocolate in a small heavy saucepan over very low heat; stir until smooth. Let cool.
6. Spread melted chocolate over top of chilled fudge; let stand until chocolate is set. Cut into small pieces; remove from pan. Makes 48 to 64 pieces.

# Chocolate Stars

*Cookies:*
1/2 cup butter or margarine, room temperature
3/4 cup sugar
1 egg
1 tablespoon milk
2 teaspoons grated orange peel
1-1/2 cups sifted all-purpose flour
1/4 cup cornstarch
1/4 cup unsweetened cocoa powder
1/2 teaspoon salt

*Icing:*
1 (16-oz.) box powdered sugar, sifted
1/4 cup orange juice
Few drops orange food coloring
2 tablespoons unsweetened cocoa powder
2 tablespoons boiling water

1. Preheat oven to 350F (175C). Grease 2 baking sheets.
2. In a medium bowl, beat butter or margarine and sugar until light and fluffy. Beat in egg, milk and orange peel until blended.
3. Sift flour, cornstarch, cocoa and salt over sugar mixture. Gradually stir in flour mixture with a wooden spoon to make a soft dough. Knead dough in bowl 8 to 10 strokes or until smooth.
4. Divide dough in half. On a lightly floured surface, roll out 1 piece of dough to 1/4 inch thick. Cut dough with a floured 3-inch star cookie cutter. Place cookies about 1 inch apart on greased baking sheets. Repeat with remaining dough.
5. Bake in preheated oven 12 to 14 minutes or until firm. Remove from baking sheets; cool completely on wire racks.
6. To make icing, in a medium bowl, blend powdered sugar and orange juice until smooth. Spoon 1/2 cup icing into a small bowl; tint with a few drops of orange food coloring.
7. In a small bowl, blend cocoa and boiling water into a smooth paste. Stir cocoa paste into plain icing. If necessary, add a little more powdered sugar to make icing a good consistency for spreading.
8. Spread chocolate icing over tops of cookies. Spoon orange icing into a pastry bag fitted with a small plain writing tip. Pipe orange icing into 4 or 5 circles on top of each cookie. Or, pipe icing in a spiral, starting from center of each cookie.
9. With a fine metal skewer, draw orange icing from center out toward points of stars. Then draw icing back in toward center from between points to give a flower effect. Let stand until icing is set. Makes 36 to 40 cookies.

# Caramel Crunch Cookies

*Crumb Layer:*
1/2 cup butter or margarine
1/2 cup sugar
1/4 cup unsweetened cocoa powder
1 teaspoon vanilla extract
2 cups graham-cracker crumbs
1/3 cup chopped nuts

*Caramel Layer:*
1 (14-oz.) can sweetened condensed milk
2 tablespoons butter or margarine
3 tablespoons dark corn syrup
1 teaspoon vanilla extract

*Topping:*
4 oz. semisweet chocolate, chopped

1. Grease an 11" x 7" baking pan.
2. To make crumb layer, in a medium saucepan over low heat, combine butter or margarine, sugar, cocoa and vanilla. Stir until butter or margarine melts and mixture is smooth. Remove from heat. Stir in crumbs and nuts until combined.
3. Press crumb mixture onto bottom of greased pan; smooth top.
4. To make caramel layer, in a small saucepan over low heat, combine condensed milk, butter or margarine, corn syrup and vanilla. Stir until mixture comes to a boil. Boil 3 minutes, stirring constantly. Pour hot caramel over crumb layer. Spread evenly; let stand until completely cool.
5. Melt chocolate in a small heavy saucepan over very low heat; stir until smooth. Let cool. Spread cooled chocolate over caramel layer. Let stand until chocolate is set. Run a knife tip around inside of pan to loosen mixture. Cut into 25 bars. Makes 25 cookies.

Left to right: Peppermint Marble Cake, Chocolate-Fudge Bars, Chocolate-Covered Peanutty Bars

# Peppermint Marble Cake

3/4 cup butter or margarine, room temperature
1 cup granulated sugar
3 eggs
1-2/3 cups all-purpose flour
1 teaspoon baking powder
1/2 teaspoon baking soda
2 tablespoons unsweetened cocoa powder
2 teaspoons instant coffee powder
2 tablespoons boiling water
1/2 teaspoon vanilla extract
1/2 teaspoon peppermint extract
2 to 3 drops green food coloring
Powdered sugar

**1.** Preheat oven to 350F (175C). Grease a 6-1/2-cup ring mold.
**2.** In a medium bowl, beat butter or margarine and granulated sugar until light and fluffy. Beat in eggs, 1 at a time, beating well after each addition.
**3.** Sift flour, baking powder and baking soda over egg mixture; fold in. Divide batter into thirds, placing batter in 2 additional bowls.
**4.** In a small bowl, dissolve cocoa and coffee in boiling water; stir into 1 bowl of batter. Stir vanilla into second bowl of batter. Stir peppermint extract and green food coloring into third bowl of batter.
**5.** Spoon batters alternately into greased pan. Run tip of a knife through batters to create a marbled effect.
**6.** Bake in preheated oven 40 to 45 minutes or until a wooden pick inserted in center comes out clean. Cool in pan on a wire rack 5 minutes. Remove from pan; cool completely on wire rack. Place cake on a serving plate; sift powdered sugar over cake immediately before serving. Makes 8 servings.

# Chocolate-Covered Peanutty Bars

6 oz. semisweet or sweet chocolate
3 tablespoons butter or margarine
20 graham-cracker squares
1 (14-oz.) can sweetened condensed milk
3 tablespoons light corn syrup
1/4 cup crunchy peanut butter

1. Line bottom and sides of an 11" x 7" baking pan with foil, extending foil 2 inches above rim of pan all the way around.
2. Melt chocolate and 1 tablespoon butter or margarine in a small heavy saucepan over very low heat; stir until smooth. Spread 1/2 of chocolate mixture in bottom of foil-lined pan, covering bottom of pan completely. Reserve remaining chocolate mixture for topping.
3. Arrange 1/2 of graham crackers over chocolate, breaking crackers into halves and quarters to make them fit snugly. Set aside.
4. In a medium saucepan, combine remaining 2 tablespoons butter or margarine, condensed milk and corn syrup. Cook, stirring, until mixture comes to a boil. Boil 3 minutes, stirring constantly. Remove from heat; stir in peanut butter. Stir vigorously 1 minute or until mixture thickens. Pour over crackers; spread evenly.
5. Arrange remaining crackers over caramel filling, breaking crackers to fit. Press crackers down lightly. Spread reserved chocolate mixture over crackers. Refrigerate, uncovered, 1 hour or until chocolate is firm.
6. To serve, invert pan onto a flat surface. Peel off foil; cut cookies into 24 bars. Makes 24 cookies.

# Chocolate-Fudge Bars

1/4 cup light corn syrup
10 tablespoons butter or margarine
6 oz. semisweet chocolate, coarsely chopped
28 graham-cracker squares, coarsely crushed
3/4 cup flaked or shredded coconut
1/4 cup chopped red candied cherries
1/3 cup raisins

1. Line an 8-inch-square baking pan with foil. Set aside.
2. In a large saucepan over low heat, combine corn syrup, butter or margarine and chocolate. Stir until mixture is smooth. Remove from heat.
3. Stir in cracker crumbs until combined. Fold in coconut, cherries and raisins. Pour mixture into lined pan; press down firmly with back of a wooden spoon. Cool to room temperature. Refrigerate 2 to 3 hours or until firm.
4. Remove from pan; place on a flat surface. Peel off foil; cut into bars. Refrigerate during hot weather. Makes 24 to 32 bars.

# Chocolate-Topped Coconut Pyramids

*Pyramids:*
1 (14-oz.) can sweetened condensed milk
1 (12-oz.) pkg. flaked coconut (4 cups loosely packed)
2 oz. semisweet chocolate, finely chopped

*To decorate:*
3 oz. sweet or milk chocolate, chopped
Flaked coconut
Red candied cherries, quartered

---

**1.** Preheat oven to 375F (190C). Line 2 baking sheets with parchment paper.
**2.** In a large bowl, stir condensed milk, coconut and chocolate with a wooden spoon until combined.
**3.** Shape mixture into large walnut-sized balls. Place balls about 1-1/2 inches apart on lined baking sheets.
**4.** Bake in preheated oven 15 to 18 minutes or until golden brown. Cool on baking sheets on wire racks 5 minutes. Remove from baking sheets; cool completely on wire racks.
**5.** To decorate, melt chocolate in a small heavy saucepan over very low heat; stir until smooth. Let cool. Dip tops of coconut pyramids into melted chocolate. Decorate with coconut and cherries. Let stand until chocolate is set. Makes about 36.

---

Treasure Cups can also be used to serve individual helpings of Chunky-Fudge Ice Cream, page 443. For an elegant finale to a dinner party, serve Treasure Cups filled with a rich chocolate mousse, such as Rum & Raisin Mousse, page 436, topped with a dollop of whipped cream.

# Chocolate Treasure Cups

8 oz. semisweet chocolate, chopped
6 double-foil cupcake cases, about 2-1/2 inches in diameter

*Filling:*
6 teaspoons raspberry jam or strawberry jam
1 (11-oz.) can mandarin-orange sections
1-1/2 cups sponge-cake crumbs
1 teaspoon unflavored gelatin powder

*To decorate:*
Red, green and yellow candied cherries, quartered

---

**1.** Melt chocolate in a small heavy saucepan over very low heat; stir until smooth. Let cool.
**2.** Spoon about 1 heaping tablespoon melted chocolate into bottom of 1 foil cupcake case. Spread chocolate over bottom and up side of case with back of spoon, covering inside of case completely. Place in muffin pan. Repeat with remaining chocolate and foil cases. Refrigerate 30 minutes or until firm.
**3.** Recoat insides of cases with remaining melted chocolate; refrigerate until firm.
**4.** To make filling, spoon 1 teaspoon jam into bottom of each chocolate cup.
**5.** Drain orange sections, reserving juice. Reserve 4 or 5 orange sections for decoration. Finely chop remaining sections. In a medium bowl, combine chopped orange sections and cake crumbs.
**6.** In a small saucepan, combine gelatin and reserved orange syrup. Stir well; let stand 3 minutes. Stir over low heat until gelatin dissolves; let cool. Stir cooled gelatin mixture into crumb mixture; stir until blended.
**7.** Spoon mixture into chocolate cups. Refrigerate 1 to 2 hours or until set.
**8.** To serve, carefully peel foil cases off chocolate cups, using tip of sharp knife to loosen foil from chocolate. Coarsely chop reserved orange sections. Decorate cups with candied cherries and chopped orange sections. Makes 6 servings.

**Variation**
Substitute 1 (8-ounce) can crushed pineapple for mandarin oranges. Make as directed above.

# Chocolate & Honey Toffee

**3/4 cup honey**
**1/3 cup firmly packed light-brown sugar**
**1/2 cup butter or margarine**
**2 teaspoons ground cinnamon**
**3 oz. semisweet or sweet chocolate, chopped**

1. Butter an 8-inch-square pan.
2. In a medium saucepan over low heat, stir honey and brown sugar until sugar dissolves.

3. Stir in butter or margarine until melted. Increase heat; boil until mixture reaches soft-crack stage 270F to 290F (132C to 143C) on a candy thermometer. Remove from heat.
4. Stir in cinnamon until blended. Pour into buttered pan; let stand in a cool place until almost firm. Score into 32 (2" x 1") pieces. When cold, invert onto a flat surface; cut along scored lines.
5. Melt chocolate in a small heavy saucepan over very low heat; stir until smooth. Let cool.
6. Dip each piece of toffee halfway into cooled chocolate. Place on a sheet of waxed paper or foil; let stand until chocolate is set. Makes 32 pieces.

Clockwise from left: Chocolate-Topped Coconut Pyramids, Chocolate & Honey Toffee, Chocolate Treasure Cups

# Chocolate & Apricot Dream

**3 tablespoons unsweetened cocoa powder**
**2 tablespoons cornstarch**
**3/4 cup granulated sugar**
**1-1/4 cups milk**
**2 egg yolks, beaten**
**1 (17-oz.) can apricot halves, well drained**
**2 tablespoons apricot brandy**
**1/2 pint whipping cream (1 cup)**
**2 tablespoons powdered sugar**

*To decorate:*
**Chocolate triangles, page 423**

1. In a medium saucepan, combine cocoa, cornstarch and granulated sugar. Gradually stir in milk. Cook over medium heat, stirring, until mixture thickens and comes to a boil. Remove from heat.

2. Stir 1/4 cup hot milk mixture into egg yolks until blended. Return mixture to saucepan; stir well. Cook, stirring, until thickened. Do not boil. Pour chocolate custard into a medium bowl. Cool slightly.

3. Set 2 apricot halves aside for decoration. In a blender or food processor fitted with a steel blade, process remaining apricots until pureed. Stir apricot puree and brandy into cooled chocolate custard.

4. Cover surface of custard with a sheet of waxed paper to prevent a skin from forming. Refrigerate 1 hour.

5. In a medium bowl, beat cream until soft peaks form. Beat in powdered sugar. Spoon 2/3 cup whipped-cream mixture into a pastry bag fitted with a star or rosette tip; refrigerate. Fold remaining whipped-cream mixture into chocolate mixture. Pour into a 4-cup serving bowl; smooth top. Refrigerate until served.

6. To serve, pipe chilled whipped-cream mixture into rosettes on top of chocolate mixture. Cut reserved apricots into thin slices. Decorate rosettes with apricot slices and chocolate triangles. Makes 6 to 8 servings.

Chocolate & Apricot Dream

# Chocolate-Butterscotch Sauce

1/3 cup firmly packed light-brown sugar
2 tablespoons chocolate-flavored drink mix
1/4 cup butter or margarine
3/4 cup milk

1. In a small saucepan over low heat, combine brown sugar, drink mix and butter or margarine. Cook, stirring, until sugar dissolves.
2. Increase heat to medium; cook 2 minutes.
3. Remove from heat; stir in milk. Return to heat; boil 2 minutes. Serve warm or cover and refrigerate until chilled. Makes about 1 cup.

# Special Chocolate Sauce

4 oz. semisweet chocolate, broken into pieces
1/2 cup half and half
1/4 cup butter or margarine, cubed
2 egg yolks
1 tablespoon strong coffee
1 tablespoon rum

1. In a small saucepan over low heat, combine chocolate and half and half. Cook, stirring, until mixture is smooth. Do not boil.
2. Remove from heat; slowly beat in butter or margarine, 1 piece at a time, until melted.
3. Beat in remaining ingredients until smooth. Serve warm or cover and refrigerate until chilled. Makes about 1 cup.

# Fudge Sauce

3 oz. semisweet chocolate, broken into pieces
2 tablespoons butter or margarine
1 (5.3-oz.) can evaporated milk
1/3 cup firmly packed light-brown sugar
1/4 teaspoon vanilla extract

1. In a medium saucepan over low heat, combine all ingredients. Cook, stirring, until chocolate melts and sugar dissolves. Do not boil.
2. Serve hot or warm. Makes about 1 cup.

# Quick Chocolate Sauce

2 tablespoons unsweetened cocoa powder
1/4 cup corn syrup or honey
1/4 cup butter or margarine
1/2 cup milk
1/2 teaspoon vanilla extract

1. In a small saucepan over low heat, combine all ingredients. Cook, stirring, until smooth.
2. Increase heat. Boil 2 to 3 minutes or until slightly reduced. Serve hot or cover and refrigerate until chilled. Makes about 1 cup.

---

### To Make Chocolate Sauces

1. For a smooth chocolate sauce, stir constantly while cooking. If lumps form, beat with a whisk.
2. If a sauce contains cocoa, cook to eliminate any starchy taste. For a quick sauce that needs no cooking, use a chocolate-flavored drink mix. Drink mixes are already sweetened; sweeten to taste using corn syrup or honey.
3. Most chocolate sauces thicken when cooled. Thin with a little milk, cream or a liqueur, such as Tia Maria.

# Chocolate Pavlova

AUSTRALIA

*Meringue:*
3 egg whites
1 cup superfine sugar
1/4 cup unsweetened cocoa powder
2 tablespoons cornstarch
1 teaspoon lemon juice or white vinegar

*Filling:*
1/2 pint whipping cream (1 cup)
1 teaspoon vanilla extract
2 tablespoons powdered sugar
2 oz. semisweet chocolate, grated
1 pint fresh strawberries, washed, hulled (2 cups)
Powdered sugar

---

*Pavlova, an Australian dessert, was created in honor of Mme. Pavlova, the famous ballerina. The center of the meringue is hollowed out slightly before baking. The cooled pavlova is usually filled with whipped cream and fruit.*

**1.** Preheat oven to 300F (150C). Line a baking sheet with parchment paper. Draw an 8-inch circle on parchment paper.
**2.** In a large bowl, beat egg whites until stiff peaks form. Beat in superfine sugar, 1 tablespoon at a time, until meringue is stiff and glossy.
**3.** Sift cocoa and cornstarch over meringue; fold into meringue with lemon juice or vinegar.
**4.** Spoon meringue inside circle on lined baking sheet. Spread evenly; hollow out center slightly, pushing meringue toward edge of circle.
**5.** Bake in preheated oven 1 hour 30 minutes to 2 hours or until meringue is crisp on the outside. Cool on baking sheet on a wire rack 15 minutes. Carefully peel off lining paper; cool completely on wire rack.
**6.** To make filling, in a medium bowl, beat cream until soft peaks form. Beat in vanilla and powdered sugar. Fold in chocolate. Spoon chocolate-cream mixture into center of cooled meringue; spread to edge of hollowed-out center. Arrange strawberries on top of cream mixture. Refrigerate until served. Sift powdered sugar over strawberries immediately before serving. Fill and serve meringue the same day. Makes 4 to 6 servings.

# Viennese Chocolate Spritz

AUSTRIA

*Cookies:*
2 oz. unsweetened chocolate
1 cup butter or margarine, room temperature
1 cup sugar
1 teaspoon vanilla extract
1/4 teaspoon salt
2 egg yolks
2-1/2 cups sifted all-purpose flour

*To decorate:*
6 oz. semisweet chocolate, melted, cooled
Powdered sugar

---

**1.** Preheat oven to 375F (190C). To make cookies, melt chocolate in a small heavy saucepan over very low heat; stir until smooth. Let cool.
**2.** In a medium bowl, beat butter or margarine and sugar until light and fluffy. Beat in vanilla, salt and egg yolks until blended.
**3.** Beat in cooled chocolate. Gradually stir in flour with a wooden spoon until thoroughly combined.
**4.** Spoon dough into a large pastry bag fitted with a 3/4-inch star tip. Pipe out dough in S shapes about 1 inch apart on ungreased baking sheets.
**5.** Bake in preheated oven 8 to 10 minutes or until firm when lightly pressed. Remove from baking sheets; cool completely on wire racks.
**6.** To decorate, dip 1 end of cooled cookies into chocolate. Place on foil or waxed paper; let stand until chocolate is set. Sift powdered sugar over other ends of cookies. Makes 54 to 60 cookies.

Top to bottom: Chocolate Pavlova, Viennese Chocolate Spritz

# Creole Cake

CARIBBEAN

---

1/3 cup dried apricots, finely chopped
1/4 cup dark rum
1 recipe Cocoa Layer Cake, page 447
1 cup flaked coconut
4 oz. semisweet chocolate, chopped
1 tablespoon butter or margarine
1 tablespoon instant coffee powder
2 tablespoons light-brown sugar
1/4 cup boiling water
1/4 cup apricot jam
1-1/2 cups whipping cream
2 tablespoons powdered sugar

*To decorate:*
Chocolate bark, page 424

---

1. In a medium bowl, combine apricots and rum. Let stand at room temperature 4 hours.
2. Preheat oven to 350F (175C). Grease and flour 2 (8-inch) square baking pans.
3. Prepare Cocoa Layer Cake as directed on page 447, folding 2/3 cup coconut into batter. Pour batter into prepared pans.
4. Bake in preheated oven 25 to 30 minutes or until centers spring back when lightly pressed. Cool in pans on wire racks 5 minutes. Remove from pans; cool completely on wire racks.
5. Melt chocolate and butter or margarine in a small heavy saucepan over very low heat; stir until smooth. Let cool. Stir in remaining 1/3 cup coconut.
6. In a medium bowl, blend coffee, brown sugar and boiling water until smooth.
7. Finely crumble 1 cake layer. Fold 1/3 of cake crumbs into apricot-rum mixture, 1/3 into chocolate-coconut mixture and remaining 1/3 into coffee mixture.
8. Cut remaining layer in half horizontally. Place 1/2 of layer on a serving plate; spread with 2 tablespoons apricot jam. Spread crumb-apricot mixture over jam; smooth top. Spread crumb-chocolate mixture over apricot mixture; smooth top. Spread crumb-coffee mixture over chocolate mixture; smooth top. Spread cut side of second half with remaining 2 tablespoons apricot jam. Place layer, jam-side down, on top of last filling layer; press down lightly.
9. In a medium bowl, beat cream until soft peaks form. Beat in powdered sugar. Spread whipped-cream mixture around sides and over top of cake, covering completely. Decorate cake with chocolate bark. Refrigerate until served. Makes 9 servings.

Left to right: Creole Cake, Danish Spice Cake, Chocolate Posset

# Danish Spice Cake
DENMARK

*Cake:*
3/4 cup butter or margarine
1 cup sugar
1 egg
1 cup all-purpose flour
1/4 cup unsweetened cocoa powder
2 teaspoons ground allspice

*Topping:*
2 oz. semisweet chocolate, chopped
1/4 cup chopped, toasted, blanched almonds

*Filling:*
1-1/2 cups whipping cream
1 teaspoon vanilla extract
3 tablespoons powdered sugar
3/4 cup chopped, toasted, blanched almonds

1. Cut out 6 (8- or 9-inch) parchment-paper circles. Set 4 parchment circles aside. Turn 2 (8- or 9-inch) round cake pans upside down; grease outside bottom surface. Place 1 parchment circle on greased surface of each pan. Lightly grease parchment paper. Set aside.
2. Preheat oven to 375F (190C).
3. In a medium bowl, beat butter or margarine and sugar until light and fluffy. Beat in egg until blended.
4. Sift flour, cocoa and allspice over egg mixture; fold in.
5. Spread about 1/3 cup mixture on each paper-covered cake pan, starting from center and spreading mixture toward edge.
6. Bake in preheated oven 10 minutes. Cool layers on pans 2 minutes. Slide off pan carefully; cool completely on wire racks. Do not remove lining paper. Prepare pans again; repeat with remaining mixture 2 more times to make a total of 6 layers. Layers are very fragile; do not stack.
7. To make topping, melt chocolate in a small saucepan over low heat; stir until smooth. Peel lining paper off 1 layer; place on a flat surface. Spread melted chocolate over layer; sprinkle with almonds. Let stand until set.
8. To make filling, in a medium bowl, beat cream until soft peaks form. Beat in vanilla and powdered sugar. Fold in almonds. Carefully peel lining paper off remaining 5 layers. Place 1 layer on a serving plate; spread with a thin layer of cream mixture. Top with second layer; spread with cream mixture. Repeat with remaining layers and cream mixture, ending with layer of cream mixture. Place chocolate-covered layer on top. Refrigerate until served. Makes 8 to 10 servings.

# Chocolate Posset
ENGLAND

1 pint whipping cream (2 cups)
6 tablespoons chocolate-flavored drink mix
3 tablespoons sugar
1 teaspoon ground cinnamon
6 to 8 tablespoons gin
3 egg whites

*To decorate:*
Chocolate curls, page 423

1. In a large bowl, beat cream until soft peaks form. Beat in drink mix, sugar and cinnamon until blended. Do not overbeat; mixture should not be stiff.
2. Stir in gin, 1 tablespoon at a time, to taste.
3. In a medium bowl, beat egg whites until stiff but not dry. Fold beaten egg whites into chocolate-cream mixture. Refrigerate several hours or overnight.
4. To serve, whisk chilled mixture until thick and fluffy. Spoon into wine glasses or individual dessert dishes. Decorate with chocolate curls. Makes 6 to 8 servings.

# Chocolate Bakewell Tart

ENGLAND

*Pastry:*
1-1/2 cups all-purpose flour
1/4 teaspoon salt
1/4 cup butter or margarine
1/4 cup vegetable shortening
1 egg yolk
2 to 3 tablespoons iced water

*Filling:*
3 tablespoons seedless raspberry jam
1/3 cup butter or margarine, room temperature
1/2 cup sugar
2 eggs
1 teaspoon almond extract
2 tablespoons unsweetened cocoa powder
1/3 cup finely ground almonds
1/3 cup sponge-cake crumbs
1/4 cup sliced almonds

1. To make pastry, in a medium bowl, combine flour and salt. With a pastry blender or 2 knives, cut in butter or margarine and shortening until mixture resembles coarse crumbs. In a small bowl, beat egg yolk and 2 tablespoons water until blended; sprinkle over flour mixture. Stir with a fork until mixture binds together, adding more water if necessary. Shape into a flattened ball. Wrap in waxed paper; refrigerate 30 minutes.
2. On a lightly floured surface, roll out pastry to a 13" x 9" rectangle. Use pastry to line an 11" x 7" baking pan, pressing pastry about 1 inch up sides of pan. Lightly prick bottom of pastry with a fork.
3. Preheat oven to 350F (175C). To make filling, spread jam over pastry. In a medium bowl, beat butter or margarine and sugar until creamy. Beat in eggs and almond extract until blended. Sift cocoa into a small bowl; stir in grounds almonds. Fold cocoa mixture and cake crumbs into egg mixture. Spread mixture evenly over jam. Sprinkle with sliced almonds.
4. Bake in preheated oven 30 to 40 minutes or until center is slightly firm when lightly pressed. Cool completely in pan on a wire rack. Cut into rectangles to serve. Makes 8 to 10 servings.

# Truffles

FRANCE

1 tablespoon instant coffee powder
2 tablespoons boiling water
8 oz. semisweet chocolate, chopped
1/2 cup butter or margarine, cubed
2 tablespoons dark rum
Powdered sugar
Chocolate sprinkles

*Truffles improve with standing. Make them at least 2 to 3 days before serving.*

1. In top of a double boiler set over a pan of simmering water, dissolve coffee in boiling water. Add chocolate; stir until smooth. Remove top of double boiler from heat. With a wooden spoon, gradually beat in butter or margarine until melted and mixture is smooth and thick. Stir in rum until blended.
2. Pour mixture into a medium bowl; refrigerate 2 to 3 hours or until firm. Place chocolate sprinkles in a wide shallow dish. Dust your hands with powdered sugar. Using your sugar-coated hands, roll chocolate mixture into walnut-sized balls.
3. Roll truffles in sprinkles to coat completely; place in small paper cases. Refrigerate until served. Makes about 24 truffles.

Left to right: Truffles, Chocolate Bakewell Tart, Finnish Gâteau

# Finnish Gâteau
FINLAND

1 recipe Cocoa Layer Cake, page 447

*Filling:*
2 tablespoons cornstarch
1/3 cup sugar
1-1/4 cups milk
2 egg yolks, beaten
1 teaspoon vanilla extract
1 tablespoon butter or margarine, room temperature
1 cup chunk-style applesauce

*Icing:*
1-1/2 cups sugar
2/3 cup half and half
2 tablespoons light corn syrup
2 oz. unsweetened chocolate, chopped
2 tablespoons butter or margarine
About 1/2 cup chopped, toasted, blanched almonds

**1.** Prepare and bake cake layers through step 4 as directed on page 447. Cut each layer in half horizontally.
**2.** To make filling, in a medium saucepan, combine cornstarch and sugar. Gradually stir in milk. Cook over low heat, stirring, until mixture thickens and comes to a boil. Remove from heat.
**3.** Stir 1/4 cup hot milk mixture into egg yolks. Return mixture to pan; stir well. Cook, stirring, until mixture is thickened. Do not boil. Pour into a medium bowl. Stir in vanilla and butter or margarine until butter or margarine melts. Cover surface of custard with a sheet of waxed paper to prevent a skin from forming. Refrigerate 2 to 3 hours or until completely chilled.
**4.** Place 1 cake layer on a serving plate; spread with 1/2 of chilled custard. Top with second layer; spread with applesauce. Top with third layer; spread with remaining custard. Top with fourth layer; lightly press down on cake.
**5.** To make icing, in a medium saucepan over medium heat, combine sugar, half and half, corn syrup and chocolate. Cook, stirring, until chocolate melts and sugar dissolves. Boil rapidly, without stirring, to soft-ball stage 234F (113C) on a candy thermometer. Remove from heat; stir in butter or margarine. Cool to lukewarm.
**6.** Beat cooled icing with a wooden spoon until icing thickens and loses its gloss. Spread icing over side and top of cake with a flat spatula. Press almonds lightly into icing around side of cake. Makes 6 to 8 servings.

# Bûche de Noël

FRANCE

### Cake:
**4 eggs, separated**
**1/2 cup granulated sugar**
**1/2 teaspoon vanilla extract**
**1/2 cup sifted cake flour**
**1/4 cup unsweetened cocoa powder**
**1/2 teaspoon salt**
**Powdered sugar**

### Filling & Frosting:
**Double recipe Chocolate Buttercream, page 447**
**1 tablespoon instant coffee powder**
**2 tablespoons boiling water**

### To decorate:
**Red and green candied cherries**
**Powdered sugar**

---

**1.** Preheat oven to 400F (205C). Grease a 15" x 10" jelly-roll pan. Line bottom of pan with waxed paper; grease paper.

**2.** To make cake, in a medium bowl, beat egg yolks until creamy. Beat in granulated sugar until thick and lemon-colored. Beat in vanilla. Sift flour, cocoa and salt over egg-yolk mixture; fold in.

**3.** In a medium bowl, beat egg whites until stiff but not dry. Fold beaten egg whites into egg-yolk mixture. Spread mixture in prepared pan; smooth top.

**4.** Bake in preheated oven 12 to 15 minutes or until center springs back when lightly pressed.

**5.** Sift powdered sugar over a clean towel; invert cake onto sugared towel. Peel off lining paper; trim crusty edges. Starting from short end, roll up cake in towel. Cool completely on a wire rack.

**6.** To make filling, prepare buttercream as directed on page 447, omitting half and half. In a small bowl, dissolve coffee in boiling water. Cool slightly. Beat cooled coffee into buttercream until blended.

**7.** Unroll cooled cake; spread 1/2 of buttercream over cake to within 1/2 inch of edges. Reroll cake, without towel; place, seam-side down, on a serving plate. Completely cover cake with remaining buttercream. Draw prongs of a fork over icing to create a bark effect. Decorate with candied cherries. Refrigerate until served. Sift powdered sugar over roll immediately before serving. Makes 10 to 12 servings.

Left to right: Bûche de Noël, Piped Mocha Truffles, Pacific Gold

# Piped Mocha Truffles

FRANCE

**Chocolate Cases:**
4 oz. semisweet chocolate, chopped
16 foil petits-four cases

*Filling:*
1 teaspoon instant coffee powder
1 tablespoon hot water
5 oz. semisweet or sweet chocolate, chopped
2 tablespoons whipping cream
1/4 cup butter or margarine, cubed
2 egg yolks, beaten
1 to 2 tablespoons dark rum

*To decorate:*
Crystallized candy violets

1. To make chocolate cases, melt chocolate in a small heavy saucepan over very low heat; stir until smooth. Cool slightly.

2. Spoon about 1 teaspoon melted chocolate into each foil case. Spread chocolate over bottom and up side of cases with back of spoon or your fingertip, covering insides completely. Place on a baking sheet; refrigerate about 20 minutes or until chocolate is completely set. Recoat inside of cases with remaining melted chocolate; let stand until chocolate is set.
3. Peel foil cases off chocolate cups carefully, using a knife tip to loosen chocolate from foil.
4. To make filling, in top of a double boiler set over a pan of simmering water, dissolve coffee in boiling water. Add chocolate; stir until smooth. Stir in cream until mixture is smooth and thickened. Remove top of double boiler from heat.
5. Gradually beat in butter or margarine, a little at a time, beating until butter or margarine melts. Beat in egg yolks and rum until thoroughly blended. Refrigerate about 30 minutes or until mixture is completely cool and thickened. Mixture should still be soft enough to pipe.
6. Spoon chocolate filling into a pastry bag fitted with a medium star tip; pipe filling into chocolate cups. Decorate with violets. Makes 16 truffles.

# Pacific Gold

PACIFIC

1/2 recipe Chocolate-Cookie Ice Cream, page 443, or
    other ice cream
1 fresh small or medium pineapple
2 egg whites
1/2 cup sugar
1/2 teaspoon vanilla extract

1. Make and freeze ice cream according to directions on page 443.
2. Preheat oven to 475F (220C). Carefully cut a thin slice from top and bottom of pineapple. Reserve top; cut away any peel from around leaves. Peel pineapple; with a small knife or end of a vegetable peeler, remove eyes.
3. Cut pineapple into 4 to 6 slices; cut out center core.
4. Soften ice cream slightly. Reassemble pineapple, placing ice cream between each slice and in center hole. Place in a baking pan; freeze while preparing meringue.
5. In a medium bowl, beat egg whites until soft peaks form. Gradually beat in sugar, beating until meringue is stiff and glossy. Beat in vanilla.
6. Spoon meringue into a large piping bag fitted with a 3/4-inch star tip; pipe stars over chilled pineapple, completely covering pineapple down to baking pan.
7. Bake in a preheated oven about 3 minutes or until meringue tips are lightly browned.
8. Insert reserved leaves into position on top of meringue-covered pineapple. Serve immediately. Makes 4 to 6 servings.

Left to right: Russian Cake, Chocolate-Topped Shortbread, Mazariner

# Russian Cake

RUSSIA

1 (10-3/4-oz.) pkg. frozen pound cake, thawed
5 tablespoons sweet sherry
1/4 cup raspberry jam or strawberry jam
3 tablespoons red-currant jelly
1 (7-oz.) pkg. marzipan
4 oz. semisweet chocolate, chopped
1 tablespoon butter or margarine

**1.** Remove cake from foil pan. Carefully wash and dry pan. Grease clean pan.
**2.** Cut cake horizontally into 3 layers. Place bottom layer in greased pan; sprinkle with 2 tablespoons sherry. Spread with 2 tablespoons jam; top with middle layer. Sprinkle with 2 tablespoons sherry; spread with remaining jam. Top with top layer; sprinkle with remaining 1 tablespoon sherry.

**3.** Place a sheet of waxed paper over cake; press down gently. Place a similar-sized loaf pan on top of cake; fill 1/3 full of pie weights or dried beans. Refrigerate overnight.
**4.** In a small saucepan over low heat, melt jelly; let cool. Remove weighted pan and waxed paper from cake. Invert cake onto a flat surface. Remove pan. Brush top and sides of cake with cooled jelly.
**5.** Roll out marzipan between 2 sheets of waxed paper to a rectangle large enough to cover top and sides of cake. Peel off 1 sheet of waxed paper; place marzipan over cake, covering cake completely. Peel off waxed paper. Press marzipan around cake; trim bottom edges.
**6.** Melt chocolate and butter or margarine in a small heavy saucepan over very low heat; stir until smooth. Let cool.
**7.** Spread cooled chocolate mixture over top and around sides of marzipan-covered cake, covering completely. Let stand until chocolate is set. Place cake on a serving plate; refrigerate until served. Makes 6 to 8 servings.

1. Preheat oven to 325F (165C). Grease an 8-inch-square baking pan. Line pan with waxed paper; grease paper.
2. To make shortbread, in a medium bowl, beat butter or margarine and sugar until light and fluffy. Stir in ground almonds and mixed fruit, if desired. Stir in flour to make a soft dough. Knead dough in bowl 8 to 10 strokes or until smooth. Press dough into prepared pan; smooth top.
3. Bake in preheated oven 30 to 35 minutes or until golden. Cool in pan on a wire rack 10 minutes. Remove from pan; peel off lining paper. Cool completely on wire rack. When cooled, return shortbread to pan.
4. To make icing, in a small saucepan over low heat, combine butter or margarine, milk and granulated sugar. Cook, stirring, until butter or margarine melts. Bring mixture to a boil; remove from heat. Sift cocoa and powdered sugar into a medium bowl. Beat in hot milk mixture until icing is stiff and completely cool. Spread icing over shortbread in pan. Make wavy lines in icing with prongs of a fork. Let stand until icing is set. Cut into bars; remove from pan. Makes 14 to 16 bars.

## Mazariner
SWEDEN

---

Double recipe of pastry for Chocolate Chiffon Pie, page 432
1/4 cup butter or margarine, room temperature
1/2 cup sugar
1 egg
1/3 cup almonds, ground
Few drops almond extract
Green food coloring
4 oz. semisweet chocolate, broken into pieces
About 12 blanched almonds, toasted

---

1. Preheat oven to 350F (175C). Prepare pastry through step 1 as directed on page 432. On a lightly floured surface, roll out pastry to about 1/4 inch thick; cut out 12 (5-inch) circles. Use pastry to line 12 (3-inch) tart pans. Prick pastry with a fork.
2. In a medium bowl, beat butter or margarine and sugar until light and fluffy. Beat in egg. Carefully fold in ground almonds, almond extract to taste and enough green food coloring to make a pastel green. Fill each tart two-thirds full.
3. Bake in preheated oven about 15 minutes or until filling puffs. Cool on a wire rack.
4. Melt chocolate in a small heavy saucepan over very low heat; stir until smooth. Spread melted chocolate over cooled tarts. Place an almond on each tart; let stand until chocolate is set. Make 12 tarts.

## Chocolate-Topped Shortbread
SCOTLAND

---

*Shortbread:*
1/2 cup butter or margarine, room temperature
1/2 cup sugar
1/4 cup finely ground blanched almonds
1/4 cup candied mixed fruit, if desired
1 cup all-purpose flour

*Icing:*
3 tablespoons butter or margarine
2 tablespoons milk
2 tablespoons granulated sugar
2 tablespoons unsweetened cocoa powder
1-1/2 cups powdered sugar

---

# Chocolate-Muesli Bars
SWITZERLAND

*Bars:*
1/3 cup honey
1/2 cup butter or margarine
1/3 cup firmly packed light-brown sugar
1-3/4 cups muesli, see box below
1/3 cup raisins or semisweet chocolate pieces
1/3 cup chopped almonds

*Topping:*
4 oz. semisweet chocolate, chopped
1 tablespoon butter or margarine

**1.** Preheat oven to 350F (175C). Grease an 8-inch-square baking pan. Line pan with foil; grease foil.
**2.** In a large saucepan over low heat, combine honey, butter or margarine and brown sugar. Cook, stirring, until butter or margarine and sugar are melted. Remove from heat. Stir in muesli, raisins or chocolate pieces and nuts until distributed. Press mixture evenly into bottom of prepared pan.
**3.** Bake in preheated oven 25 to 30 minutes or until golden brown. Cool completely in pan on a wire rack.
**4.** To make topping, melt chocolate and butter or margarine in a small heavy saucepan over very low heat; stir until smooth. Let cool.
**5.** Remove cooled muesli mixture from pan; peel off foil. Place on a flat surface; spread chocolate mixture over top. Let stand until chocolate is set. Cut into 16 bars. Makes 16 cookies.

---

**Muesli** was one of the best known items in the raw-food diet devised by Switzerland's Dr. Bircher-Brenner in the 1930's. He originally intended the diet to be rich in fruit. The modern version contains a lot more cereal. Although muesli is best known as a breakfast food, it makes a good meal at any time when combined with fresh fruit and milk or yogurt. Muesli is made from a selection of cereals, such as rolled oats, cracked wheat, rye flakes, wheat germ and bran. Dried fruits, nuts and sometimes sugar are added to this base. Muesli is available in some supermarkets and specialty shops.

# Rum & Chocolate Cake
SWITZERLAND

1 recipe Cocoa Layer Cake, page 447

*Syrup:*
1 cup water
1/2 cup firmly packed light-brown sugar
2 tablespoons unsweetened cocoa powder
1/4 cup dark rum

*Filling:*
4 oz. semisweet chocolate, chopped
2 tablespoons whipping cream
1 egg, beaten
1 teaspoon vanilla extract
Powdered sugar

**1.** Preheat oven to 350F (175C). Grease 2 (8-inch) round cake pans. Prepare and bake Cocoa Layer Cake as directed on page 447.
**2.** Cool cake layers in pans on wire racks 5 minutes. Remove from pans; cool completely on wire racks.
**3.** To make syrup, in a small saucepan over low heat, combine water, brown sugar and cocoa. Cook, stirring, until sugar dissolves. Bring to a boil. Remove from heat; stir in rum.
**4.** Wash and dry cake pans. Return cake layers to clean pans, top-side up. Poke holes in top of each layer with a fork or metal skewer. Spoon syrup over layers; let stand 2 to 3 hours.
**5.** To make filling, melt chocolate in a small heavy saucepan over very low heat; stir until smooth. Whisk in cream, egg and vanilla until mixture is smooth. Cool slightly; refrigerate until completely cool and almost firm.
**6.** Remove cake layers from pans; place 1 layer, bottom-side up, on a serving plate. Spread with cooled chocolate filling; top with second layer, bottom-side down.
**7.** Place a lace doily on top of cake; sift powdered sugar over doily. Carefully remove doily. Makes 6 to 8 servings.

Top to bottom: Rum & Chocolate Cake, Chocolate-Muesli Bars

# Chinese

Trade and cultural exchanges between China and the outside world took place as early as the time of the Roman Empire. However, Chinese culinary art was comparatively unknown in the West until recent times.

Many people have always wanted to try Chinese cooking. However, they have been discouraged by the thought of exotic ingredients and complicated techniques. These are unfounded fears. Basic Chinese cooking is really quite simple. In this section there are recipes representing a wide range of China's various regional styles. Also included are a number of dishes that could be termed specialties. They are not elaborate or time-consuming.

An authentic Chinese meal is a multi-course affair. For this reason, menu planning is different from planning a Western menu. In China, several dishes may be served at the same time. Recipes in this section give a brief overview of Chinese cooking. Dishes may be used for an all-Chinese meal or as part of a Western-style meal.

Since not all Chinese ingredients are available in this country, adequate substitutes are suggested when possible. A Chinese cook, anywhere in the world, can always produce a Chinese meal, using only local ingredients. The authentic Chinese flavor of the food depends more on how it is prepared and cooked, not what ingredients are used.

## REGIONAL COOKING STYLES

The fundamentals of Chinese cooking remain the same throughout China. All food is prepared and cooked in accordance with the same principles. These principles include careful preparation of ingredients before cooking, heat control and harmonious blending of different flavors. This is true from Peking cuisine in the north to Cantonese cooking in the south. What distinguishes one region from the other is the staple food and special seasoning. For example, in the north, people eat more wheat products, such as noodles, dumplings and pancakes. In the south, more rice and rice products are the foundation of the diet.

Traditionally, the various styles of cooking are classified into four major groups according to locality.

**The eastern region** is represented by China's largest city, Shanghai, with a population of well over 12 million. The cuisine of Shanghai is strongly influenced by the regional styles from the Yangtse River delta, particularly by the sophisticated school known as Huaiyang. The characteristics of this region can be best summarized as exquisite in appearance, rich in flavor and sweet in taste.

**The southern region** is represented by China's most diverse school of cuisine, originating from Canton in the Pearl River delta. Because Canton was the first Chinese port opened for trade, foreign influences are particularly strong in its cooking. Together with the neighboring province of Fujian, Canton is the origin of many Chinese emigrants. Therefore, this is also the best-known style of Chinese cooking abroad.

**The western region** is characterized by the richly flavored and piquant food of Szechuan. Before the discovery of chili pepper in the New World, the less pungent but numbing Szechuan peppercorn was the dominant spicy flavor. Now chili peppers and peppercorns are both used extensively. The neighboring province of Hunan is also renowned for hot, peppery cooking.

**The northern region** is centered around Peking, China's capital for many centuries. Because it is the political and cultural center of China, Peking has accumulated the best cooking styles from all the other regions. It has become China's culinary center in addition to creating a cuisine of its own. Fermented sauces are important in this region. Lamb is more popular here than in other regions.

You will find recipes from each of these regions in this book. A few recipes have been slightly adapted for practical reasons, but the majority are unaltered to preserve their authenticity.

## PREPARATION & COOKING TECHNIQUES

**Slicing**—This is probably the most common form of cutting in Chinese cooking. To slice, ingredients are cut into 1/8-inch slices. The slices are then cut into 1-1/2-inch by 1-inch pieces. It is easier to slice uncooked meats if they are first partially frozen.

**Shredding**—Shredding is similar to the julienne technique. To shred, first cut ingredients into thin slices. Stack slices; cut into thin strips about size of wooden matchsticks (1/8 inch by 1/8 inch).

**Dicing**—To dice, first cut ingredients into coarse strips about 1/4 inch by 1/4 inch; then dice into 1/4-inch cubes.

**Diagonal cutting**—This method is used for cutting vegetables, such as carrots, celery, zucchini or asparagus. Make a vertical diagonal cut; roll vegetable half a turn before making next cut.

**Mincing or finely chopping**—Chop ingredients into small bits. Although a food processor or blender can be used, flavor and texture will not be quite the same.

**Flower-cutting**—First diagonally score surface of each piece in a crisscross pattern. Then cut into small pieces. When cooked, each piece will open up and resemble ears of corn or flowers, hence the name *flower*. Kidneys, squid and tripe are usually cut in this manner.

**Chopping**—To cut a whole cooked chicken or duck across the bones, follow these directions:

**1.** Remove wings, legs and thighs.

**2.** Separate breast from back.

**3.** Chop back into about 8 pieces; place on bottom of a serving dish. Chop each wing into 2 or 3 pieces; place on each side of back pieces.

**4.** Chop each leg and thigh into 3 or 4 pieces; place on edge of serving dish.

**5.** Split breast lengthwise; cut each half into 3 or 4 pieces. Arrange on top of back pieces.

After cutting, the next step in Chinese food preparation is seasoning or coating. The basic method for coating fish or chicken is to combine fish or chicken with salt, egg white and cornstarch. This technique, known as *velveting*, preserves the natural delicate texture during cooking in hot oil. Meat is combined with salt, sugar, soy sauce, rice wine and cornstarch.

To achieve the desired texture or textures in any dish, use the correct cooking method. There are four basic cooking techniques: water-cooking, oil-cooking, steam-cooking and fire-cooking.

## SPECIAL INGREDIENTS & SEASONINGS

To produce a Chinese meal, special ingredients are not always needed. However, there are certain items that are commonly available that will add an exotic touch to everyday cooking.

**Bamboo shoots**—Ivory-colored shoots of bamboo plants. They are available canned. After opening, cover with water, seal and refrigerate up to a week.

Map of the four main culinary regions of China

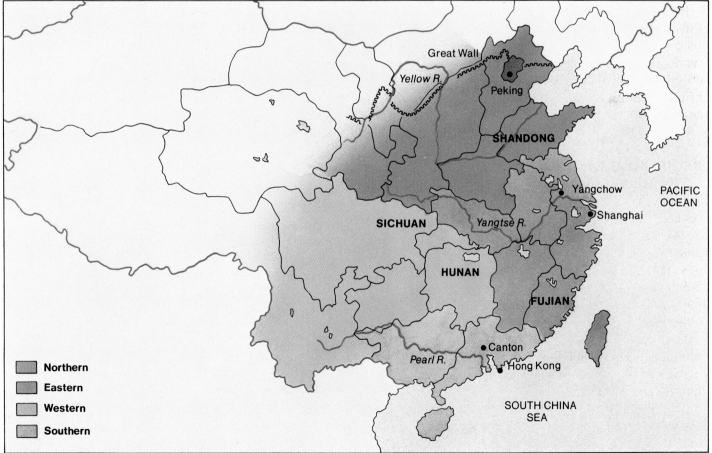

**Bean curd**—Also known as dofu or tofu. This custard-like preparation of pureed and pressed soybeans is exceptionally high in protein. In China, it is known as the "poor man's meat." It is sold in cakes about 3 inches square and 1 to 3 inches thick. It is available in Oriental markets and supermarkets. Cover it with water and store in the refrigerator. Use within a few days. Change water daily.

**Bean sprouts**—Sprouts from mung beans. Fresh bean sprouts are widely available in most supermarkets. Refrigerate two to three days. Do not use canned bean sprouts. They do not have the crunchy texture that is characteristic of this popular vegetable.

**Cellophane or transparent noodles**—Dried noodles made from mung beans. They are sold in dried bundles weighing from 2 ounces to 1 pound. Soak in warm water 5 minutes before using.

**Hot bean paste**—Fermented bean paste mixed with salt, flour and hot chilies. It is sold in jars. Chili sauce mixed with crushed yellow-bean sauce is a substitute. The amount of chili sauce used depends entirely on personal taste.

**Chili sauce**—Hot red sauce made from chilies, vinegar, sugar and salt. Use sparingly in cooking or as a dipping sauce. Substitute hot-pepper sauce, if desired.

**Dried Chinese mushrooms**—Widely used in many dishes for flavor and aroma. Soak in warm water 20 to 30 minutes, or in cold water several hours or until softened. When mushrooms are softened, rinse and squeeze dry. Discard hard stems before using. Dried European mushrooms, though of slightly different flavor and fragrance, can be substituted.

**Cooking oil**—In China, usually peanut oil. Use any good vegetable oil.

**Dried shrimp**—Salted and sun-dried shrimp. They are available in various sizes. Soak in warm water about 30 minutes or until softened. Drain and rinse before using. Store indefinitely in a dry, air-tight container.

**Five-spice powder**—A mixture of star anise, fennel seeds, cloves, cinnamon and Szechuan pepper. It is very piquant; use sparingly. Keep tightly covered.

**Gingerroot**—Sold fresh in most supermarkets. Refrigerated, it will keep for weeks. Do not substitute powdered ginger.

**Hoisin sauce**—Also known as *barbecue sauce*. This piquant sauce is made from soy sauce, sugar, flour, vinegar, salt, garlic, chili and sesame oil. Refrigerated, it will keep several months.

**Oyster sauce**—Thickish brown sauce made from

Top to bottom: above bowl, cellophane noodles; bamboo shoots; light soy sauce; bean sprouts; soaked and dry wood ears; hot bean paste; egg noodles.

oysters and soy sauce. This bottled sauce will keep several months if refrigerated.

**Red-bean paste**—Reddish-brown paste made from pureed red beans and sugar. It is sold in cans. Once opened, transfer to a covered container. It will keep in the refrigerator several months. Substitute sweetened chestnut puree.

**Rice wine**—Also known as *Shaohsing wine*. It is made from glutinous rice. Substitute dry sherry.

**Salted black beans**—Very salty indeed! Also known as *fermented black beans*. They are sold in plastic bags, jars or cans. Crush with water or rice wine before using. They will keep indefinitely in a tightly covered jar.

**Sesame paste**—Sold in jars covered with oil. It resembles clay in color and consistency, but is aromatic, rich and tasty. Stir to incorporate oil before using. Substitute peanut butter creamed with sesame oil.

**Sesame oil**—Oil from sesame seeds. It is sold in bottles. In China, it is widely used for seasoning rather than cooking. The refined yellow-sesame oil sold in Middle Eastern stores is not as aromatic, has less flavor and is not a very satisfactory substitute.

**Szechuan peppercorns**—Also known as *hua chiao*. This reddish-brown peppercorn is much stronger and more fragrant than black or white peppercorns. They are sold in plastic bags. Store peppercorns in a tightly sealed container.

**Szechuan preserved vegetable**—Specialty of Szechuan. It is the root of a special variety of mustard greens that is pickled in salt and chilies. It is sold in cans. Once opened, preserved vegetable should be transferred, unwashed, to a tightly covered container. Refrigerated, it will keep for months.

**Soy sauce**—Made from fermented soybeans, wheat, yeast, salt and sugar. Sold in bottles or cans, this popular Chinese sauce is used for cooking and at the table. Use light soy sauce for light meats, chicken and fish. Dark soy sauce is usually sweeter and is used for red meats. It will discolor food more than light soy sauce.

**Water chestnuts**—Available fresh or in cans. Canned water chestnuts are already peeled. They will keep refrigerated several weeks in fresh water in a covered jar.

**Wood ears or cloud ears**—Dried black fungus. Soak in warm water 20 minutes; then rinse in fresh water before using. They have a crunchy texture and a mild but subtle flavor.

**Yellow-bean sauce**—Thick sauce made from crushed yellow beans, flour and salt. It is sold in cans or jars. After opening, transfer to a jar with a lid. It will then keep in the refrigerator for months.

## WOKS & OTHER EQUIPMENT

The most frequently used cooking method in China is quick or rapid stir-frying. Use a wok for the best results.

The wok has three main advantages. First, because of its shape, a wok heats evenly. This decreases cooking time. Second, after stirring, ingredients always return to the center. The final advantage is that a smaller amount of oil is needed to cook in a wok than a skillet. The traditional iron wok keeps a steady and intense heat. Woks may also be made of heavy steel.

A new wok should be seasoned before use. First, wash it in hot soapy water; then dry by placing it over medium heat. When dry, add 1 to 2 tablespoons vegetable oil. Carefully rotate and tilt the hot wok to distribute the oil. Leave on the heat about 5 minutes. Turn off heat; leave wok to cool. A note of caution: do not leave a hot wok unattended. When it is cool, wipe excess oil from wok with paper towels.

After each use, always wash the wok immediately. To prevent rusting, dry thoroughly over a medium heat before putting wok away. Follow above directions if your wok needs to be seasoned again.

Besides stir-frying, use the wok for deep-frying, shallow-frying, steaming, braising, stewing and boiling. The type with a single handle is best suited to stir-frying; the two-handled type is better for all other purposes, as it rests more steadily on the burner. Flat-bottomed woks are available for use on electric elements. Flat-bottomed woks are less likely to tip; this is an advantage when deep-frying. Electric woks are a comparatively recent innovation. An electric wok is useful as a second wok or for use at the table. It is safer to use than a charcoal-burning fire-pot when cooking Chinese Hot-Pot. Some electric woks may not reach a high enough temperature for stir-frying.

It is useful to have a bamboo steamer. The advantage of a bamboo steamer over a metal one is that the bamboo lid is not airtight. This allows a small amount of evaporation, which prevents condensation forming inside the lid. Substitute a rack or a metal steamer if a bamboo steamer is not available.

A cleaver is one of the few essential tools in a Chinese kitchen. It may appear to be dangerous and awkward to use. In reality, it is light, steady and not dangerous to use provided you handle it correctly and with care. With practice, it will be easy and simple to use. Use it as a cutting knife and not a chopper. Special heavy cleavers are available for chopping bones.

清 湯

# Basic Stock for Soups

1 (3- to 4-lb.) stewing chicken or 3 lbs. pork spareribs
11 cups water
4 to 6 thin gingerroot slices
3 or 4 green onions

1. Place all ingredients in a large saucepan. Bring to a boil, skimming off any foam from top. Reduce heat. Cover; simmer 2 to 2-1/2 hours.
2. Strain stock when slightly cooled; refrigerate. Discard chicken or spareribs; no flavor remains in them. Discard gingerroot and onions.
3. Lift fat from top of cold stock before using. Stock will keep in refrigerator 3 or 4 days. Freeze if storing for a longer period. Makes 7 to 8 cups.

白菜肉片湯

# Sliced Pork & Cabbage Soup

4 oz. lean pork
1 tablespoon rice wine or dry sherry
1 tablespoon soy sauce
1/2 medium Chinese cabbage
2 cups Basic Stock, above, using chicken
1 teaspoon salt

1. Thinly slice pork. In a medium bowl, combine wine or sherry and soy sauce. Add sliced pork; let stand 10 minutes.
2. Cut cabbage in 1-inch lengths.
3. In a medium saucepan, bring stock to a boil. Add seasoned pork, stirring to keep slices separate. Boil 30 seconds; add sliced cabbage and salt. Reduce heat; simmer 1-1/2 to 2 minutes. Cabbage should remain crisp. Makes 4 servings.

Left to right: Sliced Pork & Cabbage Soup, Chinese Mushroom Soup
On chopping block with cleaver, left to right: gingerroot, shredded cabbage, sliced gingerroot, dried Chinese mushrooms

冬菇湯

# Chinese Mushroom Soup

6 medium dried Chinese mushrooms or
    4 oz. fresh mushrooms
2 teaspoons cornstarch
1 tablespoon cold water
3 egg whites
2 teaspoons salt
2 cups Basic Stock, opposite

*To garnish:*
1 teaspoon finely chopped green onion

1. Soak dried mushrooms in warm water 20 minutes or until softened. Rinse; squeeze dry. Discard hard stems; cut caps into thin slices. If using fresh mushrooms, wipe with damp paper towels; thinly slice.
2. In a small bowl, combine cornstarch and cold water; set aside. Stir egg whites with a fork to blend; do not froth. Add a pinch of salt.
3. In a medium saucepan, bring stock to a boil; add sliced mushrooms. Boil 1 minute. Stir in cornstarch mixture; stir constantly until thickened.
4. Add remaining salt. Slowly pour egg whites into soup, stirring constantly. Cook 1 minute.
5. Serve hot. Garnish with onion. Makes 4 servings.

蛋花湯

# Egg-Drop Soup

2 eggs
1 teaspoon salt
2 cups Basic Stock, opposite
2 teaspoons finely chopped green onion

1. In a small bowl, beat eggs with a pinch of salt; set aside.
2. In a medium saucepan, bring stock to a boil. Slowly pour beaten eggs into boiling stock, stirring constantly. Cook 1 minute.
3. Place remaining salt and onions in a serving bowl. Add soup; serve hot. Makes 4 servings.

# 炝明虾

## Peking Poached Shrimp

8 oz. peeled, deveined uncooked shrimp
2 cups water
2 tablespoons rice wine or dry sherry
1 teaspoon salt
2 teaspoons sesame oil

*To garnish:*
1 tablespoon thinly shredded gingerroot

---

1. If shrimp are frozen, thaw before using. Rinse shrimp. Cut each shrimp in half lengthwise.
2. In a medium saucepan, bring water to a boil. Add shrimp; cook until pink. Drain shrimp; cool in a bowl of cold water a few seconds. Drain well; place shrimp on a small serving dish.
3. In a small bowl, combine wine or sherry, salt and sesame oil; pour mixture evenly over shrimp.
4. Garnish with gingerroot. Serve cold by itself or as part of assorted hors d'oeuvres. Makes about 12 appetizers.

# 油爆虾

## Rapid-Fried Shrimp in Shells

8 oz. unpeeled uncooked shrimp
Vegetable oil for deep-frying
2 tablespoons rice wine or dry sherry
1/2 teaspoon salt
2 tablespoons soy sauce
2 teaspoons sugar
1 teaspoon finely chopped green onion
1 teaspoon finely chopped gingerroot

*To garnish:*
1 tablespoon finely chopped fresh coriander or parsley

---

*It is easier to eat these shrimp with chopsticks or your fingers than with a fork.*

1. Rinse shrimp; remove legs. Do not peel. Pat dry with paper towels.
2. Heat oil in a wok or saucepan over high heat. Deep-fry shrimp until bright pink; quickly remove with a slotted spoon. Carefully pour oil from wok or saucepan; reserve for another use, if desired.
3. Return shrimp to same wok or saucepan; add wine or sherry, salt, soy sauce, sugar, onion and gingerroot. Stir over medium heat until each shrimp is coated with sauce.
4. Neatly arrange shrimp on a serving dish. Garnish with coriander or parsley. Serve hot or cold. Makes about 12 appetizers.

# 熟炝虾仁

## Hot Mixed Shrimp

8 oz. peeled, deveined uncooked shrimp
2 cups water

*Sauce:*
2 teaspoons cornstarch
1 tablespoon water
1 tablespoon sesame oil
2 tablespoons soy sauce
1 teaspoon sugar

*To garnish:*
2 teaspoons finely chopped gingerroot

---

1. Rinse shrimp with cold water.
2. In a medium saucepan, bring 2 cups water to a boil. Remove from heat; immediately add shrimp. Cover; steep shrimp 2 to 3 minutes or until pink.
3. Drain shrimp. Place in a serving dish.
4. For sauce, in a small bowl, combine cornstarch and water. Warm sesame oil in a wok or saucepan over medium heat. Stir in soy sauce and sugar until sugar dissolves. Stir in cornstarch mixture. Cook sauce until thickened, stirring constantly. Pour sauce evenly over shrimp.
5. Garnish with gingerroot. Serve cold. Makes about 12 appetizers.

Clockwise from top: Rapid-Fried Shrimp in Shells, light soy sauce, Peking Poached Shrimp, Hot Mixed Shrimp

鴛鴦虾仁

## Red & White Shrimp with Green Vegetable

2 teaspoons salt
1 lb. peeled, deveined uncooked shrimp
1 egg white
1 tablespoon cornstarch
1 cup vegetable oil
8 oz. Chinese pea pods, trimmed, or broccoli flowerets
2 green onions, finely chopped
2 teaspoons finely chopped gingerroot slices
2 tablespoons rice wine or dry sherry
1 tablespoon tomato paste
About 1 tablespoon chili sauce

---

*This colorful dish is perfect for special occasions. As a starter, it serves 8 to 10 people. As a main dish served with 1 or 2 other dishes, it serves 4 to 6 people. Its Chinese name is Yuanyang Shrimp or Mandarin Ducks Shrimp. Mandarin ducks, also known as "love birds," are often used as symbols of affection and happiness.*

**1.** In a medium bowl, combine a pinch of salt and shrimp. Stir in egg white; then stir in cornstarch.
**2.** Preheat a wok or large skillet over high heat. Add 3 tablespoons oil. When oil is hot, add pea pods or broccoli and 1 teaspoon salt. Stir-fry pea pods 1-1/2 to 2 minutes. Stir-fry broccoli 2-1/2 to 3 minutes. Place stir-fried pea pods or broccoli in center of a serving platter.
**3.** Wash and dry wok or skillet; place wok or skillet over high heat. Add remaining oil. When oil is hot, add coated shrimp; deep-fry 1 minute. Remove shrimp with a slotted spoon; drain on paper towels.
**4.** Pour off oil, leaving about 1 tablespoon in wok or pan. Add onions and gingerroot; stir-fry a few seconds. Add drained shrimp, remaining salt and wine or sherry; stir to blend. Remove half of shrimp; place at end of platter containing pea pods or broccoli.
**5.** Add tomato paste and chili sauce, to taste, to shrimp remaining in wok or skillet; stir a few seconds to blend sauce. Spoon shrimp mixture on other end of platter. Serve hot. Makes 4 servings.

### Variation
If desired, substitute a milder Szechuan chili and tomato sauce for tomato paste and chili sauce.

糖醋大虾

## Cantonese Sweet & Sour Prawns

8 oz. unpeeled prawns
1 egg white
1 tablespoon cornstarch
Vegetable oil for deep-frying
1 green onion, finely chopped
2 teaspoons finely chopped gingerroot
2 tablespoons sugar
1 tablespoon rice wine or dry sherry
1 tablespoon soy sauce
1 tablespoon vinegar
2 teaspoons cornstarch combined with
   2 tablespoons water

---

*Like Rapid-Fried Shrimp in Shells, page 480, eat this dish with chopsticks or your fingers. Prawns are large shrimp.*

**1.** Remove legs from prawns, but do not peel. Cut each prawn into 2 or 3 pieces. In a medium bowl, combine egg white and cornstarch. Add prawns; stir to coat.
**2.** Heat oil in a wok or deep saucepan over medium heat. Add coated prawn pieces, one at a time; deep-fry until golden. Remove prawns with a slotted spoon; drain on paper towels.
**3.** Pour off oil, leaving about 1 tablespoon in wok or pan. Add onion and gingerroot; stir-fry a few seconds. Add sugar, wine or sherry, soy sauce and vinegar. Stir constantly until sugar dissolves. Add cooked prawns; blend well. Stir in cornstarch and water mixture; stirring constantly, cook until thickened. Serve hot. Makes 4 servings.

### Variation
Although it is more authentic to cook prawns unpeeled, peel before cooking, if desired.

Top to bottom: Cantonese Sweet & Sour Prawns, Red & White Shrimp with Green Vegetable

# 炸蟹丸

## Deep-Fried Crabme...

1 lb. fresh, frozen or canned crabmeat
2 oz. pork fat, minced
4 to 6 water chestnuts, minced
1 egg
1 tablespoon rice wine or dry sherry
1 teaspoon salt
1 tablespoon finely chopped gingerroot
1 teaspoon finely chopped green onion
2 tablespoons cornstarch
Vegetable oil for deep-frying
Lettuce leaves

1. In a medium bowl, combine crabmeat, pork fat, water chestnuts, egg, wine or sherry, salt, gingerroot, onion and cornstarch.
2. Chill mixture 1 hour to firm. Shape into 24 (1-inch) balls.
3. Heat oil in a wok or deep saucepan over medium heat. When oil is hot, add crabmeat balls, one at a time. Deep-fry until light golden. Remove crabmeat balls with a slotted spoon.
4. Increase heat to high. Return cooked crabmeat balls to oil; deep-fry a few seconds or until golden brown. Place lettuce leaves on a serving plate. Arrange hot crabmeat balls over lettuce. Makes 24 small balls.

### Variations
Make and cook crabmeat balls through step 3 the day before serving. Warm as in step 4. Or, place crabmeat balls in 1/2 cup boiling stock in a wok or saucepan. Bring to a boil. Simmer 5 minutes. Thicken sauce with a mixture of 2 teaspoons cornstarch and a little water or stock. Garnish with 1 tablespoon finely chopped ham.

Substitute shrimp or a mixture of crabmeat and shrimp for crabmeat.

## ...reribs in Cantonese ...& Sour Sauce

1-1/2 lbs. pork spareribs
1/2 teaspoon salt
Freshly ground Szechuan or black pepper
1 teaspoon sugar
1 tablespoon cornstarch
1 egg yolk
Vegetable oil for deep-frying
2 tablespoons all-purpose flour
1 small green bell pepper, shredded
1 small red bell pepper, shredded
1 tablespoon soy sauce
3 tablespoons sugar
3 tablespoons vinegar
1 tablespoon cornstarch blended with
   3 tablespoons water

---

*The sauce is bright and translucent, not too sweet or too sour, and the meat is succulent.*

**1.** Cut spareribs into individual ribs. With a cleaver, chop each rib into 2 or 3 pieces. In a large bowl, combine chopped spareribs, salt, pepper, sugar and cornstarch. Stir in egg yolk until distributed. Let stand 10 minutes.
**2.** Heat oil in a wok or deep saucepan over medium heat. Coat each sparerib piece with flour before deep-frying. Add coated sparerib pieces to hot oil, one at a time. Separate with chopsticks, if necessary. Deep-fry until crisp and golden; remove spareribs with a slotted spoon.
**3.** Heat oil until bubbling. Add deep-fried spareribs; deep-fry again 30 seconds or until golden brown. Remove with a slotted spoon or strainer; drain on paper towels.
**4.** Pour off oil, leaving about 1 tablespoon in wok or saucepan. Place wok or saucepan over high heat. When oil is hot, add bell peppers; stir-fry 30 seconds. Add soy sauce, sugar and vinegar. Stir a few times. Stir in cornstarch mixture. Stirring constantly, cook until sauce thickens; add spareribs. Stir well; serve immediately. Makes 4 servings.

## 滑溜里脊片
## Pork Slices with Chinese Vegetables

8 oz. lean pork
1 tablespoon soy sauce
1 tablespoon rice wine or dry sherry
1 tablespoon cornstarch
Water
1/2 oz. wood ears
4 oz. Chinese pea pods, trimmed, or broccoli flowerets
1/4 cup vegetable oil
2 green onions, cut into 1-inch lengths
4 oz. bamboo shoots, sliced
4 oz. water chestnuts, sliced
1 teaspoon salt
1 teaspoon sugar
1 teaspoon sesame oil

---

**1.** Cut pork into small, thin slices. In a medium bowl, combine sliced pork, soy sauce, wine or sherry and 1/2 tablespoon cornstarch. In a small bowl, combine remaining cornstarch with a little water to make a paste; set aside.
**2.** Soak wood ears in warm water 15 to 20 minutes or until softened; rinse. Discard any hard parts. Coarsely chop. If pea pods are large, cut in half. If using broccoli, cut flowerets into small pieces.
**3.** Preheat a wok or large skillet over high heat. Add vegetable oil. When hot, add seasoned pork; stir-fry 1 minute or until color changes. Remove pork with a slotted spoon.
**4.** To oil remaining in wok or skillet, add onions and pea pods or broccoli. Stir-fry 2 minutes. Stir in bamboo shoots, chopped wood ears, water chestnuts, salt and sugar. Add cooked pork; stir-fry 1 minute. Stir in cornstarch mixture; stirring constantly, cook until thickened. Stir in sesame oil; serve hot. Makes 4 servings.

Top to bottom: Pork Slices with Chinese Vegetables, Pork Spareribs in Cantonese Sweet & Sour Sauce

# 清炖獅子頭

## Yangchow "Lion's Head" (Pork Meatballs with Chinese Cabbage)

1-1/4 lbs. ground pork
2 teaspoons finely chopped gingerroot
2 green onions, finely chopped
1 teaspoon salt
2 tablespoons rice wine or dry sherry
1 tablespoon cornstarch
1 medium Chinese cabbage
2 tablespoons vegetable oil
1 cup beef stock

*This famous dish originated from Yangchow in the Yangtse River delta. Pork meatballs are supposed to resemble the shape of a lion's head, with the cabbage its mane, hence the name.*

**1.** In a large bowl, combine pork, gingerroot, onions, salt, wine or sherry and cornstarch. Shape mixture into 4 to 6 meatballs.
**2.** Cut cabbage into large chunks. Heat oil in a large saucepan. Add cabbage; stir-fry 1 minute. Place meatballs on top of cabbage; add stock. Bring to a boil. Cover; simmer 45 minutes. Serve hot. Makes 4 to 6 servings.

### Variation
Add 2 tablespoons soy sauce and 1 tablespoon sugar to meatball mixture. Reduce salt to 1/2 teaspoon. Meat will have a darker, richer appearance.

# 五香排骨

## Five-Spice Pork Spareribs

1-1/2 to 1-3/4 lbs. pork spareribs
1 teaspoon salt
1 tablespoon sugar
2 tablespoons rice wine or dry sherry
2 tablespoons soy sauce
1 teaspoon five-spice powder
1 tablespoon Hoisin or barbecue sauce

**1.** Cut pork into individual ribs. With a cleaver, chop each rib into 2 or 3 small pieces. In a shallow ovenproof dish, combine ribs and remaining ingredients. Cover and let stand 1 hour, turning once or twice.
**2.** Preheat oven to 400F (205C).
**3.** Bake seasoned spareribs in preheated oven 40 to 45 minutes or until tender, turning once.
**4.** Or barbecue ribs on a grill 15 to 20 minutes or until brown and crispy, turning once or twice. Makes 4 servings.

### Variation
Substitute a mixture of 1 teaspoon chili sauce, 1 teaspoon vinegar, 2 teaspoons cornstarch and 1 crushed garlic clove for Hoisin or barbecue sauce.

# 豉汁蒸排骨

## Cantonese Steamed Pork Spareribs in Black-Bean Sauce

1 lb. pork spareribs
1 garlic clove, finely chopped
1 teaspoon finely chopped gingerroot
1 tablespoon black-bean sauce
1 tablespoon soy sauce
1 tablespoon rice wine or dry sherry
1 teaspoon sugar
1 teaspoon cornstarch

*To garnish:*
2 green onions, cut into short lengths
1 small hot red pepper, thinly shredded
1 teaspoon sesame oil

**1.** Cut pork into individual ribs. With a cleaver, chop spareribs into small pieces.
**2.** In a large bowl, combine garlic, gingerroot, black-bean sauce, soy sauce, wine or sherry, sugar and cornstarch. Add chopped spareribs; let stand 15 to 20 minutes.
**3.** Place seasoned spareribs on a heatproof plate; put into a steamer. Steam 25 to 30 minutes or until tender.
**4.** Garnish with onions and red pepper. Sprinkle with sesame oil. Serve hot. Makes 2 to 3 servings.

Left to right: Yangchow "Lion's Head," Five-Spice Pork Spareribs, Cooked Rice

豉 椒 牛 肉

## Beef & Green Peppers in Cantonese Black-Bean Sauce

1 (8- to 10-oz.) beef-flank steak
1/4 teaspoon salt
1 tablespoon soy sauce
1 tablespoon rice wine or dry sherry
1 teaspoon sugar
1 tablespoon cornstarch
1 small green bell pepper
1 medium onion
1/4 cup vegetable oil
2 teaspoons shredded gingerroot
2 green onions, shredded
1 or 2 green or red chilies, shredded
1-1/2 tablespoons fermented black beans crushed in
   1 tablespoon rice wine or dry sherry

*Although pork is the most popular meat in China, beef is an important part of the diet of Chinese Moslems. There are about four million Chinese Moslems widely distributed throughout China.*

**1.** Cut beef into thin slices about 1-1/2 inches across. In a medium bowl, combine sliced beef, salt, soy sauce, wine or sherry, sugar and cornstarch.
**2.** Slice green pepper and onion into 1-inch squares.
**3.** Preheat a wok or large skillet over high heat. Add oil. When oil smokes, add seasoned beef; stir-fry a few seconds. Remove beef with a slotted spoon. To same oil, add gingerroot, green onions, chilies and green-pepper and onion squares; stir-fry a few seconds. Add crushed black-bean mixture and cooked beef. Stir-fry 1 minute. Serve immediately. Makes 4 servings.

### Variation
Substitute purchased black-bean sauce for black-bean-and-wine mixture. Flavor will be slightly different.

干 炒 牛 肉 絲

## Szechuan Dry-Fried Shredded Beef

2 tablespoons sesame oil
1 (10-oz.) beef-flank steak, shredded
2 tablespoons rice wine or dry sherry
1 tablespoon hot bean paste
1 tablespoon Hoisin sauce or barbecue sauce
1 garlic clove, finely chopped
1/2 teaspoon salt
1 tablespoon sugar
2 carrots, shredded
2 green onions, finely chopped
2 teaspoons finely chopped gingerroot
1/2 teaspoon freshly ground Szechuan or black pepper
1 teaspoon chili oil

*Dry-frying is a cooking method unique to Szechuan cuisine. Main ingredients are slowly stir-fried over low heat with any seasonings. Additional ingredients are added, and the mixture quickly stir-fried over high heat.*

**1.** Heat a wok or skillet over high heat. Add sesame oil. When hot, add beef with 1 tablespoon wine or sherry; stir-fry until beef shreds separate.
**2.** Reduce heat. Pour off excess liquid; stir gently until beef is completely dry. Stir in bean paste, Hoisin or barbecue sauce, garlic, salt, sugar and remaining wine or sherry. Stir a few times.
**3.** Increase heat to high. Add carrots; stir-fry 1 minute. Add onions, gingerroot, pepper and chili oil; stir-fry 1 minute. Serve hot. Makes 4 servings.

### Variation
Substitute 3 or 4 shredded celery stalks for carrots, or use half carrots and half celery.

Clockwise from top: Cantonese Beef in Oyster Sauce, Beef & Green Peppers in Cantonese Black-Bean Sauce, Szechuan Dry-Fried Shredded Beef

# 蚝油牛肉

## Cantonese Beef in Oyster Sauce

1 (8- to-10 oz.) beef-flank steak
Salt
1/2 teaspoon freshly ground pepper
1 teaspoon sugar
1 tablespoon light soy sauce
2 tablespoons rice wine or dry sherry
1 tablespoon cornstarch
1 egg
1 small Chinese cabbage
1/4 cup vegetable oil
1 green onion, finely chopped
2 teaspoons finely chopped gingerroot
1-1/2 tablespoons oyster sauce

**1.** Cut beef into thin slices about 1-1/2 inches across. In a medium bowl, combine sliced beef, a pinch of salt, pepper, sugar, soy sauce, wine or sherry, cornstarch and egg. Let stand 20 to 30 minutes.
**2.** Cut each Chinese-cabbage leaf into 2 or 3 pieces.
**3.** Preheat a wok or large skillet over high heat. Add 2 tablespoons oil. When oil smokes, add cabbage pieces; stir-fry 1-1/2 to 2 minutes or until leaves become limp. Quickly remove with a slotted spoon; place cabbage in a serving dish.
**4.** Wash and dry wok or skillet. Add remaining oil. When oil smokes, add onion and gingerroot; stir-fry a few seconds. Add seasoned beef; stir-fry 1 minute. Add oyster sauce; stir-fry 1 minute. Spoon beef mixture over cabbage. Makes 4 servings.

# 魚香茄子

## Eggplant with Szechuan "Fish Sauce"

3 to 6 dried red chilies
1 (1-lb.) eggplant
Vegetable oil for deep-frying
3 or 4 green onions, finely chopped
1 teaspoon finely chopped gingerroot
1 garlic clove, finely chopped
1 teaspoon sugar
1 tablespoon soy sauce
1 tablespoon vinegar
1 tablespoon hot bean paste
2 teaspoons cornstarch mixed with 2 tablespoons water
1 teaspoon sesame oil

*No fish is used in this recipe. The sauce normally is used for fish dishes, hence the name "fish sauce."*

**1.** Soak chilies in water to cover 5 to 10 minutes. Drain; cut into small pieces, discarding stalks. If small, chilies can be left whole. Peel eggplant; cut into 1-1/2-inch diamond-shaped pieces.
**2.** Heat vegetable oil in a wok or deep saucepan over medium heat. Add eggplant pieces; deep-fry 1-1/2 to 2 minutes or until soft. Remove eggplant with a slotted spoon; drain on paper towels.
**3.** Pour off oil; return cooked eggplant to wok or pan. Add soaked chilies, onions, gingerroot and garlic; stir-fry a few seconds. Add sugar, soy sauce, vinegar and bean paste; stir-fry 1 minute. Stir in cornstarch mixture; stirring constantly, cook until thickened. Sprinkle with sesame oil. Serve either hot or cold. Makes 4 servings.

### Variation
Add 4 ounces thinly shredded pork at beginning of step 3 before returning cooked eggplant to wok or saucepan.

Top to bottom: Stir-Fried Spinach & Bean Curd, Eggplant with Szechuan "Fish Sauce," Braised Broccoli, Stir-Fried Mixed Vegetables

菠菜炒豆腐

## Stir-Fried Spinach & Bean Curd

8 oz. spinach
8 oz. bean curd
1/4 cup vegetable oil
1 teaspoon salt
1 teaspoon sugar
1 tablespoon soy sauce
1 teaspoon sesame oil

1. Wash spinach well; shake off excess water.
2. Cut bean curd into 16 pieces.
3. Heat vegetable oil in a wok or large skillet over high heat. Add bean-curd pieces; stir-fry until golden, gently turning. Remove bean curd with a slotted spoon.
4. Add spinach to wok or skillet; stir-fry 30 seconds or until leaves are limp. Add bean curd, salt, sugar and soy sauce; stir-fry 1 to 1-1/2 minutes or until blended. Sprinkle with sesame oil; serve hot. Makes 4 servings.

油燜西芝

## Braised Broccoli

1 lb. broccoli or cauliflower
3 tablespoons vegetable oil
1 teaspoon salt
1 teaspoon sugar
3 tablespoons water

1. Cut broccoli or cauliflower into flowerets; peel and thinly slice stalks.
2. Preheat a wok or skillet over high heat. Add oil. When oil is hot, add broccoli or cauliflower flowerets and sliced stalks; stir-fry 30 seconds. Add salt, sugar and stock or water; cook 2 to 3 minutes, stirring constantly. Serve hot. Makes 4 servings.

炒鮮蔬

## Stir-Fried Mixed Vegetables

4 oz. fresh bean sprouts
2 carrots
4 oz. Chinese pea pods, trimmed, or broccoli flowerets
3 tablespoons vegetable oil
4 oz. bamboo shoots, sliced
1 teaspoon salt
1 teaspoon sugar
1 tablespoon water

*This dish should have harmonious contrast in color and texture.*

1. Wash bean sprouts in cold water; discard bits and pieces that float to the surface.
2. Cut carrots into thin slices. If pea pods are large, cut into 2 or 3 pieces.
3. Preheat a wok or large skillet over high heat. Heat oil in preheated wok or skillet. When oil is hot, add sliced carrots, pea pods or broccoli and bamboo shoots; stir-fry 1 minute. Add washed bean sprouts, salt and sugar. Stir-fry 1 to 2 minutes, adding stock or water, if necessary. Do not overcook because vegetables will lose their crunchiness. Serve hot. Makes 4 servings.

### Variations
If fresh sprouts are not available, do not used canned bean sprouts. Substitute thinly shredded celery for fresh bean sprouts.

Substitute cabbage, zucchini or cauliflower for bamboo shoots.

For stir-frying, choose the freshest vegetables available. Use as soon as possible after purchasing. To prevent loss of vitamins into water, wash vegetables before cutting. To avoid vitamin destruction by exposure to air, cook vegetables soon after cutting. Never overcook vegetables or use too much water in cooking. Do not use a lid over the wok or pan when cooking green vegetables unless specified. This will spoil the bright green color.

# 豉油鷄（廣東式）

## Cantonese Soya Braised Chicken

1 (3- to 3-1/2-lb.) roasting chicken
2 tablespoons freshly ground Szechuan or black pepper
2 tablespoons finely chopped gingerroot
5 tablespoons dark soy sauce
3 tablespoons rice wine or dry sherry
2 tablespoons sugar
3 tablespoons vegetable oil
1/2 cup water or chicken stock
1 small head lettuce, shredded

*This bright brown chicken is seen in restaurant windows in China. Serve hot or cold.*

**1.** Pat chicken dry with paper towels. Rub inside and out with pepper and gingerroot.
**2.** In a large bowl, combine soy sauce, wine or sherry and sugar. Add chicken; let stand at least 45 minutes, turning several times. Remove chicken from liquid, reserving liquid. Pat chicken dry with paper towels.
**3.** Heat oil in a wok or large saucepan over medium heat. Add seasoned chicken; sauté until browned. Add reserved liquid and water or stock. Bring to a boil; reduce heat. Cover; simmer 45 minutes, turning chicken several times during cooking without breaking skin.
**4.** Chop chicken into small pieces. Spread lettuce on a medium platter. Arrange chopped chicken neatly over lettuce. Pour 2 tablespoons cooking liquid over chicken. Refrigerate until ready to serve. Makes 4 to 6 servings.

Left to right: Soya Duck, Szechuan Bang-Bang Chicken

# 棒棒鶏

## Szechuan Bang-Bang Chicken

2 boneless chicken breasts
Salt
Water
1 head lettuce, shredded

*Sauce:*
1 tablespoon sesame-seed paste
1 tablespoon light soy sauce
2 tablespoons vinegar
About 1 teaspoon chili sauce
1 teaspoon sugar
2 tablespoons chicken stock or water

---

*This popular Peking and Szechuan restaurant dish is extremely simple to cook. If sesame-seed paste is not available, an acceptable substitute is peanut butter creamed with a little sesame oil. Chicken is pounded after cooking, hence the name.*

**1.** Place chicken and salt in a medium saucepan; add water to cover. Bring to a boil. Reduce heat; simmer 10 minutes.
**2.** Remove chicken; discard cooking liquid. With a rolling pin, pound cooked chicken until soft.
**3.** Place shredded lettuce on a serving dish. Shred chicken with your fingers; place on lettuce.
**4.** For sauce, in a small bowl, combine all sauce ingredients using chili sauce to taste. Pour sauce over chicken. Serve cold. Makes 4 servings.

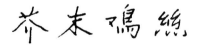

## Shredded Chicken in Mustard Sauce

2 tablespoons dry mustard
Water
2 boneless chicken breasts, shredded
1/2 teaspoon salt
2 egg whites, slightly beaten
1 tablespoon cornstarch
1/2 cup vegetable oil
1 tablespoon light soy sauce
1 tablespoon vinegar
2 teaspoons sesame oil

---

**1.** In a small bowl, blend dry mustard with enough cold water to form a thin paste. Let stand 30 minutes before using.
**2.** In a medium bowl, combine chicken, salt, egg whites and cornstarch.
**3.** Preheat a wok or large skillet over medium heat. Add vegetable oil. When hot, add chicken. Separate chicken shreds with chopsticks or a fork. Stir until chicken turns white. Remove chicken with a slotted spoon. Drain on paper towels. Arrange cooked chicken in a serving dish.
**4.** For sauce, in a small bowl, combine mustard mixture, soy sauce, vinegar and sesame oil. Pour sauce over chicken. Serve cold. Makes 4 servings.

## Soya Duck

1 (4-1/2- to 5-lb.) duck
About 4 cups water
2 teaspoons salt
4 green onions
4 thin gingerroot slices
1 teaspoon five-spice powder
3 tablespoons rice wine or dry sherry
6 tablespoons dark soy sauce
2/3 cup packed brown sugar
1 tablespoon sesame oil

---

**1.** Remove and discard excess fat and tail from duck. Reserve giblets for another use.
**2.** In a large saucepan, bring water to a boil. Add duck; boil 1 minute. Remove duck from cooking liquid. Pat duck dry with paper towels. Rub 1 teaspoon salt inside duck.
**3.** Add remaining salt, onions, gingerroot and five-spice powder to cooking liquid remaining in saucepan. Bring to a boil.
**4.** Return duck to saucepan; add wine or sherry, soy sauce and sugar. Reduce heat. Cover; simmer duck 1-1/2 hours. Lift out duck; rub with sesame oil.
**5.** Boil cooking liquid until slightly reduced. Baste duck with reduced cooking liquid several times. Chop duck into small pieces, page 475. Serve hot or cold. Makes 4 servings.

# 青椒炒鷄絲

## Shredded Chicken Breast with Green Peppers

2 boneless chicken-breast halves, shredded
1 teaspoon salt
1 egg white
1 tablespoon cornstarch
Water
1/4 cup vegetable oil
1 green onion, finely chopped
2 teaspoons finely chopped gingerroot
1 large green bell pepper, shredded
2 tablespoons rice wine or dry sherry
1 teaspoon sesame oil

---

*Do not overcook this dish. When correctly done, chicken should be tender and peppers should be crunchy and shining.*

**1.** In a medium bowl, combine chicken and 1/2 teaspoon salt. Stir in egg white; then stir in 2 teaspoons cornstarch. In a small bowl, combine remaining cornstarch and a little water to make a paste; set aside.
**2.** Preheat a wok or large skillet over medium heat. Add vegetable oil. When oil is warm, add coated chicken; stir-fry until white. See box, below. Remove chicken with a slotted spoon.
**3.** Increase heat to high. When oil is very hot, add onion and gingerroot. Stir-fry a few seconds. Add green peppers; stir-fry 30 seconds. Add cooked chicken, remaining salt and wine or sherry. Stir 30 seconds. Stir in cornstarch mixture; cook until thickened. Stir in sesame oil. Serve hot. Makes 4 servings.

---

Combining chicken with salt, egg white and cornstarch prior to cooking is a technique known as *velveting.* The coating forms a barrier between the chicken and hot oil. This preserves chicken's natural delicate texture. Oil should not be too hot (about 325F, 165C) in the first cooking stage; use medium heat. The second cooking is done over high heat. Fresh rather than frozen chicken is preferred.

# 辣子鷄丁

## Chicken Cubes with Walnuts Szechuan-Style

8 to 10 oz. boneless chicken, cut into 1/2-inch cubes
1/2 teaspoon salt
1 egg white
1 tablespoon cornstarch
1/4 cup vegetable oil
2 green onions, finely chopped
2 teaspoons finely chopped gingerroot
1/2 cup coarsely chopped walnuts
1 tablespoon crushed yellow-bean sauce
1 green bell pepper, cut into 1-inch pieces
2 teaspoons sugar
2 tablespoons rice wine or dry sherry
About 1 tablespoon chili sauce
2 teaspoons cornstarch blended with 1 tablespoon water

---

**1.** In a medium bowl, combine chicken and salt. Stir in egg white; then stir in cornstarch.
**2.** Preheat a wok or large skillet over medium heat. Add oil. When oil is warm, add coated chicken; stir-fry 10 seconds. Remove chicken with a slotted spoon.
**3.** Increase heat to high. When oil is hot, add onions, gingerroot and walnuts; stir-fry a few seconds. Add bean sauce; stir-fry a few seconds. Add green pepper and cooked chicken; stir-fry a few seconds. Add sugar, wine or sherry and chili sauce, to taste; stir-fry 30 seconds. Stir in cornstarch mixture; stirring constantly, cook until thickened. Serve hot. Makes 4 servings.

**Variation**
Substitute almonds, cashews or peanuts for walnuts.

Clockwise from top: Chicken Cubes with Walnuts Szechuan-Style, Shredded Chicken Breast with Green Peppers, Cooked Rice

# 醬爆鶏脯丁

## Diced Chicken in Peking Bean Sauce

1 egg white
1 tablespoon cornstarch
Water
Vegetable oil for deep-frying
2 boneless chicken breasts, cut into 1/2-inch cubes
2 tablespoons crushed yellow-bean sauce
1 tablespoon sugar
1 tablespoon rice wine or dry sherry
1 teaspoon sesame oil

1. In a shallow bowl, lightly beat egg white. In a small bowl, blend cornstarch and 2 tablespoons water into a smooth paste.
2. Heat vegetable oil in a wok or deep saucepan over medium heat until warm. Dip chicken cubes in egg white, then in cornstarch mixture. Gently drop coated chicken into warm oil; see box, opposite page. Deep-fry over medium heat a few seconds. Remove chicken with a slotted spoon; drain on paper towels.
3. Pour off all oil. Place wok or saucepan over high heat. Add bean sauce; stir a few times. Add sugar; stir until sugar dissolves. Add wine or sherry and sesame oil; stir constantly until well blended. Add 1 tablespoon water, if necessary. Add drained chicken; stir until coated with sauce.
4. Serve hot. Makes 4 servings.

# 金华玉樹雞

## Cantonese Chicken, Ham & Greens

1 (2-1/2- to 2-3/4-lb.) broiler-fryer chicken
Water
2 thin gingerroot slices
2 green onions
2 teaspoons salt
8 oz. cooked ham
2 tablespoons vegetable oil
8 oz. broccoli flowerets or bok choy, chopped

*Serve cold as a starter or as part of a buffet. Or serve it hot as a main course. When served on its own with rice or noodles, this dish is ample for 4 to 6 people.*

**1.** Place chicken in a large saucepan; cover with cold water. Add gingerroot, onions and 1-1/2 teaspoons salt. Bring to a boil. Cover; simmer 25 to 30 minutes. Turn off heat; keep pan covered. Let steep in hot water at least 1 hour. *Do not* lift lid. Lifting lid will let heat escape, and chicken will not cook properly.
**2.** Heat 2 tablespoons oil in a wok or skillet. Add broccoli or bok choy and a little salt; stir-fry 2 to 3 minutes. Arrange cooked broccoli or bok choy around edge of a serving dish.
**3.** To serve, drain chicken. Gently pull meat from bone; cut into small pieces. Cut ham into thin slices same size as chicken pieces.
**4.** Arrange chicken and ham slices in alternate layers in center of serving dish. Makes 4 to 6 servings.

红 烧 鸡 块

# Shanghai Braised Chicken

1 (3- to 3-1/2-lb.) broiler-fryer chicken
2 thin gingerroot slices
2 green onions
2 tablespoons vegetable oil
2 tablespoons rice wine or dry sherry
3 tablespoons soy sauce
1 tablespoon sugar
1/2 cup beef stock or water
4 or 5 dried Chinese mushrooms
8 oz. bamboo shoots, sliced

*Substitute 4 chicken quarters for whole chicken.*

**1.** Cut chicken into 12 to 14 pieces. Cut gingerroot and onions into small pieces.
**2.** Heat oil in a wok or saucepan over high heat. Add gingerroot and onions; stir-fry a few seconds. Add chicken pieces; stir-fry 5 minutes or until chicken is lightly browned. Add wine or sherry, soy sauce, sugar and stock or water. Reduce heat; simmer 20 to 25 minutes, stirring occasionally.
**3.** Meanwhile, soak mushrooms in warm water 20 minutes or until softened; rinse. Squeeze dry; discard hard stems. Add mushrooms and bamboo shoots to chicken mixture. Increase heat to high; cook 10 minutes or until liquid has almost evaporated. Serve hot. Makes 4 to 6 servings.

**Variation**
Substitute carrots for bamboo shoots. If dried Chinese mushrooms are not available, substitute fresh mushrooms.

烩 鸡 翅

# Chicken Wings Assembly

12 chicken wings, wing-tips removed
1/4 teaspoon salt
1 tablespoon sugar
2 tablespoons soy sauce
2 tablespoons rice wine or dry sherry
1 tablespoon cornstarch
2 tablespoons vegetable oil
1 garlic clove, crushed
3 green onions, cut into short lengths
3 to 4 tablespoons water
1 teaspoon sesame oil, if desired

**1.** Cut wings in half at joints as shown below. Combine wing pieces, salt, sugar, soy sauce, wine or sherry and cornstarch. Let stand 10 minutes, turning once or twice.
**2.** Preheat a wok or skillet over high heat. Add vegetable oil; heat. Add seasoned wings; stir-fry 1 to 2 minutes or until wings start to brown. Remove with a slotted spoon.
**3.** Add garlic and onions to wok or skillet to flavor oil. Add wings and a little stock or water. Stir; cover. Cook over a medium-high heat 5 minutes. Listen carefully for sizzling to make sure it is not burning. Add more stock or water, if necessary. Occasionally stir gently to prevent wings sticking to bottom of skillet or wok.
**4.** Cover; cook 5 to 10 minutes longer or until sauce is almost entirely absorbed. Add sesame oil, if desired, stirring to blend. Serve hot. Makes 4 to 6 servings.

1/Using a sharp knife, cut off wing-tip of each chicken wing.

2/Cut between remaining joint to make 2 pieces.

Clockwise from bottom: Chicken Wings Assembly, Shanghai Braised Chicken, Cantonese Chicken, Ham & Greens

# Party Time

This chapter lets you have fun with food. Eating is necessary, but it doesn't have to be boring! Essentially, food should be fun—fun to prepare, and fun to eat. Many children may start to cook by playing with pastry or cookie dough. Their products often end up limp and grey. No matter, if children are involved in food preparation at an early age, their interest in food and cooking grows.

Too often food preparation is left to one member of the household, but cooking can be a family affair. Children, husbands and even guests can get involved in meal preparation. The idea of this chapter is to add a little extra sparkle and imagination to everyday eating by involving other members of the family and guests when possible. Although some of the recipes are out of the ordinary, all of them are geared to family eating and entertaining. They are imaginative without being difficult.

## FAMILY FUN

This section contains unusual and colorful food ideas for the whole family. Some would make ideal presents to give at Christmas or other special occasions. If there is some supervision from an adult, many of the recipes are simple enough for children to make for themselves.

For that special birthday party when the cake must be impressive, make one of the spectacular children's fantasy cakes—*Ozzy Owl* or *Barney Bee* will make any birthday memorable.

## CHRISTMAS

However it is celebrated, Christmas is always a time of gaiety and celebration. It is also a time when special foods are prepared and served. This section has suggested menus for Christmas dinner and for parties during the holidays. This will provide new ideas, and perhaps, create some new family favorites.

## THE GREAT OUTDOORS

This section includes food ideas for family picnics and barbecues in the backyard. There are many appropriate foods to choose from. Picnics can be elegant or casual, but picnic foods need to be sturdy and easily transported. There is a wide range of special equipment for keeping foods hot or cold, such as ice chests and vacuum bottles. These may be worth the investment if you picnic a lot. Remember that fresh air tends to increase appetites; make sure that you provide generous quantities of everything.

## FOOD ON A SKEWER

Food on a skewer is another novel way of presenting a meal for family or friends. Many foods, such as good-quality steak, chicken and seafood, cook quickly. When these are cut into small pieces and threaded on skewers, they cook quickly on the outside but are still succulent and moist in the center. Fruit kabobs make appetizing dishes and are a change from the more traditional main-dish kabobs.

Skewers come in a variety of sizes, but an 11-inch skewer is the one most commonly used. This is the size skewer that has been used in most of the recipes in this book. Small metal and bamboo skewers are available. If using bamboo skewers, soak in water 30 minutes before using to prevent the bamboo from scorching during cooking.

Do not pack food tightly when threading it on a skewer. Otherwise, it will cause the food to cook unevenly and affect cooking time. Foods on the skewer should touch, but not be pressed together.

Kabobs can be cooked under a broiler or over an outside barbecue grill. Remember to preheat grill or broiler before using. The distance the food is from the source of heat determines the speed at which it will cook. Ideally, a kabob should cook about 4 inches away from the heat source; this ensures thorough cooking, without the food becoming charred. If your broiler is much higher than this, then raise the food on a baking pan or something of a convenient size that is heatproof. Alternatively, you can cook kabobs on a barbecue. Remember that food usually cooks faster on a barbecue. Reduce the cooking time slightly, and watch the food carefully to prevent burning. Use special wood chips or mesquite charcoal to add interesting flavors to barbecued foods.

Baste grilled meats with a flavorful mixture during cooking. Try these barbecue, mustard or marmalade sauces for enviable results.

**Mustard Sauce:** In a small bowl, combine 1 tablespoon wine vinegar, 1 tablespoon prepared mustard and 1/2 cup packed brown sugar.

**Barbecue Sauce:** In a small bowl, combine 1 tablespoon prepared mustard, 2 teaspoons brown sugar, 1 tablespoon wine vinegar and 1 tablespoon ketchup.

**Marmalade Sauce:** In a small bowl, combine 2 tablespoons marmalade, 2 teaspoons soy sauce and 1 tablespoon orange juice.

Clockwise from bottom left: Pear Dumpling, Peanut Sandwich Balls, Banana Pops

# Party Lights

*Ice Cubes:*
**Green food coloring**
**Maraschino cherries**

*Lemonade:*
**1/3 cup lemon juice**
**3/4 cup sugar**
**1 qt. water (4 cups)**
**Yellow food coloring, if desired**

---

*Kids love bright colors, especially in drinks. Brightly colored drinks can be made with very little effort. For an extra touch, add contrasting colored ice cubes.*

**1.** To make green ice cubes, measure capacity of ice-cube tray by filling it with water. Pour water into a measuring cup.
**2.** Add enough green food coloring to water to give desired color.
**3.** Place a maraschino cherry in each ice-cube compartment; pour in green water. Freeze until solid.
**4.** In a pitcher, combine ingredients for lemonade. Stir until sugar dissolves. Refrigerate until chilled.
**5.** Place 2 to 3 green ice cubes into each glass; fill with lemonade. Makes 4 servings.

# Peanut Sandwich Balls

---

**1 (8-oz.) pkg. cream cheese, room temperature**
**2 tablespoons peanut butter**
**1/2 cup finely chopped ham**
**3 tablespoons fresh bread crumbs**
**1/4 cup finely chopped peanuts**

---

**1.** In a medium bowl, beat cream cheese and peanut butter with a wooden spoon until smooth.
**2.** Beat in ham and bread crumbs.
**3.** Shape mixture into about 24 small balls. Roll each ball in chopped peanuts until evenly coated.
**4.** Insert a wooden pick into each ball. Makes 24 balls.

# Coconut Funny Faces

**6 tablespoons butter or margarine, room temperature**
**1/3 cup sugar**
**3 egg yolks**
**1/2 teaspoon vanilla extract**
**1-1/4 cups sifted all-purpose flour**
**1 cup flaked or shredded coconut**

*To decorate:*
**6 to 8 tablespoons apple jelly or orange marmalade**
**1/4 cup flaked or shredded coconut**
**1 tablespoon unsweetened cocoa powder**
**12 red candied cherries**
**Assorted candies**

---

*These cookies are guaranteed to put a smile on anyone's face.*

**1.** In a large bowl, beat butter or margarine and sugar until light and fluffy. Beat in egg yolks and vanilla until blended.
**2.** Fold in flour and coconut. Shape dough into a flattened ball; wrap in plastic wrap or foil. Refrigerate 30 minutes.
**3.** Preheat oven to 350F (175C). Grease 2 baking sheets. On a lightly floured surface, roll out chilled dough to 1/8 inch thickness. Cut dough into 24 rounds with a plain 2-1/2- inch cookie cutter. Place cookies on greased baking sheets.
**4.** Bake in preheated oven 12 to 15 minutes or until golden brown. Remove from baking sheets; cool on wire racks.
**5.** To decorate, spread jelly or marmalade over flat side of 1/2 of cookies; top with remaining cookies.
**6.** In a small bowl, toss coconut and cocoa powder together until coconut is blended.
**7.** Spread a little jelly or marmalade around top edge of each cookie sandwich; sprinkle with cocoa-coated coconut for hair.
**8.** Cut cherries in half; attach to cookies with a dab of jelly or marmalade for eyes. Make mouth and nose with small candies. Makes 12 cookies.

Clockwise from left: Party Lights, Coconut Funny Faces, Peanut Sandwich Balls

Left to right: Flying Saucers, Cheesy Twists, Marbled Eggs, Tub O'Beans

## Flying Saucers

**Pastry for a double-crust pie**
**1 cup chopped ham**
**1 cup shredded cheese (4 oz.)**
**3 tablespoons ketchup**
**Freshly ground pepper**
**1/2 cup chopped peanuts, if desired**
**1 egg, beaten**

*To garnish:*
**4 pickled onions**
**Thin cucumber slices**
**Pimentos, cut into leaf shapes**

---

**1.** Preheat oven to 375F (190C). On a lightly floured surface, roll out pastry to 1/8 inch thick. Cut out 8 (5-inch) circles.
**2.** Line 4 (4-1/4-inch) tart pans with pastry.
**3.** In a medium bowl, combine ham, cheese, ketchup, pepper and peanuts, if desired.
**4.** Divide filling among pastry-lined pans. Brush pastry edges with beaten egg.
**5.** Lay remaining pastry circles over filling. Press edges together to seal. Glaze top surface of pastry with beaten egg. Place tarts on a baking sheet.
**6.** Bake in preheated oven 30 to 35 minutes or until pastry is golden brown.
**7.** Decorate as shown in photo with onions, cucumber and pimentos. Serve hot or cold. Makes 4 servings.

## Cheesy Twists

**4 oz. puff pastry, thawed, if frozen**
**1 egg, beaten**
**3/4 cup grated Parmesan cheese (2 oz.)**
**2 tablespoons sesame seeds**

---

**1.** On a lightly floured board, roll out pastry to a 12-inch square.
**2.** Cut pastry into 2 equal rectangles.
**3.** Brush 1 pastry rectangle with beaten egg; sprinkle with cheese.
**4.** Top with second pastry rectangle. Roll lightly to press 2 pastry rectangles together.
**5.** Brush top surface of pastry lightly with beaten egg; sprinkle with sesame seeds.
**6.** Cut into 6 (6- x 1/2-inch) strips.
**7.** Twist each strip 2 or 3 times, bringing ends together to form a circle. Press ends to seal. Rinse a baking sheet with water. Place circles on damp baking sheet. Refrigerate 30 minutes.
**8.** Preheat oven to 425F (220C).
**9.** Bake in preheated oven 12 minutes or until golden brown. Makes 24 rings.

# Marbled Eggs

**6 eggs**
**About 2 teaspoons food coloring**

*These attractive mottled eggs are very simple to make. They add interest to a packed school lunch or picnic. Use your choice of colors.*

**1.** Place eggs in a medium saucepan; add enough cold water to completely cover.
**2.** Bring water to a boil; simmer eggs 3 minutes. Remove eggs carefully with a slotted spoon.
**3.** Add enough food coloring to cooking water to tint it a deep color.
**4.** Tap eggs all over with back of a spoon to crack shells.
**5.** Return eggs to colored water; simmer 7 minutes.
**6.** Fill a medium bowl 1/2 full of iced water; add 2 teaspoons additional food coloring. Place eggs in iced water.
**7.** When cool, peel eggs. Makes 6 hard-cooked eggs.

# Tub O'Beans

**8 individual round whole-wheat-bread loaves**
**Vegetable oil**
**1 (15-oz.) can baked beans**
**1 (11-oz.) can whole-kernel corn, drained**
**4 large frankfurters, chopped**

**1.** Preheat oven to 375F (190C). Cut a thin slice from top of each loaf. Carefully hollow out centers, leaving shells about 1/2 inch thick. Use centers for bread crumbs, if desired.
**2.** Brush inside of hollowed loaves with oil.
**3.** Place loaves on a baking sheet. Bake in preheated oven 10 minutes or until loaves are crisp.
**4.** Meanwhile, in a medium saucepan, combine beans, corn and frankfurters. Stir over medium heat until hot.
**5.** Divide bean mixture among baked loaves; wrap each filled loaf in foil.
**6.** Bake 10 minutes.
**7.** Remove foil; serve warm. Makes 8 servings.

# Banana Pops

6 large firm bananas, peeled
12 wooden skewers or wooden ice-cream sticks
12 oz. semisweet or milk chocolate

***To decorate:***
Colored shot or chocolate sprinkles
Frosting
Candied fruit

---

*The banana with a difference! Let children decorate their own Banana Pops. Some suggestions are a child's name piped in icing, a face made from small colored candies, or numbers to celebrate a birthday.*

**1.** Cut each banana in half crosswise.
**2.** Insert a wooden skewer or stick at least 2 inches inside each banana half.
**3.** Place skewered bananas on a piece of foil. Freeze 1 hour or until firm.
**4.** Break chocolate into pieces. Place chocolate pieces in the top of a double boiler over simmering water. Stir until chocolate melts.
**5.** Taking 1 banana from freezer at a time, hold it over chocolate. Spoon melted chocolate over banana until evenly coated. If bananas are frozen, chocolate coating will start to set immediately.
**6.** As soon as each banana is coated with chocolate, sprinkle with colored shot, chocolate sprinkles or any decoration of your choice.
**7.** When each banana has been coated with chocolate and decorated, lay it carefully on a sheet of lightly oiled waxed paper. Or, push wooden handles into a large block of florist foam.
**8.** As soon as chocolate coating has set on bananas and decorations are firmly in place, wrap banana pops lightly in foil or freezer wrap. Return to freezer. Serve without thawing. Makes 12 servings.

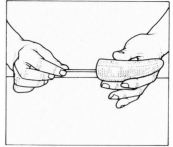

1/Insert a wooden skewer or stick at least 2 inches inside each banana half.

2/Spoon melted chocolate over banana until evenly coated.

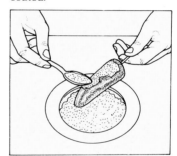

3/Sprinkle with colored shot, chocolate sprinkles or any decoration of your choice.

4/Push wooden handles into a large block of florist foam.

Banana Pops

# Orange-Banana Floats

5 small bananas, peeled
Juice of 1 lemon
2 tablespoons honey
1 qt. orange juice (4 cups)
Ice cubes
6 scoops vanilla ice cream
6 thin orange slices, if desired

---

*This makes a delicious party drink for kids. Serve it with spoons so that none of the ice cream is wasted at the bottom of the glass.*

1. Chop bananas. In a blender or food processor fitted with a steel blade, process chopped bananas, lemon juice and honey until smooth.
2. Add 1/2 of orange juice; process until blended.
3. Pour orange-and-banana mixture into a large pitcher; stir in remaining orange juice. Add a few ice cubes.
4. Place a scoop of ice cream into each of 6 tall tumblers. Pour over orange-and-banana mixture.
5. Make a small cut in each orange slice; place over rim of each glass, if desired. Serve immediately with straws and long-handled spoons. Makes 6 servings.

# Animal Sandwiches

6 whole-wheat-bread slices
Butter or margarine, room temperature
2 (4-1/2-oz.) cans deviled ham
2 small pkgs. potato chips

---

*If you use small animal-cookie cutters, you should be able to get 4 open sandwiches from each slice of bread. If you don't have animal shapes, use any other decorative cookie cutters.*

1. Spread slices of bread with butter or margarine; then spread with a thin layer of deviled ham.
2. Crush potato chips with a rolling pin. Press crushed chips onto ham-covered bread slices.
3. Cut animal shapes from potato chip-topped bread, using animal-cookie cutters. Makes 18 to 24 small sandwiches depending on size of cutter.

# Butterfly-Wing Cookies

3 egg yolks
1/2 cup sugar
1/2 cup half and half
2 teaspoons vanilla extract
2-2/3 cups all-purpose flour
Vegetable oil for deep-fat frying
Powdered sugar, if desired

---

1. In a large bowl, beat egg yolks, sugar, half and half and vanilla until blended.
2. Stir in flour to make a smooth dough.
3. On a lightly floured surface, roll out dough to a 16" x 10" rectangle. Cut out 24 diamond shapes with a fluted pastry wheel.
4. Cut a small slit in center of each diamond. Tuck opposite points of diamond through slit and pull through slightly, as shown below.
5. Heat oil in a deep-fryer or saucepan to 375F (190C) or until a 1-inch bread cube turns golden brown in 50 seconds. Carefully place 4 to 6 cookies into hot oil. Deep-fry 3 to 4 minutes or until golden and crisp.
6. Remove deep-fried cookies with a slotted spoon; drain on paper towels. Repeat with remaining cookies. Sprinkle with sifted powdered sugar, if desired. Makes 24 cookies.

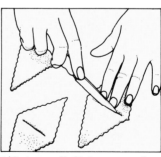 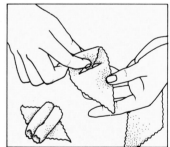

1/Cut a small slit in center of each diamond.

2/Tuck opposite points of diamond through slit and pull through slightly.

Clockwise from left: Butterfly-Wing Cookies, Orange-Banana Floats, Animal Sandwiches

# Orange-Cup Trifles

8 large navel oranges
1 (3-oz.) pkg. orange-flavored gelatin
4 pound-cake or sponge-cake slices
1 (16-oz.) can sliced peaches or pears, drained
1-1/2 cups sweetened whipped cream

*To decorate:*
Candied orange slices
Candied lemon slices

---

*These orange cups can be filled the day before you plan to serve them. Decorate with whipped cream just before serving. Use large oranges, if available.*

1. Cut a thick slice from stem end of each orange; discard slices.
2. Carefully hollow out oranges with a grapefruit spoon. Remove seeds, membrane and white pith from orange pulp. Chop pulp, reserving juice. Measure juice; add enough water to make 1 cup. Pour juice mixture into a small saucepan; bring to a boil.
3. Place orange gelatin in a medium bowl; pour in hot orange-juice mixture. Stir until gelatin is completely dissolved. Stir in 1 cup cold water. Refrigerate until gelatin is thick and syrupy.
4. Cut cake slices and peaches or pears into small cubes. In a medium bowl, combine cake cubes, peach or pear cubes and chopped oranges. Spoon mixture evenly into orange shells; pack down lightly. Spoon orange gelatin over filled oranges. Refrigerate until gelatin is completely set, about 3 hours.
5. Pipe or spoon whipped cream decoratively on top of orange cups. Decorate with candied orange and lemon slices. Makes 8 servings.

# Coffee Shortbread Cookies

1/2 cup finely ground almonds
1-1/4 cups all-purpose flour, sifted
3/4 cup powdered sugar
2 tablespoons instant coffee powder
3/4 cup butter or margarine, room temperature
Granulated sugar

---

1. In a large bowl, combine almonds, flour, powdered sugar and coffee until blended. Add butter or margarine; beat at medium speed until blended, scraping down side of bowl occasionally.
2. Shape dough into a ball. Wrap in plastic wrap or foil; refrigerate 30 minutes.
3. Preheat oven to 350F (175C). On a lightly floured surface, roll out dough to about 1/4 inch thick. Cut dough with a 1-1/2- to 2-inch-floured plain or fluted cookie cutter.
4. Place cookies about 1 inch apart on ungreased baking sheets. Sprinkle with granulated sugar.
5. Bake 10 to 12 minutes or until edges are just firm. Remove from baking sheets; cool on wire racks. Makes 60 to 66 cookies.

# Chocolate Refrigerator Bars

1/2 cup butter or margarine
1/3 cup sugar
5 tablespoons unsweetened cocoa powder
1 egg, beaten
1 teaspoon vanilla extract
1 cup shredded or flaked coconut
1/3 cup chopped pecans
8 whole graham crackers, crushed

*Butter Icing:*
1/4 cup butter or margarine, room temperature
1-3/4 cups powdered sugar, sifted
1 egg

*Chocolate Topping:*
6 oz. semisweet chocolate
1 tablespoon butter, room temperature

---

1. Grease a 9-inch-square baking pan.
2. Melt butter or margarine and sugar in a small saucepan over low heat, stirring until smooth.
3. Stir in cocoa, egg and vanilla. Cook until mixture thickens, stirring constantly.
4. Remove from heat; stir in coconut, pecans and crushed crackers. Press mixture evenly into greased pan. Refrigerate 1 hour.
5. To make Butter Icing, in a small bowl, beat butter or margarine, powdered sugar and egg until smooth and creamy. Spread over refrigerated chocolate mixture. Return to refrigerator until icing is firm.
6. To make Chocolate Topping, melt chocolate and butter in a small heavy saucepan over low heat, stirring until smooth. Swirl chocolate over icing. Refrigerate 3 to 4 hours. Cut into squares. Makes 16 to 20 squares.

# Carrot Cookies

1/2 cup butter or margarine, room temperature
1/2 cup sugar
1 egg
1/4 cup orange marmalade
1-1/2 cups grated carrots (about 2 medium carrots)
1-1/3 cups all-purpose flour
1/2 teaspoon salt
1/2 teaspoon baking powder
1/2 cup chopped raisins

**1.** Preheat oven to 350F (175C). Lightly grease 2 baking sheets.
**2.** In a medium bowl, beat butter or margarine and sugar until light and fluffy. Beat in egg until blended. Stir in marmalade and carrots.
**3.** Sift flour, salt and baking powder over butter mixture. Fold in dry ingredients and raisins. Drop rounded teaspoons of mixture, about 1-1/2 inches apart, on greased baking sheets.
**4.** Bake in preheated oven 12 to 15 minutes or until golden around edges. Remove from baking sheets; cool on wire racks. Makes about 48 cookies.

Left to right: Orange-Cup Trifles, Chocolate Refrigerator Bars

# Barney Bee

**1 recipe Quick Chocolate Cake, page 516**
**1 recipe Chocolate Buttercream, page 447**
**Chocolate sprinkles**
**5 oz. semisweet chocolate, chopped**
**1/4 cup light corn syrup**
**10 oz. white chocolate, chopped**
**Yellow food coloring**
**3 oz. marzipan**
**Powdered sugar**

**1.** Preheat oven to 350F (175C). Grease an 8" x 4" loaf pan and a 3-cup heatproof bowl. Line bottom of bowl with a circle of waxed paper; grease paper.

**2.** Prepare Quick Chocolate Cake as directed on page 516. Pour batter into prepared pan and bowl, filling each about two-thirds full.

**3.** Bake both cakes at the same time. Position smaller cake near front of oven so it can be quickly removed when done. Bake in preheated oven 45 to 50 minutes for loaf cake and 50 to 60 minutes for bowl cake or until a wooden pick inserted in centers comes out clean. Cool in containers on wire racks 5 minutes. Invert onto wire racks; remove containers and paper. Cool completely on wire racks.

**4.** Prepare Chocolate Buttercream as directed on page 447.

**5.** Cut cooled loaf cake in half lengthwise; sandwich together with a little buttercream. Place cake on a flat surface. Cut bowl cake from top to bottom making 1 piece two-thirds of cake. Spread buttercream over cut edge of large piece of cake; press against 1 end of loaf cake. Spread buttercream over cut edge of small piece of cake; press against opposite end of loaf cake. Trim sides even with loaf cake.

**6.** Set aside 1 tablespoon buttercream. Spread remaining buttercream over top and sides of cake, covering cake completely. Press chocolate sprinkles around large end of cake to make the head. Place cake on a decorative 14-inch-square cake board.

**7.** Melt 4 ounces semisweet chocolate in a small heavy saucepan over very low heat; stir until smooth. Stir in 2 tablespoons corn syrup. Pour chocolate mixture onto a small baking sheet. Refrigerate 25 minutes or until set. Remove chocolate from baking sheet with a dough scraper. On a flat surface, knead vigorously 3 minutes. Shape into a flattened ball; wrap in plastic wrap. Let stand at room temperature 40 minutes. Divide into 2 equal pieces; knead each piece vigorously 1 minute. Flatten each piece. Turn pasta machine to widest setting; pass each piece of chocolate through machine 3 times, folding chocolate into thirds before running through machine. Adjust machine to next widest setting; run chocolate through without folding. Place chocolate strips on a flat surface; cut into 4 ribbons, each 1 inch wide and 9 inches long.

**8.** To make 4 yellow ribbons, melt 4 ounces white chocolate in a small heavy saucepan over very low heat; stir until smooth. Stir in remaining 2 tablespoons corn syrup and a few drops yellow food coloring. Follow chilling, rolling and cutting directions above for making chocolate ribbons.

Barney Bee

**9.** Starting behind head, place alternate strips of yellow and chocolate ribbons over body. Gather dark chocolate scraps; knead until smooth. Flatten and roll out with a rolling pin. Place over tail at end of body. Trim edges of yellow and chocolate ribbons even with bottom of cake, if necessary.

**10.** Draw 2 wings on a sheet of parchment paper, each about 7 inches long and 3 inches wide. Melt remaining 6 ounces white chocolate in a small heavy saucepan over very low heat; stir until smooth. Pour white chocolate inside wing outlines; spread evenly. Let stand until completely set. Melt remaining 1 ounce semisweet chocolate in a small heavy saucepan over very low heat; stir until smooth. Spoon into a pastry bag fitted with a small plain writing tip. Pipe narrow chocolate lines on wings to represent veins. Let stand until chocolate is completely set.

**11.** Place marzipan in a small bowl; knead in a few drops of yellow food coloring. Knead until marzipan is smooth. Add powdered sugar if marzipan is too soft to shape. Divide marzipan into 2 pieces, making 1 piece 2/3 of marzipan. Cut large piece of marzipan into 6 equal pieces. Roll out each piece with palm of your hand to make 6 ropes, each 6 inches long. Dab a little buttercream at 1 end of each rope. Press onto body of wasp for legs, bending each stick; see photo. Cut remaining piece of marzipan into 5 pieces. Use 2 small pieces to make eyes; attach to head with buttercream. Roll 1 piece into a thin stick for mouth; attach to face with buttercream. Shape remaining 2 pieces of marzipan around 2 small wooden picks, leaving 1/4 of pick uncovered; insert uncovered part into head for antennae.

**12.** Cut slit on each side of body for inserting wings. Carefully remove wings from paper. Gently insert 1 white-chocolate wing into each slit. Support backs of wings with popsicle sticks. Refrigerate until served. Remove antennae before serving to prevent anyone eating wooden picks by mistake. Makes 8 to 10 servings.

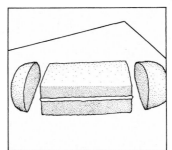

1/Cut cake in half lengthwise; sandwich together with a little buttercream.

2/Starting behind head, place alternate strips of yellow and chocolate ribbons over body.

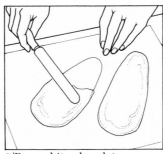

3/Pour white chocolate over wing outlines; spread evenly.

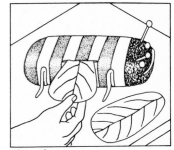

4/Gently insert 1 white-chocolate wing into each slit.

# Ozzy Owl

1 recipe Quick Chocolate Cake, page 516
1 recipe Chocolate Buttercream, page 447
1 sugar ice-cream cone
5 oz. marzipan
Red and green food coloring
1 oz. white chocolate
8 oz. dark semisweet- or sweet-chocolate buttons

---

**1.** Preheat oven to 350F (175C). Grease a 3-cup heatproof bowl and a 6-cup heatproof bowl. Line bottoms of bowls with waxed paper; grease paper. Prepare Quick Chocolate Cake as directed on page 516. Pour 2/3 of batter into prepared large bowl and remaining batter into prepared small bowl.

**2.** Bake both cakes at the same time. Position smaller cake near front of oven so it can be quickly removed when done. Bake small bowl in preheated oven 40 to 45 minutes and large bowl 1 hour 10 minutes or until a wooden pick inserted in centers comes out clean. Cool in bowls on wire racks 5 minutes. Invert on wire racks; remove bowls and paper. Cool completely on wire racks.

**3.** Prepare Chocolate Buttercream as directed on page 447. Cut both cakes in half horizontally. Sandwich layers together with a little buttercream. Place large cake, flat-side down, on a cake board. Spread a little buttercream on top; place small cake, flat-side down, on top. Trim sides of cakes as needed to make edges smooth and even. Set aside about 1/3 cup buttercream. Spread remaining buttercream around side and over top of cake, covering cake completely.

**4.** Cut ice-cream cone about 2 inches from tip, discarding tip. With kitchen scissors, cut cone in half lengthwise. Trim halves with a sharp knife or scissors to make ears for owl. Spread buttercream over ears; place ears on top of cake.

**5.** Place marzipan in a small bowl; add a few drops of red and green food coloring. Knead until marzipan is an even shade of brown. Remove a small piece of marzipan; shape into a small hooked beak. Use about 1/4 of remaining marzipan to make 2 feet with 3 claws each. Divide remaining marzipan in half; shape into 2 ovals for wings. Press wings onto sides of lower part of owl; curve wings around body, leaving small space between wings and body. Spread with buttercream.

**6.** Melt white chocolate in a small heavy saucepan over very low heat; stir until smooth. Draw 2 small oval egg-size shapes on a sheet of waxed paper. Spread melted white chocolate inside ovals. Place a chocolate button on each oval for eyes. Let stand until completely set. Attach ovals to head of owl with a dab of buttercream.

**7.** Place a row of chocolate buttons around bottom edge of owl; repeat rows of buttons, slightly overlapping, until body and head of owl is completely covered. Do not cover face. Press beak between eyes; place feet at bottom of owl. Makes 8 to 10 servings.

# Thomas Toad

1 recipe Quick Chocolate Cake, page 516
1 recipe Chocolate Buttercream, page 447
About 3/4 cup chocolate sprinkles
2 chocolate-covered marshmallow cookies
5 small round white candies
Red licorice rope
1/2 cup flaked coconut
Blue, green and yellow food coloring
4 oz. marzipan

---

**1.** Preheat oven to 350F (175C). Grease a 3-cup heatproof bowl and a 6-cup heatproof bowl. Line bottoms of bowls with waxed paper; grease paper. Prepare Quick Chocolate Cake as directed on page 516. Pour 2/3 of batter into prepared large bowl and remaining batter into prepared small bowl.

**2.** Bake both cakes at the same time. Position smaller cake near front of oven so it can be quickly removed when done. Bake small bowl in preheated oven 40 to 45 minutes and large bowl 1 hour 10 minutes or until a wooden pick inserted in centers comes out clean. Cool in bowls on wire racks 5 minutes. Invert on wire racks; remove bowls and paper. Cool completely on wire racks.

**3.** Prepare Chocolate Buttercream as directed on page 447. Cut both cakes in half horizontally. Sandwich layers together with a little buttercream. Place large cake, flat-side down, on a cake board. Spread a little buttercream on top; place small cake, flat-side down, on top. Trim sides of cakes as needed to make edges smooth and even. Set aside about 1/3 cup buttercream. Spread remaining buttercream around side and over top of cake, covering cake completely.

**4.** Spread some of reserved buttercream on bottom of marshmallow cookies; place cookies on top of cake to make eyes. Spread backs of 2 white candies with some of reserved buttercream; arrange center of cookies to make eyes. Place cake on a 10-inch-round cake board.

**5.** Cut out a half-moon wedge halfway down cake beneath eyes to make mouth. Remove wedge; place a small piece of red licorice across bottom of mouth.

**6.** In a small bowl, toss coconut with a few drops blue food coloring. Spread coconut on cake board around toad.

**7.** Divide marzipan into 2 pieces, making 1 piece 2/3 of marzipan. In a small bowl, knead a few drops green food coloring into large piece of marzipan; knead until smooth. In a small bowl, knead yellow food coloring into small piece of marzipan. Divide green marzipan into 9 small pieces; flatten each piece into a small circle. Arrange circles on top of coconut in groups of 3 to make 3 lily pads.

**8.** Divide yellow marzipan in thirds. Flatten into 3 circles. Snip out small triangles around edge of each circle to make water lilies. Curve snipped edges up slightly; place on lily pads. Place white candy in center of each water lily. See variation for Chocolate-Frog Pond, opposite page, for remaining decorations. Makes 8 to 10 servings.

# Chocolate-Frog Pond

**1 (6-oz.) pkg. lime-flavored gelatin**
**1/4 cup whipping cream, whipped**
**About 12 miniature chocolate eggs, unwrapped**
**Colored candy flowers**
**1 (2-oz.) strip of angelica**

**1.** Prepare gelatin as directed on package. Pour into a large shallow dish. Refrigerate until firm.

**2.** Spoon whipped cream into a pastry bag fitted with a fine writing tip. Pipe dots for eyes and a strip for a mouth on 1 end of each egg. Stick onto gelatin with a dollop of whipped cream.
**3.** Place candy flowers in groups on firm gelatin.
**4.** Cut angelica into fine strips; stick into gelatin for reeds. Chill before serving. Makes 6 to 8 servings.

## Variation
Use large creme-filled chocolate eggs. Use candied-cherry halves for eyes and chocolate buttons for feet.

Top to bottom: Ozzy Owl, Chocolate-Frog Pond, Thomas Toad

Top to bottom: Choc Around the Clock, Meringue Cookies

# Quick Chocolate Cake

3/4 cup butter or margarine, room temperature
1-1/4 cups sugar
4 eggs
1 teaspoon vanilla extract
1-1/2 cups all-purpose flour
1/4 cup unsweetened cocoa powder
1 teaspoon baking powder
1/4 teaspoon baking soda
1/2 teaspoon salt
1/3 cup milk

1. Preheat oven to 350F (175C). Grease and flour 2 (8-inch) round cake pans.
2. In a medium bowl, beat butter or margarine and sugar until light and fluffy. Beat in eggs and vanilla until blended.
3. Sift flour, cocoa, baking powder, baking soda and salt into a medium bowl. Add to egg mixture alternately with milk; beat until blended. Beat 1 minute with an electric mixer at medium speed, scraping side of bowl occasionally. Pour batter into prepared pans; smooth tops.
4. Bake in preheated oven 30 to 35 minutes or until a wooden pick inserted in center comes out clean. Cool in pans on wire racks 5 minutes. Remove from pans; cool completely on wire racks. Fill and frost as desired. Makes 6 to 8 servings.

# Choc Around the Clock

2 cups self-rising flour
1/2 cup unsweetened cocoa powder
1/4 cup cornstarch
1-1/2 cups sugar
4 eggs, separated
3/4 cup vegetable oil
1 cup water

*To decorate:*
1 recipe Chocolate Buttercream, page 447
About 60 chocolate-covered finger cookies
1 cup powdered sugar, sifted
1 tablespoon warm water
2 chocolate-covered marshmallow cookies
Meringue Cookies, opposite, if desired

1. Preheat oven to 375F (190C). Grease 3 (9-inch) square baking pans.
2. Sift flour, cocoa and cornstarch into a large bowl; stir in sugar until blended. In a small bowl, beat egg yolks, oil and water until blended. Add to flour mixture; beat with an electric mixer at low speed until thoroughly blended, scraping down side of bowl occasionally.
3. In a medium bowl, beat egg whites until stiff but not dry. Fold beaten egg whites into chocolate mixture. Divide batter equally among greased pans; smooth tops.
4. Bake in preheated oven 20 to 25 minutes or until centers spring back when lightly pressed. Cool in pans on wire racks 5 minutes. Remove from pans; cool completely on wire racks.
5. Prepare Chocolate Buttercream as directed on page 447. Set aside 1/3 of buttercream for decoration. Place 1 cake layer on a flat surface; spread with a thin layer of buttercream. Top with a second layer; spread with buttercream. Place third layer on top. Spread remaining buttercream around sides of cake. Press chocolate fingers into buttercream around sides.
6. Position cake at center of top edge of a 14-inch-square white cake board.
7. Mark a 7-inch circle in center of cake with a knife tip. In a small bowl, blend powdered sugar and water until mixture is smooth. Spread inside marked circle; let stand until completely set.
8. Spoon all but 2 tablespoons reserved buttercream into a pastry bag fitted with a small open-star tip. Pipe buttercream in small stars around edge of circle and over remaining top of cake. If desired, pipe additional buttercream stars around edge of cake board.
9. Spoon remaining buttercream into a small pastry bag fitted with a small plain writing tip. Pipe numbers and hands on white circle for face of clock and 2 chains of tiny circles below clock, making 1 chain slightly longer than other. Place marshmallow cookie at bottom of each chain. Decorate board with fanciful Meringue Cookies, opposite, if desired. Makes 9 to 12 servings.

# Meringue Cookies

4 egg whites
1/2 cup sugar
1 cup powdered sugar
1/4 cup unsweetened cocoa powder

*To decorate:*
**Whole cloves**
**Flaked almonds**
**Slivered almonds**

1. Preheat oven to 300F (150C). Line baking sheets with parchment paper.
2. In a medium bowl, beat egg whites until soft peaks form. Beat in sugars until stiff and glossy. Sift cocoa over meringue; fold in.
3. Spoon meringue into a pastry bag fitted with a coupling. Using the appropriate tip suggested below, pipe shapes on paper-lined baking sheets; see directions below.
4. Bake meringues in preheated oven about 45 minutes to 1 hour, depending on size, or until completely dried out. Cool on baking sheets on wire racks. Carefully remove cooled meringues from paper. Meringue shapes can be stored up to 2 weeks in an airtight container at room temperature. Makes 50 to 70 cookies depending on size.

**Shaping Instructions:**
**Snails:** Using a 1/2-inch plain tip, pipe a short straight length of meringue to form a head; from straight line, make a circle. Continue piping in a spiral to form shell. Insert 2 whole cloves in head to make feelers.
**Mice:** Using a 1/2-inch plain tip, pipe about 1 inch of meringue. Then pipe a large bulb of meringue back over top, releasing pressure into a long-drawn-out point. At pointed end, insert 2 whole cloves into meringue for eyes and 2 almonds flakes for ears.
**Hedgehogs:** Using a 3/4-inch star tip, pipe about 1 inch of meringue. Then pipe back over this, releasing pressure to form a sharp point. Insert 2 whole cloves into pointed end of meringue to form eyes; insert halved slivered almonds all over back to form spines.
**Stars:** Using a 3/4-inch star tip, hold bag vertically; squeeze out a star of meringue. Release pressure quickly to avoid a long point.
**Rosettes:** Using a 3/4-inch star or rosette tip, pipe meringue in a circle; finish by bringing tip into center of circle. Release quickly.

## Christmas Day

Roast Turkey & Stuffing*
Gravy
Steamed Brussels Sprouts
Orange-Cranberry Sauce
Brown-Sugar Meringues*
Christmas Pudding, page 404

*Recipe included in book

## Roast Turkey & Stuffing

1 (10- to 12-lb.)
  oven-ready turkey,
  with giblets
1 small onion, peeled,
  quartered
About 7 cups favorite
  stuffing
3 tablespoons butter or
  margarine, softened
2 tablespoons vegetable
  oil
Salt
Freshly ground black
  pepper

*To serve:*
Gravy, if desired
Oven-roasted potatoes
1 lb. small sausages,
  broiled
8 to 16 rolled bacon
  slices, broiled

*To garnish:*
Watercress or parsley
  sprigs

1. In a medium saucepan, combine giblets and onion; cover with cold water. Bring to a boil; reduce heat. Cover and simmer 1 hour. Strain stock; cool slightly. Refrigerate until needed for gravy.
2. Preheat oven to 350F (175C). Stuff turkey with stuffing. Secure neck skin with a skewer; lightly truss stuffed turkey.
3. Place turkey on a rack in a roasting pan; rub all over with butter or margarine. Season turkey with salt and pepper.
4. Roast in preheated oven about 3-1/2 hours or until a thermometer inserted in inner thigh area, without touching bone, reads 180F (85C). Juices will be clear when pierced with a skewer in inner thigh area. Baste occasionally with pan drippings while roasting.
5. Transfer turkey to a large platter. Remove fat from pan drippings. Remove fat from reserved stock. Thicken drippings and stock with cornstarch to make gravy, if desired.
6. Arrange oven-roasted potatoes, sausages and bacon rolls around turkey. Garnish with watercress or parsley. Makes 8 servings.

## Brown-Sugar Meringues

4 egg whites
1/2 cup granulated sugar
1/2 cup firmly packed
  light-brown sugar

1/2 pint whipping cream
  (1 cup), if desired,
  whipped

1. Preheat oven to 250F (120C). Line 2 baking sheets with parchment paper. In a medium bowl, beat egg whites until soft peaks form. Gradually beat in sugars until stiff and glossy.

Left to right: Christmas Pudding, page 404; Brown-Sugar Meringues; Steamed Brussels sprouts; Roast Turkey

**2.** Spoon meringue mixture into a pastry bag fitted with a star tip. Pipe into twists or whirls on lined baking sheets.

**3.** Bake in preheated oven about 2 hours or until meringues are firm and dry. Remove from oven; cool completely on baking sheet on wire racks. Carefully peel off paper; store at room temperature in an airtight container up to 2 weeks.

**4.** Immediately before serving, sandwich meringues together with whipped cream, if desired. Makes 20 meringues.

*Recipe included in book

# Mulled Wine

| | |
|---|---|
| 3 (750ml.) bottles burgundy or other red wine | 10 whole cloves |
| 1/2 cup brandy | 1 teaspoon cardamom seeds, if desired |
| 1 cup raisins | 1 (3-inch) cinnamon stick |
| 3/4 cup sugar | Thin peel of 2 lemons |

1. In a large saucepan over low heat, combine all ingredients. Stir until sugar dissolves.
2. Simmer 30 minutes. Remove and discard cloves, cinnamon, cardamom and lemon peel. Makes 20 (1/2-cup) servings.

# Cheese Sables

| | |
|---|---|
| 1-1/4 cups sifted all-purpose flour | 1/2 cup butter or margarine |
| 1/2 teaspoon salt | 1 egg yolk, beaten |
| 1/8 teaspoon pepper | 3 tablespoons iced water |
| 1/8 teaspoon red (cayenne) pepper | About 3 tablespoons milk |
| 3/4 cup shredded Cheddar cheese (3 oz.) | 2 tablespoons finely chopped walnuts or pecans |
| 1/4 cup grated Parmesan cheese | |

1. In a medium bowl, combine flour, salt, pepper and cayenne. Stir in cheeses until blended. With a pastry blender or 2 knives, cut in butter or margarine until mixture resembles coarse crumbs. Sprinkle with egg yolk and iced water; toss with a fork until mixture binds together. Knead dough in bowl 8 to 10 strokes or until smooth.
2. Divide dough in half. Shape each piece into a 7 x 1-1/4-inch roll. Wrap separately; refrigerate 1 hour.
3. Preheat oven to 375F (190C). Line baking sheets with parchment paper.
4. Cut rolls into 1/4-inch-thick slices. Place slices, cut-side down, about 1 inch apart on lined baking sheets. Brush tops with milk; sprinkle with chopped nuts.
5. Bake in preheated oven 10 to 12 minutes or until golden. Remove from baking sheets; cool completely on wire racks. Makes 56 pastries.

# Cheese Dip

| | |
|---|---|
| 1/2 cup crumbled blue cheese (6 oz.), room temperature | 1 teaspoon paprika |
| | 1 teaspoon sugar |
| 1 small onion, finely chopped | 1 tablespoon lemon juice |
| 2 celery stalks, chopped | 1 tablespoon white-wine vinegar |
| 1 hard-cooked egg, chopped | About 1/4 cup milk |
| Salt | |
| | *To serve:* |
| | Crudités |

1. In a blender or food processor fitted with a steel blade, process cheese, onion. celery and egg until smooth. Add remaining ingredients; process again until smooth. Add additional milk if necessary to give a good consistency for dipping.
2. Serve with crudités such as celery sticks, sliced carrots, bell-pepper strips, green onions and raw cauliflowerets. Makes about 2 cups.

# Celery & Peanut Boats

1/4 cup crunchy peanut butter
2 tablespoons butter or margarine, room temperature
Salt
Freshly ground pepper
1 tablespoon finely chopped green-onion tops or chives

Pinch of dried leaf thyme
Pinch of garlic salt, if desired
1/4 cup fresh bread crumbs
A few drops of lemon juice
6 celery stalks, trimmed

**1.** In a small bowl, beat peanut butter and butter or margarine until smooth. Season with salt and pepper. Stir in onion tops or chives, thyme and garlic salt, if desired. Stir in bread crumbs; stir in enough lemon juice to give a good consistency for spreading.
**2.** Spoon mixture into celery stalks.
**3.** Cut filled celery into 1-inch lengths. Arrange on a plate. Cover and refrigerate until served. Makes about 40 appetizers.

# Sausage & Shrimp Bacon Rolls

20 bacon slices
20 cocktail sausages

20 cooked, deveined, peeled shrimp

**1.** Preheat broiler. Lay bacon slices on a flat surface; stretch slightly with back of a knife. Cut each piece in half crosswise.
**2.** Wrap a half slice of bacon around each sausage; wrap remaining bacon around shrimp. Secure with wooden picks.
**3.** Cook under preheated broiler 4 or 5 inches from heat 5 to 10 minutes, turning once, until bacon is crisp. Serve hot. Makes 40 appetizers.

Clockwise from left: Cheese Dip, Cheese Sables, Crudités, Mulled Wine, Celery & Peanut Boats, Sausage & Shrimp Bacon Rolls

# White-Wine Cup

| | |
|---|---|
| 4 (750ml.) bottles dry white wine, chilled | 1 orange, thinly sliced |
| 4 to 6 tablespoons orange-flavored liqueur | 1 apple, cored, sliced |
| 1/4 medium cucumber, thinly sliced | *To serve:* Crushed ice 1 qt. soda water, chilled |

1. Combine wine, liqueur, cucumber, orange and apple in a large bowl. Refrigerate until chilled.
2. To serve, put crushed ice in a punch bowl or large pitcher. Add chilled wine mixture and soda water. Serve immediately. Makes about 30 (1/2-cup) servings.

# Cheese Twists

| | |
|---|---|
| 1/2 (17-1/2-oz.) pkg. frozen puff pastry, thawed | 3 tablespoons grated Parmesan cheese |
| About 3 tablespoons milk | |

1. Preheat oven to 425F (220C). Grease 2 baking sheets. On a lightly floured surface, roll out pastry to a 12-inch square about 1/8-inch thick. Trim edges neatly with a sharp knife. Cut pastry into quarters; cut each quarter into 1/2- to 3/4-inch-wide strips.
2. Brush strips with milk. Sprinkle with cheese. Give each strip 1 or 2 twists. Place on greased baking sheets.
3. Bake in preheated oven about 12 minutes or until lightly browned. Remove from baking sheet; cool on wire racks. Serve warm or cold. Store in an airtight container. Makes about 36 twists.

# Chicken Pinwheels

| | |
|---|---|
| 1 cup finely chopped cooked chicken | 1 tablespoon chopped fresh parsley, if desired |
| 1 (8-1/2-oz.) can water chestnuts, drained, finely chopped | 1 unsliced whole-wheat-bread loaf, crust removed |
| 2 tablespoons finely chopped onion | *To garnish:* |
| Freshly ground pepper | Parsley sprigs |

1. In a medium bowl, combine all ingredients except bread.
2. Cut loaf lengthwise into 4 equal slices.
3. Spread bread slices with chicken mixture, spreading mixture almost to edges. Starting with a long side, roll up each slice, jelly-roll style. Wrap rolls tightly in plastic wrap. Refrigerate at least 1 hour or overnight.
4. Cut rolls crosswise into thin slices. Arrange on a plate. Garnish with parsley sprigs. Makes about 45 pinwheels.

**Variation**
**Olive & Ham Rolls:** Spread bread with 1/2 cup room-temperature butter or margarine. Arrange 1/2 pound thinly-sliced ham over butter or margarine. Place a roll of pimento-stuffed green olives along 1 long edge of each bread slice. Starting from edge with olives, roll up, jelly-roll style. Finish as directed above.

# Cocktail Canapés

| | |
|---|---|
| 1/4 cucumber, sliced | 1 (4-oz.) carton whipped cream cheese, room temperature |
| 24 small crackers | |
| 4 hard-cooked eggs | |
| 4 oz. deveined, peeled, cooked medium shrimp | 2 oz. smoked-salmon pieces |
| Fresh parsley sprigs | 12 cooked asparagus tips |

1. Cut cucumber slices in half. On each of 12 crackers, place a hard-cooked-egg slice, half a cucumber slice, a shrimp and a parsley sprig.
2. Roll salmon into 12 small rolls. On each of 12 remaining crackers, place a small smoked-salmon roll in center. Spoon cream cheese into a pastry bag fitted with a star tip. Pipe a row of cream cheese on each side of salmon. Top with an asparagus spear. Makes 24 appetizers.

# Curry Puffs with Watercress Dip

| | |
|---|---|
| 1/2 recipe Choux Paste, page 349 | *Watercress Dip:* |
| 2 tablespoons butter or margarine | 1/4 cup mayonnaise |
| 1 onion, finely chopped | 2 tablespoons plain yogurt |
| 2 teaspoons curry powder | 1 bunch watercress, finely chopped |
| Vegetable oil for deep-frying | Grated peel of 1/2 lemon |

**1.** Make Choux Paste as directed on page 349 in steps 2 and 3, reducing sugar to 1 tablespoon. Melt butter or margarine in a small saucepan over low heat. Add onion; sauté about 7 minutes or until lightly browned. Stir in curry powder; cool slightly. Beat curry mixture into choux paste.
**2.** In a large saucepan, heat oil to 375F (190C) or until a 1-inch bread cube turns golden brown in 40 seconds.
**3.** Drop small teaspoons of choux mixture into oil, about 6 at a time. Fry 3 to 4 minutes, turning if necessary, until puffed and golden brown. Drain on paper towels; keep warm. Repeat with remaining dough.
**4.** To make dip, in a small bowl, combine dip ingredients. Garnish with a sprig of watercress, if desired. Place bowl containing watercress dip on a large plate; surround with warm puffs. Makes about 25 puffs.

Clockwise from upper left: White-Wine Cup, Curry Puffs with Watercress Dip, Olive & Ham Rolls, Chicken Pinwheels, Cocktail Canapés, Cheese Twists

This is an attractive assortment of supper dishes for a traditional New Year's Eve party. The cream puffs and soufflé can be made ahead and frozen.

## Bean-Sprout Salad

| | |
|---|---|
| 4 oz. fresh mushrooms, thinly sliced | 4 carrots, julienned |
| 1 cup French dressing | 2 cups thinly shredded red cabbage |
| 2 lb. fresh bean sprouts (about 8 cups) | 3 cartons radish sprouts or alfalfa sprouts |

**1.** Place mushrooms in a large salad bowl; stir in French dressing. Let stand 30 minutes.
**2.** Add remaining ingredients; toss to combine. Serve immediately. Makes 20 servings.

Clockwise from top right: Lasagna Verde, Bean-Sprout Salad, Smoked-Fish & Olive Pâté, Whole-wheat rolls, Apple-Cabbage Salad

# Lasagna Verde

1 tablespoon vegetable oil
Salt
1 lb. green lasagna
  noodles

*Meat Sauce:*
1-1/2 lb. lean ground beef
2 lb. lean ground pork
8 oz. chicken livers,
  finely chopped
2 onions, finely chopped
2 garlic cloves, crushed
1-1/4 cups finely
  chopped carrots
1/4 cup tomato paste
2 (1-lb.) cans tomatoes
1-1/2 cups tomato juice
2 tablespoons
  Worcestershire sauce

1/2 teaspoon ground
  nutmeg
8 oz. mushrooms, if
  desired, chopped
Freshly ground pepper

*White Sauce:*
1/2 cup butter or
  margarine
1/2 cup all-purpose flour
1 qt. milk (4 cups)
2 teaspoons dry mustard
2 cups shredded
  mozzarella cheese
  (8 oz.)

1. Add 1 tablespoon oil to a large saucepan of boiling salted water. Add noodles, 3 or 4 at a time; cook according to package directions until tender. Drain; rinse with cold water. Lay out flat. Repeat with remaining noodles.
2. To make meat sauce, in a large heavy saucepan over medium heat, cook beef and pork, without added fat, until browned. Stir to break up meat. Stir in chicken livers, onions, garlic and carrots; cook about 10 minutes, stirring frequently. Drain off excess fat.
3. Stir in tomato paste, tomatoes, tomato juice, Worcestershire sauce, nutmeg and mushrooms, if desired. Season with salt and pepper. Bring to a boil; reduce heat. Cover and simmer 30 minutes, stirring occasionally.
4. To make white sauce, melt butter or margarine in a medium saucepan over medium heat. Stir in flour; cook 1 minute, stirring. Gradually stir in milk; bring to a boil, stirring. Reduce heat; simmer 2 minutes. Season with salt and pepper. Stir in mustard and 1/2 of cheese. Stir until cheese melts.
5. Preheat oven to 400F (205C). Grease 2 (13" x 9") baking dishes. Alternate layers of noodles, meat sauce and white sauce, ending with white sauce. Sprinkle with remaining cheese.
6. Bake in preheated oven 40 to 50 minutes or until hot and bubbly. Serve hot. Makes 20 servings.

# Smoked-Fish & Olive Pâté

1 onion, chopped
4 hard-cooked eggs,
  chopped
12 pimento-stuffed green
  olives, sliced
1-1/2 lb. smoked
  whitefish, chopped
Freshly ground pepper
1 to 2 garlic cloves,
  crushed

3/4 cup plain yogurt

*To garnish:*
2 tablespoons chopped
  fresh parsley
16 pimento-stuffed green
  olives, sliced

1. In a blender or food processor fitted with a steel blade, process onion and eggs until finely chopped. Add olives and whitefish; process until smooth.
2. Season with pepper. Add garlic and yogurt; process until smooth.
3. Stir in more yogurt if too thick to spread.
4. Spoon pâté into 2 serving dishes; sprinkle with chopped parsley. Arrange sliced olives around edge. Serve with cocktail rounds or crackers. Makes 20 servings.

# Apple-Cabbage Salad

2 green-skinned apples,
  cored, thinly sliced
2 tablespoons lemon juice
2 heads Chinese cabbage,
  finely sliced
1 cucumber, diced
2 green peppers, thinly
  sliced

1 bunch green onions,
  chopped
1 bunch celery, thinly
  sliced
2 bunches watercress,
  coarsely chopped
1 cup French dressing

1. In a large salad bowl, toss apples with lemon juice.
2. Add all remaining ingredients except dressing. Cover and refrigerate up to 8 hours.
3. Pour French dressing over salad; toss to coat with dressing. Serve immediately. Makes 20 servings.

# Mocha-Filled Cream Puffs

24 Cream Puffs

*Filling:*
2 qts. mocha ice cream, softened

*Easy Chocolate Sauce:*
6 tablespoons cocoa powder
3/4 cup corn syrup

3/4 cup butter or margarine
1-1/2 cups half and half
2 teaspoons vanilla

---

**1.** Fill each cream puff with about 3 tablespoons ice cream. If making ahead, place in freezer until about 15 minutes before serving.
**2.** To make sauce, in a medium saucepan over low heat, combine all ingredients. Cook, stirring constantly, until smooth. Boil 3 minutes or until slightly reduced. Serve hot or refrigerate until chilled.
**3.** To serve, arrange filled cream puffs in a serving dish. Spoon a little chocolate sauce over each cream puff. Serve remaining sauce separately. Makes about 48 cream puffs.

# Lemon & Lime Soufflé

2 (1/4-oz.) envelopes unflavored gelatin (2 tablespoons)
1/2 cup water
Grated peel and juice of 3 lemons
Grated peel and juice of 2 limes
8 eggs, separated

1-1/2 cups superfine sugar
1-3/4 cups whipping cream

*To decorate:*
Kiwifruit slices
Lime slices

---

**1.** In a small saucepan, combine gelatin and water. Stir well; let stand 3 minutes. Stir over low heat until gelatin dissolves; set aside to cool.
**2.** Reserve lemon peel and lime peel. In a large bowl, beat lemon juice, lime juice, egg yolks and 1 cup sugar until foamy. Place bowl over pan of simmering water; cook, beating constantly, until mixture thickens and coats back of a spoon. Remove bowl from water; stir in gelatin mixture. Add reserved lemon peel and lime peel; stir until combined. Refrigerate until mixture mounds when dropped from a spoon.
**3.** Cut a piece of foil large enough to wrap around outside of a 2-quart soufflé dish and extend 2 to 3 inches above rim of dish. Secure foil to dish with kitchen string or tape.
**4.** In a medium bowl, beat cream until soft peaks form. Fold whipped cream into lemon-lime mixture. In a medium bowl, beat egg whites until stiff but not dry. Gradually beat in remaining 1/2 cup sugar; beat until stiff and glossy. Fold beaten egg whites into lemon-lime mixture. Pour mixture into prepared dish; smooth top. Refrigerate several hours or until set. Carefully remove foil collar; decorate soufflé with kiwifruit slices and lime slices. Makes 18 to 20 servings.

Left to right: Mocha-Filled Cream Puffs, Lemon & Lime Soufflé

# Barbecue Bites

Juice of 2 lemons
1/4 teaspoon ground ginger
Salt
Freshly ground pepper
2 firm avocados, halved, peeled
18 bacon slices

*These small bacon and avocado bundles make a perfect appetizer while everyone is waiting impatiently for steaks or hamburgers to grill.*

1. Preheat grill. In a medium bowl, combine lemon juice, ginger, salt and pepper. Cut each avocado half into 9 equal pieces. It does not matter if they are not all quite the same shape. Toss avocado cubes in the lemon-juice mixture.
2. Cut each bacon slice in half crosswise. Roll up each cube of avocado in a piece of bacon. Thread on 6 small skewers.
3. Place on preheated grill. Cook 2 to 3 minutes or until bacon is crisp. Makes 6 servings.

# Barbecued Spareribs

4 lb. pork spareribs

*Marinade:*
6 tablespoons soy sauce
1/4 cup vegetable oil
3 garlic cloves, crushed
1 teaspoon grated gingerroot or 1/4 teaspoon
    ground ginger
Grated peel of 1 lemon
Few drops of hot-pepper sauce
1/2 teaspoon ground cinnamon
Salt
Freshly ground pepper
1/4 cup honey

*There is not much meat on spareribs. If they are to be served as a main course, allow about one pound per person. To cook spareribs more quickly, separate into individual ribs.*

1. Preheat grill. Cut spareribs into individual ribs, if desired.
2. To make marinade, in a small bowl, combine all ingredients except honey.
3. Place spareribs on preheated grill, bone-side down; brush with marinade. Cook about 10 minutes. Turn ribs over; brush with more marinade. Cook 15 minutes more.
4. Turn ribs again; brush with marinade and honey. Cook 10 to 15 minutes more or until ribs are tender. Makes 4 main-dish servings.

# Arabian Orange Salad

4 oranges, peeled
1 medium onion, cut into thin rings
1/4 cup sliced black olives

*Dressing:*
6 tablespoons olive oil
Juice of 1/2 lemon
1 tablespoon chopped fresh mint
1 tablespoon chopped pine nuts or blanched almonds
1 tablespoon chopped raisins
Salt
Freshly ground pepper

1. Remove white bitter pith from oranges. Cut into thin slices, discarding any seeds. Arrange orange slices, onion and olives in a shallow dish.
2. To make dressing, in a small bowl, combine oil, lemon juice, mint, nuts, raisins, salt and pepper. Spoon evenly over orange mixture. Cover; refrigerate 1 hour for flavors to blend.
3. To take on a picnic, pack salad in a tightly covered container. Makes 4 servings.

Top to bottom: Barbecued Spareribs, Barbecue Bites, Arabian Orange Salad

# Swedish Meat Patties

3 white-bread slices, crusts removed
1/2 cup club soda
8 oz. ground veal
8 oz. ground pork
2 oz. ham, finely chopped
1 teaspoon juniper berries, crushed
2 egg yolks
Salt
Freshly ground pepper
Vegetable oil

*To serve:*
4 large rye-bread slices, spread with unsalted butter
1 medium onion, cut into thin rings
2 dill pickles, cut into wedges
2 tablespoons capers
1/2 cup dairy sour cream

1. Break bread into small pieces. In a small bowl, combine bread pieces and club soda. Let stand 20 minutes.
2. Preheat grill. In a medium bowl, combine veal, pork, ham, juniper berries and egg yolks. Season with salt and pepper. Stir in bread mixture until smooth. Form into 4 flat patties. Refrigerate 30 minutes.
3. Brush patties with oil. Place on preheated grill. Cook 4 minutes. Turn patties; brush with oil. Cook 4 minutes more or until juices are no longer pink.
4. Place a rye-bread slice on each serving plate. Place a grilled patty on each slice. Garnish with a few onion rings, dill pickles and a small spoonful of capers. Add a dollop of sour cream to each plate. Makes 4 servings.

---

Scandinavians are masters at making meatballs and meat patties. They combine a variety of ground meats with subtle seasonings, such as juniper berries, dill seed and ground allspice. One secret is the addition of club soda to the basic mixture to lighten the texture. Meatballs are often served slightly rare or pink. If pork is used in the meat mixture, cook until well-done. Bread slices are used to absorb the delicious meat juices.

---

# Maple Chicken

4 chicken legs
*Marinade:*
2/3 cup unsweetened orange juice
1 medium onion, thinly sliced
1 garlic clove, crushed
Salt
Freshly ground pepper
Freshly grated nutmeg
1/4 cup maple syrup

---

*Maple syrup gives chicken a pronounced maple flavor. If desired, substitute a mild honey. The flavor is enhanced by marinating overnight.*

1. Pierce chicken legs at regular intervals with a fine skewer. Place pierced chicken in a shallow dish. Add orange juice, sliced onion and garlic. Season with salt, pepper and nutmeg. Cover; refrigerate 8 hours or overnight.
2. Preheat grill.
3. Remove chicken from marinade, allowing excess to drip off. Place on preheated grill; cook 15 minutes. Turn over; brush with maple syrup. Cook 15 to 20 minutes or until chicken is tender. Test chicken by piercing in thickest part with a small skewer. If juices run clear, chicken is done. Serve hot. Makes 4 servings.

# Orange & Watercress Salad

4 oranges
1 bunch watercress, washed, shaken dry
1 small onion, finely chopped
1/4 cup olive oil
2 tablespoons chopped fresh chives or parsley
Salt
Freshly ground pepper

---

1. Grate peel and squeeze juice from 1 orange. Peel remaining oranges with a small sharp knife. Section peeled oranges.
2. Cut watercress into sprigs. Place orange sections and watercress sprigs into a shallow serving dish; sprinkle with onion. In a small bowl, combine orange juice, orange peel, olive oil and chives or parsley. Season with salt and pepper. Spoon dressing over salad. Makes 4 servings.

Top to bottom: Swedish Meat Patties, Maple Chicken with Orange & Watercress Salad

# Cheesy Meat Loaf

3/4 lb. lean ground beef
3/4 lb. lean ground pork
2-1/2 cups fresh bread crumbs
1 egg, beaten
1/2 cup beer
1 teaspoon dried rosemary, crushed
Salt
Freshly ground pepper
1 small onion, finely chopped
1 cup diced Edam cheese

*To garnish:*
Radish halves
Green onions
Watercress

---

*This meat loaf is cooked on a rack rather than in a loaf pan to allow the fat from the pork to drain off during cooking. Since this meat loaf is served cold, it is important to remove the fat.*

**1.** Preheat oven to 350F (175C). In a medium bowl, combine beef and pork until blended.
**2.** Place bread crumbs in another medium bowl. Stir in egg, beer, rosemary, salt and pepper. Pour over meat; stir in bread-crumb mixture, onion and cheese.
**3.** Shape mixture into loaf; smooth top. Place on a rack in a baking pan.
**4.** Bake in preheated oven 1-1/2 hours.
**5.** Discard fat. Cool meat loaf to room temperature. When cool, wrap in plastic wrap or foil; refrigerate until thoroughly chilled.
**6.** To take on a picnic, unwrap. Slice meat loaf; rewrap. Keep chilled until ready to serve. When ready to serve, arrange on a serving plate; garnish with radishes, green onions and watercress. Makes 6 servings.

# Tomato Vichyssoise

3 tablespoons butter or margarine
1 medium onion, finely chopped
2 cups peeled, coarsely chopped potatoes
2 cups coarsely chopped tomatoes
1 garlic clove, crushed
1 tablespoon tomato paste
1 tablespoon chopped fresh basil or 1 teaspoon
    dried leaf basil
1-1/2 cups chicken stock
1-1/2 cups milk
Salt
Freshly ground pepper
1/2 cup whipping cream

*To garnish:*
Chopped fresh parsley or basil

---

*This soup makes a delicious starter for a barbecue meal. Or, pack chilled soup in a thermos to take on a picnic.*

**1.** Melt butter or margarine in a medium saucepan. Add onion; sauté 3 minutes. Add potatoes, tomatoes, garlic, tomato paste, basil, stock and milk. Season with salt and pepper. Bring to a boil; simmer 25 to 30 minutes or until potatoes are tender.
**2.** Press soup through a sieve. Or, process soup in a blender or food processor fitted with a steel blade until smooth. Cool pureed soup; stir in cream.
**3.** Refrigerate until chilled. Garnish with chopped parsley or basil. Serve with crusty bread, if desired. Makes 6 servings.

Left to right: Cheesy Meat Loaf, Strawberry-Cheese Mousse

# Strawberry-Cheese Mousse

1 (15-oz.) container whole-milk ricotta cheese (2 cups)
1/2 cup sugar
1 teaspoon vanilla extract
2 eggs, separated
1/2 pint whipping cream (1 cup)
1 (1/4-oz.) envelope unflavored gelatin (1 tablespoon)
1/4 cup water
1 pint strawberries, washed, hulled

*To decorate:*
Sweetened whipped cream, if desired

1. Lightly oil an 8-inch heart-shaped pan.
2. In a medium bowl, beat ricotta cheese, sugar, vanilla, egg yolks and cream until smooth and blended.
3. In a small saucepan, combine gelatin and water. Stir well; let stand 3 minutes. Stir over low heat until gelatin dissolves; set aside to cool. Beat into cheese mixture. Refrigerate until mixture mounds when dropped from a spoon.
4. Set 8 large strawberries aside for decoration. Coarsely chop remaining strawberries.
5. In a medium bowl, beat egg whites until stiff but not dry. Fold beaten egg whites and chopped strawberries into cheese mixture. Pour mixture into oiled pan; refrigerate 3 to 4 hours or until set.
6. Unmold on a flat serving plate. Decorate with reserved strawberries and whipped cream, if desired. Makes 6 to 8 servings.

# Potted Blue Cheese

3 cups crumbled Stilton cheese or other
   blue cheese (12 oz.)
1/2 cup unsalted butter, room temperature
Freshly ground pepper
Pinch of grated nutmeg
3 tablespoons port
2 tablespoons chopped blanched almonds, toasted
Few whole toasted almonds

1. In a medium bowl, blend cheese and butter.
2. Season with pepper and nutmeg. Beat in port and chopped almonds.
3. Press cheese mixture into a small crock or other serving dish. Top with whole almonds.
4. Refrigerate to store. Bring to room temperature before serving. Makes about 3 cups.

# Middle-Eastern-Style Kabobs

1 medium eggplant
Salt
8 small white onions
2 medium zucchini, cut into rings 1/2 inch thick
1 red bell pepper, cut into cubes
8 cherry tomatoes
1/2 cup plain yogurt
1 garlic clove, crushed
1/2 teaspoon ground ginger
3 tablespoons olive oil
Salt
Freshly ground black pepper

*To serve:*
Mozzarella-cheese or feta-cheese slices
Olive oil

---

*These kabobs are rather crunchy. If you prefer vegetables that are more tender, blanch them before grilling.*

**1.** Cut eggplant roughly into 1-inch cubes. Place eggplant cubes in a colander; sprinkle with salt. Let stand 30 minutes.
**2.** Simmer onions in boiling water 5 minutes. Drain onions.
**3.** Rinse eggplant cubes; pat dry with paper towels.
**4.** Thread rinsed eggplant, cooked onions, zucchini, bell pepper and tomatoes on 4 kabob skewers.
**5.** In a small bowl, combine yogurt, garlic, ginger, olive oil, salt and pepper.
**6.** Place kabobs in a large shallow dish. Spoon yogurt mixture over kabobs. Cover and refrigerate 3 hours.
**7.** Preheat broiler or grill. Gently shake kabobs to remove excess yogurt mixture.
**8.** Broil kabobs about 4 minutes on each side, brushing with a little yogurt mixture.
**9.** Sprinkle mozzarella-cheese or feta-cheese slices with olive oil. Serve with hot kabobs. Makes 4 servings.

# Mixed Fruit Kabobs

*Coconut Cream:*
3 tablespoons shredded coconut
1/4 cup boiling water
1/2 cup whipping cream, thickly whipped
*Kabobs:*
1/2 cup fresh orange juice
Juice of 2 lemons
5 tablespoons sugar
1 pear, peeled, cut into 8 pieces
2 small firm bananas, peeled, cut into 4 pieces
2 fresh or canned pineapple slices, cut into 8 pieces
8 pitted cherries or seedless grapes
4 small preserved stem-ginger pieces
2 tablespoons warm honey
Brown sugar
2 tablespoons flaked almonds

---

*This could be called fruit salad on a stick! Children will love it. It is equally suitable for an informal dinner party.*

**1.** To make Coconut Cream, in a small bowl, combine coconut and boiling water. Let stand 30 minutes. Strain through a sieve, pressing coconut to extract flavor and liquid. Whisk coconut milk into thickly whipped cream. This can be prepared ahead.
**2.** In a medium bowl, combine orange juice, lemon juice and sugar.
**3.** Stir in pear, bananas, pineapple, cherries or grapes, and preserved ginger until evenly coated in juice mixture. The juice prevents fruit discoloration.
**4.** Preheat broiler. Drain fruit thoroughly; thread alternately on 4 kabob skewers.
**5.** Put fruit kabobs on a broiler-pan rack. Brush with honey; sprinkle with brown sugar and almonds.
**6.** Broil 3 to 4 minutes or until kabobs are light golden.
**7.** Serve immediately with Coconut Cream. Makes 4 servings.

Top to bottom: Middle-Eastern-Style Kabobs, Mixed Fruit Kabobs with Coconut Cream

Top to bottom: Chicken-Liver & Water-Chestnut Kabobs,
Apple-Sausage Kabobs

## Apple-Sausage Kabobs

1/4 cup dry bread crumbs
1/4 teaspoon rubbed sage
1 teaspoon dried onion flakes
1/2 cup boiling water
1 lb. bulk pork sausage
1 egg yolk
Salt
Freshly ground pepper
2 red-skinned apples, cut into wedges
Juice of 1 lemon
Vegetable oil

**1.** In a medium bowl, combine bread crumbs, sage, onion flakes and water. Let stand until water has been absorbed.
**2.** Stir in sausage and egg yolk. Season with salt and pepper.
**3.** Shape into small balls about the size of a walnut; refrigerate 1 hour.
**4.** In a medium bowl, toss apple wedges in lemon juice.
**5.** Preheat broiler. Thread sausage balls and apple wedges alternately on 4 kabob skewers.
**6.** Place kabobs on a broiler-pan rack. Brush with oil. Broil 5 minutes. Turn; brush with oil. Broil 5 to 6 minutes or to desired doneness. Makes 4 servings.

# Chicken-Liver & Water-Chestnut Kabobs

1 lb. chicken livers, rinsed, dried
8 bacon slices
8 water chestnuts, halved
2 tablespoons soy sauce
1/4 cup vegetable oil
Freshly ground pepper

---

*Bacon slices will roll easily if you stretch them slightly on a flat surface.*

1. Cut chicken livers into 16 equal pieces.
2. Cut bacon slices in half crosswise.
3. Roll up 1 piece of chicken liver and 1 water chestnut half in a half-slice of bacon.
4. Thread bacon rolls on 4 kabob skewers.
5. In a small bowl, combine soy sauce, oil and pepper.
6. Preheat broiler. Put kabobs on a broiler-pan rack. Spoon soy-sauce mixture over kabobs.
7. Broil 4 to 5 minutes. Turn kabobs; spoon remaining sauce over kabobs. Broil 4 to 5 minutes or until livers are done.
8. Serve kabobs with hot cooked rice or risotto and a green salad. Or, serve as an appetizer. Makes 4 main-dish servings.

**Variation**
Substitute calves' liver for chicken livers, if desired.

# Brunch Kabobs

6 precooked sausage links, halved crosswise
8 oz. ham, cut in 1-inch chunks
16 button mushrooms
Vegetable oil
Freshly ground pepper
2 medium cooking apples, peeled, cut into
1/4-inch-thick rings
1/4 cup butter or margarine, melted
2 tablespoons sugar

---

1. Thread sausage, ham and mushrooms alternately on 4 kabob skewers.
2. Preheat broiler. Brush kabobs generously with oil; sprinkle with pepper.
3. Put kabobs on a broiler-pan rack. Broil about 3 minutes. Turn kabobs; broil 3 minutes more or until sausage is no longer pink.
4. Meanwhile, to make apple rings, in a large skillet, combine apples and melted butter or margarine. Cook over low heat 1 minute. Turn apple rings; increase heat to high. Sprinkle with sugar; cook 1 to 2 minutes.
5. Serve broiled kabobs over buttered apple rings. Makes 4 servings.

# Scallops en Brochette

Salt
Freshly ground white pepper
6 tablespoons fresh bread crumbs
Finely grated peel of 1/2 lemon
1 lb. bay scallops
1 tablespoon all-purpose flour
Melted butter or margarine

*Lemon-Cream Sauce:*
1/2 cup whipping cream
Grated peel of 1/2 lemon
2 tablespoons finely chopped fresh parsley
Salt
Freshly ground pepper

---

1. Preheat broiler. In a shallow bowl, combine salt, white pepper, bread crumbs and lemon peel.
2. Coat scallops lightly in flour; dip coated scallops into melted butter or margarine. Roll buttered scallops in crumb mixture.
3. Thread on 4 kabob skewers. Place kabobs on a broiler-pan rack. Brush with additional melted butter or margarine.
4. Broil about 3 minutes. Turn kabobs; brush with additional melted butter or margarine. Broil 2 to 4 minutes or until scallops are done.
5. To make Lemon-Cream Sauce, in a small saucepan, heat cream until hot; stir in lemon peel and parsley. Season with salt and pepper. Serve sauce separately. Makes 4 servings.

# Fish Kabobs

1 lb. firm-textured white fish, cod, halibut,
   monkfish, etc.
1/4 cup lime or lemon juice
6 tablespoons olive oil
Salt
Freshly ground pepper
1 tablespoon chopped fresh rosemary or
   1 teaspoon dried rosemary
4 small onions, cut into thick slices
1 lemon, cut into thin wedges

*Use a firm-textured fish for kabobs to prevent fish falling
apart during cooking. Fish kabobs keep their shape better
if they are cooked on a baking sheet or large shallow pan,
rather than a rack.*

1. Cut fish into 1-inch cubes. Place fish cubes in a shallow
dish.
2. In a small bowl, combine lime or lemon juice, olive oil,
salt, pepper and rosemary. Spoon over fish. Cover; refrigerate 4 hours.
3. Preheat broiler. Thread marinated fish on 4 kabob skewers alternately with onion slices and lemon wedges. Place
kabobs on a baking sheet or large shallow pan. Brush with
marinade.
4. Broil 3 to 4 minutes. Turn kabobs; brush with marinade.
Broil 3 to 4 minutes or until fish is cooked through.
5. Serve with warm pita bread and a green salad. Makes 4
servings.

# Mixed Grill on a Skewer

8 oz. lamb, cut into 1-inch cubes
4 lamb's kidneys, skinned, quartered, cored
12 small cocktail sausages
12 button mushrooms

*Basting Sauce:*
1 tablespoon Worcestershire sauce
3 tablespoons chili sauce
2 tablespoons vegetable oil
1 garlic clove, crushed
Juice of 1/2 lemon
Salt
Freshly ground pepper

1. Thread lamb, kidneys, sausages and mushrooms alternately on 4 kabob skewers.
2. To make sauce, in a small bowl, combine sauce
ingredients.
3. Preheat broiler. Put kabobs on a broiler-pan rack. Brush
1/2 of sauce over kabobs.
4. Broil 5 minutes.
5. Turn kabobs; brush with remaining sauce. Broil 5 minutes or until meats are tender.
6. Serve with sautéed potatoes and a green vegetable.
Makes 4 servings.

# Sole & Anchovy Roll-Ups

12 small sole fillets
Anchovy paste
All-purpose flour

*Batter:*
2/3 cup all-purpose flour
Salt
Freshly ground pepper
1 egg
1/2 cup milk
Vegetable oil for deep-frying

*Parsley Mayonnaise:*
1/2 cup mayonnaise
3 tablespoons dairy sour cream
3 tablespoons finely chopped fresh parsley

1. Cut each fillet in half crosswise.
2. Spread 1 side thinly with anchovy paste; roll up jelly-
roll style.
3. Thread 6 sole rolls on each of 4 metal kabob skewers.
4. Dust lightly on all sides with flour.
5. To make batter, in a medium bowl, combine flour, salt
and pepper. Stir in egg and a little milk. Beat in remaining
milk until smooth.
6. Place kabobs in a long shallow dish without touching.
Spoon batter over kabobs until coated.
7. Fill a long pan 1/3 full of oil; heat to 375F (190C) or until
a 1-inch bread cube turns golden brown in 50 seconds.
Carefully lower kabobs into hot oil. Deep-fry 5 to 6 minutes or until fish is crisp and golden. Remove kabobs with
tongs; metal skewers will be hot. Drain kabobs on paper
towels.
8. To make mayonnaise, in a small bowl combine
mayonnaise, sour cream and parsley. Serve with hot
kabobs. Makes 4 servings.

*Clockwise from top: Mixed Grill on a Skewer, Fish Kabobs, Sole
& Anchovy Roll-Ups with Parsley Mayonnaise*

# Grilled Chicken

2 (2-1/2- to 3-lb.) broiler-fryer chickens
6 tablespoons vegetable oil
1 tablespoon Worcestershire sauce
2 garlic cloves, crushed
Juice of 1/2 lemon
1 tablespoon prepared brown mustard
Salt
Freshly ground pepper

1. Place 1 chicken on a cutting board, breast-side down.
2. Cut through backbone with poultry shears or a sharp knife.
3. Remove backbone completely.
4. Open out chicken; place skin-side up on a cutting board. Pound with a meat mallet or rolling pin to flatten. Be careful not to splinter bones or tear flesh.
5. Fold wing tips under wings so they lie flat.
6. Insert 2 skewers, crisscross fashion, through chicken to hold it rigid. Repeat steps 1 through 6 for other chicken.
7. Place prepared chickens in a shallow dish.
8. In a small bowl, combine oil, Worcestershire sauce, garlic, lemon juice, mustard, salt and pepper. Spoon over chickens. Cover; refrigerate 4 to 6 hours, or preferably overnight.
9. Preheat grill. Place chickens, skin-side down, on grill rack. Grill 25 minutes.
10. Turn chickens; baste with remaining marinade. Grill 20 to 30 minutes or until tender. Makes 4 to 6 servings.

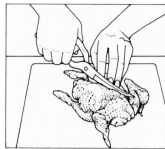

1/Cut through backbone with poultry shears or a sharp knife.

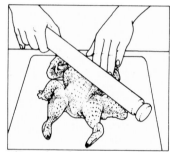

2/Remove backbone completely.

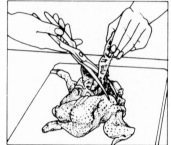

3/Pound with a meat mallet or rolling pin to flatten.

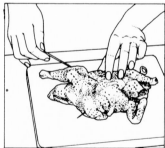

4/Insert 2 skewers, crisscross fashion, through each chicken to hold it rigid.

Grilled Chicken

# Special Beef Kabobs

*Marinade:*
6 tablespoons vegetable oil
Grated peel of 1 orange
2 tablespoons brandy
2 tablespoons chopped fresh rosemary or
   2 teaspoons dried rosemary
1 garlic clove, crushed
Salt
Freshly ground pepper

*Kabobs:*
1 lb. lean beef, cut into 1-inch cubes
2 medium zucchini, about 8 oz., sliced
1 small orange, cut into 8 wedges

---

1. To make marinade, in a medium bowl, combine marinade ingredients.
2. Add beef to marinade; stir until coated. Cover; refrigerate 4 hours.
3. Remove beef from marinade; pat dry with paper towels.
4. Preheat broiler. Thread marinated beef on 4 kabob skewers alternately with zucchini and orange.
5. Place kabobs on a broiler-pan rack. Brush with marinade. Broil 5 to 6 minutes.
6. Turn kabobs; brush with additional marinade. Cook 5 to 6 minutes or to desired doneness.
7. Serve hot with rice and a green salad. Makes 4 servings.

# Veal & Prune Kabobs

12 large pitted prunes
About 1/2 cup dry white wine
1-1/4 lb. lean veal, in 1 piece
3 ham slices
3 tablespoons honey
3 tablespoons white-wine vinegar
Salt
Freshly ground pepper
Vegetable oil

---

1. Place prunes in a shallow dish; add enough wine to cover. Let stand overnight or until plumped.
2. Cut veal into 1-inch cubes.
3. Cut each ham slice into 4 strips. Roll up each wine-soaked prune in a strip of ham.
4. Thread veal cubes and ham rolls on 4 kabob skewers.
5. Preheat broiler. In a small pan, heat honey and wine vinegar until honey dissolves. Season with salt and pepper.
6. Brush kabobs with oil; then brush with honey mixture.
7. Place kabobs on a broiler-pan rack. Broil about 6 minutes. Turn kabobs; brush with honey mixture. Broil 6 minutes or to desired doneness.
8. Serve hot. Makes 4 servings.

# Pork Saté

3 tablespoons smooth or crunchy peanut butter
2 tablespoons soy sauce
1 tablespoon vinegar
1 tablespoon chicken stock or water
Salt
Freshly ground pepper
1 teaspoon curry powder
1 lb. pork-loin tenderloin

*To serve:*
2 lemons, cut into wedges

---

*Saté are usually served as appetizers with drinks, or as part of an hors d'oeuvre. Use small bamboo or metal skewers.*

1. In a small saucepan, combine peanut butter, soy sauce, vinegar, stock or water, salt, pepper and curry powder. Stir over low heat until blended. Set aside to cool.
2. Cut pork into 1/2-inch cubes.
3. Stir pork cubes into peanut-butter sauce. Cover; refrigerate 4 hours.
4. Preheat broiler. Thread marinated pork cubes on 12 small skewers. Place on a broiler-pan rack.
5. Broil about 2 minutes. Turn; broil 2 minutes more or until pork is no longer pink.
6. Serve with lemon wedges. Makes 6 servings.

Top to bottom: Pork Saté with peanut sauce, Special Beef Kabobs

Left to right: Ham & Cheese Kabobs, Skewered Meatballs

## Ham & Cheese Kabobs

1 (12-oz.) 1-inch-thick cooked ham slice
8 oz. Edam cheese
All-purpose flour
1 egg, beaten
3 tablespoons fresh bread crumbs
Freshly ground pepper
1/4 cup red-currant jelly
Juice of 1/2 orange

**1.** Preheat broiler. Cut ham into 1-inch cubes.
**2.** Cut cheese into 3/4-inch cubes.
**3.** Dust cheese cubes lightly with flour. Dip floured cheese cubes into beaten egg; roll in bread crumbs until evenly coated.
**4.** Thread ham and coated cheese cubes alternately on 4 kabob skewers. Place on a broiler-pan rack; season with pepper.
**5.** In a small saucepan, combine jelly and orange juice. Stir over low heat until jelly melts. Spoon jelly mixture over kabobs.
**6.** Broil about 4 minutes. Turn kabobs; spoon over additional jelly mixture. Broil 4 minutes or until heated through.
**7.** Serve hot with Orange & Watercress Salad, page 530. Makes 4 servings.

# Skewered Meatballs

1 lb. ground beef or lamb
1 medium onion, finely chopped
2 teaspoons fresh thyme or 1/2 teaspoon
   dried leaf thyme
Salt
Freshly ground pepper
2 garlic clove, crushed
2 egg yolks
1 large red bell pepper, halved
1 large green bell pepper, halved
5 tablespoons vegetable oil
1/8 teaspoon ground ginger
Pinch of ground turmeric

*Yogurt & Cucumber Sauce:*
1/2 cucumber, peeled, grated
1/2 teaspoon dill seeds
1/4 teaspoon sugar
1/2 cup plain yogurt
1 tablespoon chopped fresh mint

**1.** In a medium bowl, combine meat, onion, thyme, salt, pepper, garlic and egg yolks.
**2.** Shape into 24 small meatballs about the size of a walnut. Cover; refrigerate 3 to 4 hours to firm up texture of meatballs.
**3.** Cut bell peppers into 1-inch-square pieces.
**4.** Thread chilled meatballs and bell-pepper pieces alternately on 4 kabob skewers. Place kabobs into a shallow dish.
**5.** In a small bowl, combine oil, ginger, turmeric, salt and pepper. Brush kabobs with oil mixture. Cover; refrigerate 1 hour.
**6.** Preheat broiler.
**7.** To make sauce, squeeze grated cucumber in a dish towel to remove excess moisture. In a small bowl, combine cucumber, dill seeds, sugar, yogurt, mint, salt and pepper.
**8.** Place kabobs on a broiler-pan rack; brush with oil mixture. Broil 6 to 8 minutes.
**9.** Turn kabobs; brush with oil mixture. Broil 6 minutes or to desired doneness. Serve hot with sauce and a pasta salad. Makes 4 servings.

# Quick & Easy

Preparing and cooking a meal for family and friends is an exciting challenge—and one which this chapter will help you meet successfully, again and again. Whether you are looking for speedy new ideas for family snacks, need inspiration when you have only minutes between dashing home and serving a meal, or want something simple yet impressive to offer your guests—read on!

The title has been taken literally. Recipes were chosen and written to be quick and easy. Preparation time may vary according to your expertise, but the times listed can be used as planning guides. At a glance, you can choose the section to suit the occasion—whether you have fifteen, thirty, forty-five or sixty minutes; want to prepare one dish or a complete meal in advance; or want a balanced menu already planned for you.

Inventory your kitchen equipment occasionally to see if replacements or new items are needed. Take good care of nonstick cooking surfaces. Keep appliances in good working order. Make sure that everything is conveniently located. Just moving your most frequently used gadgets from one drawer to another nearer the sink or range, and making space for the mixer on the countertop, can save steps and time. Adding a few inexpensive tools could be the key to more leisure time over the years.

## KITCHEN EQUIPMENT

**Knives**—Choose the best you can afford and keep them sharp. Non-stainless-steel knives remain sharp longer. You need straight-edged blades for chopping, dicing and shredding. Scalloped- or serrated-edged ones are best for the sawing motion needed to slice bread, meat, frozen foods, fruit and vegetables, especially those with tough skins, like tomatoes. Use stainless-steel knives for cutting acidic foods, such as lemons.

**Hand tools**—Time-savers include: good-quality kitchen scissors for snipping everything from marshmallows to chives; an apple corer, which also cuts decorative butter pats and carrots slices; a slicer to cut wafer-thin slices of vegetables that will cook quickly or to slice cucumbers for salads; a fruit zester to scrape rapidly across lemon and orange peel; a wire whisk to leave the other hand free for pouring; a stiff vegetable brush to brush along the grain to clean celery and to scrub root vegetables; and a salad spinner to make short work of drying lettuce and other salad greens.

**Weights and measures**—A set of accurate kitchen scales may be helpful. Standard measuring cups for dry and liquid ingredients and a set of standard measuring spoons are essentials for kitchen success. Extra sets of these are handy when making several recipes at once.

**Utensils**—Flameproof casseroles save time and dishwashing. The casserole can be used on the stove top and in the oven, as well as on the table. One-pot cooking was invented for the busy cook! Nonstick pans and bakeware of all kinds make flipping, tossing and turning easier. Again, buy the best you can afford. This is where quality really counts.

## ELECTRICAL EQUIPMENT

**Blenders** crumb bread and cookies, grate nuts and cheese, make fruit and vegetable purees, stir batters and sauces and make creamy pâtés and foolproof mayonnaise.

**Electric mixers,** with their many speeds and attachments, whip, whisk, cream, beat, chop, slice, shred, mince, grind and sieve.

**Food processors,** with the various discs, cope with almost every step of food preparation except beating egg whites, whipping cream and sieving foods.

**Slow-cookers** cook casseroles, puddings, stews, soups and vegetables slowly and surely. This is a perfect way to cook at a controlled temperature when you are away from home.

**Pressure cookers,** the original fast-cookers, are especially time-saving for less-tender cuts of meat, root vegetables, dried beans and peas and steamed puddings. Foods which take a long time to cook can have cooking time reduced by half when cooked in a pressure cooker.

**Steamers and rice cookers** cook rice and keep it hot. Rice cookers will soft-cook or hard-cook eggs to perfection. Steamers and rice cookers also steam meat, fish, fruit and vegetables.

**Microwave ovens** are useful for cooking foods quickly. They also can be used to defrost frozen items and to reheat leftovers. Many models offer features that make cooking practically foolproof. As with any electrical applicance, follow the manufacturer's directions. There is cookware on the market that can be used in both microwave and conventional ovens. Check labels to be sure. Many conventional recipes can be adapted for the microwave oven.

## THINGS TO HAVE ON HAND

It's reassuring to keep a carefully chosen stock of the canned, packaged and frozen foods you use most often. Here are some reminders.

**Canned goods**—Peeled tomatoes are time savers for sauces, soups and casseroles. Consommé makes a good instant soup with a dash of sherry and a tastier beef stock than bouillon cubes. The condensed kind doubles for a meat glaze and, when chilled, can be chopped and mixed with cold meats, even melon, as a salad. Tuna turns green salad into a French-style meal and makes a marvelous sauce for pasta or rice or a filling for pastry. All canned fruits are useful; some are more versatile than others. For example, grapefruit sections mixed with sliced avocado make a great salad in a hurry. Peach or apricot halves broiled or baked with a stuffing take on a touch of glamour that belie their usual image.

**Dry goods**—Check stocks regularly, or store in clear containers so you can tell at a glance when to buy more. Add variety with brown and white rice and whole-wheat and vegetable pasta in all shapes and sizes. Choose from a wide selection of dried legumes. Try lentils, red kidney beans, pinto beans or navy beans; reduce the cooking time by cooking in a pressure cooker.

**Frozen foods**—Keep a selection of frozen vegetables in your freezer to add variety in shape and color to your meals. Broccoli, green peas, carrots, corn, green beans, spinach and even potatoes will add a quick side dish.

Quick-thawing fruits, such as raspberries, strawberries, blueberries and peaches, make easy desserts. Ice cream can be a dessert by itself, or serve it with cookies, cake or fruit. Frozen pie crust and puff pastry save time; bake and add a filling for a dessert in minutes. Keep yeast rolls in the freezer. Or, freeze yeast dough; bake before guests arrive to give your kitchen that warm, delicious aroma of home-baked bread. Freeze foods in serving sizes that are right for your family. It's easy to open two packages for guests.

Ingredients for garnishes

## HELPFUL HINTS

● A day or two in advance, chop herbs for garnishes; slice or chop mushrooms, onions or carrots. Do not chop vegetables such as potatoes that turn brown. Store prepared vegetables in tightly covered containers in the refrigerator.

● Section or slice oranges and grapefruit; squeeze orange juice or lemon juice. Grate citrus peel up to 2 days ahead.

● Make sugar syrup for fruit salad; add a bay leaf or orange-peel twist. Refrigerate up to 4 days.

● Use small, clean containers with lids for storing prepared items. But, remember to label them clearly. A frantic last-minute search for chopped parsley saves neither time nor temper!

● Make extra cookies, sheet cakes or pie crusts; freeze for an easy dessert later.

● Chop or grind nuts. Toast nuts while using the oven or broiler. Store nuts in tightly covered containers in the refrigerator.

● Prepare two casseroles at the same time—one to serve and one to freeze for later. This saves preparation and cleanup time.

● When measuring honey or syrup, use the cup to measure the shortening first. The honey or syrup will slide out easily.

● Dip peaches or tomatoes into boiling water for a few seconds before peeling them.

● Never waste anything. Make stock from bones left from deboning a roast or chicken. Combine bones, chopped onion, carrots, celery and herbs in a large stockpot. Simmer 1 to 2 hours. Cool and strain. Freeze up to 3 months.

● Use leftover wine and spices to poach apples or pears. Or, use wine instead of water in sugar syrup for extra-special fruit salads. Wine can also be frozen in ice-cube trays.

● A heat diffuser that fits over a heating unit on the range allow you to simmer stews and casseroles on very low heat. This frees you to do other things without worrying that your dish will burn.

● To cool hot foods quickly, place container in a larger pan or sink of cold water. Be careful that the water does not enter the food. Or, pour liquid foods into a shallow pan to cool more quickly.

## IN FIFTEEN MINUTES

Rushing in from work or shopping? Unexpected guests to cook for? What can you cook in fifteen minutes? Lots of things, from simple dishes like *Pan-Fried Danish Egg & Bacon* and *Apple Stacks*, to really super main dishes that are fit for a party. You will enjoy trying *Shrimp in Garlic Butter* or *Steak with Anchovies.*

When time is so precious, it's best to spend it all on the main dish and keep the side dishes simple. Quick-cooking rice and pasta come to the rescue.

And for dessert? Even as the minutes tick away, there's time for *Banana & Rum Flambé*, chilled *Raspberry Cream* or *Ginger-Soufflé Omelet.* All in fifteen minutes or less!

## IN THIRTY MINUTES

After cooking a main dish in a quarter of an hour, thirty minutes seems quite a luxury! Using quick-cooking meats, such as pork tenderloin, ham steaks, liver or fish fillets, you can produce tempting meals. The secret is in simple, but good, sauces. These include *Orange & Ginger Sauce, Pimento Mayonnaise* and *Cucumber Sauce.* The little extras make all the difference; recipes include herbs, spices and flavored butters for cooking and glazing.

Wrapping food in foil reduces cleanup time. Try foil-wrapped *Sole & Mushrooms in Sweet & Sour Sauce.*

Fresh fruit is a positive boon when time is at a premium. *Peach Caramels* and *Poached Pears with Chocolate Sauce* are two more ideas for glamorous presentations.

## IN FORTY-FIVE MINUTES

In this amount of time, there is an opportunity to use the oven, to prepare fresh vegetables and to make warm and welcome desserts. Mixing and matching these ideas, you can easily prepare two courses well within your deadline. While thin, tender beef strips are cooking in red wine, you could make *Honey Cream.* With *Blue-Cheese Soufflé* in the oven, *Peaches in Marmalade Sauce* could be sizzling to spicy perfection at the same time.

A few extra minutes spent in preparing a dish can more than pay dividends when it comes to cooking. Cut vegetables into flowerets or slices. Cut meat into small strips, or use prepared chicken or turkey cutlets. Reducing the size of the food also reduces the cooking time.

## IN SIXTY MINUTES

An hour to produce a main dish or a complete meal gives you a little breathing space. It gives you time to prepare the dish and start it cooking. You can set the table, put away the groceries or do last-minute picking up before guests arrive. The recipes in this chapter do not require your full attention while they cook.

While the *Honeyed Lamb* is cooking to succulence, you have time to make a batch of crepes for *Crepe Gâteau with Cherry Sauce.* While the brown rice is simmering to a delicious nutty tenderness and the vegetables are steaming, there's plenty of time to whip up a dessert from one of the earlier sections. And while a tangy *Steamed Lemon & Raisin Pudding* is steaming away, you could be turning your attention to one of the quick broiled or pan-fried dishes.

## MENUS

When you are entertaining friends at lunch or dinner, it isn't always possible to spend as much time as you would like preparing and cooking the meal. Our menus make allowance for this. Each menu includes at least one course prepared ahead, reassuringly ready to serve or to finish at mealtime. In many cases this made-ahead dish is the first course. *Potato & Sausage Salad, Smoked Mackerel & Cream-Cheese Pate* or *Pears with Camembert Sauce* are examples of this. Many of these starters have other possibilities, too. With crudités and a basket of hot, crusty rolls or a French-bread loaf, they make a perfect light lunch or supper dish.

In all menu planning, balance is the key word—balance of the nutritional values, colors, textures and flavors. Fruit and vegetables feature strongly in many of the menus; they add bright colors, crunchy textures and important vitamins and minerals. Cost is another consideration in meal planning. If one dish calls for an expensive ingredient, balance your budget by planning less-expensive side dishes.

Whether you plan a low-cost family supper or a special dinner for your guests, the same principles apply. This careful selection of dishes allows you more time to relax with family and friends. Last-minute attention to details in the kitchen is minimized.

# Shrimp in Garlic Butter

1/2 cup butter or margarine
1 medium onion, finely chopped
3 garlic cloves, finely chopped
12 oz. peeled, uncooked shrimp, thawed, if frozen
2 tablespoons chopped fresh parsley
Pinch of salt
Freshly ground black pepper
Pinch of red (cayenne) pepper
1/4 teaspoon lemon juice

*To garnish:*
1 lemon, quartered

*Preparation and cooking time: 15 minutes*

**1.** Melt butter or margarine in a medium skillet over medium heat. Add onion; sauté 4 minutes, stirring once or twice. Stir in garlic and shrimp; reduce heat to low. Cook over low heat 5 minutes, stirring occasionally.
**2.** Stir in 1/2 of parsley, salt, black pepper, red pepper and lemon juice.
**3.** Garnish with remaining parsley and lemon wedges. Serve hot with crusty rolls. Makes 4 servings.

# Poached Trout

4 medium rainbow trout, ready to cook
1/2 cup white wine or cider
Few parsley sprigs
1 medium onion, sliced
2 lemon slices
6 peppercorns
1/2 cup whipping cream
Salt
Freshly ground pepper

*To garnish:*
Parsley sprigs

*Preparation and cooking time: 15 minutes*

**1.** In a skillet, combine trout, wine or cider, parsley, onion, lemon and peppercorns. Cover; simmer 10 minutes or until fish tests done. Place cooked trout on a platter; keep warm.
**2.** Strain cooking liquid into a small saucepan; bring to a boil. Immediately reduce heat; stir in cream. Heat until hot. Season sauce with salt and pepper.
**3.** Pour sauce over fish; garnish with parsley sprigs.
**4.** Serve with small new potatoes for a perfect accompaniment. Makes 4 servings.

# Smoked-Mackerel & Orange Kabobs

1 cup quick-cooking rice
Salt
1 tablespoon butter or margarine
Juice and peel of 1/2 orange
4 medium smoked-mackerel fillets or other
    smoked-fish fillets, skinned
1 teaspoon lemon juice
Freshly ground pepper
3 large oranges, peeled, sectioned
2 tablespoons blanched almonds

*To garnish:*
1 bunch watercress, trimmed

*Preparation and cooking time: 15 minutes*

**1.** Cook rice according to package directions. Stir in salt, butter or margarine, orange juice and orange peel. Keep rice mixture warm.
**2.** Preheat broiler. While rice is cooking, cut fish fillets crosswise into 1-inch strips; toss strips in lemon juice. Sprinkle with pepper. Thread mackerel strips and orange sections alternately on 4 skewers. Broil under preheated broiler 5 minutes, turning skewers once.
**3.** Place almonds on a dry baking sheet; toast under broiler 2 minutes, turning once.
**4.** Immediately before serving, stir toasted almonds into rice. Place skewers on rice; garnish with watercress. Makes 4 servings.

Top to bottom: Poached Trout, Boiled potatoes, Smoked-Mackerel & Orange Kabobs

# Pan-Fried Danish Egg & Bacon

6 bacon slices
4 large tomatoes, sliced
1/2 teaspoon Italian seasoning
1 teaspoon vegetable oil
1 tablespoon all-purpose flour
6 tablespoons milk
6 eggs
Salt
Freshly ground pepper
1 tablespoon butter or margarine

*To garnish:*
Parsley sprigs

*Preparation and cooking time: 10 minutes*

**1.** Preheat broiler. Place bacon on a broiler-pan rack. Broil under preheated broiler 2 minutes; turn slices.
**2.** Place tomatoes on rack with bacon; sprinkle tomato slices with 1/2 of Italian seasoning and oil. Broil 3 minutes. Keep warm.
**3.** While bacon and tomatoes are cooking, prepare eggs. Place flour in a medium bowl; stir in milk. Beat in eggs until blended. Stir in salt, pepper and remaining Italian seasoning.
**4.** Melt butter or margarine in a large skillet. Pour in egg mixture; cook over medium heat 4 to 5 minutes, lifting edges occasionally with a spatula.
**5.** When eggs are set, arrange broiled bacon in a wheel pattern on top with broiled tomatoes overlapping around edge. Garnish with parsley sprigs. Cut into quarters; serve hot. Makes 4 servings.

Pan-Fried Danish Egg & Bacon

Apple Stacks

## Apple Stacks

4 large cooking apples
1/4 cup honey
3/4 cup shredded Cheddar cheese (3 oz.)
1/2 small head lettuce, shredded
2 tablespoons walnut halves

*Preparation and cooking time: 15 minutes*

**1.** Preheat broiler. Line a broiler pan with foil.
**2.** Peel and core apples; cut each crosswise into 3 or 4 rings. Arrange rings close together on foil; spread with 1/2 of honey.
**3.** Broil under preheated broiler 3 minutes. Using a spatula, turn apple rings; spread with remaining honey. Broil 3 minutes. Sprinkle cheese over apples; broil 2 minutes.
**4.** Stack cooked slices into 4 apple shapes; see below. Place lettuce on 4 plates. Place apples on lettuce; garnish with walnut halves. Makes 4 servings.

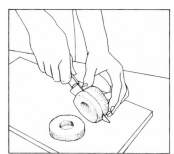
1/Cut apples crosswise into 3 or 4 slices.

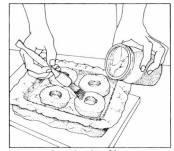
2/Spread with 1/2 of honey.

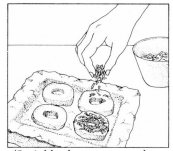
3/Sprinkle cheese over apples.

4/Stack cooked slices into 4 apple shapes.

## Spaghetti with Cream Sauce

12 oz. whole-wheat spaghetti
Salt
1/4 cup butter or margarine
6 oz. button mushrooms, sliced
2 to 3 tablespoons chopped fresh herbs
Freshly ground pepper
1/2 pint whipping cream (1 cup)
2 egg yolks
1/2 cup shredded sharp Cheddar cheese (2 oz.)

*Preparation and cooking time: 15 minutes*

**1.** Cook spaghetti in boiling salted water according to package directions until tender.
**2.** While spaghetti is cooking, prepare sauce. Melt butter or margarine in a medium skillet. Add mushrooms; sauté over medium heat 3 minutes. Stir in 2 tablespoons herbs, salt and pepper; cook 1 minute.
**3.** In a medium saucepan, heat cream over low heat; do not boil. Beat in egg yolks; stir in cheese, salt and pepper.
**4.** Drain spaghetti; return to pan. Stir in mushroom mixture. Turn pasta into a warm serving dish; pour cream sauce over spaghetti. Sprinkle with remaining herbs, if desired. Serve immediately. Makes 4 servings.

## Eggs with Blue-Cheese Mayonnaise

6 hard-cooked eggs
2/3 cup mayonnaise
1/2 cup crumbled Danish blue cheese (2 oz.)
1/4 cup soft farmer's cheese (2 oz.)
6 tablespoons whipping cream
Freshly ground pepper
1 small head lettuce
1 bunch watercress, trimmed
2 tablespoons chopped mint

*To garnish:*
2 tomatoes, quartered

*Preparation: 15 minutes*

**1.** Peel eggs; cut peeled eggs into halves.
**2.** In a small bowl, combine mayonnaise, cheeses and cream. Stir until blended; season with pepper.
**3.** Finely shred lettuce. In a medium bowl, combine shredded lettuce, watercress and mint.
**4.** Divide salad among 4 plates; arrange 3 egg halves on each plate, cut-sides down. Spoon mayonnaise mixture over eggs. Garnish with tomato wedges. Makes 4 servings.

# Ham Steaks with Cucumber Sauce

2 smoked-ham center slices, about 1 lb. total weight
1 teaspoon vegetable oil

*Cucumber Sauce:*
1 medium cucumber, peeled, diced
Salt
1-1/2 tablespoons butter or margarine
3 tablespoons all-purpose flour
1 cup milk
2 tablespoons whipping cream
1 tablespoon chopped chives
Ground white pepper
Pinch of red (cayenne) pepper

*Preparation and cooking time: 15 minutes*

**1.** Preheat broiler. Brush ham with oil; place on a broiler-pan rack. Broil under preheated broiler 4 to 5 minutes per side. While ham is cooking, prepare sauce.
**2.** To prepare sauce, in a medium saucepan, cook cucumber in boiling salted water 3 minutes; drain thoroughly. Pat dry with paper towels.
**3.** In a medium saucepan, melt butter or margarine; stir in flour. Cook over medium heat 1 minute, stirring constantly. Gradually stir in milk; bring sauce to a boil. Simmer 3 minutes. Stir cooked cucumber, cream and chives into sauce. Season with salt, white pepper and red pepper.
**4.** Cut broiled ham into serving pieces. Arrange on a serving plate; spoon a little sauce over ham to garnish. Serve remaining sauce separately.
**5.** Serve with small new potatoes and a green vegetable, such as broccoli spears. Makes 4 servings.

# Turkey in Sweet & Sour Sauce

1 lb. turkey breast
2 teaspoons cornstarch
2 tablespoons vegetable oil
1 tablespoon butter or margarine
4 oz. mushrooms, thinly sliced

*Sweet & Sour Sauce:*
6 tablespoons water
1-1/2 teaspoons cornstarch
1-1/2 tablespoons light-brown sugar
1-1/2 tablespoons honey
3 tablespoons red-wine vinegar
3 tablespoons tomato paste
3 tablespoons orange juice
3 tablespoons soy sauce

*To serve:*
About 2 cups hot cooked white rice

*Preparation and cooking time: 15 minutes*

**1.** Cut turkey into 5 (2-inch x 1/2-inch) strips. In a medium bowl, toss turkey strips with cornstarch.
**2.** Heat oil in a large skillet over medium heat. Add coated turkey strips; sauté 3 minutes. Remove from skillet with a slotted spoon; drain on paper towels. Melt butter or margarine in same skillet. Add mushrooms; sauté 2 minutes.
**3.** To prepare sauce, in a medium saucepan, combine water and cornstarch into a smooth paste. Stir in remaining ingredients. Bring sauce to a boil, stirring constantly. Simmer 1 minute; stir in drained turkey. Simmer 5 minutes.
**4.** Stir sautéed mushrooms into turkey mixture. Serve hot over rice. Makes 4 servings.

# Liver with Fresh Sage

1 lb. calves' liver, cut into thin slices
1-1/2 tablespoons all-purpose flour
Salt
Freshly ground pepper
1/2 teaspoon rubbed sage or 1 teaspoon chopped fresh sage
2 tablespoons butter or margarine
1 tablespoon vegetable oil
About 12 fresh sage leaves
1/2 cup condensed consommé
1 teaspoon lemon juice
Hot cooked rice

*To garnish:*
4 sage sprigs

*Preparation and cooking time: 15 minutes*

**1.** Cut liver slices into 1/2-inch strips. In a plastic bag, combine flour, salt, pepper and rubbed sage or chopped sage. Add liver strips to seasoned flour; toss to coat.
**2.** Heat butter or margarine and oil in a large skillet. Add coated liver; sauté over medium heat 2 minutes. Turn liver; add sage leaves. Cook 2 minutes. With a spatula, remove liver from skillet; discard sage leaves. Set liver aside; keep warm.
**3.** Add consommé and lemon juice to skillet. Increase heat; bring sauce quickly to a boil, stirring constantly. Season with salt and pepper.
**4.** Spoon rice into a serving dish; top with cooked liver. Pour sauce over liver. Garnish with sage sprigs. Makes 4 servings.

Clockwise from top left: Liver with Fresh Sage, Turkey in Sweet & Sour Sauce, Ham Steaks with Cucumber Sauce

# Steak with Anchovies

1 (1-1/2-lb.) beef-loin top sirloin steak
Freshly ground pepper
3 tablespoons butter or margarine, room temperature
1 tablespoon vegetable oil
1 tablespoon chopped fresh parsley
2 drops lemon juice
1 (2-oz.) can anchovy fillets, drained

*To garnish:*
Parsley sprigs
Tomato roses, box, opposite page

*Preparation and cooking time: 15 minutes*

**1.** Season steak with pepper.
**2.** Heat 1 tablespoon butter or margarine and oil in a large skillet over medium-high heat. Add steak; cook 2 minutes. Turn steak. Cook 2 minutes.
**3.** Reduce heat to medium; cook 1 to 3 minutes on each side or until steak is cooked to desired doneness.
**4.** While meat is cooking, in a small bowl, beat remaining butter or margarine, parsley, lemon juice and pepper until blended. Shape into a roll; freeze a few minutes.
**5.** To serve, cut steak into serving pieces. Arrange anchovy fillets on steak pieces. Immediately before serving, cut parsley-butter roll into 4 to 6 pieces; place parsley-butter pieces on steak. Garnish with parsley and tomato roses.
**6.** Serve with cooked spinach blended with sour cream and freshly grated nutmeg. Makes 4 to 6 servings.

Steak with Anchovies

# Rarebit with Mushrooms

4 large bread slices
1/4 cup butter or margarine
6 oz. mushrooms, sliced
1 tablespoon chopped fresh parsley
3 tablespoons all-purpose flour
1/2 cup dark ale or cider
2 teaspoons prepared mustard
2 cups shredded sharp Cheddar cheese (8 oz.)
2 eggs, slightly beaten
Salt
Freshly ground black pepper
Pinch of red (cayenne) pepper

*Preparation and cooking time: 15 minutes*

**1.** Preheat broiler. Toast bread in a toaster or broiler.
**2.** Melt 2 tablespoon butter or margarine over low heat. Add mushrooms; sauté 5 minutes. Stir in parsley; set aside.
**3.** Melt remaining butter or margarine in a medium saucepan over medium heat. Stir in flour; cook 1 minute, stirring constantly. Gradually stir in ale or cider; bring to a boil. Simmer 2 minutes. Remove pan from heat; stir in mustard, cheese and eggs. Season with salt, black pepper and red pepper. Stir until cheese melts.
**4.** Place toast in a 9-inch-square baking pan. Spoon mushrooms over toast; spoon cheese mixture over mushrooms. Broil under preheated broiler until brown and bubbling. Makes 4 servings.

## Variations

This melt-in-the-mouth savory is delicious with other quick-cooking foods, too. Substitute cooked ham slices or cooked shrimp for mushrooms. Or, serve rarebit with broiled bacon and tomatoes or with poached eggs.

# Sausage Rolls

8 precooked sausage links
8 bacon slices
16 prunes, pitted
4 pita-bread rounds, split, warmed

*Preparation and cooking time: 15 minutes*

**1.** Preheat broiler. Cut each sausage in half crosswise.
**2.** Stretch bacon slices on a work surface. Cut each slice in half crosswise.
**3.** Roll each sausage half and a prune in a bacon piece. Thread 4 rolls on a short skewer. Repeat with remaining rolls.
**4.** Place skewers on a broiler-pan rack. Broil under preheated broiler 5 to 6 minutes or until bacon is crisp, turning once.
**5.** Remove skewers; divide sausage rolls among pieces of pita. Serve hot. Makes 4 servings.

---

## Tomato Roses

Using a vegetable peeler, peel firm-skinned tomatoes in a single strip. Peel should have a little flesh on it. Loosely roll the peel as shown, making a rose. Add smooth parsley for leaves. Tomato roses enhance the appearance of cold platters and salads. Use the remaining tomato flesh as platter or salad ingredient.

---

Left to right: Banana & Rum Flambé, Raspberry Cream, Ginger
Soufflé Omelet, Fruity Yogurt Dessert

## Banana & Rum Flambé

**3 tablespoons butter or margarine**
**4 ripe bananas, peeled, halved lengthwise**
**1/3 cup packed light-brown sugar**
**2 tablespoons blanched almonds**
**2 tablespoons rum**

*To serve:*
**Whipped cream or ice cream**

*Preparation and cooking time: 10 minutes*

**1.** Melt butter or margarine in a shallow flameproof dish;
add bananas in 1 layer. Sprinkle with sugar and almonds.
**2.** Sauté bananas over medium heat 3 minutes; turn. Sauté
until golden brown.
**3.** In a small saucepan, warm rum. Pour over bananas;
carefully ignite rum. Serve while flaming. Serve with
whipped cream or ice cream. Makes 4 servings.

## Raspberry Cream

**1/2 pint whipping cream (1 cup)**
**1/3 cup sugar**
**1 tablespoon Marsala, if desired**
**2 egg whites**
**8 oz. fresh raspberries, or frozen raspberries, thawed**
**5 macaroons, broken into 4 pieces each**

*Preparation: 10 minutes, plus thawing if using frozen
raspberries*

**1.** In a medium bowl, whip cream until stiff peaks form.
Beat in sugar and Marsala, if desired.
**2.** In a medium bowl, beat egg whites until stiff but not
dry. Fold beaten egg whites into cream mixture.
**3.** Reserve a few berries to decorate. Just before serving,
stir raspberries and macaroons into cream mixture. Spoon
into 4 sherbet or wine glasses; decorate with reserved
fruit. Makes 4 servings.

# Ginger Soufflé Omelet

6 eggs, separated
3 tablespoons granulated sugar
2 tablespoons butter or margarine
2 tablespoons chopped stem ginger preserved in syrup
1/4 cup apricot jam
1 tablespoon powdered sugar, sifted

*Preparation and cooking time: 15 minutes*

**1.** In a medium bowl, beat egg yolks and granulated sugar until combined. In a medium bowl, beat egg whites until stiff but not dry. Fold beaten egg whites into egg-yolk mixture.
**2.** Melt butter or margarine in a large skillet over medium heat. Pour in egg mixture, spreading evenly over skillet bottom. Cook omelet about 3 minutes or until bottom is golden brown.
**3.** Preheat broiler. Stir stem ginger into jam.
**4.** Broil omelet under preheated broiler 2 minutes or until firm and golden brown on top. Spread with jam mixture; broil 1 minute.
**5.** Decorate top with sifted powdered sugar. Cut into wedges; serve immediately. Makes 4 servings.

# Fruity Yogurt Dessert

2 egg whites
2 tablespoons light-brown sugar
1 (8-oz.) carton peach or other fruit yogurt
1 large banana, peeled, chopped
1 teaspoon lemon juice
2 tablespoons mixed dried fruit
1 tablespoon chopped mixed candied fruit
2 tablespoons chopped nuts

*Preparation time: 10 minutes*

**1.** In a medium bowl, beat egg whites until soft peaks form. Beat in brown sugar until stiff and glossy. Fold in yogurt.
**2.** In a small bowl, toss banana in lemon juice. Fold banana, dried fruit and candied fruit into yogurt mixture.
**3.** Spoon mixture into 4 sherbet or wine glasses; sprinkle with nuts.
**4.** Refrigerate 15 to 30 minutes; this dessert needs to be eaten soon after making. Makes 4 servings.

# Melon, Pimento & Ham Salad

*Pimento Mayonnaise:*
1/2 cup mayonnaise
1 tablespoon dairy sour cream
2 canned pimentos, drained
1 tablespoon tomato paste
Salt
Freshly ground pepper

*Salad:*
8 oz. cooked ham, diced
4 oz. seedless green grapes
8 to 10 walnut halves
1/2 honeydew or other melon, chilled

*To garnish:*
Lettuce leaves

---

*Preparation: 30 minutes*

**1.** To prepare mayonnaise, in a blender or food processor fitted with a steel blade, process mayonnaise, sour cream, pimentos, tomato paste, salt and pepper until smooth.
**2.** In a medium bowl, combine Pimento Mayonnaise with ham, grapes and walnuts.
**3.** Discard seeds from melon; make melon balls, using a melon baller or teaspoon. Or, peel melon; cut into small cubes.
**4.** Arrange lettuce leaves in a serving dish. Place ham salad in center of lettuce; surround with a ring of melon balls or cubes. Makes 4 servings.

**Variation**
Substitute diced cooked chicken for ham. Chicken is excellent combined with Pimento Mayonnaise.

---

### Melon Bowl

For a special presentation, use a melon as a container. It looks especially attractive filled with fruit salad or frosty fruit sherbet decorated with mint sprigs.

To make a melon bowl, cut a slice from top of melon; scoop out and discard seeds. Remove part of melon pulp, leaving a thin wall. Use a teaspoon or a grapefruit knife with a curved blade to remove pulp. Cut zigzag points around top of melon. Use melon pulp as part of salad, if desired. Fill melon with fruit salad or sherbet.

---

# Skillet Pizza

1-1/2 cups self-rising flour
Freshly ground pepper
1/2 teaspoon Italian seasoning
1/4 cup water
1/4 cup olive oil
1/3 cup tomato sauce
2 medium tomatoes, peeled, sliced
1 tablespoon chopped fresh basil or parsley
4 oz. thinly sliced salami
12 pimento-stuffed olives, sliced
4 to 5 slices mozzarella cheese

---

*Preparation: 30 minutes*

**1.** Preheat broiler. In a medium bowl, combine flour, pepper and Italian seasoning. Stir in water and 2 tablespoons olive oil to form a soft dough.
**2.** On a lightly floured surface, knead dough until smooth. Roll out dough to a 9-inch circle.
**3.** Heat 1 tablespoon of remaining oil in a large skillet. Add dough circle; cook over medium heat 5 minutes. Remove from skillet. Add remaining 1 tablespoon oil to skillet. Return dough circle to pan; cook on other side 5 minutes.
**4.** When crust is golden brown on both sides, remove pan from heat. If skillet handle is not flameproof, transfer pizza crust to a baking sheet. Spread crust with tomato sauce; cover with sliced tomatoes. Sprinkle with basil or parsley.
**5.** Arrange salami slices, slightly overlapping, on tomatoes. Top with sliced olives. Arrange cheese slices in center of pizza.
**6.** Broil under preheated broiler 5 minutes or until cheese is melted. Cut into wedges; serve hot. Makes 2 servings.

**Variation**
**Seafood Pizza:** Cook pizza dough as directed above. Cover with tomato sauce, sliced tomatoes and chopped herbs. Substitute 1 (4-oz.) can drained shrimp and 1 (4-oz.) jar mussels or smoked oysters for salami. Sprinkle with freshly ground black pepper and a pinch of red (cayenne) pepper. Top with olives and cheese. Broil as directed above.

Top to bottom: Skillet Pizza, Melon, Pimento & Ham Salad

# Cottage-Cheese Salad & Muffins

*Muffins:*
2 cups all-purpose flour
2 tablespoons sugar
2-1/2 teaspoons baking powder
1 teaspoon salt
2 eggs
3/4 cup milk
3 tablespoons vegetable oil

*Salad:*
1 cup cream-style cottage cheese
1/2 pint dairy sour cream (1 cup)
1 cup finely diced radishes, cucumber or green onions
Salt
Freshly ground pepper
Lettuce leaves

*Preparation and cooking time: 30 minutes*

**1.** Preheat oven to 400F (205C). Grease a 12-cup muffin pan or line with paper baking cups.
**2.** In a large bowl, combine flour, sugar, baking powder and salt.
**3.** Beat eggs in a small bowl. Beat in milk and oil until well blended. Pour milk mixture into flour mixture; stir until flour is moistened. Batter will be lumpy. Spoon batter into prepared muffin cups.
**4.** Bake in preheated oven 20 to 25 minutes or until lightly browned. Remove muffins from pan immediately.
**5.** Prepare salad while muffins are baking. In a medium bowl, combine cottage cheese and sour cream. Stir in vegetables, salt and pepper.
**6.** Line individual serving dishes with lettuce. Spoon cottage-cheese mixture over lettuce; serve with hot muffins. Makes 4 servings.

**Variations**
**Whole-Wheat Muffins:** Substitute 1 cup all-purpose flour and 3/4 cup whole-wheat flour for all-purpose flour. Increase sugar to 1/4 cup and baking powder to 1 tablespoon.
**Herbed Muffins:** Add 2 teaspoons Italian seasoning and 1/4 teaspoon dry mustard to dry ingredients.

# Scrambled Eggs with Peppers

1 green bell pepper, halved
6 bread slices
8 eggs
2 teaspoons prepared mustard
Salt
Freshly ground pepper
1 tablespoon butter or margarine
1/2 (8-oz.) pkg. cream cheese, room temperature
2 tablespoons whipping cream

*Preparation and cooking time: 20 minutes*

**1.** Preheat broiler. Place pepper, cut-side down, on a broiler-pan rack. Broil under preheated broiler 4 to 5 minutes or until skin turns black and blisters. Cool broiled pepper; peel off skin. Cut peeled pepper lengthwise into thin strips.
**2.** Toast bread under broiler or in a toaster. Cut each slice into 4 triangles. Remove crusts, if desired.
**3.** In a medium bowl, beat eggs and mustard. Season with salt and pepper.
**4.** Melt butter or margarine in a large skillet over medium heat. Add egg mixture; stir 3 to 4 minutes or until eggs begin to set.
**5.** Stir in cheese; cook about 2 minutes or until mixture is softly set. Stir in cream.
**6.** Spoon egg mixture into a serving dish; arrange toast around edge. Crisscross pepper strips over top. Serve immediately. Makes 4 servings.

# Stir-Fried Chicken

4 chicken-breast halves, boneless
2 tablespoons cornstarch
3 tablespoons soy sauce
5 tablespoons vegetable oil
2 garlic cloves, finely chopped
4 green bell peppers, sliced
3 tablespoons blanched almonds
Salt
Freshly ground black pepper

*Preparation and cooking time: 25 minutes*

**1.** Cut chicken into small cubes. In a medium bowl, combine chicken cubes and cornstarch. Stir in 2 tablespoons soy sauce and 2 tablespoons oil.
**2.** In a large skillet, heat remaining oil. Add garlic, bell peppers and almonds. Stir-fry 3 minutes. Remove with a slotted spoon; keep warm.
**3.** Drain chicken; add to oil remaining in skillet. Stir-fry 4 to 5 minutes or until chicken is done.
**4.** Return bell-pepper mixture to skillet; stir in remaining soy sauce. Season with black pepper.
**5.** Serve hot over hot cooked noodles or rice. Makes 4 servings.

Top to bottom: Scrambled Eggs with Peppers, Stir-Fried Chicken

# Pork in Orange & Ginger Sauce

2 pork-loin tenderloins, about 1-1/2 lb. total weight
4 teaspoons all-purpose flour
Salt
Freshly ground pepper
1/4 teaspoon dried leaf thyme
2 tablespoons butter or margarine
2 oranges
2 tablespoons ginger-flavored brandy
1 teaspoon grated fresh gingerroot
1/4 cup whipping cream

*Preparation and cooking time: 30 minutes*

**1.** Cut pork into 1-inch slices. In a plastic bag, combine flour, salt, pepper and thyme.
**2.** Melt butter or margarine in a large skillet. Add pork; sauté over medium-high heat 2 minutes per side. Reduce heat to medium; cover pan with lid or foil. Cook 10 minutes, turning once.
**3.** Grate peel and squeeze juice from 1 orange. Cut remaining orange into 8 wedges for garnish.
**4.** With tongs, place pork on a serving dish; keep warm. Add 2 tablespoons orange juice and orange peel to skillet; stir in brandy and gingerroot. Season mixture with salt and pepper. Stir in cream; heat until hot. Do not boil.
**5.** Pour sauce over pork; garnish with orange wedges. Serve with hot cooked rice and a green salad. Makes 4 servings.

---

### Oranges and Lemons

To extract the last drop of juice from an orange or lemon, place fruit on a table. Using flat palm of your hand, roll it firmly backwards and forwards a few times. This releases juice and ensures that none is wasted. Let fruit reach room temperature before squeezing.

---

# Marinated Pork Chops

4 pork chops
2/3 cup beer or apple juice
3 medium onions, sliced
1 bay leaf
6 peppercorns
1 tablespoon molasses
1 tablespoon lemon juice
Freshly ground pepper
2 tablespoons vegetable oil

*Preparation and cooking time: 25 minutes, plus at least 2 hours marinating time*

**1.** Place chops, beer or apple juice, 1 sliced onion, bay leaf and peppercorns in a shallow dish. Cover and refrigerate at least 2 hours.
**2.** Preheat broiler. Remove chops from marinade; strain sauce into a medium saucepan. Bring sauce to a boil; boil 4 minutes or until mixture is reduced by 1/2.
**3.** Stir in molasses, lemon juice and pepper.
**4.** Brush 1 side of chops with sauce; broil under preheated broiler 4 to 5 minutes. Turn chops; brush other side with sauce. Broil 4 to 5 minutes or until pork is no longer pink.
**5.** Heat oil in a medium skillet over medium heat. Add remaining onions; sauté 2 minutes. Add remaining sauce; simmer 5 minutes.
**6.** To serve, spoon glazed onions over broiled chops. Makes 4 servings.

---

### Marinating

Here's a simple way to marinate meat and fish. Place meat or fish into a heavy plastic bag. Be sure to check bag for holes before using. Add marinade. Seal bag with a twist tie. Turn bag occasionally to distribute marinade. This method works well for marinating a piece of meat that is large or odd shaped, or for cubes of meat or fish that need to be turned frequently.

# Crispy-Coated Liver

**6 tablespoons butter or margarine**
**1 large onion, sliced into rings**
**1/4 cup all-purpose flour**
**Salt**
**Freshly ground pepper**
**1/2 teaspoon Italian seasoning**
**1 egg**
**1 tablespoon milk**
**1 lb. calves' liver, thinly sliced diagonally**
**3/4 cup regular rolled oats**
**1/2 cup medium sherry**
**1/2 cup chicken stock**

*To garnish:*
**Parsley sprigs**

*Preparation and cooking time: 25 minutes*

**1.** Melt 2 tablespoons butter or margarine in a large skillet over medium heat. Add onion; sauté 5 to 6 minutes, turning occasionally. Remove onion from skillet; keep warm.
**2.** In a shallow bowl, combine flour, salt, pepper and Italian seasoning. In a shallow bowl, beat egg and milk until combined. Pat liver dry with paper towels. Dip liver first into seasoned flour until coated on both sides, then dip into egg mixture. Finally, coat with oats, pressing in oats to coat evenly.
**3.** Melt remaining butter or margarine in skillet used for onions. Add coated liver; sauté over medium heat 3 minutes per side or until coating is crisp and brown. Liver should be slightly pink inside; pierce with point of a sharp knife to test.
**4.** Remove liver from pan with tongs; keep warm. Stir any remaining seasoned flour into fat remaining in skillet. Stir 1 minute. Gradually stir in sherry and stock; bring to a boil. Season with salt and pepper.
**5.** Arrange liver in a heated serving dish; scatter cooked onion over liver. Spoon sauce over liver and onion. Garnish with parsley. Makes 4 servings.

Crispy-Coated Liver

# Sole in Sweet & Sour Sauce

**4 sole fillets, about 6 oz. each**
**4 oz. mushrooms, sliced**
**1 red bell pepper, thinly sliced**
**2 tablespoons sliced blanched almonds**

*Sauce:*
**1 tablespoon cornstarch**
**1/4 cup orange juice**
**Grated peel of 1 orange**
**1 tablespoon light-brown sugar**
**1 tablespoon honey**
**1 tablespoon cider vinegar**
**1 tablespoon tomato paste**
**1 tablespoon soy sauce**
**1 tablespoon sweet sherry**
**1 tablespoon vegetable oil**
**1 teaspoon hot-pepper sauce**
**Salt**
**Freshly ground pepper**

*To garnish:*
**Lemon slices**
**Parsley sprigs**

*Preparation and cooking time: 20 minutes*

**1.** Cut 4 (12" x 8") foil pieces; brush centers with a little oil. Trim fish; arrange each fillet on an oiled foil piece. Scatter mushrooms, bell pepper and almonds over fish. Bring up sides of foil to make a dish shape.
**2.** To prepare sauce, in a medium bowl, combine cornstarch and orange juice. Stir in remaining sauce ingredients.
**3.** Pour sauce over fish. Fold and seal edges of foil firmly to make watertight packages. Place in a steamer or colander over boiling water; steam 20 minutes.
**4.** Serve fish in foil parcels, if desired. Or, carefully remove from package; place on individual plates. Garnish with lemon and parsley.
**5.** Serve with hot cooked rice or noodles. Makes 4 servings.

# Chicken Cutlets with Vegetable Kabobs

**6 tablespoons butter or margarine, room temperature**
**1 teaspoon paprika**
**1 teaspoon tomato paste**
**1/4 teaspoon Worcestershire sauce**
**Salt**
**Freshly ground black pepper**
**4 chicken cutlets**
**3 tablespoons vegetable oil**
**1 tablespoon red-wine vinegar**
**4 small zucchini, cut into 3/4-inch slices**
**4 oz. small mushrooms**
**1 red or yellow bell pepper, cut into 1-1/4-inch squares**

*Preparation and cooking time: 30 minutes*

**1.** In a small bowl, beat butter or margarine, paprika, tomato paste, Worcestershire sauce, salt and black pepper until combined.
**2.** Spread 1/2 of mixture on both sides of cutlets. Shape remaining butter or margarine mixture into 8 pats; refrigerate.
**3.** Preheat broiler. In a small bowl, combine oil and vinegar; season with salt and black pepper. Add zucchini, mushrooms and bell pepper; toss to coat. Drain vegetables; thread on 4 small skewers.
**4.** Place chicken breasts on a broiler-pan rack. Broil under preheated broiler 15 minutes. Turn chicken; place kabobs on rack with chicken. Broil 6 minutes, turning kabobs once. Baste kabobs with remaining oil-and-vinegar mixture.
**5.** Serve hot with 2 chilled butter pats on each chicken piece. Makes 4 servings.

# Trout with Apples

**4 large rainbow trout, ready to cook**
**Freshly ground pepper**
**1 tablespoon lemon juice**
**4 fresh rosemary sprigs or 2 teaspoons dried rosemary**
**1/4 cup butter or margarine**
**2 apples, cored, thickly sliced**

*To garnish:*
**1 lemon, quartered**

*Preparation and cooking time: 25 minutes*

**1.** Sprinkle inside each trout with pepper and lemon juice; place a rosemary sprig inside each trout. Or, sprinkle inside each trout with 1/2 of dried rosemary.
**2.** Melt butter or margarine in a large skillet over medium heat. Add trout; cook 6 minutes. Using spatulas, turn fish, taking care not to break skin. Add apples. Cook 6 to 8 minutes or until fish tests done and apples are golden brown, turning apples once. Transfer to a warm serving dish.
**3.** Serve fish surrounded by apples; garnish with lemon wedges. Makes 4 servings.

Sole in Sweet & Sour Sauce, Cooked spaghetti

# Peach Caramels

4 large ripe peaches, peeled, halved
2 teaspoons lemon juice
1 tablespoon ground almonds
2 to 3 drops almond extract
1 tablespoon sugar
3/4 cup whipping cream, whipped
2 tablespoons chopped blanched almonds, toasted

*Sauce:*
2/3 cup packed light-brown sugar
2 tablespoons butter or margarine
1 tablespoon milk

*Preparation and cooking time: 20 minutes*

**1.** In a medium bowl, toss peaches in lemon juice. Stir ground almonds, almond extract and sugar into whipped cream.
**2.** Fill peach cavities with almond cream, reserving a little for decoration. Sandwich peach halves together; arrange on a serving dish.
**3.** To prepare sauce, in a medium saucepan, combine brown sugar, butter or margarine and milk. Bring to a boil; simmer over low heat 7 minutes. Remove from heat; beat with a wooden spoon 1 minute or until sauce is smooth.
**4.** Slowly spoon sauce over peaches; do not cover completely.
**5.** When sauce has cooled, spoon or pipe remaining cream on peaches; top with toasted almonds. Makes 4 servings.

# Poached Pears with Chocolate Sauce

1-1/2 cups water
1/2 cup sugar
1/4 teaspoon vanilla extract
4 large ripe pears, peeled
4 oz. semisweet chocolate

*Preparation and cooking time: 20 to 25 minutes*

**1.** In a medium saucepan, combine water, sugar and vanilla; bring to a boil.
**2.** Add pears; poach pears over medium heat 10 minutes or until tender, turning occasionally. With a slotted spoon, carefully remove pears from poaching liquid; keep warm.
**3.** Break chocolate into pieces; add to poaching liquid. Stir until melted. Beat until smooth; simmer 10 minutes or until sauce is thick enough to coat a spoon.
**4.** Serve pears warm; serve sauce separately.
**5.** Or, refrigerate pears until chilled. Serve with hot or cold chocolate sauce and whipped cream. Makes 4 servings.

# Drop Scones with Blueberry Sauce

*Scones:*
3/4 cup all-purpose flour
2 teaspoons baking powder
Pinch of salt
1 egg, beaten
1/2 cup milk
Vegetable oil for cooking
2/3 cup dairy sour cream

*Blueberry Sauce:*
1 cup fresh or frozen blueberries
2 tablespoons blueberry jam or blackberry jam
1 teaspoon lemon juice
1 tablespoon sugar, if necessary

*Preparation and cooking time: 30 minutes*

**1.** Sift flour, baking powder and salt into a medium bowl. Stir in egg; gradually beat in milk. Beat until batter is smooth.
**2.** Lightly grease a heavy skillet with vegetable oil; place over medium heat. Drop batter, 1 tablespoon at a time, into hot skillet. Leave 2 to 3 inches between scones to allow spreading.
**3.** Cook over medium heat 2 to 3 minutes or until bubbles appear on surface. Turn; cook 2 to 3 minutes or until golden brown. Repeat with remaining batter. Keep warm.
**4.** To prepare sauce, combine blueberries, jam and lemon juice in a medium saucepan. Bring to a boil. Simmer 2 minutes. Add sugar, if necessary.
**5.** Place warm scones on a serving plate. Serve with sauce and sour cream separately. Makes 12 to 16 scones.

Clockwise from top left: Peach Caramels, Poached Pear with Chocolate Sauce, Drop Scones with Blueberry Sauce

# Broiled Chicken with Cheese

4 chicken-breast halves, boneless
1/4 cup vegetable oil
1 tablespoon lemon juice
1 teaspoon dried leaf thyme
Salt
Freshly ground pepper
4 oz. cooked ham, thinly sliced
2 oz. Swiss cheese, thinly sliced
2 large tomatoes, sliced

*Preparation and cooking time: 45 minutes*

**1.** Preheat broiler. Cut 4 (12-inch-square) foil pieces.
**2.** With a sharp knife, cut 3 slits in each chicken breast. Lay on foil.
**3.** In a small bowl, combine oil, lemon juice, thyme, salt and pepper.
**4.** Draw foil up around chicken. Pour oil mixture over chicken; carefully seal packages.
**5.** Cook chicken packages under preheated broiler, turning once, 35 minutes or until juices run clear when chicken is pierced with a skewer.
**6.** Carefully open packages; arrange ham, cheese and finally tomatoes on chicken breasts. Spoon cooking juices over tomatoes. Broil 3 to 4 minutes or until cheese is bubbling.
**7.** Serve with hot corn-on-the-cob, if desired. Makes 4 servings.

# Veal & Mushroom Rolls

4 veal cutlets, about 3 oz. each
6 tablespoons butter or margarine
2 oz. mushrooms, finely chopped
2 tablespoons raisins
1 tablespoon chopped fresh parsley
2 tablespoons shredded Cheddar cheese
Salt
Freshly ground pepper
2 teaspoons all-purpose flour
3/4 cup red wine

***To garnish:***
**Parsley sprigs**

*Preparation and cooking time: 45 minutes*

**1.** Pound cutlets with a meat mallet or rolling pin until flattened. Cut each cutlet in half.
**2.** Melt 2 tablespoons butter or margarine in a medium skillet. Add mushrooms; sauté 2 minutes. Cool slightly; stir in raisins, parsley, cheese, salt and pepper.
**3.** Divide filling among veal pieces; press firmly. Roll up veal; tie with kitchen string.
**4.** Melt remaining butter or margarine in a large skillet over medium heat. Add veal rolls; sauté about 8 minutes or until evenly browned, turning occasionally.
**5.** Remove veal rolls from skillet with tongs; keep warm. Stir flour into fat remaining in skillet; cook 1 minute. Gradually stir in wine; bring to a boil. Season with salt and pepper. Return veal rolls to skillet. Cover; simmer 10 minutes, turning once.
**6.** To serve, remove strings; garnish with parsley. Makes 4 servings.

Top to bottom: Broiled Chicken with Cheese, Veal & Mushroom Rolls

Left to right: Carrot & Corn Casserole, Bacon & Corn Chowder

## Carrot & Corn Casserole

1 lb. carrots, sliced
1 tablespoon butter or margarine
2 teaspoons honey
3 tablespoons chicken stock
Salt
Freshly ground pepper
1 (12-oz.) can whole-kernel corn, drained
1 tablespoon chopped fresh parsley

*Topping:*
3/4 cup whole-wheat flour
1/2 teaspoon salt
5 tablespoons butter or margarine
1/2 cup fresh bread crumbs
Pinch of ground ginger

*Preparation and cooking time: 40 minutes*

**1.** Preheat oven to 375F (190C). Grease a 1-1/2-quart casserole.
**2.** Place carrots in a medium saucepan; add enough water to almost cover. Cook over medium heat 10 minutes or until crisp-tender. Drain carrots; stir in butter or margarine, honey, chicken stock, salt and pepper.
**3.** Spread carrot mixture in greased casserole. Cover with corn; sprinkle with parsley.
**4.** To prepare topping, in a small bowl, combine flour and salt. With a pastry blender or 2 knives, cut in butter or margarine until mixture resembles coarse crumbs. Stir in bread crumbs and ginger. Sprinkle topping over vegetables.
**5.** Bake in preheated oven 20 minutes or until topping is crisp and brown. Serve hot. Makes 4 servings.

## Bacon & Corn Chowder

4 bacon slices, diced
1 medium onion, sliced
1 medium leek, sliced
2 celery stalks, sliced
2 medium carrots, thinly sliced
1 cup chicken stock
1-1/2 cups diced potatoes
1 (12-oz.) can whole-kernel corn, drained
1-1/2 cups milk
Salt
Freshly ground black pepper
Pinch of red (cayenne) pepper
6 tablespoons whipping cream

*To garnish:*
1 tablespoon chopped fresh parsley

*Preparation and cooking time: 45 minutes*

**1.** Sauté bacon in a medium saucepan over medium heat 3 minutes or until browned.
**2.** Stir in onion, leek, celery and carrots; cook 4 minutes.
**3.** Add stock; bring to a boil. Add potatoes; return to a boil. Cover pan; simmer 20 minutes.
**4.** Add corn and milk; heat to the simmering point. Simmer 3 minutes; season with salt, black pepper and red pepper.
**5.** Stir in cream; heat until hot.
**6.** Garnish with parsley. Serve hot with hot crusty rolls. Makes 4 servings.

# Cheese & Olive Puffs

2 cups shredded sharp Cheddar cheese (8 oz.)
2 eggs, separated
2 tablespoons beer
1/4 teaspoon salt
Freshly ground pepper
1/3 cup all-purpose flour
1 teaspoon baking powder
24 pimento-stuffed olives
Vegetable oil for deep-frying

*Salad:*
2 medium, firm tomatoes, sliced
2 green onions, sliced
1 tablespoon freshly chopped basil
5 tablespoons prepared French dressing

*Preparation and cooking time: 30 minutes, plus 30 minutes standing.*

1. In a medium bowl, beat cheese, egg yolks and beer until blended. Add salt and pepper.
2. Sift flour and baking powder; stir into cheese mixture.
3. In a medium bowl, beat egg whites until stiff but not dry; fold beaten egg whites into cheese mixture. Cover bowl; let stand 30 minutes.
4. To prepare salad, arrange tomato slices around edge of a serving plate; sprinkle with onions and basil. Pour French dressing over salad. Refrigerate until served.
5. Dust hands with flour; shape cheese mixture into 24 walnut-sized balls. Gently push 1 olive into center of each ball. Shape cheese mixture around olive until completely enclosed.
6. Heat oil to 375F (190C) in a deep saucepan or deep-fryer. Deep-fry, a few at a time, 2 to 3 minutes or until puffed and golden. Drain on paper towels. Repeat with remaining balls. Place balls in a small bowl; place bowl in center of salad. Serve immediately. Makes 4 servings of 6 puffs each.

Cheese & Olive Puffs

# Mixed-Vegetable Curry

1 small cauliflower, cut into flowerets
1-1/3 cups diced carrots
1-1/4 cups diced potatoes
Water
1-1/2 cups green peas
3 tablespoon butter or margarine
1 large onion, sliced
1 tablespoon curry powder
1 tablespoon all-purpose flour
Salt
2 tablespoons mango chutney
Water or chicken stock
2/3 cup half and half
2 tablespoons blanched almonds

*To garnish:*
4 hard-cooked eggs, cut into wedges
Pinch of paprika

*Preparation and cooking time: 40 minutes*

**1.** Steam cauliflower, carrots and potatoes over boiling water 6 minutes or until crisp-tender. Bring 1 cup water to a boil in a medium saucepan; add peas. Cook peas 5 minutes.
**2.** Drain vegetables, reserving cooking liquid from peas. Keep cooked vegetables warm.
**3.** Melt butter or margarine in a large saucepan. Add onion; sauté over low heat 5 minutes. Stir in curry powder, flour and salt; cook 1 minute. Stir in chutney.
**4.** Pour cooking liquid into a 2-cup measuring cup; add enough water or chicken stock to make 2 cups. Gradually stir into curry mixture; bring to a boil. Simmer 5 minutes; stir in half and half.
**5.** Stir in vegetables; heat until hot. Stir in almonds.
**6.** Serve hot; garnish with egg wedges and paprika. Serve with hot cooked rice. Makes 4 servings.

# Blue-Cheese Soufflé

Parmesan cheese or seasoned dry bread crumbs
2-1/2 tablespoons butter or margarine
3 tablespoons all-purpose flour
1 cup milk
Red (cayenne) pepper
Salt
Freshly ground black pepper
1 cup crumbled blue cheese or Roquefort cheese (4 oz.)
4 egg yolks
5 egg whites

*Preparation and cooking time: 45 minutes*

**1.** Preheat oven to 375F (190C). Heavily grease a 6-cup soufflé dish; sprinkle bottom and side with Parmesan cheese or bread crumbs. Shake out excess cheese or crumbs.
**2.** Melt butter or margarine in a medium saucepan. Stir in flour; cook over low heat 2 minutes. Gradually stir in milk; cook until thickened, stirring constantly. Stir in red pepper, salt and black pepper.
**3.** Stir in cheese. Cook over low heat 1 to 2 minutes or until cheese is melted.
**4.** Remove saucepan from heat; beat in egg yolks, 1 at a time, beating well after each addition.
**5.** Beat egg whites until stiff but not dry. Stir 2 tablespoons beaten egg whites into sauce. Fold in remaining egg whites. Spoon mixture into prepared soufflé dish.
**6.** Bake in preheated oven 30 to 35 minutes or until soufflé is firm and golden on top.
**7.** Serve immediately with sliced tomatoes and a tossed green salad. Makes 4 servings.

---

### Cooking Vegetables

Vegetables can be steamed or cooked in boiling water. Steaming has several advantages over cooking vegetables in boiling water. Fewer nutrients are lost in the cooking water; vegetables also have a better texture, color and flavor. Steaming is a good method to use when, as in the recipe for *Mixed-Vegetable Curry*, several vegetables are cooked at once. If the vegetables have different cooking times, add the shorter-cooking ones last.

Always have the water in the steamer or saucepan boiling before adding the vegetables. Leaving the lid off for a few minutes will make green vegetables brighter in color. Vegetable cooking liquid can be used for soup or sauce.

Buy an inexpensive collapsible steamer that fits any saucepan, or improvise with a colander or strainer and a large pan.

Salami & Pasta Salad

# Salami & Pasta Salad

1 cup whole-wheat macaroni
Salt
8 oz. new potatoes, scrubbed
1/4 cup prepared French dressing
3 green onions, sliced
1/4 cup walnut halves
1 tablespoon chopped chives
4 oz. salami, diced
4 oz. Swiss cheese, cubed, if desired
6 tablespoons dairy sour cream
1 teaspoon prepared mustard
Freshly ground pepper

*Preparation and cooking time: 45 minutes, including cooling*

1. Cook macaroni in boiling, salted water according to package directions until tender. Do not overcook. Drain well.
2. At same time, in another saucepan, cook potatoes in boiling, salted water 12 to 15 minutes or until tender. Do not overcook.
3. Drain potatoes; cool until they can be handled. Peel; cut into cubes.
4. While pasta and potatoes are still warm, in a medium bowl, combine with French dressing. Set aside to cool.
5. When pasta and potatoes are cool, stir in green onions; walnuts, reserving a few for garnish; chives; salami; and cheese, if desired.
6. In a small bowl, combine sour cream, mustard and pepper. Stir dressing into salad.
7. Arrange salad in a serving bowl; garnish with reserved walnuts.
8. Serve with chilled melon slices or cubes for a delightful contrast. Makes 4 servings.

# Marinated Sirloin Steak

1-1/2 lb. beef sirloin steak
1 medium onion, thinly sliced
1 garlic clove, crushed
2 tablespoons olive oil
1 tablespoon tomato paste
1 tablespoon soy sauce
1 teaspoon hot-pepper sauce
1 tablespoon dark-brown sugar
2 tablespoons thawed frozen orange-juice concentrate
Salt
1 (16-oz.) can tomatoes
1 tablespoon butter or margarine
4 oz. mushrooms, thinly sliced

*To garnish:*
1 tablespoon chopped fresh parsley

---

*Preparation and cooking time: 45 minutes, plus extra marinating, if possible*

**1.** Cut steak into 4 portions; remove any excess fat.
**2.** In a glass or stainless-steel bowl, combine onion, garlic, olive oil, tomato paste, soy sauce, hot-pepper sauce, sugar, orange juice and salt. Add steak pieces; turn to coat thoroughly. Let marinate a few minutes or a few hours, as time permits.
**3.** Place tomatoes in a large saucepan; add steak and marinade. Simmer, uncovered, over medium heat 20 to 25 minutes or until steak is tender and sauce has thickened. Spoon steak and sauce into a warm serving dish.
**4.** Melt butter or margarine in a small skillet over medium heat. Add mushrooms; sauté 3 to 4 minutes. Spoon over steak mixture. Garnish with parsley.
**5.** This is a hearty dish, full of flavor. Serve with boiled potatoes and a green vegetable, such as cabbage, lightly simmered in chicken stock and flavored with sesame or caraway seeds. Makes 4 servings.

**Variation**
When time is not as important, substitute a less-tender cut of meat for the steak. Substitute beef stew cubes or round steak. Cook 1-1/2 to 2 hours. Flavor is even better and meat is more tender if meat is marinated several hours before cooking. This makes a great informal party dish.

# Prune-Stuffed Pork Tenderloin

2 pork-loin tenderloins, about 1-1/2 lb. total weight
8 pitted prunes, halved
2 tablespoons raisins
1 tablespoon honey
1 tablespoon butter or margarine
1 teaspoon all-purpose flour
1 cup cider or apple juice
Salt
Freshly ground pepper

---

*Preparation and cooking time: 45 minutes*

**1.** Trim pork; cut each tenderloin lengthwise without cutting completely through.
**2.** Arrange prune halves along 1 side of each tenderloin. Cover prunes with 1 tablespoon raisins and honey. Close tenderloins over fruit. Secure with wooden picks or tie with kitchen string.
**3.** Melt butter or margarine in a medium skillet. Add stuffed tenderloins; sauté until brown. Remove from skillet; set aside.
**4.** Stir flour into fat remaining in skillet; cook 1 minute. Gradually stir in cider or apple juice; bring to a boil.
**5.** Season with salt and pepper; add remaining raisins. Return tenderloins to skillet. Cover with a lid or foil; simmer 30 minutes, turning once.
**6.** Serve with hot cooked rice and a green salad. Makes 4 servings.

1/Cut each tenderloin lengthwise without cutting completely through.

2/Cover prunes with 1 tablespoon raisins and honey.

3/Close tenderloins over fruit.

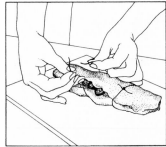
4/Secure with wooden picks or tie with kitchen string.

# Chicken Cutlets on Spinach

6 chicken cutlets
2 tablespoons vegetable oil
3 tablespoons butter or margarine
2 lb. fresh spinach
2/3 cup dairy sour cream
1 teaspoon lemon juice
Salt
Freshly ground pepper

*To garnish:*
1 lemon, quartered

*Preparation and cooking time: 45 minutes*

**1.** Roll each chicken cutlet; tie with kitchen string.
**2.** Heat oil and 1 tablespoon butter or margarine in a large skillet over medium-high heat. Add rolled cutlets; sauté 4 minutes, turning to brown evenly.
**3.** Reduce heat to low; cook about 10 minutes or until chicken is tender and golden brown.
**4.** While chicken is cooking, wash spinach; remove tough stems. Place washed spinach in a medium saucepan over medium heat. Cook spinach in water clinging to leaves 8 minutes or until tender.
**5.** Stir remaining butter or margarine, sour cream and lemon juice into cooked spinach. Season with salt and pepper. Stir over medium heat until spinach and cream makes a smooth thick puree.
**6.** Spoon spinach mixture into a serving dish; arrange cooked chicken rolls on spinach mixture. Garnish with lemon wedges.
**7.** Serve with boiled new potatoes. Makes 4 servings.

Prune-Stuffed Pork Tenderloin

Left to right: Pear & Ginger Sponge, Peaches in Marmalade Sauce, Fruit Bake

## Honey Cream

**3 eggs, separated**
**3 tablespoons honey**
**1/2 pint whipping cream (1 cup)**
**2 tablespoons medium sherry**
**2 tablespoons chopped nuts**

*Preparation and cooking time: 45 minutes, including cooling*

**1.** Combine egg yolks and honey in a medium heatproof bowl. Beat over a pan of hot water 5 minutes or until mixture is light and foamy. Remove bowl from pan; place in a larger bowl of cold water. Stir 2 minutes.
**2.** In a small bowl, whip cream until stiff peaks form. In a medium bowl, beat egg whites until stiff but not dry.
**3.** When egg-yolk mixture is cool, stir in sherry. Fold in whipped cream. Fold in beaten egg whites.
**4.** Spoon mixture into 4 sherbet or wine glasses; sprinkle with nuts. Refrigerate 20 to 30 minutes or until chilled. Makes 4 servings.

## Peaches in Marmalade Sauce

**4 large ripe peaches, halved**
**1/4 cup orange marmalade**
**3 tablespoons butter or margarine**
**1/4 teaspoon ground cinnamon**
**2 tablespoons blanched almonds**

***To serve:***
**Whipped cream**

*Preparation and cooking time: 45 minutes*

**1.** Preheat oven to 350F (175C). Arrange peach halves, cut-side up, in a shallow baking dish.
**2.** In a small saucepan, combine marmalade, butter or margarine and cinnamon. Stir over low heat until marmalade melts; pour over peaches. Sprinkle with nuts. Cover with foil.
**3.** Bake in preheated oven 35 minutes. Serve hot with whipped cream. Makes 4 servings.

### Variation
Substitute canned peach halves for fresh peaches. Drain canned peaches well before using.

# Fruit Bake

3 tart apples (about 1 lb.), peeled, thinly sliced
1/4 cup packed light-brown sugar
2 tablespoons orange juice
1/4 cup diced pitted dates
2 firm bananas, thickly sliced
1 teaspoon lemon juice

*Topping:*
1-1/2 cups all-purpose flour
1/4 teaspoon ground ginger
2 teaspoons baking powder
2 tablespoons butter or margarine
2/3 cup milk
Grated peel of 1 orange
1 teaspoon orange juice
Milk for brushing

*Preparation and cooking time: 45 minutes*

**1.** Preheat oven to 425F (220C). Place apples in a 1-quart casserole. Sprinkle with sugar. Pour orange juice over apples. Stir in dates.
**2.** Sprinkle bananas with lemon juice; place on top of apple mixture.
**3.** To prepare topping, sift flour, ginger and baking powder into a medium bowl. With a pastry blender or 2 knives, cut in butter or margarine until mixture resembles coarse crumbs.
**4.** Combine milk, orange peel and orange juice in a small bowl; stir into flour mixture until blended. Knead dough in bowl 10 strokes or until smooth.
**5.** On a lightly floured surface, roll out dough to 1/2 inch thick. Cut dough into 8 to 10 rounds with a floured round 2-inch cutter.
**6.** Arrange rounds over fruit. Brush tops with milk.
**7.** Bake in preheated oven 25 minutes or until topping is golden brown. Serve hot. Makes 4 servings.

# Pear & Ginger Sponge

1 lb. very firm pears, peeled, sliced
1/4 cup packed light-brown sugar
1/2 teaspoon ground ginger
2 pieces stem ginger preserved in syrup, thinly sliced

*Sponge Topping:*
1/4 cup butter or margarine, room temperature
1 cup all-purpose flour, sifted
1/4 cup packed light-brown sugar
1-1/2 teaspoons baking powder
1 teaspoon ground ginger
1 egg, beaten
1/3 cup milk

*To serve:*
Vanilla custard sauce or sweetened whipped cream

*Preparation and cooking time: 45 minutes*

**1.** Preheat oven to 400F (205C). Grease an 8-inch cake pan or 1-1/2-quart baking dish. Arrange pear slices in bottom of greased pan or dish. Combine sugar, ground ginger and stem ginger in a small bowl; sprinkle over pears.
**2.** To prepare sponge, beat butter or margarine, flour, sugar, baking powder, ginger, egg and milk in a large bowl at low speed until blended. Increase speed to high; beat 2 minutes. Spread batter evenly over pears.
**3.** Bake in preheated oven 30 minutes or until cake tester inserted in center of cake comes out clean. Serve hot with custard sauce or sweetened whipped cream. Makes 4 servings.

# Brown Rice with Crisp Vegetables

2 tablespoons olive oil
1 medium onion, sliced
1 garlic clove, crushed
1-1/2 cups uncooked long-grain brown rice
3-3/4 cups hot chicken stock
Salt
Freshly ground pepper
1 small cauliflower, cut into small flowerets
2 cups diced carrots
2 leeks, sliced
1 cup green peas
2 tablespoons butter or margarine
1 cup shredded Cheddar cheese (4 oz.)
1 tablespoon chopped fresh mint
1 tablespoon chopped fresh parsley

*To serve:*
Grated Parmesan cheese

*Preparation and cooking time: 1 hour*

1. Heat olive oil over medium heat in a medium saucepan. Add onion and garlic; sauté 2 minutes, stirring once or twice. Stir in rice; cook 1 minute.
2. Stir in stock, salt and pepper; bring to a boil. Cover pan; reduce heat. Simmer 40 minutes. Rice should be tender and all stock absorbed.
3. While rice is cooking, steam cauliflower, carrots, leeks and peas 6 to 8 minutes or until crisp-tender. Do not overcook.
4. Melt butter or margarine in a large skillet. Add steamed vegetables; sauté, stirring frequently, about 4 minutes or until glazed but not brown.
5. Stir glazed vegetables, Cheddar cheese and mint into cooked rice. Garnish with parsley; serve immediately. Serve Parmesan cheese separately.
6. Serve with French bread spread with garlic butter, wrapped in foil and then baked in a 350F (175C) oven 15 minutes. Makes 4 servings.

### Variation
**White Rice with Crisp Vegetables:** Substitute long-grain white rice for brown rice. Reduce chicken stock to 3 cups. Cook about 20 minutes.

# Lentil & Watercress Patties

3 tablespoons vegetable oil
1 large onion, finely chopped
1 garlic clove, crushed
1 cup plus 2 tablespoons lentils (8 oz.), washed, drained
2 cups chicken stock
Few parsley sprigs
2 tablespoons tomato paste
1 cup chopped blanched almonds
1 bunch watercress, finely chopped
1 tablespoon chopped fresh mint
Salt
Freshly ground pepper
2 tablespoons all-purpose flour
Vegetable oil for frying

*Preparation and cooking time: 1 hour*

1. Heat 3 tablespoons oil in a medium saucepan over medium heat. Add onion and garlic; sauté 2 minutes, stirring once or twice. Stir in lentils until coated with oil.
2. Stir in stock and parsley; bring to a boil. Reduce heat; cover saucepan. Simmer 40 minutes or until lentils are soft and stock is completely absorbed. Remove from heat; discard parsley.
3. Beat lentils with a wooden spoon until blended; beat in tomato paste, almonds, watercress and mint. Season with salt and pepper.
4. Shape mixture into 12 flat patties. Coat with flour.
5. Heat oil in a large skillet over medium heat. Add enough patties to fill skillet; sauté about 5 minutes per side or until crisp. Drain on paper towels. Repeat with remaining patties. Serve hot or cold.
6. Serve hot patties with creamy mashed potatoes and a green vegetable. Serve cold patties with a salad for an unusual picnic snack. Makes 4 servings.

Top to bottom: White Rice with Crisp Vegetables, Lentil & Watercress Patties

# Shrimp Mille-Feuille

**1/2 (17-1/2-oz) pkg. puff pastry, thawed, if frozen**

*Filling:*
**6 tablespoons butter or margarine, room temperature**
**1/4 cup all-purpose flour**
**1 cup milk**
**8 oz. shrimp, cooked, peeled, deveined**
**1 teaspoon lemon juice**
**Few drops of hot-pepper sauce**
**Salt**
**Freshly ground white pepper**
**Pinch of red (cayenne) pepper**
**3/4 cup whipping cream, whipped**

*To garnish:*
**2 tablespoons canned condensed consommé**
**2 tablespoons dairy sour cream**
**4 mushrooms, thinly sliced**

---

*Preparation and cooking time: 1 hour, including cooling*

**1.** Preheat oven to 425F (220C). Divide pastry into 3 equal pieces. Roll each piece to a 10" x 5" rectangle. Rinse a baking sheet with cold water; place pastry rectangles on damp baking sheet. Prick pastry with a fork.

**2.** Bake pastry in preheated oven 12 to 15 minutes or until puffed and golden brown. Cool on a wire rack.

**3.** Prepare filling while pastry is cooking. Melt 3 tablespoons butter or margarine in a medium saucepan over medium heat. Stir in flour; cook 1 minute. Gradually stir in milk. Bring to a boil; simmer 3 minutes, stirring constantly. Remove from heat; place saucepan in a bowl of cold water. Let cool.

**4.** In a medium bowl, beat remaining butter or margarine until softened. Stir in shrimp, reserving 6 for garnish. Fold shrimp mixture into cooled sauce. If sauce is not completely cool, the butter or margarine will melt. Stir in lemon juice, hot-pepper sauce, salt, white pepper, red pepper and whipped cream.

**5.** Sandwich pastry layers together with shrimp filling.

**6.** In a small bowl, beat consommé and sour cream until smooth. Spread over top of filled pastry; arrange sliced mushrooms and reserved shrimp down center of sour-cream topping. Refrigerate until served. Do not assemble more than 1 hour before serving to prevent a soggy pastry. Makes 4 servings.

Shrimp Mille-Feuille

# Chicken Goulash

6 to 8 chicken-breast halves, skinned
Salt
Freshly ground pepper
4 teaspoons paprika
2 tablespoons vegetable oil
2 medium onions, thinly sliced
2 green bell peppers, sliced
3 tablespoons tomato paste
1-1/4 cups plain yogurt
6 oz. mushrooms, sliced

*To garnish:*
Parsley sprigs

*Preparation and cooking time: 1 hour*

**1.** Sprinkle chicken with salt, pepper and 1 teaspoon paprika. Heat oil in a large skillet over medium heat. Add chicken; sauté 3 minutes per side.
**2.** Remove chicken with tongs; set aside. Add onions and bell peppers; sauté 4 minutes, stirring once or twice. Stir in remaining paprika, tomato paste and yogurt.
**3.** Return chicken to skillet; bring sauce to a boil. Reduce heat; cover. Simmer 35 minutes, turning chicken once.
**4.** Add mushrooms; cook 10 minutes or until chicken is tender. Garnish with parsley sprigs.
**5.** Serve with hot cooked rice or noodles tossed with butter or margarine and 1 teaspoon caraway seeds. Makes 4 servings.

# Beef Strips in Red Wine

3 tablespoons butter or margarine
1 tablespoon vegetable oil
4 oz. mushrooms, sliced
1 medium onion, chopped
2 tablespoons all-purpose flour
Salt
Freshly ground pepper
1/2 teaspoon Italian seasoning
1-1/2 lb. beef round steak, cut into thin strips
1 garlic clove, crushed
1 tablespoon port
1/2 cup beef stock
1/2 cup red wine

*Preparation and cooking time: 50 minutes*

**1.** Heat butter or margarine and oil in a large skillet over medium heat. Add mushrooms; sauté 2 minutes. Remove cooked mushrooms with a slotted spoon; set aside. Add onion to skillet; sauté 4 minutes, stirring once or twice. Remove cooked onions with a slotted spoon; set aside.
**2.** In a plastic bag, combine flour, salt, pepper and Italian seasoning. Add beef, shake to coat. Shake excess flour from beef; add to fat remaining in skillet. Sauté 5 minutes, stirring frequently.
**3.** Stir in cooked mushrooms, cooked onions, garlic, port, stock and wine; bring to a boil.
**4.** Reduce heat to low. Cover pan; simmer 25 minutes.
**5.** Serve with boiled new potatoes and a green vegetable. Makes 4 servings.

# Tandoori-Style Chicken

4 chicken legs with thighs attached, skinned
1 teaspoon salt
1 garlic clove, crushed
1 tablespoon tomato paste
1 tablespoon curry powder
2 bay leaves, finely crumbled
Juice of 1/2 lemon
1 (16-oz.) carton plain yogurt (2 cups)
6 tablespoons butter or margarine, melted
2 tablespoons paprika

*To garnish:*
1 lemon, quartered
Watercress sprigs

*Preparation and cooking time: 1 hour*

**1.** Preheat oven to 400F (205C). Slash chicken in several places with a sharp knife. Place chicken pieces in a casserole large enough to hold chicken in 1 layer.
**2.** In a small bowl, combine salt, garlic, tomato paste, curry powder, bay leaves and lemon juice; stir in yogurt. Pour yogurt mixture over chicken. Top with melted butter or margarine. Cover casserole.
**3.** Bake in preheated oven 50 minutes or until chicken is tender.
**4.** Pour off sauce; keep warm. Sprinkle paprika over baked chicken. Bake, uncovered, 5 minutes. Garnish with lemon and watercress. Serve sauce separately.
**5.** Serve with side dishes of bell-pepper rings, thin onion rings, banana slices dipped in lemon juice and rolled in shredded coconut and orange slices. Makes 4 servings.

### Variation
To improve flavor, pour yogurt mixture over chicken; cover and refrigerate overnight. Add melted butter or margarine immediately before baking chicken.

Clockwise from top left: Tandoori-Style Chicken with coconut-coated banana slices, bell-pepper rings and onion rings; Beef Strips in Red Wine; Chicken Goulash

# Beef Fricassee

1-1/2 lb. beef stew cubes, cut into 1-inch cubes
3 tablespoons butter or margarine
1 tablespoon vegetable oil
2 medium onions, thinly sliced
1 garlic clove, crushed
Grated peel of 1 lemon
1 tablespoon all-purpose flour
1 cup hot chicken stock
Salt
Freshly ground pepper
3 egg yolks
3 tablespoons lemon juice
1 tablespoon chopped fresh parsley

*Preparation and cooking time: 1 hour*

**1.** Trim off and discard any fat from beef.
**2.** In a large skillet, heat butter or margarine and oil over medium heat. Add onions and garlic; sauté 3 to 4 minutes. Remove with a slotted spoon.
**3.** Add beef to fat remaining in skillet; sauté until brown. Stir in lemon peel and flour; cook 1 minute.
**4.** Gradually stir in stock; season with salt and pepper. Return onions and garlic to skillet; bring to a boil. Reduce heat; cover. Simmer 45 minutes or until beef is tender.
**5.** In a small bowl, beat egg yolks and lemon juice; stir in 1/4 cup of stock mixture. Pour egg mixture into skillet. Stir well; heat about 4 minutes. Do not boil.
**6.** Garnish with parsley. Serve hot. Serve with broccoli, cauliflower or Brussels sprouts and new potatoes. Makes 4 servings.

# Honeyed Lamb

1-1/2 lb. lamb stew cubes, cut into 1-inch cubes
2 medium onions, sliced
2 medium carrots, sliced
2 celery stalks, thinly sliced
1/2 teaspoon dried leaf thyme
1/2 cup cider or apple juice
2 tablespoons honey
1 tablespoon red-wine vinegar
Salt
Freshly ground pepper
1/2 tablespoon butter or margarine, room temperature
1 teaspoon all-purpose flour

*Preparation and cooking time: 1 hour*

**1.** Preheat oven to 400F (205C). Trim off and discard any fat from lamb. Place onions, carrots and celery into a 2-quart casserole; top with lamb cubes. Sprinkle with thyme.
**2.** In a small saucepan, heat cider or apple juice and honey. When honey dissolves, stir in vinegar; pour over lamb and vegetables. Season with salt and pepper. Cover casserole.
**3.** Bake in preheated oven 45 minutes or until lamb is tender.
**4.** In a small bowl, beat butter and flour to a smooth paste. Stir paste into cooking juices in casserole; bake 5 minutes.
**5.** Serve with mashed potatoes. Makes 4 servings.

# Pork Chops in Normandy Sauce

4 pork chops
2 tablespoons butter or margarine
1 tablespoon vegetable oil
2 medium onions, sliced
1 garlic clove, crushed
2 medium cooking apples, peeled, thickly sliced
1/2 teaspoon dried leaf thyme
1 cup cider or apple juice
1 tablespoon honey
1 tablespoon brandy, if desired
Salt
Freshly ground pepper
1/4 cup whipping cream

*Preparation and cooking time: 1 hour*

**1.** Preheat oven to 375F (190C). Trim excess fat from chops. Heat 1 tablespoon butter or margarine and oil in a large skillet over medium heat. Add chops; sauté 3 minutes per side. Transfer to a shallow casserole large enough to hold chops in 1 layer.
**2.** Add remaining butter or margarine to skillet. Add onions and garlic; sauté over medium heat 3 minutes. Transfer to casserole with a slotted spoon.
**3.** Add apple slices; sauté 1 minute per side. Transfer to casserole with a slotted spoon.
**4.** Add thyme, cider or apple juice, honey and brandy, if desired to skillet. Season with salt and pepper. Stir until honey melts. Pour mixture over pork chops. Cover casserole.
**5.** Bake in preheated oven 35 minutes or until chops are tender. Skim fat from surface; stir in cream. Serve hot.
**6.** Serve with fresh vegetables, such as tiny carrots, whole green beans or green peas. Makes 4 servings.

# Meatballs in Horseradish Sauce

1 bread slice
1/4 cup water
1 lb. lean ground beef
Salt
Freshly ground pepper
1/4 teaspoon dry mustard
1 egg, beaten
3 tablespoons butter or margarine

*Sauce:*
2 teaspoons all-purpose flour
1 cup chicken stock
2 tablespoons prepared horseradish sauce
1/2 teaspoon lemon juice

*To garnish:*
1 tablespoon chopped fresh parsley

*Preparation and cooking time: 50 minutes*

**1.** In a small bowl, soak bread in water a few minutes; squeeze dry.
**2.** In a medium bowl, combine soaked bread and ground beef, mashing it vigorously with a wooden spoon until it forms a paste. Beat in salt, pepper, dry mustard and egg. Or, place all ingredients in a food processor fitted with a steel blade; process until blended.
**3.** With floured hands, shape meat mixture into balls about 1-1/2 inches in diameter. Melt butter or margarine in a large skillet. Add meatballs; sauté 6 to 8 minutes or until brown and crisp, turning frequently. Remove meatballs from skillet with a slotted spoon; drain on paper towels.
**4.** To prepare sauce, stir flour into fat remaining in skillet; cook 1 minute. Gradually stir in stock. Bring to a boil; stir in horseradish sauce and lemon juice. Season with salt and pepper.
**5.** Return meatballs to pan. Cover and simmer over low heat 3 minutes.
**6.** Garnish with parsley; serve hot. Makes 4 servings.

Left to right: Beef Fricassee, Meatballs in Horseradish Sauce

# Orange Bread & Butter Pudding

1/4 cup butter or margarine, room temperature
6 thin bread slices, crusts removed
Grated peel of 2 oranges
1/3 cup raisins
2 eggs, separated
2-1/2 cups milk
3 tablespoons sugar
1/4 teaspoon ground cinnamon
1/2 teaspoon vanilla extract

*To decorate:*
1 orange, thinly sliced
2 tablespoons red-currant jelly

*To serve:*
1 cup sweetened whipped cream

---

*Preparation and cooking time: 1 hour*

Clockwise from left: Orange Bread & Butter Pudding, Steamed
Lemon & Raisin Pudding, Crepe Gâteau with Cherry Sauce

**1.** Preheat oven to 375F (190C). Grease a 1-quart baking dish.
**2.** Spread butter or margarine on bread; cut each slice into 4 triangles. Arrange triangles on bottom of greased baking dish. Sprinkle with grated orange peel and raisins.
**3.** In a medium bowl, beat egg yolks, milk, sugar, cinnamon and vanilla until blended. In a medium bowl, beat egg whites until stiff but not dry. Fold beaten egg whites into milk mixture; pour over bread.
**4.** Bake in preheated oven 40 to 45 minutes or until pudding has risen and is golden brown.
**5.** Arrange orange slices on top of pudding. Spoon jelly over orange slices. Serve pudding hot with sweetened whipped cream. Makes 4 servings.

# Crepe Gâteau with Cherry Sauce

1-1/4 cups all-purpose flour
1/4 cup sugar
1/4 teaspoon salt
3 eggs
1-1/2 cups milk
1/3 cup unsalted butter or margarine, melted
Butter or margarine for cooking crepes

*Cherry Sauce:*
1 cup grape juice
1 cup water
2 tablespoons honey
1 tablespoon lemon juice
1 lb. fresh or frozen dark sweet cherries, pitted
1/4 cup cornstarch

*To serve:*
Sweetened whipped cream, if desired

*Preparation and cooking time: 45 minutes, plus 1 hour standing*

1. Place flour, sugar, salt, eggs and milk in a blender or food processor fitted with a steel blade; process until smooth, scraping down sides as necessary. With motor running, pour melted butter slowly into batter; process until combined. Pour batter into a large measuring cup or small pitcher. Cover and refrigerate 1 hour.
2. To prepare sauce, combine grape juice, water, honey and lemon juice in a medium saucepan. Add cherries; bring to a boil. Simmer 10 minutes or until cherries are softened.
3. Remove cherries with a slotted spoon; set aside. Pour liquid into a 2-cup measuring cup; add enough water to make 2 cups. In a small bowl, stir enough liquid into cornstarch to make a smooth paste. Pour liquid mixture into saucepan; stir in cornstarch mixture. Stir until blended. Cook over medium heat until sauce boils. Boil 2 minutes or until sauce clears and thickens, stirring constantly. Return cherries to sauce; set aside.
4. To cook crepes, melt 1 tablespoon butter or margarine in a 6- or 7-inch skillet or crepe pan. Pour in just enough batter to cover bottom of pan in a thin layer. Cook over medium heat 1-1/2 minutes or until small bubbles begin to form on surface of crepe. Turn crepe; cook 1-1/2 minutes. Remove to a flat plate; repeat process with remaining batter. Add additional butter or margarine to skillet as necessary.
5. Gently reheat sauce. Line up 4 serving plates. Place 1 crepe on each plate. Spoon a little sauce over each crepe. Repeat with 3 more crepes and more sauce on each plate, making a stack of 4 crepes with sauce between each layer.
6. Serve warm with remaining sauce on the side and sweetened whipped cream, if desired.

### Variation
Substitute 1 (17-ounce) can pitted dark sweet cherries for fresh cherries. Use cherry juice instead of grape juice, adding as much water as necessary. Do not add cherries to sauce in step 2, but add them at the end of step 3. There will be fewer cherries in the sauce, but it will still be delicious.

# Steamed Lemon & Raisin Puddings

3/4 cup all-purpose flour
1-1/2 teaspoons baking powder
1/2 cup sugar
1/2 cup butter or margarine, room temperature
2 eggs
Grated peel of 2 lemons
3 tablespoons lemon juice
2/3 cup raisins

*Sauce:*
1/4 cup honey
Grated peel of 2 lemons
1/4 cup lemon juice
2 tablespoons water
3 tablespoons raisins
1 tablespoon dark rum or brandy, if desired

*To decorate:*
Lemon slices

*Preparation and cooking time: 1 hour*

1. Grease 6 (5-ounce) dariole molds or ramekins. Sift flour and baking powder into a medium bowl. Add sugar, butter or margarine, eggs, lemon peel and lemon juice; beat until blended and smooth. Stir in raisins.
2. Spoon mixture into greased molds or ramekins. Cover tops with greased foil. Place molds on a trivet in a large saucepan. Add enough boiling water to come halfway up sides of molds. Bring to a boil. Cover; reduce heat until water simmers. Simmer 40 to 45 minutes, adding more water as necessary to maintain water level.
3. To prepare sauce, combine honey, lemon peel, lemon juice, water, raisins and rum or brandy, if desired, in a small saucepan. Cook over low heat 5 to 6 minutes, stirring constantly.
4. Run tip of a knife around inside edge of each mold; invert on a serving plate. Remove molds. Spoon a little sauce over puddings. Serve remaining sauce separately. Decorate with lemon slices. Makes 6 servings.

## Pork Chops with Marjoram Sauce

2 tablespoons butter or margarine
1 tablespoon vegetable oil
4 large pork chops
1 medium onion, finely chopped
1 garlic clove, finely chopped
3 tablespoons chicken stock
3 tablespoons dry vermouth
1 tablespoon chopped fresh marjoram or 1 teaspoon
   dried leaf marjoram
Salt
Freshly ground pepper
1/4 cup whipping cream

*Preparation and cooking time: 1 hour*

**1.** Heat butter or margarine and oil in a flameproof casserole over medium heat. Add pork chops; sauté 4 minutes per side. Remove chops with tongs; keep warm.
**2.** Add onion and garlic to fat remaining in casserole. Sauté 3 minutes, stirring occasionally; stir in stock and vermouth. Return chops to casserole; add marjoram, salt and pepper.
**3.** Bring to a boil. Cover; reduce heat. Simmer 30 minutes or until pork chops are tender and no longer pink.
**4.** Increase heat; bring to a boil again. Boil until liquid is slightly reduced. Stir in cream; heat through. Makes 4 servings.

## Raspberries in Melba Sauce

1 lb. raspberries, fresh or thawed frozen
*Sauce:*
12 oz. raspberries, fresh or thawed frozen
1 teaspoon lemon juice
1 cup powdered sugar, sifted

*To serve:*
1/4 teaspoon ground cinnamon
1/4 cup powdered sugar, sifted
2/3 cup whipping cream, whipped
1 egg white, stiffly beaten

*Preparation time: 20 minutes, plus thawing time for frozen raspberries*

**1.** Place 1 pound raspberries in a serving dish.
**2.** To prepare sauce, press 12 ounces raspberries through a sieve into a medium bowl. Stir lemon juice and 1 cup powdered sugar into puree. Pour over whole raspberries; gently stir to combine. Cover bowl and refrigerate until served.
**3.** To serve, stir cinnamon and 1/4 cup powdered sugar into whipped cream; fold in beaten egg white. Serve separately with raspberries. Make topping immediately before serving. Makes 4 servings.

## Smoked-Mackerel & Cream-Cheese Pâté

1/2 cup butter or margarine, room temperature
2 (3-oz.) pkgs. cream cheese, room temperature
12 oz. smoked mackerel or other
   smoked fish, skinned, flaked
2 teaspoons lemon juice
1 tablespoon chopped chives
Freshly ground pepper

*To garnish:*
4 small bay leaves

*Preparation time: 20 minutes*

**1.** In a medium bowl, cream 6 tablespoons butter or margarine and cream cheese. Stir in fish, lemon juice, chives and pepper. Beat until mixture is smooth.
**2.** Divide pâté among 4 individual ramekin dishes; smooth tops. Melt remaining butter or margarine in a small saucepan. Pour melted butter or margarine over pâté. Tip dishes to form a thin, even layer. Garnish each pâté with a bay leaf.
**3.** Cover with plastic wrap; refrigerate up to 2 days. Makes 4 servings.

Clockwise from left: Pork Chop with Marjoram Sauce, Raspberries in Melba Sauce, Smoked-Mackerel & Cream-Cheese Pâté

*Green Beans Greek-Style*
*Beef Paprika with Rice*
*Steamed Spinach*
*Oranges in Raisin Syrup*

# Green Beans Greek-Style

1/4 cup olive oil
1 garlic clove, finely chopped
1 medium onion, finely chopped
1/2 cup dry white wine
1/2 cup water
1 tablespoon tomato paste
8 coriander seeds, crushed
Fresh parsley
Salt
Freshly ground pepper
1 lb. green beans, trimmed
4 oz. button mushrooms, sliced

---

*Preparation and cooking time: 1 hour*

**1.** Heat olive oil in a large saucepan over low heat. Add garlic and onion; sauté 10 minutes, stirring frequently. Add wine, water, tomato paste, coriander, parsley, salt and pepper. Bring to a boil. Cover; simmer 5 minutes.
**2.** Add beans and mushrooms. Cover; simmer 20 to 25 minutes or until beans are crisp-tender.
**3.** Spoon mixture into a serving dish; cool. Cover and refrigerate until served.
**4.** Serve chilled. Makes 4 servings.

# Beef Paprika with Rice

2 tablespoons vegetable oil
1 medium onion, thinly sliced
1 garlic clove, crushed
2 celery stalks, thinly sliced
1 lb. lean ground beef
1 tablespoon all-purpose flour
1 tablespoon paprika
Salt
Freshly ground pepper
1 bay leaf
1 cup chicken stock
1-1/3 cups uncooked long-grain white rice
2 tablespoons butter or margarine
4 oz. button mushrooms, sliced
3 tablespoons dairy sour cream

*To garnish:*
1 tablespoon chopped fresh parsley

---

*Preparation and cooking time: 1 hour 20 minutes*

**1.** Heat oil in a large skillet over medium heat. Add onion, garlic and celery; sauté 4 minutes, stirring once or twice. Add ground beef; sauté 8 minutes, stirring to break up meat and brown evenly. Drain off excess fat. Stir in flour and paprika; cook 2 minutes.
**2.** Add salt, pepper, bay leaf and stock; bring to a boil. Cover; lower heat. Simmer about 50 minutes. Dish can be made ahead to this point and refrigerated, if desired.
**3.** Cook rice according to package directions while meat is simmering.
**4.** Melt butter or margarine in a small skillet over medium heat. Add mushrooms; sauté 3 to 4 minutes.
**5.** Remove bay leaf from meat. Stir in sour cream; heat through. Do not boil.
**6.** Spoon meat and sauce in the center of a heated serving dish; surround with hot cooked rice. Place mushrooms over meat; garnish with parsley. Serve with steamed spinach. Makes 4 servings.

# Oranges in Raisin Syrup

1/4 cup honey
5 tablespoons water
1 tablespoon lemon juice
1/3 cup raisins
1 tablespoon dark rum, if desired
6 seedless oranges, peeled, thinly sliced

*To decorate:*
6 to 8 walnut halves

---

*Preparation and cooking time: 20 minutes*

**1.** In a small saucepan, combine honey and water. Stir over low heat until honey dissolves. Boil 2 minutes; add lemon juice, raisins and rum, if desired. Boil 5 minutes.
**2.** Place oranges in a medium bowl. Pour hot sauce over oranges. Let stand until cool. Cover and refrigerate.
**3.** Serve chilled. Decorate with walnuts. Makes 4 servings.

Clockwise from top left: Oranges in Raisin Syrup, Green Beans Greek-Style, Beef Paprika with Rice

## Stir-Fried Beef

1 lb. lean beef top-round steak
2 tablespoons soy sauce
4 teaspoons cornstarch
Salt
2 tablespoons vegetable oil
1 garlic clove, finely chopped
1 (1/2-inch) piece fresh gingerroot,
   peeled, finely chopped
1 cup chicken stock
2 tablespoons dry sherry
8 green onions, thinly sliced

*Golden Rice:*
1 cup uncooked long-grain white rice
1 teaspoon ground turmeric

*To garnish:*
2 green onions

*Preparation and cooking time: 30 minutes, plus marinating*

**1.** Trim excess fat from beef. Cut beef into thin slices; cut slices into 1/2-inch strips.
**2.** In a medium bowl, combine 1 tablespoon soy sauce, 1 teaspoon cornstarch and a pinch of salt. Add beef; toss to coat with marinade. Cover; let stand at room temperature 2 hours or refrigerate overnight. Drain beef, reserving marinade.
**3.** Heat oil in a large skillet or wok over medium-high heat. Add garlic and ginger; stir-fry 1 minute. Stir in marinated beef; stir-fry 2 minutes. Stir in stock, sherry and remaining soy sauce; bring to a boil. Reduce heat; simmer 10 minutes.
**4.** In a small bowl, combine remaining cornstarch and reserved marinade.
**5.** Stir cornstarch mixture and sliced green onions into beef mixture. Stir over low heat 1 to 2 minutes or until sauce thickens.
**6.** Prepare Golden Rice while beef is marinating. Cook rice and turmeric according to package directions. Spoon Golden Rice into a serving dish; spoon stir-fried beef mixture over rice. Garnish with green onions. Serve immediately. Makes 4 servings.

## Broccoli & Yogurt Salad

1-1/2 lb. broccoli, fresh or frozen
Salt
3/4 cup plain yogurt
2 teaspoons olive oil
1 teaspoon lemon juice
Freshly ground pepper
2 oz. mushrooms, thinly sliced
4 to 6 walnut halves

*Preparation and cooking time: 25 minutes*

**1.** Cut broccoli into 1-inch pieces. In a medium saucepan, cook broccoli in boiling, salted water until crisp-tender. Drain and cool.
**2.** To prepare dressing, in a small bowl, combine yogurt, olive oil, lemon juice, salt and pepper. If making ahead, refrigerate dressing and cooked broccoli in separate covered containers.
**3.** Place broccoli and mushrooms in a serving bowl. Add dressing. Toss lightly to combine; garnish with walnuts. Salad is best served cool but not cold. Makes 4 servings.

## Strawberries in Butterscotch Sauce

1-1/2 lb. fresh or partially-thawed frozen strawberries
*Sauce:*
1 cup packed light-brown sugar
1 cup corn syrup
1/2 cup whipping cream
3 or 4 drops vanilla extract

*Preparation and cooking time: 15 minutes*

**1.** Place strawberries in individual serving dishes.
**2.** To prepare sauce, combine brown sugar and corn syrup in a medium saucepan. Stir over low heat until sugar dissolves. Cook 5 minutes.
**3.** Remove pan from heat; stir in cream and vanilla. Beat about 2 minutes or until sauce is smooth and glossy. Top strawberries with warm sauce. Or, make sauce ahead; refrigerate until served. Do not reheat; serve chilled. Makes 4 servings.

Clockwise from top left: Strawberries in Butterscotch Sauce, Broccoli & Yogurt Salad, Stir-Fried Beef with Golden Rice

1. Cut melon in half; scoop out and discard seeds. Using a melon baller or a small teaspoon, make melon balls. Place melon balls in a serving dish.
2. To prepare sauce, in a small bowl, combine yogurt, ginger syrup, stem ginger and nutmeg. Pour sauce over melon balls; stir to combine. Cover dish; refrigerate until served. Or, refrigerate melon balls and sauce separately. Place melon balls in individual serving dishes; top with sauce.
3. Garnish with orange slices. Makes 4 servings.

# Duck with Honey & Grape Sauce

**4 duck quarters, weighing about 14 oz. each**
**Salt**

*Sauce:*
**1/4 cup honey**
**Grated peel and juice of 1/2 orange**
**8 oz. seedless grapes**
**1 tablespoon butter or margarine**

*To garnish:*
**Watercress sprigs**

*Preparation and cooking time: 1 hour 30 minutes*

1. Preheat oven to 350F (175C). Prick duck pieces all over with a fork. Rub salt into skin. Place prepared duck, skin-side up, on a rack in a roasting pan.
2. Roast in preheated oven about 1-1/4 hours or until duck is tender and juices run clear when duck is pierced with a skewer.
3. While duck is roasting, in a small saucepan, combine honey, orange peel, orange juice, grapes and butter or margarine; bring to a boil.
4. Transfer duck to an ovenproof serving dish; pour sauce over duck; bake 5 minutes. Serve hot. Makes 4 servings.

# Melon Balls in Ginger Sauce

**1 medium cantaloupe or honeydew melon**
*Sauce:*
**8 oz. plain yogurt**
**4 teaspoons ginger syrup from preserved stem ginger**
**1 tablespoon finely chopped stem ginger**
**    preserved in syrup**
**Pinch of grated nutmeg**

*To garnish:*
**4 orange slices**

*Preparation time: 20 minutes*

# Nutty Cream Cones

**1/4 cup butter or margarine, room temperature**
**1/4 cup sugar**
**1/3 cup all-purpose flour, sifted**
**1/8 teaspoon salt**
**1 egg, beaten**

*Cream Filling:*
**1/2 pint whipping cream (1 cup)**
**2 tablespoons powdered sugar**
**1/2 teaspoon vanilla extract**
**2 tablespoons toasted, chopped almonds**
**3 tablespoons toasted, sliced almonds**

*Preparation and cooking time: 50 minutes*

1. Preheat oven to 400F (205C). Grease and flour 2 large baking sheets. Draw 8 (4-inch) circles on each sheet.
2. In a medium bowl, beat butter or margarine and sugar until light and fluffy. Fold in flour and salt. Stir in egg until thoroughly blended.
3. Drop 1-1/2 teaspoons batter into each circle on prepared baking sheets. Spread batter evenly with a small spatula to fill circles.
4. Bake in preheated oven, 1 baking sheet at a time, 4 minutes or until edges of cookies are golden.
5. Remove from oven; quickly shape each cookie around the handle of a wooden spoon to make a cone. Cool on spoon 1 minute. Remove from spoon; cool completely on a wire rack.
6. Repeat with remaining cookies. Cookies can be stored in airtight containers up to 2 days.
7. To make filling, in a medium bowl, whip cream until soft peaks form. Beat in powdered sugar and vanilla; beat until stiff peaks form. Fold in chopped almonds.
8. Spoon cream filling into rolled cookies; sprinkle with almonds. Makes 16 cones.

Top to bottom: Melon Balls in Ginger Sauce, Duck with Honey & Grape Sauce, Nutty Cream Cones

Curried Apple Soup
Whole-Wheat Spaghetti with Tuna Sauce
Green Salad
Blueberry Kissel

# Curried Apple Soup

3 tablespoons butter or margarine
1 lb. cooking apples, peeled, chopped
1 medium onion, sliced
2 celery stalks, thinly sliced
2 teaspoons curry powder
1 tablespoon chopped fresh mint
Juice of 1 lemon
2 cups chicken stock
2 tablespoons semolina
1-1/4 cups milk or plain yogurt
Salt
Freshly ground pepper

*To garnish:*
4 teaspoons shelled sunflower seeds
Chopped fresh parsley

*Preparation and cooking time: 45 minutes*

**1.** Melt butter or margarine in a large skillet over low heat. Add apples, onion and celery; cook 5 minutes, stirring occasionally. Increase heat to medium. Stir in curry powder; cook 3 minutes. Stir in mint, lemon juice and stock. Bring to a boil. Cover; simmer 20 minutes or until apples are tender.
**2.** In a blender or food processor fitted with a steel blade, process apple mixture until smooth. Place semolina in a medium saucepan; gradually stir in apple puree. Stir in milk or yogurt; bring slowly to a simmer. Do not boil. Season with salt and pepper.
**3.** Serve soup hot or refrigerate until chilled. Garnish with sunflower seeds and parsley. Makes 4 servings.

# Whole-Wheat Spaghetti with Tuna Sauce

12 oz. whole-wheat spaghetti
1/4 cup butter or margarine
2 tablespoons olive oil
1 garlic clove, finely chopped
2/3 cup chicken stock
3 tablespoons dry sherry
1 (6-1/2-oz.) can tuna, drained, flaked
3 tablespoons chopped fresh parsley
Salt
Freshly ground pepper
2 tablespoons whipping cream

*Preparation and cooking time: 30 minutes*

**1.** Cook spaghetti according to package directions. Drain; return to pan. Stir in 1/2 of butter or margarine; keep warm.
**2.** Heat olive oil and remaining butter or margarine in a medium saucepan over medium heat. Add garlic; sauté 2 minutes. Stir in stock and sherry; boil 5 minutes to slightly reduce liquid. Stir in tuna and 2 tablespoons parsley. Season with salt and pepper; stir in cream.
**3.** Place spaghetti in a heated serving dish; add sauce. Toss to combine. Garnish with remaining parsley. Makes 4 servings.

Clockwise from top left: Blueberry Kissel, Curried Apple Soup,
Whole-Wheat Spaghetti with Tuna Sauce

# Blueberry Kissel

**1-1/2 lb. fresh or frozen blueberries**
**1/2 cup packed light-brown sugar**
**1/4 cup red wine**
**Juice and grated peel of 1/2 orange**
**1 tablespoon arrowroot or cornstarch**
**2 tablespoons granulated sugar**

*To serve:*
**1/4 cup toasted sliced almonds**
**Whipped cream**
**Cookies**

*Preparation and cooking time: 20 minutes*

**1.** In a medium saucepan, combine blueberries, brown sugar, wine, orange juice and orange peel. Cook over low heat about 8 to 10 minutes or until blueberries are almost tender.
**2.** In a small bowl, stir a little juice from fruit into arrowroot or cornstarch to make a smooth paste. Stir into fruit; simmer about 2 minutes or until mixture thickens.
**3.** Pour blueberry mixture into a heatproof serving dish; sprinkle with granulated sugar to prevent a skin forming on top.
**4.** Arrange almonds decoratively over pudding. Serve warm or cold with whipped cream and cookies. Any leftover kissel makes a delicious sauce with ice cream. Makes 4 servings.

# Chicken Breasts in Egg & Lemon Sauce

4 chicken-breast halves, boneless
1 tablespoon vegetable oil
1/4 cup butter or margarine
4 oz. mushrooms, thinly sliced

*Sauce:*
2 tablespoons butter or margarine
2 tablespoons all-purpose flour
1 cup chicken stock
2 eggs
2 tablespoons lemon juice
1 tablespoon water
Salt
Freshly ground pepper

*To garnish:*
1 tablespoon chopped fresh parsley

---

*Preparation and cooking time: 40 minutes*

**1.** Remove skin from chicken; cut chicken on the diagonal into 3/4-inch slices. Heat oil and 1/4 cup butter or margarine in a large skillet over medium heat. Add chicken slices; sauté 4 minutes per side.
**2.** Add mushrooms; cook 4 minutes, turning chicken once. Remove chicken and mushrooms with a slotted spoon; keep warm.
**3.** To prepare sauce, melt 2 tablespoons butter or margarine in same skillet. Stir in flour; cook 1 minute. Gradually stir in stock; bring to a boil, stirring constantly. Reduce heat to low.
**4.** In a small bowl, beat eggs until frothy; beat in lemon juice and water.
**5.** Remove sauce from heat; add about 5 tablespoons hot sauce to beaten egg mixture. Stir mixture into sauce remaining in pan. Cook over low heat until sauce thickens; do not boil because sauce may curdle. Season with salt and pepper.
**6.** Add chicken and mushrooms to sauce; serve immediately. Garnish with parsley. Makes 4 servings.

# Fennel & Apple Salad

2 medium fennel bulbs, trimmed, thinly sliced
2 Red Delicious apples, cored, thinly sliced

*Dressing:*
2/3 cup dairy sour cream
1 teaspoon cider vinegar
Grated peel of 1/2 orange
1 tablespoon orange juice
Pinch of sugar
Salt
Freshly ground pepper

*To garnish:*
2 tablespoons raisins

---

*Preparation time: 15 minutes*

**1.** Place fennel and apples in a serving bowl. Toss to combine.
**2.** To prepare dressing, in a small bowl, combine all ingredients. Spoon dressing over fennel and apples. Toss immediately to prevent browning of apples.
**3.** Garnish with raisins. Makes 4 servings.

# Chocolate Pots with Cherry Brandy

1-1/2 cups half and half
4 oz. semisweet chocolate
4 egg yolks
1/4 cup sugar
1/8 teaspoon salt
2 tablespoons cherry-flavored brandy

*To serve:*
Cookies

---

*Preparation and cooking time: 35 minutes, plus chilling*

**1.** Heat half and half in a medium saucepan until tiny bubbles form around inside of saucepan. Do not boil.
**2.** Melt chocolate in top of a double boiler over simmering water. Remove from heat.
**3.** Add egg yolks to melted chocolate; beat until smooth. Stir in sugar and salt.
**4.** Gradually stir hot half and half into chocolate mixture. Return to heat; cook over simmering water about 15 minutes, stirring constantly. Stir in brandy.
**5.** Pour into 4 individual dessert dishes; set aside to cool. When cool, refrigerate several hours or until set.
**6.** Serve with cookies. Makes 4 servings.

Clockwise from left: Fennel & Apple Salad, Chocolate Pot with Cherry Brandy, Chicken Breasts in Egg & Lemon Sauce

Clockwise from left: Turkey Cutlets with Anchovies, Pear with Camembert Sauce, Pineapple Rings with Almond Meringue

---

*Pears with Camembert Sauce*
*Turkey Cutlets with Anchovies*
*Broiled Tomatoes & Mushrooms*
*Pineapple Rings with Almond Meringue*

---

## Pears with Camembert Sauce

4 ripe dessert pears, peeled, halved, cored
1 tablespoon lemon juice
1/2 cup dairy sour cream
2 tablespoons whipping cream
2 oz. Camembert cheese, room temperature
Pinch of red (cayenne) pepper

*To garnish:*
Mint sprigs

---

*Preparation time: 15 minutes*

**1.** Brush pear with lemon juice to prevent browning; arrange pears, cut-side up, in a shallow serving dish.
**2.** In a blender or food processor fitted with a steel blade, process sour cream, whipping cream, cheese and red pepper until smooth.
**3.** Top each pear with sauce; garnish with mint. Makes 4 servings.

# Turkey Cutlets with Anchovies

Juice of 1 lemon
2 tablespoons vegetable oil
1 teaspoon dried leaf oregano
Salt
Freshly ground pepper
4 turkey-breast cutlets, about 4 oz. each
2 tablespoons all-purpose flour
1-1/2 cups fresh bread crumbs
Grated peel of 1 lemon
2 tablespoons chopped fresh mint or parsley
1 egg
1 tablespoon milk
1/4 cup vegetable oil for sautéing

*To garnish:*
8 anchovy fillets
8 pimento-stuffed green olives
2 hard-cooked eggs, sliced

*Preparation and cooking time: 30 minutes, plus marinating*

1. In a shallow dish, combine lemon juice, 2 tablespoons oil, oregano, salt and pepper. Add turkey cutlets; turn to coat. Cover; marinate 1 hour at room temperature or overnight in refrigerator, turning once.
2. Drain marinated turkey; pat dry with paper towels. In a shallow dish, combine flour, salt and pepper. Dip turkey into seasoned flour to coat.
3. In another shallow dish, combine bread crumbs, lemon peel and mint or parsley. In another shallow dish, beat egg and milk until combined.
4. Dip floured turkey slices into egg mixture, then into bread-crumb mixture.
5. Heat 1/4 cup oil in a large skillet over medium heat. Add coated turkey cutlets; sauté 3 to 4 minutes per side or until golden brown.
6. Arrange cooked cutlets on a heated serving dish. Roll anchovies around olives. Garnish cutlets with olives and hard-cooked-egg slices. Serve hot. Makes 4 servings.

# Pineapple Rings with Almond Meringue

8 (1/2-inch-thick) fresh or canned pineapple slices
3 tablespoons butter or margarine, melted
2 tablespoons dark rum

*Meringue:*
2 egg whites
1/2 cup packed light-brown sugar
1/2 cup ground almonds

*Preparation and cooking time: 30 minutes*

1. Preheat broiler. Drain canned pineapple, if using; pat dry with paper towels. Place on a broiler-pan rack. Brush pineapple slices on 1 side with 1/2 of butter or margarine.
2. Broil under preheated broiler 4 minutes. Turn pineapple; brush with remaining butter or margarine. Broil 3 to 4 minutes or until pineapple is lightly browned and bubbling. Brush with rum.
3. In a medium bowl, beat egg whites until soft peaks form. Gradually beat in sugar until stiff and glossy. Fold in ground almonds.
4. Spoon meringue mixture over rings; with back of a spoon, make peaks in meringue. Broil 2 minutes or until lightly browned. Serve immediately. Makes 4 servings.

### Variation
Substitute 2/3 cup shredded coconut for ground almonds. Sprinkle extra coconut over meringue before broiling. The coconut forms a crisp, toasted crust that contrasts perfectly with the soft, chewy meringue.

<table>
<tr><td>

*Potato & Sausage Salad*
*Leek & Cheese Flan*
*Tomatoes*
*Hot French Bread*
*Baked Apples with Apricot*

</td></tr>
</table>

# Potato & Sausage Salad

1 lb. new potatoes
Salt
6 to 8 green onions, thinly sliced
2 tablespoons chopped chives
1 tablespoon chopped chervil or fresh parsley
1/2 cup dairy sour cream
1 tablespoon white-wine vinegar
Freshly ground pepper
6 oz. summer sausage, in 1 piece

*Preparation and cooking time: 40 minutes*

**1.** In a large saucepan, cook potatoes in boiling, salted water until tender. Drain; let stand until cool enough to handle. Peel; cut into thick slices or quarter.
**2.** In a medium bowl, combine onions, herbs and sour cream; stir in vinegar and pepper. Stir in potatoes until coated.
**3.** Remove and discard skin from sausage; cut in 1/2-inch cubes. If making ahead, refrigerate potato salad and sausage cubes in separate covered containers.
**4.** Immediately before serving, stir sausage cubes into potato salad. Makes 4 servings.

# Leek & Cheese Flan

1-1/4 cups all-purpose flour
1/2 teaspoon salt
6 tablespoons chilled shortening
3 to 4 tablespoons iced water

*Filling:*
2 tablespoons butter or margarine
4 medium leeks, thinly sliced
1 tablespoon snipped chives
1 cup shredded Swiss, Gruyère or Cheddar cheese (4 oz.)
3 eggs
1-1/2 cups half and half
Salt
Freshly ground pepper

*To serve:*
Tomato halves

*Preparation and cooking time: 1 hour*

**1.** Combine flour and salt in a medium bowl. With a pastry blender or 2 knives, cut in shortening until mixture resembles coarse crumbs.
**2.** Sprinkle with 3 tablespoons water; toss with a fork until mixture begins to hold together. Add remaining water, if necessary. Gather dough into a ball; shape into a flattened round. Wrap in plastic wrap; refrigerate 30 minutes.
**3.** Preheat oven to 400F (205C).
**4.** On a lightly floured surface, roll out dough to a 12-inch circle. Use pastry to line a 9-inch quiche or flan pan with a removable bottom. Trim pastry edge. Prick bottom and side of pastry with a fork. Line with foil; fill foil with pie weights or dried beans.
**5.** Bake 10 minutes. Remove foil and pie weights; bake 5 minutes. Reduce oven temperature to 375F (190C).
**6.** To prepare filling, melt butter or margarine in a medium skillet. Add leeks; sauté 4 minutes. With a slotted spoon, transfer cooked leeks to baked pie crust. Sprinkle with chives and 1/2 of cheese.
**7.** In a medium bowl, beat eggs, half and half, salt and pepper until blended. Pour over leeks and cheese. Sprinkle with remaining cheese.
**8.** Bake 30 to 35 minutes or until center is set. Serve warm.
For a special touch, cut tomato halves with a zigzag cutter. Makes 6 servings.

# Baked Apples with Apricot

**4 medium cooking apples**
**1/2 cup chopped dried apricots**
**1/3 cup packed light-brown sugar**
**Pinch of ground coriander**
**1/2 cup apple juice**
**1/4 cup butter or margarine**

*To serve:*
**Whipped cream or ice cream**

*Preparation and cooking time: 1 hour*

**1.** Preheat oven to 350F (175C). Core apples; cut a shallow slit around center of each apple to prevent skin from bursting. Arrange apples in a shallow ovenproof dish.
**2.** In a small bowl, combine apricots, sugar and coriander. Pack apricot mixture tightly into apples. Sprinkle remaining filling around apples for sauce. Add apple juice; dot apples with pieces of butter or margarine.
**3.** Bake apples, uncovered, in preheated oven about 40 minutes or until tender. Do not overcook, or they will collapse and lose their shape. Serve hot or cold with whipped cream or ice cream. Makes 4 servings.

Clockwise from top left: Potato & Sausage Salad, Baked Apple with Apricot, Leek & Cheese Flan

# Make-Ahead Meals

Today's busy lifestyle is less hectic if meals are planned and prepared ahead. Prepare dishes for entertaining when you have time to enjoy making them. There are no last-minute surprises; you already know how the dish turned out. Cleanup is also done in advance; this leaves the kitchen clean and tidy for entertaining. Make double batches of favorite recipes; one to serve now, one to freeze for later. Maximize the use of your freezer and refrigerator.

## REFRIGERATING PREPARED FOODS

If necessary, cool prepared foods 30 minutes at room temperature. Most soups, appetizers and main dishes can be refrigerated safely one to two days. Baked products can be stored longer. Cover food to prevent loss of moisture and absorption of flavors from other foods. There is a wide variety of containers designed for storing foods. Some containers can go directly from the refrigerator to the microwave oven or regular oven. Others require that the food be transferred to another container before heating. Read labels to determine which type you have.

## FREEZING PREPARED FOODS

Freezing is an excellent way of preserving food. But it is essential to use good ingredients, to prepare food correctly and to package and store it carefully. Here are a few reminders of the basic rules.

**Cooling**—Recipes prepared for freezing should be cooled as quickly as possible after cooking. To cool food quickly, place hot food in its pan in a larger pan or sink containing iced water. Or, pour hot food into a large shallow pan. Cool up to 30 minutes before freezing. Do not leave meat dishes, soups or appetizers at room temperature longer than 30 minutes to prevent bacterial growth and food spoilage.

**Open Freezing**—Some foods, such as frosted cakes, are difficult to wrap before freezing. Freeze these, unwrapped, on a baking sheet or plate. When frozen, wrap and label. Use the open freezing method for chopped onions, shredded cheese or cookies. After freezing, pack these in plastic freezer bags or rigid freezer containers for storage. Since these are frozen individually, you can remove the amount needed without thawing the entire package.

**Seasoning**—Lightly season dishes for freezing with salt and pepper. Taste and adjust seasoning immediately before serving. Some flavors change during storage. Garlic, bell peppers, celery and cloves intensify during storage, but the flavor of onion decreases.

**Storage**—As a rule, use frozen prepared dishes within three months. During this time, there should be no significant change in flavors. However, there are some exceptions to this rule. Store cured meats, fatty fish, leftovers, sandwiches, gelatin dishes, unbaked doughs and highly spiced foods one month or less.

**Packaging**—Food must be carefully packaged before freezing to prevent changes in flavor and texture. If not properly wrapped, food will lose moisture and become dry and tasteless. Or, food may absorb odors from other foods.

Special freezer paper, heavyweight foil, plastic freezer bags, boilable bags and rigid containers are suitable for freezing food.

*Plastic freezer bags* are available in several sizes. Do not use regular plastic bags; they are too thin to prevent freezer burn. Always seal bags securely with twist ties.

*Rigid plastic containers* with tight-fitting lids are suitable for most foods. Square-shaped containers take less space than round ones.

*Foil* is malleable and easily formed around awkwardly shaped food. It makes a good barrier for strong flavors, but does tear readily. Use a layer of plastic wrap inside the foil, or put the foil package into a freezer bag. Do not rely on foil alone for anything with sharp bones; pad them first with plastic wrap or waxed paper. Food containing acid, garlic, onion or dried fruit can cause foil to dissolve and discolor food. To prevent this, use a protective wrapping of plastic wrap or waxed paper.

*Boilable plastic bags* are small pouches that are heat-sealed with a special appliance. If you freeze food on a regular basis, you might want to invest in this equipment. Food frozen in these bags can be dropped into boiling water without thawing. This saves time in cooking and cleanup.

*Freezer-to-oven casseroles* are suitable for preparing main dishes for freezing. If desired, turn food out after freezing by loosening it with a knife or by quickly dipping the casserole into hot water. Or, line the casserole with foil before cooking the dish. After freezing, lift the foil and food from the casserole; wrap food completely in foil.

**Labeling and Storing**—It is very important to label food, because once frozen, many foods lose their identity. The label should include the date the food was frozen, recipe name, number of servings and a use-by date. If desired, include the cookbook name and page number or instructions for finishing the dish. For example, a label could say *Make-Ahead Meals, page 14.* Or, *add 1/2 cup milk; heat 20 minutes.* This simplifies cooking and serving.

Keep the freezer well organized. Keep a record of what is frozen and when it should be used to prevent waste. This is also helpful in meal planning.

**Thawing**—For most recipes, thaw before final cooking or heating, either in the refrigerator or at room temperature. Do not leave casseroles, soups or main dishes at room temperature any longer than is necessary for thawing. If you have a microwave oven, follow the manufacturer's directions for defrosting. Do not use metal or foil containers for heating or thawing in a microwave oven. Many foods can be cooked without thawing. Heat frozen creamed dishes, soups or stews in the top of a double boiler to prevent scorching. Frozen fruits have better texture and flavor if only partially thawed before serving.

**Garnishes and Decoration**—Garnishes and decorations add interest and color to foods. Add them immediately before serving.

Packaging materials for freezing

# Old-Fashioned Chicken Pie

Basic Pastry, page 251

6 tablespoons butter or margarine
1 onion, chopped
8 oz. mushrooms, thinly sliced
1/4 cup all-purpose flour
1-1/2 cups milk
1 cup chicken stock
2 cups diced cooked potatoes
2-1/2 cups diced cooked chicken
Salt
Freshly ground pepper
1 egg beaten with 1 tablespoon milk for glaze

1. Prepare Basic Pastry through step 2, page 251.
2. For filling, melt 2 tablespoons butter or margarine in a medium skillet over medium heat. Add onion; sauté until transparent. Add mushrooms; sauté 5 minutes. Set aside.
3. Melt remaining 1/4 cup butter or margarine in a large saucepan. Stir in flour; cook over low heat 1 minute, stirring constantly. Gradually stir in milk and stock or bouillon; cook over low heat until mixture is thickened, stirring constantly. Stir in reserved mushroom mixture, potatoes, chicken, salt and pepper. Spoon into a deep 9-inch pie plate or 2-quart casserole; set aside.
4. Preheat oven to 400F (205C). Roll out dough on a lightly floured surface to an 11-inch circle. Carefully fold dough over rolling pin; place over chicken filling. Trim excess dough; reserve for decoration. Crimp and flute pastry edge.
5. Gather dough scraps into a ball. Roll out dough to 1/8 inch thick. Cut out oval shapes as pictured for decoration. Make a hole in center of pie for a pie bird, or cut steam vent in center. Brush bottoms of decorations with water; place around center vent. Brush with egg mixture.
6. Place pie on a baking sheet. Bake in preheated oven 25 to 30 minutes or until pastry is golden brown. Cool on a wire rack. Refrigerate overnight, or freeze.
**To freeze:** Open freeze. When frozen, wrap in foil; label. Freeze up to 3 months. Thaw unwrapped pie in refrigerator overnight.
**To serve after refrigerating or thawing:** Place unwrapped pie on a baking sheet; heat in preheated 350F (175C) oven about 30 minutes or until hot and bubbly. If necessary, cover crust with foil to keep it from overbrowning. Makes 1 pie.

# Golden Chicken Casserole

1 (15-oz.) can tomatoes
1/4 cup all-purpose flour
Salt
Freshly ground black pepper
1 (2-1/2- to 3-lb.) chicken, cut into quarters
1/4 cup vegetable oil
2 tablespoons butter or margarine
1 large onion, quartered, sliced
1 teaspoon turmeric
1 cup cider or apple juice
1/2 cup whole-kernel corn
1 small yellow bell pepper, sliced
1 small red bell pepper, sliced
1 Golden Delicious apple, cored, sliced

*Turmeric has very little flavor, but gives a glowing golden color to this casserole. Yellow bell peppers are available in many large supermarkets. If they are not available, use a green bell pepper.*

1. Preheat oven to 350F (175C). Drain tomatoes, reserving juice. Set tomatoes aside.
2. In a plastic bag, combine flour, salt and black pepper. Add chicken; shake to coat. Heat oil in a large skillet over medium heat. When oil is hot, add coated chicken; sauté until lightly browned on all sides. Using tongs, place browned chicken in a 2-quart casserole.
3. Add butter or margarine to skillet. Add onion; sauté until golden. Stir in any remaining seasoned flour and turmeric; cook 1 minute, stirring constantly.
4. Stir in reserved tomato juice and cider or apple juice. Cook until thickened, stirring constantly.
5. Cut drained tomatoes into quarters. Add tomato quarters, corn, bell peppers and apple to casserole. Pour sauce over chicken and vegetables. Cover casserole; bake in preheated oven about 40 minutes or until chicken is tender. Serve immediately, or cool 30 minutes. Refrigerate overnight, or freeze.
**To freeze:** Pack cooled chicken mixture into a rigid freezer container or freeze in casserole. Cover and label. Freeze up to 2 months. Thaw at room temperature 3 to 4 hours.
**To serve after refrigerating or thawing:** Return to casserole, if necessary. Cover and heat in a preheated 350F (175C) oven about 30 minutes. Taste and adjust seasoning. Makes 4 servings.

Top to bottom: Old-Fashioned Chicken Pie, Golden Chicken Casserole

# Shepherd's Pie

1/3 recipe Savory Hamburger Mix, page 252
2 carrots, shredded
1/2 cup fresh or frozen green peas
2 celery stalks, sliced
2 tomatoes, sliced
4-1/2 cups diced, peeled potatoes,
   cooked (1-1/2 lb.)
2 tablespoons butter or margarine
2 tablespoons milk
Salt
Freshly ground pepper
Vegetable oil

**1.** In a large bowl, combine beef mixture, carrots, peas and celery. Spoon into a shallow 1-quart casserole. Cover with tomato slices.
**2.** In a large bowl, using a potato masher, mash potatoes with butter or margarine and milk until light and fluffy. Season with salt and pepper; spread mashed potatoes over tomatoes. Using the tines of a fork, decorate potatoes. Cool 30 minutes. Refrigerate overnight, or freeze.
**To freeze:** Cover cooled casserole with foil; label. Freeze up to 3 months. Thaw at room temperature 3 to 4 hours.
**To serve immediately or after refrigerating or thawing:** Uncover; brush potatoes with a little oil. Bake in a preheated 375F (190C) oven about 1-1/4 hours or until heated through and potatoes are browned.

### Variation
Substitute 1 (8-ounce) can baked beans in tomato sauce, for carrots, peas and celery. Stir 1/2 cup (2 ounces) shredded Cheddar cheese into mashed potatoes.

Left to right: Shepherd's Pie, Turkey & Noodle Ring

# Turkey & Noodle Ring

8 oz. egg noodles
Salt
5 tablespoons butter or margarine

*Filling:*
1 cup chicken stock
1 bay leaf
1 onion
4 whole cloves
3 tablespoons butter or margarine
1/3 cup all-purpose flour
3/4 cup milk
Salt
Freshly ground pepper
1-1/2 cups cubed cooked turkey
2 canned pimentos, drained, sliced
1 tablespoon chopped fresh parsley
3 tablespoons half and half

*To garnish:*
Finely chopped fresh parsley

1. Cook noodles in a large saucepan according to package directions until almost tender. Drain well; return to saucepan. Add salt and butter or margarine; stir until melted. Pack buttered noodles into a ring mold; set aside to cool.
2. In a medium saucepan, combine stock, bay leaf and onion studded with cloves. Bring to a boil; reduce heat. Simmer 10 minutes. Strain stock, discarding onion and bay leaf.
3. To make filling, in a medium saucepan, melt butter or margarine. Stir in flour; cook 1 minute, stirring constantly. Whisk in seasoned stock and milk. Cook until thickened and smooth, stirring constantly. Stir in salt, pepper, turkey, pimentos and parsley. Simmer 5 minutes; cool 30 minutes. Refrigerate overnight, or freeze.
**To freeze:** Pack cooled filling into a rigid freezer container. Cover and label. Wrap ring mold in foil; label. Freeze filling and noodles up to 2 months. Thaw ring mold at room temperature 3 to 4 hours. Thaw filling only until it can be removed from container.
**To serve immediately or after refrigerating or thawing:** Unwrap ring mold; place in a roasting pan. Add enough boiling water to pan to come half-way up side of mold. Bake in a preheated 325F (165C) oven about 30 minutes or until heated through. Meanwhile, place filling in a saucepan; bring to a boil over medium heat, stirring occasionally. Stir in half and half; heat but do not boil. Turn out noodle ring onto a heated serving dish. Spoon hot filling into center. Sprinkle with chopped parsley. Makes 4 servings.

# Filled Pasta Shells

1 lb. lean ground beef
2 tablespoons butter or margarine
1 onion, chopped
2 eggs, beaten
2 cups shredded mozzarella cheese (8 oz).
8 oz. cup ricotta cheese (1 cup)
3/4 cup grated Parmesan cheese (2-1/4 oz.)
1/4 cup dry bread crumbs
1 teaspoon Italian seasoning
Salt
Freshly ground pepper
6 cups spaghetti sauce, homemade or prepared
1 (12-oz.) pkg. jumbo pasta shells, cooked, drained

1. In a medium skillet, sauté beef, without added fat, until no longer pink. Drain off fat; spoon cooked beef into a large bowl. Melt butter or margarine in same skillet. Add onion; cook until transparent. Stir cooked onion, eggs, mozzarella cheese, ricotta cheese, 1/2 cup Parmesan cheese, bread crumbs, Italian seasoning, salt and pepper into cooked beef.
2. Preheat oven to 350F (175C). Spoon about 1 cup spaghetti sauce over bottom of an 11" x 7" baking dish. Repeat with a second baking dish.
3. Fill cooked shells with meat filling; place 15 filled shells in a single layer in each dish. Pour 2 cups sauce over filled shells in each dish. Sprinkle each dish with 2 tablespoons of remaining Parmesan cheese.
4. Bake in preheated oven 25 to 30 minutes or until cheese is melted. Serve immediately or cool. Refrigerate overnight, or freeze.
**To freeze:** Wrap in foil; label. Freeze up to 3 months. Thaw overnight in refrigerator.
**To serve after refrigerating or thawing:** Heat in a preheated 350F (175C) oven 30 minutes or until sauce is bubbling and shells are heated through. Makes 2 casseroles, 6 servings each.

# Winter Beef Stew

3 tablespoons vegetable oil
1-1/2 lb. beef stew cubes
2 onions, cut into 8 pieces each
2 carrots, sliced
1 parsnip, chopped
1 turnip, chopped
1 celery stalk, sliced
2 tablespoons all-purpose flour
1 (8-oz.) can tomatoes
1/2 teaspoon Italian seasoning
1 teaspoon prepared brown mustard
2 cups beef stock
Salt
Freshly ground pepper

*To serve:*
2 tablespoons sherry
Chopped fresh parsley

1. Heat oil in a large heavy saucepan. Add beef cubes in 3 batches; sauté until browned. Using a slotted spoon, remove browned cubes from pan. Drain on paper towels.
2. Add vegetables to pan; sauté gently 5 minutes.
3. Stir in flour; stirring often, cook 5 minutes or until flour is golden brown.
4. Stir in undrained tomatoes, Italian seasoning, mustard and stock. Bring to a boil; cook until thickened and smooth. Season with salt and pepper.
5. Return beef to pan. Cover; simmer about 1-1/2 hours or until beef is tender, stirring occasionally. Cool 30 minutes. Refrigerate overnight, or freeze.
**To freeze:** Pack cooled stew into a rigid freezer container. Cover and label. Freeze up to 2 months. Thaw at room temperature 4 to 6 hours.
**To serve after refrigerating or thawing:** Lift off and discard any fat. Bring stew to a boil in a large saucepan, stirring occasionally. Add sherry; adjust seasoning. Sprinkle with parsley. Makes 4 to 6 servings.

### Variation
**Beef & Mushroom Crumble:** Substitute 8 ounces chopped mushrooms for carrots, parsnip, turnip and celery. Use only 1/2 cup stock. After cooking, cool stew. Spoon into a casserole. Top with *Crumble Topping.* To make Crumble Topping, in a medium bowl, cut 5 tablespoons firm butter or margarine into 1-1/4 cups all-purpose flour; season with salt and pepper. Stir in 1/2 cup (2 ounces) shredded Cheddar cheese. Sprinkle topping over stew.
**To freeze:** Cover and label. Freeze up to 2 months. Thaw at room temperature 4 to 5 hours.
**To serve after thawing:** Uncover; bake thawed casserole in a preheated 375F (190C) oven 50 minutes or until topping is golden brown.

# Easy Chili con Carne

2 lb. lean ground beef
2 large onions, finely chopped
2 garlic cloves, crushed
6 tablespoons all-purpose flour
2 tablespoons tomato paste
2 (16-oz.) cans tomatoes with juice, chopped
2 (15-oz.) cans kidney beans, undrained
2 teaspoons dried leaf oregano
1 teaspoon ground cumin
2 tablespoons chili powder
Hot-pepper sauce

1. In a large heavy saucepan over medium heat, sauté beef, without added fat, until no longer pink. Add onions and garlic; sauté until onion is tender. Drain off fat.
2. Stir flour into cooked beef mixture. Cook 1 minute, stirring constantly. Stir in tomato paste, tomatoes with juice, kidney beans, oregano, cumin, chili powder and hot-pepper sauce to taste.
3. Simmer 30 minutes. Cool 30 minutes. Refrigerate overnight, or freeze.
**To freeze:** Pack cooled chili into 2 rigid freezer containers. Cover and label. Freeze up to 1 month. Thaw overnight in refrigerator.
**To serve after refrigerating or thawing:** In a large saucepan over medium heat, bring chili to a boil, stirring frequently. Makes 8 servings.

# Spiced Brisket

1 (2-lb.) rolled beef brisket
2-1/2 cups beef stock
1 small onion, sliced
6 strips lemon peel
1 bay leaf
1 tablespoon pickling spice
Salt
Freshly ground pepper
3 fresh parsley sprigs

1. Preheat oven to 325F (165C).
2. Place roast into a deep casserole or Dutch oven. Add stock, onion, lemon peel and bay leaf. Tie pickling spice in cheesecloth; add to roast. Add salt, pepper and parsley sprigs.
3. Cover; roast in preheated oven about 2 hours or until roast is tender.
4. Carefully lift out roast; place in a bowl or dish that will hold it snugly. Cover with a plate; place a heavy weight on plate. Refrigerate overnight.
5. Strain cooking liquid, discarding vegetables; reserve for another use, if desired.
**To serve after refrigerating:** Thinly slice roast. Serve with pickles or salads. Roast is excellent for sandwiches. Makes 6 to 8 servings.

# Make-Ahead Beef Burgundy

2 tablespoons vegetable oil
1-1/2 lb. beef-round steak, cut in 1-inch cubes
2 medium onions, chopped
2 garlic cloves, crushed
1 cup red wine
3/4 cup beef stock
1 bay leaf
1 teaspoon Italian seasoning
Salt
Freshly ground pepper
6 oz. mushrooms, sliced
3 tablespoons all-purpose flour

*This is an excellent dish to have on hand for unexpected guests. Double recipe, if desired.*

**1.** Heat oil in a large heavy saucepan. Add beef; sauté until browned. Add onions and garlic; sauté until softened.
**2.** Add wine, 1/2 cup stock, bay leaf and Italian seasoning. Season with salt and pepper. Cover; simmer over low heat 40 minutes. Add mushrooms; simmer 15 minutes longer or until beef is tender.
**3.** In a small bowl, blend flour and remaining stock into a paste. Stir into hot stew. Cook until thickened, stirring frequently. Discard bay leaf. Cool 30 minutes. Refrigerate overnight, or freeze.
**To freeze:** Spoon stew into a rigid freezer container. Cover and label. Freeze up to 2 months. Thaw overnight in refrigerator.
**To serve after refrigerating or thawing:** Heat in a large saucepan until hot and bubbling. Serve with French bread and a green salad. Makes 4 servings.

Clockwise from upper left: Easy Chili con Carne, Confetti Rice without corn, page 618; Make-Ahead Beef Burgundy

# Sweet & Sour Ham Steaks

4 (4- to 6-oz.) ham steaks
Vegetable oil
4 teaspoons brown sugar

*Sauce:*
1 (8-oz.) can pineapple chunks (juice pack)
1 tablespoon vegetable oil
1 onion, finely chopped
1 tablespoon all-purpose flour
1 tablespoon soy sauce
1 tablespoon wine vinegar
1 tablespoon ketchup
Freshly ground pepper

*Confetti Rice:*
1 cup uncooked long-grain white rice
1/4 cup frozen or fresh peas
1/4 cup frozen or canned whole-kernel corn, if desired
2 tablespoons water

---

**1.** Preheat broiler. Place ham steaks on a rack in a broiler pan. Brush lightly with oil; broil under preheated broiler 5 minutes.
**2.** Turn steaks. Brush with oil; sprinkle with brown sugar. Broil until sugar melts and caramelizes.
**3.** To make sauce, drain juice from pineapple into a measuring cup. Add enough water to make 1 cup.
**4.** Heat oil in a medium saucepan. Add onion; sauté until softened. Stir in flour; cook 1 minute, stirring constantly.
**5.** Stir juice mixture, soy sauce, vinegar and ketchup into flour mixture. Cook, stirring constantly, until sauce thickens. Stir in pineapple chunks. Season with pepper. Pour sauce over broiled ham; cool. Refrigerate overnight, or freeze.
**6.** To make Confetti Rice, cook rice according to package directions until almost tender. Stir in peas and corn, if desired. Cook until rice is tender and liquid is absorbed. Cool. Refrigerate overnight, or freeze.
**To freeze:** Pack ham and sauce into a rigid freezer container. Cover and label. Pack cooled rice into a rigid freezer container. Cover and label. Freeze ham and rice up to 1 month. Thaw 2 to 3 hours at room temperature.
**To serve after refrigerating or thawing:** Place ham and sauce into an ovenproof dish. Cover; heat in a preheated 350F (175C) oven until hot and bubbling. Heat rice mixture in a medium saucepan with 2 tablespoons water. Cock over low heat until water is absorbed and rice is hot. Serve with ham. Makes 4 servings.

Clockwise from left: Sweet & Sour Ham Steaks with Confetti Rice, Pork Paprika, Pork Patties & Red Cabbage

# Pork Paprika

2 tablespoons vegetable oil
1/4 cup butter or margarine
1 (1-lb.) pork-loin tenderloin, sliced
1 onion, chopped
1 garlic clove, crushed
2 tablespoons paprika
3 tablespoons all-purpose flour
1/2 cup cider or white wine
1/2 cup beef stock
1 tablespoon tomato paste
Salt
Freshly ground pepper
6 oz. small button mushrooms, halved

*To serve:*
1/2 cup dairy sour cream

---

## Pork Patties & Red Cabbage

1 lb. lean ground pork
1 medium onion, finely chopped
2 tablespoons dry bread crumbs
1 teaspoon dried leaf thyme
1 tablespoon finely chopped fresh parsley
1 egg, beaten
Salt
Freshly ground pepper
1/4 cup butter or margarine
2 tablespoons vegetable oil

*Red Cabbage:*
3 tablespoons butter or margarine
2 lb. red cabbage, finely sliced
1/4 cup packed brown sugar
1/4 cup water
1/4 cup wine vinegar
Salt
Freshly ground pepper
1 cooking apple, peeled, cored, chopped

---

**1.** In a large bowl, combine pork, onion, bread crumbs, thyme, parsley, egg, salt and pepper until blended. With floured hands, shape pork mixture into 8 oval patties. Chill 1 hour.
**2.** Heat butter or margarine and oil in a large skillet. Add patties, 4 at a time; sauté over a medium heat about 8 minutes per side or until well browned. Remove browned patties from pan; sauté remaining patties. Cool. Refrigerate overnight, or freeze.
**3.** To make red cabbage, melt butter or margarine in a heavy saucepan. Add cabbage, brown sugar, water, vinegar, salt and pepper. Cover tightly; cook over low heat about 30 minutes, shaking pan and stirring occasionally.
**4.** Add apple; cook 15 minutes longer. Cool. Refrigerate overnight, or freeze.
**To freeze:** Pack pork patties and cabbage into separate freezer containers. Cover and label. Freeze up to 1 month. Thaw at room temperature 2 to 3 hours.
**To serve after refrigerating or thawing:** Place cabbage in a casserole. Cover; heat in a preheated 350F (175C) oven about 30 minutes or until hot. Place pork patties on a greased baking sheet. Heat in same oven 30 minutes. Serve with boiled new potatoes tossed in melted butter and finely chopped parsley. Makes 4 servings.

### Variation

Substitute *Mock Sauerkraut* for *Red Cabbage.* To make Mock Sauerkraut, finely shred white cabbage. Cook as above except substitute 1 tablespoon granulated sugar for 1/4 cup brown sugar; add 1/2 teaspoon caraway seeds. Be careful that cabbage does not brown.

---

**1.** Heat oil and butter or margarine in a large heavy saucepan. Add pork slices; brown on both sides. Using tongs, remove from pan.
**2.** Add onion, garlic and paprika to pan; sauté about 2 minutes. Stir in flour; cook 1 minute, stirring constantly.
**3.** Stir in cider or wine, stock and tomato paste. Bring to a boil; cook until thickened and smooth, stirring constantly.
**4.** Season with salt and pepper. Return pork to saucepan; cover. Simmer 15 minutes. Add mushrooms; cook 5 minutes. Cool 30 minutes. Refrigerate overnight, or freeze.
**To freeze:** Pack cooled pork and sauce into a rigid freezer container. Cover and label. Freeze up to 1 month. Thaw at room temperature 3 to 4 hours.
**To serve immediately or after refrigerating or thawing:** Bring pork and sauce to a boil in a large saucepan, stirring occasionally. Stir in sour cream; heat but do not boil. Adjust seasonings. Serve with small boiled potatoes and green vegetables. Makes 4 servings.

# Pork & Pineapple Casserole

2 tablespoons vegetable oil
1-1/2 lb. lean pork cubes, trimmed
1 tablespoon cornstarch
1 tablespoon sugar
1/4 cup water
1/4 cup soy sauce
1/4 cup red-wine vinegar
2 tablespoons dry sherry
1 tablespoon Worcestershire sauce
1/2 teaspoon ground ginger
1 (15-1/4-oz.) can pineapple chunks (juice pack)
1 red or green bell pepper, cut into 1-inch pieces
1 cup macadamia nuts

**1.** Preheat oven to 350F (175C).
**2.** Heat oil in a medium skillet. Add pork; sauté over medium heat until browned on all sides. Using a slotted spoon, place browned pork in a 1-1/2-quart casserole.
**3.** In a medium bowl, combine cornstarch and sugar. Stir in water until smooth. Stir in soy sauce, vinegar, sherry, Worcestershire sauce and ginger. Drain syrup from pineapple; stir syrup into cornstarch mixture. Set pineapple aside.
**4.** Pour cornstarch mixture over browned pork; stir until pork is coated. Cover; bake in preheated oven 30 minutes.
**5.** Add reserved pineapple, bell pepper and macadamia nuts to pork. Stir well; replace cover. Bake 30 minutes longer or until pork is thoroughly cooked. Cool 30 minutes. Refrigerate overnight, or freeze.
**To freeze:** Wrap cooled casserole in foil; label. Freeze up to 1 month. Thaw at room temperature 3 to 4 hours.
**To serve after refrigerating or thawing:** Cover; bake in a preheated 350F (175C) oven 20 minutes or until heated through. Makes 4 to 6 servings.

Left to right: Leek Pie, Lamb with Pineapple

# Leek Pie

*Pastry:*
1-1/2 cups all-purpose flour
1/4 teaspoon salt
1/2 cup butter or margarine
4 to 5 tablespoons iced water

*Filling:*
6 tablespoons butter or margarine
6 to 8 medium leeks, rinsed, trimmed, sliced
3 tablespoons all-purpose flour
3/4 cup chicken stock
3/4 cup milk
2 eggs
6 crisp-cooked bacon slices, crumbled
Salt
Freshly ground pepper
Milk

---

1. To make pastry, in a medium bowl, combine flour and salt. With a pastry blender or 2 knives, cut in butter or margarine until mixture resembles coarse crumbs. Sprinkle with water, 1 tablespoon at a time, tossing with a fork until mixture holds together. Form dough into a ball. Wrap in waxed paper or plastic wrap; refrigerate 30 minutes.
2. To make filling, melt 3 tablespoons butter or margarine in a large skillet. Add leeks; sauté 5 minutes or until softened. Remove from heat; set aside.
3. Melt remaining 3 tablespoons butter or margarine in a medium saucepan. Stir in flour; cook 1 minute. Gradually stir in stock and 3/4 cup milk; bring to a boil, stirring constantly. In a small bowl, beat eggs with a whisk. Whisk 3 tablespoons sauce into beaten eggs until blended. Pour mixture back into saucepan; cook over low heat until sauce is thickened, stirring constantly. Do not boil. Remove from heat; stir in bacon and sautéed leeks. Season with salt and pepper. Cool. Spoon leek mixture into a 9-inch pie pan or 1-1/2-quart casserole.
4. Preheat oven to 400F (205C). Roll out dough on a lightly floured surface to an 11-inch circle. Fold dough over rolling pin; place over leek filling. Trim excess dough; reserve for decoration. Crimp and flute pastry edge.
5. Gather dough scraps into a ball; roll out to 1/8 inch thick. Cut out decorations. Make a hole in center of pie to let steam escape. Brush bottom of decorations with water; place on top of pie. Brush top of pie with milk.
6. Place pie on a baking sheet; bake in preheated oven 25 to 30 minutes or until pastry is golden brown. Cool completely on a wire rack. Refrigerate overnight, or freeze.
**To freeze:** Open freeze. When frozen, wrap in foil; label. Freeze up to 1 month. Thaw unwrapped pie at room temperature 3 to 4 hours.
**To serve after refrigerating or thawing:** Place on a baking sheet. Bake in a preheated 350F (175C) oven about 30 minutes or until hot and bubbly. Makes 6 servings.

# Lamb with Pineapple

2 to 2-1/2 lb. lean lamb stew cubes
1 (8-oz.) can pineapple chunks (juice pack)
About 1 cup beef stock
2 tablespoons vegetable oil
12 small white onions
1/4 cup all-purpose flour
1/4 teaspoon Chinese five-spice powder
2 tablespoons tomato paste
Salt
Freshly ground pepper
8 oz. button mushrooms

*To garnish:*
Chopped fresh parsley

---

*If five-spice powder is unavailable, substitute a pinch each of ground nutmeg and coriander, 1 to 2 teaspoons soy sauce and 1 tablespoon sherry.*

1. Preheat oven to 350F (175C). If necessary, trim lamb. Drain juice from pineapple into a 2-cup measuring cup. Add enough stock to make 1-1/2 cups.
2. Heat oil in a large skillet. Add onions; sauté until lightly browned. Add lamb cubes; sauté until lightly browned. Using a slotted spoon, place browned onions and lamb in a 2-1/2-quart casserole.
3. Stir flour and five-spice powder into skillet; cook 1 minute, stirring constantly. Stir juice mixture into flour mixture. Cook until thickened and smooth, stirring constantly. Stir in tomato paste. Season with salt and pepper. Pour sauce over lamb and onions.
4. Cover; bake in preheated oven 1-1/4 hours or until lamb is tender. Stir in mushrooms and drained pineapple. Cool 30 minutes. Refrigerate overnight, or freeze.
**To freeze:** Pack cooled lamb mixture into a rigid freezer container. Cover and label. Freeze up to 1 month. Thaw overnight in refrigerator.
**To serve after refrigerating or thawing:** Return to casserole; cover. Bake in a preheated 350F (175C) oven about 45 minutes or until hot and bubbling. Adjust seasoning. Sprinkle with parsley. Serve with hot cooked rice and green vegetables. Makes 6 servings.

## Variation
Substitute 1 (15-ounce) can lima beans with liquid, and 1 tablespoon chopped fresh mint for pineapple. Serve with chow-mein noodles.

# Sausage-Stuffed Beef Rolls

4 oz. bulk pork sausage
1 egg, beaten
4 bread slices, made into bread crumbs
1 teaspoon Italian seasoning
1 teaspoon prepared brown mustard
Salt
Freshly ground pepper
1 (1-1/2-lb.) beef-flank steak
1 large potato, peeled, diced
2 carrots, sliced
1 parsnip, diced
1 turnip, diced
1 onion, chopped
2 tablespoons all-purpose flour
1 cup beef stock

---

1. Preheat oven to 325F (165C).
2. In a medium bowl, combine sausage, egg, bread crumbs, Italian seasoning, mustard, salt and pepper. Spread evenly over steak. Roll up steak from long side; tie with kitchen string.
3. Place all vegetables into a large roasting pan; sprinkle with flour, salt and pepper. Pour in stock. Lay stuffed steak on top.
4. Cover with foil; bake in preheated oven 2 hours. Cool 30 minutes. Refrigerate overnight, or freeze.
**To freeze:** Wrap cooled steak roll in foil; label. Pack vegetables into a rigid freezer container. Cover and label. Freeze up to 1 month. Thaw in refrigerator overnight.
**To serve after refrigerating or thawing:** Cut steak into thick slices. Place vegetables in an oval ovenproof serving dish; arrange steak slices on top. Cover with foil; heat in a preheated 350F (175C) oven about 30 minutes or until heated through. Makes 4 servings.

# Beef Curry

1/4 cup vegetable oil
1 large onion, chopped
1 garlic clove, crushed
1 (1/2-inch) piece gingerroot, peeled, finely chopped
1/4 cup cream of coconut
2 to 4 teaspoons curry powder
2 cups beef stock
Salt
Freshly ground pepper
1 lb. beef stew cubes
1/4 teaspoon ground coriander
2 tablespoons apricot jam

---

*Everyone who likes curry has their own favorite recipe. This basic sauce can be used with meat, shrimp or eggs. Add curry powder to taste.*

1. Heat 2 tablespoons oil in a large saucepan. Add onion and garlic; sauté until lightly browned. Stir in ginger and cream of coconut; cook 2 minutes.
2. Stir in curry powder and stock. Season with salt and pepper. Bring to a boil; simmer 15 minutes.
3. Meanwhile, heat remaining oil in a large skillet. Add beef; season with salt, pepper and coriander. Sauté until well browned.
4. Place browned beef in sauce. Cook over low heat 1 hour or until beef is tender. Stir in jam. Cool 30 minutes. Refrigerate overnight, or freeze.
**To freeze:** Pack beef mixture into a rigid freezer container. Cover and label. Freeze up to 1 month. Thaw at room temperature 3 to 4 hours.
**To serve after refrigerating or thawing:** Heat beef curry in a saucepan. Bring to a boil, stirring occasionally. Adjust seasoning. Serve with hot cooked rice, sliced-tomato-and-onion salad and grated cucumber combined with plain yogurt. Makes 4 servings.

---

To make your own curry powder, combine 4 teaspoons ground coriander, 1 teaspoon ground turmeric, 2 teaspoons ground cumin, 1 teaspoon freshly ground pepper, 2 to 4 teaspoons chili powder and 1 teaspoon ground cloves. Or, if you have a spice mill, grind whole spices and combine as desired. Store curry powder in a tightly covered container.

Fresh gingerroot is much milder in flavor than ground ginger. To keep gingerroot fresh, store peeled slices covered with sherry in a tightly sealed jar 1 to 2 months. Or, open freeze grated or sliced fresh gingerroot on a baking sheet. When frozen, pack in a small plastic freezer bag. Freeze up to 3 months.

# Pork & Root-Vegetable Bake

2 carrots, chopped
1 small rutabaga, chopped
1 small parsnip, chopped
1 small turnip, chopped
1/2 teaspoon salt
Water
2 tablespoons vegetable oil
4 thick pork chops, trimmed
1 onion, chopped
Freshly ground pepper
4-1/2 cups sliced, peeled potatoes, cooked 5 minutes

**1.** Place carrots, rutabaga, parsnip, turnip and salt into a medium saucepan. Cover with water; bring to a boil. Simmer 3 minutes. Drain, reserving 1 cup liquid.
**2.** Place cooked vegetables in bottom of a 2-quart casserole.
**3.** Heat oil in a large skillet. Add chops; sauté 5 minutes on each side. Using tongs, remove browned chops from skillet; set aside. Add onion to skillet; sauté until softened.
**4.** Scatter cooked onion over vegetables in casserole. Lay browned chops on vegetables. Sprinkle with salt and pepper. Pour reserved cooking liquid over chops.
**5.** Cover chops with overlapping potato slices. Brush with drippings from skillet. Cool 30 minutes. Refrigerate overnight, or freeze.
**To freeze:** Cover casserole tightly. Label. Freeze up to 1 month. Thaw at room temperature 3 to 4 hours.
**To serve after refrigerating or thawing:** Uncover; bake in a preheated 325F (165C) oven 1 to 1-1/2 hours or until pork is tender and potatoes are tender and browned. Serve with a green vegetable. Makes 4 servings.

Sausage-Stuffed Beef Rolls

# Chicken-Liver Pan-Fry

2 tablespoons vegetable oil
2 bacon slices, chopped
1 onion, finely chopped
1 small green bell pepper, sliced
1 lb. chicken livers, trimmed
4 oz. mushrooms, quartered
1 to 2 teaspoons rubbed sage

*To serve:*
6 tablespoons dry vermouth or white wine
Salt
Freshly ground pepper

---

**1.** Heat oil in a large skillet. Add bacon and onion; sauté until bacon is lightly browned.
**2.** Add bell pepper and chicken livers; sauté 5 minutes. Stir in mushrooms and sage; sauté 5 minutes longer. Cool 30 minutes. Refrigerate overnight, or freeze.
**To freeze:** Pack liver mixture in a rigid freezer container. Cover and label. Freeze up to 1 month. Thaw in refrigerator overnight.
**To serve immediately or after refrigerating or thawing:** Return to pan, add vermouth or wine. Bring to a boil, stirring occasionally. Season with salt and pepper. Serve with hot cooked white or brown rice and a green salad. Makes 4 servings.

# Liver Stroganoff

1/4 cup butter or margarine
1 tablespoon vegetable oil
1 large onion, thinly sliced
1 lb. calves' liver, cut into thin strips
1 tablespoon tomato paste
1/2 cup beef stock
1 teaspoon prepared brown mustard

*To serve:*
1/2 cup dairy sour cream
Salt
Freshly ground pepper

---

**1.** Heat butter or margarine and oil in a large skillet. Add onion; sauté until softened.
**2.** Add liver; sauté about 5 minutes or until liver is barely done.
**3.** Stir in tomato paste and stock; cook 2 minutes. Stir in mustard. Cool 30 minutes. Refrigerate overnight, or freeze.
**To freeze:** Pack liver mixture in a rigid freezer container. Cover and label. Freeze up to 1 month. Thaw overnight in refrigerator.
**To serve immediately or after refrigerating or thawing:** Heat liver stroganoff in a medium saucepan. Bring to a boil, stirring frequently. Stir in sour cream; heat but do not boil. Season to taste with salt and pepper. Serve immediately with hot cooked noodles or rice. Makes 4 servings.

Left to right: Chicken-Liver Pan-Fry, Liver Stroganoff

# Oxtail Stew with Dumplings

5 tablespoons all-purpose flour
Salt
Freshly ground pepper
1 oxtail, cut up
2 tablespoons vegetable oil
3 cups beef stock
1 tablespoon prepared horseradish
1 large onion, sliced
2 carrots, sliced
2 celery stalks, sliced
1 small parsnip, diced
1 bay leaf

*Dumplings:*
1 cup cake flour
2 teaspoons baking powder
1/2 teaspoon salt
1 teaspoon Italian seasoning
1 egg
Milk

---

*Oxtail is an inexpensive cut that is ideally suited to braising. The meat becomes tender and the flavor is superb.*

**1.** Preheat oven to 325F (165C).
**2.** In a plastic bag, combine flour, salt and pepper. Add oxtail pieces; shake to coat.

**3.** Heat oil in a large skillet. Add oxtail pieces; sauté until browned all over. With a slotted spoon, remove browned oxtail pieces; set aside.
**4.** Add any remaining seasoned flour to skillet; stirring, cook 1 minute or until browned. Stir in stock; stirring constantly, cook until thickened and smooth. Stir in horseradish.
**5.** Place all vegetables in bottom of a 2-quart casserole. Add bay leaf. Arrange browned oxtail pieces over vegetables.
**6.** Pour horseradish sauce over oxtail pieces. Cover; bake in preheated oven 3 hours. Cool; spoon off any fat from surface. Discard bay leaf.
**7.** To make dumplings, combine cake flour, baking powder, salt and Italian seasoning. Beat egg in a 1-cup measuring cup; add enough milk to make 1/2 cup. Stir egg mixture into dry ingredients. Add more milk, if necessary, but keep batter stiff. If refrigerating stew overnight before serving, make dumplings while stew heats.
**To freeze:** Put cooled stew into a rigid freezer container. Cover and label. Freeze up to 1 month. Drop dumplings by tablespoonfuls onto a greased baking sheet. Open freeze dumplings. When frozen, pack in a plastic bag or container; label. Freeze up to 1 month. Thaw stew overnight in refrigerator. Cook dumplings frozen.
**To serve immediately or after refrigerating or thawing:** Lift off and discard any fat. Return stew to casserole. Cover; bake in a preheated 350F (175C) oven about 1 hour or until hot and bubbly. Top with fresh or frozen dumplings; replace cover. Bake 20 minutes longer or until dumplings are firm when touched. Makes 4 servings.

# Haddock & Anchovy Puff

1 (12-oz.) haddock fillet
1/2 cup milk
1/2 cup water
2 tablespoons butter
3 tablespoons all-purpose flour
4 anchovy fillets, chopped
1 hard-cooked egg, minced
Salt
Freshly ground pepper
1/2 (17-1/4-oz.) package frozen puff pastry, thawed
1 egg yolk beaten with 1 tablespoon water for glaze

*If you find the salty flavor of anchovies too strong, use chopped parsley and some lemon peel instead. Mince the egg white, or it will be rubbery after freezing.*

**1.** Place fish, milk and water in a medium saucepan. Cover; simmer 10 minutes.
**2.** Remove poached fish from pan; reserve cooking liquid in pan. Remove and discard skin and bones from fish. Flake fish.
**3.** Combine butter and flour into a paste. Cut in small pieces; stir into reserved cooking liquid. Bring to a boil, stirring until thickened and smooth. Stir in flaked fish, anchovies and hard-cooked egg. Season with salt and pepper.
**4.** Roll out pastry dough on a lightly floured board to a 12-inch square. Trim edges. Turn pastry so a corner is pointing toward you.
**5.** Put fish mixture in center of square. Fold pastry like an envelope. Fold the bottom corner to center, 2 side corners to center, then top corner down to cover. Brush all edges with beaten egg as you fold; press to seal. Refrigerate overnight, or freeze.
**To freeze:** Put pastry on a baking sheet; open freeze. When frozen, wrap in foil; label. Freeze up to 1 month. Thaw unwrapped filled pastry on a baking sheet at room temperature 2 to 3 hours.
**To serve immediately or after refrigerating or thawing:** Brush with egg-yolk glaze; bake in a preheated 400F (205C) oven 45 to 50 minutes or until raised, golden brown and heated through.

Top to bottom: Haddock & Anchovy Puff, Stuffed Fish Fillets

# Stuffed Fish Fillets

**4 (4- to 6-oz.) fish fillets with skin**
*Stuffing:*
**2 tablespoons butter or margarine**
**1 small onion, chopped**
**1 small cooking apple, peeled, cored, grated**
**Grated peel and juice of 1/2 lemon**
**1 tablespoon chopped parsley**
**1/4 cup dry bread crumbs**
**Salt**
**Freshly ground pepper**
**6 tablespoons apple juice**

*To garnish:*
**Lemon slices**
**Parsley sprigs**

1. Preheat oven to 350F (175C). Wipe fillets with damp paper towels.
2. To make stuffing, melt butter or margarine in a medium skillet. Add onion; sauté until softened. Stir in apple, lemon peel, lemon juice, parsley, bread crumbs, salt and pepper.
3. Lay fillets on a flat surface, skin-side down. Divide stuffing among fillets; roll up, starting at tail end.
4. Put rolls into a freezer-to-oven dish large enough to hold rolls in 1 layer. Spoon apple juice over top.
5. Cover with buttered waxed paper and foil; bake in preheated oven about 15 minutes. Cool 30 minutes. Remove waxed paper and foil. Cover with fresh waxed paper and foil. Refrigerate overnight, or freeze.
**To freeze:** Label. Freeze up to 1 month. Do not thaw before reheating.
**To serve after refrigerating or freezing:** Heat frozen fish in a preheated 350F (175C) oven about 30 minutes or until heated through. If refrigerated, heat 10 to 15 minutes. Garnish with lemon slices and parsley. Makes 4 servings.

# Smoky Fish Cakes

**12 oz. smoked haddock or other smoked fish fillets**
**1/2 cup milk**
**2 tablespoons butter or margarine**
**3/4 cup mashed potatoes**
**1 tablespoon chopped parsley**
**Freshly ground pepper**
**1 small package onion-and-sour-cream-flavored potato chips**
**1/4 cup dry bread crumbs**
**1 egg, beaten**
**Vegetable oil for deep-frying**

1. Place fish and milk in a medium saucepan. Simmer 10 minutes. Drain, reserving 2 tablespoons liquid. Remove and discard any skin and bones from poached fish; flake fish.
2. In a small bowl, beat reserved poaching liquid and butter or margarine into potatoes. Stir in flaked fish, parsley and pepper. With lightly floured hands, shape fish mixture into 8 round cakes. Refrigerate until firm.
3. Put potato chips into a plastic bag; finely crush with a rolling pin. In a shallow bowl, combine crushed chips and bread crumbs.
4. Dip fish cakes into beaten egg to coat; then press into crumb mixture. Refrigerate overnight, or freeze.
**To freeze:** Open freeze on a baking sheet. When frozen, pack in a rigid freezer container. Cover and label. Freeze up to 1 month. Do not thaw before cooking.
**To serve immediately or after refrigerating or freezing:** Heat oil to 375F (190C) or until a 1-inch bread cube turns golden brown in 50 seconds. Deep-fry frozen cakes in hot oil about 8 minutes or until golden and heated through. If cooking immediately or after refrigerating, reduce cooking time. Serve with green vegetables or a salad. Makes 4 servings.

---

*Open freeze* foods such as fish cakes, meatballs or meat patties. Place unwrapped items to be frozen on a baking sheet. Freeze until firm. Place frozen items in plastic freezer bags or rigid freezer containers. The amount needed can be removed without thawing, because items will not be frozen together. Reseal and return remaining food to freezer.

# Cold Poached Trout with Hazelnut Mayonnaise

4 (7-oz.) trout, cleaned
2 bay leaves
Parsley sprigs
Salt
Freshly ground pepper

*Hazelnut Mayonnaise:*
1 egg
1 cup ground hazelnuts or walnuts
1/4 cup wine vinegar
4 to 6 tablespoons water
Salt
Freshly ground white pepper

*To serve:*
Parsley sprigs
Cucumber balls or small cubes

*Some people object to seeing heads on cooked fish. Remove heads before serving, if desired.*

**1.** Preheat oven to 350F (175C).
**2.** Trim trout fins. Put trimmed trout into a large shallow baking dish or roasting pan large enough to hold fish in 1 layer.
**3.** Cover with boiling water. Add bay leaves, parsley, salt and pepper. Cover with foil; bake in preheated oven 10 minutes. Cool in cooking liquid. When cool, drain cooked trout, discarding liquid and herbs. Slit skin from head to tail along back and stomach; carefully remove skin. Cover skinned trout tightly; refrigerate up to 2 days. Do not freeze.
**4.** To make mayonnaise, in a blender, process egg, nuts, vinegar and 1/4 cup water. Blend until smooth, adding more water if too stiff. Season with salt and white pepper. Cover and refrigerate.
**To serve immediately or after refrigerating:** Arrange skinned, cooked trout on a platter. Garnish with parsley and cucumber. Serve with Hazelnut Mayonnaise. Makes 4 servings.

Left to right: Cold Poached Trout with Hazelnut Mayonnaise, Seafood Continental with Spiced Rice

# Seafood Continental with Spiced Rice

2 tablespoons vegetable oil
2 garlic cloves, crushed
1 lb. tomatoes (3 or 4 small tomatoes), peeled, chopped
2 canned pimentos, drained, chopped
1/4 teaspoon dried leaf oregano
3 tablespoons white wine or water
8 oz. cod or other white-fish fillet, skinned, chopped
6 oz. deveined, peeled uncooked large shrimp
4 oz. deveined, peeled uncooked small shrimp

*Spiced Rice:*
1 tablespoon vegetable oil
6 cardamom pods
1 (3-inch) cinnamon stick
1 cup uncooked long-grain white rice
2-1/4 cups boiling water
Salt

**1.** Heat oil in a medium saucepan. Add garlic; sauté 1 minute. Stir in tomatoes, pimentos, oregano and wine or water. Cover; simmer 20 minutes.
**2.** Add fish and shrimp. Replace cover; cook 10 minutes longer. Cool 30 minutes. Refrigerate overnight, or freeze.
**3.** To make rice, heat oil in a medium saucepan. Stir in spices. Add rice, water and salt; bring to a boil. Simmer 15 minutes or until water is absorbed and rice is tender. Cool.
**To freeze:** Pack fish mixture and rice in separate rigid freezer containers. Cover and label. Freeze up to 1 month. Thaw frozen fish mixture and rice at room temperature until partially thawed. Do not thaw completely.
**To serve immediately or after refrigerating or thawing:** Fish and shrimp are completely cooked; be careful not to overcook when heating. Heat fish mixture in a saucepan over low heat; bring to a boil, stirring occasionally. In another saucepan, combine rice and 2 tablespoons water. Cover; heat until water has been absorbed. Remove spices. Serve hot fish mixture over hot rice. Makes 4 servings.

# Cod Steaks with Nutty Cheese Topping

4 (1/2-inch-thick) cod steaks
1/4 cup butter or margarine, room temperature
1 cup shredded Cheddar cheese (4 oz.)
1/2 cup chopped peanuts
2 teaspoons milk

**1.** Preheat broiler. Grease a broiler pan.
**2.** Place cod steaks in greased broiler pan; broil 5 minutes per side.
**3.** In a medium bowl, blend remaining ingredients; spread 1/2 over each steak.
**4.** Broil 5 to 10 minutes longer or until cheese topping has browned. Cool 30 minutes. Refrigerate overnight, or freeze.
**To freeze:** Pack cooled fish into a rigid freezer container. Cover and label. Freeze up to 1 month. Do not thaw before heating.
**To serve after refrigerating or freezing:** Place frozen fish in a greased baking dish. Cover with foil; heat in a preheated 350F (175C) oven about 20 minutes or until heated through. Reduce cooking time for refrigerated fish. Place under broiler to brown top, if desired. Serve with baked tomatoes and mashed potatoes. Makes 4 servings.

# Lamb Strudel

2 tablespoons butter or margarine
1 onion, finely chopped
1 lb. lean ground lamb
1/2 pint dairy sour cream (1 cup)
2 egg yolks
3/4 cup dry bread crumbs
2 tablespoons chopped fresh dill
Salt
Freshly ground pepper
4 filo leaves
1/4 cup butter or margarine, melted
1-1/2 cups tomato sauce, homemade or prepared

1. Melt butter or margarine in a medium skillet. Add onion; sauté until onion is transparent. Add ground lamb; sauté until no longer pink. Drain off fat; spoon lamb mixture into a large bowl.
2. In a medium bowl, beat sour cream and egg yolks until smooth. Stir in bread crumbs, dill, salt and pepper. Stir sour-cream mixture into lamb mixture.
3. Unfold filo leaves; place on a slightly damp towel. Cover with another damp towel. Remove 2 leaves; place on a dry towel, slightly overlapping. Brush with melted butter. Place remaining 2 leaves on top of buttered leaves; brush with melted butter.
4. Spoon lamb mixture 1/4 inch from 1 long edge of buttered filo leaves. Fold long narrow edge of dough up over meat mixture; fold in edges at short ends. Use towel to roll strudel over, jelly-roll style, until completely enclosed in dough. Brush seam with water; press to seal. Lift in towel; roll onto ungreased baking sheet, seam-side down. Brush with melted butter. Cover with plastic wrap; refrigerate until ready to bake.
**To serve immediately or after refrigerating:** Uncover strudel; bake in preheated 350 (175C) oven 20 to 25 minutes or until golden. Turn over; bake 20 minutes longer. Heat tomato sauce in a small saucepan; pour into a serving dish. Slice strudel; serve with sauce. Makes 6 to 8 servings.

# Double Rack of Lamb

2 lamb rib roasts, 6 to 8 ribs each, oven ready
*Stuffing:*
1/3 cup dried apricots
Water
2 tablespoons butter
2 medium leeks, cut into rings
1/2 cup uncooked long-grain white rice
1-1/2 cups chicken stock
2 tablespoons pine nuts
1/4 cup raisins
Salt
Freshly ground pepper

*Ask your butcher to prepare the lamb for you. If paper frills are unavailable, make foil frills.*

1. Place the racks of lamb together to form an arch. Crisscross bones. Refrigerate overnight, or freeze.
2. To make stuffing, soak apricots in water 30 minutes. Drain apricots, discarding water; chop soaked apricots. Melt butter in a medium saucepan. Add leeks; sauté until barely softened. Stir in rice; sauté 1 minute.
3. Stir in stock; bring to a boil. Cover; cook about 15 minutes or until rice is tender and all liquid has been absorbed.
4. Stir in chopped apricots, pine nuts and raisins. Add salt and pepper to taste. Set aside to cool. Refrigerate overnight, or freeze.
**To freeze:** Spoon cooled stuffing into a rigid freezer container. Cover and label. Wrap rib-bone ends with plastic wrap or waxed paper. Wrap roast in foil; label. Freeze stuffing and roast up to 1 month. Thaw overnight in refrigerator.
**To serve immediately or after refrigerating or thawing:** Spoon stuffing into center of roast. Cover rib ends with foil. Season with salt and pepper. Roast in preheated 400F (205C) oven 40 minutes or until desired doneness. Place cutlet frills on ends of bones, if desired. Makes 6 to 8 servings.

# Pork-Chop & Vegetable Casserole

8 pork chops
1/2 teaspoon dried leaf oregano
2 large onions, thickly sliced
1 small red bell pepper, cut into strips
1 small green bell pepper, cut into strips
1 zucchini, sliced
4 large tomatoes, peeled, sliced
1 teaspoon sugar
Salt
Freshly ground black pepper
1 cup red wine

1. Remove and discard bones from chops. Shape deboned chops into rounds, securing each with a wooden pick or string.
2. Grease a deep freezer-to-oven casserole; sprinkle with oregano. Arrange onions, bell peppers, zucchini and tomatoes in layers in casserole. Sprinkle with sugar; add salt and pepper to taste. Pour wine over vegetables.
3. Arrange boned chops on vegetables. Cover; bake in preheated oven about 1 hour. Cool 30 minutes. Skim off excess fat. Refrigerate overnight, or freeze.
**To freeze:** Cover and label. Freeze up to 1 month. Thaw at room temperature 3 to 4 hours or overnight in refrigerator.
**To serve immediately or after refrigerating or thawing:** Discard any fat from top of casserole. Heat in a preheated 350F (175C) oven about 45 minutes or until hot. Serve with new potatoes and a green salad. Makes 4 servings.

Pork-Chop & Vegetable Casserole

# Bacon & Brazil-Nut Stuffing

3/4 cup chopped cooked ham
1 small onion, finely chopped
2 cups fresh whole-wheat bread crumbs
2 tomatoes, peeled, chopped
1 Golden Delicious apple, peeled, grated
1/2 cup chopped Brazil nuts
2 tablespoons chopped fresh herbs
1 egg, beaten
Freshly ground pepper

**1.** In a medium bowl, combine all ingredients.
**2.** Refrigerate overnight, or freeze.
**To freeze:** Spoon stuffing into a rigid freezer container. Cover and label. Freeze up to 3 weeks. Thaw overnight in refrigerator.

# Prune & Almond Stuffing

1 tablespoon butter or margarine
1 small onion, chopped
4 oz. lean ground pork
2/3 cup raisins, chopped
1 cup fresh bread crumbs
1/2 cup chopped blanched almonds
1 egg, beaten
Salt
Freshly ground pepper

**1.** Melt butter or margarine in a large skillet. Add onion and pork; sauté until pork is grey, stirring frequently. Drain off and discard fat. Stir in remaining ingredients. Cool.
**2.** Refrigerate overnight, or freeze.
**To freeze:** Spoon stuffing into a rigid freezer container. Cover and label. Freeze up to 3 weeks. Thaw overnight in refrigerator.

# Cranberry & Rice Stuffing

2 tablespoons butter or margarine
4 green onions, thinly sliced
1 chicken or turkey liver, chopped
2 celery stalks, thinly sliced
2/3 cup cooked long-grain white rice
3 tablespoons cranberry sauce
1 egg, beaten
Salt
Freshly ground pepper

**1.** Melt butter or margarine in a large skillet. Add onions, liver and celery; sauté 5 minutes. Stir in remaining ingredients. Cool 30 minutes.
**2.** Refrigerate overnight, or freeze.
**To freeze:** Spoon stuffing into a rigid freezer container. Cover and label. Freeze up to 3 weeks. Thaw overnight in refrigerator.

# Roast Stuffed Chicken

1 (3- to 4-lb.) roasting chicken
*Stuffing:*
12 oz. lean ground pork
1 small onion, minced
3/4 cup fresh bread crumbs
2 eggs, beaten
1/2 teaspoon dried leaf tarragon
Salt
Freshly ground pepper
1/4 cup butter or margarine
8 oz. chicken livers, trimmed

*To garnish:*
Watercress

---

*Remove all bones except leg and wing bones. Leave them in to give chicken its usual shape. Carving is so easy that your guests will be impressed. To carve, cut off legs and wings; slice across body through meat and stuffing.*

**1.** With a sharp knife, cut along length of backbone through tail. Cutting close to bone, gradually ease away meat and skin from around body carcass, as shown below. When you reach joint connecting thigh bone and body, break it away from socket, leaving bones in leg. Repeat with wing joints.

**2.** Be careful not to slit skin over top of breast bone. When breast bone has been cut free, lift out body carcass. Lay chicken flat, skin-side down.

**3.** To make stuffing, in a medium bowl, combine pork, onion, bread crumbs, eggs, tarragon, salt and pepper.

**4.** Melt 2 tablespoons butter or margarine in a small skillet. Add livers: sauté gently 5 minutes. Set aside to cool. Coarsely chop cooled livers.

**5.** Spread 1/2 of pork mixture down center of chicken. Spread with chopped livers; cover livers with remaining pork mixture.

**6.** Bring cut edges of chicken together again; sew with needle and kitchen string to enclose stuffing completely. Shape chicken into its usual form; truss to hold legs and wings in place.

**To freeze:** Do not stuff chicken. Package and freeze boned chicken, chopped livers and stuffing separately. Freeze up to 3 weeks. Thaw frozen chicken, livers and stuffing overnight in refrigerator. Stuff, as directed above, immediately before roasting.

**To serve after refrigerating or thawing:** Place stuffed chicken in a roasting pan. Spread chicken with remaining 2 tablespoons butter or margarine; season with salt and pepper. Roast in preheated 350F (175C) oven 1-1/2 hours or until a thermometer inserted in stuffing registers 170F (75C) and juices run clear when chicken is pierced with a knife between breast and thigh. Carve by cutting off legs and wings, then slicing across body through stuffing and meat. Garnish with watercress. Makes 6 to 8 servings.

Left to right: Roast Stuffed Chicken, Anniversary Chicken Pastries

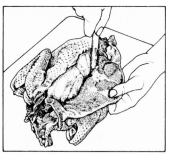

1/With a knife, separate meat from bone.

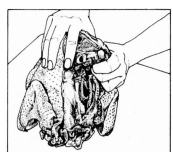

2/Break joint between thigh and body.

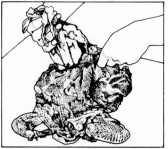

3/Cut breast bone free from meat.

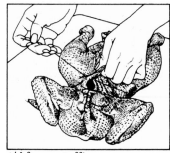

4/After stuffing, sew up chicken.

*These are fun to make for a wedding anniversary or Valentine's Day dinner party.*

**1.** To make pastry, in a medium bowl, combine flour and salt. Using a pastry blender or 2 knives, cut in butter or margarine and cream cheese until mixture resembles coarse crumbs. Sprinkle with 6 tablespoons water; toss with a fork until dough sticks together. Add more water, if necessary. Refrigerate dough 1 hour.

**2.** To make filling, melt butter or margarine in a large skillet. Add chicken; sauté 4 to 5 minutes or until lightly browned on both sides. Set aside to cool. In a medium bowl, combine almonds. cranberry sauce and onion. Season with salt and pepper.

**3.** To complete, cut chilled dough into 4 equal pieces. Roll out each dough piece on a lightly floured surface into a 9" x 8" rectangle.

**4.** Cut 1 dough rectangle in half crosswise. Lay a cooked chicken breast in center of 1 half. Spread chicken with 2 tablespoons cranberry mixture. Top with remaining dough half. Cut into a heart shape. Seal edges; crimp and flute. Place pastry heart on an ungreased baking sheet. Repeat with remaining dough, chicken and cranberry mixture, making 4 hearts.

**5.** Make decorative leaves or initials of anniversary guests with pastry trimmings. Moisten bottoms of decorations with water. Place decorations on pastry hearts. Refrigerate overnight, or freeze.

**To freeze:** Open freeze on baking sheets. When frozen, wrap in foil; label. Freeze up to 1 month. Thaw unwrapped pastry hearts on an ungreased baking sheet at room temperature 3 to 4 hours.

**To serve after refrigerating or thawing:** Brush with egg glaze. Bake in a preheated 425F (220C) oven 35 to 40 minutes or until golden brown. Serve hot. Makes 4 servings.

---

To *open freeze* means to freeze before wrapping. Place foods on a baking sheet or a plate, or freeze in pan or dish. This method is useful since many foods are difficult to package or wrap before freezing. Freezing firms the items and makes them more manageable.

---

# Anniversary Chicken Pastries

*Pastry:*
2-1/4 cups all-purpose flour
1 teaspoon salt
1/2 cup butter or margarine
1/2 (8-oz.) pkg. cream cheese, room temperature
6 to 8 tablespoons iced water
1 egg beaten with 1 tablespoon milk for glaze

*Chicken Filling:*
2 tablespoons butter or margarine, melted
4 boneless chicken-breast halves, skinned
5 tablespoons finely ground almonds
5 tablespoons cranberry sauce
1 tablespoon grated onion
Salt
Freshly ground white pepper

# Lamb Curry

2 tablespoons vegetable oil
1-1/2 lb. lamb stew cubes
1 medium onion, chopped
1 garlic clove, crushed
1 tablespoon ground coriander
2 teaspoons curry powder
1 teaspoon ground turmeric
1/2 teaspoon ground cumin
1/4 teaspoon chili powder
1/4 teaspoon ground cinnamon
1/4 teaspoon ground ginger
1/4 teaspoon freshly grated or ground nutmeg
1 tablespoon all-purpose flour
1 tablespoon tomato paste
1 teaspoon lemon juice
1 tablespoon shredded coconut
2 tablespoons raisins
1-1/2 cups hot chicken stock
Salt
Freshly ground pepper

**1.** Heat oil in a large skillet. Add lamb, onion and garlic. Sauté until browned. Stir in spices and flour until lamb is coated.
**2.** Stir in tomato paste, lemon juice, coconut, raisins and stock. Simmer about 30 minutes or until lamb is tender. Season with salt and pepper. Cool 30 minutes. Refrigerate overnight, or freeze.
**To freeze:** Spoon into a rigid freezer container. Cover and label. Freeze up to 1 month. Thaw overnight in refrigerator.
**To serve after refrigerating or thawing:** Heat curry in a medium saucepan; bring to a boil. Serve with hot cooked rice. Makes 4 servings.

Top to bottom: Lamb Curry, Moussaka

# Moussaka

1 large eggplant, sliced
Salt
About 3 tablespoons olive oil
1 lb. ground lamb or beef
2 medium onions, thinly sliced
2 garlic cloves, crushed
3 tablespoons all-purpose flour
3 tablespoons tomato paste
1 teaspoon Italian seasoning
1/2 cup beef stock
Freshly ground pepper

*Topping:*
2 tablespoons butter or magarine
3 tablespoons all-purpose flour
1 teaspoon dry mustard
1 cup milk
1/2 cup shredded Cheddar cheese (2 oz.)
1 egg, beaten

---

1. Place eggplant slices in a colander; sprinkle with salt. Let stand 30 minutes. Rinse with cold water; drain.
2. Heat 2 tablespoons olive oil in a large skillet. Add drained eggplant slices, in batches; cook 3 minutes, turning once. Add more oil, if necessary. Using tongs, place cooked eggplant on paper towels to drain.
3. Add lamb or beef, onions and garlic to same skillet; sauté until meat is browned. Stir in flour until blended. Stir in tomato paste, Italian seasoning and stock. Cook until thickened, stirring constantly. Season with salt and pepper.
4. To make topping, melt butter or margarine in a medium saucepan. Stir in flour and mustard; cook 1 minute, stirring constantly. Stir in milk; cook until thickened. Remove from heat; stir in cheese until melted. Stir in egg.
5. In a large shallow casserole, alternate layers of meat mixture and cooked eggplant, beginning and ending with eggplant. Pour topping over last eggplant layer. Cool. Refrigerate overnight, or freeze.
**To freeze:** Cover casserole with foil; label. Freeze up to 1 month. Thaw overnight in refrigerator.
**To serve immediately or after refrigerating or thawing:** Bake in a preheated 350F (175C) oven 35 minutes or until hot and bubbly. Serve with a green salad and bread. Makes 4 servings.

# Chicken with Apples & Cream

2 tablespoons butter or margarine
1 tablespoon vegetable oil
4 boneless chicken breasts, skinned
1 medium onion, finely chopped
2 Golden Delicious apples, peeled, sliced
1/2 cup apple juice
4 crisp-cooked bacon slices, crumbled
Salt
Freshly ground pepper

*To serve:*
2 Golden Delicious apples, cored, cut into rings
2 tablespoons brown sugar
1/4 cup butter or margarine
2 tablespoons Calvados or other brandy, warmed
1/2 cup whipping cream

---

1. Preheat oven to 375F (190C). Heat butter or margarine and oil in a flameproof casserole. Add chicken; sauté until browned.
2. With tongs, remove browned chicken from casserole; set aside. Add onion to casserole; sauté until softened. Add sliced apples, apple juice, bacon, salt and pepper.
3. Return chicken to casserole. Cover casserole; bake in preheated oven about 25 minutes or until chicken is tender. Cool 30 minutes. Refrigerate overnight, or freeze.
**To freeze:** Spoon sauce mixture into bottom of a rigid freezer container; add chicken breasts. Cover and label. Freeze up to 1 month. Thaw overnight in refrigerator or at room temperature 2 to 3 hours.
**To serve immediately or after refrigerating or thawing:** Place chicken, without sauce, in a baking dish; cover with foil. Heat in a preheated 350F (175C) oven about 20 minutes or until heated through. Meanwhile, coat apple rings in sugar. Melt butter or margarine in a large skillet. Add apple rings; sauté until browned. Remove from skillet; keep hot. Add sauce mixture to skillet; bring to a boil, stirring occasionally. Simmer until reduced by 1/3. Add Calvados or brandy; ignite. Shake pan until flames die. Stir in cream; adjust seasoning. Heat, but do not boil. Arrange hot chicken in a serving dish; top with sauce. Garnish with sautéed apple rings. Makes 4 servings.

# Individual Beef Wellingtons

4 (6-oz.) beef-loin tenderloin steaks
Vegetable oil
1 garlic clove, crushed
4 oz. soft liver pâté
1 (17-1/4-oz.) pkg. frozen puff pastry, thawed
1 egg, beaten for glaze

1. Preheat broiler. Brush steaks with oil. Broil under preheated broiler 5 minutes per side. Cool.

2. In a small bowl, mash garlic into pâté.
3. Cut each pastry sheet in half crosswise. Roll out each half-sheet on a lightly floured surface into a rectangle large enough to enclose 1 steak.
4. Place 1 steak in center of each rectangle. Spread steaks with garlic-flavored pâté. Dampen edges of pastry; fold to enclose steaks. Press edges to seal. Decorate with pastry leaves cut from trimmings. Refrigerate overnight, or freeze.

**To freeze:** Open freeze on a baking sheet. When frozen, wrap in foil; label. Freeze up to 1 month. Thaw in refrigerator 4 to 6 hours.

**To serve immediately or after refrigerating or thawing:** Place unwrapped packets on a baking sheet; brush with beaten egg. Bake in preheated 425F (220C) oven 20 to 25 minutes or until crust is puffed and golden brown. Serve hot. Makes 4 servings.

Individual Beef Wellington

# Beef Steaks Chasseur

1/4 cup butter or margarine
2 tablespoons vegetable oil
1 large onion, thinly sliced
1 lb. mushrooms, finely chopped
1/2 cup white wine
Salt
Freshly ground pepper

*To serve:*
6 (6-oz.) sirloin or porterhouse steaks, cut 1 inch thick
Parsley sprigs

**1.** Heat butter or margarine and oil in a medium skillet. Add onion; sauté until soft. Add mushrooms; sauté 8 to 10 minutes or until softened.

**2.** Stir in wine, salt and pepper. Cook 5 minutes longer; cool. Refrigerate overnight, or freeze.

**To freeze:** Spoon mushroom mixture into a rigid freezer container. Cover and label. Freeze up to 1 month. Thaw at room temperature 2 to 3 hours.

**To serve immediately or after refrigerating or thawing:** Preheat broiler or grill. Heat mushroom mixture in a medium saucepan until hot. Broil steaks to desired doneness. Place broiled steaks on individual plates; top with hot mushroom mixture. Garnish with parsley. Makes 6 servings.

Beef Steaks Chasseur

# Beef & Ham Loaf

1-1/2 lb. lean ground beef
8 oz. ground cooked ham
1 large onion, minced
1-1/2 cups fresh whole-wheat bread crumbs
2 eggs
1 teaspoon dried mixed herbs, any combination
1 tablespoon chopped parsley
1 teaspoon salt
Freshly ground pepper

*Topping:*
3 large tomatoes, peeled, chopped
1 (7-oz.) can pimentos, drained, chopped
1 medium onion, thinly sliced

---

1. Preheat oven to 350F (175C).
2. In a large bowl, combine beef, ham, minced onion, bread crumbs, eggs, mixed herbs, parsley, salt and pepper.
3. To make topping, combine tomatoes, pimentos and sliced onion in a medium saucepan. Simmer 10 minutes or until vegetables are barely tender, stirring occasionally.
4. Spread topping in bottom of a 9" x 5" non-stick loaf pan or use a generously greased loaf pan. Spoon meat mixture over topping, spreading evenly. Cover with waxed paper and foil.
5. Place pan in a roasting pan containing about 1 inch water. Bake in preheated oven 1-1/2 hours. Remove waxed paper and foil. Cool 30 minutes. Refrigerate overnight, or freeze.
**To freeze:** Cover with fresh foil; label. Freeze up to 1 month. Thaw overnight in refrigerator.
**To serve after refrigerating or thawing:** Place covered loaf pan in a roasting pan containing water. Heat in a preheated 350F (175C) oven about 1 hour. Invert on a platter; remove pan. Serve with scalloped potatoes and green vegetables. To serve cold, line a platter with lettuce leaves; invert cold loaf onto lined platter. Makes 6 servings.

## Variation

**Pâté en Croûte:** Do not make topping. Make pastry for a 9-inch double-crust pie. Line loaf pan with 2/3 of pastry. Fill with meat mixture; cover with remaining pastry. Brush with beaten egg. Bake in a preheated 400F (205C) oven 30 minutes. Reduce heat to 325F (165C); bake 45 minutes longer. Cool 30 minutes. Wrap as above; freeze. Thaw overnight in refrigerator. Serve warm or cold with a tomato sauce.

# Roast Beef with Ale Sauce

1 (2-1/2-lb.) beef bottom-round roast
Salt
Freshly ground pepper
3 tablespoons all-purpose flour
1 cup light ale or beer
1 tablespoon tomato paste

*To serve:*
2 tablespoons butter or margarine
2 large leeks, cut into 1/2-inch rings
3 celery stalks, sliced

*To garnish:*
Celery leaves

---

1. Preheat oven to 325F (165C).
2. Place roast on a rack in a roasting pan. Season with salt and pepper.
3. Roast in preheated oven 1 to 1-1/2 hours for medium done, 160F (70C) internal temperature, or to desired degree of doneness.
4. Remove roast from pan; set aside. Spoon off excess fat from pan drippings. In a small bowl, blend flour and 1/4 cup ale or beer into a paste. Add remaining ale or beer to roasting pan; bring to a boil, scraping up browned bits for sauce. Stir in tomato paste and flour paste. Cook sauce until thickened, stirring constantly. Set aside to cool. Slice roast. Refrigerate overnight, or freeze.
**To freeze:** Pack roast slices in a rigid freezer container. Cover and label. Freeze up to 2 months. Pour sauce into a separate rigid freezer container. Cover and label. Freeze up to 2 months. Thaw frozen meat and sauce overnight in refrigerator.
**To serve immediately or after refrigerating or thawing:** Place meat in a shallow casserole. Cover; heat in a preheated 325F (165C) oven 20 minutes or until heated through. While meat is heating, melt butter or margarine in a large skillet. Add leeks and celery; sauté until softened. Heat sauce in a medium saucepan; bring to a boil, stirring occasionally. Pour hot sauce over hot meat. Serve with sautéed leeks and celery. Garnish with celery leaves. Makes 6 to 8 servings.

## Variation

If desired, freeze meat and sauce in the same container. To serve, thaw and heat together in a medium saucepan over low heat.

Top to bottom: Beef & Ham Loaf, Roast Beef with Ale Sauce

# Pork Strips with Sage

**2 cups fresh white bread crumbs**
**4 teaspoons rubbed sage**
**1 teaspoon salt**
**Freshly ground pepper**
**2 (10-oz.) pork-loin tenderloins**
**2 eggs, beaten**
**Vegetable oil for deep-frying**
**Applesauce**

*Serve these for a dinner party with scalloped potatoes and broccoli.*

**1.** In a shallow bowl, combine bread crumbs, sage, salt and pepper.
**2.** Cut pork into 1/4-inch slices. Cut each slice in half lengthwise to make strips.
**3.** Dip pork strips into eggs; coat evenly in crumb mixture. Place coated strips in a single layer on a baking sheet. Refrigerate overnight, or freeze.

**To freeze:** Open freeze on a baking sheet. When frozen, pack in a freezer container or plastic freezer bag. Cover and label. Freeze up to 1 month. Do not thaw.

**To serve immediately or after refrigerating or freezing:** In a deep saucepan or deep-fryer, heat oil to 375F (190C) or until a 1-inch bread cube turns golden brown in 50 seconds. Deep-fry frozen pork strips 5 to 8 minutes or until browned, crisp and cooked through. Reduce cooking time for unfrozen strips. Drain on paper towels. Serve with applesauce. Makes 6 servings.

Left to right: Pork Strips with Sage, Pork with Orange & Onion Stuffing

# Pork with Orange & Onion Stuffing

2 tablespoons butter or margarine
1 large onion, thinly sliced
Grated peel and sections of 2 large oranges
1/2 cup dry bread crumbs
Salt
Freshly ground pepper
1 (3-lb.) boneless pork loin
1 tablespoon brown sugar

*To garnish:*
Orange slices
Lettuce leaves
Watercress

1. Preheat oven to 350F (175C).
2. To make stuffing, melt butter or margarine in a large skillet. Add onion; sauté until lightly browned. Stir in orange peel and orange sections, bread crumbs, salt and pepper.
3. Lay pork flat; spread with stuffing. Roll up to enclose stuffing; tie with kitchen string.
4. Place stuffed roast on a rack in a roasting pan. Rub with sugar, salt and pepper.
5. Roast in preheated oven 1-1/2 to 2 hours or until a thermometer inserted into center of stuffing registers 170F (75C). Juices should run clear when meat is pierced. Cool 30 minutes. Refrigerate overnight, or freeze.
**To freeze:** Wrap in plastic wrap and foil, or put into a freezer container; label. Freeze up to 1 month. Thaw in refrigerator 12 hours.
**To serve immediately or after refrigerating or thawing:** To serve cold, slice meat; arrange on a serving dish. Garnish with sliced oranges, lettuce leaves and watercress. Serve with a salad or pickles and hot baked potatoes. To serve hot, place in a roasting pan. Heat in a preheated 350F (175C) oven about 45 minutes. If desired, make a gravy from pan juices and 2 to 3 tablespoons fresh orange juice. Garnish as for serving cold. Makes 6 to 8 servings.

# Deviled Pork Chops

6 large pork chops
Salt
Freshly ground pepper
1 (8-oz.) can tomatoes
3 tablespoons ketchup
1 tablespoon soy sauce
2 tablespoons Worcestershire sauce
2 teaspoons prepared brown mustard
2 tablespoons wine vinegar
1 tablespoon brown sugar

*Hot cooked rice is a good accompaniment to this spicy dish. Double the recipe, if desired.*

1. Preheat broiler.
2. Place chops on a broiler-pan rack. Sprinkle with salt and pepper. Broil until browned on both sides, about 10 minutes per side. Cool 30 minutes.
3. In a blender or food processor fitted with a steel blade, puree tomatoes with their juice. Stir in ketchup, soy sauce, Worcestershire sauce, mustard, vinegar and brown sugar.
**To freeze:** Place cooled chops in a rigid freezer container; pour tomato mixture over chops. Cover and label. Freeze up to 1 month. Thaw at room temperature 3 to 4 hours.
**To serve immediately or after refrigerating or thawing:** Place chops and sauce in an ovenproof serving dish. Cover; cook in a preheated 350F (175C) oven about 45 minutes or until heated through and bubbling. Makes 6 servings.

**Variation**
Omit tomato mixture. In a medium saucepan, combine 1 cup unsweetened apple juice, 3 tablespoons red-currant jelly and 1/2 teaspoon rubbed sage. Heat until jelly dissolves. Simmer 2 to 3 minutes to thicken sauce slightly. Pour over cooked chops. Freeze and serve as above.

# Veal Marsala

2 tablespoons all-purpose flour
Salt
Freshly ground white pepper
Grated peel of 1 small orange
4 veal cutlets, beaten until thin
5 tablespoons butter or margarine
1 tablespoon vegetable oil
8 oz. button mushrooms, thinly sliced

*To serve:*
1/2 cup Marsala
1/2 cup dairy sour cream
Milk
Cooked zucchini strips, if desired

---

*Turkey cutlets are a good substitute for veal. Substitute sweet sherry for Marsala, if desired.*

1. In a shallow bowl, combine flour, salt, white pepper and orange peel. Coat cutlets with seasoned flour.
2. Heat 1/4 cup butter or margarine with oil in a large skillet. Add coated cutlets; sauté over low heat about 4 minutes on each side.
3. Remove cooked cutlets from skillet; set aside to cool. Add remaining tablespoon butter or margarine to skillet. Add mushrooms; sauté 3 minutes, turning gently. Cool. Refrigerate overnight, or freeze.
**To freeze:** Place cooled cutlets into a rigid freezer container. Add cooled mushrooms. Cover and label. Freeze up to 1 month. Thaw at room temperature 2 to 3 hours.
**To serve immediately or after refrigerating or thawing:** Place cutlets and mushrooms into an ovenproof serving dish. Add Marsala. Cover; bake in a preheated 350F (175C) oven 25 to 30 minutes or until heated through. Thin sour cream with a little milk, if necessary; spoon over heated cutlets. Serve with zucchini, if desired. Makes 4 servings.

### Variation

**Veal Grand Marnier:** Substitute 2 teaspoons dried leaf tarragon for orange peel in step 1. Grate peel from 2 large oranges. Juice 1 orange; section other orange. Cook cutlets as in step 2. In step 3, omit mushrooms. Add remaining butter or margarine, grated orange peel and orange juice; bring to a boil. Add orange sections and 2 tablespoons Grand Marnier. Bring back to a boil. Serve cooked cutlets topped with a spoonful of orange sauce.

# Ham & Cheese Pie

*Pastry:*
3 cups all-purpose flour
1 teaspoon salt
1 cup vegetable shortening
1 egg yolk
1/2 cup iced water
*Filling:*
16 oz. small-curd cottage cheese or
    ricotta cheese (2 cups)
2 eggs
1 teaspoon Italian seasoning
Salt
Freshly ground pepper
1-1/2 cups chopped cooked ham
1 (10-oz.) pkg. frozen chopped spinach,
    thawed, well drained
1/2 cup grated Parmesan cheese (1-1/2 oz.)
1 egg yolk beaten with 1 tablespoon milk for glaze

---

1. Preheat oven to 375F (190C).
2. To prepare pastry, in a medium bowl, combine flour and salt. Using a pastry blender or 2 knives, cut in shortening until mixture resembles coarse crumbs. Blend egg yolk and water; sprinkle over flour mixture. Toss with a fork until mixture begins to stick together.
3. Gather pastry; shape into a ball. Divide pastry into 2 pieces, making 1 piece 2/3 of dough. Roll out larger piece of pastry to a 14-inch circle on a lightly floured surface. Line an 8-inch springform pan with pastry. Press onto bottom and up side of pan. Do not trim pastry edge.
4. To make filling, in a blender or food processor fitted with a steel blade, process cottage cheese or ricotta cheese, eggs, Italian seasoning, salt and pepper until smooth. Stir in 3/4 cup ham.
5. Spoon filling into bottom of pastry-lined pan. Scatter spinach over filling; sprinkle with 1/4 cup Parmesan cheese. Top with remaining ham and Parmesan cheese. Brush edge of pastry with water.
6. Roll out remaining pastry to a 9-inch circle on a lightly floured surface. Place over filling. Crimp and flute pastry edges to seal. Slash center of pastry for steam vent. Brush pastry with egg-yolk glaze.
7. Bake in preheated oven 1-1/2 hours or until top is golden brown. Cool completely in pan on a wire rack. Refrigerate overnight, or freeze.
**To freeze:** Open freeze in pan. When frozen, remove pie from pan. Wrap in foil; label. Freeze up to 1 month. Thaw wrapped pie at room temperature 2 to 3 hours or in refrigerator overnight.
**To serve after refrigerating or thawing:** If desired, place on a baking sheet; heat in preheated 300F (150C) oven 20 to 30 minutes or until warm. Serve warm or cold with a tossed green salad. Makes 4 to 6 servings.

Clockwise from upper left: Brandied Chicken Livers & Noodles,
Ham & Cheese Pie, Veal Marsala

# Brandied Chicken Livers & Noodles

**1/2 cup butter or margarine**
**1 shallot, finely chopped**
**1 lb. chicken livers, trimmed, halved**
**4 oz. button mushrooms, quartered**
**Salt**
**Freshly ground pepper**

*To serve:*
**8 oz. egg noodles**
**2 tablespoons butter or margarine**
**6 tablespoons brandy, warmed**
**1/2 pint whipping cream (1 cup)**

*To garnish:*
**Chopped parsley**

**1.** Melt butter or margarine in a large skillet. Add shallot; sauté until softened. Add livers; sauté 3 minutes or until livers are no longer pink in center.

**2.** Add mushrooms; sauté 5 minutes longer. Season with salt and pepper. Cool 30 minutes. Refrigerate overnight, or freeze.

**To freeze:** Spoon cooled liver mixture into a rigid freezer container. Cover and label. Freeze up to 1 month. Thaw at room temperature 3 to 4 hours.

**To serve immediately or after refrigerating or thawing:** Heat liver mixture in a medium saucepan; bring to a boil, stirring occasionally. Meanwhile, cook noodles according to package directions until tender. Drain cooked noodles; toss with butter or margarine. Pour warmed brandy over livers; ignite brandy. When flames die, add cream. Heat but do not boil. Adjust seasoning. Serve brandied livers over hot noodles. Sprinkle with parsley. Makes 4 servings.

# Princess Sole

1 (15-oz.) can asparagus spears, drained
4 sole fillets (about 1-1/2 lb.), skinned
1 shallot, finely chopped
5 tablespoons dry white wine
5 tablespoons fish stock or clam juice
1/4 cup butter, cut in 6 pieces
1/2 cup whipping cream
Salt
Freshly ground pepper

*If you ask, fish markets will often give you fish bones to make stock. Cover fish bones with water; add a little parsley, lemon peel, salt and pepper. Simmer about 15 minutes. Strain before using.*

**1.** Preheat oven to 350F (175C). Grease a shallow baking dish.
**2.** Reserve 8 asparagus spears for garnish. Chop remaining spears.
**3.** Lay sole fillets, skinned-side up, on a board. Divide chopped asparagus among fillets; roll to enclose asparagus.
**4.** Sprinkle greased baking dish with shallot; arrange rolled fillets in dish. Pour over wine and fish stock or clam juice. Cover with foil; bake in preheated oven 10 minutes. Cool 30 minutes. Lay 2 reserved asparagus spears on each rolled fillet. Refrigerate overnight, or freeze.
**To freeze:** Wrap dish in foil; label. Freeze up to 2 months. Thaw wrapped fillets in refrigerator 6 to 8 hours.
**To serve immediately or after refrigerating or thawing:** Heat in a preheated 350F (175C) oven about 10 minutes. Drain liquid into a medium saucepan; boil to reduce liquid by 1/2. Beat in butter, a piece at a time. Beat until each piece is incorporated before adding more. Whip cream lightly; fold into sauce. Season with salt and pepper. Pour seasoned sauce over fish. Brown top of dish under a preheated broiler, if desired. Serve with mashed potatoes and green beans. Makes 4 servings.

# Salmon Mousse

1 (15-1/2-oz.) can red sockeye salmon or pink salmon
1 (1/4-oz.) envelope unflavored gelatin
  (1 tablespoon)
1/4 cup cold water
1/2 (8-oz.) pkg. cream cheese, room temperature
2/3 cup mayonnaise
2/3 cup plain yogurt
2 tablespoons lemon juice
1/3 cup finely chopped dill pickle
1 teaspoon dried dill weed

*For garnish:*
1 hard-cooked egg
Thinly sliced pimento-stuffed olives
Chopped fresh parsley
Shredded lettuce leaves

**1.** Lightly oil an 8" x 4" loaf pan; set aside.
**2.** Drain salmon, reserving liquid in a 1-cup measuring cup. Add enough water to salmon liquid to measure 1/2 cup. Place salmon in a medium bowl. Remove and discard bones, if desired. Mash salmon with a fork; set aside.
**3.** In a small saucepan, combine gelatin and water. Stir well; let stand 3 minutes. Stir over low heat until gelatin dissolves. Add reserved salmon liquid; stir until blended. Set aside to cool.
**4.** In a medium bowl, beat cream cheese until smooth. Beat in mayonnaise and yogurt. Fold in mashed salmon, lemon juice, dill pickle, dill weed and cooled gelatin mixture. Spoon salmon mixture into oiled loaf pan; smooth top. Cover and refrigerate until set. Do not freeze.
**To serve after refrigerating:** Wet a clean dish towel with hot water; squeeze dry. Wrap hot wet towel around loaf pan 30 seconds. Invert mousse onto a serving plate; remove pan. Cut hard-cooked egg in half; remove yolk. Sieve yolk; finely chop egg white. Decorate top of mousse with rows of sliced olives, parsley, sieved egg yolk and chopped egg white. Surround with shredded lettuce leaves. Serve with a cucumber salad and boiled new potatoes. Makes 6 servings.

# Seafood Salad

4 large scallops, fresh or frozen
1 bay leaf
4 (1-inch) lemon-peel strips
Salt
Freshly ground white pepper
3/4 cup cooked long-grain white rice
4 oz. deveined, peeled cooked shrimp
1 tablespoon chopped fresh parsley
1 tablespoon lemon juice
1/4 cup sliced almonds
2 celery stalks, thinly sliced
6 tablespoons thick mayonnaise
4 cleaned scallop shells

*To serve:*
1/4 cup mayonnaise
Cooked unpeeled shrimp
4 parsley sprigs
Paprika
Lettuce leaves, if desired

1. Place scallops in a saucepan with bay leaf, lemon peel, salt and white pepper. Cover with water. Simmer 5 minutes. Drain cooked scallops, discarding bay leaf and lemon peel. Chop cooked scallops; set aside to cool.
2. In a medium bowl, combine chopped scallops, rice, shrimp, chopped parsley, lemon juice, almonds, celery and mayonnaise. Season with salt and pepper. Chill before serving.
**To serve:** Spoon salad into scallop shells. Top each salad with mayonnaise, 1 whole shrimp, 1 parsley sprig and a little paprika. Garnish plate with lettuce, if desired. Serve with hot rolls. Makes 4 servings.

Left to right: Seafood Salad, Salmon Mousse

# Microwave

## GETTING TO KNOW YOUR MICROWAVE OVEN

This guide will help you enjoy the full potential of the most revolutionary addition to today's kitchen—the microwave. Revised standard recipes and delicious new ones demonstrate the time-saving versatility of this exciting appliance.

In-depth information and full-color how-to photographs will enable you to make the microwave work for you as never before. You will find many useful tips for adapting your favorite recipes so they can be cooked in the microwave.

This incredible appliance is geared to your busy lifestyle. Get to know it with the help of this book. The following questions and answers give information that is basic to cooking a wide range of foods in your microwave.

**Q. What are the main advantages of cooking with a microwave?**

**A.** Compared with conventional cooking, the greatest advantage is fast cooking time for all but a few items. This in turn saves energy and reduces the heat output into your kitchen, a tremendous plus during the summer. The fast cooking encourages maximum retention of vitamins and flavor in vegetables and other foods.

**Q. Can you stir or check food in the microwave while the oven is operating?**

**A.** The microwave power will automatically shut off when you open the oven door. Check on the food, close the oven door and then restart the microwave. Or, if the food is done, turn the timer to OFF.

**Q. Can you change power levels while the microwave is operating?**

**A.** You certainly can. If food is boiling too hard, for example, change the power to a lower level to cook more slowly. It's similar to using a burner on top of the range.

**Q. What are microwave hot spots?**

**A.** Most microwaves have one area that has a concentration of microwaves and consequently cooks food more quickly. This explains why it is necessary to stir and rearrange foods or turn dishes during cooking. This action rotates the food through the hot spot and contributes to even cooking. Some rearranging is also recommended for ovens with the carousel or rotating feature.

**Q. How do you know where the hot spot is in a particular microwave?**

**A.** Watch which area of food in a large casserole starts to bubble first or which area of cheese on a casserole melts first. This is a good indication of where the hot spot is.

**Q. Why does the amount of food affect the microwave cooking time?**

**A.** Unlike conventional cooking, 6 baked potatoes will not cook in the same length of time in the microwave as 2 potatoes. Foods have to absorb microwave energy in order to cook. More food absorbing microwave energy means less microwave energy is available for each item. The same is true for the contents of a casserole. The amount in a large casserole takes longer to heat than the amount in a small casserole.

**Q. What other factors affect microwave cooking times?**

**A.** The starting temperature of food affects the cooking time. Frozen peas, for example, take longer to cook than canned peas that start at room temperature. The shape of food also affects microwave cooking times. Microwave ovens cook food from the outside toward the inside. Therefore, thin foods cook faster than thick foods. The center of a dish heats more slowly than the edges. Select foods that are uniform in size and shape for more even microwave cooking. The composition of foods also affects the microwave cooking time. Foods high in fat and sugar cook faster in the microwave.

**Q. Which utensils can be used in the microwave?**

**A.** Refer to your manufacturer's use-and-care guide. Generally, ovenproof glass, ceramic and pottery dishes, including clay pots, with no metallic trim or parts, oven cooking bags and frozen-food pouches can all be used for microwave cooking. Paper should be used only for short cooking times. Plastics vary widely; check the plastic cookware package description to find plastic utensils recommended for microwave cooking. Some will melt or distort, especially if used with foods high in fat or sugar content. Baskets and wooden boards without any metal parts can be used in the microwave for brief reheating of foods such as rolls. Many specially designed microwave utensils are available. They include browning skillets, plastic or ceramic meat-roasting racks, fluted tube dishes, muffin dishes and ring molds.

**Q. Which utensils cannot be used in the microwave?**

**A.** Metal in any form should not be used unless the manufacturer of your oven states otherwise. This includes metal twist ties and dishes with decorative metal trim. There are two reasons for this. The most important is that it may cause *arcing* which looks and sounds like lightning or sparks inside the oven. The other reason for not using metal is that it reflects microwaves away from itself rather than allowing them to pass through the material and cause the food to become hot. This shielding effect of metal can be used to advantage when cooking large items such as roast meat or poultry. During the longer cooking time required for these items, some areas tend to cook faster than others. To prevent overbrowning, these areas can be shielded with small pieces of foil held in place with wooden picks. Never allow the foil to touch the oven walls.

**Q. How do you know if a dish is safe to use in a microwave?**

A. Place 1 cup of cool water in the microwave beside the dish you are testing. Microwave at 100% (HIGH) for 1 minute. If the dish is warm, it is absorbing microwave energy and should not be used in the microwave.

## SOUPS & SAUCES

**Q. What are the advantages of cooking soups and sauces in the microwave?**

A. Individual servings of soup can be heated in moments in mugs or bowls. Big batches of soup made on top of the range can be frozen in family-size portions and reheated in the microwave. Sauces don't need to be stirred constantly as they do on top of the range. And there's an added bonus; they don't stick to the dish!

**Q. Which soups or sauces do not cook satisfactorily in the microwave?**

A. Dried-bean and pea soups can be cooked successfully in the microwave, but not much time is saved. When a sauce depends on eggs for thickening, it is difficult to prevent it from curdling.

**Q. How do you know when soups and sauces are done?**

A. Soups should be at least 170F (75C) before serving. Be sure to stir soups before serving to help equalize the temperature throughout the soup. Remember that soups bubble around the edges long before the center is hot. Thickened sauces also start to bubble at the edges partway through the cooking time. Don't stop cooking then! Stir the sauce often with a whisk to prevent lumping; continue cooking according to the recipe until the sauce is thickened and smooth.

## MEATS

**Q. What are the advantages of cooking meat in the microwave?**

A. Most meats can be cooked in the microwave with a good time saving. In addition, there are fewer preparation dishes and no baked-on mess to clean up.

**Q. What are the disadvantages of cooking meat in the microwave?**

A. A few meats, such as pot roast, take almost as long to cook in the microwave as they would conventionally. In addition, these meats usually require more attention from the cook when the microwave is used. Unless the microwave is the only cooking device available, it may be less trouble to cook these recipes conventionally. Roasts may be cooked considerably faster in the microwave. But they also require more attention and should be a uniform and compact shape. When considering cost, time and convenience, many cooks may feel more comfortable cooking them conventionally.

**Q. Which meats do not cook satisfactorily in the microwave?**

A. Meats cannot be deep-fried in the microwave. Extra-large roasts and pot roasts are difficult to cook in the microwave because it is not easy to achieve an even doneness.

## POULTRY
The natural tenderness of poultry makes it ideal for fast microwave cooking.

**Q. Why do you rearrange chicken pieces during microwave cooking?**

A. Chicken pieces are rearranged to promote even cooking. Move the center pieces of chicken to the outside of the dish and the ones from the outside edges to the center. Whole birds are turned over partway through the cooking time for the same reason.

**Q. Will poultry brown in the microwave?**

A. Poultry cooks so quickly in the microwave that the browning often needs a little assistance. Sauces and glazes enhance the appearance of whole birds. Chicken pieces can be cooked in sauce or crumbs for color.

## FISH & SEAFOOD
Use the microwave oven to produce delicious summer dishes without heating up your kitchen.

**Q. How is fish cooked in the microwave?**

A. Because fish is already tender, most varieties cook very satisfactorily at 100% (HIGH) in the microwave.

**Q. What are the disadvantages of cooking fish in the microwave?**

A. Shellfish becomes tough if overcooked in the microwave. Watch shellfish carefully and test for doneness before the end of the cooking time.

**Q. Can fish be pan-fried in the microwave?**

A. Breaded fish can be cooked quickly and successfully in the microwave with special browning skillets. The opposite is true for batter-coated fish which tends to get soggy when cooked in the browning skillet. Frozen fish portions and fish sticks that are breaded give particularly good results.

**Q. How do you know when fish is done?**

A. Using the tines of a fork, gently lift up the flesh in the center of the fish. The flesh should be beginning to flake. It will continue cooking during the standing time. Shellfish usually turns from translucent in its raw state to opaque when cooked.

## EGGS & CHEESE

**Q. How are eggs cooked in the microwave?**

A. Because eggs are already tender, most egg dishes cook at 100% (HIGH). The exceptions are quiches and layered casseroles. They are cooked at a lower power so the centers will get done without overcooking the edges.

**Q. Which egg dishes do not cook satisfactorily in the microwave?**

**A.** Never try to cook an egg in the shell in the microwave. The egg will explode, making a considerable mess in the oven. To cook whole eggs out of the shell, prick the yolk with a fork or wooden pick. The yolk has a high fat content and consequently attracts microwaves more than the white. In addition, the yolk has an outer membrane that has the same effect as the egg shell, so unpricked yolks are likely to explode. Egg dishes that rely on the puffiness of beaten egg whites are not successful in the microwave. Soufflés or puffy omelets puff beautifully while they are being cooked in the microwave, but they fall immediately when removed. Even using low power levels, the outside edges will be tough and overcooked by the time the center of the soufflé is done.

### Q. How do you know when eggs are done?

**A.** For most egg dishes in large casseroles, a knife inserted in the center should feel hot. Cooking casseroles is deceiving; the edges will bubble vigorously before the center is even warm. That is why bringing the edges of the casserole to the center promotes more even heating.

## VEGETABLES & SALADS

### Q. What are the advantages of cooking vegetables in the microwave?

**A.** Vegetables have more flavor when cooked in the microwave because they cook more quickly. They usually require little or no water that might dilute some of the flavor. Studies indicate that vegetables cooked in the microwave actually retain more vitamins and minerals.

### Q. Which vegetable dishes do not cook satisfactorily in the microwave?

**A.** Vegetable soufflés do not work in the microwave because the egg structure cannot be set without overcooking the edges of the soufflé. Commercially frozen vegetable soufflés can be reheated in the microwave because the structure is already set.

## BREADS, GRAINS, PASTA & SANDWICHES

### Q. What are the advantages of cooking breads and grains in the microwave?

**A.** Convenience breads defrost and heat in a matter of minutes. Keep a variety of breads and rolls on hand for sandwiches. Use the microwave to defrost only the number of slices or rolls needed. You can cook and eat hot cereals right in the heat-proof serving bowls.

### Q. What are the disadvantages of cooking breads and grains in the microwave?

**A.** Compared with conventionally baked bread, yeast breads baked in the microwave are pale, low in volume and tough. Quick breads end up pale and raise and cook unevenly. Microwaved breads do not brown, but this can be partially overcome by using toppings, frostings and dark flours. It is easy to overcook breads in the microwave. This results in a dry, tough and hard product. Although rice and pasta do not cook any faster in the microwave, they can be cooked successfully.

### Q. How do you reheat breads and grains in the microwave?

**A.** Reheat breads on a white paper towel so the bottom won't get soggy. You can reheat breads and rolls in a straw basket if the basket has no metal parts. Anything sugary, such as raisins, jelly filling or frosting, will become hot very quickly. Baked breads, rolls and sandwiches should be heated only until warm. If they are heated beyond this point in the microwave, they will become tough and hard.

## DESSERTS

### Q. Which kinds of desserts are most suitable for the microwave?

**A.** Puddings cooked this way are extra smooth and creamy. All fruit-based desserts have an excellent fresh flavor because of the fast cooking.

### Q. Which desserts do not cook satisfactorily in the microwave?

**A.** Drop cookies cook so unevenly that they are not recommended. Some are burned while others are still doughy. The pastry in a two-crust pie does not cook but the filling heats rapidly. The solution is to make deep-dish pies, or microwave the pastry shell first. The top crust is microwaved separately; then the pie is assembled before serving. Custard in a large pie plate and dessert soufflés overcook on the edges before the center sets. It is difficult to obtain consistently good results with cakes made from scratch. Microwave baking results are more predictable with pudding-type cake mixes. Cream puffs, angel-food cakes, chiffon cakes and meringues should not be attempted because they never give good results.

**Give dish a half turn**—When the skillet is given a half turn, the tomato will be in the same position as the tomato in the top skillet.

**Pierce or prick**—Pierce foods with membranes or tight skins such as egg yolks, oysters, chicken livers and baked potatoes.

**Browning skillets**—A special substance on the outside bottom of these skillets causes this area to become extremely hot.

**Pie plates**—Both pie plates are marked as 10-inch plates but one holds 7 cups and the other holds 4-1/2 cups!

**Ring molds**—Ovenproof glass, plastic and ceramic rings are available. Or, place a glass or ceramic baking cup in center of a pie plate.

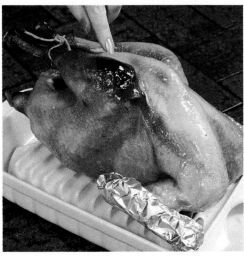

**Shielding**—Use small pieces of foil secured with wooden picks to cover areas that are over-browning or becoming warm during defrosting.

**Cover**—Use a casserole lid unless the recipe states to cover in some other manner. Or, cover with vented plastic wrap.

**Cover with paper towel**—Use white paper towels to cover foods that might spatter and require only a loose cover.

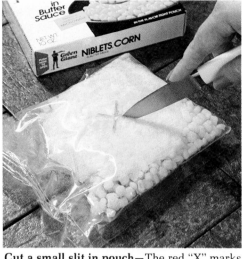

**Cut a small slit in pouch**—The red "X" marks a 1-inch slit that should be cut with a knife to vent frozen pouches.

**Cover with waxed paper**—Use waxed paper for a loose-fitting cover that allows steam to escape.

**Stir**—Always stir outside edges toward center and center toward outside edge. The outside edges will cook first.

**Cover with vented plastic wrap**—Either fold back a corner as on the squash rings or cut a few small slits with a knife.

**Rearrange**—Move items from the center to the outside edge, and items at the edge to the center.

# Savory Cheese-Stuffed Mushrooms

1/2 cup herb-seasoned stuffing mix
1/2 cup shredded Swiss cheese (2 oz.)
1/4 cup chopped parsley
1/4 cup finely chopped water chestnuts
2 tablespoons chopped pimento
3 tablespoons water
1/2 teaspoon chicken-bouillon granules
12 fresh mushrooms, 1-1/2 inches in diameter
2 tablespoons butter or margarine

*To garnish:*
Pimento strips

1. In a medium bowl, combine stuffing mix, cheese, parsley, water chestnuts and pimento.
2. In a 1-cup glass measuring cup, combine water and bouillon granules. Microwave at 100% (HIGH) 30 seconds or until water boils and granules have dissolved. Add bouillon to stuffing mixture. Toss with a fork until mixed well.
3. Wash mushrooms; pat dry on paper towels. Remove stems from mushrooms; reserve for another use.
4. Place butter or margarine in a glass baking cup. Microwave at 100% (HIGH) 45 seconds or until melted. Dip mushrooms in butter or margarine. Fill mushrooms with cheese stuffing. Arrange mushrooms in a circle on a round 12-inch microwave platter, propping mushrooms up along edge of plate. Drizzle with any remaining butter or margarine. Garnish with pimento strips.
5. Microwave at 100% (HIGH) 4 to 5 minutes or until heated through; give platter a half turn after 2 minutes. Remove any smaller mushrooms as soon as they are cooked; keep warm. Continue microwaving remaining mushrooms. Makes 4 servings.

# Tomato Tang

2 (12-oz.) cans vegetable-tomato juice cocktail (3 cups)
1 (14-1/2-oz.) can beef broth
1 tablespoon lemon juice
1 teaspoon Worcestershire sauce
1 teaspoon prepared horseradish
Dash hot-pepper sauce

*To garnish:*
6 thin lemon slices, halved, with a parsley sprig on each

1. In a deep 2-quart casserole with lid, combine vegetable-tomato juice cocktail, beef broth, lemon juice, Worcestershire sauce, horseradish and hot-pepper sauce. Cover. Microwave at 100% (HIGH) 8 to 10 minutes or until mixture is boiling.
2. Stir. Cover. Microwave at 30% (MEDIUM LOW) 10 to 12 minutes to blend flavors; stir once. Garnish with lemon slices topped with parsley sprigs. Makes 4 servings.

# Bacon-Nut-Stuffed Artichokes

8 bacon slices
1/4 cup bacon drippings
1/2 cup chopped onion
1/2 cup chopped pecans, toasted
2/3 cup seasoned dry bread crumbs
2 tablespoons dry white wine
2 (14-oz.) cans artichoke bottoms, drained (about 12 bottoms)
3 tablespoons butter or margarine
1 teaspoon lemon juice

*To garnish:*
Pecan halves

1. Place bacon on a microwave rack in a 12-inch-square microwave baker. Cover bacon with a white paper towel. Microwave at 100% (HIGH) 7 to 9 minutes or until crisp; give dish a half turn after 4 minutes. Remove bacon. Drain on paper towels; crumble drained bacon.
2. Remove rack from baking dish. Drain off all but 1/4 cup drippings. Add onion to baking dish. Microwave at 100% (HIGH) 3 to 4 minutes or until tender; stir once.
3. Add chopped pecans, bread crumbs, wine and crumbled bacon. Toss lightly to mix well.
4. Rinse artichoke bottoms; pat dry with paper towels. Place butter or margarine in a 1-1/2-cup bowl. Microwave at 100% (HIGH) 45 to 60 seconds or until melted. Stir in lemon juice.
5. Dip artichokes in butter or margarine mixture. Top artichokes with bacon mixture. Arrange in a circle in a 12-inch-square microwave baker. Drizzle with any remaining butter or margarine mixture. Garnish with pecan halves. Microwave at 100% (HIGH) 5 to 7 minutes or until heated through; give dish a half turn after 3 minutes. Makes 6 servings.

Top to bottom: Savory Cheese-Stuffed Mushrooms; Bacon-Nut-Stuffed Artichokes; Spinach-Stuffed Appetizer Oysters, page 657

# Hearty Pizza Dip

8 oz. bulk pork sausage
2 tablespoons sliced green onion
2 tablespoons chopped green bell pepper
1 (8-oz.) can pizza sauce
1/2 teaspoon fennel seed
1/2 teaspoon dried leaf oregano
1/2 teaspoon dried leaf basil
2 cups shredded process American cheese (8 oz.)

*To serve:*
Crackers

1. In a deep 1-quart casserole with lid, combine sausage, green onion and green pepper. Microwave at 100% (HIGH) 3 to 4 minutes or until sausage is no longer pink and vegetables are tender, stirring twice. Drain well.
2. Stir in pizza sauce, fennel seed, oregano and basil. Microwave at 100% (HIGH) 2 minutes or until boiling. Stir in cheese in 2 batches. When all cheese has been added, cover.
3. Microwave at 30% (MEDIUM LOW) 8 to 10 minutes or until cheese is melted and mixture is heated through; stir 3 times. Serve hot with crackers as dippers. Makes 2-1/3 cups.

# Traditional Hot Cocoa

1/4 cup unsweetened cocoa powder
1/4 cup sugar
1/4 cup hot water
3-1/2 cups milk
1/2 teaspoon vanilla extract
3 or 4 large marshmallows

1. In a deep 1-1/2-quart casserole with lid, thoroughly blend cocoa powder and sugar. Whisk in hot water until blended. Cover and microwave at 100% (HIGH) 2 minutes.
2. Gradually whisk in milk. Cover. Microwave at 100% (HIGH) 7-1/2 to 8-1/2 minutes or until heated through; whisking every 2 minutes. Whisk in vanilla.
3. Ladle cocoa into 3 or 4 mugs. Top each serving with a marshmallow. Arrange mugs in a circle in microwave oven. Microwave at 100% (HIGH) 1-1/2 to 2 minutes or until marshmallows are puffed. Makes 3 to 4 servings.

# Curried-Chicken Snack Sandwiches

1 cup finely diced cooked chicken
1/2 cup finely chopped apple
1/4 cup raisins
2 tablespoons chopped celery
2 tablespoons chopped green onion
2 tablespoons chopped peanuts
2 tablespoons mayonnaise or salad dressing
2 tablespoons plain yogurt
1 teaspoon curry powder
5 or 6 (4-inch diameter) pita-bread rounds, halved
    crosswise, or 12 to 14 slices party rye bread or Melba
    toast

*To garnish:*
Apple slices

1. In a medium bowl, combine chicken, chopped apple, raisins, celery, green onion and peanuts.
2. In a small bowl, mix together mayonnaise or salad dressing, yogurt and curry powder. Combine chicken mixture and mayonnaise mixture; toss lightly to mix well.
3. Spoon filling into pita-bread halves or spread on party rye bread or Melba toast. Place in a circle on a round 12-inch microwave platter. Microwave at 100% (HIGH) 2-1/2 to 3 minutes or until filling is heated through; give platter a half turn after 1-1/2 minutes. Garnish with apple slices. Makes 5 to 6 servings.

# Nut Nibblers

2 tablespoons butter or margarine
1 teaspoon celery salt
1 teaspoon chili powder
1 teaspoon onion powder
3-1/2 cups mixed pecan halves, cashews, almonds
    (13 oz.)

1. In a 1-cup glass measuring cup, combine butter or margarine, celery salt, chili powder and onion powder. Microwave at 100% (HIGH) 30 seconds or until butter or margarine melts.
2. Place nuts in a 12" x 7" baking dish. Stir butter or margarine mixture; pour over nuts. Toss until coated thoroughly. Microwave at 30% (MEDIUM LOW) 20 minutes or until toasted: stir every 7 minutes. Cool completely. Store in a plastic bag or airtight container. Makes 3 cups.

# How to Make Spinach-Stuffed Appetizer Oysters

1/Pierce oysters with a large fork to break membrane. This prevents oysters from bursting during microwaving.

2/Dip oysters in melted butter or margarine mixture. Rinse and reuse oyster shells. Place butter-dipped oysters in rinsed oyster shells.

## Spinach-Stuffed Appetizer Oysters

1/2 (12-oz.) pkg. frozen spinach soufflé
3 tablespoons seasoned dry bread crumbs
3 tablespoons grated Parmesan cheese
1 tablespoon butter or margarine
1/2 teaspoon lemon juice
8 fresh shucked oysters, drained

*To garnish:*
Pimento strips

1. Remove frozen soufflé from package, Cut in half with a sharp knife. Return 1/2 of soufflé to freezer. Place remaining 1/2 of frozen soufflé in a 1-quart bowl. Microwave at 30% (MEDIUM LOW) 3 minutes or until thawed; break up with a fork after 1-1/2 minutes. Let stand 3 minutes. Stir bread crumbs and Parmesan cheese into soufflé.
2. Place butter or margarine in a glass baking cup. Microwave at 100% (HIGH) 45 seconds or until melted. Stir in lemon juice.
3. Pat oysters dry on paper towels. Pierce with a large fork. Dip oysters in melted butter or margarine mixture; place in rinsed shells. Top oysters with spinach mixture. Drizzle with any remaining butter or margarine mixture.
4. Arrange in a circle on a round 12-inch microwave platter. Top oysters with pimento strips. Microwave at 50% (MEDIUM) 4 to 5 minutes or until heated through and oysters are tender; give platter a half turn after 2 minutes. Let stand 1 minute before serving. Makes 4 servings.

---

### Cooking Appetizers

Many precooked appetizers, such as cocktail meatballs and stuffed vegetables are ideal for reheating in the microwave.

Do not attempt to deep-fry any kind of food, such as deep-fried appetizers. Dips made with cream cheese should only be heated until warm to prevent curdling.

The microwave is perfect for cooking individual servings of soups and beverages. Stir to distribute the heat. Soups and beverages without eggs should be heated to 170F (75C).

# Chicken-Liver & Bacon Appetizers (Rumaki)

4 oz. chicken livers
2 tablespoons soy sauce
1 tablespoon dry sherry
1 garlic clove, minced
1 teaspoon grated fresh gingerroot
1/2 (8-oz.) can water chestnuts, drained
9 bacon slices

1. Cut chicken livers in 1-inch pieces. Pierce with a large fork. In a medium bowl, combine soy sauce, sherry, garlic and gingerroot. Mix well. Place chicken livers in marinade. Cover and marinate at room temperature 30 minutes.
2. Cut water chestnuts in half. Cut bacon slices in half crosswise. Remove chicken livers from marinade; drain on paper towels. Place bacon on a rack in a 12-inch-square microwave baker. Cover with white paper towels. Microwave at 100% (HIGH) 4 minutes or until bacon is partially cooked. Drain off fat from dish.
3. Place 1 piece of water chestnut and 1 piece of chicken liver on 1 half-slice of bacon. Roll up and secure with a wooden pick. Place on rack in same baker. Repeat with remaining water chestnuts, chicken livers and bacon.
4. Microwave at 100% (HIGH) 5-1/2 to 6-1/2 minutes or until bacon is crisp and liver is slightly pink in center. Turn livers over and rearrange once during cooking. Makes 18 pieces.

### Variation
To cook 8 ounces of chicken livers, cook in 2 batches using directions above. Do not attempt to microwave 36 Rumaki at once.

# Dilly Ham Dip

1 (8-oz.) pkg. cream cheese
1 tablespoon milk
1 teaspoon Worcestershire sauce
2 tablespoons chopped green onion
Dash freshly ground pepper
3 tablespoons prepared sandwich spread
1 cup finely chopped cooked ham
3 tablespoons chopped dill pickle, drained
2 teaspoons prepared mustard

*To garnish:*
Green- and red-bell pepper strips
Parsley sprig

*To serve:*
Fresh vegetables or crackers

1. Place cream cheese in a 1-1/2-quart bowl. Microwave at 10% (LOW) 1-1/2 to 2 minutes or until softened.
2. Add milk, Worcestershire sauce, green onion and pepper. Beat with an electric mixer on medium speed until blended.
3. Stir in sandwich spread, ham, dill pickle and mustard. Spoon into a 9-inch serving dish. Cover with vented plastic wrap. Microwave at 70% (MEDIUM HIGH) 3 to 3-1/2 minutes or until heated through; stir twice. Garnish with pepper strips and parsley. Serve warm with fresh vegetables or crackers as dippers. Makes 2 cups.

# Bacon-Olive Cracker Melts

1 (5-oz.) jar process-cheese spread
1/4 cup chopped pimento-stuffed green olives
3 bacon slices, crisp-cooked, crumbled
Dash red (cayenne) pepper
24 Melba-toast rounds or crackers

*To garnish:*
Olive slices, if desired

1. Place cheese spread in a 1-quart bowl. Microwave at 10% (LOW) 1 minute or until soft. Stir in olives, bacon and cayenne.
2. Place Melba toast or crackers in a circle on a round 12-inch microwave platter. Spread about 1 teaspoon cheese mixture on each cracker. Garnish each cracker with an olive slice, if desired.
3. Microwave at 100% (HIGH) 45 to 60 seconds or until cheese melts; give plate a half turn after 30 seconds. Makes 24 appetizers.

Clockwise from top left: Tomato Tang, page 654; Dilly Ham Dip; Curried-Chicken Snack Sandwiches, page 656; Bacon-Olive Cracker Melts; Chicken-Liver & Bacon Appetizers

# Old-Fashioned Vegetable Soup

2 lb. beef neck bones
1 large onion, chopped
2 celery stalks, chopped
1 bay leaf
1 tablespoon Worcestershire sauce
1 (12-oz.) can vegetable-tomato juice cocktail
1 (28-oz.) can tomatoes, chopped (1-1/2 cups)
1 (10-oz.) pkg. frozen mixed vegetables (2 cups)

1. In a 4-quart casserole with lid, place neck bones, meaty-side down. Add onion, celery, bay leaf and Worcestershire sauce. Pour in vegetable-tomato juice cocktail and tomatoes. Cover.
2. Microwave at 100% (HIGH) 15 minutes or until boiling. Microwave at 30% (MEDIUM LOW) 1-1/2 hours or until meat is tender; stir twice. Let stand covered 20 minutes. Remove bones. Cover bones tightly; set aside.
3. Add mixed vegetables to liquid in casserole with lid. Break apart vegetables with a large fork. Cover. Microwave at 100% (HIGH) 15 minutes or until vegetables are almost tender.
4. While vegetables are cooking, cut meat from bones; discard bones. Stir meat into soup. Cover. Microwave at 100% (HIGH) 10 minutes or until heated through. Skim off excess fat. Makes 4 servings.

# Spicy All-Purpose Tomato Sauce

2 tablespoons olive oil
1/4 cup chopped onion
1/4 cup chopped green bell pepper
1/4 cup chopped celery
2 (16-oz.) cans tomatoes, drained, chopped (1-2/3 cups, drained)
2 teaspoons brown sugar
1/4 teaspoon salt
1/4 teaspoon dried leaf oregano
1/4 teaspoon dried leaf basil
1/8 teaspoon garlic powder

1. In a deep 1-1/2-quart casserole with lid, combine olive oil, onion, green pepper and celery. Microwave at 100% (HIGH) 3 minutes or until vegetables are tender; stir after 1-1/2 minutes.
2. Stir in tomatoes, brown sugar, salt, oregano, basil and garlic powder. Cover. Microwave at 100% (HIGH) 5 minutes or until mixture boils. Stir well; cover. Microwave at 30% (MEDIUM LOW) 15 to 20 minutes or until sauce reaches desired consistency; stir after 10 minutes. Makes 1-1/2 cups.

# Split Pea Soup

8 oz. dried split peas (about 1-1/4 cups)
8 oz. bulk pork sausage
1/2 cup chopped onion
1/2 cup chopped celery
5 cups chicken broth
1 teaspoon fennel seed

*To garnish:*
Chopped ham
Croutons
Chopped parsley

1. Rinse and drain split peas; set aside. In a deep 4-quart casserole with lid, combine sausage, onion and celery. Microwave at 100% (HIGH) 5 to 7 minutes or until sausage is no longer pink; stir after 3 minutes. Drain off fat.
2. Stir in peas, broth and fennel seed; cover. Microwave at 100% (HIGH) 22 to 25 minutes. Stir and cover. Microwave at 30% (MEDIUM LOW) 50 to 60 minutes or until peas are tender; stir occasionally. Skim off excess fat. Garnish with chopped ham, croutons and parsley. Makes 4 servings.

# Quick & Creamy Chicken Chowder

1 (10-3/4-oz.) can condensed cream of chicken soup
1-1/2 soup cans milk
1 (10-oz.) pkg. frozen broccoli, carrots and pasta twists with sauce cubes
1/8 teaspoon rubbed sage
1 cup diced cooked or canned chicken

*To garnish:*
Chopped watercress or parsley

1. In a deep 2-quart casserole with lid, combine soup and milk. Whisk until smooth. Stir in frozen vegetables with sauce cubes and sage. Cover.
2. Microwave at 100% (HIGH) 5 minutes. Stir until sauce cubes dissolve. Add chicken. Cover. Microwave at 100% (HIGH) 10 to 12 minutes or until heated through; stir after 5 minute. Let stand, covered, 2 minutes.
3. Stir before serving. Garnish each serving with watercress or parsley. Makes 3 to 4 servings.

Spicy All-Purpose Tomato Sauce

# Shortcut Minestrone

1 lb. ground beef
1 cup chopped onion
1/2 cup chopped green bell pepper
1 (16-oz.) can tomatoes
1 (16-oz.) jar Italian cooking sauce (2 cups)
1 cup Chianti wine
1 (15-1/2-oz.) can chili beans with gravy
1/2 cup spaghetti, broken in 1-inch pieces
2 oz. thinly sliced pepperoni
1 teaspoon dried leaf basil

*To garnish:*
**Croutons, if desired**
**Grated Parmesan cheese, if desired**

1. In a deep 3-quart casserole with lid, combine ground beef, onion and green pepper. Microwave at 100% (HIGH) 5 to 6 minutes or until meat is no longer pink and vegetables are tender; stir after 2 minutes. Drain off fat.
2. Chop tomatoes, reserving juice. Stir in cooking sauce, chopped tomatoes with juice, wine, beans with gravy, spaghetti, pepperoni and basil. Cover. Microwave at 100% (HIGH) 10 minutes or until boiling. Stir well. Cover.
3. Microwave at 30% (MEDIUM LOW) 35 minutes or until spaghetti is tender; stir twice. To serve, top each serving with croutons and grated Parmesan cheese, if desired. Makes 6 servings.

# French Onion Soup

6 tablespoons butter or margarine
4 medium onions, thinly sliced (4 cups)
2 teaspoons all-purpose flour
1 tablespoon sugar
1 teaspoon dry mustard
2 (10-3/4-oz.) cans condensed chicken broth
1/4 cup dry white wine
2 teaspoons Worcestershire sauce
1 cup croutons
1/4 cup shredded Parmesan cheese (1 oz.)
1 cup shredded mozzarella cheese (4 oz.)

1. Place butter or margarine in a deep 3-quart casserole. Microwave butter or margarine at 100% (HIGH) 1-1/2 minutes or until melted. Stir in onions. Microwave at 100% (HIGH) 25 to 30 minutes or until onions are browned and caramelized; stir every 5 minutes.
2. Stir in flour, sugar and mustard; microwave at 100% (HIGH) 2 minutes or until mixture bubbles. Gradually stir in broth, wine and Worcestershire sauce. Microwave at 100% (HIGH) 9 to 10 minutes or until mixture thickens slightly and bubbles; stir every 3 minutes.
3. Ladle into 4 bowls. Top each serving with croutons. Sprinkle with Parmesan cheese and mozzarella cheese. Microwave at 100% (HIGH) 2 to 2-1/2 minutes or just until cheese melts; turn bowls after 1 minute. Makes 4 servings.

# Lazy-Day Vichyssoise

1 (9-oz.) pkg. frozen small onions with cream sauce
2/3 cup water
1 tablespoon chicken-bouillon granules
1 tablespoon butter or margarine
1 cup milk
3/4 cup instant mashed-potato buds
1/2 cup whipping cream

*To garnish:*
**Chopped chives**

1. In a deep 1-quart casserole with lid, combine frozen onions, water, bouillon granules and butter or margarine. Cover. Microwave at 100% (HIGH) 3 minutes. Stir until sauce is smooth. Stir in milk. Cover. Microwave at 100% (HIGH) 4 minutes or until onions are tender. Stir in potato buds.
2. In a food processor or blender, process mixture until smooth. Process in 2 batches, if necessary. Stir in whipping cream. Press mixture through a fine sieve, if desired. Cover and refrigerate 8 hours or overnight.
3. Serve icy cold in small bowls or icers. Top with chives. Makes 3 to 4 servings.

# How to Make No-Fail Hollandaise Sauce

1/In a blender container, combine egg yolks, lemon juice, salt and white pepper, if you have it. Otherwise substitute black pepper.

2/Blend egg yolks and lemon juice until frothy. Then with blender running at high speed, slowly pour in melted butter or margarine. Blend until sauce is thick and creamy.

3/Pour sauce into a glass measuring cup or sauce boat. Set sauce in a large bowl. Pour hot water into bowl. This water bath helps keep sauce from curdling.

4/Microwave sauce just until warm—it will curdle if it becomes hot. Spoon sauce over omelets, Eggs Benedict, vegetables, fish or poultry dishes.

## No-Fail Hollandaise Sauce

**3 egg yolks**
**2 tablespoons lemon juice**
**Dash salt**
**Dash white pepper**
**1/2 cup butter or margarine, cut up**
**1/4 teaspoon dried leaf tarragon**
**1/4 teaspoon grated fresh lemon peel**

**1.** In a blender container, combine egg yolks, lemon juice, salt and pepper. Cover and blend at low speed until frothy. Place butter or margarine in a 2-cup glass measuring cup. Microwave at 100% (HIGH) 1 to 1-1/2 minutes or until melted.
**2.** With blender at high speed, slowly pour in melted butter or margarine, blending constantly until mixture is very thick. Stir in tarragon and lemon peel.
**3.** To warm, pour into same glass measuring cup or a sauce boat; set in bowl of hot water. The hot water should be at the same level as the sauce. Microwave at 30% (MEDIUM LOW) 5 minutes, or until warm; stir every 2 minutes. Stir before serving. Refrigerate any leftover sauce. Makes 1 cup.

# Curried Asparagus Bisque

2 tablespoons butter or margarine
1/4 cup chopped onion
1/2 teaspoon celery salt
1 teaspoon curry powder
1 (10-3/4-oz.) can condensed chicken broth
1 (8-oz.) pkg. frozen cut asparagus
1-1/2 teaspoons lemon juice
1/2 cup plain yogurt

*To garnish:*
1/2 avocado, sliced
1/4 cup plain yogurt
Chopped chives or red caviar

1. Place butter or margarine in a deep 2-quart casserole. Microwave at 100% (HIGH) 30 seconds or until melted. Add onion. Microwave at 100% (HIGH) 2 to 2-1/2 minutes or until tender.
2. Stir in celery salt and curry powder. Stir in chicken broth. Add asparagus; cover. Microwave at 100% (HIGH) 7 to 8 minutes or until tender.
3. Stir in lemon juice. Process mixture in a food processor or blender until smooth. Process in 2 batches, if necessary.
4. In same casserole, blend yogurt and a little hot soup mixture. Gradually blend in remaining hot soup. Cover and refrigerate 8 hours or overnight. Serve icy cold in small bowls or icers. Top each serving with a fan of avocado slices, a dollop of yogurt and a sprinkling of chives or caviar. Makes 4 servings.

# Oriental Chicken Soup

1 boneless chicken breast
2 (14-1/2-oz.) cans chicken broth
1/4 cup thinly sliced celery
1/4 cup thinly sliced green onions
2 tablespoons dry sherry
1/2 cup chopped watercress leaves

1. Remove skin from chicken breast, if necessary. Cut chicken into 1-inch slivers; set aside. Pour broth into a deep 2-quart casserole with lid. Cover. Microwave at 100% (HIGH) 8 to 10 minutes or until boiling.
2. Add chicken pieces. Cover. Microwave at 100% (HIGH) 3 to 4 minutes or until chicken is almost done. Add celery, green onions and sherry. Microwave at 100% (HIGH) 3 to 5 minutes or until vegetables are crisp-tender.
3. Divide watercress leaves among 4 to 6 soup cups. Pour in hot soup. Makes 4 to 6 servings

# Tuna Chowder Florentine

1 (9-oz.) pkg. frozen creamed spinach in a pouch
2 cups milk
1 (6-1/2-oz.) can tuna, drained, broken up
2 hard-cooked eggs, chopped
2 tablespoons chopped pimento
2 teaspoons snipped chives
2 teaspoons Dijon-style mustard
1 teaspoon lemon juice

*To garnish:*
1 hard-cooked egg, sliced
Paprika

1. Remove creamed spinach from pouch. Place in a deep 2-quart casserole with lid. Cover. Microwave at 100% (HIGH) 7 minutes. Stir in milk. Stir in tuna, eggs, pimento, chives, mustard and lemon juice. Cover.
2. Microwave at 100% (HIGH) 8 minutes or until hot; stir after 4 minutes. Garnish with hard-cooked egg; sprinkle with paprika. Makes 4 servings.

# Swiss Corn Chowder

1 (10-3/4-oz.) can condensed cream of onion soup
1-1/2 soup cans milk
1 (8-3/4-oz.) can cream-style corn
1 (7-oz.) can whole-kernel corn
1/4 cup chopped pimento
1/2 cup shredded Swiss cheese (2 oz.)

1. In a deep 2-quart casserole with lid, whisk together soup, milk and cream-style corn. Stir in whole-kernel corn with liquid and pimento. Cover.
2. Microwave at 100% (HIGH) 10 minutes or until heated through; stir after 5 minutes. Stir in cheese. Microwave, uncovered, at 70% (MEDIUM HIGH) 2 minutes or until cheese is melted; stir after 1 minute. Makes 4 servings.

Tuna Chowder Florentine

# Speedy Stew

1 lb. beef chuck, or lamb, pork or veal shoulder
2-2/3 cups water
1 (1.5-oz.) envelope seasoning mix for stew
1 (24-oz.) pkg. frozen stew vegetables
1 cup frozen green peas
3 tablespoons all-purpose flour
1/3 cup water

**1.** Pierce meat deeply on all sides with a large fork. Cut into 1-inch cubes. Place meat in a deep 3-quart casserole with lid. Add 2-2/3 cups water and seasoning mix. Mix well, making sure meat is covered by liquid. Cover. Microwave at 100% (HIGH) 10 minutes. Stir; cover. Microwave at 30% (MEDIUM LOW) 30 minutes.
**2.** Stir in frozen stew vegetables, making sure meat is still covered by liquid. Cover. Microwave at 30% (MEDIUM LOW) 45 minutes or until meat and vegetables are almost tender.
**3.** Stir in peas; mix well. Cover. Microwave at 30% (MEDIUM LOW) 15 minutes or until meat and vegetables are tender. Meat is done when it can be easily pieced with a fork. Vegetables should be tender when pierced with a fork. Let stand, covered, 10 minutes.
**4.** Shake together flour and water in a screw-top jar. Stir into stew. Microwave, uncovered, at 100% (HIGH) 2 to 3 minutes or until thickened and bubbly; stir 3 times. Makes 3 to 4 servings.

# Simmered Barbecued Ribs

3 to 3-1/2 lb. pork loin back ribs or beef short ribs, 2-1/2 inches long and 1/2- to 1-inch thick
1 large onion, sliced, separated into rings
1 large bay leaf
2 (12-oz.) cans beer, room temperature
2 tablespoons Worcestershire sauce
2-1/2 cups bottled barbecue sauce

**1.** Cut pork ribs into 2-rib portions. Cut thick beef short ribs in half lengthwise. Pierce ribs all over with a large fork. Place, bone-side up, in a deep 4-quart casserole with lid. Add onion and bay leaf. Pour in beer and Worcestershire sauce.

**2.** Cover and microwave at 100% (HIGH) 10 minutes. Microwave at 30% (MEDIUM LOW) 30 minutes. Rearrange ribs, bringing ribs in center of casserole to outside edge. Be sure ribs are bone-side up and meaty-side is under liquid. Cover. Microwave at 30% (MEDIUM LOW) 60 to 75 minutes.
**3.** Let ribs stand, covered, 20 minutes. Meat is done when it can be easily pierced with a fork. Pour off pan juices from casserole. Turn ribs meaty-side up. Pour barbecue sauce over ribs, coating well. Cover. Microwave at 30% (MEDIUM LOW) 10 minutes or until heated through. Serve ribs with onion and sauce. Makes 3 to 4 servings.

# New England Boiled Dinner

2-1/2 to 3 lb. boneless corned-beef brisket
4 cups ginger ale
2 potatoes, cut up (2 cups)
2 medium onions, cut up
2 medium carrots, cut up
1/2 large rutabaga, peeled, cubed
1/2 small cabbage, cut in 4 wedges

**1.** Slash fat edges of roast. Score fat on top and bottom of roast. Place roast, fat-side down, in a floured roasting bag set in a deep 4-quart casserole. Choose the size roasting bag and baking dish that allows the meat to be as totally immersed in liquid as possible.
**2.** Add spices from corned-beef package, if any. Add ginger ale to cover roast. Tie roasting bag with string, leaving a 2-inch opening to vent steam. Microwave at 100% (HIGH) 10 minutes. Microwave at 30% (MEDIUM LOW) 30 minutes.
**3.** Carefully open roasting bag; turn roast over. Add potatoes, onions, carrots and rutabaga. Tie bag, leaving a 2-inch opening. Microwave at 30% (MEDIUM LOW) 60 minutes or until meat can be pierced with a fork with little resistance.
**4.** Open roasting bag; let steam escape. Add cabbage wedges. Tie roasting bag, leaving a 2-inch opening. Microwave at 30% (MEDIUM LOW) 30 minutes.
**5.** Allow steam to escape before testing for doneness. Meat is done when it can be easily pieced with a fork. When meat and vegetables are done, tie bag tightly. Let stand 20 minutes. Reserve cooking liquid. Carve meat in thin slices diagonally across the grain. Arrange on a warm serving platter with vegetables. Refrigerate any leftover corned beef and vegetables in cooking liquid. Makes 4 servings.

New England Boiled Dinner

# How to Make Pot Roast with Vegetables

1/Slash fat edges of roast with a sharp knife. This helps to keep meat flat during cooking. Cut roast in serving-size pieces. This makes meat easier to arrange in casserole, and helps meat cook more evenly.

2/Pierce pieces deeply all over on both sides with a large fork. This has the same effect as pounding other cuts of meat. It makes pot roast more tender and juicy.

## Easy Swiss Steak

1-1/2 lb. beef round steak, 1/2 inch thick
3 tablespoons all-purpose flour
1 (8-oz.) can tomato sauce
1 cup water
1 (1-oz.) envelope Swiss-steak seasoning mix

1. Cut meat in 5 or 6 pieces. Slash fat edges of meat. Coat meat with flour. With a meat mallet, pound meat until it is 1/4 inch thick.
2. In a 3-quart casserole with lid, mix tomato sauce, water and Swiss-steak seasoning mix. Add steak pieces, making sure all meat is covered by liquid. Cover and let stand 10 minutes.
3. Microwave at 100% (HIGH) 10 minutes. Microwave at 30% (MEDIUM LOW) 30 minutes. Turn steak over; give casserole a half turn. Microwave at 30% (MEDIUM LOW) 20 minutes. Let stand, covered, 10 minutes. Meat is done when it can be easily pierced with a fork. Makes 5 to 6 servings.

## Meat Loaf

1 lb. ground beef chuck
1 egg
1/4 cup quick-cooking rolled oats
2 tablespoons chopped onion
1 (8-oz.) can tomato sauce
1/4 teaspoon dried leaf thyme
1/4 teaspoon dried leaf marjoram
1/2 teaspoon celery salt
1 tablespoon brown sugar
1 teaspoon Worcestershire sauce
1 teaspoon prepared mustard

1. In a medium bowl, thoroughly combine meat, egg, oats, onion, 1/2 of tomato sauce, thyme, marjoram and celery salt. Press meat mixture into a loaf in a 9" x 5" loaf dish; shape loaf so meat does not touch sides of dish.
2. Cover with waxed paper. Microwave at 100% (HIGH) 5 minutes. Pour off juices.
3. Stir brown sugar, Worcestershire sauce and mustard into remaining tomato sauce. Spoon tomato glaze over loaf, coating entire top and sides. Give dish a half turn. Cover with waxed paper. Microwave at 30% (MEDIUM LOW) 17 to 20 minutes or until a microwave meat thermometer inserted in center of loaf registers 170F (75C).
4. Cover with foil; let stand 5 minutes. Temperature will rise about 10F (5C) during standing time. Makes 4 servings.

# Cutlets

1 egg
1 tablespoon water
2 tablespoons all-purpose flour
3/4 cup dry seasoned bread crumbs
1/2 teaspoon dried leaf marjoram
1 tablespoon dried parsley flakes
4 (4- to 5-oz.) pork or veal cutlets, pounded
3 tablespoons vegetable oil

1. In a pie plate, whisk egg and water until frothy. Place flour in a pie plate or on waxed paper. In another pie plate or on waxed paper, mix bread crumbs, marjoram and parsley flakes. Coat cutlets on both sides with flour. Dip both sides in egg mixture, then in crumb mixture, coating generously. Press crumb mixture into meat with fingers.
2. Preheat a 10-inch microwave browning skillet, uncovered, at 100% (HIGH) 4 minutes. Add oil to hot browning skillet. Using hot pads, tilt skillet to coat evenly with oil. Quickly add cutlets. Microwave at 100% (HIGH) 3-1/2 minutes.
3. Turn cutlets over. Microwave at 100% (HIGH) 3-1/2 minutes or until done. Let stand 1 minute. Meat should no longer be pink when cut. Makes 4 servings.

# Chinese Tacos

1 lb. ground beef or pork
1/4 cup chopped green onion
1/4 cup chopped water chestnuts
2 teaspoons cornstarch
2 tablespoons soy sauce
1 teaspoon vinegar
1/2 teaspoon dry mustard
1/2 teaspoon ground ginger
1/2 teaspoon beef-bouillon granules
1/3 cup water
5 or 6 large crisp iceberg-lettuce leaves
1 (3-oz.) can canned fried rice noodles or chow mein
   noodles

1. Crumble meat into a deep 2-quart casserole. Add green onion. Cover with waxed paper. Microwave at 100% (HIGH) 5 minutes or until meat is no longer pink; stir twice. Pour off juices. Add water chestnuts.
2. In a small bowl, mix cornstarch, soy sauce and vinegar. Stir in dry mustard and ginger until smooth. Stir into meat mixture; mix well. Add bouillon granules and water; stir until well mixed. Cover. Microwave at 100% (HIGH) 3 minutes or until thickened and bubbly; stir once.
3. To serve, spoon meat mixture into center of lettuce leaves. Top with noodles. Fold up, envelope-style, to eat. Serve with additional soy sauce. Makes 5 to 6 servings.

# Pot Roast with Vegetables

2 lb. beef chuck roast, about 1-1/4 to 1-1/2 inches thick
1 teaspoon dried leaf thyme
1 cup unsweetened apple juice
1 to 1-1/2 cups beef broth
2 tablespoons vinegar
2 potatoes, cut up (2 cups)
4 carrots, cut up (2 cups)
2 medium onions, cut up

1. Trim off large fat edges from roast. Slash remaining fat edges of roast at 1-inch intervals. Cut in 4 serving pieces. Pierce pieces deeply all over on both sides with a large fork. Place in a deep 3-quart casserole with lid; pieces should lie flat. Sprinkle with thyme.
2. Combine apple juice, beef broth and vinegar in a medium bowl or glass measuring cup. Pour over roast. Roast must be completely covered with liquid to cook evenly. Add additional broth to cover, if necessary. If time permits, cover meat and let marinate several hours or overnight in the refrigerator. This gives added tenderness and flavor.
3. Cover roast with lid. Microwave at 100% (HIGH) 10 minutes. Microwave at 30% (MEDIUM LOW) 30 minutes. Turn pieces of roast over. Add vegetables and cover. Other vegetables can be substituted, such as turnips, celery, rutabaga and parsnips.
4. Microwave at 30% (MEDIUM LOW) 60 to 75 minutes. Turn top vegetables over in broth. Let stand, covered, 20 minutes. Standing time is very important; do not omit this step. Meat is done when it can be easily pieced with a fork. Vegetables should be tender when pierced with a fork. Makes 4 servings.

# Easy Paella

4 bacon slices
2 (10-oz.) pkgs. frozen Spanish-style rice
6 tablespoons water
1 cup cubed, cooked pork or ham (4 oz.)
1 (4-1/2-oz.) can large shrimp, drained
1 large tomato, cut in wedges

1. Place bacon in a 2-quart casserole with lid. Cover with white paper towels. Microwave at 100% (HIGH) 4 minutes or until crisp. Remove bacon from casserole, leaving drippings in casserole. Drain bacon on paper towels. Crumble drained bacon; set aside.
2. Stir contents of seasoning pouch from rice into bacon drippings in casserole. Stir in water. Add frozen rice. Cover. Microwave at 100% (HIGH) 6 minutes.
3. Stir in pork or ham, shrimp and tomato wedges; cover. Microwave at 100% (HIGH) 8 minutes or until rice is tender and meat is heated through. Top with crumbled bacon. Makes 4 to 6 servings.

# How to Make Creamy Onion-Smothered Chops

1/Place coated chops in a deep casserole. Whisk together onion soup, milk, bouillon granules, steak sauce and any remaining flour mixture.

2/Top chops with onion rings. Arrange chops in casserole so small tenderloin portion is toward center of casserole. The thicker loin portion is to outside of casserole because it takes longer to cook.

3/Pour sauce mixture over chops and onion. Make sure all chops are coated with sauce. Partway through cooking time, chops are turned over and pushed back under sauce.

4/After cooking and standing, chops should be tender when pierced with a fork. Serve chops and pan gravy over mashed potatoes, noodles or rice. Garnish with parsley.

## Creamy Onion-Smothered Chops

4 (4- to 6-oz.) pork loin chops, 1/2 inch thick
3 tablespoons all-purpose flour
1 teaspoon ground sage
1 large onion, sliced, separated into rings
1 (10-1/2-oz.) can condensed cream of onion soup
1/2 soup can milk
2 teaspoons beef-bouillon granules
2 tablespoons steak sauce

*To garnish:*
Chopped parsley

1. Slash fat edges of chops. In a shallow bowl, mix flour and sage. Coat meat with flour mixture. Place in a deep 2-quart casserole with lid, with tenderloin portion toward center of dish. Top with onion.
2. In a medium bowl, whisk soup, milk, bouillon granules, steak sauce and any remaining flour mixture until smooth. Pour mixture over chops, being sure to coat all chops. Cover and microwave 30 minutes at 30% (MEDIUM LOW). After 15 minutes, turn chops over and rearrange. Push chops under liquid. Cover and microwave for remaining time or until tender. Let stand, covered, 10 minutes. Chops are done when they have no pink color when cut in center.
3. Skim off any fat. Serve pan juices over chops. Garnish with parsley. Makes 4 servings.

# Spaghetti & Meat Sauce

1 lb. ground beef chuck
1 cup chopped onion
1/2 cup chopped green bell pepper
1 (16-oz.) can tomatoes
1 (8-oz.) can tomato sauce
1 (6-oz.) can tomato paste
1/4 cup water
1 bay leaf
2 teaspoons dried leaf oregano
1 teaspoon dried leaf basil
1 tablespoon Worcestershire sauce

*To serve:*
**Hot cooked spaghetti**
**Grated Parmesan cheese**

**1.** Crumble meat into a deep 3-quart casserole. Add onion and green pepper. Cover with waxed paper. Microwave at 100% (HIGH) 5 to 6 minutes or until meat is no longer pink; stir twice.
**2.** Pour off pan juices. Chop tomatoes, reserving juice. Stir in chopped tomatoes with juice, tomato sauce, tomato paste, water, bay leaf, oregano, basil and Worcestershire sauce. Cover. Microwave at 100% (HIGH) 10 minutes or until boiling.
**3.** Stir well. Microwave at 30% (MEDIUM LOW) 45 minutes or until sauce reaches desired consistency; stir occasionally. Serve over hot cooked spaghetti. Sprinkle with Parmesan cheese. Makes 4 servings.

# Ham Ring

1/2 lb. ground cooked ham
1/2 lb. ground pork
1 egg
1/4 cup quick-cooking rolled oats
1/4 cup chili sauce
2 tablespoons chopped onion
2 tablespoons chopped green bell pepper
1/2 teaspoon dry mustard
1/4 cup chili sauce
1 tablespoon brown sugar
1/4 teaspoon dry mustard

**1.** In a medium bowl, thoroughly mix ham, pork, egg, oats, 1/4 cup chili sauce, onion, green pepper and 1/2 teaspoon dry mustard. Press into a ring in a 10-inch pie plate. Shape ring around custard cup in center of pie plate. Shape ring so meat does not touch sides of dish. Cover with waxed paper. Microwave at 100% (HIGH) 5 minutes.
**2.** Combine 1/4 cup chili sauce, brown sugar and 1/4 teaspoon mustard. Spread over ring, coating entire top and sides. Give dish a half turn. Microwave at 30% (MEDIUM LOW) 9 to 10 minutes Cover with foil; let stand 5 minutes. A microwave meat thermometer inserted in center of ring should register 170F (75C). Makes 4 servings.

# Easy Scalloped Potatoes & Ham

1 tablespoon butter or margarine
1/2 cup cheese-cracker crumbs or poppy-seed cracker crumbs
2 tablespoons butter or margarine
1/2 cup chopped celery
1/4 cup chopped onion
2 (10-oz.) pkgs. frozen creamed peas and potatoes
1-1/2 cups milk
1/4 cup chopped pimento
2 teaspoons prepared mustard
2 cups cooked ham (8 oz.), cut in 1/2-inch cubes

*To garnish:*
**Watercress**

**1.** In a small bowl, melt 1 tablespoon butter or margarine at 100% (HIGH) 30 seconds. Stir in cracker crumbs; set aside.
**2.** In a 2-quart casserole with lid, combine 2 tablespoons butter or margarine, celery and onion. Cover. Microwave at 100% (HIGH) 3 minutes; stir once.
**3.** Add frozen creamed peas and potatoes, milk, pimento and mustard. Cover. Microwave at 100% (HIGH) 6 minutes. Stir until sauce is smooth.
**4.** Stir in ham. Cover. Microwave at 100% (HIGH) 6 to 7 minutes or until heated through. Stir. Sprinkle buttered crumbs around edge of dish. Garnish with watercress. Makes 6 servings.

# Easy Oven Chicken

1 (3-lb.) broiler-fryer chicken, cut up, without backs
Water or milk to moisten
1 (2-3/8-oz.) envelope seasoned coating mix for chicken

1. Make a small slit in skin on each piece of chicken. Dip chicken pieces in milk or water; drain off excess liquid. Following package directions, shake in coating mix in shaker bag provided.
2. Place chicken, skin-side up, on a microwave rack in a 12" x 7" baking dish. Arrange meaty portions toward outside of dish. Microwave, uncovered, at 100% (HIGH) 19 to 21 minutes. Rearrange chicken pieces once during cooking.
3. Check doneness toward end of cooking time; remove any done pieces. Juices run clear when chicken is pierced in thickest part. Continue cooking remaining pieces. Makes 3 to 4 servings.

# Oven-Fried Chicken

2 tablespoons butter or margarine
1 (3-lb.) broiler-fryer chicken, cut up, without backs
1 egg
1 tablespoon water
1 (4.2-oz.) pkg. seasoned crumb-coating chicken

1. Place butter or margarine in a 12" x 7" baking dish. Microwave at 100% (HIGH) 30 seconds or until melted. Set aside.
2. Make a small slit in skin on each piece of chicken. In a pie plate, whisk together egg and water. Dip chicken pieces in egg mixture; then dip in coating mix according to package directions.
3. Place chicken, skin-side down, in butter or margarine with meaty portions toward outside of dish. Microwave at 100% (HIGH) 12 minutes.
4. Turn chicken pieces over. Microwave at 100% (HIGH) 10 minutes. Let stand 5 minutes. Check doneness toward end of cooking time; remove any done pieces. Juices should run clear when chicken is pierced in thickest part. Continue cooking remaining pieces. Makes 3 to 4 servings.

# Roasting Bag Chicken

1 (2-1/2- to 3-lb.) broiler-fryer chicken, cut up
1 (1.37-oz.) envelope seasoning mix

1. Make a small slit in the skin on each piece of chicken. Roll pieces in seasoning mix according to package directions.
2. Place chicken pieces, skin-side up, in a single layer in the roasting bag included with mix. Place bag in a 12" x 7" baking dish. Tie bag with string, leaving a 1-inch opening to allow steam to escape. Cut 4 small slits in top of bag.
3. Microwave at 100% (HIGH) 25 to 30 minutes; give dish a half turn after 15 minutes. Let stand in closed roasting bag 5 minutes. Carefully open bag; juices should run clear when chicken is pierced in thickest part. If not, microwave 30 seconds more; test again. Makes 3 to 4 servings.

# Sherried Chicken Rolls

1/4 cup butter or margarine
1/2 (2-1/2-oz.) jar sliced mushrooms, drained
1/2 cup shredded Swiss cheese (2 oz.)
2 tablespoons chopped parsley
1 teaspoon rubbed sage
6 whole chicken breasts, skinned, boned
2 onions, sliced, separated into rings
1 (10-3/4-oz.) can condensed creamy
   chicken-mushroom soup
1 cup dry sherry

*To serve:*
Hot cooked rice

1. Place butter or margarine in a 12" x 7" baking dish. Microwave at 100% (HIGH) for 1 minute or until melted.
2. In a small bowl, toss together mushrooms, Swiss cheese, parsley and sage. Lay chicken breasts on a flat surface, boned-side up. Spoon mushroom mixture over chicken breasts. Roll up or fold over. Secure with wooden picks. Place in baking dish. Turn chicken pieces over in butter or margarine to coat. Top with sliced onion.
3. In a medium bowl, whisk together soup and sherry. Pour over chicken, coating completely. Cover with vented plastic wrap. Microwave at 100% (HIGH) 10 minutes.
4. Give dish a half turn; rearrange chicken rolls. Microwave at 30% (MEDIUM LOW) 40 minutes or until tender. Let stand, covered, 5 minutes. Place chicken on a serving plate. Stir sauce well; spoon some of sauce over chicken. Serve chicken and sauce with hot cooked rice. Makes 6 servings.

Sherried Chicken Rolls

# Roast Broiler-Fryer Chicken

**1 recipe Golden Soy Glaze, below**
**1 (3- to 3-1/4-lb.) whole broiler-fryer chicken**

**1.** Prepare glaze, below. Twist wing tips behind back. Tie legs together tightly with string. Make a small slit in back skin for release of steam. Brush whole chicken with glaze.
**2.** Place chicken, breast-side down, on a microwave rack in a 12" x 7" baking dish. Cover with a tent of greased waxed paper. Microwave at 100% (HIGH) 10 minutes.
**3.** Turn chicken breast-side up. Brush with more glaze. Give dish a half turn. Cover with a tent of waxed paper. Microwave at 100% (HIGH) 12 to 14 minutes. Let stand 5 minutes. Juices should run clear when chicken is pierced with a fork between leg and thigh. A microwave meat thermometer inserted between leg and thigh should register 180F (80C).
**4.** When done, brush chicken with more glaze. Cover tightly with foil; let stand 3 to 5 minutes. Makes 3 to 4 servings.

## Variations

**Stuffed Broiler-Fryer Chicken:** Lightly pack 1-1/4 to 1-1/2 cups stuffing of your choice into body and neck cavities. Skewer openings closed with wooden picks. Microwave as above. Stuffed chicken may need up to 2 minutes longer cooking time. A microwave meat thermometer inserted in center of stuffing must register 165F (75C). If not, continue cooking until this temperature is reached.
**Roasting Chicken:** A 3-1/2- to 3-3/4-pound roasting chicken without giblets will need about 2 minutes longer microwave cooking time than the unstuffed broiler-fryer chicken. If you want to stuff the chicken, use 2 cups stuffing. Microwave stuffed roasting chicken as above, increasing cooking time to 15 minutes on the first side and to 15 to 20 minutes on the second side. A microwave meat thermometer inserted in center of stuffing must register 165F (75C). If not, continue cooking until this temperature is reached.

# Roast Turkey

**1 recipe Golden Soy Glaze, below**
**1 (6- to 8-lb.) frozen whole self-basting turkey, thawed**

**1.** Prepare glaze, below. Remove giblets from turkey. Twist wing tips behind back. Tie legs together tightly with string or replace under band of skin, if present. Make a small slit in back skin for release of steam. Brush whole turkey with glaze.
**2.** Place turkey, breast-side down, on a microwave rack in a 12" x 7" baking dish. Cover with a tent of greased waxed paper. Microwave at 100% (HIGH) 12 to 15 minutes.
**3.** Turn turkey breast-side up. Brush with more glaze. Give dish a half turn. Shield wings, ends of drumsticks and top of breast with small pieces of foil if these areas are browning faster than the rest of the bird. Secure foil with wooden picks, if necessary. Cover with a tent of waxed paper.
**4.** Microwave at 50% (MEDIUM) 65 to 75 minutes; give dish a half turn after 30 minutes. Let stand 5 to 10 minutes. Juices should run clear when turkey is pierced with a fork between leg and thigh. A microwave meat thermometer should register 180F (80C) between leg and thigh and at thickest part of breast meat. When done, brush turkey with more glaze; cover tightly with foil. Let stand 5 minutes. Makes 8 to 10 servings.

## Variation

**Roast Stuffed Turkey:** Lightly pack 2-1/2 to 3 cups stuffing into body cavity and 3/4 to 1-1/4 cups into neck cavity. Skewer openings closed with wooden picks. Microwave as above. A microwave meat thermometer inserted in center of stuffing must register 165F (75C). If not, continue microwaving until this temperature is reached.

# Golden Soy Glaze

**1 teaspoon cornstarch**
**2 tablespoons soy sauce**
**1/3 cup water**

**1.** Combine cornstarch and soy sauce in a small bowl. Stir until blended. Stir in water. Microwave at 100% (HIGH) 1-1/2 to 2 minutes or until thickened; stir every 30 seconds.
**2.** Brush soy glaze on poultry. Grease waxed paper. Place waxed paper, greased-side down, over glazed poultry, forming a tent. Makes about 1/2 cup.

# How to Make Herbed-Chicken Pot Pies

1/Prepare Chicken à la King; stir thawed frozen peas, thyme and sage into hot mixture.

2/Spoon chicken mixture into individual casseroles; heat through. Top each with a pastry round; heat briefly in microwave.

## Herbed-Chicken Pot Pies

**2 sticks pie-crust mix**
**1 cup frozen green peas, thawed**
**1/2 teaspoon dried leaf thyme**
**1/2 teaspoon dried rubbed sage**
**4 cups hot Chicken à la King, opposite**

---

**1.** Prepare pie-crust mix according to package directions. On a lightly floured board, roll out pastry to 1/8 inch thick. Cut in 4 circles 1 inch larger than tops of 4 individual casseroles. Fold under edges of pastry; flute so pastry will fit inside tops of casseroles. Pierce pastry with a fork or use a cookie cutter to make a chicken-shape cutout in center of each round.
**2.** Place pastry rounds on a 12-inch platter. Microwave at 70% (MEDIUM HIGH) 7-1/2 to 8 minutes or until barely done; give platter a half turn after 4 minutes. Cool pastry rounds on a wire rack.
**3.** Stir peas, thyme and sage into hot Chicken à la King. Spoon hot chicken mixture into individual casseroles. Cover with vented plastic wrap. Microwave at 100% (HIGH) 6 to 7 minutes or until heated through, rearranging once.
**4.** Uncover casseroles; stir fillings. Top each casserole with a pastry round. Microwave, uncovered, at 100% (HIGH) 2 minutes or until pastry is warm. Makes 4 servings.

## Chicken à la King

**1/4 cup butter or margarine**
**1/4 cup shredded carrot**
**1/4 cup chopped celery**
**1/4 cup chopped onion**
**1/4 cup all-purpose flour**
**1/2 teaspoon salt**
**1 cup chicken broth**
**1 cup half and half**
**2 cups cubed cooked chicken or turkey**
**1/2 (2-1/2-oz.) jar sliced mushrooms, drained**
**1/4 cup chopped pimento**

*To serve:*
**Patty shells, toast triangles or mashed potatoes**

---

**1.** In a deep 2-quart casserole, combine butter or margarine, carrot, celery and onion. Microwave at 100% (HIGH) 5 minutes or until vegetables are tender; stir after 2-1/2 minutes.
**2.** Blend in flour and salt. Microwave at 100% (HIGH) 30 seconds. Stir in broth and half and half. Microwave at 100% (HIGH) 4 to 5 minutes or until thickened and bubbly; stir every minute. Mixture should be thick and smooth.
**3.** Stir in chicken or turkey, mushrooms and pimento; cover. Microwave at 100% (HIGH) 3 minutes or until heated through. Stir; serve in patty shells, or over toast triangles or mashed potatoes. Makes 4 servings.

# Hearty Fish Stew

2 tablespoons butter or margarine
1/2 cup cubed peeled rutabaga
1/4 cup chopped onion
1-1/2 cups strained fish stock or chicken broth
2 tomatoes, peeled, quartered
2 ears corn-on-the-cob, cut in 1-1/2-inch pieces
1/2 teaspoon dried leaf basil
1/2 teaspoon dried leaf oregano
1/2 teaspoon salt
1 lb. fish fillets or steaks, poached, chilled
1 medium zucchini, cut in 1-inch pieces

1. In a deep 2-quart casserole with lid, combine butter or margarine, rutabaga and onion. Cover. Microwave at 100% (HIGH) 5 minutes or until onion is tender.
2. Stir in fish stock or chicken broth, tomatoes, corn, basil, oregano and salt. Cover. Microwave at 100% (HIGH) 18 to 20 minutes or until vegetables are barely tender; stir after 9 minutes.
3. Break fish into chunks. Add fish to casserole with zucchini. Cover. Microwave at 100% (HIGH) 3 to 4 minutes or until fish is heated through and zucchini is crisp-tender. Makes 3 to 4 servings.

# Luncheon Seashells

1 tablespoon butter or margarine
3 tablespoons dry bread crumbs
3 tablespoons grated Parmesan cheese
1 tablespoon chopped parsley
3 tablespoons butter or margarine
3 tablespoons all-purpose flour
1/2 teaspoon dried leaf thyme
1/4 teaspoon celery salt
1/8 teaspoon pepper
1 cup fish stock or chicken broth
1/2 cup half and half
1 lb. fish or scallops, poached, cubed (2-1/4 cups cubed)
1 (14-oz.) can artichoke hearts, drained, quartered
1 (2-1/2-oz.) jar sliced mushrooms, drained

1. Place 1 tablespoon butter or margarine in a 2-cup bowl. Microwave at 100% (HIGH) 30 seconds or until melted. Stir in bread crumbs, Parmesan cheese and parsley; set aside.
2. Place 3 tablespoons butter or margarine in a 1-quart glass measuring cup. Microwave at 100% (HIGH) 1 minute or until melted. Stir in flour, thyme, celery salt and pepper.
3. Microwave at 100% (HIGH) 30 seconds. Stir in fish stock or chicken broth and half and half. Microwave at 100% (HIGH) 3 to 4 minutes or until thickened and bubbly; stir every minute. Mixture should be thick and smooth.
4. Fold in fish or scallops, artichoke hearts and mushrooms. Spoon into 4 (5-1/2-inch) baking shells or individual casseroles. Microwave at 100% (HIGH) 6 to 8 minutes or until heated through; rearrange shells after 3 minutes. Sprinkle with crumb mixture. Makes 4 servings.

---

### Cooking Fish

Cook fish until it is starting to flake when a fork is inserted into the thickest part. Another guide is to cook fish until it turns from translucent to opaque. Fish will continue to cook during the standing time. Overcooked fish is tough and dry.

Hearty Fish Stew

# Creamy Scalloped Oysters

1/2 cup butter or margarine
2 cups oyster crackers, crushed
2 tablespoons chopped parsley
1 tablespoon chopped chives
1/4 teaspoon paprika
1 pint shucked oysters
3/4 cup whipping cream
1/4 teaspoon hot-pepper sauce
1/4 teaspoon freshly ground pepper

---

**1.** Place butter or margarine in a 1-1/2-quart bowl. Micro-wave at 100% (HIGH) 1-3/4 minutes or until melted. Stir cracker crumbs, parsley, chives and paprika into melted butter or margarine. Reserve 1/3 of cracker mixture for topping.
**2.** Drain oysters, reserving 2 tablespoons liquor. Add oys-ters to remaining cracker mixture. In a small bowl, com-bine oyster liquor, whipping cream, hot-pepper sauce and pepper. Mix well. Stir into oyster mixture.
**3.** Spoon into a 8-inch-round baking dish. Cover with vented plastic wrap. Microwave at 50% (MEDIUM) 9 to 10 minutes or until heated through; stir every 3 minutes. Stir again and top with reserved crumb mixture. Microwave, uncovered, at 50% (MEDIUM) 1 minute or until crumbs are heated through. Makes 4 servings.

# Creamy Stuffed Manicotti

*Zucchini Sauce:*
1/4 cup butter or margarine
2 cups coarsely chopped zucchini
1/2 cup sliced green onion
1/2 cup chopped pimento
1/4 cup all-purpose flour
1 teaspoon celery salt
1/4 teaspoon pepper
1-3/4 cups milk

*Filling:*
1 egg
1 cup (8 oz.) cream-style cottage cheese
1 (9-1/4-oz.) can tuna, drained, flaked
1/2 cup herb-seasoned stuffing mix
1/2 cup chopped ripe olives
1/4 cup grated Parmesan cheese
2 tablespoons chopped parsley
1 teaspoon chopped chives
8 manicotti shells, cooked, drained

***To garnish:***
Snipped chives

---

**1.** To make sauce, in a 1-1/2-quart casserole, combine butter or margarine, zucchini and green onion. Microwave at 100% (HIGH) 3 to 5 minutes or until barely tender. Stir in pimento. Blend in flour, celery salt and pepper.
**2.** Microwave at 100% (HIGH) 30 seconds. Whisk in milk. Microwave at 100% (HIGH) 5 to 7 minutes or until mixture thickens and bubbles; stir every 2 minutes. Mixture should be thick and smooth.
**3.** Pour 1/2 of sauce into a 12" x 7" baking dish. Set aside remaining sauce.
**4.** Beat egg in a medium bowl. Stir in cottage cheese, tuna, stuffing mix, olives, Parmesan cheese, parsley and chives. Mix well. Spoon about 1/2 cup cottage cheese mixture into each manicotti shell. Place manicotti on top of sauce in baking dish.
**5.** Pour remaining sauce over manicotti, coating all pasta. Cover with vented plastic wrap. Microwave at 50% (MEDIUM) 20 to 25 minutes or until heated through, giving dish a half turn once. At the end of cooking time, stir sauce and spoon over manicotti shells. Let stand, covered, 5 minutes. Garnish with additional chopped chives. Makes 4 to 6 servings.

# How to Make Easy Herbed-Halibut Steaks

1/Arrange halibut steaks with thickest portions toward outside of baking dish; spread with cheese mixture.

2/Serve herbed-halibut steaks with buttered green beans, canned spiced peaches and hot blueberry muffins.

## Easy Herbed-Halibut Steaks

1/2 (4-oz.) carton semi-soft natural cheese with garlic and herbs
1/4 cup Tangy Tartar Sauce, opposite, or prepared tartar sauce
4 (6-oz.) halibut steaks, 3/4 inch thick
12 cucumber slices
1/2 cup shredded Cheddar cheese (2 oz.)
1 tablespoon chopped chives

1. In a small bowl, whisk together semi-soft cheese and tartar sauce. Arrange halibut steaks in a 12" x 7" baking dish, placing larger pieces and thicker portions toward outside of dish. Spread steaks with cheese mixture.
2. Cover with vented plastic wrap. Microwave at 100% (HIGH) 7 to 8 minutes or until center of fish is beginning to flake when tested with a fork. Give dish a half turn after 4 minutes.
3. Top steaks with cucumber slices. Sprinkle with Cheddar cheese and chopped chives. Microwave, uncovered, at 100% (HIGH) 2-1/2 minutes or until cheese melts. Let stand, covered, 5 minutes. Makes 4 servings.

## Tangy Tartar Sauce

1/4 cup plain yogurt
1/4 cup mayonnaise or salad dressing
1/4 cup chopped dill pickle
1/4 cup sliced pimento-stuffed green olives
1/8 teaspoon onion powder
1/8 teaspoon freshly ground pepper

1. In a medium bowl, combine all ingredients. Mix well.
2. Cover and refrigerate until serving time. Serve with hot or cold fish dishes. Makes about 1 cup.

# Shrimp Creole

2 bacon slices, diced
1/3 cup chopped celery
1/3 cup chopped onion
1 large garlic clove, minced
1 (28-oz.) can tomatoes
1 cup chili sauce
1-1/2 teaspoons dried leaf thyme
1/4 teaspoon salt
1/4 teaspoon pepper
1/4 teaspoon hot-pepper sauce
3-1/2 cups cooked peeled shrimp

*To serve:*
Hot cooked rice

---

**1.** In a deep 3-quart casserole, combine bacon, celery, onion and garlic. Microwave at 100% (HIGH) 5 minutes or until vegetables are tender; stir after 2 minutes. Chop tomatoes, reserving juice. Stir in chopped tomatoes with juice, chili sauce, thyme, salt, pepper and hot-pepper sauce. Mix well. Cover.
**2.** Microwave at 100% (HIGH) 6 minutes or until boiling. Stir. Cover. Microwave at 30% (MEDIUM LOW) 20 minutes. Stir in shrimp. Cover. Microwave at 100% (HIGH) 4 to 5 minutes or until heated through; stir after 2 minutes. Serve over hot cooked rice. Makes 6 servings.

# Pan-Fried Fish Fillets

1/4 cup milk
1/4 cup yellow cornmeal
1/4 cup packaged biscuit mix
1/4 cup all-purpose flour
1 tablespoon sesame seeds
1/2 teaspoon paprika
1/2 teaspoon celery salt
1/8 teaspoon onion powder
1 lb. fish fillets, 1/4 to 1/2 inch thick
1/4 cup vegetable oil

---

**1.** Pour milk into a pie plate. In another pie plate, mix together cornmeal, biscuit mix, flour, sesame seeds, paprika, celery salt and onion powder. Dip fish fillets in milk to moisten both sides; drain off excess milk. Dip in cornmeal mixture; coat both sides. Place breaded fish on a rack; set aside.
**2.** Preheat a 10-inch microwave browning skillet, uncovered, at microwave 100% (HIGH) 4 minutes. Add oil to skillet. Using hot pads, tilt skillet so entire surface is coated with oil. Quickly add fish. If fillets have skin, place skin-side up. Microwave on first side at 100% (HIGH) 1-1/2 minutes.
**3.** Turn fish over and give dish a half turn. Microwave at 100% (HIGH) 1-1/2 to 2 minutes or until browned and center of fish is beginning to flake when tested with a fork. Makes 3 or 4 servings.

**Variation**
**Pan-Fried Filleted Trout:** Tie whole trout together with string. Use milk and breading mixture as above. Preheat browning skillet 4 minutes. Add 1/4 cup oil as above. Microwave 2 (8-ounce) trout at 100% (HIGH) 2 minutes. Turn trout over. Microwave at 100% (HIGH) 2 minutes or until center of fish is beginning to flake when tested with a fork.

---

### Purchasing Fish & Shellfish

Fish and shellfish are extremely perishable. Purchase them the day they are to be eaten if possible. Fresh fish should have a mild aroma. The *fishy* smell develops with age. Flesh should be firm and spring back when pressed. Check packages of frozen fish and shellfish for signs of damage and thawing. Keep frozen until needed. For many recipes, fish can be cooked frozen or partially thawed.

# How to Make Fish in a Clay Pot

1/Chop leeks, radishes and fennel, to use as a stuffing mixture. This two-level cutting board makes chopping easier.

2/Spoon vegetable stuffing into fish cavity. It may be necessary to remove head and tail so fish will fit clay pot.

3/Tie fish cavity closed with string. Soak sorrel or spinach leaves in hot water to make them pliable and easy to wind around fish.

4/Place stuffed fish on a microwave rack or inverted saucers in clay pot; drizzle with wine and butter sauce.

## Fish in a Clay Pot

Sorrel or spinach leaves
1 (3- to 3-1/2-lb.) cleaned whole fish
Garlic salt to taste
1/4 cup chopped fennel
1/4 cup sliced leeks
1/4 cup chopped radishes
3 tablespoons butter or margarine
3 tablespoons dry white wine

1. Soak a 4-quart clay pot and lid in cold water 20 minutes or according to manufacturer's directions. Soak sorrel or spinach leaves in hot water. Sprinkle cavity of fish with garlic salt.
2. In a small bowl, combine fennel, leeks and radishes. Stuff fennel mixture into cavity of fish. Tie fish cavity with string to hold in stuffing. Drain sorrel or spinach. Wrap sorrel or spinach leaves around entire fish.
3. Place fish on a microwave rack or inverted saucers in soaked clay pot. Place butter or margarine in a glass baking cup. Microwave at 100% (HIGH) 45 to 60 seconds or until melted. Stir in wine. Drizzle butter or margarine mixture over fish. Cover with clay-pot lid.
4. Microwave at 100% (HIGH) 40 to 45 minutes or until center of fish is beginning to flake when tested with a fork. Give clay pot a half turn after 20 minutes. Serve fish with cooking juices. Makes 6 servings.

# Chicken Quiche

2 cups Gruyère cheese (8 oz.)
1 (10-inch) baked, unpricked pastry shell
1 tablespoon butter or margarine, room temperature
1 cup cubed cooked chicken
1/4 cup chopped green onion
1/3 cup cooked drained whole-kernel corn
1 pint half and half (2 cups)
1/4 teaspoon salt
1/2 teaspoon rubbed sage
1/2 teaspoon dried leaf thyme
5 eggs, beaten

1. Sprinkle shredded cheese into baked pastry shell.
2. In a 1-quart casserole, combine butter or margarine, chicken, green onion and corn. Cover with waxed paper. Microwave at 100% (HIGH) 2 to 3 minutes or until onion is tender. Drain very well. Add well-drained filling to pastry shell; set aside.
3. In a 1-quart glass measuring cup, combine half and half, salt, sage and thyme. Microwave at 100% (HIGH) 2-1/2 to 3-1/2 minutes or until almost boiling.
4. Gradually stir half-and-half mixture into eggs. Pour into pastry shell. Microwave, uncovered, at 50% (MEDIUM) 17 to 19 minutes or until a knife inserted off-center comes out clean. Give quiche a quarter turn every 9 minutes. Let stand 10 minutes. Knife inserted just off center should come out clean. Center should jiggle slightly. Quiche will set upon standing. Makes 8 servings.

# Overnight Brunch Casserole

2 tablespoons butter or margarine
2 tablespoons all-purpose flour
1-1/4 cups milk
1 (4-oz.) carton semi-soft natural cheese with garlic and herbs
8 oz. bulk pork sausage
1/4 cup chopped green onions
1/4 cup chopped pimento-stuffed green olives
1 cup drained cooked whole-kernel corn or green peas
12 eggs, beaten

*To garnish:*
Tomato wedges
Chopped parsley

1. Place butter or margarine in a 1-quart glass measuring cup. Microwave at 100% (HIGH) 45 seconds or until melted. Stir in flour. Microwave at 100% (HIGH) 30 seconds. Whisk in milk. Microwave at 100% (HIGH) 2-1/2 to 3 minutes or until mixture thickens and bubbles; stir every minute. Mixture should be thick and smooth. Stir in cheese. Microwave at 100% (HIGH) 1 minute or until cheese melts. Stir until smooth; set aside.
2. In a 12" x 7" baking dish, combine sausage and green onions. Microwave at 100% (HIGH) 5 minutes or until sausage is browned and done; stir every 2 minutes. Drain well.
3. Stir in olives, corn or peas and eggs. Cover with vented plastic wrap. Microwave at 70% (MEDIUM HIGH) 8 minutes or until eggs are almost set; stir every 3 minutes. Fold in cheese sauce.
4. Cover with plastic wrap; refrigerate overnight. To serve, vent plastic wrap. Microwave at 70% (MEDIUM HIGH) 8 to 10 minutes or until heated through; stir twice. Top with tomato wedges. Microwave at 70% (MEDIUM HIGH) 2 to 3 minutes or until tomatoes are warmed. Sprinkle with parsley. Makes 8 servings.

---

### Cooking Cheese

Because most cheeses are high in fat, they attract the microwaves. This causes cheese to melt quickly. If cheese is used as a topping, add it toward the end of the cooking time. Cheese stirred into a casserole cooks more slowly because it is mixed with other ingredients. Overcooked cheese is tough and stringy.

Chicken Quiche

# Scrambled Eggs

4 eggs
1/4 cup milk
Dash salt
Dash pepper
2 teaspoons butter or margarine, cut in pieces

---

**1.** In a deep 1-quart bowl, whisk together eggs, milk, salt and pepper. Dot with butter or margarine. Cover with vented plastic wrap. Microwave at 70% (MEDIUM HIGH) 2-1/2 minutes or until about half set; stir.
**2.** Microwave at 70% (MEDIUM HIGH) 1-1/4 to 1-1/2 minutes or until almost set. Stir. Let stand, covered, 1 minute before serving. Makes 2 servings.

# Bacon & Eggs

2 bacon slices, halved
2 eggs

---

**1.** Preheat a 10-inch microwave browning skillet, uncovered, at microwave 100% (HIGH) 3 minutes. Quickly add bacon to 1 end of skillet. Microwave, uncovered, at 100% (HIGH) 30 to 60 seconds.
**2.** Turn bacon over. Using hot pads, tilt skillet to coat with drippings. Break eggs into a cup. Gently add eggs to other end of skillet. Prick yolks with a fork or wooden pick. Microwave, uncovered, at 100% (HIGH) 1-1/2 to 2 minutes or until eggs are done as desired. Let stand, covered, 1 minute. Makes 2 servings.

# Scrambled Eggs Deluxe

6 tablespoons butter or margarine
3 cups sliced fresh mushrooms
1/3 cup chopped green onions
1 medium garlic clove, minced
1 (14-oz.) can artichoke hearts, drained, halved
6 eggs, beaten
1-1/2 cups shredded Cheddar cheese (6 oz.)
2-1/2 cups cubed cooked ham (13 oz.)
1/3 cup seasoned dry bread crumbs
1 (3-oz.) can French-fried onions

---

**1.** In a 12" x 7" baking dish, combine butter or margarine, mushrooms, green onions and garlic. Cover with vented plastic wrap. Microwave at 100% (HIGH) 5 to 6 minutes or until onion is tender; stir after 3 minutes.
**2.** Stir in artichoke hearts, eggs, cheese, ham and bread crumbs. Mix well. Cover with vented plastic wrap. Microwave at 70% (MEDIUM HIGH) 12 to 14 minutes or until eggs are almost set; stir after 6 minutes.
**3.** Top with French-fried onions. Microwave, uncovered, at 100% (HIGH) 2 minutes or until onions are warm. Makes 6 servings.

# Sunshine Omelet Filling

2 teaspoons butter or margarine
1/2 cup chopped zucchini
2 tablespoons shredded carrot
2 tablespoons chopped green onion
1/4 teaspoon dried leaf basil
6 cherry tomatoes, halved
2 teaspoons sunflower kernels

---

**1.** In a 1-quart casserole, combine butter or margarine, zucchini, carrot, green onion and basil. Microwave, uncovered, at 100% (HIGH) 2-1/2 to 3 minutes or until vegetables are tender; stir once. Add tomatoes.
**2.** Microwave at 100% (HIGH) 45 to 60 seconds or until heated through. Stir in sunflower kernels. Use mixture as filling for French Omelet, opposite, or other omelet. Makes 2/3 cup.

# How to Make French Omelet

1/Pour beaten egg mixture into melted butter in a pie plate. Cover pie plate completely with plastic wrap. Do not vent plastic wrap or portions of omelet will not cook. Microwave at 70% 1-1/2 minutes.

2/Gently lift cooked edges; let uncooked egg flow underneath. Cover with unvented plastic wrap; continue microwaving. Fill with Sunshine Omelet Filling, opposite, or Bacon Omelet Filling, below.

## French Omelet

2/3 cup Bacon Omelet Filling, opposite, or
    Sunshine Omelet Filling, opposite
1 tablespoon butter or margarine
3 eggs
3 tablespoons milk
Dash salt
Dash pepper

1. Prepare filling for omelet; set aside. Place butter or margarine in a 9-inch pie plate. Microwave at 100% (HIGH) 30 seconds or until melted.
2. Beat together eggs, milk, salt and pepper. Add to pie plate. Cover completely with plastic wrap; do not vent. Microwave at 70% (MEDIUM HIGH) 1-1/2 minutes.
3. Remove wrap. Gently lift cooked egg edges, allowing uncooked egg to flow underneath. Cover completely with unvented plastic wrap. Microwave at 70% (MEDIUM HIGH) 1-1/2 to 1-3/4 minutes or until almost set. Let stand, covered, 1 minute.
4. Fill with prepared filling. Fold over; serve immediately. Makes 2 servings.

## Bacon Omelet Filling

4 bacon slices
4 thin onion slices, separated in rings
4 green-bell-pepper rings
1/2 teaspoon dried leaf Italian herbs

1. Place bacon on a microwave rack in a 12" x 7" baking dish. Cover with a white paper towel. Microwave at 100% (HIGH) 3-1/2 to 4 minutes or until crisp. Drain bacon on paper towels, reserving pan drippings. Crumble bacon; set aside.
2. Remove microwave rack. Discard all but 4 teaspoons bacon drippings. Stir in onion, green-pepper rings and Italian herbs. Microwave, uncovered, at 100% (HIGH) 3-1/2 to 4-1/2 minutes or until tender; stir once. Drain off excess drippings.
3. Stir in crumbled bacon. Use mixture as filling for French Omelet, opposite, or other omelet. Makes 2/3 cup.

## Smoky Eggs à la King

2 tablespoons butter or margarine
1/2 cup chopped zucchini
3 tablespoons chopped onion
2 tablespoons all-purpose flour
1/2 cup milk
1/2 cup chicken broth
1/2 (2-1/2-oz.) pkg. sliced smoked beef, snipped
2 hard-cooked eggs, sliced
2 tablespoons chopped pimento

*To serve:*
**Chow mein noodles, warmed**

---

**1.** In a deep 1-quart casserole, combine butter or margarine, zucchini and onion. Microwave at 100% (HIGH) 3 minutes or until vegetables are tender; stir once. Stir in flour; mix well. Microwave at 100% (HIGH) 30 seconds or until bubbly.
**2.** Whisk in milk and broth. Microwave at 100% (HIGH) 2-1/2 to 3-1/2 minutes or until thickened and bubbly; stir every minute. Mixture should be thick and smooth.
**3.** Stir in beef, eggs and pimento. Cover. Microwave at 100% (HIGH) 2 to 2-1/2 minutes or until heated through; stir after 1 minute. Stir; serve over chow mein noodles. Makes 3 to 4 servings.

## Mushroom-Macaroni Bake

2 tablespoons butter or margarine
2 cups fresh mushroom slices
1/2 cup chopped red or green bell pepper
1/4 cup chopped onion
1 (10-3/4-oz.) can condensed cream of onion soup
3/4 cup milk
1/2 teaspoon dried dill weed
2 cups shredded Edam cheese (8 oz.)
2 cups medium-shell macaroni (7 oz.), cooked, drained
1 (9-oz.) pkg. frozen Italian green beans, cooked, drained

*To garnish:*
**Sunflower kernels, if desired**
**Chopped parsley, if desired**

---

**1.** In a deep 2-quart casserole, combine butter or margarine, mushrooms, red or green pepper and onion. Cover. Microwave at 100% (HIGH) 4 to 5 minutes or until vegetables are just tender; stir once.
**2.** Stir in soup, milk and dill weed. Mix well. Stir in cheese, macaroni and green beans. Cover. Microwave at 100% (HIGH) 10 to 12 minutes or until heated through; stir once. Stir before serving.
**3.** Garnish with sunflower kernels and parsley, if desired. Makes 5 to 6 servings.

## Cheese Lover's Lasagna

1 egg
2 tablespoons all-purpose flour
1 cup cream-style cottage cheese
1/2 cup grated Parmesan cheese (1-1/2 oz.)
1/4 cup shredded carrot
1/4 cup chopped celery
1/4 cup chopped pimento
1/4 cup chopped green onions
1 (10-oz.) pkg. frozen chopped spinach, cooked, drained well
2 tablespoons all-purpose flour
1/2 cup plain yogurt
1 (10-3/4-oz.) can condensed cream of onion soup
6 plain or whole-wheat lasagna noodles, cooked, drained well
8 oz. sliced sharp process American cheese

---

**1.** Butter a 12" x 7" baking dish; set aside. In a medium bowl, beat egg. Stir in 2 tablespoons flour, cottage cheese and Parmesan cheese. Fold carrot, celery, pimento, green onions and spinach into cottage-cheese filling; set aside.
**2.** In a medium bowl, whisk 2 tablespoons flour into yogurt. Whisk in soup, mixing well. In buttered baking dish, layer 1/2 of noodles, then 1/2 each of the cottage-cheese mixture, process cheese and yogurt sauce. Repeat layers.
**3.** Cover with vented plastic wrap. Microwave at 50% (MEDIUM) 25 to 30 minutes or until hot in center, giving dish a half turn once. Let stand, uncovered, 10 minutes. Makes 6 servings.

## Old-Fashioned Cheese Rarebit

3/4 cup half and half
1/2 cup shredded process American cheese (2 oz.)
1/2 cup shredded process Swiss cheese (2 oz.)
1 tablespoon all-purpose flour
1/2 teaspoon dry mustard
1 teaspoon Worcestershire sauce
1 egg yolk, beaten

---

**1.** Pour half and half into a 1-quart bowl. Microwave at 100% (HIGH) 1-1/2 to 2 minutes or until almost boiling. Toss together cheeses, flour and dry mustard. Gradually add cheese mixture to hot half and half, whisking well after each addition. Whisk in Worcestershire sauce.
**2.** Microwave at 100% (HIGH) 1 to 1-1/2 minutes or until cheeses are melted; stir 3 times. Whisk until smooth. Gradually stir half the hot sauce into egg yolk; mix well. Stir yolk mixture into remaining hot sauce in bowl.
**3.** Microwave at 100% (HIGH) 45 to 60 seconds or until thickened and heated through; stir every 15 seconds. Serve over toasted English muffins or open-face sandwiches. Makes 2 servings.

# How to Make Cheese Lover's Lasagna

1/Press cooked spinach in a sieve to remove excess moisture. Spinach must be well-drained or filling will be watery.

2/Shredded carrot, chopped celery, pimento, green onion and spinach are folded into cottage-cheese filling.

3/Whisk flour into yogurt. Whisk in onion soup. Flour helps keep yogurt from curdling.

4/Layer 1/2 of lasagna noodles; then 1/2 each of cottage-cheese filling, cheese slices and yogurt sauce. Repeat layers. Microwave lasagna until hot.

# Shirred Eggs

4 teaspoons butter or margarine
4 eggs
Dash seasoned salt
1/4 cup shredded Cheddar cheese (1 oz.)

*To garnish:*
**Chopped parsley**

**1.** Butter insides of 4 (6-ounce) glass baking cups. Place 1 teaspoon butter or margarine in bottom of each cup. Microwave at 100% (HIGH) 20 seconds or until melted.
**2.** Gently slip 1 egg into each cup. Prick yolks with a pin or wooden pick. Sprinkle with seasoned salt, cheese and parsley. Cover each cup with vented plastic wrap. Microwave at 70% (MEDIUM HIGH) 3 to 3-1/2 minutes or until eggs are just set; rearrange cups after 1 minute. Give them a half turn after 2 minutes. Let stand, covered, 1 minute. Makes 4 servings.

# Blanched & Butter-Cooked Asparagus

1-1/4 lb. fresh asparagus spears
1/4 cup water
2 tablespoons butter or margarine

1. Wash asparagus. Grasp stalk at either end and bend in a bow shape. Stalk will break where tender part of stalk starts. Discard tough part of stalk.
2. Place spears in a 2- to 3-quart casserole with lid. Add water. Cover. Microwave at 100% (HIGH) 6 minutes or until crisp-tender; rearrange spears after 3 minutes. Drain in a colander; run cold water over asparagus. Wrap and refrigerate.
3. At serving time, melt butter or margarine in same casserole at 100% (HIGH) 30 seconds. Add asparagus, stirring to coat. Cover. Microwave at 100% (HIGH) 4 to 5 minutes or until heated through; stir once. Let stand, covered, 2 minutes. Makes 4 to 5 servings.

# Zesty Brussels Sprouts

1 (10-oz.) pkg. frozen Brussels sprouts
1/4 cup chopped green onions
1/4 cup chopped celery
1/4 cup chopped carrots
2 tablespoons water
2 tablespoons butter or margarine
1 cup cherry tomatoes
1/2 cup plain yogurt
1 tablespoon all-purpose flour
2 teaspoons Dijon-style mustard
1 teaspoon prepared horseradish

1. In a deep 1-1/2-quart casserole with lid, combine Brussels sprouts, green onions, celery, carrots and water. Cover. Microwave at 100% (HIGH) 8 minutes or until almost tender; stir once. Drain well.
2. Stir in butter or margarine. Add cherry tomatoes. Cover. Microwave at 100% (HIGH) 2 to 3 minutes or until heated through. Let stand, covered, while making sauce.
3. In a small bowl, combine yogurt, flour, mustard and horseradish; whisk to mix well. Microwave at 30% (MEDIUM LOW) 3 minutes or until hot and thickened; stir every minute. Stir sauce; spoon over vegetables. Makes 3 to 4 servings.

# Confetti Asparagus Bake

2 (10-oz.) pkgs. frozen asparagus spears
1/4 cup butter or margarine
2 tablespoons seasoned dry bread crumbs
3 tablespoons finely chopped onion
3 tablespoons finely chopped celery
1 tomato, chopped, drained
1/4 teaspoon dried leaf basil, crushed
1/4 teaspoon dried leaf thyme, crushed
2 tablespoons grated Parmesan cheese

1. Loosen wrapping on asparagus packages. Place packages in microwave oven on paper towels. Microwave at 100% (HIGH) 3 minutes. On a round 12-inch microwave platter, arrange asparagus spears, spoke-fashion, with tips pointing to center.
2. In a small bowl, microwave butter or margarine at 100% (HIGH) 1 minute or until melted. Combine 1 tablespoon melted butter or margarine with bread crumbs; set aside.
3. Sprinkle onion, celery and tomato pieces over asparagus; drizzle with remaining melted butter or margarine. Sprinkle with basil and thyme. Cover with vented plastic wrap. Microwave at 100% (HIGH) 10 to 11 minutes or until asparagus is tender, giving platter a half turn after 5 minutes. Sprinkle with Parmesan cheese and buttered crumbs. Makes 6 servings.

# Blanched & Butter-Cooked Broccoli

1 lb. fresh broccoli
1/4 cup water
1 tablespoon butter or margarine

1. Wash broccoli; cut into flowerets, leaving 1 to 2 inches of stalk. Place in a 1-quart casserole with lid, with stems toward outside of dish. Add water. Cover. Microwave at 100% (HIGH) 6 to 7 minutes or until starting to get tender.
2. Drain in a colander; rinse under running water. Wrap and refrigerate. At serving time, melt butter or margarine in same casserole at 100% (HIGH) 45 seconds. Add broccoli; stir to coat. Cover. Microwave at 100% (HIGH) 4 to 5 minutes or until tender and heated through; stir once. Let stand, covered, 2 minutes. Makes 4 servings.

*Confetti Asparagus Bake*

# Green Beans Italiano

1 (9-oz.) pkg. frozen Italian green beans
2 tablespoons water
1/2 (16-oz.) can garbanzo beans, drained
2 tablespoons chopped pimento
2 tablespoons sliced ripe olives
2 tablespoons chopped pepperoni
2 tablespoons olive oil
1/2 teaspoon dried leaf oregano, crushed
1/8 teaspoon garlic powder

**1.** In a deep 1-1/2-quart casserole with lid, combine Italian beans and water. Cover. Microwave at 100% (HIGH) 7 minutes or until tender; stir once. Drain well.
**2.** Add garbanzo beans, pimento, olives, pepperoni, olive oil, oregano and garlic powder; mix well. Cover. Microwave at 100% (HIGH) 2 minutes or until heated through; stir once. Makes 3 to 4 servings.

# Glazed Beets

2 (16-oz.) cans whole tiny beets, drained
2 tablespoons firmly packed brown sugar
2 teaspoons cornstarch
2/3 cup cranberry-juice cocktail
2 tablespoons white vinegar
1 teaspoon prepared horseradish
1/4 cup cranberry-orange relish

**1.** Place beets in a 2-quart casserole with lid; set aside. In a 2-cup glass measuring cup, mix brown sugar and cornstarch until well combined. Stir in cranberry-juice cocktail, vinegar and horseradish.
**2.** Microwave at 100% (HIGH) 2 to 2-1/2 minutes or until mixture thickens and bubbles; stir every minute. Stir in cranberry-orange relish. Gently mix sauce into beets. Cover. Microwave at 100% (HIGH) 7 minutes or until heated through. Makes 6 servings.

# Maple Baked Beans

1 lb. dried pea beans (2 cups)
2 qts. water
1/4 teaspoon baking soda
6 cups water
1 teaspoon salt
8 crisp-cooked bacon slices, crumbled
1/2 cup firmly packed brown sugar
1/2 cup maple-flavored syrup
2 teaspoons instant minced onion
2 teaspoons Worcestershire sauce
1 teaspoon ground cinnamon
2 apples, cored, sliced

**1.** Sort and rinse beans. In a deep 4-quart casserole with lid, combine beans and 2 quarts water. Stir in baking soda. Cover and let stand overnight.
**2.** Drain and rinse beans. Return beans to casserole. Add 6 cups water and salt. Cover and microwave at 100% (HIGH) 18 to 20 minutes or until boiling. Stir. Cover and microwave at 30% (MEDIUM LOW) 60 to 70 minutes or until beans are tender; stir every 20 minutes. Drain, reserving liquid.
**3.** Stir bacon, brown sugar, maple-flavored syrup, onion, Worcestershire sauce and cinnamon into beans. Add 1 cup reserved cooking liquid; reserve remaining liquid. Cover. Microwave at 30% (MEDIUM LOW) 80 to 90 minutes or until beans are very tender and flavors blend; stir every 20 minutes. Add more reserved cooking liquid, if necessary. Top with a ring of apple slices. Cover. Microwave at 30% (MEDIUM LOW) 15 to 20 minutes or until apples are tender; give dish a half turn after 10 minutes. Makes 6 to 8 servings.

# Brussels Sprouts

1 lb. fresh Brussels sprouts
1/4 cup water

**1.** Trim off wilted outer leaves and excess stem from Brussels sprouts. Wash sprouts. Cut a X in bottom of each sprout. Halve any large sprouts.
**2.** In a 1-quart casserole with lid, combine sprouts and water. Cover. Microwave at 100% (HIGH) 8 to 9 minutes or until tender; stir once. Let stand, covered, 2 minutes. Drain. Makes 4 servings.

Green Beans Italiano

# Carrot Coins

**1 lb. carrots**
**1/4 cup water**

**1.** Halve thick portion of carrots lengthwise. Slice 1/2 inch thick. In a 1-quart casserole with lid, combine carrots and water. Cover.
**2.** Microwave at 100% (HIGH) 11 to 12 minutes or until tender; stir after 5 minutes. Let stand, covered, 2 minutes. Drain. Makes 4 servings.

# Fresh Cauliflowerets

**1 (1-1/2-lb.) head cauliflower**
**1/4 cup water**

**1.** Cut into flowerets. Place in a 1-1/2-quart casserole with lid, with stems toward outside of dish. Add water; cover.
**2.** Microwave at 100% (HIGH) 7 to 8 minutes or until tender; stir after 4 minutes. Let stand, covered, 2 minutes. Drain. Makes 5 to 6 servings.

# Crisp Fried Eggplant

**1/2 medium eggplant (8 oz.)**
**1/2 cup all-purpose flour**
**1/2 cup milk**
**1 egg white**
**1/4 teaspoon onion salt**
**Seasoned dry bread crumbs**
**9 tablespoons vegetable oil**

**1.** Cut eggplant crosswise into 12 to 14 thin slices, about 1/8 inch thick. Set aside.
**2.** Preheat a 10-inch microwave browning skillet, uncovered, at microwave 100% (HIGH) 4 minutes.
**3.** In a pie plate, beat together flour, milk, egg white and onion salt. Place bread crumbs in a pie plate. Dip eggplant in batter, then in bread crumbs; press crumbs in with fingers. Place crumb-coated slices on a wire rack over waxed paper.
**4.** Add 3 tablespoons oil to preheated browning skillet. Quickly add 4 to 5 eggplant slices in a single layer. Microwave, uncovered, at 100% (HIGH) 1 minute. Turn slices; microwave at 100% (HIGH) 30 seconds or until tender.
**5.** Keep warm in a 200F (95C) oven while preparing remaining slices. Wipe out browning skillet with paper towels, being careful not to touch hot skillet.
**6.** Preheat browning skillet at 100% (HIGH) 3 minutes. Add 3 tablespoons oil. Quickly add 4 to 5 more crumb-coated slices; microwave as before. Repeat with remaining slices and oil, wiping out and preheating browning skillet as before. Makes 6 servings.

# Fresh Mushroom Slices

**2 tablespoons butter or margarine**
**2 cups sliced fresh mushrooms**

**1.** Place butter or margarine in a 1-quart casserole with lid. Microwave at 100% (HIGH) 45 seconds or until melted.
**2.** Add mushrooms. Toss to coat. Cover. Microwave at 100% (HIGH) 3 to 4 minutes or until tender; stir after 2 minutes. Makes 2 servings.

# How to Make Peas à la Francaise

1/Line a deep casserole with large lettuce leaves. In lettuce-lined casserole, gently combine frozen peas and onions, shredded lettuce, butter and sugar. The leaves provide moisture for cooking peas.

2/Serve peas with dollops of sour cream for a delightful sweet and sour flavor. Sprinkle chives over sour cream.

## Peas à la Francaise

**Several large iceberg-lettuce leaves**
**2 (10-oz.) pkgs. frozen peas and onions**
**2 cups shredded iceberg lettuce**
**2 tablespoons sugar**
**1/4 cup butter or margarine**

*To garnish:*
**Dairy sour cream**
**Chopped chives**

**1.** Line a deep 2-quart casserole with a lid with large lettuce leaves. Break apart peas and onions with a fork. In lettuce-lined casserole, gently combine peas and onions, shredded lettuce, sugar and butter or margarine. Cover.
**2.** Microwave at 100% (HIGH) 10 minutes or until peas are tender, tossing gently after 5 minutes. Let stand, covered, 2 minutes. Serve topped with a dollop of sour cream and chives. Makes 6 servings.

## Baked Potatoes

**4 (6- to 8-oz.) baking potatoes**

**1.** Pierce each potato several times with a large fork to allow steam to escape. Arrange potatoes, spoke-fashion, in a circle in microwave oven.
**2.** Microwave at 100% (HIGH) 10 to 12 minutes or until potatoes are soft when gently squeezed. Turn potatoes over and rearrange once after 5 minutes. Wrap in foil; let stand 5 minutes. Makes 4 servings.

# How to Make Confetti-Stuffed Peppers

1/For precooking, pepper halves are placed cut-side down against baking dish to capture steam and speed cooking. Turn peppers cut-side up; drain before filling with creamed vegetable mixture.

2/Cook peppers until they are crisp-tender and filling is heated through. Slip a silver knife into center of filling to check if it is hot. Sprinkle with cracker crumbs after cooking; this prevents crumbs from getting soggy.

## Confetti-Stuffed Peppers

1 tablespoon butter or margarine
1/4 cup cheese-cracker crumbs
1 (8-oz.) pkg. frozen mixed vegetables with onion sauce
1/2 cup milk
1 tablespoon butter or margarine
1/4 cup instant-cooking rice
2 tablespoons chopped pimento
1/4 teaspoon dried leaf thyme, crushed
2 medium green bell peppers, halved lengthwise

1. Place 1 tablespoon butter or margarine in a small bowl. Microwave at 100% (HIGH) 30 seconds or until melted. Stir in cracker crumbs; set aside.
2. In a 1-1/2-quart casserole with lid, combine frozen vegetables, milk and 1 tablespoon butter or margarine. Cover and microwave at 100% (HIGH) 6 minutes. Stir sauce after 3 minutes until smooth. When vegetables are tender, quickly stir in rice, pimento and thyme. Let stand, covered, 5 minutes.
3. Arrange peppers, cut-side down, in an 8-inch-square baking dish. Cover with vented plastic wrap. Microwave at 100% (HIGH) 5 minutes. Turn peppers cut-side up; drain off juices. Spoon creamed vegetables into peppers. Cover dish with vented plastic wrap. Microwave at 100% (HIGH) 4 minutes or until peppers are crisp-tender and filling is heated through. Slip a silver knife into center of filling to check that it is hot. Sprinkle with buttered cracker crumbs. Makes 4 servings.

## Taco Salad

6 cups torn mixed salad greens
1 (15-oz.) can red beans, drained, rinsed
1 avocado, sliced
2 tomatoes, cut in wedges
1/2 cup ripe olives, sliced
1 lb. ground beef
1/4 cup chopped green onions
2 to 4 tablespoons canned diced green chilies
1 cup taco sauce
1 cup shredded Cheddar cheese (4 oz.)

*To garnish:*
Corn chips

1. In a 4-quart salad bowl, arrange greens, beans, avocado, tomatoes and olives. Cover and refrigerate until serving time.
2. At serving time, crumble ground beef into a deep 1-1/2-quart casserole. Stir in green onions. Microwave at 100% (HIGH) 4 to 5 minutes or until meat is no longer pink and onion is tender; stir after 2 minutes. Drain.
3. Stir in chilies and taco sauce. Microwave at 100% (HIGH) 3 to 4 minutes or until boiling.
4. Pour over salad. Toss until combined. Garnish with cheese and corn chips. Serve immediately. Makes 6 servings.

# Pina Colada Salad Mold

1 (8-oz.) can pineapple chunks, juice pack
1 (3-oz.) pkg. lemon-flavored gelatin
1/2 cup non-alcoholic Pina Colada drink mix
1/4 cup rum
2 tablespoons lemon juice
1/4 cup shredded coconut
1/4 cup chopped macadamia nuts

*To garnish:*
Lettuce leaves
Lime slices

---

1. Lightly oil a 3-cup mold. Drain pineapple, reserving juice. Add water to juice to make 1 cup. In a 1-1/2-quart bowl, microwave juice mixture at 100% (HIGH) 2-1/2 minutes or until boiling.
2. Stir in gelatin until completely dissolved. Stir in Pina Colada mix, rum and lemon juice. Refrigerate until almost set.
3. Fold in pineapple, coconut and nuts. Pour into oiled mold. Refrigerate until firm. Unmold on lettuce leaves; garnish with lime slices. Makes 4 servings.

# Fresh Spinach

1 lb. fresh spinach (12 cups)

---

1. Wash and drain spinach. Trim off tough stem ends. Place spinach with water that clings to leaves in a deep 5-quart casserole with lid. Cover.
2. Microwave at 100% (HIGH) 9 to 10 minutes or until tender; stir after 4 minutes. Makes 4 servings.

# Baked Sweet Potatoes or Yams

4 (6- to 8-oz.) sweet potatoes or yams

---

1. Pierce each potato several times with a large fork for steam to escape. Arrange potatoes, spoke-fashion, in a circle in microwave oven.
2. Microwave at 100% (HIGH) 11 to 14 minutes; turn potatoes over and rearrange after 5 minutes. When done, potatoes are soft when gently squeezed. Wrap in foil. Let stand 5 minutes. Makes 4 servings.

# Spaghetti Squash Straw & Hay

1/4 cup butter or margarine
6 cups hot cooked spaghetti squash with shell, below
3/4 cup sliced cooked ham strips
1/2 cup cooked green peas
1 (2-1/2-oz.) jar sliced mushrooms, drained
2 egg yolks, beaten
1/2 pint whipping cream (1 cup)
1 cup grated Parmesan cheese (4 oz.)

---

1. In a large bowl, stir butter or margarine into hot squash until melted. Fold in ham, peas and mushrooms. In a small bowl, whisk egg yolks and cream until foamy. Slowly add cream mixture to squash mixture; mix well. Stir in 1/2 of Parmesan cheese.
2. Drain juices from baking dish used to cook squash. Mound squash mixture into 1 of the squash shells in a 13" x 9" baking dish. Cover with vented plastic wrap.
3. Microwave at 100% (HIGH) 7 to 10 minutes or until heated through and sauce has thickened; toss every 3 minutes. Top with remaining Parmesan cheese. Makes 6 servings.

# Spaghetti Squash

1 (4-1/4-lb.) spaghetti squash
1/3 cup water

---

1. Place whole squash in a 13" x 9" baking dish. Microwave at 100% (HIGH) 10 minutes. Halve squash lengthwise. Remove seeds and membrane. Place squash, cut-side up, in same baking dish. Add water. Cover with vented plastic wrap.
2. Microwave at 100% (HIGH) 12 minutes; give dish a half turn after 6 minutes. Let stand, covered, 2 minutes. Squash should feel tender when pierced with a large fork and strands of squash should start to pull away from the shell. Makes 6 servings.

# Succotash Scallop

1 (10-oz.) pkg. frozen baby lima beans
1 cup water
1 tablespoon butter or margarine
1/4 cup seasoned dry bread crumbs
2 tablespoons butter or margarine
2 tablespoons chopped onion
2 tablespoons chopped green bell pepper
2 teaspoons all-purpose flour
1/2 cup milk
1 cup shredded Monterey Jack cheese (4 oz.)
1 (8-3/4-oz.) can whole-kernel corn, drained
1/2 (8-oz.) can water chestnuts, drained, sliced
2 tablespoons chopped pimento
1/2 teaspoon celery seed

---

**1.** Combine lima beans and water in a deep 1-1/2-quart casserole with lid. Cover and microwave at 100% (HIGH) 11 minutes or until tender, stirring once. Drain. Cover and set aside.
**2.** In a small bowl, microwave 1 tablespoon butter or margarine at 100% (HIGH) 30 seconds or until melted. Stir in bread crumbs; set aside.
**3.** In same casserole, microwave 2 tablespoons butter or margarine, onion and green pepper at 100% (HIGH) 2-1/2 to 3 minutes or until vegetables are tender; stir after 1 minute. Stir in flour until blended; microwave at 100% (HIGH) 1 minute or until mixture bubbles. Gradually add milk.
**4.** Microwave at 100% (HIGH) 1-1/2 to 2 minutes or until thickened and bubbly; stir after 1 minute. Gradually add cheese; stir until melted. Stir in limas, corn, water chestnuts, pimento and celery seed. Cover. Microwave at 100% (HIGH) 6 minutes or until heated through. Top with buttered crumbs. Makes 4 servings.

# Hot Slaw Mexicana

1/8 medium head cabbage
1/2 medium carrot
1/4 medium green bell pepper
1/2 cup cherry tomatoes
1/4 cup pitted ripe olives
1/4 cup whole-kernel corn, cooked, drained
1/2 cup shredded process pepper cheese or sharp process cheese (2 oz.)
1 tablespoon milk
1/2 teaspoon celery seed
1/8 teaspoon dry mustard
1/2 avocado, sliced

---

**1.** Using thin slicing blade on a food processor, slice cabbage, carrot, green pepper, cherry tomatoes and olives. Or slice finely by hand. Toss with corn in a deep 2-quart bowl; set aside.
**2.** In a medium bowl, combine cheese, milk, celery seed and dry mustard. Microwave at 30% (MEDIUM LOW) 2 to 2-1/2 minutes or until cheese has melted; stir every minute. Stir until smooth. Pour cheese dressing over cabbage mixture. Toss gently.
**3.** Cover with vented plastic wrap. Microwave at 100% (HIGH) 2 to 3 minutes or until heated through; stir once. Garnish with avocado slices. Serve salad hot. Makes 3 to 4 servings.

# French Tossed Salad Mold

1 (1/4-oz.) envelope unflavored gelatin (1 tablespoon)
1-1/2 cups water
1/2 cup sweet red French dressing
1/2 cup finely chopped lettuce
2 tablespoons shredded carrot
2 tablespoons chopped green bell pepper
2 tablespoons chopped celery
2 tablespoons sliced ripe olives
2 tablespoons chopped green onion

*To garnish:*
**Cherry tomatoes**
**Ripe olives**
**Celery leaves**

---

**1.** Lightly oil a 2-1/2 cup ring mold. In a 1-quart bowl, combine gelatin and water. Let stand 3 minutes. Microwave at 100% (HIGH) 1-1/2 to 2 minutes or until gelatin dissolves. Stir in French dressing. Refrigerate until almost set.
**2.** Fold in lettuce, carrot, green pepper, celery, olives and green onion. Turn into oiled mold. Refrigerate until set.
**3.** Unmold on a platter. Garnish with cherry tomatoes, olives and celery leaves. Makes 4 servings.

Hot Slaw Mexicana

# Herbed French Loaf

1 (8-oz.) loaf French bread
1/2 cup butter or margarine
2 teaspoons dried leaf oregano
2 teaspoons dried leaf basil
1 teaspoon celery seed
1/2 teaspoon onion powder
1/2 teaspoon sesame seeds

1. Cut French bread in 1-inch slices, cutting to, but not quite through, bottom of loaf.
2. In a small bowl, microwave butter or margarine at 10% (LOW) 1-1/2 to 2 minutes or until softened. Stir in oregano, basil, celery seed and onion powder. Spread between bread slices and over top of loaf. Sprinkle with sesame seeds.
3. Line a platter with paper towels. Place loaf on paper-towel-lined platter. Microwave at full power (HIGH) 1 to 1-1/2 minutes or until warm. Makes 4 to 6 servings.

# Taco Hot Dogs

2 tablespoons taco sauce
1/2 cup shredded Cheddar cheese (2 oz.)
2 tablespoons chopped onion
2 tablespoons chopped canned green chilies
4 hot dogs
4 taco shells

*To serve:*
**Shredded lettuce**
**Marinated garbanzo beans, drained**
**Frozen guacamole dip, thawed**

1. In medium bowl, combine taco sauce, cheese, onion and chilies. Slit hot dogs lengthwise, but not quite through. Stuff with 3/4 of cheese mixture. Place in taco shells. Stand stuffed taco shells upright in a 11" x 7" baking dish. If needed, support shells with crumpled waxed paper.
2. Spoon remaining cheese mixture over top. Microwave at full power (HIGH) 1-1/2 to 2 minutes or until heated through. To serve, top with shredded lettuce, garbanzo beans and guacamole dip. Makes 4 servings.

### Variation
**Beef Tacos:** For 4 servings, crumble 1/2 pound ground beef into a 1-quart casserole. Cover loosely with waxed paper. Microwave at full power (HIGH) 4 minutes or until meat is no longer pink; stir after 2 minutes. Drain well. Stir in 1/4 cup taco sauce, 1/2 cup shredded Cheddar cheese, 2 tablespoons chopped onion and 2 tablespoons chopped green chilies. Spoon into 4 taco shells. Microwave and serve as above.

# Crab Sandwiches Supreme

1 (7-1/2-oz.) can Alaskan king crab, drained, flaked
1/4 cup diced celery
1/2 (4-oz.) carton semi-soft natural cheese with garlic and herbs
2 tablespoons minced green onion
2 tablespoons grated Parmesan cheese
2 tablespoons lemon juice
2 tablespoons capers, drained
2 tablespoons mayonnaise or salad dressing
Dash pepper
6 hamburger buns, split

1. In a medium bowl, combine crab, celery, semi-soft cheese, green onion, Parmesan cheese, lemon juice, capers, mayonnaise and pepper. Mix well. Spread 1/4 cup of mixture on each of 4 hamburger buns using about 1/4 cup mixture for each.
2. Replace tops of buns; wrap each in a paper towel. Place wrapped buns on a microwave platter or tray. Microwave at full power (HIGH) 2-1/2 minutes or until heated through; give plate a half turn after 1-1/2 minutes. Makes 6 servings.

# Swiss Club Sandwiches

1 cup diced cooked chicken
1/4 cup chopped celery
1/4 cup sliced pimento-stuffed green olives
1 tablespoon chopped green onion
2 tablespoons crumbled blue cheese
1/4 cup mayonnaise or salad dressing
8 slices plain toast zwieback, 3-1/2 x 1-1/2 inches or 4 plain rusks, 3-1/2 inches in diameter
4 tomato slices
12 cooked asparagus spears, well-drained
2 Swiss-cheese slices, halved crosswise
6 crisp-cooked bacon slices

1. In a medium bowl, combine chicken, celery, olives, green onion, blue cheese and mayonnaise or salad dressing. Mix gently.
2. Arrange 2 zwieback or 1 rusk for each serving in a 11" x 7" baking dish. Spoon chicken mixture onto zwieback or rusks. Top each with tomato slices, asparagus spears and Swiss-cheese slices. Crumble bacon over each serving. Microwave at full power (HIGH) 3-1/2 to 4 minutes or until heated through. Makes 4 servings.

*Swiss Club Sandwich*

# Spanish Rice

6 bacon slices
1/2 cup chopped onion
1/2 cup chopped green bell pepper
1 (28-oz.) can tomatoes
1/2 teaspoon celery salt
3/4 cup long-cooking rice
1/2 cup shredded process American cheese (2 oz.)

*To garnish:*
Green-bell-pepper rings

**1.** Place bacon on a microwave rack in a 12" x 7" baking dish. Cover with a white paper towel. Microwave at full power (HIGH) 4 to 5 minutes or until crisp. Measure about 1/4 cup bacon drippings into a deep 2-quart casserole with lid. Crumble bacon; set aside.
**2.** Add onion and green pepper to drippings in casserole. Microwave at full power (HIGH) 5 minutes or until tender; stir after 3 minutes. Drain tomato juice into a 2-cup measuring cup; add enough water to make 1-1/2 cups. Chop tomatoes. Stir in tomatoes, tomato-juice mixture and celery salt. Cover. Microwave at full power (HIGH) 6 to 8 minutes or until boiling.
**3.** Add rice. Stir until moistened. Cover. Microwave at 30% (MEDIUM LOW) 25 to 30 minutes or until rice is tender; stir every 10 minutes. Sprinkle bacon and cheese over mixture. Garnish with green-pepper rings. Microwave, uncovered, at full power (HIGH) 1 minute or until cheese is melted. Makes 4 to 6 servings.

# Quick-Cooking Rolled Oats

3 cups hot water
1-1/2 cups quick-cooking rolled oats
1/2 teaspoon salt

*To serve:*
Milk or half and half
Brown sugar
Cinnamon or nutmeg

**1.** Measure hot water into a deep 2-quart casserole. Stir in cereal and salt.
**2.** Microwave at full power (HIGH) 4-1/2 minutes or until water is nearly all absorbed. Stir well every 2 minutes. Stir before servings. Makes 4 servings.

# Strawberry-Jam Kuchen

*Streusel Topping:*
1/2 cup all-purpose flour
1/4 cup granulated sugar
1/4 cup firmly packed brown sugar
1 teaspoons ground cinnamon
3 tablespoons butter or margarine
1 egg yolk

*Kuchen:*
2 cups packaged biscuit mix
2 tablespoons sugar
1 egg
2/3 cup milk
1/2 cup strawberry jam

*To serve:*
Powdered sugar
Strawberries, if desired

**1.** To prepare topping, in a medium bowl, mix flour, granulated sugar, brown sugar and cinnamon. With a pastry blender or 2 knives, cut in butter or margarine and egg yolk until crumbly. Set aside.
**2.** Grease bottom of a round 8-inch baking dish. In a medium bowl, combine biscuit mix, sugar, egg and milk; mix well. Beat vigorously by hand 30 seconds. Spread batter in greased baking dish.
**3.** Spoon jam in dollops over batter. Swirl through with a knife to marble. Sprinkle topping over batter. Microwave, uncovered, at 30% (MEDIUM LOW) 7 minutes; give dish a half turn after 4 minutes. Microwave at full power (HIGH) 3 minutes or until a wooden pick inserted in center of cake comes out clean; give dish a half turn after 1-1/2 minutes.
**4.** Cool cake on a flat counter 15 minutes. Cut cake in wedges while warm. To serve, sprinkle with powdered sugar; garnish with strawberries, if desired. Makes 6 to 8 servings.

# Long-Cooking Rice

2-1/4 cups hot water
1 tablespoon butter or margarine
1/4 teaspoon salt
1 cup long-cooking rice

**1.** In a deep 2-quart casserole with lid, combine hot water, butter or margarine and salt. Cover. Microwave at full power (HIGH) 4 to 5 minutes or until boiling. Stir in rice; cover. Microwave at 30% (MEDIUM LOW) 20 minutes or until tender; stir after 10 minutes. Let stand, covered, 5 minutes. Fluff with a fork. Makes 4 to 5 (1-cup) servings.

# How to Make Strawberry-Jam Kuchen

1/Spread batter in a round, 8-inch baking dish. Spoon strawberry jam over top of batter. Then, with a knife, swirl through batter to marble jam.

2/For Streusel Topping, use a pastry blender or 2 knives to cut butter or margarine and egg yolk into flour, sugar and cinnamon. Topping should resemble fine crumbs.

3/Sprinkle Streusel Topping evenly over top of batter.

4/Garnish cake with fresh strawberries and powdered sugar. Cut in wedges; serve with hot coffee or tea.

# Parmesan-Spaghetti Ring

1/4 cup butter or margarine
10 oz. spaghetti, cooked, drained
2/3 cup grated Parmesan cheese
3 eggs, beaten
1 (3-1/2-oz.) can chopped mushrooms, drained
2 tablespoons chopped parsley
1 (16-oz.) jar spaghetti sauce

1. Oil a 5-cup microwave ring mold. In a large bowl, add butter or margarine to hot cooked spaghetti. Using 2 forks, gently lift spaghetti until butter or margarine is melted.

Stir in Parmesan cheese; then stir in eggs. Stir in mushrooms and parsley.
2. Turn into oiled mold. Cover with vented plastic wrap. Microwave at full power (HIGH) 5 minutes or until set. Cover with foil to keep warm.
3. Pour spaghetti sauce into a 1-quart casserole with lid. Cover. Microwave at full power (HIGH) 5 minutes or until heated through; stir after 2-1/2 minutes. Slide knife around edge of mold to loosen spaghetti ring. Turn ring out onto a serving plate. Serve with spaghetti sauce. Makes 6 servings.

# Peach-Parfait Pie

1 Baked Pastry Shell, page 704, or Crumb Crust, below
1 (3-oz.) pkg. lemon-flavored gelatin
1-1/4 cups water
1 pint peach ice cream
1 cup thawed frozen whipped topping

*To garnish:*
**Whipped topping**
**Peach slices**
**Mint sprig**

1. Cook pastry or crumb crust in a 9-inch pie plate; set aside.
2. In a 2-quart bowl, combine gelatin and water. Microwave at 100% (HIGH) 2 to 3 minutes or until gelatin dissolves; stir every minute. Add several scoops of ice cream to hot gelatin. Stir until ice cream is melted. Stir in remaining ice cream.
3. Stir whipped topping; stir into ice-cream mixture. Whisk until smooth. Refrigerate 40 to 45 minutes or until mixture mounds when dropped from a spoon.
4. Spoon into pastry shell or crumb crust. Refrigerate 8 hours or overnight or until firm. Garnish with whipped topping, peach slices and a mint sprig. Makes 6 servings.

## Variations

**Raspberry-Parfait Pie:** Substitute raspberry-flavored gelatin for lemon gelatin and frozen raspberry yogurt or sherbet for peach ice cream. Garnish with fresh or frozen raspberries.

**Lime-Parfait Pie:** Substitute lime-flavored gelatin for lemon gelatin and lime sherbet for peach ice cream. Garnish with fresh lime slices.

# Devonshire Cheesecake Cups

6 vanilla wafers
1 (8-oz.) pkg. cream cheese
1/3 cup firmly packed brown sugar
1 egg
1/2 teaspoon vanilla extract

*To garnish:*
**Dairy sour cream**
**Green grapes or strawberries**
**Brown sugar**

1. Place paper baking cups in 6 (6-ounce) custard cups. Place a vanilla wafer in each paper baking cup; set aside.
2. Unwrap cream cheese; place in a 1-1/2-quart bowl. Microwave at 10% (LOW) 1-1/2 to 2 minutes or until softened. Add brown sugar, egg and vanilla. Beat with an electric mixer on high speed until smooth.
3. Pour into paper baking cups. Arrange in a circle in microwave. Microwave at 30% (MEDIUM LOW) 7 to 8 minutes; rearrange cups after 4 minutes. Remove any cheesecake cups that are set in center or those in which a knife inserted off-center comes out clean.
4. Microwave remaining cheesecake cups at 30% (MEDIUM LOW) 1 minute or until done. Cool on a wire rack 1 hour. Refrigerate. Serve topped with dollops of sour cream, green-grape clusters or strawberries and a sprinkling of brown sugar. Makes 6 servings.

# Crumb Crust

6 tablespoons butter or margarine
1-1/2 cups fine graham-cracker, vanilla-cookie or
    chocolate-wafer crumbs
3 tablespoons sugar

1. Lightly butter a 9-inch pie plate. Place butter or margarine in a 1-1/2-quart bowl. Microwave at 100% (HIGH) 45 to 60 seconds or until melted. Stir in crumbs and sugar until all crumbs are moistened. Spoon crumb mixture over bottom and side of pie plate. Press crumbs firmly and evenly over bottom and side of pie plate.
2. Microwave at 100% (HIGH) 1-1/2 to 2 minutes or until set; give dish a half turn after 1 minute. Quickly press crumbs firmly against pie plate again. Cool before filling. Makes a (9-inch) crust.

Devonshire Cheesecake Cups

# Peanut-Brickle Layer Bars

1/4 cup butter or margarine
1 cup peanut-butter-cookie crumbs
1 cup peanut-butter-flavored baking pieces
1 (6-oz.) pkg. almond-brickle baking pieces (1-1/4 cups)
1 (3-1/2-oz.) can flaked coconut (1-1/3 cups)
1/2 cup salted peanuts, chopped
1 (14-oz.) can sweetened condensed milk (1-1/3 cups)

1. Place a 2-inch diameter jar in center of a 12" x 7" baking dish. Place butter or margarine in baking dish. Microwave at 100% (HIGH) 1 minute or until melted. Stir in cookie crumbs. Press into bottom of baking dish around jar.
2. Sprinkle with peanut-butter pieces, almond-brickle pieces, coconut and peanuts. Spoon condensed milk evenly over all. Microwave, uncovered, at 100% (HIGH) 7 to 8 minutes or until set in center when lightly touched; give dish a half turn after 4 minutes. Cool completely on a wire rack; cut into bars. Makes 48 bars.

# Baked Pastry Shell

1-1/2 sticks pie-crust mix
3 tablespoons water

1. Prepare pie-crust mix with water according to package directions. On a lightly floured surface, roll out dough 1/8 inch thick. Cut circle of dough 2 inches larger than top of pie plate. Gently fit pastry in pie plate. Fold under edge and flute. Prick all over bottom and side of pastry with a fork.
2. Microwave at 70% (MEDIUM HIGH) 7 to 9 minutes or until done; give dish a half turn after 4 minutes. If dough puffs up during cooking, gently prick with a fork. Cool on a wire rack before filling. Makes 1 (9- or 10-inch) shell.

# Toasted-Almond Cake Roll

2 cups slivered blanched almonds (7-1/2 oz.)
3/4 teaspoon baking powder
4 egg whites
4 egg yolks
1/2 cup powdered sugar
1 teaspoon vanilla extract
1/4 teaspoon almond extract
Powdered sugar

*Cocoa-Fluff Filling:*
1 envelope dessert-topping mix
1/2 cup cold milk
1/2 teaspoon vanilla extract
1/4 cup chocolate-drinking mix

1. Spread almonds in a 12-inch-square microwave baker. Microwave at 100% (HIGH) 4 to 5 minutes or until toasted; stir every 1-1/2 minutes. Cool to room temperature. Grind almonds or process until fine in a food processor fitted with the steel blade in 2 or 3 batches. Measure 1-1/2 cups. Stir baking powder into ground almonds; set aside.
2. Line same microwave baker with waxed paper cut long enough to extend over ends of baking dish. Butter top-side of waxed paper where it touches bottom of dish.
3. In a large bowl, beat egg whites with an electric mixer on high speed until stiff but not dry. In a large bowl, combine egg yolks, 1/2 cup powdered sugar, vanilla and almond extract. With an electric mixer on high speed, beat mixture 3 to 5 minutes or until thick and lemon-colored. Stir nut mixture into yolk mixture. Fold in beaten egg whites. Spread batter evenly in prepared baking dish.
4. Microwave at 100% (HIGH) 6 minutes or until a wooden pick inserted in center of cake comes out clean. Let stand 1 minute. Using extended ends of waxed paper, lift cake out of dish. Place on a wire rack. Immediately cover with a damp cloth towel. Cool 50 to 60 minutes.
5. To prepare filling, in a deep bowl, combine dessert-topping mix, milk, vanilla and drink mix. Beat with an electric mixer on high speed until peaks form. Beat about 2 minutes or until smooth and fluffy.
6. To serve, remove towel. Spread filling on cake. Roll up, jelly-roll style, peeling off waxed paper as cake is rolled. Be careful not to roll too tightly. Sprinkle top of roll with additional powdered sugar. Makes 6 to 8 servings.

# How To Make Bananas-Foster Chiffon Pie

1/Thoroughly combine unflavored gelatin and brown sugar. Mixing gelatin with sugar helps prevent lumping. Stir in egg-yolk mixture; microwave until mixture begins to boil.

2/Beat egg whites until soft peaks form. Beat in brown sugar.

3/Beat brown sugar into egg whites until stiff and glossy. At stiff-peak stage, a rubber spatula should leave a clean trough through egg whites.

4/Garnish with whipped cream, banana slices and mint. To loosen crumb crust, wrap a hot wet towel around pie plate for a few minutes before serving.

## Bananas-Foster Chiffon Pie

1 (9-inch) Crumb Crust, page 702, made with vanilla
  wafers
1 (1/4-oz.) envelope unflavored gelatin (1 tablespoon)
2/3 cup firmly packed brown sugar
4 egg yolks
1/2 cup mashed ripe bananas
1/4 cup dark rum
1 teaspoon grated lemon peel
4 egg whites
1/4 teaspoon cream of tartar
2/3 cup firmly packed brown sugar
1 cup banana-flavored yogurt

*To garnish:*
**Whipped cream**
**Sliced bananas dipped in lemon juice**
**Mint sprig**

1. Prepare crust using vanilla wafers; set aside.
2. In a 1-1/2-quart bowl, thoroughly combine gelatin and 2/3 cup brown sugar; set aside.
3. In a medium bowl, with an electric mixer on medium speed, beat egg yolks, bananas, rum and lemon peel until blended. Stir into gelatin mixture. Microwave at 30% (MEDIUM LOW) 6 to 7 minutes or until mixture almost boils and gelatin is dissolved; stir every 1-1/2 minutes. Refrigerate until mixture mounds when dropped from a spoon.
4. In another medium bowl, with an electric mixer on high speed, beat egg whites and cream of tartar until soft peaks form. Gradually add 2/3 cup brown sugar; beat until stiff and glossy. Fold banana mixture into egg-white mixture. Fold in banana yogurt. Spoon into pie crust. Refrigerate 8 hours or overnight or until set.
5. Garnish with whipped cream, banana slices and mint. Makes 6 servings.

# Luscious Strawberry Trifle

1 (4-1/2-oz.) pkg. golden egg-custard mix
3 cups milk
1/2 teaspoon orange-flavored extract
1/4 teaspoon grated orange peel
8 (1-oz.) sponge-cake dessert cups
1/4 cup orange-flavored liqueur
1/4 cup orange marmalade
4 cups sliced fresh strawberries
2 cups thawed frozen whipped topping

*To decorate:*
Whipped topping, if desired
Fresh whole strawberries

1. Empty custard mix into a bowl. Gradually stir in milk. Microwave, uncovered, at 100% (HIGH) 5 minutes. Stir well. Microwave at 100% (HIGH) 3 minutes or until mixture comes to a boil; stir once; sauce will be thin. Stir in orange extract and orange peel. Refrigerate only 15 minutes.
2. Arrange 4 sponge-cake dessert cups in a 2-1/2-quart glass serving bowl; cut cakes as necessary to fit dishes. Prick cakes all over with a fork. Drizzle with 1/2 of orange-flavored liqueur.
3. Spread with 1/2 of orange marmalade. Top with 1/2 of strawberries. Pour 1/2 of custard sauce over strawberries, being sure part of custard flows through to cake layer. Repeat layers of cake, liqueur, marmalade, strawberries and custard sauce. Spread top with whipped topping. Refrigerate several hours.
4. Immediately before serving, decorate with additional whipped topping, if desired and whole strawberries. Makes 8 to 10 servings.

# Café au Lait Soufflé

2 teaspoons unflavored gelatin powder
2 tablespoons sugar
2 egg yolks
1/2 cup cold strong coffee
2 tablespoons coffee-flavored liqueur
2 egg whites
1/8 teaspoon cream of tartar
2 tablespoons sugar
1/2 cup whipping cream, whipped

*To garnish:*
Whipped cream, if desired
Chocolate curls, if desired

1. In a 1-quart bowl, thoroughly mix gelatin and 2 tablespoons sugar. In a medium bowl, with an electric mixer at low speed, beat egg yolks and coffee until blended. Stir into gelatin mixture. Microwave at 30% (MEDIUM LOW) 4 to 4-1/2 minutes or until mixture almost boils and gelatin is dissolved; stir every minute. Stir in liqueur. Refrigerate 1 to 1-1/2 hours or until mixture mounds when dropped from a spoon; stir frequently.
2. In another medium bowl, with an electric mixer at high speed, beat egg whites and cream of tartar until soft peaks form. Gradually add remaining 2 tablespoons sugar; beating until stiff and glossy. Fold coffee mixture into egg-white mixture. Fold in whipped cream. Spoon into a 1-quart soufflé dish or 3 to 4 (10-oz.) cups. Refrigerate 3 to 4 hours or until firm.
3. Garnish with whipped cream and chocolate curls, if desired. Makes 3 to 4 servings.

# Baked Apples

4 (6- to 7-oz.) baking apples
1/4 cup raisins
1/2 cup firmly packed brown sugar
Ground cinnamon
Ground nutmeg
1/4 cup bourbon or apple juice
Vanilla ice cream or whipping cream

1. Core apples, being careful not to cut through bottoms. Peel a small strip around top of each apple. Set apples, stem-side up, in an 8-inch-square baking dish. Spoon raisins into center of each apple. Mound brown sugar on apples. Sprinkle with cinnamon and nutmeg. Drizzle with bourbon or apple juice.
2. Cover with vented plastic wrap. Microwave at 100% (HIGH) 7 to 9 minutes; give dish a half turn after 4 minutes. Let stand, covered, 10 minutes. Apple should be tender when pierced with a fork. If not, recover and microwave 1 to 2 minutes more. Spoon pan juices over apples. Serve with vanilla ice cream or cream. Makes 4 servings.

Café au Lait Soufflé

# Metric Charts

## Comparison to Metric Measure

| When You Know | Symbol | Multiply By | To Find | Symbol |
|---|---|---|---|---|
| teaspoons | tsp | 5.0 | milliliters | ml |
| tablespoons | tbsp | 15.0 | milliliters | ml |
| fluid ounces | fl. oz. | 30.0 | milliliters | ml |
| cups | c | 0.24 | liters | l |
| pints | pt. | 0.47 | liters | l |
| quarts | qt. | 0.95 | liters | l |
| ounces | oz. | 28.0 | grams | g |
| pounds | lb. | 0.45 | kilograms | kg |
| Fahrenheit | F | 5/9 (after subtracting 32) | Celsius | C |

## Liquid Measure to Milliliters

| | | |
|---|---|---|
| 1/4 teaspoon | = | 1.25 milliliters |
| 1/2 teaspoon | = | 2.5 milliliters |
| 3/4 teaspoon | = | 3.75 milliliters |
| 1 teaspoon | = | 5.0 milliliters |
| 1-1/4 teaspoons | = | 6.25 milliliters |
| 1-1/2 teaspoons | = | 7.5 milliliters |
| 1-3/4 teaspoons | = | 8.75 milliliters |
| 2 teaspoons | = | 10.0 milliliters |
| 1 tablespoon | = | 15.0 milliliters |
| 2 tablespoons | = | 30.0 milliliters |

## Liquid Measure to Liters

| | | |
|---|---|---|
| 1/4 cup | = | 0.06 liters |
| 1/2 cup | = | 0.12 liters |
| 3/4 cup | = | 0.18 liters |
| 1 cup | = | 0.24 liters |
| 1-1/4 cups | = | 0.3 liters |
| 1-1/2 cups | = | 0.36 liters |
| 2 cups | = | 0.48 liters |
| 2-1/2 cups | = | 0.6 liters |
| 3 cups | = | 0.72 liters |
| 3-1/2 cups | = | 0.84 liters |
| 4 cups | = | 0.96 liters |
| 4-1/2 cups | = | 1.08 liters |
| 5 cups | = | 1.2 liters |
| 5-1/2 cups | = | 1.32 liters |

## Fahrenheit to Celsius

| F | C |
|---|---|
| 200—205 | 95 |
| 220—225 | 105 |
| 245—250 | 120 |
| 275 | 135 |
| 300—305 | 150 |
| 325—330 | 165 |
| 345—350 | 175 |
| 370—375 | 190 |
| 400—405 | 205 |
| 425—430 | 220 |
| 445—450 | 230 |
| 470—475 | 245 |
| 500 | 260 |

# Index